FEDERAL INCOME TAXATION OF BUSINESS ENTERPRISES

CASES, STATUTES, RULINGS

FIFTH EDITION

RICHARD A. WESTIN
Professor of Law, Emeritus
University of Kentucky College of Law

BEVERLY I. MORAN
Professor of Law
Vanderbilt University

Vandeplas Publishing
UNITED STATES OF AMERICA

Westin, Richard A. & Moran, Beverly I.

Federal Income Taxation of Business Enterprises
Cases, Statutes and Rulings

Fifth Edition 2019

Published by:

Vandeplas Publishing LLC – 2019

801 International Parkway, 5th Floor
Lake Mary, FL 32746
USA

www.vandeplaspublishing.com

ISBN: 978-1-60042-304-8

Preface

Albert Einstein once said that "things should be as simple as possible, but no simpler." That wise observation applies to the teaching of federal income taxation, among other things. In recent years, the Internal Revenue Code has become ever more complex, as has the teaching of the taxation of business enterprises. The practical problem is that the law student who plans a career in business law is in an unpleasant predicament. He or she must either avoid federal income tax courses, and bear the guilty knowledge that a large area of relevant law has been overlooked, with significant implications in terms of personal feelings of inadequacy, or face the burden of taking a large dose of notoriously difficult courses in corporate and partnership taxation. This book is designed to alleviate that Hobson's choice. Whether it has succeeded is for the instructor and student to decide.

This book provides teaching materials for a basic income taxation course dealing with the taxation of partnerships, corporations, S corporations, and limited liability companies. In addition, it alludes to a short list of other business enterprises. It can definitely be completed in the usual three hours assigned to such courses, on the assumption that students will spend two hours of preparation for each hour in the classroom.

The book begins with the study of partnerships, moves to C corporations, then to S corporations, then to limited liability companies. In general, we take a cradle-to-grave approach to each subject. Our teaching of the course out of these materials convinces us that the order is realistic and effective.

The cases have been extensively edited, and most footnotes in the original cases have been eliminated (and in one case, split) without any explicit reference to the fact of their elimination, other than the words in this paragraph. Case and statute citations of the court and commentators, as well as footnotes, have been omitted without so specifying; numbered footnotes are from the original materials but do not retain the original numbering, except by accident.

The book is fairly rich with problems that are scattered along the way, rather than at the end of each chapter. They are not especially difficult and are designed to build confidence while at the same time forcing at least some review of the central Code provisions and pertinent regulations. We do not view this as a "problems" book, and we advise students that if they find themselves struggling unduly with a problem, to drop it, but always at least take a crack at the problems, because if they do not, the colloquy in class in which the answer is revealed will pass over their heads.

Richard A. Westin
Lexington, Kentucky, 2018

Summary Table of Contents

Table of Contents

Chapter 1

THE TAX CHARACTER OF PARTNERSHIPS

A. INTRODUCTION

1. STATE LAW CHARACTERISTICS

A partnership is a contractually-based relationship among owners of an enterprise organized for a profit. Partnerships fall into the following two broad categories: general partnerships and limited partnerships.

General partnerships can arise orally and may be informal, although most operate under a written partnership agreement, which is to say a foundational contract among its owners. By contrast, limited partnerships are creatures of state law that must satisfy filing requirements, usually with a Secretary of State, in order to come into being, and that must have at least one general partner.

The defining characteristic of a general partnership is that each partner bears unlimited personal liability to third parties for the partnership's obligations. Limited partners, on the other hand, like shareholders in a corporation, are liable to third parties only to the extent of their actual contributions to the limited partnership, plus any promised additional contributions. Again, like shareholders, limited partners as such are generally precluded from managing the partnership. Limited partnership interests, like shares of stock, are fairly easy to market, whereas it is difficult to market general partnership interests.

There is one related concept that merits mentioning at this point – the "joint venture." This is non-tax terminology for a state law partnership that has a limited purpose, such as to build and sell a single apartment project.

2. TAX BACKGROUND

The partnership tax rules appear in §§ 701-777 of the Code, known as Subchapter K. After careful study, Subchapter K was enacted in 1954 in order to straighten out the confusion that had arisen under earlier tax laws. The Senate Finance Committee Report in support of the new framework provided:

> "The existing tax treatment of partners and partnerships is among the most confused in the entire income tax field. The present statutory provisions are wholly inadequate. The published Regulations, rulings, and court decisions are incomplete and frequently contradictory. As a result, partners today cannot form, operate or dissolve a partnership with any assurance as to tax consequences.
>
> This confusion is particularly unfortunate in view of the great number of business enterprises and ventures carried on in partnership form. It should also be noted that the partnership form of organization is much more commonly employed by small businesses and in farming operations than the corporate form.
>
> Because of the vital need for clarification, the House and our committee have undertaken the first comprehensive statutory treatment of partners and partnerships in the history of the income tax laws. In establishing a broad pattern applicable to partnerships, generally, the principal objectives have been simplicity, flexibility, and equity as between partners."[1]

---

[1] S. Rep. No. 1622 83d Cong., 2d Sess. 89 (1954).

Whether these goals have actually been achieved seems doubtful, and Subchapter K has a well-deserved reputation for complexity despite the deceptively simple appearance of both the Code sections and the reporting forms.[2]

Some basic principles may be seen in the forms. Begin by looking at the annual partnership return (Form 1065) which appears as an appendix to this book. No tax payment accompanies the Form 1065, which is why it is called an information return. However, each Form 1065 is accompanied by at least two Forms K-1; this is the form on which a report of the individualized results of a partnership's year is made for each particular partner. The partnership's tax return preparer transmits a completed K-1 to each partner at the end of the partnership's taxable year, and it is used by each partner in preparing his own personal return. A Schedule K-1 appears immediately after the Form 1065 as an appendix.

These forms illustrate a basic tension that runs through Subchapter K, namely that a partnership is both an aggregate of individual partners who pay taxes directly on their share of the partnership's profits, but at the same time is also a separate entity for a variety of other purposes, such as filing the tax return, having a distinct taxable year, and adopting an accounting method to compute its profits or losses. The former is referred to as the "aggregate theory"; the latter is known as the "entity theory." The tax law in some instances treats a partnership as if it were an entity and in others as if it were an aggregation of individuals.

B. THE GROWING POPULARITY OF PARTNERSHIPS

The partnership form of doing business (where feasible) is often favored over incorporation. In large measure this preference comes from federal tax laws.

The Internal Revenue Code of 1986 inverted the historic relationship between individual and corporate marginal tax rates in which top individual income tax rates used to exceed top corporate rates. As a result, the corporate form naturally became less desirable. In the early 21st Century, the rate differential between the top personal and corporate federal income rates all but disappeared. In fact, the most recent tax reform caps corporate tax rates at 21%. But rates are not the only reason for preferring non-corporate form. Corporations also suffer from the enduring problem of the double tax.

Because corporations are separate legal and taxable entities, doing business in corporate form presents a "double tax" problem, in the sense that the corporation first pays its own tax on its profits, and then, when it distributes those same profits as dividends, the shareholders must pay a second tax on those same profits. By contrast, a partnership is not subject to the separate U.S. income tax on corporations; instead, all partnership items of income deduction or credit pass through to the partners, and, when a partnership distributes its profits, there is no second round of taxes. On the other hand, since the George W. Bush administration the corporate double tax has softened by making most dividends taxable at favorable long-term capital gains rates.

---

[2] Little did the 1954 legislators imagine how deep the conflict between simplicity and flexibility could go, and how complicated Subchapter K would turn out to be in practice. The late Professor Boris Bittker seems to have thought the effort was a failure. B. Bittker, Federal Taxation of Income, Estates and Gifts, Vol. 3 at 85.1.2 (1981). Much of the reason for these complications seems to be the exploitation by clever tax advisors of rules designed for simple and straightforward transactions by inappropriately applying them to complicated tax-driven transactional formats for which the rules were not intended. That in turn triggers reactions by Congress and the Internal Revenue Service that are themselves overly complex, if not sometimes paranoid. On a deeper level, however, the underlying problems are probably inherent in the structural ambiguities of Subchapter K itself. In the end, Subchapter K may simply be inappropriate for businesses of any degree of complexity.

Starting in 2018, taxpayers can receive a deduction of up to 20% against their Qualified Business Income (QBI) from pass-through entities. Combined with reduced rates, the deduction can result in substantial tax savings.

Example:

The ABC partnership earns $300,000 of QBI. ABC's three equal partners are single taxpayers with no income from other sources.

For ease of computation, assume that each partner is subject to a flat tax rate of 28% in 2017 (the rate for $100,000 of income for a single taxpayer) and a flat rate of 22% in 2018 (the rate for $80,000 of income for a single taxpayer). Further, again for ease of computation, assume no other offsetting deductions or credits, including no standard deduction.

In 2017, each partner reports $100,000 of income and is liable for $28,000 of income tax at the 28% rate.

Starting in 2018 and through tax year 2025, each partner deducts 20% off his taxable income from the partnership. With the deduction, each partner reports only $80,000 of the $100,000 pass through and owes only $17,600 of tax (22% x $80,000). Each partner has a $10,400 savings over his 2017 tax liability.

Detailed analysis

The 2017 law added a tax deduction for "qualified business income" (QBI) which is only available to non-corporate taxpayers. The deduction is popularly known as the the the "pass-through deduction," because it benefits not only partners in partnerships, but also members of LLCs taxed as partnerships, shareholders of S corporations (shareholders subject to a single tax on corporate income), owners of single-member LLCs and sole proprietors not operating through any legal entity. The new law is intended to give non-corporate business owners a reduction similar to the new corporate income tax rates of 21 percent. The details follow. The new law, embodied in § 199A is set to expire ("sunset") in 2025. Nevertheless, do not be surprised if it is made a permanent feature of the federal tax law before then.

The formal statement of §199A is that non-corporate taxpayers who have QBI" from a partnership, S corporation, or sole proprietorship may deduct 20% of his or her QBI. The 20% deduction is afflicted by complicated formulae and various limitations discussed below. In general, the deduction cannot exceed 20% of the excess of the taxpayer's taxable income over net capital gain, making the realization of big net capital gains a potential problem.

What is QBI?

QBI is generally the net amount of "qualified items of income, gain, deduction, and loss" relating to any "qualified trade or business" of the taxpayer, but only to the extent that these items are connected to the conduct of an American trade or business. In general, QBI is the ordinary operating income of the business. In a twist that is easy to forget, if this year's QBI is negative, the loss carries over and reduces QBI in the succeeding tax year.

Investment income is not QBI, e.g., capital gains or losses, dividends, and interest income except interest allocable to the business. Compensation paid to employees and guaranteed payments to a partner for services to the partnership are also not QBI.

How big is the deduction?

The deduction is 20% of QBI before various limitations whittle it down.

Limitations that reduce the deduction

1. Taxpayers with large incomes

Taxable income limit. For single taxpayers with 2018 taxable incomes under $157,500, or married filing jointly taxpayers with incomes under $315,000, the only limitation on the 20% deduction is that the deduction cannot exceed taxable income, excluding net capital gain. In a Darwinian move, net capital losses must be added back to taxable income, hence the 20% deduction may decline because of increased capital gains. This will call for more tax planning when selling capital assets.

Phased-in limits. For taxpayers with 2018 taxable income above $207,500 (filing single) or $415,000 (filing jointly) there is more trouble in that intricate further limits regarding *certain business activities* and the amount of wages and assets are applied to the 20% deduction against QBI. These limitations phase in for taxpayers with 2018 taxable income between $157,500 - $207,500 (filing single) and $315,000 - $415,000 (married filing jointly). We will call this "top incomes" for convenience.

Businesses that cannot take the deduction. Service businesses such as health, law, accounting, actuarial science, performing arts, consulting, athletics, financial services, brokerage services, including investing and investment management, trading, or dealing in securities, partnership interests, or commodities, and any trade or business where the principal asset of such trade or business is the reputation or skill of one or more of its employees are not eligible for the deduction.

Wage and asset limits. For people with top incomes the QBI deduction is capped at the lesser of:

A. 50% of W-2 wages related to the qualified business (no employees means no deduction) or

B. The sum of 25% of such W-2 wages plus 2.5% of the unadjusted basis of all qualified property, meaning tangible depreciable property of the qualified business, with a favorable mark-up beyond the scope of this writing.

One computes the wage and asset limitations separately for each source of one's QBI and one cannot combine operating results from one source of QBI source another. This prevents opportunistic aggregation of profitable and losing businesses.

C. PARTNERSHIP STATUS

The first major inquiry is whether an entity organized as a partnership under local law stands up as such, or whether it has to be reclassified as another form of organization for federal income tax purposes. For federal income tax purposes all business or investment entities that are not sole proprietorships fall into one of the following basic classifications: corporation; trust or estate; or partnership. Reg. §§ 301.7701-2 through 301.7701-4. Thus, for example, even the most obscure or novel foreign entity must be forced into one of these three pigeonholes for U.S. federal income tax purposes if it has to deal with the IRS. (There are some specialized entities, such as farmers' cooperatives that fall into unique categories, but only because Congress carved out special rules for them.)

Conversely, many relationships that appear to involve no entity at all, such as landlord and tenant or debtor and creditor, have the potential for inadvertently producing a partnership for federal income tax purposes.

The Supreme Court shaped the process of classifying entities for federal income tax purposes in *Morrissey v. Commissioner*, 296 U.S. 344 (1935). The facts involved a trust that was organized to form and operate a golf course for a profit. The Court evaluated the question in terms of whether the trust more closely resembled a corporation or a traditional trust. Finding a preponderance of corporate characteristics, it declared the entity to be taxable as a corporation.

In later years, physicians took advantage of the tendency of the case law to treat a state law limited partnership as a corporation if it had a "preponderance of corporate characteristics," thereby allowing them to get the benefit of the more generous pension plan arrangements formerly available only to corporations. The Treasury Department counterattacked with the so-called Kintner Regulations, named after the *Kintner* case, which strove to ensure that a limited partnership would be treated as a partnership and not as a corporation. Tax shelter promoters in turn latched onto the generously pro-limited partnership rules and marketed their wares as limited partnership interests, with deductions passing through to the limited partners.

The Regulations required two preliminary factors to exist in order to find either a partnership or a corporation. They required that there be "associates" who joined together in order to conduct a profit-making enterprise, and that they did so with a view to sharing in those profits. There was an acknowledged possible exception for a one-shareholder corporation.

Assuming those two factors existed, then the question became whether the enterprise had three or more of the following characteristics, in which event it was characterized as a corporation for federal income tax purposes:

1. Continuity of life, meaning the entity does not legally dissolve if a member transfers an interest in the entity;

2. Centralization of management, meaning that the power to make managerial decisions is concentrated in less than all the members;

3. Free transferability of interests, meaning the owners can transfer their interests in income and capital of the enterprise; and

4. Limited liability, meaning there is not even one owner who has unlimited liability for the obligations of the enterprise.

Curiously, the government did not amend these Regulations during the tax shelter era. Instead, it took a litigating position that limited partnerships are generally taxable as corporations, as the *Larson* case (next) exemplifies. It was a failure. What follows is a heavily edited version of the Larson decision, which utterly defeated the government. The Kintner Regulations have recently been rewritten, and the four-factor analysis has been obliterated, but the concept of limited liability remains important under the new Regulations with respect to the default rules for foreign entities. Accordingly, the discussion of that concept in *Larson* remains important.

LARSON v. COMMISSIONER
66 T.C. 159 (1976)

[The taxpayers owned limited partnership interests in two real estate syndications (Mai Kai and Soumis) organized under the California Uniform Limited Partnership Act. The general partner in each partnership was a corporation (GHL) that was independent of the limited partners and was organized for the purpose of promoting and managing the syndications. Under California law the partnerships could be dissolved by the bankruptcy of the general partner. The general partner invested no money in the partnerships and held interests that were subordinated to those of the limited partners. The limited partners could vote to remove the general partner. The limited partners could transfer their income rights with the consent of the general partner, which consent could not unreasonably be withheld. A transferee of a limited partner's capital interest, if the transfer was at fair market value, had the right to become a substituted limited partner without the consent of any member. There were clearly "associates" and a "joint profit intent." There was centralized management; interests were found freely transferable on the facts; the entity did legally dissolve if a general partner went bankrupt. The remaining issue was whether the entity had the corporate characteristic of limited liability. The facts as to that point were that the general partner was a corporation with only modest assets and was owned by persons unrelated to the limited partners.]

TANNENWALD, J.

3. Limited Liability

Unless some member is personally liable for debts of, and claims against, an entity . . . the entity possesses the corporate characteristic of limited liability. The regulation provides that "in the case of a limited partnership subject to a statute corresponding to the Uniform Limited Partnership Act, personal liability exists with respect to each general partner, except as provided in subparagraph (2) of this paragraph." The first sentence of subparagraph (2) establishes a conjunctive test, under which a general partner is considered not to have personal liability only "when he has no substantial assets (other than his interest in the partnership) which could be reached by a creditor of the organization and when he is merely a 'dummy' acting as the agent of the limited partners." In other words, personal liability exists if the general partner either has substantial assets or is not a dummy for the limited partners . . . . Although the purpose of subparagraph (2) was ostensibly to delineate the conditions under which personal liability of a general partner does not exist, practically all the remaining material in the subparagraph outlines the conditions under which such personal liability does exist. In several examples, personal liability is said to exist, either because the general partner has substantial assets or because he is not a dummy for the limited partners. . . . In no instance is there a suggestion that both conditions established by the first sentence of subparagraph (2) need not be satisfied.

* * *

While it may be doubtful that GHL could be considered to have had substantial assets during the years in issue, we find it unnecessary to resolve this question since it is clear that GHL was not a dummy for the limited partners of Soumis and Mai-Kai. Respondent contends that GIL fell within the "dummy" concept because it was subject to removal by the limited partners, and thus was subject to their ultimate control. While it is true that a mere "dummy" would be totally under the control of the limited partners, it does not follow that the presence of some control by virtue of the power to remove necessarily makes the general partner a "dummy." It seems clear that the limited partners' rights to remove the general partner were designed to give the limited partners a measure of control over their investment without involving them in the "control of the business"; the rights were not designed to render GHL a mere dummy or to empower the limited partners "to direct the business actively through the general partners." *Glensder Textile Co.*, 46 B.T.A. at 183. Moreover, the record indicates that the limited partners did not use GHL as a screen to conceal their own active involvement in the conduct of the business; far from being a rubber stamp, GHL was the moving force in these enterprises. With a minor exception, the persons controlling GHL were independent of and unrelated to the limited partners.

In view of the foregoing we conclude that personal liability existed with respect to GHL, and the partnerships lack the corporate characteristic of limited liability.

NOTES

1. **The IRS's next moves.** In Rev. Rul. 79-106, 1979-1 C.B. 448, the Service accepted the outcome in *Larson* and in effect gave up the fight. Then, almost twenty years later, the IRS promulgated the "check-a-box" regulations (also commonly referred to as "check-the-box" regulations) that let taxpayers elect whether they want to treat unincorporated business entities as partnerships or corporations for federal income tax purposes. Reg. § 301.7701-1 through 3. True trusts cannot make the election. Does this make *Larson* unimportant? Not entirely.

    The concept of "limited liability" in *Larson* is a key issue in determining whether to classify a foreign business entity as a corporation or as a partnership or sole proprietorship.

    An appendix at the back of the book contains a flow chart distinguishing among sole proprietorships, partnerships, and corporations, and the impact of the check-the-box election. In addition, a copy of Form 8832 (Entity Classification Election) is attached as an appendix at the end of the book. Reg. § 301.7701-2(a) defines "business entity."

2. **But state law changed.** The Revised Uniform Limited Partnership Act (RULPA) is not the same as the UPA contemplated by the *Larson* court. *See* RULPA §§ 402, 801. It became possible to have the partners agree that the partnership will continue despite the bankruptcy of a general partner by means of selecting a new general partner within a ninety-day window period. This makes partnerships less vulnerable to technical legal dissolutions. You will look at the impact of dissolutions later in the book.

3. **Trusts.** Prior to the check-a-box regulations, if a trust had the power to conduct business, it was treated as a corporation. This was because, in addition to having a business purpose and associates (namely, the beneficiaries, the grantor, or both combined), centralized management, and limited liability, trusts commonly have free transferability and unlimited life; hence, trusts were generally doomed to corporate status if they had a business purpose. *See* Reg. § 301.7701-4(a).

    If a trust does not have a power to conduct business, it is simply a trust. Under the check-a-box system, if a trust does have a power to conduct business (and if it has "associates"), it becomes a "business entity," and can elect to be taxed as a partnership or a corporation. See the Preamble to the Proposed Regulations, issued May 13, 1996. As a result, one can add a business power to a trust document (which would make it a corporation) and then elect to treat the business trust as a partnership.

4. **Associates in a testamentary trust setting.** *Bedell v. Commissioner*, 86 T.C. 1207 (1987), held that a testamentary trust that operated a bedding factory for profit was not to be treated as a corporation, on the theory that there were no "associates." The beneficiaries, who were heirs of the decedent, had no managerial authority and had no hand in forming the trust. The case may offer a blueprint for the wicked who would rather operate under the trust rules than the partnership rules.

5. **Liquidating trusts.** There is another group of trusts that can qualify as trusts despite a business flavor. These consist of liquidating trusts, which are used temporarily to take control of the assets of a corporation that is in the process of being dismantled, and bondholders' protective trusts, which are vehicles by which bondholders take temporary claim to a debtor's assets pursuant to powers granted them by the terms of the debt instrument. As long as their primary purposes are not submerged by the conduct of business, bondholders' trusts and liquidating trusts can retain their income tax status as trusts, despite their possible profitability. Reg. § 301.7701-4(d). Likewise, investment trusts sold to the public and holding portfolios of income-producing assets can retain their status as long as their reinvestment powers are highly circumscribed. Reg. § 301.7701-4(c). These are commonly referred to as "unit investment trusts" and are frequently advertised in business sections of newspapers.

6. *Per se* **corporations.** Regulations identify the following eight specific business organizations that each will be deemed a "*per se* corporation" for federal tax purposes: all statutory corporations; joint-stock companies; associations; insurance companies subject to Subchapter L; state-chartered banks that have deposits insured by the Federal Deposit Insurance Act; state-owned entities; non-§ 7701(a)(3) entities (*e.g.*, publicly traded partnerships subject to § 7704); and specified foreign business entities (*i.e.*, eighty different foreign entities designated by name). Reg. § 301.7701-2(b).

7. **Grandfather rules.** The check-a-box regulations generally apply only to entities formed on or after January 1, 1997. The regulations promise to respect the partnership classification of any domestic eligible entity that was in existence before 1997 if three conditions are met: (i) the entity had a reasonable basis for partnership classification; (ii) the entity and all owners of the entity recognized the federal tax consequences of any change in the entity's classification after 1991; and (iii) neither the entity nor any member was notified by the IRS in writing on or before May 8, 1996, that the entity's classification was under audit. Reg. § 301.7701-3(h)(2). There was also limited grandfathering for foreign entities.

8. **Election and Default rules.** If the entity is a business entity (and not a trust), then it may be a per se corporation. If it is not, then it falls into the residual group of business entities, which is the topic of the rest of this paragraph. (If the business enterprise existed before 1997, it is likely to be grandfathered.)

Assuming it is not grandfathered, then the owners are free to make the check-a-box election. Let's assume they do not elect. What then? If it is a U.S. business entity, then the "default" outcome is that it is a sole proprietorship if there is only one owner and a partnership if there are several owners. Reg. § 301.7701-3(b)(1). If it is foreign business entity and no one has personal liability, then the default result is that it is a corporation for federal income tax purposes; if at least one person has personal liability, then the enterprise is a sole proprietorship if there is only one owner and a partnership if there are several owners. Reg. § 301.7701-3(b)(2). An election must be made by all the owners, and may not be changed again for five years.

9. **State law and entity classification**. Just because an entity achieves a particular status for federal income tax purposes does not mean that the same status will apply for state tax law purposes. For example, at least at one point the California Franchise Tax Board stated that it would not follow the check-a-box classification structure and would continue to rely on the *Kintner* four-factor test to determine whether an entity is a partnership for California state tax purposes. BNA Daily Tax Report, at G-8 (Feb. 3, 1997); 18 Cal. Code Reg. § 23038. Likewise, Texas taxes limited liability companies under its franchise tax, regardless of whether they elect to be taxed as partnerships, and recently imposed the franchise tax on state law limited partnerships. Texas Tax Code Chapter 171.

10. **Partner?** Even if an entity is a partnership, that does not determine whether everyone who is engaged in it is a partner. *See, e.g.,* Rev. Rul. 77-332, 1977-2 C.B. 484 (even though such arrangements are illegal under state law, a non-accountant may be treated as a member of an accounting partnership for federal income tax purposes).

REV. RUL. 75-374
1975-2 C.B. 261

Advice has been requested whether, under the circumstance described below, the co-owners of an apartment project would be treated as a partnership for Federal income tax purposes.

X, a life insurance company, and Y, a real estate investment trust, each own an undivided one-half interest in an apartment project. X and Y entered into a management agreement with Z, an unrelated corporation, and retained it to manage, operate, maintain, and service the project.

Generally, under the management agreement Z negotiates and executes leases for apartment units in the project; collects rents and other payments from tenants; pays taxes, assessments, and insurance premiums payable with respect to the project; performs all other services customarily performed in connection with the maintenance and repair of an apartment project; and performs certain additional services for the tenants beyond those customarily associated with maintenance and repair. Z is responsible for determining the time and manner of performing its obligations under the agreement and for the supervision of all persons performing services in connection with the carrying out of such obligations.

Customary tenant services, such as heat, air conditioning, hot and cold water, unattended parking, normal repairs, trash removal, and cleaning of public areas are furnished at no additional charge above the basic rental payments. All costs incurred by Z in rendering these customary services are paid for by X and Y. As compensation for the customary services rendered by Z under the agreement, X and Y each pay Z a percentage of one-half of the gross rental receipts derived from the operation of the project.

Additional services, such as attendant parking, cabanas, and gas, electricity, and other utilities are provided by Z to tenants for a separate charge. Z pays the costs incurred in providing the additional services, and retains the charges paid by tenants for its own use. These charges provide Z with adequate compensation for the rendition of these additional services.

Section 761(a) of the Internal Revenue Code of 1954 provides that the term "partnership" includes a syndicate, group, pool, joint venture or other unincorporated organization through or by means of which any business, financial operation, or venture is carried on, and which is not a corporation or a trust or estate.

9

Section 1.761-1(a) of the Income Tax Regulations provides that mere co-ownership of property that is maintained, kept in repair, and rented or leased does not constitute a partnership. Tenants in common may be partners if they actively carry on a trade, business, financial operation, or venture and divide the profits thereof. For example, a partnership exists if co-owners of an apartment building lease space and in addition provide services to the occupants either directly or through an agent.

The furnishing of customary services in connection with the maintenance and repair of the apartment project will not render a co-ownership a partnership. However, the furnishing of additional services will render a co-ownership a partnership if the additional services are furnished directly by the co-owners or through their agent. In the instant case by reason of the contractual arrangement with Z, X and Y are not furnishing the additional services either directly or through an agent. Z is solely responsible for determining the time and manner of furnishing the services, bears all the expenses of providing these services, and retains for its own use all the income from these services. None of the profits arising from the rendition of these additional services are divided between X and Y.

Accordingly, X and Y will be treated as co-owners and not as partners for purposes of section 761 of the Code.

1. PARTNER IN A PARTNERSHIP OR A LENDER?

It is sometimes difficult to distinguish common commercial relationships from partnerships for federal income tax purposes. The following early case deals with the knotty question of sorting a lending arrangement from a partnership.

DORZBACK v. COLLISON
195 F.2d 69 (3d Cir. 1952), *aff'g* 93 F. Supp. 935 (D. Del. 1950)

MARIS, CIRCUIT JUDGE

This is an appeal from a judgment for the plaintiff taxpayer in an action brought in the United States District Court for the District of Delaware for the recovery of income taxes and interest paid to the defendant Collector pursuant to deficiency assessments made by the Commissioner of Internal Revenue for the years 1943, 1944 and 1945.

The facts are these. On May 14, 1941 the taxpayer's wife loaned to the taxpayer from her own funds the sum of $8,500 to pay off an existing indebtedness of his in that amount and to evidence his resulting indebtedness to her the taxpayer gave her his bond in that amount bearing interest at 5% per annum. On January 4, 1943 the taxpayer and his wife entered into a written agreement in which they agreed that in lieu of the interest she had been receiving on this indebtedness she should share in the net profits derived from the taxpayer's retail business by receiving 25% of the net profits after the payment of an annual salary of $4,000 to the taxpayer. It was further agreed that the wife should continue to be a creditor and not a partner of the taxpayer but that her standing as a creditor should be subordinated to the rights of all general business creditors of the taxpayer.

Under this agreement the taxpayer's wife received $6,892.33 for 1943, $7,681.63 for 1944 and $10,346.32 for 1945. In computing their taxable net incomes for these years these amounts were reported as income by the wife and deducted by the taxpayer as interest paid. The Commissioner of Internal Revenue disallowed taxpayer's interest deductions of 25% of net profits, allowing deductions only in the amount of 5% of the principal sum of $8,500. The present action was instituted to recover the deficiencies assessed and paid by reason of the disallowance of these deductions.

At the trial, the district judge directed the jury to bring in a verdict for the taxpayer on the ground that there was no evidence of lack of a bona fide debtor creditor relationship between the taxpayer and his wife as a result of the agreement of January 4, 1943. The question whether or not the 25% share of net profits could legally be construed as a payment of interest was reserved and decided, as a matter of law, in favor of the taxpayer by the district judge. Alternatively, the district judge concluded that the taxpayer and his wife were joint adventurers and accordingly taxable on their respective shares in the profits of the business for the years involved. The defendant's motions for judgment n. o. v. and for a new trial were accordingly denied. D.C., 93 F. Supp. 935. This appeal followed.

The defendant contends that the district judge erred in not submitting to the jury the question whether a debtor-creditor relationship existed between the taxpayer and his wife and in concluding that the payments made by the taxpayer to his wife in 1943, 1944 and 1945 were deductible interest payments.

Section 23(b) of the Internal Revenue Code provides that in computing net income there shall be allowed as a deduction "All interest paid or accrued within the taxable year on indebtedness." The taxpayer contends that under the express terms of this section he is entitled to the whole of the deductions which he claimed. For, he says, he was indebted to his wife and the amounts he paid her were interest on that indebtedness. The defendant contends, on the other hand, that there was evidence from which the jury might have found that the 1943 agreement did not create a debtor-creditor relationship but was merely a scheme to reallocate family income and that therefore the taxpayer was not entitled to deduct as interest the amounts paid his wife during 1943, 1944 and 1945.

The defendant points to the following facts to which the taxpayer testified: The year 1942 had been fairly profitable for the taxpayer; the arrangement agreed upon would be advantageous to him in reporting his income; his wife desired a larger return on her money than 5%; he felt grateful to her because of the fact that in 1932, when his bank was pressing him for payment of his debt in the amount of $25,000, she had endorsed his note to provide additional security. The defendant urges that these circumstances surrounding the 1943 agreement show the arrangement to be a device to reallocate income among the family group and therefore raised an issue as to the bona fides of the agreement and whether a bona fide debtor-creditor relationship resulted from it. The defendant, however, does not deny that prior to January 4, 1943 the taxpayer was unconditionally indebted to his wife in the amount of $8,500. Nor does he contend that the controlling state law does not recognize inter-spouse indebtedness. The agreement of January 4, 1943 expressly provided that the wife should continue to be a creditor of the taxpayer. We think that the evidence would support no other finding than that the indebtedness which resulted from the wife's loaning of her own money to her husband in 1941 continued after the agreement of 1943.

We have not overlooked the principle that transactions between husband and wife calculated to reallocate family income or reduce family taxes are subject to careful scrutiny. But here, as we have pointed out, the wife had a personal stake of her own, the $8,500 of her own money which she had loaned the taxpayer, upon which she was entitled to a return. Indeed the defendant concedes this since the Commissioner allowed the deduction of interest at 5% for the years in question, a position clearly inconsistent with the denial of any debtor-creditor relationship.

We think that the district judge rightly held that the agreement of 1943 did not change that relationship. For that agreement concerned only the return which the wife was to receive on her loan. It did not change her status as a creditor. Nor did it affect her relationship as a creditor when she agreed to subordinate her claim to the claims of the general business creditors. *Commissioner of Internal Revenue v. O.P.P. Holding Corp.*, 2 Cir., 1935, 76 F.2d 11, 12. And even if the 1943 agreement had operated to change the wife's status from creditor to partner or joint adventurer the result, taxwise, would have been the same, as the district judge concluded.

11

For in that situation the wife would still have been taxable on her 25% share of the profits of the business. We accordingly conclude that the district judge rightly held that the evidence established the existence of a bona fide debtor-creditor relationship between the taxpayer and his wife during the years in question.

The other question to be determined is whether the taxpayer was entitled to deduct the payments made under the 1943 agreement "in lieu of interest" as interest payments under Section 23(b). The defendant contends that the payments of 25% of net profits, which amounted almost to the amount of the principal in 1943 and 1944 and in 1945 were greater than the actual indebtedness, could not be considered to be interest under that section. He claims that it was error for the district judge to determine as a matter of law that payments of a share in the net profits of the business made in lieu of interest were deductible as interest payments.

Interest on indebtedness has been defined to mean "compensation for the use or forbearance of money." *Deputy v. Du Pont*, 308 U.S. 488, 498 (1940). The word must be given the "usual, ordinary and everyday meaning of the term." *Old Colony R. Co. v. Commissioner*, 1932(a), 284 U.S. 552, (a). In the Old Colony case the Supreme Court said [284 U.S. at page 560]: "And as respects 'interest,' the usual import of the term is the amount which one has contracted to pay for the use of borrowed money. He who pays and he who receives payment of the stipulated amount conceives that the whole is interest."

The defendant contends that although Section 23(b) provides that "All interest paid" shall be deductible, yet when payments are made in lieu of interest at such high rates as are present in this case they are so unreasonable that they must be held not to be allowable interest deductions but rather a subterfuge to reallocate business profits. We are not, however, persuaded that a payment made "in lieu of interest" is not the equivalent of "interest." The phrase "in lieu of" means "instead of." Webster's New International Dictionary, 2d Ed., p. 1427. In *Kena, Inc., v. Commissioner*, 1941, 44 B.T.A. 217, 219-220, 221, the Board of Tax Appeals said:

> It is axiomatic that the language used to describe a thing does not determine its character. The contract of December 13, 1932, denominated the amount to be paid to the petitioner as "an additional sum in lieu of interest." The word "lieu" means "place or stead." It does not imply that the character of the payment was different from interest but indicates that the method of computation was not in accord with the usual method of computing interest, the percentage of profit being employed as a substitute. The contract itself must be examined to determine whether the sum so designated was actual interest or was something else. . . .

It is not essential that interest be computed at a stated rate, but only that a sum definitely ascertainable shall be paid for the use of borrowed money, pursuant to the agreement of the lender and borrower.

Generally speaking, payments made for the use of money "in lieu of interest" are deductible as interest under Section 23(b).

Throughout the ages lenders have exacted all they could from borrowers for the use of money. How much has been exacted has depended upon the desperation of the borrower and the exigency of the moment. There is no requirement in Section 23(b) that deductible interest be ordinary and necessary or even that it be reasonable. Hence the phrase "All interest paid" contained in that section must be taken in its plain and literal meaning to include whatever sums the taxpayer has actually had to pay for the use of money which he has borrowed. *Arthur R. Jones Syndicate v. Commissioner of Internal Revenue*, 7 Cir., 1927, 23 F. 2d 833. We conclude that the district judge did not err in holding that the payments made by the taxpayer to his wife in 1943, 1944 and 1945 were interest paid on indebtedness and deductible under Section 23(b) of the Internal Revenue Code.

The judgment of the district court will be affirmed.

NOTES

1. **Bifurcation of debt and equity**. In *Farley Realty Corp. v. Commissioner*, 279 F.2d 701 (2d Cir. 1960), the court held that what the taxpayer claimed was "contingent interest," payable out of the appreciation in value of a building the taxpayer financed, was not interest at all, but instead reflected an equity (ownership) interest in the building. The court stopped short of declaring the arrangement a partnership, but it did deny interest expense deductions with respect to the equity component. The case is commonly seen as the first major pruning back of *Dorzback v. Collison*.

2. **The IRS's position on shared appreciation mortgages**. *Farley Realty* is an early example of an effort to create a shared appreciation mortgage (SAM). Such mortgages became popular in the 1970s when interest rates and inflation were especially high and lenders sought to share in the increases in property values caused by high rates of inflation that made lending money a more difficult business than in more stable times. In Rev. Rul. 83-51, 1983-1 C.B. 48, the IRS stated that a borrower's obligation to pay the lender a portion of the increase in value of the taxpayer's principal residence constituted deductible interest under § 163. The ruling is limited to the underlying situation, namely a fixed date for payment of both the contingent interest and the principal amount, a method for calculating the interest specified in the mortgage contract, an intent to create a debtor-creditor relationship, and payment that is made in cash or with funds borrowed from a different lender. The ruling is limited to residential loans, leaving commercial lenders in the dark as to the IRS's position on this important matter.

3. **Other relationships**. There are numerous other arrangements that may produce a partnership for federal income tax purposes. For some nondefinitive definitions, *see* I.R.C. §§ 761(a), 6231. 6031(a), 7701(a)(2). It is difficult to generalize about the factors that will cause a court to characterize the arrangement one way or another, but one important factor to keep in mind is that there need not be a sharing of losses in order to classify a person as a member of a partnership. *See McDougal v. Commissioner,* 62 T.C. 720 (1974). One noteworthy case has suggested that even an attorney and his client can form a partnership for tax purposes. *See Allum v. C.I.R.*, 90 T.C.M. (CCH) 74 (T.C. 2005), *aff'd*, 231 F.Appx. 550 (9th Cir. 2007).

2. PUBLICLY TRADED PARTNERSHIPS

In the late 1980s a number of major partnerships began trading on national stock exchanges. This novel trend was motivated by two events. One was the declining attractiveness of operating in the corporate form; the other was a trend in favor of combining tax shelter partnerships into larger enterprises. Congress became mildly alarmed at the potential revenue loss, and responded by including in the Revenue Act of 1987 a new § 7704, which treats certain publicly traded partnerships as corporations. As the name implies, a publicly traded partnership is any partnership whose interests are traded on an established securities market or readily tradable on a secondary market (or its equivalent). § 7704(b). There is a major exception for partnerships at least 90% of whose income is from passive investment sources or from certain natural resource related activities, or from both combined. § 7704(c). The exceptions are best explained as lobbying triumphs.

The 1997 Act softened the rules for pre-existing publicly traded partnerships by enacting one of the few income taxes on gross income. Specifically, a publicly traded partnership in existence in 1997 could elect to be subject to a tax on gross income from the active conduct of a trade or business. If it elects, then the rule of present law treating a publicly traded partnership as a traditional corporation does not apply. The tax is 3.5% of the partnership's gross income from the active conduct of a trade or business. This could be a bargain for older publicly traded partnerships with high profit margins. § 7704(g).

PROBLEM 1-1

Which of the following arrangements constitute a partnership for federal income tax purposes?

1) Harry and Igor jointly own a warehouse, which they lease to the Acme Brick Company. They provide no services aside from paying the taxes and maintaining the warehouse. They share the revenues and expenses. *See* Reg. § 301.7701-1(a)(2).

2) Would the result differ if Harry and Igor drafted a contract to reflect this arrangement and declared in that document that it was a partnership agreement?

3) They also jointly own the H&I Hotel and share the profits and losses 50:50. The hotel has the usual guest services.

4) Same as 3) immediately above, but Igor shares in profits, but not in losses.

5) Allie recently lent the H&I hotel business $100,000 dollars for five years. Her return is based on 5% per year plus 10% of the hotel's net profits. Is Allie a partner?

6) Allie and her friend from architecture school days, Sally, occupy office space that they rent. Each has her own clients and each bills separately, but they share the cost of a secretary, furniture, equipment, supplies and mailing (which are all their costs). Are they partners in a business partnership?

7) Allie left architecture and became a sharecropper, using the owner's land to plant wheat and paying for the right to plant on the land with 10% harvests. Is this sharecropping arrangement a partnership for federal income tax purposes?

8) Allie could not stand sharecropping anymore. She left and became an associate at the Very Big Architecture Firm, which is a partnership for federal income tax purposes. It pays her a good salary plus a "bonus" equal to 10% of her billings every year. Is Allie a partner of Very Big Architecture Firm for federal income tax purposes?

9) Is a "Berhad," organized in Malaysia, a sole proprietorship, partnership, or corporation for federal income tax purposes? See Reg. § 301.7701-2(b)(8).

10) Bob, a U.S. citizen residing in Tulsa, signs an Oklahoma limited partnership agreement with the Berhad, known as Bob-Berhad Partners, Ltd. The partnership agreement is properly filed pursuant to Oklahoma law. Bob is the limited partner, and the Berhad is the general partner.

    a)   The partners elect to treat the entity as a corporation, filing a Form 8832 on time. *See* Reg. § 301.7701-3(a).

    b)   The partners make no election. *See* Reg. § 301.7701-3(b).

c) Instead, the Berhad and Bob contribute the same assets to a Delaware corporation. Can the corporation be electively rendered a partnership for federal income tax purposes? *See* Reg. § 301.7701-2(b).

11) a) Bob contributes his partnership interest in Bob-Berhad Partners, Ltd. to an irrevocable trust (not a grantor trust under §§ 671-679) formed pursuant to California law.

b) The trust will hold the limited partnership interest and will distribute the earnings of the limited partnership to Bob. *See* Reg. § 301.7701-2(a).

c) Same as "11)(a)", but the trust is empowered to and does conduct business. *See id.* and Reg. § 301.7701-4.

d) Same as "11)(b)," but the trust elects to be taxed as a corporation. *See* Reg. § 301.7701-3(b).

e) Same as "11)(a)", but the trust is revocable at will.

12) For many years Bob has run a cigar store as a sole proprietor. On the advice of his lawyer, he contributes the assets of the store to a limited liability company ("LLC"), which assures him he has no personal liability beyond what he contributes to the LLC. Can the LLC elect to be treated as:

a) A corporation? *See* Reg. §§ 301.7701-1(a)(4) and 301.7701-2(a).

b) A partnership? *See* Reg. § 301.7701-2(a).

c) Sole proprietorship? *Id.*

d) Assume that Bob transfers the assets to a Ruritanian LLC (a foreign limited liability company), which assures him limited liability. He makes no tax elections of any sort. *See* Reg. § 301.7701-3(b). He is the sole owner of the LLC.

e) Same as "(d)." Can the Ruritanain LLC elect to be taxed as a partnership or sole proprietorship? *See* Reg. § 301.7701-3(a).

13) Bob has capitalized brilliantly on the cigar craze and has recently admitted thousands of customers as partners. The partnership trades on the New York Stock Exchange. Is it a partnership or something else? How is it taxed? *See* § 7704 and Reg. § 301.7701-2(b)(7).

3. ELECTION AGAINST PARTNERSHIP STATUS
Read § 761(a) and Reg. § 1.761-2(a)-(b).

Section 761(a) and the Regulations thereunder allow a partnership that is teetering on the brink of being a mere collection of individuals to elect out of Subchapter K, hence eliminating partnership status for purposes of that part of the Code. The statute identifies three situations in which this can be done: (1) where the entity operates solely as an investment vehicle, (2) where it operates solely for the joint extraction or joint use of property, or (3) where securities dealers join forces to engage in a particular underwriting transaction.

The first and third cases are easy to understand. The second case is designed to assist passive co-owners of oil, gas or mineral properties who depend on an active operating company for their revenues. This avoids the need to file partnership tax returns and permits the co-owners to make specialized individual elections. For example, electing out of partnership status may allow a partner to make an otherwise impermissible like-kind exchange of partnership interests. The congressional quid pro quo is that in all cases it must be possible to calculate each member's individual tax liability without the need to compute "partnership taxable income." Conversely, it is possible for an enterprise that is a partnership for tax purposes to be a co-ownership arrangement for state law purposes. Such entities are known as "tax partnerships," as the next case illustrates.

MADISON GAS & ELECTRIC CO. v. COMMISSIONER
72 T.C. 521 (1979), *aff'd* 633 F.2d 512 (7th Cir. 1980)

SCOTT, JUDGE

[The taxpayer is a regulated public utility that entered into a cooperative effort to build a nuclear power plant and to share the plant's output among its three principals. There was no agreement to share profits, only to take a share of the electric output.]

The second issue in this case involves deductions claimed by petitioner as ordinary and necessary business expenses under section 162(a) for certain training costs and other expenses paid in connection with its interest in Plant 2, the nuclear power plant.

Petitioner takes the position that the amounts paid in connection with its interest in the nuclear power plant for which it claims a deduction meet all the requirements of section 162(a) for deductible ordinary and necessary business expenses and are not capital expenditures within the meaning of section 263. Petitioner argues that these expenses were incurred in carrying on its trade or business and were not "start-up costs of a new business." Petitioner's primary position is that its agreement of joint ownership of its nuclear plant with WPS and WPL does not create a partnership and that even if it does the expenses which it paid are ordinary and necessary business expenses of the partnership.

Respondent takes the position that although the expenses which petitioner seeks to deduct would be ordinary and necessary expenses in its production of electricity if the construction of the nuclear plant were solely for use in its own business, these expenses are not deductible since they were incurred as pre-operating expenses of a partnership formed through petitioner's agreement with WPS and WPL. . . .

Thus, the determination of whether expenses are related to an existing trade or 'business of the taxpayer is essential. Although the taxpayer may actively be engaged in a trade or business, the start-up costs or pre-operating expenses of another activity, not a part of such trade or business are not deductible under section 162(a) as they are not incurred in the carrying on of a trade or business.

It initially appears that all additional expenses involved in the present case were expended in the conduct of Petitioner's existing trade or business, the production of electricity.

16

Although the means of production in the case of the nuclear facility may be radically different from conventional methods, the end product, electricity, is the same.

However, closer analysis reveals that all additional expenses claimed are in fact incurred in the initial activity of the partnership formed through Petitioner's agreement with WPS and WPL.

Respondent argues that the fact that the partners have elected under section 761(a) of the Code and section 1.761-1(a) (2), Income Tax Regs., for the partnership to be excluded from the application of Subchapter K of the Code is an admission that petitioner's arrangement with WPS and WPL is a partnership. Respondent argues that irrespective of this election the agreement and relationship between petitioner, WPS and WPL creates a partnership within the meaning of section 7701(a)(2). Respondent contends that the expenses which petitioner claims to be deductible are start-up costs which must be capitalized and not [current] expenses, relying primarily on *Richmond Television Corp. v. United States, supra.*

The question on which the parties initially join issue is whether the arrangement between petitioner, WPS and WPL creates a partnership as defined in section 7701. While we agree with petitioner that the fact that the partners elected under section 761(a) not to be subject to the provisions of Subchapter K is not an admission that the arrangement is a partnership, the definition of partnership contained in sections 761(a) and 7701 (a) (2) are the same.[3] It is therefore necessary for us to decide whether the arrangement between petitioner, WPS and WPL is a partnership as defined by section 7701(a)(2).

While petitioner denies that filing an election out under section 761(a) is an admission that a partnership exists for tax purposes, it does not contend that because of this election under section 761(a) no partnership exists for the purposes of determining what constitutes deductible expenses under section 162.

The clear import of petitioner's brief is that if we conclude that its arrangement with WPS and WLP is a partnership as defined in section 7701, then the deductibility of the expenses here involved is dependent upon whether those expenses are deductible by the partnership. Respondent makes no argument with respect to the election-out of the partnership under section 761(a) but merely cites his Rev. Rul. 65-118, 1965-1 C.B. 30. Respondent does not cite or discuss *Bryant v. Commissioner*, 46 T.C. 848 (1966), aff'd. 399 F.2d 800 (5th Cir. 1968), although in that case we in effect approved Rev. Rul. 65-118, supra, specifically pointing to the definition of partnership in section 7701(a)(2) "when used in this title" and the fact that section 48(c)(2)(D) (involved in the *Bryant* case and the revenue ruling) contained a specific provision with respect to limitations in the case of a partnership. We have found no case dealing with an election-out under section 761(a) when the controlling statute outside of Subchapter K makes no reference to partnerships. In texts on partnerships we have found statements which indicate that an election-out in such a situation is not controlled by the *Bryant* decision and other indications in the same text that it is. . . .

It is petitioner's position that a profit motive of the partnership as an entity is a requirement of partnership status and that such a motive is lacking from the arrangement present

---

[3] Respondent in Rev. Rul 68-344, 1968-1 C.B. 569, concludes that a venture formed by four electrical power companies substantially similar to the arrangement here of petitioner, WPS and WPL is properly classified as a partnership for federal tax purposes. The ruling then proceeds to discuss the provision of section 761(a) and concludes that the members of the venture may elect under section 761(a) to have the venture excluded from the application of Subchapter K. The parties stipulated in this case that it was the intention of the co-tenants – petitioner, WPS and WPL – that they created only a co-tenancy and not a partnership and that they be taxed as co-tenants and not partners. This stipulation is followed by the stipulated statement: To that end WPS filed a federal partnership return, Form 1065, and an election out of the provision of Subchapter K of the [Code].

in this case. Petitioner argues that only a co-ownership and expense-sharing arrangement was created from its agreement with WPS and WPL.

Petitioner notes that section 1.761-1(a), Income Tax Regs., and section 301.7701-3(a), Proced. & Admin. Regs., provide that "a joint undertaking merely to share expense is not a partnership" and that mere co-ownership of property is not a partnership. Petitioner also points out that these regulations provide that "Tenants in common, however, may be partners if they actively carry on a trade, business, financial operation, or venture and divide the profits thereof." Petitioner relies, in support of its position of the necessity of a profit motive by the entity for partnership status, on *Cooperative Power Plant v. Commissioner*, 41 B. T. A. 1143 (1940), and *Co-operative Insurance v. Commissioner*, 41 B. T. A. 1151 (1940), in which arrangements somewhat similar to those in the instant case were held not to be associations taxable as corporations because gain was not an objective of the arrangement. In our view, these cases have no bearing on whether the arrangement here involved created a partnership under the definition of section 7701(a)(2).

In addition, petitioner cites Wisconsin State law to support his view that the arrangement in this case is not a partnership. It is clear, however, that state law is in no way controlling on the question of whether an unincorporated activity is a partnership for Federal tax purposes. *Luna v. Commissioner*, 42 T.C. 1067, 1077 (1964).

Petitioner argues that respondent's Rev. Rul. 68-344, 1968-1 C.B. 569, is erroneous in concluding that an arrangement similar to the one here is a partnership. The essence of petitioner's argument is that the construction and operation of the nuclear power plant in this case is equivalent to a joint undertaking to share expenses such as that described in the regulations and therefore does not constitute a partnership. Section 1.761-1(a) and section 301.7701-3(a), Income Tax Regs., declare that "if two or more persons jointly construct a ditch merely to drain surface water from their properties, they, are not partners." In our view, petitioner's arrangement with WPS and WPL is in no way comparable to the joint construction of a drainage ditch.

Prior to 1954, the following definition of a partnership for Federal tax purposes was found in section 3797(a)(2), I.R.C. 1939:

(2) Partnership and Partner. The term "partnership" includes a syndicate, group, pool, joint venture, or other unincorporated organization, through or by means of which any business, financial operation, or venture is carried on, and which is not, within the meaning of this title, a trust or estate or a corporation; and the term "partner" includes a member in such a syndicate, group, pool, joint venture, or organization. . . .[4]

As petitioner points out, it has long been recognized that mere co-ownership of property will not create a partnership. *Estate of Appleby v. Commissioner*, 41 B.T.A. 18 (1940). In that case co-owners of inherited property, at the suggestion of automotive dealers, erected a garage on the property and rented the space to defray the expenses of owning the inherited property, primarily real estate taxes. We held that the erection and renting of the garage was not a group, joint venture or other organization within the partnership definition of the 1939 Code. Whether co-ownership of property gives rise to a partnership for Federal tax purposes is determined by "the degree of business activities of the co-owners or their agents. . . ." *See Hahn v. Commissioner*, 22 T.C. 212 (1954), which held the requisite activities not to be present. The regulations set forth this test in slightly different words and it is the wording of the regulations as interpreted by petitioner, which it would have us follow in equating the construction of a drainage ditch with the construction and operation of a nuclear power plant. Section 1.761-1(a), Income Tax Regs., and section 301.7701-3(a), Proced. & Admin. Regs., as noted above, declare that "Tenants in common, however, may be partners if they actively carry on a trade, business, financial operation, or venture and divide the profits thereof." Petitioner, relying on this regulation, contends that a partnership must have a profit motive for the partnership entity and that, because petitioner received the electricity from the nuclear power plant in kind, such a profit motive did not exist in its arrangement with WPL and WPS. We do not agree.

First, the statute does not require a profit motive; rather it merely requires "an unincorporated organization, through or by means of which any business, financial operation, or venture is carried on . . . " The business activity or profit motive test is important in distinguishing partnerships from the mere co-ownership of property. However, this test is not the only test for what constitutes a partnership for Federal tax purposes. Second, the test of business activity or profit motive for purposes of finding a Federal tax partnership is clearly met in the situation at hand where a group of business organizations decide to band together to produce with economies of scale a common product to be distributed to the members of the venture in kind. In *Bentex Oil Corp. v. Commissioner,* 20 T.C. 565, 571 (1953), we found without any extended discussion that an organization formed to extract oil under an operating agreement which called for distribution of the oil in kind was a partnership for Federal tax purposes. The agreement in the *Bentex* case was analogous to the agreement in the instant case. That an agreement such as the one here under consideration creates a partnership is implicit in the holdings in *Cooperative Power Plant, supra, and Cooperative Insurance, supra* . . . Joint construction of a drainage ditch simply does not require the business activity or contain the profit motive found in the joint extraction of oil or the joint production of electricity by a nuclear power plant.

Following the *Cooperative* cases and the *Bentex* case, Congress reenacted the definition of partnership in the 1954 Code. In addition to carrying the definition forward in section 7701(a)(2) without change, Congress also placed the definition within Subchapter K, section

---

[4] The definition was first placed in the Code by sec. 1111(a)(3) of the Revenue Act of 1932. The purpose of this provision was to broaden the Federal partnership definitions to include therein a number of arrangements that under state law were not partnerships, such as joint ventures. *See* S. Rep. No. 665, 72nd Cong., 1st Sess. (1932), 1939-1 (Part 2) C.B. 496, 538. In the 1954 Code, this definition of partnership was unchanged and is contained in the following two sections: section 761(a) and section 7701(a)(2).

761(a), with the added caveat allowing certain organizations to elect to be excluded from the application of Subchapter K. Section 761 (a) reads as follows:

(a) Partnership. For purposes of this subtitle, the term "partnership" includes a syndicate, group, pool, joint venture, or other unincorporated organization through or by means of which any business, financial operation, or venture is carried on, and which is not, within the meaning of this title, a corporation or a trust or estate. Under regulations the Secretary may, at the election of all the members of an unincorporated organization, exclude such organization from the application of all or part of this Subchapter, if it is availed

(1) for investment purposes only and not for the active conduct of a business, or

(2) for the joint production, extraction, or use of property, but not for the purpose of selling services or property produced or extracted, if the income of the members of the organization may be adequately determined without the computation of partnership taxable income.

If distribution in kind of jointly produced property was enough to avoid partnership status, we do not see how such distribution could be used as a test for allowing an election to be excluded from the partnership provisions of Subchapter K. Although there is no discussion of the reason for the "election-out" provision of section 761(a) in the legislative history of the section, it has been generally considered that this provision was enacted as Congressional approval of the *Bentex* case coupled with a recognition of the hardships caused by that decision.[5]

In sum, we hold that petitioner's arrangement with WPS and WPL was an unincorporated organization carrying on a business, financial operation or venture. To the extent a profit motive may be required for an unincorporated organization to be a partnership for Federal tax purposes, we hold that it is present in this case with the in kind distribution of electricity produced by the nuclear power plant.

NOTES

1. **IRS position**. The IRS continues to believe that joint production for separate sale is the same as "joint profit." *See* Flower & Holbrook, *Partners and Co-owners: The Use of Undivided Interests in Equipment Leasing,* 41 Tax Law. 733 (1988). Naturally, this conclusion has no bearing on whether there is a partnership for state law purposes.

2. **The "tax partnership."** Note that the product of the *Madison Gas* case is a so-called tax partnership, an entity that is a co-ownership at state law, but a partnership for federal income tax purposes. These are common in the oil patch, where they are used in connection with joint oil and gas operating agreements. The advantages are: no need to negotiate a partnership agreement; a simple (often one page) agreement as to allocations; ability of each owner to encumber his or her own interest (as opposed to the difficult process of encumbering a partnership interest); and no participant with unlimited liability. If the

---

[5] Thus, Congress afforded such organizations an election to be excluded from the provisions of Subchapter K. Petitioner makes some interesting arguments as to the policy reasons for not penalizing it because economies of scale have forced it to combine forces with other utilities to enjoy the advantages of nuclear power. These arguments, however, are misplaced with respect to the question of the definition of a partnership. Instead, they should have been addressed with respect to the effect of the sec. 761(a) election to be excluded from the application of Subchapter K. . . .

partnership in *Madison Gas* had managed to elect out of Subchapter K, it would then have been a co-ownership for federal income tax purposes as well.

3. **Expense sharing.** What if the taxpayer's deal with the other two utilities had merely involved sharing expenses for maintaining a common facility? Clearly, there would be no partnership because there would be no sharing of revenues in cash or in kind. Reg. § 301.7701-3(a). What if they shared revenues from a commonly-owned rental property? Now it is getting more difficult. However, the same regulation tells us that there is still no partnership, but that if the co-owners provide significant services to the tenants in connection with renting the property, there is a partnership. *Id.*

4. **Failure to file by small partnerships.** Small partnerships often fail to file their federal income tax forms. Section 6698 of the Code imposes a $50 per partner penalty on failure to file a partnership return, but contains a built-in loophole in that it excuses the penalty if there is reasonable cause for nonfiling, and Rev. Proc. 84-35, 1984-1 C.B. 509 presumes the existence of reasonable cause if the miscreant is a domestic partnership with not over ten partners, all of whom are U.S. individuals (or their estates) who have adequately reported their shares of the partnership's profits or losses, and each partner reported a simple pro-rata share of each item of partnership income, deduction, and so forth. That probably wipes thousands of simple partnership returns off the tax rolls.

5. **Lack of coordination with Subchapter K.** The entity-aggregate distinction can be a serious problem when partnership tax issues overlap with non-partnership tax law questions. The explanation is fairly simple. Congress does not always consider the impact on the partnership rules when a new tax provision is added or an old one is tampered with. Indeed, it may take years for the lack of coordination between the partnership tax law and some other part of the tax law to show up. In general, it is usually best to apply the aggregate approach to partnerships outside of Subchapter K unless there are strong policy reasons not to do so.

6. **The lack of coordination between Subchapter K and the rest of the Code is chronic.** To take just a few simple examples, under § 453A there is an interest charge when a non-dealer sells property on the installment obligation for a price exceeding $150,000 if the seller also has total installment obligations outstanding at year end in excess of $5 million. § 453A(b)(1)-(2). The IRS asserts that the $5 million threshold is applied at the partner level. Notice 88-81, 1988-2 C.B. 397. By contrast under § 179(d)(8), annual expensing of $500,000 under § 179 is explicitly limited at both the partner and partnership levels. (Here, the IRS does not have to assert; it *knows.*) Thus, if a ten-person equal partnership had $40,000 of § 179 expenses, the partners would each report only $4,000.

4. RETROACTIVE AMENDMENTS OF PARTNERSHIP AGREEMENT

The partnership agreement generally controls the tax incidents associated with being a partner, but what if the agreement is amended? Can the amendment have retroactive force? Perhaps surprisingly, § 761(c) declares that the controlling agreement can be amended as late as the prescribed filing date for the entity's federal tax return (March 15 for a calendar year partnership), as long as the amendment is valid under local law. This means that the partners can wait up to the filing date to modify the agreement and, subject to some limits to be discussed later in this book, have the modifications stick for the year reported on the tax return. Reg. § 1.761-1(c). However, extensions of time granted to extend the filing date cannot extend the mandatory cut-off date for amending the partnership agreement.

D. IRS AUDITS

NEW PARTNERSHIP AUDIT PROCESS STARTING IN 2018 "THE CENTRALIZED PARTNERSHIP AUDIT REGIME"

Under new procedures promulgated in 2018, the Service audits the partnership's items of income, gain, loss, deduction, and credit, and the partners' distributive shares for a particular partnership year (the "reviewed year") and then forces the partnership to make partnership level adjustments in the year that the audit or any judicial review is completed (the "adjustment year").

The government assesses and collects any "imputed underpayment" at the partnership level. The partnership generally has nine months to submit information to the IRS in order to modify the imputed underpayment amount after the partnership receives a notice of proposed partnership adjustment.

An eligible partnership with 100 or fewer qualifying partners can elect out of the new regime. Qualifying partners cannot be trusts, other partnerships or other disregarded entities.

The partners can reduce the imputed underpayment by filing amended returns and paying their share of the tax; or, the partnership can elect to "push out" adjustments to its reviewed year partners, provided the partnership elects within 45 days after the date of the notice in which case the reviewed year partners pay their shares.

The partners can designate a partnership representative that does not have to be a partner, who can bind the partnership and partners. The partnership must designate the partnership representative for each tax year and make the designation on the partnership's return for that year. Only the partnership representative can raise defenses to penalties, additions to tax, or additional amounts.

When a Partnership Adjustment results in an Imputed Underpayment

When a partner's return requires adjustment, the partnership makes its calculations at the partnership level and pays the liability in the form of an imputed underpayment. Section 6225 does not provide for an offsetting allocation of taxable income to the partner. However, without adjustments to outside basis to reflect the partnership adjustments that caused the imputed underpayment, a partner might be taxed twice on the same income—once indirectly on the payment of the imputed underpayment and again upon a disposition of the partnership interest or a distribution of cash by the partnership. Proposed regulations provide for adjustment to a partner's basis in its interest, and certain other tax attributes that depend on basis, in order to prevent effective double taxation or other distortions.

Partnership Adjustments Not Resulting in Imputed Underpayment

Proposed Reg. §1.704-1(b)(4)(xiii) provides that allocations of items arising from partnership adjustments that do not result in an imputed underpayment cannot have substantial economic effect. Those allocations are deemed in accordance with the partners' interests in the partnership if allocated in the manner they have been allocated in the reviewed year. We will look at the concept of "substantial economic effect," a means of controlling opportunistic tax allocations in Chapter 5.

Circle of history

Before 1982, partnerships posed serious examination and collection problems because the Service conducted separate audits of each partner. Separate partner-by-partner examinations led to inconsistent treatment between partners, either because the audits produced different results or because some partners escaped audit completely. Further, each partner had a separate right to challenge each audit thus creating opportunities for further inconsistencies

The Tax Equity and Fiscal Responsibility Act of 1982 ("TEFRA") addressed inconsistencies between partners by allowing administrative adjustments to "partnership items" in a single partnership-level proceeding. Once the partnership-level proceeding was final, the Service adjusted each partner's individual return. Although partners were allowed to raise defenses to non-partnership items in separate, partner-level proceedings, they generally could not challenge partnership items determined in the partnership-level proceeding.

Since 1982, partnerships have increased in size and complexity making it difficult for the Service to audit large partnerships or even to locate partners. Congress enacted the new centralized partnership audit rules to address these shortcomings. The TEFRA rules are repealed prospectively. In the end, the audit system has come full circle in that small partnerships are not audited under the new audit system. Instead, the partners are audited one-by-one, as in pre-TEFRA days.

PROBLEM 1-2

Travis H. Harbaugh and his family own a productive oil and gas property operated by an unrelated oil company. The family elects out of partnership status under § 761(a) and Reg. § 1.761-2(b). The family members own the property as tenants-in-common, and they are legally free to dispose of their individual interests. Absent the election out, the Harbaugh family's arrangement is a partnership for federal income tax purposes. Travis is the 60% partner/owner, and each of his other family members has 10% of the oil-producing property.

1) Can each owner use his or her own tax year (*i.e.*, a calendar year) to report the profits or losses from the property regardless of the tax year used by the partnership (*i.e.*, suppose that the partnership uses a fiscal year)? *See* § 706(b)(1)(A).

2) Prior to the election out, does the Harbaugh family's arrangement constitute a "tax partnership"?

3) Can Travis engage in a tax-free exchange of his interest in the real estate under § 1031?

4) In Rev. Rul. 58-465, 1958-2 C.B. 376, the IRS ruled that an election out could not affect the limitation found in § 704(d). Is the ruling still viable?

5) Assume there is no election out and that in year 2 the family decides it wants to alter the partnership agreement. Assuming the partnership uses a calendar year tax year, must the amendment be made by March 15, the usual latest filing date for filing its partnership return, or can it be amended after that? *See* Reg. § 1.761-2(b).

Chapter 2

PARTNERSHIP FORMATION

A. CONTRIBUTIONS OF CAPITAL
Read §§ 721, 722, and 723.

The essence of a new business in partnership form involves two or more persons who pool some combination of their services, goods, real estate, or cash for a mutual business objective. Each will make some contribution to the enterprise, even if it is just a promise of future services. In exchange, each will receive an interest in the enterprise; the interest in a partnership itself is personal property for nontax purposes. *See* UPA § 26; RULPA § 701. In a partnership setting, the initial income tax issues are whether a partner's contribution of property will result in a taxable gain or a deductible loss to the contributor, the partnership, or the other partners, and whether the receipt of a partnership interest in exchange for a partner's contribution of services will produce taxable income to the service provider, the partnership, or the other partners. The final income tax issue is what basis will each side take in contributed property?

1. NONRECOGNITION OF GAIN

As a basic matter of tax policy, it is desirable to have a tax environment that does not impede business start-ups or changes in the form of doing business. Section 721(a) implements that policy with respect to partnerships by providing that no gain or loss is recognized by a partnership or its partners when a "contribution of property [is made] to the partnership in exchange for an interest in the partnership." This nonrecognition treatment is available for a partner's contributions to newly-formed partnerships and existing partnerships alike. As you will see later, § 351 performs much the same function with respect to corporations.

The grant of nonrecognition applies only to contributions of property, not services. Cash, tangible personal and real property, and intangibles such as patents, copyrights, and accounts receivable, have all been regarded as "property" at one time or another for purposes of § 721. The term "property" is not restricted to the category of "capital assets" as defined in § 1221. This discrepancy opens the door to conversions of ordinary income into capital gain via contributions of noncapital assets in exchange for a partnership interest, which itself is a capital asset. § 741.   As you read the following case, ask yourself what the court required in order to find "property" for purposes of § 721.

UNITED STATES v. STAFFORD
727 F.2d 1043 (11th Cir. 1984), *rev* g 552 F. Supp. 311 (M.D. Ga. 1982)

Before ANDERSON and CLARK, CIRCUIT JUDGES and DUMBAULD, DISTRICT JUDGE.

ANDERSON, CIRCUIT JUDGE:

Taxpayers Demean and Flora Stafford appeal the district court's summary judgment in favor of the government on their refund action for allegedly overpaid taxes. The refund action involves the Staffords' 1969 tax return, in which they did not account for their receipt of a limited partnership interest valued at $100,000. The taxpayers argue that the partnership share qualified for nonrecognition treatment under I.R.C. § 721(a) because it was received in "exchange" for "property" they contributed to the partnership. The district court held that nonrecognition was not available because the taxpayers' contribution of a letter of intent to the partnership did not meet the exchange and property requirements of the statute . . .

2. History of the Case

[Mr. Stafford, the taxpayer, was a real estate developer who obtained an unenforceable letter of intent from Life of Georgia (LOG) written to him, promising a favorable interest rate and lease terms in connection with a hotel project. Stafford and his associates thereafter formed a partnership of which Stafford was the sole general partner. He bought two partnership shares and received a third share for contributing the letter of intent to the partnership. He claims it was a contribution of property, protected from taxation by § 721.] . . .

* * *

4. Exchange and Property Requirements

1. The Exchange Requirement

B. *Generally*

The district court held that Stafford's contribution of the letter of intent to the limited partnership was not an "exchange" for purposes of § 721. The court defined exchange as "a mutual or reciprocal transfer of one thing for another" and suggested that each side to the transaction must have a choice as to whether or not they desire the transfer. . . . Because the transfer of the letter of intent to the partnership was part of the partnership agreement as drafted by the taxpayers' attorneys, the court found that the limited partners never had a choice as to whether or not the transfer would take place. . . .

The district court's opinion on this element lacks support in the language and principles of § 721. The regulations under § 721 specify that each partner "is entitled to be repaid his contributions of money or other property to the partnership (at the value placed upon such property by the partnership at the time of the contribution) whether made at the formation of the partnership or subsequent thereto." Treas. Reg. § 1.721-4(b)(1). That Stafford's contribution of the letter of intent was part of the partnership agreement at formation in no way undermines his argument that the contribution was part of an exchange with the partnership under § 721.

Furthermore, the purpose of § 721 is to facilitate the flow of property from individuals to partnerships that will use the property productively. . . . By analogy, § 351 of the Internal Revenue Code allows nonrecognition for individuals transferring property to corporations. Indeed, post-transfer control of the transferee corporation by the contributing shareholder is a prerequisite to tax-free treatment under § 351. We therefore reject the district court's assumption that individual members of the transferee limited partnership must agree to the transfer before an exchange can occur under § 721.

The district court opinion focused on the lack of agreement between Stafford and the limited partners. Viewed properly, the exchange that took place was between Stafford and the partnership, not the limited partners as individuals. . . The assignment of January 21, 1969, tends to establish that such an exchange occurred. Stafford contributed the letter of intent and other items; the partnership issued the third share to Stafford. Again, that this exchange occurred at the formation of the partnership and without a formal partnership vote does not alter our conclusion that an exchange took place.

[The discussion of whether Stafford owned the letter of intent is omitted. That issue was decided in Stafford's favor.]

2. The Property Requirement

The district court alternatively held that Stafford had not received his third partnership share as the result of a contribution of "property." The court correctly stated that "the key to the benefit of nonrecognition afforded by I.R.C. § 721(a) is that *property* must be exchanged for an interest in the partnership." 552 F. Supp. at 314 (emphasis in original). The district court then stated as its test for property under § 721:

"After having carefully considered the arguments of counsel in conjunction with the opinion of the court of appeals, it is the opinion of the court that both value and enforceability are necessary to a conclusion that a document is 'property' for purposes of § 721." ...

Finding as a matter of law that the letter of intent was not enforceable, the court concluded that it was not property and the taxpayers were not eligible for nonrecognition under § 721.

We agree with the district court's conclusion that the letter of intent was not enforceable. Under Georgia law, an agreement becomes enforceable when there is a meeting of the parties' minds "at the same time, upon the same subject matter, and in the same sense." *Cox Broadcasting v. National Collegiate Athletic Ass 'n, 250* Ga. 391, 297 S.E.2d 733, 737 (1982). In the present case, the July 2 letter of intent and Stafford's subsequent acceptance on August 30 did reflect an agreement on many essential terms; in particular, the parties were in agreement on the interest rate for the loan and the formula for calculating lease terms. However, the July 2, 1968, letter of intent acknowledged that: "there were many details to be worked out" and stated only that "we [LOG] would like to continue our negotiations along the following general lines." The July 3 letter from LOG may have converted the proposal to negotiate to a firm proposal of major terms, but Stafford's response again made the execution of final lease and loan agreements expressly "subject to further negotiations" on several items. "Where it is evident from a written instrument, that the parties contemplated that it was incomplete, and that a binding agreement would be made subsequently, there is no agreement."

The agreement in the present case unambiguously contemplated resolution of additional items before execution of the final contract. "An agreement to reach an agreement is a contradiction in terms and imposes no obligations on the parties thereto," *Well v. H. W. Lay Co.,* 78 Ga. App. 364, 50 S.E.2d 755, 758 (1949); as such, the agreement between Stafford and LOG embodied in the letter of intent and acceptance letter was unenforceable. . . Stafford's contention that the parties intended to carry through with the terms of agreement set forth in the letter of intent is unavailing. Where, as here, the parties' written documents clearly and definitely make final agreement subject to mutually satisfactory future negotiations, we must decide as a matter of Georgia law that "the parties did not intend the letter agreement to be a binding, enforceable contract." *Dumas v. First Federal Savings & Loan Ass'n,* 654 F.2d 359, 361 (5th Cir. 1981) (applying Georgia contract law).

Nevertheless, notwithstanding its lack of legal enforceability, we still must determine whether the letter of intent was "property" within the meaning of § 721. The previous panel opinion stated that "enforceability of any agreement evidenced by the letter of intent, while perhaps not dispositive of the question, is important and material." 611 F. 2d at 996 n. 6. We agree. An enforceable contract would perhaps be assured of property status; but the absence of enforceability does not necessarily preclude a finding that document, substantially committing the parties to the major terms of a development project, is property.

Several nonenforceable obligations may rise to the level of property for purposes of § 721 or § 351. Unpatented know-how, which results from services and is not enforceable, nevertheless can be deemed property. . . (Rev. Rul. 64-56,1964-1 (Part 1) C.B. 133 (the term property under § 351 includes unpatented secret processes and formulas); Rev. Rul. 71-564, 1972-2 C.B. 179 (transfer of exclusive right to use trade secret is property under § 351)).

The instant transfer of the letter of intent outlining the major terms of a proposed loan and lease agreement to which both parties felt morally bound is closely analogous to a transfer of goodwill, which although clearly unenforceable, nevertheless has been treated as property. *See* Taxation of Partnerships, *supra* note 10, P4.02[1], n.18:

> "If goodwill is associated with a going business that is transferred to a partnership, there should be no question about the applicability of § 721. Furthermore, even if goodwill is associated with an individual who will remain active in the transferred business. an effective contribution of goodwill may be made. Citing Rev. Rul. 70-45, 1970-1 C.B. 17 (for the proposition that a professional person realizes capital gain on partial sale of goodwill to newly admitted partner); *see also* Rev. Rul. 79-288, 1979-2 C.B. 139 (transfer of trade name and goodwill to newly formed foreign corporation is transfer of property for purposes of § 351); Rev. Rul. 70-45, 1970-1 C.B. 17 (goodwill of a one-man personal service business can be capital asset; whether it is an anticipatory assignment of income or a transfer of goodwill is a question of fact)."

Thus, we conclude that the district court's requirement of legal enforceability as an absolute prerequisite to finding property status under § 721 was improper.

For purposes of our discussion as to whether the instant letter of intent is "property," we will assume arguendo that the fact finder on remand determines that the letter had value. Under the appropriate legal standard and under the circumstances peculiar to this case, we conclude that the letter of intent encompassed a sufficient bundle of rights to constitute "property" within the meaning of § 721.

Although the Internal Revenue Code does not define property for purposes of § 721 or § 351, the courts have given the term rather broad application. *See E. L DuPont de Nemours & Co. v. United States,* 471 F. 2d 1211, 1218, 200 Ct. Cl. 391 (1973). In *Hempt Bros., Inc. v. United States, aff'd,* 490 F.2d 1172 (3d Cir.) . . . the court stated "that the term [property for purposes of § 351] encompasses whatever may be transferred."

The transfer of a taxpayer's full interest in a venture further supports a conclusion that the transferred item was property. *Cf* Rev. Rul. 64-56, 1964-1 C.B. 133, 137 (evaluating the transfer of technical know-how from a United States corporation to a newly organized foreign corporation and stating that "[t]he transfer of all substantial rights and property of the kind hereinbefore specified [technical know-how] will be treated as a transfer or property for purposes of § 351 of the code"). *See also 3* J. Mertens, *supra* P20.47 at 165. . . .

A conclusion that the letter of intent is "property" under the instant circumstances comports with the purpose of § 721. Stafford exerted personal efforts on his own behalf in negotiating with LOG. When LOG and Stafford exchanged the letter of intent and acceptance in 1968, the government had not suggested that Stafford recognized taxable income. He could have completed the project as a sole proprietor without recognition of income based on his receipt of the letter. The purpose of §§ 721 and 351 is to permit the taxpayer to change his individual business into partnership or corporate form; the Code is designed to prevent the mere change in form from precipitating taxation. In keeping with this purpose, we can discern no reason to exclude Stafford's transfer of the letter of intent from the protective characterization as "property."

Stafford through his business reputation and work efforts was able to negotiate a very promising development project with LOG. He obtained from LOG officials a written document, morally, if not legally, committing LOG to the major terms of a proposed loan and lease. The transferability of the letter is undisputed and Stafford transferred his full interest in the project

28

to the partnership. We conclude that the letter encompassed a sufficient bundle of rights and obligations to be deemed property for purposes of § 721.

For the foregoing reasons, we have concluded that Stafford's transfer of the letter of intent to the partnership met both the "exchange" and "property" requirements of § 721. However, the factual dispute identified by the previous panel remains unresolved on the record before us and, accordingly, we must remand.

5. The Quid Pro Quo for Stafford's Receipt of the Partnership Share

The previous panel remanded for the fact finder to determine: "what was the quid pro quo for Stafford's receipt of the twenty-first partnership interest?" . . . The panel was concerned that a jury might find that Stafford received the partnership share wholly or partially in exchange for the services he was to provide as general partner. *Id.* Thus, even though Stafford contributed the letter to the partnership, the panel was unable to conclude that Stafford's contribution of the letter was responsible for his receipt of the third partnership share. This dispute remains; from the record we cannot ascertain whether the partnership was compensating Stafford for services to be rendered or for contribution of the letter of intent, or partially for both.

* * *

On remand the fact finder could determine that Stafford received the partnership share wholly in exchange for the letter of intent he contributed to the partnership. If so, the nonrecognition principles of § 721 apply and Stafford is entitled to his refund. *See Ungar v. Commissioner,* 22 T.C.M. 766 (1963) (the taxpayer had negotiated contracts embodying the sale, financing and leasing of real property and he transferred those contracts to a newly formed corporation in exchange for stock; the court held that the stock received in exchange for the contracts qualified for nonrecognition treatment under § 351). To support such a finding in this case, the jury necessarily must conclude that the letter of intent was worth at least $100,000 to the partnership.

On the other hand, it might be determined on remand that Stafford received the partnership share wholly as compensation for services, in which case the government's tax assessment was proper. *See* Treas. Reg. § 1.721-1(b)(1) ("the value of an interest in such partnership capital so transferred to a partner as compensation for services constitutes income to the partner under § 61").

* * *

The district court's summary judgment in favor of the government is reversed and remanded for disposition not inconsistent with this opinion.

NOTES

1. **Sorting out the rulings.** The *Stafford* decision referred to a number of revenue rulings involving transfers of intangible assets to partnerships and corporations, but the judge did not describe the facts in detail. Here is a brief summary of some of those rulings. In Rev. Rul. 64-56, technical "know how" in the form of a secret process transferred to a new corporation along with a patent was treated as property, provided the secret process enjoyed "substantial legal protection against unauthorized disclosure." The ruling went on to permit taxpayers to treat services that are merely incidental to the transfer of property as "property." Rev. Rul. 71-564 treated the transfer of an exclusive right to use a trade secret for its legally protected life as a transfer of property, by analogy to the general rule for patent transfers. Finally, in Rev. Rul. 79-288 a corporation transferred its registered name to a new corporation, along with a document reciting that the new corporation would get all the goodwill associated with the name, in exchange for stock of the new corporation. The IRS

ruled that the name and goodwill were property for federal income tax purposes, provided the rights were legally protectible.

2. **Swap funds.** Taxable gain or loss will occur on the contribution of property to a partnership if § 721(b) applies. The purpose of that subsection is to prevent the nontaxable formation of what are commonly known as "swap funds," *i.e.*, partnerships formed by investors who pool their paper assets so as to stabilize and diversify the values of their investment portfolios. Section 721(b) seems to have stamped them out. The swap fund rules do not apply to such transactions as pooling direct investments in real estate.

2. BASIS EFFECTS
Read §§ 705, 722, and 723.

In order to ensure that nonrecognition treatment results in tax postponement rather than an exemption, § 722 declares that the contributing partner's basis in his or her partnership interest (generally known by its less awkward term "outside basis") will be the same as the basis of the property contributed by that partner. This leaves the partner facing an identical potential gain or loss on any later taxable disposition of the partnership interest. The amount of the partner's gain or loss from such a disposition will be the same, at least initially, as was inherent in the property he contributed to the partnership.

Likewise, § 723 makes the partnership's basis in the property which it receives (a.k.a. "inside basis") the same as the contributing partner's basis in that property. If the partnership promptly sold the property, it would recognize gain (or loss) in the same amounts as each of the contributing partners would have at the time of making their contributions of property to the partnership.

If and when the partnership recognizes this gain or loss, the outside basis of each of the respective contributing partners will be adjusted up or down, respectively, to prevent a double counting of the same gain or loss on any later sale of a partnership interest. Section 705 also states that a partner's basis in the partnership will rise with partnership profits (which are taxable to the partners), and fall with partnership losses (which are deductible) and distributions (returns of capital up to outside basis) from the partnership, among other factors. The symmetry between inside and outside basis is discussed in more detail in Chapter 3.

a. Impact of Section 704(c) on Contributed Property
Read § 704(c).

Consider the situation where one partner contributes appreciated property as to which there is a substantial gain waiting to be recognized, while another equal partner contributes cash or property with a basis equal to its value. Under these typical circumstances, even if the pre-tax value of each partner's contribution is the same, there will be a significant difference in the net after-tax values of their contributions.

The partners might want to strike a balance between the respective fractional interests and distributive shares they each receive in the partnership, so as to account for the net after-tax values of their contributions. If the appreciated property is unlikely to be sold in the foreseeable future, perhaps little if any account should be taken of the taxes that would be incurred on its sale. On the other hand, suppose a piece of highly appreciated contributed property were in fact promptly sold by the partnership. It is not hard to decide which of the partners ought to be taxed on the gain recognized in that sale.

Unless the Code provided some remedial mechanism, anyone with potentially taxable gains might transfer appreciated property to a partnership and thereby partly shift the tax burden to the other partners, some of whom might have losses they could use to eliminate such gains.

In order to block this ploy (or the converse), § 704(c) requires that the partnership allocate all pre-contribution gain (or loss) on each piece of property to the partner who actually contributed that property.

To illustrate: A and B are equal partners in the AB partnership. A contributes property with a basis of $60 and a fair market value of $100 at the time of contribution. B contributes $100 in cash. Assuming that A's contribution gets non-recognition treatment, A's basis of $60 in the contributed property under § 722 becomes A's "outside basis" in the partnership interest that A receives in exchange. The "inside basis" in the property received from A under § 723 is likewise $60 (carried over from A). Now assume that shortly thereafter the partnership sells this property for $100. The partnership recognizes $40 of gain – the same amount of gain that A previously faced as owner of the property. Note that when the partnership recognizes its $40 of gain, all of which is allocated to A thanks to § 705(a)(1)(A), A's "outside basis" in the partnership will be increased to $100. This immediate step-up in A's outside basis results from the mandatory *allocation (i.e.,* attribution) to A of all pre-contribution gain recognized by the partnership, a result required by assignment of income principles that are statutorily enforced by § 704(c). If, instead, the property A contributed were sold a few years later for $120, $50 of gain would be taxed to A and $10 to B.

Note that § 704(c) does not work in reverse. That is, when a new partner contributes cash to an ongoing partnership which already holds appreciated or depreciated property, § 704(c) does not address the case. Also, there are some technical details with respect to implementing § 704(c) that are omitted here.[1]

Section 704(a) contains a twist for contributions of property having a built-in loss. In order to prevent what Congress believed was a common tax scam in which partners would contribute loss property to a partnership and then sell the partnership interest, thereby allowing the new partner to claim the former partner's pre-contribution loss, § 704(c)(1)(C) treats the property as if its value were equal to its basis.

To illustrate: A contributes property with a basis of $20 and a value of $10 to the AB Partnership. A later sells her interest to C. The BC Partnership later sells the property for $10. No loss is allowed on the sale. This magic is performed by treating the property as having a basis equal to the value ($10) it had when A contributed it.

b. **Holding Periods**
   Read § 1223(1) and (2).

Partnership's. Consistent with the theory that "nothing happens" for federal income tax purposes when a partner contributes property to a partnership, the partnership will take over the holding period of the partner who contributed that property. § 1223(2).

Partner's. Each partner's interest in the partnership must also be assigned a holding period. A partner's holding period does not necessarily begin when the partnership is formed. Literally speaking, it is impossible for a partnership interest to exist before formation of the partnership, but it is logical for the partner's holding period to be derived from the holding period that the partner had in property which the partner contributed to the partnership in

---

[1] The essential problem is that if the partnership recognizes a gain or loss on contributed property that differs from the built-in gain or loss, the awkward "ceiling rule" in Reg. § 1.704-3(b)(1) imposes a technical roadblock that taxpayers can electively break with "curative allocations" and "remedial allocations."

exchange for a partnership interest. Although a partnership interest is considered to be a single capital asset,[2] the partner will only tack the holding period from capital assets and section 1231 "quasi-capital" assets contributed to the partnership. *See* § 1223(1). Thus, the holding period of a partner who contributed only cash or other noncapital assets will begin on the day the partnership interest was received in exchange for such property.

Suppose a given partner contributes several properties, some of them capital assets or § 1231 assets and others not, to the same partnership. Even if all were capital assets, the partner may have held each of them for a different period of time. How is the partner's holding period in that single partnership interest then determined? In all likelihood, the partner's interest in the partnership will have a fragmented holding period in proportion to the relative values of the properties he or she contributed. A. Willis, J. Pennell & P. Postlewaite, Partnership Taxation ¶ 3.08 (4th ed. 1993). The partner would tack the holding period from each capital or § 1231 asset, and start afresh with that portion of the partnership interest which is seen to be received in exchange for cash or noncapital assets. Fortunately, there is rarely a need to determine the holding periods of partnership interests, because they are rarely disposed of before actually having been held for the long-term capital gain or loss period.

3. IMPACT OF DEBT ON OUTSIDE BASIS
Read § 752.

Section 752 allocates partnership liabilities among the partners. If § 752 causes an increase in a partner's share of partnership liabilities, that increase is treated as a contribution of cash by the partner, thereby increasing her outside basis. For example, if a 50:50 partnership were to borrow $100 from a bank, each partner's outside basis would rise by $50. Conversely, if the partnership were to assume the partner's liabilities, or accept a contribution subject to a nonrecourse debt, the partner would be deemed to have received a distribution of cash, correspondingly reducing her outside basis. At the same time, § 752 would apportion part of the debt to the contributing partner, which correspondingly would increase her basis, but in an amount smaller than the initial hypothetical distribution. The balance of the liabilities would be apportioned to the other partners by deeming them to have contributed an equal amount of cash, thereby increasing their outside bases. The details of just how to apportion such debt among the partners is taken up later in this part.

PROBLEM 2-1

Which of the following is <u>not</u> "property" for purposes of § 721?

1)   Real estate?

2)   An option to buy stock?

3)   Unpatented know-how and secret processes?

4)   A trade name?

5)   A partner's promise to provide future services to a partnership after she is admitted to that partnership? *See* Reg. § 1.721-1(b)(1).

---

[2] *See* Rev. Rul. 84-52, 1984-1 C.B. 157.

6)   Publicly traded shares of stock of ten different software corporations, contributed by ten different investors, each of whom formerly held shares of just one of the ten corporations.

7)   Could investors in "(6)" contribute the shares tax-free under § 721? *See* Reg. § 1.351-1(a)(3).

4. CAPITAL ACCOUNTS

The term "capital account" crops up constantly in the partnership tax area, but it is not formally defined because it is an accounting concept, not a tax concept.[3] A capital account balance represents the partner's equity in the partnership, signaling how much money the partner should receive if he were to leave the partnership. The federal income tax forms demand that the partnership maintain a capital account for each partner. *See* Form 1065, Schedule K-1, line L, reproduced in the appendix to this book.

Each partner's capital account will generally consist of contributions which the partner made to the partnership in cash or kind (using fair market values at the time of contribution, minus associated liabilities, known as "book value") adjusted for the partner's share of profits and losses over the years, and reduced by distributions to the partner. Because the § 704(b) allocation rules use fair market values in fixing capital accounts under specialized safe haven rules, practitioners are getting used to the idea of value-oriented capital accounts. So structured, the capital account measures what the partner is entitled to receive under state law if the partnership liquidates.

PROBLEM 2-2

A and B form the equal AB partnership. A contributes cash of $50. B contributes land with a basis of $20 and a gross value of $60, but subject to a $10 nonrecourse debt.

1)   What is A's capital account?

2)   What is the "book value" of B's real estate?

3)   What is B's capital account?

4)   Assuming the property were sold for $70, still subject to the debt, how much of the gain on the sale must B report because of § 704(c)?

5)   (Same as "(4)"). How much gain must A report, given that he is a member of an equal partnership?

6)   What is the impact of the sale of the property on the partners' capital accounts?

5. SECTION 724: CLOSING LOOPHOLES

---

[3] The § 704(b) regulations, which are discussed later in these materials, contain a comprehensive methodology for establishing and maintaining capital accounts, but it is only part of a complex safe harbor system established for the limited purpose of validating (or not validating) special allocations of partnership income and loss among partners. *See* Reg. § 1.704-1(b)(2)(u).

Partnerships can potentially operate as tax laundromats, turning dirty assets (such as appreciated inventory) in the hands of a contributing partner into clean ones (such as capital assets) that the partnership can sell on favorable tax terms (*i.e.*, at lower capital gain rates). Read § 724(a)-(c) and you will get the flavor of how Congress solved the problem, including the way unrealized receivables (such as accounts receivable of a cash method grocery store) are forever damned. Section 735 parallels § 724 for distributed property, branding the inventory for five years and unrealized receivables forever. Chapter 8 considers § 735 in depth, so § 724 gets short shrift here. After you master § 735, § 724 will feel comfortable.

PROBLEM 2-3

A and B formed the equal AB Partnership in year 1. It is a general partnership. A contributed factory equipment for his partnership interest. A owned the equipment for over a year, and it qualified as § 1231 property. A's adjusted basis in the equipment, which he had owned and used in his business for many years, was $50. A's equipment was worth $150 at the time of the transfer, and was subject to a $50 recourse debt, which the AB partnership assumed. B contributed cash of $100.

1) What is A's capital account and basis in his partnership interest?

2) What is A's holding period in his partnership interest?

3) What is B's capital account and basis in her partnership interest?

4) What is B's holding period in the partnership interest?

5) What is the partnership's basis in the equipment?

6) What is the partnership's holding period for the equipment?

7) Assume instead that A contributes two items of equipment, one of which is worth $50 and has a basis of $10 and the other of which is worth $100 and has a basis of $5. A has held the first item five years and the second for eight months. What is A's holding period in his partnership interest at the time of contributing these assets?

8) Assuming the AB partnership later sells the equipment in "(7)" for $160 and its collective basis is still $15 (each property has increased in value by $5), how much of the $145 gain is taxed to A? To B?

9) If A is a general partner and B is a limited partner, how would they share the debt if the partnership made itself liable for the obligation?

10) Partner X contributes property with a basis of $50 and value of $20 to the ABX partnership, and next year sells his partnership interest to Z, an unrelated person, for $20. Can the partnership report a loss if it sells the property for $20? Can Z? Why or why not?

B. CONTRIBUTIONS OF SERVICES
Read Prop. Reg. § 1.707-2.

It is common for partners to receive partnership interests for past or future "services" performed for the partnership (remember the IRS arguments in *Stafford, supra)*. These transactions have to be carefully analyzed and monitored by the partnership's tax advisor to ensure that there are no surprises.

1. CAPITAL INTEREST RECEIVED FOR SERVICES

Every partner has two interests, one in the partnership's future "profits" and one in the partnership's "capital." An interest in profits is self-explanatory; an interest in capital refers to what the partner would receive if the partnership were liquidated and the partner received his share of the net assets of the enterprise. Reg. § 1.704-1(e)(1)(v). It also refers to the net proceeds of a liquidation of the partner's interest on withdrawal from the partnership. There is generally no difference between the net proceeds on withdrawal, as opposed to liquidation of the partnership. As you will soon see, the simpler tax case arises where the services are compensated for with an interest in partnership capital (with its concomitant share of future profits), as opposed to a mere interest in future profits.

a. Impact on the Service Partner

McDOUGAL v. COMMISSIONER
62 T.C. 720 (1974), acq. 1975-2 C.B. 2

FAY, JUDGE:

Findings of Fact

Certain facts have been stipulated by the parties and are found accordingly. The stipulation of facts and exhibits attached thereto are incorporated herein by this reference.

F. C. and Frankie McDougal are husband and wife, as are Gilbert and Jackie McClanahan. Each couple filed joint Federal income tax returns for the years 1968 and 1969 with the district director of internal revenue in Austin, Texas. Petitioners were all residents of Berino, New Mexico, when they filed their petitions with this Court. F. C. and Frankie McDougal maintained farms at Lamesa, Texas, where they were engaged in the business of breeding and racing horses. Gilbert McClanahan was a licensed public horse trainer who rendered his services to various horse owners for a standard fee. He had numbered the McDougals among his clientele since 1965.

On February 21, 1965, a horse of exceptional pedigree, Iron Card, had been foaled at the Anthony Ranch in Florida. Title to Iron Card was acquired in January of 1967 by one Frank Ratliff, Jr., who in turn transferred title to himself, M. H. Ratliff, and John V. Burnett (Burnett). The Ratliffs and Burnett entered Iron Card in several races as a two-year-old; and although the horse enjoyed some success in these contests, it soon became evident that he was suffering from a condition diagnosed by a veterinarian as a protein allergy.

When, due to a dispute among themselves, the Ratliffs and Burnett decided to sell Iron Card for whatever price he could attract, McClanahan (who had trained the horse for the Ratliffs and Burnett) advised the McDougals to make the purchase. He made this recommendation because, despite the veterinarian's prognosis to the contrary, McClanahan believed that by the use of home remedy Iron Card could be restored to full racing vigor. Furthermore, McClanahan felt that as Iron Card's allergy was not genetic and as his pedigree was impressive, he would be valuable in the future as a stud even if further attempts to race him proved unsuccessful.

The McDougals purchased Iron Card for $10,000 on January 1, 1968. At the time of the purchase McDougal promised that if McClanahan trained and attended to Iron Card, a half interest in the horse would be his once the McDougals had recovered the costs and expenses of acquisition. This promise was not made in lieu of payment of the standard trainer's fee; for from January 1, 1968, until the date of the transfer, McClanahan was paid $2,910 as compensation for services rendered as Iron Card's trainer.

McClanahan's home remedy proved so effective in relieving Iron Card of his allergy that the horse began to race with success, and his reputation consequently grew to such proportion that he attracted a succession of offers to purchase, one of which reached $60,000. The McDougals decided, however, to keep the horse and by October 4, 1968, had recovered out of their winnings the costs of acquiring him. It was therefore on that date that they transferred a half interest in the horse to McClanahan in accordance with the promise which McDougal had made to the trainer. A document entitled "Bill of Sale," wherein the transfer was described as a gift, was executed on the following day.

On November 1, 1968, petitioners had concluded a partnership agreement by parol to effectuate their design of racing the horse for as long as that proved feasible and of offering him out as a stud thereafter.

Though the partnership initially filed no return for its first brief taxable year ended December 31, 1968, petitioners did make the computations which such a return would show and reported the results in their individual returns. The partnership was considered to have earned $1,314, against which was deducted depreciation in the amount of $278. Other deductions left the partnership with taxable income for the year of $737, which was allocated to the extent of $405 to the McDougals and to the extent of $332 to the McClanahans.

On their joint return for the year 1968 the McDougals reported, inter alia, gross income of $22,891 from their Lamesa farms. Against this income they deducted $1,390 representing depreciation on Iron Card for the first 10 months of 1968 and $9,213 in training fees. The McDougals appear, however, to have initially claimed no deduction by reason of the transfer to McClanahan of the half interest in Iron Card.

We shall now turn our attention to those returns and amended returns filed in April of 1970. The McDougals explicitly claimed by way of amendment to have transferred the half interest in Iron Card to McClanahan as compensation for services rendered and thus to be entitled to a $30,000 business expense deduction, computed by reference to the last offer to purchase Iron Card received prior to October 4, 1968. Furthermore, the McDougals acknowledged that they had recognized a gain on the aforesaid transfer. By charging the entire depreciation deduction of $1,390 against the portion of their unadjusted cost basis allocable to the half interest in Iron Card which they retained, the McDougals computed this gain to be $25,000 and characterized it as a long-term capital gain under section 1231(a) of the Internal Revenue Code of 1954.

The McClanahans simultaneously increased their income arising out of the transfer from $5,000 to $30,000. They could thus claim to have a tax cost basis of $30,000 in their half interest in the horse. Finally, purporting to have transferred the horse to a partnership in concert on November 1, 1968, petitioners computed the partnership's basis in the horse to be $33,610 under section 723[4]. This increase in basis led the partnership to claim a depreciation deduction

---

[4] Having charged the entire amount of the depreciation which they had claimed ($1,390) against their unadjusted cost basis of $5,000 in the half interest in Iron Card which they retained, the McDougals considered themselves to have an adjusted basis of $3,610 in that retained half. The McClanahans claimed a $30,000 tax cost basis in the half interest which they had just received. Under sec. 723 the contribution of the two halves to a partnership would therefore result in the partnership's having a basis

of $934 for 1968 instead of $278 and to report only $81 of taxable income for that year. The McDougals thereupon reduced their distributive share of partnership income for 1968 from $405 to $40, while the McClanahans reduced their share from $332 to $41. For the year 1969 the partnership claimed a deduction for depreciation on Iron Card in the amount of $5,602, closing the year with a loss of $8,911. This loss was allocated in its entirety to the McDougals, pursuant to the partnership agreement.

Ultimate Findings of Fact

The transfer of October 4, 1968, gave rise to a joint venture to which the McDougals are deemed to have contributed Iron Card and in which they are deemed to have granted McClanahan an interest in the capital and profits thereof, equal to their own, as compensation for his having trained Iron Card.

Opinion

Respondent contends that the McDougals did not recognize a $25,000 gain on the transaction of October 4, 1968, and that they were not entitled to claim a $30,000 business expense deduction by reason thereof. He further contends that were Iron Card to be contributed to a partnership or joint venture under the circumstances obtaining in the instant case, its basis in Iron Card at the time of contribution would have been limited by McDougals' cost basis in the horse, as adjusted. Respondent justifies these contentions by arguing that the transfer of October 4, 1968 constituted a gift.

In the alternative, respondent has urged us to find that at some point in time no later than the transfer of October 4, 1968, McDougal and McClanahan entered into a partnership or joint venture to which the McDougals contributed Iron Card and McClanahan contributed services. Respondent contends that such a finding would require our holding that the McDougals did not recognize a gain on the transfer of October 4, 1968, by reason of section 721, and that under section 723, the joint venture's basis in Iron Card at the time of the contribution was equal to the McDougals' adjusted basis in the horse as of that time.

A joint venture is deemed to arise when two or more persons agree, expressly or impliedly, to enter actively upon a specific business enterprise, the purpose of which is the pursuit of profit; the ownership of whose productive assets and of the profits generated by them is shared; the parties to which all bear the burden of any loss; and the management of which is not confined to a single participant.

While in the case at bar the risk of loss was to be borne by the McDougals alone, all the other elements of a joint venture were present once the transfer of October 4, 1968, had been effected. Accordingly, we hold that the aforesaid transfer constituted the formation of a joint venture to which the McDougals contributed capital in the form of the horse, Iron Card, and in which they granted McClanahan an interest equal to their own in capital and profits as compensation for his having trained Iron Card. We further hold that the agreement formally entered into on November 1, 1968, and reduced to writing in April of 1970, constituted a continuation of the original joint venture under section 708(b)(2)(A). Furthermore, that McClanahan continued to receive a fee for serving as Iron Card's trainer after October 4, 1968, in no way militates against the soundness of this holding. *See* section 707(c) and section 1.707-1(c), example 1, Income Tax Regs. However, this holding does not result in the tax consequences which respondent has contended would follow from it. *See* section 1.721-1(b)(1), Income Tax Regs.

---

of $33,610 in Iron Card.

When on the formation of a joint venture a party contributing appreciated assets satisfies an obligation by granting his obligee a capital interest in the venture, he is deemed first to have transferred to the obligee an undivided interest in the assets contributed, equal in value to the amount of the obligation so satisfied. He and the obligee are deemed thereafter and in concert to have contributed those assets to the joint venture.

The contributing obligor will recognize gain on the transaction to the extent that the value of the undivided interest which he is deemed to have transferred exceeds his basis therein. The obligee is considered to have realized an amount equal to the fair market value of the interest which he receives in the venture and will recognize income depending upon the character of the obligation satisfied. The joint venture's basis in the assets will be determined under section 723 in accordance with the foregoing assumptions. Accordingly, we hold that the transaction under consideration constituted an exchange in which the McDougals realized $30,000.

In determining the basis offset to which the McDougals are entitled with respect to the transfer of October 4, 1968, we note the following: that the McDougals had an unadjusted cost basis in Iron Card of $10,000; that they had claimed $1,390 in depreciation on the entire horse for the period January 1 to October 31, 1968; and that after an agreement of partnership was concluded on November 1, 1968, depreciation on Iron Card was deducted by the partnership exclusively.

Section 704(c) allows partners and joint venturers some freedom in determining who is to claim the deductions for depreciation on contributed property. As is permissible under the statute, petitioners clearly intended the depreciation to be claimed by the common enterprise once it had come into existence, an event which they considered to have occurred on November 1, 1968. Consistent with their intent and with our own holding that a joint venture arose on October 4, 1968, we now further hold that the McDougals were entitled to claim depreciation on Iron Card only until the transfer of October 4, 1968. Thereafter depreciation on Iron Card ought to have been deducted by the joint venture in the computation of its taxable income.

In determining their adjusted basis in the portion of Iron Card on whose disposition they are required to recognize gain, the McDougals charged all the depreciation which they had taken on the horse against their basis in the half in which they retained an interest. This procedure was improper. As in accordance with section 1.167(g)-1, Income Tax Regs., we have allowed the McDougals a depreciation deduction with respect to Iron Card for the period January Ito October 4, 1968, computed on their entire cost basis in the horse of $10,000; so also do we require that the said deduction be charged against that entire cost basis under section 1016(a)(2)(A). . . .

The joint venture's basis in Iron Card as of October 4, 1968, must be determined under section 723 in accordance with the principles of law set forth earlier in this opinion. In the half interest in the horse which it is deemed to have received from the McDougals, the joint venture had a basis equal to one half of the McDougals' adjusted cost basis in Iron Card as of October 4, 1968, i.e., the excess of $5,000 over one half of the depreciation which the McDougals were entitled to claim on Iron Card for the period January 1 to October 4, 1968. In the half interest which the venture is considered to have received from McClanahan, it can claim to have had a basis equal to the amount which McClanahan is considered to have realized on the transaction, $30,000. The joint venture's deductions for depreciation on Iron Card for the years 1968 and 1969 are to be determined on the basis computed in the above-described manner.

When an interest in a joint venture is transferred as compensation for services rendered, any deduction which may be authorized under section 162(a)(1) by reason of that transfer is properly claimed by the party to whose benefit the services accrued, be that party the venture itself or one or more venturers, section 1.721-1(b)(2), Income Tax Regs. Prior to McClanahan's receipt of his interest, a joint venture did not exist under the facts of the case at bar; the McDougals were the sole owners of Iron Card and recipients of his earnings. Therefore, they alone could have benefited from the services rendered by McClanahan prior to October 4, 1968, for which he was compensated by the transaction of that date. Accordingly, we hold that the McDougals are entitled to a business expense deduction of $30,000, that amount being the value of the interest which McClanahan received.

b. Impact on the Partnership

In *McDougal,* the transfer preceded the formation of the partnership. The case does not precisely address the more common situation in which a newcomer to the partnership exchanges services for a partnership interest.

The exchange of services for a capital interest in an existing partnership is reconstructed as the partnership using partnership assets in order to make a guaranteed payment. Reg. § 1.721-1(b)(2)(i). That implies gains or losses on the deemed sales of such partnership assets and potential section 162 or 212 deductions for the partners whose capital interests were diminished by the payment. Section 706(d)(1) and (2) imply that only the capital-providing partners will share the deductions, but prudence dictates embodying the understanding in the partnership agreement. This understanding may constitute a so-called special allocation, a matter taken up later in this part. Note that the expense might require capitalization under § 263. For example, if the payment to the service partner were for overseeing the construction of a building, the payment is capitalized into the partnership's basis in the property. *See* Reg. § 1.721-1(b). *See also Stevens v. Commissioner*, 46 T.C. 492 (1966), *aff'd per cur.*, 388 F.2d 298 (6th Cir. 1968) (expenses of training racehorse constituted part of acquisition cost of horse, adding to cost basis). Finally, observe that § 83(h) insists that the partnership cannot claim a deduction unless and until the service partner reports income from the receipt of the partnership interest. *See generally* W. McKee, W. Nelson, & R. Whitmore, Federal Taxation of Partnerships and Partners 5.03[2] (1978).

PROBLEM 2-4

1) X and Y recently formed the equal XY investment partnership. X contributed $100 in cash. Y, a cash method dentist, contributed the following items: (1) accounts receivable with a face amount and value of $40, but a basis of $0; (2) inventory of drills with a basis and value of $60. After how many years may these properties become capital assets in the partnership's hands?

2) Assume instead of contributing cash, X, already a partner with a trivial interest in income and profits (so small you can disregard it for calculation purposes), did $50 worth of services for the partnership for which she received a 50% share in the partnership's assets. The services were of a current (as opposed to capital) nature. How much income would X report, and what would be her basis in her partnership interest?

3) How much income or loss must Y report with respect to the property aspect of the transfer of a capital interest to X?

4) What would be the tax impact to Y of the transaction with respect to Y's right to claim a tax deduction with respect to the transfer? Use the reasoning of the *McDougal* case.

5) How would the result differ from "(4)" if the services that X provided were of a capital nature, such as for building a permanent structure?

2. RECEIPT OF A PROFITS INTEREST FOR SERVICES

The treatment of partners who contribute a promise of "services" for an interest in "profits" is trickier than the transfer of a "capital" interest for "services." This is an area dominated by case law. The primary issue is whether the partner has income at the time of receiving the profit share, or whether there is income only if and when the partnership makes money.

The seminal decision in the area is *Diamond v. Commissioner,* 492 F.2d 286 (7th Cir. 1974), *aff'g* 56 T.C. 530 (1971). The facts involved an individual, Sol Diamond, who agreed to obtain major financing for a real estate partnership in exchange for a 60% profit and loss share if he arranged the financing. He did. Thereafter, one Liederman agreed to buy Diamond's interest for $40,000 and to become a 50:50 partner. Within two months of receiving his partnership interest, Diamond sold out to Liederman for $40,000. The courts held Diamond to have received compensation for services in the amount of $40,000 (the value of the partnership interest) when the lender provided the financing. The exact limits of the *Diamond* decision were unclear, but the courts seemed impressed by the facts that (1) Diamond's profit share was for services rendered prior to admission as a partner, and (2) the interest was capable of valuation because it was sold in the same year it was received. The courts acknowledged that the *Diamond* result could cause double taxation – once when the profits interest is received and again when profits are earned – but suggested that the right solution was to allow the partner to amortize the value of the profits interest to reverse the double counting.

In G.C.M. 36346 (July 23, 1975) the IRS suggested that the *Diamond* case should be repudiated in favor of a more general rule that the receipt of an interest in future profits does not constitute immediate income to the recipient. The following excerpt is the linchpin to the proposal:

"As you may be aware this Office has been considering the proper treatment of the receipt of a profits interest in a partnership as compensation for services. This consideration stems from the decision in *Sol Diamond,* 56 T.C. 530 (1971), *aff'd,* 492 F.2d 286 (7th Cir. 1974), holding that the fair market value of an interest in partnership profits received as compensation for services is taxable under Int. Rev. Code of 1954, § 6l(a)(1). . . . This decision has been widely criticized as being contrary to Treas. Reg. § 1.721-1, as creating severe valuation problems and as resulting in double taxation to the recipient partner. . . . This approach was found unacceptable because it seemed to place a premium on whether the partnership is formed before or after the services are rendered. . . .

Arguably the only rationale for not taxing a profits interest received as compensation is that Treas. Reg. § 1.721-1(b) was apparently designed to reach such a result. *See A.* Willis, supra at § 11.01. It is difficult to quarrel with the Tax Court's finding that such an interest is property under Treas. Reg. § 1.61-2(d)(I). When a profits interest is defined to preclude any interest in partnership assets, as is done in the proposed revenue ruling, such an interest becomes analogous to an unfunded, unsecured promise to pay deferred compensation. Such a promise is not taxable upon receipt and, in fact, is not considered to be property. *See* Treas. Reg. § 1.83-3(e). An analogy of a partnership profits interest to an unfunded, unsecured promise to pay deferred compensation is imperfect, however, because amounts received pursuant to or upon assignment of such a promise are taxable as compensation where as the character of partnership profits or the character of the gain on a sale of a profits interest is determined under Code § 702(b) and Code § 741.

It must be emphasized that in holding that the receipt of a "profits" interest is not taxable, the proposed revenue ruling is limited to interests that give the holder no rights to existing partnership assets upon the liquidation of his interest. Correspondingly, a "capital" interest, which is taxable, includes an interest in earned but unrealized gains. This broad definition of a capital interest is simply an extension of the rule ... that property received as compensation is taxed at its fair market value. . . ."

The timing of income recognition is unfortunately convoluted because of § 83, which despite its sweeping scope, never explicitly comes to grips with partnership interests. Be that as it may, § 83 generally applies by its terms. In the interest of avoiding a treatise on the subject, the topic has been highly condensed in the following paragraphs.

Section 83 applies to transfers of property in connection with the performance of services as an employee or independent contractor. If a taxpayer receives an unrestricted right to property – and a partnership interest is generally a form of property – the value of the property is taxable when received. (This is the *Diamond* rule.) However, if the interest is appropriately restricted, taxation is deferred until the interest is transferable or is not subject to a substantial risk of forfeiture. Read § 83(a) through (c) and Reg. §§ 1.83-3(c), 1.83-6(b).

A partial solution to the problem of being taxed on a partnership interest is to elect under § 83(b) to include the value of a restricted interest in income when it is received. "Restricted" means it is both nontransferable and subject to a substantial risk of forfeiture. The advantage of the § 83(b) election is that if the interest has only a small value when it is received but will likely have a much greater value when the restrictions lapse, the difference is subject to preferential long-term capital gains treatment that is not taxed until the taxpayer disposes of the property. The disadvantages of the §83 election are that the value of the interest is taxed at once as ordinary income and that if the taxpayer forfeits the interest, there is no deduction beyond what she paid for the interest. § 83(b)(1).

One decision baldly accepted a profits interest as property for purposes of § 83, but found it to have no value, theorizing that a liquidation of the partnership would have yielded the taxpayer nothing. *St. John v. United States,* 84-1 USTC ¶ 9158 (C.D. Ill. 1984). Perhaps the court was confused by the difference between state law, which does recognize the interest as "property," and § 1.83-3(a), which treats "an unfunded and unsecured promise to pay money in the future" as not property.

Some commentators think that § 83 should simply be banished from Subchapter K, on the theory that Congress never intended § 83 to reach partnership situations. A. Willis, J. Pennell, &, P. Postlewaite, Partnership Taxation §§ 45.04 and 46.09. Be that as it may, Prop. Reg. § 1.721-1(b)(1) makes specific reference to the potential applicability of § 83.

CAMPBELL v. COMMISSIONER
943 F.2d 815 (8th Cir. 1991)

BEAM, CIRCUIT JUDGE.

[Mr. Campbell received a profits only interest in partnerships that he helped promote in exchange for services that he rendered to a different partnership, Summa T. Realty, that was in the business of forming and syndicating tax shelter limited partnerships. The interests in the tax shelter partnerships were readily marketable, and were valued by Campbell in part on the basis of the tax benefits they offered, and in part on the basis of the eventual value of the real estate they held. The Tax Court ruled Campbell taxable, which set off a firestorm of controversy in the tax bar. Many felt the case could be reconciled as one in which the partner received an interest in another partnership. The petitioner sought the advice of two tax lawyers before taking the interests; both assured him there would be no tax.]

41

Campbell argues on appeal, as he did unsuccessfully in the Tax Court, that a service partner (i.e., a partner who receives his partnership interest in exchange for services provided to the partnership) who receives a profits interest (i.e., a right to share in profits and losses only, as opposed to an interest in the capital assets of a partnership) in a partnership does not realize income upon receipt of that interest, and, therefore, no taxable event occurs. In the alternative, he argues that the interests he received had no value at the time he received them and, thus, he should not have been taxed.

At this point, the Commissioner concedes that the Tax Court erred in holding that the receipt of a profits interest in exchange for services to the partnership should be considered ordinary income to the service provider. . . . However, for the first time, the Commissioner now asserts that Campbell actually received the partnership interests in exchange for services he provided to his employer, rather than services he provided to the partnerships. According to the Commissioner, the Tax Court held that Campbell received the interests as compensation from his employer. Thus, he is not a service partner; the principles of partnership taxation do not apply; and Campbell's receipt of compensation from his employer was taxable upon receipt.

A. Employee or Partner

We make short work of the Commissioner's alternate argument. . . . The Commissioner's argument, at best, requires that we resolve a disputed question of fact. Contrary to the Commissioner's belief, the Tax Court did not hold that Campbell received his partnership interests for services he performed for his employer rather than services performed for the partnerships. . . . In any event, we decline to address this factual matter and we disregard the argument.

B. Taxing Profits Interests

Although the Commissioner concedes the Tax Court's error in taxing a service partner's profits interest, the Tax Court's holding is not without support. In fact, the only circuit court to address the issue arrived at the same conclusion. *See Diamond,* 492 F.2d 286. . . . Thus, we are reluctant to accept the Commissioner's concession without substantive review.

The Tax Court's holding was based principally on *Diamond,* and that case is analogous. However, to fully understand the concerns raised, we must review several prior cases and the underlying statutory provisions. When a service partner receives an interest in partnership capital, the cases clearly hold that a taxable event has occurred. The receipt of the capital interest must be included in the service partner's income. *See, e.g., United States v. Frazell,* 335 F.2d 487, 489 (5th Cir. 1964). . . . As an interest in intangible personal property, the receipt of a capital interest appears to be taxable under the authority of section 83 of the Internal Revenue Code. . . .

As noted, however, when the service partner receives solely a profits interest, the tax consequences are unclear. In contrast to *Diamond,* the Tax Court has held, and the Commissioner has conceded in some cases, that receipt of a profits interest by a service partner creates no tax liability. *See National Oil Co. v. Commissioner,* 52 T.C.M. (CCH) 1223, 1228 (1986) (Commissioner conceded that if taxpayer received only profits interest, no taxable event had occurred); *Kenroy, Inc. v. Commissioner,* 47 T.C.M. (CCH) 1749, 1756-59 (1984) (profits interest had no fair market value, thus no tax liability upon receipt); *Hale v. Commissioner,* 24 T.C.M. (CCH) 1497, 1502 (1965) ("Under the regulations, the mere receipt of a partnership interest in future profits does not create any tax liability. Sec. 1.721-1(b), Income Tax Regs.").

The code does not expressly exempt from taxation a service partner's receipt of a profits interest, and the courts that have held that it is not taxed upon receipt do not appear to have closely analyzed the issue. However, commentators have developed three interrelated theories in support of the proposition that it is not a taxable event: 1) based upon regulation 1.721-1(b), a profits interest is not property for purposes of sections 61 and 83; 2) a profits interest may have no fair market value; and 3) the nonrealization concepts governing transactions between partner and partnership preclude taxation. . . .

The Tax Court and the Seventh Circuit rejected at least the first two of these theories in *Diamond*. . . .

The commentators generally agree that the nonrecognition principles of section 721 do not apply to a service partner because a service partner does not contribute property in exchange for his partnership interest. . . . We also agree. However, the section 721 regulations are relied upon to tax a service partner's receipt of a capital interest. And, as with a profits interest, a service partner who receives a capital interest has not contributed property in exchange for his partnership interest. Thus, the section 721 regulations provide some guidance when reviewing whether general principles of partnership taxation provide for nonrealization in this case.

Section 721 codified the rule that a partner who contributes property to a partnership recognizes no income. . . And, regulation 1.721-1(b)(1) simply clarified that the nonrecognition principles no longer apply when the right to return of that capital asset is given up by transferring it to another partner. At that time, the property has been disposed of and gain or loss, if realized, must be recognized. As a corollary, section 1.721-1(b)(1) outlines the tax treatment of the partner who receives that capital interest. A substantial distinction, however, exists between a service partner who receives a capital interest and one who receives a profits interest. When one receives a capital interest in exchange for services performed, a shift in capital occurs between the service provider and the individual partners. . . The same is not true when a service partner receives a profits interest. In the latter situation, prior contributions of capital are not transferred from existing partners' capital accounts to the service provider's capital account. Receipt of a profits interest does not create the same concerns because no transfer of capital assets is involved. That is, the receipt of a profits interest never affects the non-recognition principles of section 721. Thus, some justification exists for treating service partners who receive profits interests differently than those who receive capital interests.

Probably more relevant to our analysis, however, is section 707 of the Internal Revenue Code, which supports Campbell's argument. . . . Generally, a partner receives a distributive share of income instead of compensation from his partnership. *See Pratt v. Commissioner,* 550 F.2d 1023, 1026 (5th Cir. 1977) (salary payments to a partner treated as a distributive share of income); . . . Except under certain circumstances, "the general statutory policy for treating partnerships for tax purposes contemplated that the income of a partnership would flow through to the individual partners." *Pratt,* 550 F.2d at 1026. Only when the transaction is treated as one between the partnership and a partner acting in a nonpartner capacity is the payment received by the partner not considered a distributive share. . . .

Section 707 provides that when a partner engages in a transaction with a partnership in a nonpartner capacity that transaction will be treated as between the partnership and one who is not a partner. I.R.C. § 707(a). When a partner receives payment for services performed for the partnership, that transaction falls under section 707(a)(1) if "the performance of such services . . . and the allocation and distribution, when viewed together, are properly characterized as a transaction occurring between the partnership and a partner acting other than in his capacity as a member of the partnership." *Id.* § 707(a)(2)(A)(iii). This exception was enacted to prevent partnerships from using direct allocations of income to individuals, disguised as service partners, to avoid the requirement that certain expenses be capitalized. . . . Arguably, section 707(a) would be unnecessary if compensatory transfers of profits interests were taxable upon receipt because, if so, every such transfer would be taxed without this section. . . .

In *Diamond,* where the service provider became a partner solely to avoid receiving ordinary income, we have no doubt that the receipt of the profits interest was for services provided other than in a partner capacity. That is, Diamond was likely to (and in fact did) receive

43

money equal to the value of his services and apparently did not intend to function as or remain a partner. Thus, the receipt of his partnership profits interest was properly taxable as easily calculable compensation for services performed. Campbell's case, however, is not so clear. Campbell's interests were not transferable and were not likely to provide immediate returns. Thus, we doubt that the Tax Court correctly held that Campbell's profits interests were taxable upon receipt.

More troubling, however, is Campbell's argument that the profits interests he received had only speculative, if any, value. We fully agree with this contention and we reverse the Tax Court. As noted by the Tax Court, "fair market value is 'the price at which property would change hands in a transaction between a willing buyer and a willing seller, neither being under compulsion to buy nor to sell and both being informed' of all the relevant circumstances. . . ."

The Tax Court relied too heavily on the fact that Class A limited partners were willing to pay substantial sums for their interests at the same time Campbell received his interest. Because of the difference in the nature of the investments, we believe that this fact is not relevant. The Class A limited partners had superior rights to cash distributions and return of capital, as well as some rights of participation. Further, the court should not have disregarded the expert's belief that the tax benefits were speculative in nature. The partnerships were taking untested positions in regard to deductions and all of them were likely to be challenged and disallowed by the IRS. In fact, many of the deductions were ultimately disallowed. Further, the predictions contained in the offering memoranda were just that – predictions. The partnerships had no track record. Any predictions as to the ultimate success of the operations were speculative. Thus, we hold that Campbell's profits interests in Phillips House, The Grand and Airport were without fair market value at the time he received them and should not have been included in his income for the years in issue.

REV. PROC. 93-27
1993-24 I.R.B. 63

SEC. 3. BACKGROUND

Under section 1.721-1(b)(1) of the Income Tax Regulations, the receipt of a partnership capital interest for services provided to or for the benefit of the partnership is taxable as compensation. On the other hand, the issue of whether the receipt of a partnership profits interest for services is taxable has been the subject of litigation. Most recently, in *Campbell v. Commissioner,* 943 F.2d 815 (8th Cir. 1991), the Eighth Circuit in dictum suggested that the taxpayer's receipt of a partnership profits interest received for services was not taxable, but decided the case on valuation. Other courts have determined that in certain circumstances the receipt of a partnership profits interest for services is a taxable event under section 83 of the Internal Revenue Code. *See, e.g., Campbell v. Commissioner,* T.C.M. 1990-236, *rev'd,* 943 F.2d 815 (8th Cir. 1991); *St. John v. United States,* No. 82-1134 (C.D. Ill. Nov. 16, 1983). The courts have also found that typically the profits interest received has speculative or no determinable value at the time of receipt. *See Campbell,* 943 F.2d at 823; *St. John.* In *Diamond v. Commissioner,* 56 T. C. 530 (1971), *aff'd,* 492 F.2d 286 (7th Cir. 1974), however, the court assumed that the interest received by the taxpayer was a partnership profits interest and found the value of the interest was readily determinable. In that case, the interest was sold soon after receipt.

SEC. 4. APPLICATION

.01 Other than as provided below, if a person receives a profits interest for the provision of services to or for the benefit of a partnership in a partner capacity or in anticipation of being a partner, the Internal Revenue Service will not treat the receipt of such an interest as a taxable event for the partner or the partnership.

.02 This revenue procedure does not apply:

1. If the profits interest relates to a substantially certain and predictable stream of income from partnership assets, such as income from high-quality debt securities or a high-quality net lease;

2. If within two years of receipt, the partner disposes of the profits interest; or

3. If the profits interest is a limited partnership interest in a "publicly traded partnership" within the meaning of section 7704(b) of the Internal Revenue Code.

REV. PROC. 2001-43
2001-2 CB 191, August 2, 2001
Clarifying: Rev. Proc. 93-27
Non-recognition of gain or loss on contribution: Limited liability companies: Contribution of services

The Service provided guidance on the tax treatment of the grant of a substantially nonvested partnership profits in return for the provision of services to the partnership. The determination under Rev. Proc. 93-27 as to whether an interest granted to a service provider is a profits interest is, under certain circumstances, tested at the time the interest is granted, even if, at that time, the interest is substantially nonvested.

Where a partnership grants a profits interest to a service provider in a transaction that meets the requirements of the new procedure and Rev. Proc. 93-27, the Service will not treat the grant of the interest or the event that causes the interest to become substantially vested as a taxable event for the partner or the partnership.

SECTION 1. PURPOSE

This revenue procedure clarifies Rev. Proc. 93-27, 1993-2 C.B. 343, by providing guidance on the treatment of the grant of a partnership profits interest that is substantially nonvested for the provision of services to or for the benefit of the partnership.

SECTION 2. BACKGROUND

Rev. Proc. 93-27 provides that (except as otherwise provided in section 4.02 of the revenue procedure), if a person receives a profits interest for the provision of services to or for the benefit of a partnership in a partner capacity or in anticipation of being a partner, the Internal Revenue Service will not treat the receipt of the interest as a taxable event for the partner or the partnership. ...

SECTION 3. SCOPE

This revenue procedure clarifies Rev. Proc. 93-27 by providing that the determination under Rev. Proc. 93-27 of whether an interest granted to a service provider is a profits interest is, under the circumstances described below, tested at the time the interest is granted, even if, at that time, the interest is substantially nonvested (within the meaning of §1.83-3(b) of the Income Tax Regulations). Accordingly, where a partnership grants a profits interest to a service provider in a transaction meeting the requirements of this revenue procedure and Rev. Proc. 93-27, the Service will not treat the grant of the interest or the event that causes the interest to become substantially vested (within the meaning of §1.83-3(b) of the Income Tax Regulations) as a taxable event for the partner or the partnership. Taxpayers to which this revenue procedure applies need not file an election under section 83(b) of the Code.

SECTION 4. APPLICATION

This revenue procedure clarifies that, for purposes of Rev. Proc. 93-27, where a partnership grants an interest in the partnership that is substantially nonvested to a service provider, the service provider will be treated as receiving the interest on the date of its grant, provided that:

.01 The partnership and the service provider treat the service provider as the owner of the partnership interest from the date of its grant and the service provider takes into account the distributive share of partnership income, gain, loss, deduction, and credit associated with that interest in computing the service provider's income tax liability for the entire period during which the service provider has the interest;

.02 Upon the grant of the interest or at the time that the interest becomes substantially vested, neither the partnership nor any of the partners deducts any amount (as wages, compensation, or otherwise) for the fair market value of the interest; and

.03 All other conditions of Rev. Proc. 93-27 are satisfied.

PROBLEM 2-5

X, Y and Z are individuals who plan to form a partnership to sell auto parts at a mall. Z has no money to speak of but a lot of talent and energy, for which X and Y are prepared to give Z a 20% interest in the partnership's profits.

1) What measures must the partnership take to assure there is no imposition of tax under the authority of Rev. Proc. 93-27?

2) Assume instead that Z promises to work for the XY partnership in exchange for a promise to receive a 33% partnership capital interest   in what will be the XYZ partnership after he works for the XY partnership for two years. The XY partnership can fire him any time it likes to. Is he taxable on the capital interest when he receives the promise? Consider § 83(a).

3) What if Z receives the interest described in "(2)" in year 1?

C. ASSIGNMENT OF INCOME PRINCIPLES

46

One can fairly argue that when a cash method taxpayer contributes accounts receivable to a partnership of which he is a member, the cash eventually received should be taxed to that taxpayer under traditional assignment of income principles. On the other hand, § 721 suggests that there should be an amnesty, and assignment of income principles should not apply, at least if the taxpayer has a good business reason for contributing the receivables, and is not just trying to pull a fast one on the government. The part of this book dealing with incorporation addresses that subject in connection with *Hempt Bros. v. United States,* 490 F.2d 1172 (3d Cir.), *cert. denied,* 419 U.S. 826 (1974). There is, however, a special twist in the partnership area in that § 704(c) will tax the contributing partner when the debtors pay down their debts to the extent of the difference between the receivables' bases and their values when contributed, which in effect prevents the assignment of income to other partners.

Chapter 3

PARTNERSHIP OPERATIONS

A. TAXATION OF PARTNERSHIP OPERATIONS
Read §§ 702(a)-(c), 703, and 704(a)-(c).

1. COMPUTING PARTNERSHIP INCOME

The key tax feature of the partnership is that it operates as a conduit that flows its income or losses through to its owners without paying income tax itself. This is the aggregate theory in full bloom. The partnership's return filing obligations are directed at ensuring that the partnership's annual operating results are recorded and carved up partner-by-partner, by means of the Schedule K-1. The partnership reports these results, misleadingly referred to as the "taxable income of the partnership" in § 703(a), on the basis of *its* taxable year and *its* accounting method, and in general, on the basis of tax elections made at the partnership level. The results themselves are determined as of the *end* of the partnership's taxable year. The partners' years may not exactly overlap with the partnership's. For example, if the partnership has a fiscal year that ends on June 30, partners preparing their 2007 calendar year tax returns will use only the information on the partnership return filed for June 30, 2007. The partnership's operating results later in 2007 will not affect the partners' calendar year 2007 taxable income but will instead appear on their 2008 returns. Consider what chaos would result if the partners were free each to choose the taxable year or accounting method of the partnership income by which each would have his or her income attributed; this necessitates using something like the concept of the "taxable income of the partnership." The concept is essential in order to centralize the measurement of income.

In a simple world the partnership's accountant could simply compute this "taxable income" and apportion it to each partner via the Schedule K-1. In fact, it is not that easy. Section 703(a) tells us that the partnership's income or loss is "computed in the same manner as in the case of an individual" and then goes on to serve up a variety of modifications. The statutory thread then moves to § 702(a)(8), which in effect tells us that this "taxable income" is shared by the partners. Section 704(a) tells us that the partnership agreement dictates just how the sharing is accomplished. Flipping back to § 702(a)(1)-(7), we find a list of items that have to be separately stated because they may affect each partner differently, due to his or her tax status or circumstances; these are excluded from the calculation of the partnership's taxable income, but flow through to the partners anyway as distinct items. In effect, nothing is lost to the partners. The effect of this segregation is only to force the partners to report these items in separate locations on their own tax returns. Each time such an item is lifted out and segregated, the "partnership taxable income" rises or falls correspondingly.

a. Separately-Stated Items

Because § 702(a)(1)-(7) is not an exclusive list, the courts are sometimes called on to see if anything else belongs on the list of separately stated items.

GERSHKOWITZ v. COMMISSIONER
88 T.C. 984 (1987)

WRIGHT, JUDGE.

[The taxpayer was a limited partner in four limited partnerships which marketed computer programs for income tax preparation, estate planning and financial planning. The partnerships bought the programs with nonrecourse notes and received nonrecourse loans from various entities, including Prentice-Hall. The partnerships liquidated in 1977, at which time each partnership was insolvent. The partners were solvent during 1977. The partnerships' loans were discharged by the lenders either by (1) forgiveness of indebtedness, or (2) conveyance of the security for the loan. The earlier *Stackhouse* case held that cancellation of indebtedness income is deemed a distribution under § 752(d). As a result, a reduction in debt that exceeded the partner's outside basis could produce a capital gain under § 731(a). Take a look at § 731(a)(1) and the last sentence of § 731(a), beginning "Any gain or loss . . . " before reading this case.]

Opinion 1. Prentice-Hall Transactions

The first issue for consideration is whether petitioners must recognize a gain on the Prentice-Hall transaction. Each partnership received loans in the aggregate amount of $250,000 from Prentice-Hall. Those loans were nonrecourse, and were secured by the 40,000 shares of COAP common stock owned by each partnership and by the account receivable of each partnership. Prentice-Hall also had subordinate security interest in the computer programs purchased by each partnership from Digitax Associates and COAP Planning, Inc. On June 20, 1977, Prentice-Hall released its security interest in the COAP stock, the computer programs and the accounts receivable of the Digitax partnerships and extinguished the $250,000 debt owed by each partnership. In exchange, each partnership paid Prentice-Hall $40,000 in cash. The fair market value of the COAP stock at that time was $2,500. The partnerships were insolvent both before and after the transaction.

In determining whether petitioners in the instant case must recognize a gain on the discharge of the Prentice-Hall indebtedness, two sets of rules must be considered. First, the general provisions of section 61(a)(12) dealing with income from discharge of indebtedness, and secondly the distribution provision of section 752(b) relating to a decrease in partnership liabilities.

In general, gross income includes income from the discharge of indebtedness. Sec. 61(a)(12); *United States v. Kirby Lumber Co.,* 284 U.S. 1 (1931). Income realized by a partnership on the discharge of indebtedness is passed through to each partner under section 702, and the partner's basis in his partnership interest is increased by his distributive share of such income. Sec. 705(a)(1). Under a judicially-created exception to this rule, however, a debtor will not recognize income under section 61(a)(12) if he is insolvent following the discharge of indebtedness. *Dallas Transfer and Terminal Warehouse Co. v. Commissioner,* 70 F.2d 95 (5th Cir. 1934); *Astoria Marine Construction Co. v. Commissioner,* 12 T.C. 798 (1949). Now see § 108(a)(1)(B). Ed.

Under Section 752(a), at the time a partnership assumes a liability, an individual partner's share of such liability is treated as a contribution of money by the partner to the partnership and increases the partner's basis in his partnership interest. Sec. 722. Conversely, any decrease in the partner's share of the partnership liabilities is treated as a distribution of money by the partnership to the partner under section 752(b) and results in the recognition of gain by the partner to the extent that such a distribution exceeds his adjusted basis in his partnership interest. Sec. 731(a)(1). The gain recognized is characterized as gain from the sale or exchange by the partner of his partnership interest, and is taken into income under section 61(a)(3) (gains derived from dealing in property).

Under section 61(a)(12), the Digitax partnerships realized income from the discharge of indebtedness when Prentice-Hall discharged the loans. This income was then passed through to the individual partners pursuant to section 702(a)(8). Petitioners argue that although income was realized, it should not be recognized in the instant case due to the insolvency exception to the discharge of indebtedness doctrine. In support of their position, petitioners cite *Stackhouse v. United States,* 441 F. 2d 465 (5th Cir. 1971). *Stackhouse* involved an insolvent partnership which settled a debt of $126,882.86 with a payment of $30,000. The Commissioner determined that the individual partners had income from the discharge of indebtedness to the extent of their solvency following the transaction. The District Court found that the partners had ordinary income under section 61(a)(12) to the extent of their solvency. *Stackhouse v. United States,* an unreported case (W.D. Tex. 1970, 27 AFTR 2d 71-414, 71-1 USTC par. 9128). The taxpayers appealed, alleging that the transaction was governed by the partnership distribution provisions of section 731 and 733. The Fifth Circuit Court of Appeals in *Stackhouse* attempted to reconcile the rules requiring recognition of discharge of indebtedness income with the partnership provisions providing for the treatment of partners on the discharge of a partnership liability. The court found that the discharge of partnership indebtedness resulted in a distribution to the partners under section 752(b) which resulted in a recognition of gain by each partner under section 731(a) to the extent that the amount distributed exceeded each partner's adjusted basis in his partnership interest. The court stated that "[s]ection 731(a) merely prescribes the rules for determining the amount of income derived from this discharge of indebtedness to be included in the taxpayers' gross income under section 61(a)12). In a sense then we are giving effect to both sections of the Code. . . ."

Petitioners maintain that the opinion in *Stackhouse* stands for the proposition that income from the discharge of indebtedness should be recognized at the partnership, rather than the partner, level, and that the insolvency exception to the discharge of indebtedness doctrine applies, therefore, to the partnership. The solvency of the individual partner is immaterial under petitioners' analysis. Petitioners fail to note, however, that the court in *Stackhouse* was not faced with the issue of whether income should be recognized at the partner or the partnership level, but rather whether such income should be treated as ordinary income under section 61(a)(12) or capital gain under section 731(a). The court noted that "[t]he United States concedes . . . that because the partnership had been insolvent before the settlement (its liabilities exceeded its assets), the gain to each partner should be recognized only to the extent of his solvency immediately after the settlement." 441 F.2d at 468. Thus, the parties in *Stackhouse* did not dispute, and the court did not consider, the level at which the insolvency exception applied, but rather the character of the partners' income.

Petitioners allege that their interpretation of *Stackhouse is* supported by the legislative history of the Bankruptcy Tax Act of 1980 (Pub. L. 96-589, December 24, 1980) ("the Act"). Section 2(a) of the Act amended section 108 of the Code to provide that the application of the code section providing for nonrecognition of discharge of indebtedness income when the taxpayer is insolvent should take place at the partner, rather than the partnership, level. Specifically, the legislative history states:

> "The bill provides that the rules of exclusion from gross income and reduction of tax attributes in section 108 of the Code (as amended by the bill) are to be applied at the partner level and not at the partnership level. S. Rept. No. 96-1035, 96th Cong., 2d Sess. 21 (1980)."

Based on this footnote, petitioners argue that Congress perceived that, prior to the Act, the insolvency exception to the recognition of discharge of indebtedness income was to be applied at the partnership level. Other than *Stackhouse,* however, petitioners cite no authority in support of this proposition, nor have we found any. As stated above, this issue was not addressed in *Stackhouse.* Further, by requiring recognition at the partner level, Congress provided for the inclusion of discharge of indebtedness income as a separately stated income item under section 702(a)(7) which would trigger an increase in each partner's basis under section 705. The court in *Stackhouse,* which treated such income as a distribution under section 731, ignored these provisions. Thus, Congress' intent to overturn *Stackhouse* related to application of sections 702 and 705 to discharge of indebtedness income, rather than to the level at which such income is recognized. The legislative history indicates that the purpose of the amendment to section 108 was to clarify the requirement that discharge of indebtedness income was considered income to the individual partners under section 702 rather than solely as a partnership distribution under section 731. To the extent that the result of such treatment results in ordinary income, rather than capital gain as the court held in *Stackhouse,* Congress chose to overrule that case.

Even if we were to assume, however, that petitioners' analysis of the legislative history of the Act was correct, we would still decline to follow the opinion of the Fifth Circuit in *Stackhouse.* While the analysis used by the Fifth Circuit is appealing in that it purports to integrate the two sets of rules dealing with the discharge of indebtedness, the court failed to recognize that income recognized by a partner pursuant to section 731(a) is included in that partner's gross income under section 61(a)(3) rather than under section 61(a)(12). Income realized by a partnership under section 61(a)(12) must be recognized by the partners as ordinary income under section 702. The recognition of such income provides each partner with an increase in the adjusted basis of his partnership interest under section 705. The distribution provision of section 752(b) serves to offset the basis increase received by each partner when the indebtedness was incurred and does not provide for the distribution of section 61(a)(12) income. Distributions under section 752(b) result in capital gain under section 731(a). The two sets of rules operate independently and simultaneously. The Fifth Circuit, in *Stackhouse,* failed to consider the ordinary income character of the income from the discharge of indebtedness under section 61(a)(12) as opposed to the capital gain recognized under section 731(a).

For the above-stated reasons, petitioners' reliance on *Stackhouse* is misplaced. The application of the insolvency exception to the discharge of indebtedness income should be made at the partner, not the partnership, level. Because each petitioner herein was solvent at the time the debts were discharged, each must recognize ordinary income with respect to his share of the partnership's income under section 702(a)(8). This income will provide each partner with an increase in basis under section 705(a)(1)(A). At the same time, each partner will receive a distribution from the partnership in an amount equal to his share of the partnership indebtedness. Sec. 752(b). This distribution will offset each partner's basis under section 733(1). Thus, the increase in basis under section 705, coupled with the distribution and decrease in basis under sections 752 and 733 result in a net change of zero in each partner's basis. The optional adjustments to basis enacted by the Bankruptcy Tax Act of 1980 were intended to change this result. S. Rept. No. 96-1035, 96th Cong., 2d Sess. 21 (1980).

Respondent argues, on brief, that the partners should not be entitled to a basis increase under section 705(a)(1)(A) because of the realization of discharge of indebtedness income. Respondent asserts that the basis increase would provide an opportunity for limited partners to bail out of crossover tax shelter partnerships without the recognition of the "phantom gain" inherent in their partnership interests, citing McKee, Nelson and Whitmire, Federal Taxation of Partnerships and Partners, par. 9.06[3] n. 144 (1977). We agree with respondent that, if the insolvency exception were to apply at the partnership level, such a step-up in basis would be abusive. In the instant case, however, we have determined that this exception must be applied at the partner level. When the loan proceeds were received by the partnerships, each partner increased his basis in his partnership interest by his distributive share of the liability. Sec. 722. This basis increase allowed the partners to deduct their distributive shares of partnership losses and deductions prior to the discharge of the loans. If the partnerships had received ordinary income instead of loan proceeds in the years 1972-74, the partners would have increased their bases in their partnership interests. Secs. 702(a)(8), 705(a)(1)(A). Because we are requiring the partners to recognize the same amounts as income in 1977, they should receive a basis increase in that year. While the partners were able to take advantage of the original basis increase on receipt of the loan proceeds in order to offset deductions during the intervening years, the mechanism for recognition of the use of such basis is contained in sections 752(b), 731(a) and 733, not in section 705. We note that because we have decided that the insolvency exception applies at the partner, not the partnership, level, we need not address respondent's contention that discharge of indebtedness income which is not recognized because the recipient of such income is insolvent does not constitute "tax-exempt receipts" for purposes of section 705(a)(1)(B).

[The court went on to conclude that each partnership realized income of $210,000 (liability of $250,000 less payment of $40,000).]

NOTE

A partnership can have debt cancellation income when it satisfies a debt with a partnership interest; there is debt cancellation income to the extent the debt exceeds the value of the partnership interest. § 108(e)(8).

To illustrate: the equal ABC partnership owes $100, which it discharges by transferring a partnership interest to the creditor worth $70. The partnership has $30 of cancellation of debt income, so A, B and C will each report $10 of cancellation of debt income as a distributive share of partnership income.

b. Disallowed Deductions

Section 703(a)(2) bars a partnership itself from deducting foreign income taxes, charitable gifts, net operating losses and depletion in determining its taxable income. This is more bark than bite, since these items will nevertheless appear on the K-1 and the partners will pick these items up on their personal returns. In addition, the same subsection disallows personal exemptions and other items that have no business on a partnership return in the first place. The reason for eliminating these deductions from the computation of "partnership taxable income" is that deductions for these items may be uniquely limited, depending on the facts and circumstances of each partner.

c. Organization, Syndication and Start-Up Expenditures
Read § 709.

Section 709(a) generally denies deductions for costs of organizing and financing a partnership. However, § 709(b) relaxes the prohibition by allowing 180-month amortization of organization, but not syndication, expenditures. It also allows the partnership to claim a current deduction of up to $5,000 of organization expenditures in the year the partnership begins business. The $5,000 declines (but not below zero) to the extent the organizational costs exceed $50,000. Review § 709 and Reg. § 1.709-2, then try the following straightforward problem.

Regardless of whether the partnership or corporate form is chosen, § 195 permits amortization of selected "start-up" costs incurred after the decision to acquire or establish a business, and prior to its commencing operations. The partnership makes the election. Start-up costs eligible for this amortization election include those paid or incurred in connection with:

(i) investigating the creation or acquisition of an active trade or business, or

(ii) creating an active trade or business, or

(iii) any activity engaged in for profit and for the production of income before the day on which the active trade or business begins, in anticipation of such activity becoming an active trade or business, and which, if paid or incurred in connection with the operation of an existing active trade or business in the same field as the trade or business referred to in paragraph "(i)" would be allowable as a deduction for the taxable year in which paid or incurred. You likely studied § 195 in the introductory tax course. It will not be dwelt upon here.

PROBLEM 3-1

L, M, and N (all individuals) formed the LMN limited partnership on December 1, year one. The partnership incurred the following costs in year one, before beginning business on January 1, year two:

Legal fees for drafting partnership agreement	$6,000.00
State filing fee	$2,000.00
Notice in newspaper, required by state to notify public	$500.00
Commissions paid to broker to sell interests in the partnership	$20,000.00

To what extent, doing everything it can to maximize its deductions, can the partnership deduct organizational costs under § 709(b) in year one? In year two?

B. PARTNERSHIP-LEVEL ELECTIONS

Partnerships are treated as separate entities for a variety of tax purposes. This flows naturally from the concept that a partnership has its own so-called taxable income even though it is not taxed on that amount. Section 703(b) lays the duty to make most elections affecting taxable income at the feet of the partnership.

1. Accounting Method

Section 703(b) implicitly obligates the partnership to select its own accounting method. Section 448 forces it onto the accrual method if it is a tax shelter or has a C corporation as a partner. Yes, a corporation can be a partner in a partnership.

Likewise, a partnership can be a partner in another partnership. These are known as "tier partnerships" in the trade and are quite common. Other Code provisions may also force the partnership onto a specified accounting method (including the accrual method), but this subject falls under the general heading of tax accounting and not partnership taxation.

PROBLEM 3-2

The A-J partnership consists of 10 partners, one of which is C Corporation that manufactures refrigerators. Neither the partnership nor the corporate partner has gross receipts that exceed $5 million. Under the Code, may the partnership use the cash method of accounting? See § 448 and § 703(b).

2. The Partnership's Tax Year
Read § 706(b).

The partnership generally selects its own taxable year, but to avoid manipulation § 706(b) places major restrictions on the choice of taxable year. The following is a useful description of the 1986 Act changes, as reported by the Staff of the Joint Committee on Taxation. The materials cover partnerships, S corporations, and personal service corporations.

"Taxable Years of Partnerships, S Corporations, and Personal Service Corporations (. . . secs. 706, 1378, 441, and 267 of the Code)

Prior Law

Partnerships. – Prior law required a partnership adopting or changing a taxable year to use the same taxable year as all of its principal partners (or the calendar year, if all of the partnership's principal partners do not have the same taxable year and the partnership is adopting a taxable year), unless the partnership established to the satisfaction of the Secretary of the Treasury a business purpose for selecting a different taxable year (sec. 706).

Deferral of income. – Under present law, partners in a partnership take into account their allocable share of income, gain, loss, deduction or credit of the partnership for their taxable year in which the partnership's taxable year ends. The items of income, gain, loss, deduction or credit are computed at the partnership level and reflect the partnership's (not the partner's) taxable year. To the extent that the partner's and the partnership's taxable years are not the same, a deferral of income can result. For example, assume a partnership has a taxable year ending in June, while an individual partner has a calendar year. The partner will include in his income tax return for the current calendar year his distributive share of partnership items that arose in the first six months of the current calendar year and his share of such items that arose in the last six months of the prior calendar year. Partnership items arising in the last six months of the current calendar year will not be included in the partner's return until the following calendar year. Thus, the recognition of six months' of partnership income has been deferred by the partner until the following taxable year.

* * *

Reasons for Change

The Congress believed that the prior law allowed an improper deferral of income for certain partners, shareholders in S corporations, and owners of personal service corporations. Where prior law allowed income earned by a partnership, S corporation or personal service corporation to be subjected to Federal income tax in a taxable year later than that in which it was earned, the value of the income earned is understated. This deferral of income was normally available only to certain types of taxpayers, resulting in preferential treatment of certain taxpayers at the overall expense of others. The Congress believed that requiring a partnership, S corporation, or personal service corporation to change its taxable year would impose less of a burden on the tax-paying public than other methods of eliminating the deferral.

Explanation of Provision

In general, the Act requires that all partnerships, S corporations, and personal service corporations conform their taxable years to the taxable years of their owners. An exception to

54

the rule is made in the case where the partnership, S corporation, or personal service corporation establishes to the satisfaction of the Secretary of the Treasury a business purpose for having a different taxable year. The deferral of income to owners for a limited period of time, such as the three months or less rule of present law, is not to be treated as a business purpose.

The Act provides that a partnership may not have a taxable year other than the taxable year of the partners owning a majority interest in partnership profits and capital. If partners owning a majority of partnership profits and capital do not have the same taxable year, the partnership must adopt the same taxable year as its principal [5% of capital or profits] partners. If the principal partners of the partnership do not have the same taxable year and no majority of its partners have the same taxable year, the partnership must adopt a calendar year as its taxable year unless a different taxable year is provided by regulations. In each case, the partnership may use a different taxable year if it establishes to the satisfaction of the Secretary of the Treasury a business purpose therefore.

For example, assume a partnership has one principal partner which is a fiscal year corporation owning an interest of 10 percent in partnership profits and capital. The remainder of the partners are individuals on a calendar taxable year, none of these individuals owns a sufficient interest in the partnership to be a principal partner. Under prior law, the partnership would have been required to adopt the fiscal taxable year of the corporate partner (*i.e.*, the taxable year of its principal partner). Under the Act, the partnership is required to adopt a calendar taxable year (*i.e.*, the taxable year of the majority of its partners).

An exception to the rules requiring a certain taxable year is provided in each case where the partnership, S corporation, or personal service corporation establishes to the satisfaction of the Secretary of the Treasury a business purpose for having a different taxable year."

To illustrate: The two partners of the AB general partnership consist of two partnerships, A and B. Each has an equal interest in the AB partnership. The A partnership consists of the Jones family, all of whom use the calendar year. The B partnership consists of two corporations, each of which is on the June 30 fiscal year. The Code suggests that unless it has a business reason for using a fiscal year, the AB partnership must use the calendar year. That is because there is no majority in interest, and because the principal partners (A and B) are not on the same taxable year. However, as you will see, Treasury has issued regulations that change the outcome.

NOTES – BUSINESS PURPOSE

As the legislative history indicates, unless the bulk of the partnership interests are owned by fiscal year taxpayers, the partnership is stuck with the calendar year, but as always, there are exceptions. The primary exception is for partnerships with a good business purpose for selecting a different year. For example, a ski resort might rightfully choose to close its books after ski season ends in the Spring. The other option is to make the so-called "Section 444 election," which permits a deferral of up to three months, but the price is that the partnership has to pay the government for the benefit of the tax deferral.

Absent a business purpose for selecting a unique year, the Code calls for the following three-level priority for setting the tax year:

- First, if one or more partners with the same tax year own over half the interests in capital and profits, use that year.

- Second, failing the above, if all the principal partners (those with 5 per cent or more of profits or capital) have the same year, use that year.

- Third, failing both of the above, use the year that results in the "least aggregate deferral." § 706(b)(1)(B)(iii) and Reg. § 1.706-1(b). The aggregate deferral for a taxable year is computed partner-by-partner by (1) multiplying each partner's percentage interest in partnership profits *times* the number of months of deferral that this taxable year causes for the partner and (2) adding these amounts together. The partnership is required to use the taxable year of the partners (or partners if there are shared years) that produces the smallest sum. The deferral period for a partner equals the number of months that elapse between the end of the partnership year being tested and the end of the partner's taxable year. For example, for a calendar-year partner, a partnership year ending May 30 produces a seven-month deferral.

Notice this curiosity about tax years; partners come and go. Each time there is a change, the tax year may have to change. To combat chaos, § 706(b)(l)(B) says that if the reason for the change had to do with a "majority interest taxable year," then the partnership can use the new year for at least three years before it must pick a new year.

PROBLEM 3-3

The BCD Partnership has the following three members with the following profit shares and tax years:

Partner	Profit share	Start of tax year
B (a corporation)	25%	October 1
C (an individual)	30%	January 1
D (a corporation)	45%	July 1

What tax year must the partnership use?

PROBLEM 3-4

C and D are the individual members of a prosperous law partnership that uses the cash method and a calendar tax year, as do the partners. The partnership has a pool of assets that the partners manage. The partnership had the following income and deductions during this year:

Gross fees	$800,000.00
Current § 162 deductions	$180,000.00
Dividends from US corporations	$1,000.00
Interest from corporate bonds	$5,000.00
Net long-term capital gains	$500.00
Net short-term capital gains	$800.00
Rental income from investment property	$6,000.00

What is the CD partnership's "taxable income" under § 703 for this year?

C. TAX CONSEQUENCES TO PARTNERS

Once the partnership's annual income or loss has been determined, one must attribute the results to each partner. § 704. This calls for determining each partner's so-called distributive share for the partnership's tax year. The term "distributive share" is carefully chosen, because the term concerns what is *imputed* to the partner, not what is *distributed* to the partner. In general, the partnership agreement controls the partner's distributive share of both partnership "taxable income" and of the items excluded from the computation of that figure.

1. Timing of Distributive Shares

In the following case, focus on the significance of the years 1933 and 1944-45.

COMMISSIONER v. GOLDBERGER'S ESTATE
213 F.2d 78 (3d Cir. 1954), *aff'g and rev'g in part* 18 T.C. 1233 (1952), *acq.* 1955-2 C.B. 6, 9

STALEY, CIRCUIT JUDGE.

In 1944 the estate of Norman S. Goldberger received $108,453.59 as a result of a judgment recovered in the United States District Court for the Southern District of New York. That receipt gave rise to these cases, the Commissioner having assessed income tax deficiencies for the year 1944 against both the estate and the beneficiary of a trust set up by Goldberger's will. The Tax Court held that there was no deficiency as to the estate but that the recovery, minus certain deductions, was income to the beneficiary The facts were stipulated and were found accordingly by the Tax Court.

In 1933 Goldberger entered into a joint venture with Bauer, Pogue & Co., Inc., a brokerage company, and George E. Tribble. The purpose of the venture was to trade in the stock of Fidelio Brewery, Inc. Each of the venturers contributed a substantial number of Fidelio shares, and Bauer, Pogue & Co., Inc., were the managers of the trading account. By the terms of the agreement, Goldberger was to receive 50/115ths of the net profits of the venture, which was active from June 8 to August 2, 1933. In September of that year, an accounting was rendered to Goldberger which showed that his share of the net profits of the venture was $71,847.58. This sum was paid to him. He died in 1936, believing that the ac-counting rendered in 1933 was correct. In 1939 his executrix, petitioner Trounstine, discovered that Bauer, Pogue & Co., Inc., had not dealt honestly with Goldberger in 1933. Trounstine brought suit in New York against Bauer, Pogue & Co., Inc., and Bauer, individually, for an accounting of the joint venture profits. Following removal of the suit, the district court found that, during the operation of the joint venture and in violation of its terms, Bauer, Pogue & Co., Inc., and Bauer and Pogue, individually, secretly traded in Fidelio shares and failed to account to Goldberger for the profits of those sales. After an accounting before a special master, the court found that in addition to the sum paid to Goldberger in 1933, he should have received $60,163.73. Final judgment was then entered in favor of the estate. In 1944 the estate received, in satisfaction of the judgment, $108,453.59, which included the $60,163.73 which Goldberger should have received in 1933, plus interest from August 11, 1933, and costs and disbursements. Expenses of the litigation amounted to $64,855.02, leaving a net recovery of $43,598.57.

Petitioner Trounstine is Goldberger's widow and the executrix of his estate. His will left his entire residuary estate in trust for his widow: The trustees were to pay to her all income from the res (with an irrelevant exception), and, if any year's income was less than $12,000, a sufficient amount from corpus to make a total annual payment of $12,000. Prior to receipt of the proceeds of the judgment, Goldberger's entire residuary estate, aggregating $79,272.61, had been paid over to her as trust beneficiary. The net recovery was deposited in an account maintained by her as ancillary executrix between December, 1944, and February, 1945. Between February and May of 1945, that amount was transferred to her domiciliary executrix account, and was transferred to her, individually, between March and May of 1945. The estate did not file a return for 1944, and Trounstine's 1944 return did not report any of the amount received on the recovery. The Commissioner assessed deficiencies against both the estate and Trounstine and a 25 per cent penalty against the estate for failure to file a return. On petitions for redetermination the Tax Court held that the recovery was gross income to the estate in 1944 but that it was entitled to deduct the litigation expenses and the net amount of the recovery, the latter because it was held to be currently distributable to Trounstine as trust beneficiary. This left no net income to the estate and taxed the net recovery to Trounstine. The result was a determination of no deficiency against the estate, rendering moot the penalty for failure to file, but a deficiency as to Trounstine larger than that assessed. . . The Commissioner supports his deficiency assessments by pointing to the general rule that the taxability of the principal amount of recovery in a law suit depends upon the nature of the claim and the basis of recovery. If the claim is for lost profits, the recovery is a taxable gain because it is in lieu of what would have been taxable had it been received without a law suit. If the claim is for loss of, or damage to, capital, the recovery is nontaxable because it is a return of capital. Here, the principal sum recovered was the amount of joint-venture profits wrongfully withheld from Goldberger and, therefore, we are told, there was taxable income. The taxpayers argue, correctly we believe, that the principal sum was taxable income to Goldberger in 1933 and is now beyond reach of the fisc because of the statute of limitations.

The Revenue Act of 1932 governs this phase of the case. [It] . . . includes a joint venture within the meaning of the term "partnership." Thus, for simplicity's sake, we will use partnership language here. That Act treated the firm and the individual partners substantially as does the present Code. That is, for income tax purposes, the common law, aggregate theory prevailed. The firm was not a taxable entity; its return was informational only. . . Its net income was computed, except as to the deduction for charitable contributions, in the same manner as that of an individual. . . The tax was imposed upon the individual partner, who must include, in computing his net income, his distributive share of the firm's net income, whether or not distributed to him. That is the determinative point here. The joint venture made certain profits in 1933, but Goldberger did not receive his entire share. Non-receipt makes no difference, taxwise. . . Once the joint venture realized net income, Goldberger became taxable upon his distributive share, in spite of the fact that he did not actually receive it in that year.

Finally, we think the Commissioner distorts the nature of the 1944 judgment. He argues that what the estate recovered in 1944 never became joint-venture profits in 1933 but were the profits of the individual wrongdoers, made in breach of their fiduciary duty. The opinion and findings of fact in the 1944 action, which are part of the stipulated facts here, and the Tax Court's opinion show, however, that joint-venture profits, made in 1933 but wrongfully withheld from Goldberger in that year, are exactly what the estate recovered in 1944. The fact of their non-appearance on the books of the venture, if it is a fact, is not determinative here, for book entries are "no more than evidential, being neither indispensable nor conclusive."

NOTES

1. **Statute of limitations and facts**. Cases like *Goldberger's Estate* illustrate the contrast between tax deficiencies, which generally terminate after three years under the statute of limitations found in § 6501, and facts, as to which there is no statute of limitations. Section 705 determines the partner's outside basis, which should be treated as a fact. Thus, even though Mr. Goldberger never reported the income that he was swindled out of, that income should have increased his outside basis. That would set the stage for a diminished gain (or enlarged loss) if he had sold his partnership interest or if he received a nontaxable distribution under § 731.

2. **Disputed computations.** Let's say a partner disagrees with some item on the K-1 she receives. Must she report the item? No. She can disagree with the K-1 and report what she thinks is right, but she must disclose the disagreement conspicuously, in fairness to the IRS, or lose important procedural protections against an immediate IRS assessment of a deficiency against her. *See* Reg. § 301.6222(b)-2T. The IRS has provided a Form 8082 that should be used to highlight the disagreement.

2. Character of Distributive Shares

Section 702(b) ensures that the tax character of each item of income, expense, deduction, and credit that the partnership generates retains the same character in the hands of the partners.

PROBLEM 3-5

Go back to Problem 3-4. If C's distributive share is 60% and D's is 40%, how much in dollars of each separately-stated item and of the partnership's "taxable income" will each report as his or her distributive share for the year?

3. The Special Case of Electing Large Partnerships

In 1997, Congress enacted §§ 771-777 in order to cope with aggregate and entity issues raised specifically by large partnerships. In 2015, Congress repealed those rules effective for returns filed for partnership tax years beginning after December 31, 2017.

Now, instead of separating out large partnerships and applying specific rules only for those entities, the new rules apply to all partnerships and assess all taxes and penalties resulting from a partnership audit at the partnership level. The Service will now examine partnership items of income, gain, loss, deduction or credit, and any partners' distributive shares of those items, at the partnership level under the so called centralized partnership audit rules. §6221(a). The Service will also make adjustments at the partnership level. Further, any tax and penalties attributable to the Service's adjustments are assessed and collected from the partnership in the year of the audit or any judicial review (the "adjustment year") not the individual partner' years. §§6232(a) and 6233(b)(2).

The new rules apply to all partnerships except eligible partnerships that elect to opt. An eligible partnership has 100 or fewer qualifying partners. A qualifying partner is a partner for whom the partnership is required to furnish a Schedule K-1 (Form 1065) for the tax year under §6031(b) see §6221(b)(1)(B). Qualifying partners are only individuals, C corporations (foreign and domestic) an S corporations, or a deceased partner's estate. §6221(b)(1)(C). Thus, the election to opt out is not available to any partnership with at least one partner that is classified as a partnership for federal tax purposes. If a partnership can opt out, the IRS will audit the partners one-by-one.

D. ADJUSTMENTS TO BASIS

It is a basic theme of partnership taxation that there is generally no taxable gain when property is either contributed to the partnership or distributed from it. §§ 721 and 731. However, a partner is taxed annually on his distributive share, regardless of whether he receives a distribution. The pent-up paper gains or losses on the contributed or distributed property remain latent in the partnership interest. When a partner dies, of course the magic of § 1014 takes over, largely eradicating pending gains and losses by changing the basis in the partnership interest to its fair market value at the partner's death. But there is always § 691 (income in respect of a decedent) to reckon with, especially as to recent income of, or from, the partnership. We will see this in a later chapter.

(1) Partner's (Outside) Basis and Partnership's (Inside) Basis

Perhaps the most important technical lesson of Subchapter K is that one has to keep an eye on two accounts at the same time. One account is the partner's basis in his or her partnership interest, which is generally referred to as the "outside basis." See § 705. A partner's interest in the partnership can be analogized to a block of stock in a corporation, but the basis of a partnership interest is far more dynamic; it increases and decreases regularly to reflect undistributed partnership income and losses. The determination of the partner's outside basis is of great importance. For example, current distributions of cash from the partnership are nontaxable (§ 731(a)(1)) but they reduce the distributee partner's outside basis. §733. Outside basis is subtracted from the amount realized in calculating the gain or loss on the sale or exchange of a partnership interest. §§ 741, 1001. The partner can deduct her share of partnership losses only to the extent of her outside basis. § 704(d). When the partnership liquidates, the partner's basis in the distributed assets will generally equal her outside basis. § 732(b).

The other account is the partnership's basis in its own properties, which is generally referred to as the "inside basis." One can think of the inside basis as existing on the opposite side of a legal membrane that separates the partnership from its owners. Inside basis will commonly diverge sharply from the *value* of assets the partnership owns; by the same token, the value of a partner's interest in the partnership is also apt to be quite different from the partner's outside basis. The partnership's basis in properties that its partners contribute to it is the transferor-partner's basis. See § 723. The "outside basis" of a partner and the "inside basis" of the partnership start out the same, but the inside-outside symmetry tends to deteriorate over time for various technical reasons.

(2) Impact of Income and Loss on a Partner's Basis

The notion that a partnership is a conduit (or "aggregate" of partners) for tax purposes does not mean that there will necessarily be any actual distributions to the partners. Allocations of partnership income, which the partners must report and on which they each will be taxed, may well involve income that the partnership retains. The managing partner typically controls distributions, making them only when the enterprise does not need surplus cash or property. If a partner is allocated partnership income, the partner's outside basis in the partnership interest will be correspondingly increased. § 705(a)(1). Absent this upward adjustment to outside basis, if the partner were to sell her interest before an actual distribution of the retained income, there could be *a second* tax on the same income that was earlier taxed to the selling partner as his or her share of partnership income. Conversely, the partner who is allocated a partnership loss deduction must reduce outside basis. § 705(a)(2)(A). Whenever the partnership makes an actual distribution to a partner, the partner's "outside basis" in his or her partnership interest is correspondingly decreased. § 705(a)(2).

An example involving money may drive home the point here. Assume that the partnership allocates a dollar of partnership income to each partner in accordance with the distributive shares of the respective partners as set out in their partnership agreement. Each partner will then be taxed on a dollar of income. The partner's taxability ensues regardless of whether any actual distribution of cash is made to that partner. Absent any actual distribution of the dollar, however, it naturally follows that a dollar-higher price will be realized on a sale of the partner's interest. After all, given the fact of undistributed partnership income, there is an additional dollar for each of the partners in the partnership's coffers. Unless each partner's outside basis in the partnership interest increases, there would be a dollar more of gain realized from the sale of any partner's interest in the partnership. Conversely, when a dollar is distributed, the partner's outside basis (and sales price) declines, symmetrically, by one dollar.

To illustrate: A is a newly admitted equal partner in the ABC business partnership, which is on the calendar year. His admission took place on January 1 of this year. A's basis in his partnership interest at the time of admission was zero. Assume the ABC partnership earned a net profit of $150,000, all of which the partnership retained in its bank account. If his share of partnership income for the year is $50,000, his outside basis also becomes $50,000. If, in contrast, the tax law made A's outside basis zero and he sold his partnership interest for its cash value of $50,000, he would suffer a double tax, once for the year the partnership earned the $50,000 allocable to A, and then a gain of $50,000 when A sold the partnership interest.

(3) Impact of Distributions on a Partner's Basis

Distributions also reduce the partner's basis in her partnership interest. Cash distributions reduce basis. § 705(a)(2). If and to the extent cash distributions exceed basis, the excess is treated as a capital gain on the sale of the partnership interest. § 731. Congress could have chosen to defer the tax by allowing negative basis, but consistent with its handling of comparable issues throughout the Code, it did not. Property distributions are more complex and are discussed in detail in Chapter 7.

(4) Outside Basis Adjustments for Partnership Income that is Tax-Exempt

When tax-exempt income, such as interest on tax-free municipal bonds, is allocated, each partner's "outside basis" must be correspondingly increased. § 705(a)(1)(B). If there were no increase in outside basis, eventually an income tax would fall on that supposedly exempt income when it was realized upon a distribution of cash or property to the partner or (especially) in the form of a greater amount realized from the sale of any partner's interest in the partnership. Of course, a partnership distribution of tax-exempt income dollars requires a lowering of each distributee-partner's outside basis, just as does any other cash distribution.

(5) Basis Adjustments for Partnership Expenses that are Nondeductible

Partnership expenditures that are nondeductible for tax purposes are nonetheless allocated among the partners in accordance with the partners' distributive shares. The partner whose distributive share is a dollar of a partnership expenses that is not deductible and not chargeable to the partnership capital account must reduce outside basis by a dollar, despite the nondeductible nature of that dollar. § 705(a)(2)(B). Otherwise, the partner could convert the nondeductible expenditure into a deduction by selling her partnership interest and thereby realizing a dollar less of gain (or a dollar more of loss).

(6) Basis Adjustments for Partnership Expenditures that are Capitalized

If the partnership's outlay is nondeductible because it has to be capitalized, it will obviously produce no deduction at the partner level until the capitalized amount produces a depreciation or amortization deduction. The capitalized sum naturally is reflected in the basis of the partnership's asset with reference to which the outlay was made. For example, if property having a basis of $100 is the subject of a $10 capital improvement, its basis is adjusted to $110, but the *aggregate* inside basis remains unchanged because the cash on hand prior to this outlay was already included in the aggregate inside basis amount; hence, no change in outside basis is needed to maintain order.

(7) Symmetry Between Inside and Outside Basis

Note how each dollar of income that the partnership earns increases both inside and outside basis by a dollar. Conversely, each dollar of loss *generally* affects inside and outside basis: as will be seen later, the symmetry breaks down over time.

PROBLEM 3-6

A is a partner of the ABC partnership, in which he has a 30% partnership interest. On January 1 of year one, A's basis in the partnership was $15,000. In year one, the partnership had operating income of $40,000, a long-term capital loss of $20,000, a § 1231 loss of $30,000, and foreign tax expense deduction of $10,000. A received a cash distribution during the year of $12,000. Apply the rules in § 705(a) and Reg. § 1.705-1(a) in the order in which they appear.

1) What is A's basis in the partnership at year-end?

2) How much capital loss will pass through to A from the partnership?

3) How much of A's share of the capital and § 1231 losses, if any, will be suspended because A's basis is insufficient to absorb them?

E. GENERAL DEFERRAL LIMITATION ON FLOW-THROUGH OF LOSSES
Read § 704(d).

As you saw, § 704(d) limits each partner's annual losses, including capital losses, to his or her outside basis, determined at the end of the partnership year in which the loss occurred. To accelerate a loss that is blocked by the § 704(d) limit, the partner can make a pre-year-end contribution, or do nothing and hope that there will be later profits that the suspended losses will offset, or make a contribution to the partnership in a later year, which will also revive the loss in that later year to the extent of the contribution. Alternatively, because the partnership's borrowings increase the partners' outside bases, a common solution to the § 704(d) limitation is for the partnership to borrow enough money to ensure that § 704(d) never becomes a problem; however, that in turn draws in the at-risk rules of § 465, which operate as a backstop to § 704(d).

SENNETT v. COMMISSIONER
752 F.2d 428 (9th Cir. 1985)

PER CURIAM:

Taxpayers William and Sandra Sennett claimed an ordinary loss deduction of $109,061 on their 1969 tax return. This loss represented William Sennett's share of the ordinary losses incurred in 1968 by Professional Properties Partnership ("PPP") when it repurchased his interest in the partnership. The Commissioner of Internal Revenue disallowed the deduction asserting inter alia that in 1969 Sennett had no basis in an interest in PPP since he had left the partnership in 1968 and is precluded by 26 U.S.C. § 704(d) and Treas. Reg. § 1.704-1(d) from claiming any loss. The Tax Court ruled against petitioners. It held that a former partner may not claim a share of a loss that is incurred by the partnership after the withdrawal from the partnership of that partner. We agree and affirm.

Facts

Sennett entered PPP as a limited partner in December 1967. PPP's total capital at that time was approximately $402,000. Sennett contributed $135,000 and received a 33.5 % interest in the partnership. In 1967 PPP reported an ordinary loss of $405,329, and Sennett reported his allowable distributive share of $135,000.

Sennett sold his interest in PPP on November 26, 1968, with an effective date of December 1, 1968. The contract provided that PPP would pay Sennett $250,000, in annual installments with interest. Sennett agreed to pay PPP within one year the total loss allocated to Sennett's surrendered interest. PPP then sold twenty percent of Sennett's interest to a third party. PPP's return in 1968 reported a negative capital account of $109,061, corresponding to the eighty percent portion of the partnership interest PPP bought from Sennett and retained.

On May 15, 1969, Sennett and PPP executed an amended agreement which reduced PPP's obligation to $240,000, Without interest if paid in full by December 31, 1969, or if paid one-half in 1969 and the rest in 1970, at seven percent interest. PPP executed a promissory note to Sennett for $240,000, which Sennett signed as paid in full. Sennett meanwhile paid PPP $109,061, which was eighty percent of his share of PPP's losses. On his 1969 return Sennett reported $240,000 long-term capital gain and $109,061 as his distributive share of PPP's ordinary loss. The Commissioner disallowed the ordinary loss and maintained that, instead, there should be a long-term capital gain reported of $130,939 ($240,000 – $109,061). The Tax Court agreed and the Sennetts took this appeal.

Analysis

In deciding whether Sennett can deduct a $109,061 loss, we must look to 26 U.S.C. § 704(d). The statute provides:

LIMITATION ON ALLOWANCE OF LOSSES. – A partner's distributive share of partnership loss (including capital loss) shall be allowed only to the extent of the adjusted basis of such partner's interest in the partnership at the end of the partnership year in which such loss occurred. Any excess of such loss over such basis shall be allowed as a deduction at the end of the partnership year in which said excess is repaid to the partnership. . .

Treas. Reg. § 1.704-1(d) – in force in 1969 and having substantively the same effect now – interprets the statute as allowing only a partner to benefit from the carryover allowed by subsection 704(d). The Commissioner relies upon this regulation in disallowing the deduction, since Sennett was not a partner in the year he repaid the excess. Sennett does not deny this. Nor does he deny that his basis was zero when PPP purchased his interest and incurred the loss in 1968. Sennett argues instead that the regulation is merely an "interpretive regulation," and entitled to little or no weight. Sennett points to statutory language which allows the taxpayer to claim a deduction in the amount of the excess of basis in the partnership. He claims he repaid the loss in 1969 and is entitled to the deduction regardless of his lack of partner status.

This circuit has held that an interpretive regulation will be given effect if "it is a reasonable interpretation of the statute's plain language, its origin, and its purpose." *First Charter Financial Corp. v. United States*, 669 F.2d 1342, 1348 (9th Cir. 1982). "[A] Treasury regulation 'is not invalid simply because the statutory language will support a contrary interpretation." Id. (quoting *United States v. Vogel Fertilizer Co.*, 455 U.S. 16, 26, 70 L. Ed. 2d 792, 102 S. Ct. 821 (1982)). As will be explained below, restricting carryover to partners is a reasonable interpretation in light of the wording of the statute and the legislative history.

Statutory language supports the Treasury Regulation. For example, the presence of the word "partner" at the beginning of subsection 704(d) strongly implies that a taxpayer must be a partner to take advantage of the carryover.

The Treasury Regulation's interpretation is also supported by a review of the legislative history of the statute. Section 704(d), as initially adopted by the House, allowed for deduction of the distributive share to the extent of adjusted basis. There was no provision for a carryover of the excess loss until the excess was repaid. H.R. Rep. No. 1337, 83d Cong., 2d Sess. 1, *reprinted in 1954* U.S. Code Cong. & Ad. News 4017, 4364. The bill the Senate passed, which was the version Congress enacted, provided for carryover. The accompanying Senate Report sums up both sentences of subsection 704(d) in a fashion that demonstrates the committee felt the subsection limited carryover to partners. It states:

"Your committee has revised subsection (d) of the House bill to provide that any loss in excess of the basis of a partner's partnership interest may be allowed as a deduction only at the end of the partnership year in which the loss is repaid, either directly, or out of future profits. Subsection (d), as amended, may be illustrated as follows. Assume that a partner has a basis of $50 for his interest, and his distributive share of partnership loss is $100. Under the subsection, the partner's distributive share of the loss would be limited to $50, thereby decreasing the basis of his interest to zero. The remaining $50 loss would not be recognized, unless the partner makes a further contribution of $50. If, however, the partner repays the $50 loss to the partnership out of his share of partnership income for the following year, then the additional $50 loss will be recognized at the end of the year in which such repayment is made. S. Rep. No.

1622, 83d Cong., 2d Sess. 1, *reprinted in* 1954 U.S. Code Cong. & Ad. News 4621, 5025. . . ."

Limiting carryovers to those who are partners at the time of repayment, as Treas. Reg. § 1.704-1(d) does, effectuates congressional intent to allow deductions only to the extent of adjusted basis. When a partner repays the excess loss, it is, as the Senate Report notes, "a further contribution" to the partnership. The partner thereby increases his basis by an amount equal to the loss and reduces it to zero by taking the loss. Nor is the partnership element merely a formal distinction, since the partner repaying the excess loss increases his interest in the partnership and his exposure to loss. Sennett's position, in contrast, was that of a debtor with rights superior to those of partners.

Conclusion

Since Sennett was not a member of the partnership and, therefore, had no basis in the partnership at the time of the loss, he was not entitled to deduct a portion of PPP's putative loss. The decision of the Tax Court rejecting the $109,061 deduction and setting taxpayer's long-term capital gain for the 1969 taxable year at $130,939 is affirmed.

PROBLEM 3-7

1) What deduction would Sennett have been allowed if he did not repay his share of the loss to the partnership? Remember the loss-limitation rule of § 704(d). Why did he agree to repay that amount?

2) According to *Oden v. Commissioner, T.C.M.* 1981-184, *aff'd in an unpublished opinion,* 679 F.2d 885 (4th Cir. 1982), a cash method partner's note takes a zero basis in the partnership's hands. But what happens if the partnership sells the note and the partner later pays it off? Will the partnership have income on the sale? Will the profit on the sale of the note be attributed to the contributing partner? When the partner pays off the note, what basis is there for claiming a deduction for those payments? The Ninth Circuit has held that a cash method shareholder does have basis in his own contributed note, but went out of its way to say that it was reluctant to extend the same rule to partnerships. *Peracchi v. Commissioner,* 143 F.3d 487 (9th Cir. 1998).

F.   OTHER RESTRICTIONS ON LOSSES

A familiar grouping of other limitations that arise outside Subchapter K operates simultaneously with the general § 704(d) limitation.

(1) Hobby Losses

Although the passive activity loss rules have generally come to overshadow the hobby loss rules as a weapon against the syndication of tax-oriented investments, § 183 remains a potent force. Curiously, § 183 is actually an allowance provision (permitting the use of deductions up to the amount of gross income from an income-generating hobby), but it is seen as a threat to loss deductions because it contains the regulations that are used to sort hobbies from real businesses.

The government has had a string of litigating successes arguing its position that § 183 must be applied at the partnership level, such that, no matter how serious about making a profit the investor limited partners may have been when they contributed to the enterprise, the partnership's right to claim deductions for operating losses depends on the promoter-general partner's motives. *Brannen v. Commissioner,* 722 F.2d 695 (11th Cir. 1984), seems to be the seminal decision here. Moreover, the courts have closed ranks behind the government and denied embezzlement or theft losses to investors for their cash investments in tax shelters unless the investors were completely naive. *See, e.g., Viehweg v. Commissioner,* 90 T.C. 1248 (1988) and Rev. Rul. 70-333, 1970-1 C.B. 38.

(2) At-Risk Rules

The at-risk rules of § 465 are apt to restrict a partner's losses when § 704(d) will not. The key target is nonrecourse debt that the partnership has incurred and that increases basis under § 752, but does not add at-risk amounts. Like § 704(d), the at-risk rules suspend losses pending further contributions or earnings.

The at-risk rules apply at the partner, not the partnership, level. § 465(a)(1). Thus, one must evaluate the extent to which the individual partner is at risk. § 465(b)(1). A favorable factor from the partners' perspective is that the obligation to make further capital contributions to the partnership is included in the amount at risk, provided outside creditors can force the partner to make the contributions: Prop. Reg. § 1.465-24. Note that § 704(d) and § 465 do not overlap perfectly and that one must, therefore, test for the applicability of each limitation every year.

The key exception to the general rule of § 465 is a special interest rule for the real estate industry, the core concept of which is that nonrecourse debt secured by real estate and obtained from an unrelated person can count as being at-risk. *See* § 465(b)(6) (qualified nonrecourse financing treated as amount at risk). Interestingly, real estate is the one kind of asset that has historically been able to attract nonrecourse financing, so this is no small loophole.

(3) Passive Activity Losses

The so-called passive loss rules of § 469 apply after the at-risk and hobby-loss rules. The passive loss rules have special consequences when applied to a partnership setting. The rules themselves are simply designed to prevent taxpayers from offsetting losses and credits from rents and so-called passive trades or business against income from portfolio investments and personal services. The general approach of the passive loss rules is to make such losses and credits available only against income from passive trades or businesses, unless and until the taxpayer disposes of his or her entire interest in the passive activity in a fully taxable transaction.

It is natural that the PAL provisions apply to partnerships, because tax shelters (the primary targets of § 469) have historically been packaged and sold in limited partnership form, with the investors (often, in fact, victims of hyperbolic claims of promoters) buying in as limited partners. This area is so thorny that it seems best simply to list the primary rules and say no more about the topic. The following are the primary rules insofar as they affect partnerships:

1. The PAL rules are applied partner-by-partner. § 469(a)(2)(A).

2. Any partner who "materially participates" is exempt from the PAL limits. (This calls for regular, continuous and substantial activity by the partner, or meeting certain more mechanical tests that operate as surrogates for the general standard.) This means a limited partner is not *per se* foreclosed from claiming loss deductions from a limited partnership. *See* Temp. Reg. § 1.469-5T(e)(2).

3. Investment income derived from a partnership is culled out and cannot be used to reduce the partnership's passive activity losses. § 469(e)(1). Service income earned from a partnership is treated the same way. § 469(e)(3).

66

4. Partnerships may have multiple activities; if so, each is broken out and tested separately.

PROBLEM 3-8

Individuals X and Y form the equal XY partnership. The individuals and the partnership all use the cash method and a calendar tax year. X and Y each contribute $100,000 to the partnership, which it uses to buy a building costing $200,000. XY's books reveal the following further transactions during year one:

Rental income	$13,000.00
Straight-line depreciation on building (assume this is correct)	$5,000.00
Operating expenses	$7,000.00
Illegal bribe paid to local official	$500.00

1) How much income or loss must each partner report?

2) What is X's year-end outside basis?

3) Next year the partnership loses $210,000. How large a loss can X claim in year two?

4) In year three, the partnership's profits amount to $50,000. How much of that $50,000 would X be taxable on?

5) In situations where § 704(d) may limit a partner's losses for the year, which of the following techniques might that partner use to mitigate the issue?

    a)   Contribute cash to the partnership before year end?

    b)   Contribute cash to the partnership after year end?

    c)   Increase partnership borrowing for the year?

    d)   Find ways to increase partnership income, such as selling rights to future income?

    e)   Contributing the partner's own notes on the partner's behalf?

Chapter 4

TRANSACTIONS BETWEEN PARTNERS AND PARTNERSHIPS AND BETWEEN COMMONLY-CONTROLLED PARTNERSHIPS
Read § 707(a)-(c).

Partners sometimes act as third parties when dealing with their partnerships. Section 707 accommodates third party relationships, but also prevents the partners from using a false relationship as a way to deduct prohibited costs.

Briefly, § 707(a)(1) recognizes the partner acting as a stranger to the partnership, but § 707(a)(2) intervenes to recharacterize some potentially *mala fide* dealings. Section 707(b) restricts losses and deductions between partners and partnerships as related taxpayers in the § 267 sense, without regard to motive, and § 707(c) creates a special hybrid, the guaranteed payment, referring to transactions in which a partner, acting as a partner, gets an assured payment for capital or services.

A. LIMITATIONS ON LOSSES IN TRANSACTIONS BETWEEN PARTNERS AND CONTROLLED PARTNERSHIPS

Section 707(b) prevents the recognition of losses between a partner and a partnership controlled by the transferor, or between commonly-controlled partnerships. The provision is necessary because without these limits taxpayers could claim losses with respect to transfers of property that they continue to control. This prohibition applies if:

1. The partner directly or indirectly owns over 50% of partnership capital *or* profits,

   or

2. The transaction is between two partnerships in which the same persons directly or indirectly own over 50% of partnership capital or profits.

The powerful constructive ownership rules of § 267(c)(l), (2), (4) and (5) apply. Reg. § 1.707-1(b)(3). Those rules deem owners of entities to own the portion of the partnership reflected by the owner's share of the entity (e.g., of a trust that owns a partnership interest). Individuals constructively own partnership interests owned by spouses, ancestors, siblings, and descendants.

The transferee-partnership can offset future gains with the disallowed loss when it later sells the property. §§ 707(b)(1), 267(d). Because the transferee may sell the property for less than the original basis in the asset, the loss may never produce a tax benefit.

To illustrate: A sells his dog to the AB partnership. The dog has a basis of $20 and a fair market value of $10. A owns 60% of the capital of the AB partnership. The loss is disallowed because A owns over 50% of partnership capital and profits. §707(b). If the partnership later sells the dog for $11, the AB partnership will not be taxed on the $1 of gain, but the remaining $9 of disallowed loss is gone forever. Conversely, if the partnership later sells the dog for $8, the original $10 loss will never produce a tax benefit.

B. CONVERSION OF CHARACTER OF ASSETS INTO ORDINARY GAIN ASSETS ON SALE TO OR BETWEEN CONTROLLED PARTNERSHIPS.
Read § 707(b)(2).

Section 707(b)(2) converts gains on assets sold to a controlled partnership (or between controlled partnerships) into ordinary gains if the property is an ordinary asset in the transferee-partnership's hands. This provision is buttressed by § 1239(a), which applies if the property is depreciable in the partnership's hands.

To illustrate: A, a dog fancier but not a dealer, sells his pet dachshund to the ABC partnership, a dealer in dogs. A has a 50.1% interest in ABC's profits. A's gain on this sale is taxable as ordinary income because A directly controls the ABC partnership.

Note how § 707(b)(2) only applies to gains. It cannot, therefore, be manipulated to turn capital losses into ordinary losses.

C. LIMITATIONS ON CURRENT DEDUCTIONS ON TRANSACTIONS BETWEEN PARTNERS AND PARTNERSHIPS

Section 267(a)(2) defers deductions from transactions with partners until the partner takes the payment into gross income. It also sweeps in transactions between the partnership and persons who are *related* to the partner. § 267(e). There is no minimum ownership level, but the deferral is proportionate to the related partner's interest in the partnership. Reg. § 1.267(b)-1(b).

PROBLEM 4-1

A is an equal member of the accrual-method ABC partnership. A owns X Corp., a cash method taxpayer, which lent ABC some money last year. ABC partnership owes interest of $300 to X Corp. as of the end of its year. ABC pays X Corp. in year 4.

1) To what extent can ABC deduct this interest in year 1?

2) What is the impact on A's outside basis? See § 705(a)(2)(B).

Conversely, if X Corp. were on the accrual method and borrowed money from the ABC partnership and ABC were on the cash method, X Corp.'s interest expense deductions would be deferred in proportion to A's interest in ABC (i.e., one-third). Reg. § 1.267(b)-1(b), Examples (1) and (2).

D. GUARANTEED PAYMENT

A partnership implies risks. It is often necessary to offer assured income to certain partners in order to induce them to do what they would otherwise be expected to do as partners. For example, a partner in a real estate venture might insist on being paid a fixed sum for collecting and depositing the monthly rents. With this in mind, read Reg. § 1.707-1(c).

This grid may help sort out guaranteed payments from other forms of compensation:

	MEASURED BY INCOME	NOT MEASURED BY INCOME
PARTNER CAPACITY	Distributive share	§ 707(c) guaranteed payment
NON-PARTNER CAPACITY	§ 707(a) payment	§ 707(a) payment

1. IMPACT ON RECIPIENT

PRATT v. COMMISSIONER
64 T.C. 203 (1975), *aff'd in part and rev 'd in part,* 550 F.2d 1023 (5th Cir. 1977)

SCOTT, JUDGE:

The issue for decision is whether management fees for services performed by petitioners for, and interest earned on, loans made by petitioners to two limited partnerships, of which petitioners were general partners, are deductible by the partnerships, and, if so, whether these amounts are includable in the income of petitioners who report income on the cash basis in the year accrued and deducted as business expenses by the partnerships which report on an accrual basis, even though petitioners did not receive payment of the amounts in the years of accrual by the partnerships. . .

Each of the limited partnership agreements contained the following provisions:

"Such General Partners shall contribute their time and managerial abilities to this partnership, and each such General Partner shall expend his best effort to the management of and for the purpose for which this partnership was formed. That for such managerial services and abilities contributed by the said General Partners, they shall receive a fee of five (5%) per cent of the Gross Base Lease Rentals of the said leases, and then the said General Partners shall receive ten (10%) per cent of all overrides and/or percentage rentals provided for in said leases as a fee for such managerial services."

The General Partners shall give their personal services to the Partnership and shall devote thereto such time as they may deem necessary, without compensation other than the managerial fees as hereinbefore set out. Any of the Partners, General or Limited, may engage in other business ventures of every nature and description, independently or with others. . . .

The general partners had agreed that the management fees would be divided equally among the general partners who performed managerial services.

Petitioners contributed managerial services to the two partnerships and management fees were credited to accounts payable to them. These fees were accrued and deducted annually by each of the partnerships. . . The amount of management fees accrued by each of the partnerships in each of the years indicated is a reasonable and proper fee to pay for the services of managing a shopping center of the type of Parker Plaza and Stephenville. A like amount of fees would have had to have been paid to a third party, not a general partner, as a fee for managing the shopping centers had such shopping centers been managed by a third party.

These management fees were not paid to petitioners, and petitioners did not report their respective management fees on their respective income tax returns for the years 1967, 1968, and 1969. . . .

70

It was the intent of all the partners in Parker Plaza and Stephenville that the management fees and interest were to be expenses to the partnerships.

In his notice of deficiency mailed to each petitioner, respondent increased the income of each of them for each of the years 1968 and 1969 and each of them except Jack for 1967 by amounts equal to his portion of management fees and by the amounts of interest credited to his account by each partnership with the following explanation:

> "It is determined that in computing the ordinary net income of the partnerships Plaza Shopping Center, Ltd. and Stephenville Shopping Center, Ltd. claimed management fees and interest are not allowed, such amounts being determined a division of partnership profits. Accordingly, your distributive share of the partnerships' income is increased for 1967, 1968, and 1969 returns as ordinary income. . . ."

Petitioners stated that without question each of the partnerships could accrue and deduct the amounts of management fees and interest credited to petitioners' accounts had the amount been due and credited to third parties rather than partners, citing *Liflans Corp. v. United States,* 390 F.2d 965 (Ct. Cl. 1968), and that such third parties would not be required to include these amounts in their income if they reported their income on a cash basis until the amounts were actually or constructively received by them.

Petitioners contend that the management fees credited to them fall within the provisions of either 707(a) or 707(c) and under either section are properly deductible by the partnership but not includable in their income for the years accrued by the partnership and credited to their accounts. Petitioners point to no provisions of the statute other than sections 707(a) and 707(c) under which management fees to partners for services to the partnership might be treated differently than such items were treated under the law prior to the enactment of the 1954 Code. Prior to the enactment of the provisions of section 707 of the 1954 Code, credits or payments to a partner for services, whether designated as fees or as salary, were not deductible by the partnership in computing the partnership income but were considered as part of the distributive share of partnership income of the partner to whom the credit or payment was made pursuant to the partnership agreement. *Frederick S. Klein,* 25 T.C. 1045 (1956). Therefore, if the management fees credited to petitioners do not qualify as transactions between a partner and a partnership, covered by section 707(a) or as guaranteed payments under section 707(c), they are part of the partners' distributive income from the partnership, includable in their distributive shares of profit or loss under section 706 for their taxable year in which the taxable year of the partnership ends and not proper deductions by the partnership in computing distributive partnership income.

In our view the management fees credited to petitioners were not "guaranteed payments" under section 707(c) even though, for reasons hereinafter discussed, we would not agree with petitioners' position that they were not required to include the amounts of the fees in their income for the years here in issue even if they were to be so considered.

Section 707(c) refers to payments "determined without regard to the income." The parties make some argument as to whether payments based on "gross rentals" as provided in the partnership agreements should be considered as payments based on "income." In our view there is no merit to such a distinction. The amounts of the management fees are based on a fixed percentage of the partnership's gross rentals which in turn constitute partnership income. To us it follows that the payments are not determined without regard to the income of the partnership as required by section 707(c) for a payment to a partner for services to be a guaranteed payment.

Since we conclude that the management fees are not guaranteed payments under section 707(c), we must decide whether the provisions for such fees in the partnership agreement might be considered as a "transaction" engaged in by petitioners with the partnership in a capacity other than as a partner within the meaning of section 707(a). Initially, it might be noted that since section 707(c) deals specifically with continuing payments to a partner for services such as salary payments or the management fees here in issue, it is far from clear that such continuing payments were ever intended to come within the provisions of section 707(a). Section 707(a) refers to "transactions" between a partner and a partnership and is susceptible of being interpreted as covering only those services rendered by a partner to the partnership in a specific transaction as distinguished from continuing services of the partner which would either fall within section 707(c) or be in effect a partner's withdrawal of partnership profits. *See F. A. Falconer,* 40 T.C. 1011, 1015 (1963), where we stated as follows with respect to section 707(c):

"Section 707(c) has no counterpart in the Internal Revenue Code of 1939. It initially appeared in the Internal Revenue Code of 1954. Since we have been unable to locate in our research any court decisions pertaining directly to the issue here presented, we approach the problem as one of the first impression. *But compare Foster v. United States,* (S.D.N.Y. 1963, 12 A.F.T.R. 2d, par. 63-5058, 63-2 U.S.T.C. par. 9588). The legislative history of section 707(c) reveals that it was specifically intended to require ordinary income treatment to the partner receiving guaranteed salary payments and to give a deduction at the partnership level."

The touchstone for determining "guaranteed payments" is whether they are payable without regard to partnership income. And, in determining whether in a particular case an amount paid by a partnership to a partner is a "drawing" or a "guaranteed payment," the substance of the transaction, rather than its form, must govern. *See* sec. 1.701-1(a), Income Tax Regs. These are both factual matters to be judged from all the circumstances. S. Rept. No. 1622 to accompany H.R. 8300, 83d Cong., 2d Sess., p. 387 (1954), contains the following explanation:

"Subsection (c) provides a rule with respect to guaranteed payments to members of a partnership. A partner who renders services to the partnership for a fixed salary, payable without regard to partnership income, shall be treated, to the extent of such amount, as one who is not a partner, and the partnership shall be allowed a deduction for a business expense. The amount of such payment shall be included in the partner's gross income, and shall not be considered a distributive share of partnership income or gain. A partner who is guaranteed a minimum annual amount for his services shall be treated as receiving a fixed payment in that amount."

However, we need not decide whether a continuing payment to a partner for services was ever contemplated as being within the provisions of section 707(a).

Section 1.707-1(a) of the Income Tax Regulations with respect to a "partner not acting in capacity as partner" states that, "In all cases, the substance of the transaction will govern rather than its form." Here, the record indicates that in managing the partnership petitioners were acting in their capacity as partners. They were performing basic duties of the partnership business pursuant to the partnership agreement. Although we have been unable to find cases arising under the 1954 Code concerning when a partner is acting within his capacity as such, a few cases arising under the provisions of the 1939 Code dealt with whether a payment to a partner should be considered as paid to him in a capacity other than as a partner. *See Leif J. Sverdrup,* 14 T.C. 859, 866 (1950); *Wegener v. Commissioner,* 119 F.2d 49 (5th Cir. 1941), *aff'g.* 41 B.T.A. 857 (1940), *cert. denied* 314 U.S. 643 (1941). In *Wegener,* a joint venture was treated as a partnership for limited purposes, and the taxpayer-partner was found to be acting outside the scope of his partnership duties and in an individual capacity as an oil well drilling contractor, so that payments he received from the "partnership" for carrying out this separate and distinct activity were income to him individually as if he were an outsider. In the *Sverdrup* case, we recognized a payment to a taxpayer by a joint venture between a partnership of which the taxpayer was a member and a third party as compensation for work done on contracts being performed by the joint venture since "This sum was not a part of the income of the partnership of which he was a member, but was paid to him as an individual for services rendered to the joint venture."

Petitioners in this case were to receive the management fees for performing services within the normal scope of their duties as general partners and pursuant to the partnership agreement. There is no indication that any one of the petitioners was engaged in a transaction with the partnership other than in his capacity as a partner. We therefore hold that the management fees were not deductible business expenses of the partnership under section 707(a). Instead, in our view the net partnership income is not reduced by these amounts and each petitioner's respective share of partnership profit is increased or loss is reduced by his credited portion of the management fees in each year here in issue. *Frederick S. Klein, supra.*

Respondent on brief argues that the interest accrued by the partnership on the promissory notes evidencing loans by each petitioner to the partnerships are "guaranteed payments" under section 707(c) includable in petitioners' income for the year accrued by the partnership under section 706(a) and section 1.707-1(c), Income Tax Regs. Petitioners agree with respondent that under section 707(c) the interest on the notes are guaranteed payments but argue that these amounts are includable in their income only when received, and that the regulation making such payments includable in income by the partners in the year paid or accrued by the partnership (section 1.707(c), Income Tax Regs.), is "an overextension of Respondent's authority."

In our view respondent's regulation is a reasonable interpretation of section 707(c) and carries out the express intention of Congress as reflected in the legislative history of section 707(c). S. Rept. No. 1622, to accompany H.R. 8300 (Pub. L. No. 591), 83d Cong., 2d Sess. 387 (1954), states in part as follows:

> It should be noted that such payments, whether for services or for the use of capital, will be includable in the recipient's return for the taxable year with or within which the partnership year in which the payment was made, or accrued, ends.

This language leaves no doubt that Congress intended to foreclose the possibility that a partnership might accrue salary and interest expenses, which expenses would reduce each partner's distributive share of net partnership income or increase his loss therefrom, while the salaried partner might never receive the payments and therefore never include the amounts in income. As we pointed out in *Andrew O. Miller, Jr.,* 52 T.C. 752, 762 (1969). These words ("but only for the purpose of section 61(a) . . . and section 162(a) . . .") were added to section 707(c) by the Senate which at the same time also amended section 706 to provide that guaranteed payments received by a partner are to be included in his income for his taxable year in which the partnership's taxable year ends. In connection with section 707(c), the Senate committee report indicates that the reason for the change was to provide that guaranteed payments are to be included in income at the same time as a partner's distributive share – not at the time when compensation would ordinarily be included in income. This is the only example in the legislative history of the need for the "but only" words. *See also Thomas Browne Foster,* 42 T.C. 974, 980 (1964). In our view, section 1.707-1(c), Income Tax Regs., is valid and in accordance with the provisions of section 707(c). Decisions will be entered for the respondent.

NOTE

Capitalized guaranteed payments. Section 707(c) is explicit that a guaranteed payment used to compensate a partner must be capitalized if the services create a capital asset. After the *Pratt* decision came down, tax lawyers noted a loophole. If the service partner were compensated with an allocation, there could be no capitalization; one never capitalizes allocations. That meant that by using the blueprint mapped out in *Pratt* and applying it to a case where the service partner was, for example, devoting his time to the building of an apartment complex, the other partners would take a smaller allocation of profits instead of a larger allocation of profits plus a nondeductible service fee.

To illustrate: Murray is a member of the Murray, Moe & Jack building partnership. His profit share is so small we will ignore it. The partnership agreement states that he is entitled to receive 10% of gross rents as compensation for overseeing the staged development of a building. Rents are $100, and he receives $10 this year. If this were an allocation, he would report $10, and the other partners would report $90. If it were a guaranteed payment, the other partners would report $100 as their distributive share, and Murray would report § 707(c) income of $10. The § 707(c) payment would be capitalized, so the partners could not reduce their distributive shares by the guaranteed payment. Murray would get $10 under either structure, but Moe and Jack are better off with an allocation.

PROBLEM 4-2

Assume that the *Pratt* partnership has no expenses and rental income of $100 and that Mr. Pratt's only income was the payment decided in the *Pratt* case. There are 3 equal partners.

1) What is the character of the 10% management fee in the opinion of the court in *Pratt*?

2) According to the *Pratt* decision, would the other partners be entitled to deduct the 10% management fee?

3) Assuming that the 10% might have been a guaranteed payment, and that it had to be capitalized, how (if at all) would B and C benefit from the *Pratt* result?

4) Assuming that the 10% must be treated as a guaranteed payment and that A (the service partner) is on the cash method, but that the partnership is in the accrual method, when would A report the 10%? When the partnership accrues the expense? When A receives the $10? Some other time?

REV. RUL. 81-300
1981-2 C.B. 143

Issue

Are the management fees paid to partners under the circumstances described below distributive shares of partnership income or guaranteed payments under section 707(c) of the Internal Revenue Code?

Facts

The taxpayers are the general partners in a limited partnership formed to purchase, develop and operate a shopping center. The partnership agreement specifies the taxpayers' shares of the profit and loss of the partnership. The general partners have a ten percent interest

74

in each item of partnership income, gain, loss, deduction, or credit. In addition, the partnership agreement provides that the general partners must contribute their time, managerial abilities and best efforts to the partnership and that in return for their managerial services each will receive a fee of five percent of the gross rentals received by the partnership. These amounts will be paid to the general partners in all events.

Pursuant to the partnership agreement, the taxpayers carried out their duties as general partners and provided the management services required in the operation of the shopping centers. The management fee of five percent of gross rentals were reasonable in amount for the services rendered.

Law and Analysis

Section 707(a) of the Code provides that if a partner engages in a transaction with a partnership other than in the capacity of a member of such partnership, the transaction shall, except as otherwise provided in this section, be considered as occurring between the partnership and one who is not a partner.

Section 1.707-1(a) of the Income Tax Regulations provides that a partner who engages in a transaction with a partnership other than in the capacity of a partner shall be treated as if the partner were not a member of the partnership with respect to such transaction. The regulation's section further states that such transactions include the rendering of services by the partner to the partnership and that the substance of the transaction will govern rather than its form.

Section 707(c) of the Code provides that to the extent determined without regard to the income of the partnership, payments to a partner for services, termed "guaranteed payments," shall be considered as made to one who is not a member of the partnership, but only for purposes of section 61(a) and, subject to section 263, for purposes of section 162(a).

In *Pratt v. Commissioner,* 64 T. C. 203 (1975), *aff 'd in part, rev 'd in part,* 550 F.2d 1023 (5th Cir. 1977), under substantially similar facts to those in this case, both the United States Tax Court and the United States Court of Appeals for the Fifth Circuit held that management fees based on a percentage of gross rentals were not payments described in section 707(a) of the Code. The courts found that the terms of the partnership agreement and the actions of the parties indicated that the taxpayers were performing the management services in their capacities as general partners. *Compare* Rev. Rul. 81-301.

When a determination is made that a partner is performing services in the capacity of a partner, a question arises whether the compensation for the services is a guaranteed payment under section 707(c) of the Code or a distributive share of partnership income under section 704. In *Pratt,* the Tax Court held that the management fees were not guaranteed payments because they were computed as a percentage of gross rental income received by the partnership. The court reasoned that the gross rental income was "income" of the partnerships and, thus, the statutory test for a guaranteed payment, that it be "determined without regard to the income of the partnership," was not satisfied. On appeal, the taxpayer's argument was limited to the section 707(a) issue and the Fifth Circuit found it unnecessary to consider the application of section 707(c).

The legislative history of the Internal Revenue Code of 1954 indicates the intent of Congress to treat partnerships as entities in the case of certain transactions between partners and their partnerships. *See* S. Rep. No. 1622, 83d Cong., 2d Sess. 92 (1954). The Internal Revenue Code of 1939 and prior Revenue Acts contain no comparable provision and the courts had split on the question of whether a partner could deal with the partnership as an outsider. *Compare Lloyd v. Commissioner,* 15 B.T.A. 82 (1929) and *Wegener v. Commissioner,* 119 F.2d 49 (5th Cir. 1941), *aff'g* 41 B.T.A. 857 (1940), *cert. denied* 314 U.S. 643 (1941). This resulted both in uncertainty and in substantial computational problems when an aggregate theory was applied and the payment to a partner exceeded the partnership income. In such situations, the fixed salary was treated as a withdrawal of capital, taxable to the salaried partner to the extent that the withdrawal was made from the capital of other partners. *See,* for example, Rev. Rul. 55-30, 1955-1 C.B. 430. Terming such treatment as unrealistic and unnecessarily complicated, Congress enacted section 707(a) and (c) of the Code of 1954. Under section 707(a) the partnership is considered an unrelated entity for all purposes. Under section 707(c), the partnership is considered an unrelated entity for purposes of sections 61 and 162 to the extent that it makes a guaranteed payment for services or for the use of capital.

Although a fixed amount is the most obvious form of guaranteed payment, there are situations in which compensation for services is determined by reference to an item of gross income. For example, it is not unusual to compensate a manager of real property by reference to the gross rental income that the property produces. Such compensation arrangements do not give the provider of the service a share in the profits of the enterprise, but are designed to accurately measure the value of the services that are provided.

Thus, and in view of the legislative history and the purpose underlying section 707 of the Code, the term "guaranteed payment" should not be limited to fixed amounts. A payment for services determined by reference to an item of gross income will be a guaranteed payment if, on the basis of all of the facts and circumstances, the payment is compensation rather than a share of partnership profits. Relevant facts would include the reasonableness of the payment for the services provided and whether the method used to determine the amount of the payment would have been used to compensate an unrelated party for the services.

It is the position of the Internal Revenue Service that in *Pratt* the management fees were guaranteed payments under section 707(c) of the Code. On the facts presented, the payments were not disguised distributions of partnership net income, but were compensation for services payable without regard to partnership income.

Holding

The management fees are guaranteed payments under section 707(c) of the Code.

NOTES

1. **Taxation of the receipt of a guaranteed payment**. We know that the beneficiary of the guaranteed payment is taxed in the year the partnership reports the deduction (whether by payment or accrual). *See* Reg. § 1.707-1(c). Presumably, there is no second tax when the beneficiary is on the cash method and the accrual method partnership pays the receivable in a later year. There is, however, no clear authority for this obvious proposition. *Cf.* Reg. § 1.704-1(b)(2)(iv)(o) (capital accounts are only adjusted downward for guaranteed payments). The income from a guaranteed payment belongs on the payee's return alone.

2. **Legislative history**. The legislative history of the Deficit Reduction Act of 1984 attempted to narrow § 707(c) in favor of § 707(a) in close cases. *See S.* Rep. 98-169, 98th Cong., 2d Sess. 226 Title I Part E(2) (1984). This issue is discussed later in the chapter in connection with § 707(a)(2)(A).

3. **Self-Employment Taxes**. Guaranteed payments limited partners receive for services are subject to SECA taxes. §1402(a)(13). General partners include guaranteed payments and distributive shares of business profits in SECA earnings. §1402(a); Reg. §1.1402(a)-1(a)(2). Limited partners remain exempt from SECA on their distributive shares of partnership income.

2. GUARANTEED PAYMENT PLUS ALLOCATION

A minimum guaranteed payment can be combined with a profit-sharing allocation. In such cases, the allocation reduces the guaranteed payment; the net positive figure, if any, is the guaranteed payment for § 707(c) purposes.

To illustrate: A is a member of the AB partnership. A has a 30% distributive share, subject to a guarantee that he will never receive less than $100. The partnership agreement says that if the 30% share is less than $100, then the guaranteed amount is to be treated as a partnership expense. Assume the partnership earns $200 this year before paying A. A's guaranteed payment is $40, according to Reg. §1.70 7-1(c):

Guarantee	$100.00
Minus 30% distributive share of $200.00	($60.00)
Section 707(c) payment	$40.00

The partnership's income for the year, after deducting the guaranteed payment, is $160. The $60 is an allocation of profits to A. The remaining $100 is B's distributive share. The partners will share each item of partnership income in a 6:10 ratio, based on the $60 allocation to A and the $100 allocation to B. Rev. Rul. 69-180, 1969-1 C.B. 183. To put it in easier terms, as long as the distributive share at least equals the guaranteed minimum, the entire amount received by the beneficiary of the guaranteed payment is a distributive share. NB: You need to read the examples in Reg. §1.707-1(c) carefully in order to appreciate certain variations, noting, inter alia, that the "offset rule" (above) does not apply to capital gains or separately-stated items.

PROBLEM 4-3

A and B each contributed $25,000 to the newly formed AB partnership to operate an existing clothing store. The partnership is on the accrual method. Their agreement provides that, in connection with A's duties as a partner, A is entitled to an annual payment of $10,000 regardless of the income of the partnership. Any profit or loss, after deducting A's guaranteed amount, shall be shared equally between A and B. The first year's operation resulted in a loss of $15,000 after deducting A's guarantee. What net income or loss from the partnership should A report on her individual income tax return, assuming she was a material participant in the business? *See* Reg. § 1.707-1(c), Example 2.

PROBLEM 4-4

a) The equal LMN general partnership is on the accrual method of accounting and is a calendar year business enterprise with various kinds of income. L is a cash method calendar year partner. L gets $10 for services of a current nature (not a capitalized type) that he rendered to the partnership. How might the $10 be characterized?

b) If the payment to L is a § 707(a) payment, when does L report the payment in income?

c) If the payment to L is a § 707(c) payment, does L have income? For a §707(c) payment, must LMN defer the deduction until L is paid? *See* § 274(e).

d) What if the partnership does not actually pay L until next year? Is L still taxed on the income this year if it is otherwise a § 707(c) payment?

e) L will be paid 10% of gross revenues for designing a new product, a duty required by the partnership agreement. In the eyes of the *Pratt* court, what is the character of this arrangement? Assume L is working in his capacity as a partner.

f) In the view of Revenue Ruling 81-300 and assuming the financial arrangement is comparable to what the partnership would have paid an outsider, what is the character of this arrangement? A is working in his capacity as a partner.

g) Applying the result in "(f)" and assuming that some of the partnership's income was tax-exempt, does that mean some of the $10 paid to L is tax exempt? Does it matter how the $10 was characterized under (5)?

h) L gets $10 as a §707(a) payment, which is capitalized. Assume unrealistically that he has no profit share. What is the allocation to M and N this year, assuming the partnership had $300 of profits before considering the § 707(a) payment to L?

i) Same as "(h)". Is the $10 §707(a) payment deductible to the partnership?

j) Assume the $10 is designed to be a distributive share, but it is a § 707(a) payment and must be capitalized. Income is $300.

- What is the result to L?

- What is the result to M and N?

k) Assume L is entitled to and receives a guaranteed payment of $10, but the partnership earns $0. How much of what he is paid is a guaranteed payment?

l) Same as "(k)" above, but the partnership earns an operating profit of $100 (calculated before the guaranteed payment amount). How much of the $10 is a distributive share and how much is guaranteed payment?

m) L is entitled to the greater of 33% of partnership profits or $200, and the partnership earns $300 (calculated before the guaranteed payment amount). How much is the guaranteed payment?

n) What is M's distributive share?

o) Same as "(m)" above, but the payment to L is a § 707(c) payment that must be capitalized. How much income do M and N have?

E. DISGUISED TRANSACTIONS

1. COMPENSATION DISGUISED AS A DISTRIBUTION
Read § 707(a)(2)(A).

Section 707(a)(2)(A) has an interesting background. Following *Cagle v. CIR,* 539 F.2d 409 aff'g 63 TC 86 (1976), tax advisors realized that guaranteed payments would have to be capitalized if the services would have to be capitalized if performed by an outsider. To avoid this result, they used the device of paying for services through "allocations" of distributive shares of partnership income, plus distributions of money to these service "partners" in place of § 707(a) or § 707(c) payments. The scheme was to let the investor partners avoid the capitalization requirement and get *a de facto* deduction in the form of a reduced allocation of profits.

Congress responded with § 707(a)(2)(A), turning such patterns of allocations and distributions into § 707(a)(1) payments, thereby indirectly forcing their capitalization. Congress identified some factors that eventual regulations would use in order to sort disguised service contracts from good-faith allocations. The primary factor is whether the service provider bears any real economic risk of nonpayment. The second most important factor is whether the putative partner is a long-term member or is expected to withdraw once the services have been provided. There are further factors, but they are not worth dwelling on. It is important to notice that this section does not depend on taxpayer motivations, which means that the innocent can be punished along with the guilty.

PROBLEM 4-5

A commercial office building constructed by a partnership is projected to generate gross income of at least $100,000 per year indefinitely. Its architect, whose normal fee for such services is $40,000, contributes cash for a 25% interest in the partnership and receives both a 25% distributive share of net income for the life of the partnership and an allocation of $20,000 of partnership gross income for the first two years of partnership operations after lease-up. The partnership is expected to have sufficient cash available to distribute $20,000 to the architect in each of the first two years, and the agreement requires such distributions. How would you treat the architect's income from the partnership?

2. SALES AND EXCHANGES DISGUISED AS DISTRIBUTIONS

The game of cops and robbers never ends in the land of taxes. Congress has enacted the following three difficult and confusingly similar reform provisions that attack potentially abusive transactions between partnerships and their partners: §§ 707(a)(2)(B), 704(c)(1)(B), and 737.

Section 707(a)(2)(B)

Because contributions to and distributions from partnerships are generally nontaxable under §§ 721 and 731, respectively, it is tempting to use partnerships as fig leaves to conceal sales or exchanges between partners, or with the partnership. In the late 1980's aggressive taxpayers noticed the opportunity and manipulated the partnership rules in order to undertake Wall Street level tax-deferred corporate acquisitions in ways never intended by Congress. The deals were known as "mixing bowl" transactions, based on the image of various parties contributing different businesses into a partnership bowl tax-free, with the partnership mixing the interests and dishing them out selectively to other partners tax-free under § 731.

There was clearly a need for reform. Congress could have applied a remedy in the form of a subjective tax-avoidance test, or it could have used rigid, objective tests that would on occasion sweep in good people along with the bad. It chose the latter.

Section 707(a)(2)(B) is a frontal attack on disguised sales and exchanges. It applies when there is a direct or indirect transfer of money or other property to a partnership, and there is *a related* distribution of money or other property to the contributing partner or to another partner. If the two transactions, viewed together, are fairly characterized as a sale or exchange of the property, then § 707(a)(2)(B) steps in and taxes the combined transaction as a sale or exchange with the partnership, or between partners, as the facts may indicate.

There is a rebuttable presumption that where a transfer of property to a partnership occurs within two years of a distribution to the contributing partner, regardless of the order of the two transactions, a sale or exchange has occurred, unless one of several minor exceptions applies. Reg. § 1.707-3(c). The primary exceptions are for a reasonable guaranteed payment for capital, meaning not over 150% of the top applicable federal rate (AFR) when the guarantee is first established; a reasonable (not over 150% of the AFR) "preference return," meaning a preferential distribution on cash flow; and certain repayments of preoperating expenses. Reg. § 1.707-4(a), (b).

One has to be on one's toes here; the distribution that triggers the deemed sale might even arise from a mere decrease in the partner's share of partnership liabilities. Make sure to understand that the contribution and distribution may be either between the partnership and the partner or between partners. You draw your conclusion as to whether this is a disguised sale or exchange by looking at the facts through the microscope of § 707(a)(2)(B).

To illustrate: At the end of this year, L contributes land with a basis of $60 and a value of $100 to the equal LC partnership, in which L and C are equal partners. C contributed cash of $100 around the same time. Eighteen months later the partnership distributes the property to C and two months later it distributes $100 to L. This is rebuttably presumed a disguised sale between the partners. § 707(a)(2)(B). L would report a $40 gain and C would take a $100 basis in the property. In contrast, if L contributed land that stayed in the partnership and shortly thereafter L got back $100 in cash in a related transaction, that would be recharacterized as a sale from L to the partnership.

To the extent that § 707(a)(2)(B) does not apply, distributions of property (not cash) are subject to § 704(c)(1)(B) and § 737.

Section 704(c)(1)(B)

Recall § 704(c), which forces partners to report built-in gains or losses when the partnership sells property they contributed. However, a distribution is normally a nontaxable transaction to the partnership, because the § 704 allocation rules are generally independent of the distribution rules.

Now for the catch: if property with built-in gain or loss is merely distributed to a *different* partner within seven years of the contribution, § 704(c)(1)(B) creates a deemed sale of the property, thereby triggering the special § 704(c) allocation to the contributing partner to the extent it would have been triggered had it *really* been sold at its then fair market value.

To illustrate: This year, P contributes property with basis of $60 and a value of $100 to the PR partnership, in which P and R are equal partners. Six years later, when the property is still worth $100, the partnership distributes the property to R. There is no distribution to P. P is taxed as if P had sold the property to R. The allocable § 704(c) gain is whatever that gain would have been if the partnership had sold the property at its then value, namely $40 of gain. (Had the property lost value since it was contributed, the § 704(c) gain would have been correspondingly diminished.) R gets a $100 cost basis in the property under § 704(c)(l)(B)(iii). This would hold true whether or not P or R were out to avoid income taxes. P's outside basis rises by $40. *Id.*

Section 737

It is not over yet. Section 737 taxes a partner who contributed built-in gain property and to whom *a different property* was distributed within seven years. §737(b). The gain is the lesser of the §704(c) gain or the "excess distribution," meaning the value of the distributed property minus the partner's pre-distribution outside basis. Motives are irrelevant and it does not matter whether the partner's interest in the partnership is reduced by the distribution. Conf. Rep. No. 1018, 102d Cong. 2d Sess 428 (1992). This restricts mixing-bowl transactions in cases where the partnership would be willing to continue to hold property that is subject to the § 704(c) allocation.

To illustrate: This year, P contributes land with basis of $60 and a value of $100 to the PR partnership in which P and R are equal partners. R contributes stock, which has a basis and value of $100. Six years later, the partnership distributes the stock to P. There is no distribution to R. Assume P has a $60 outside basis. Section 737 taxes P on the lesser of: the $100 value of the stock minus P's $60 outside basis just before the distribution, viz., $40, or P's net precontribution gain of $40. So, either way P's § 737 gain is $40, and its character is the same as if the PR partnership had sold the property. §§ 704(c)(1)(B)(ii), 737(a). P's outside basis increases by $40 under § 737(c)(l). PR's basis in the land rises by $40. § 737(c)(2).

Now step back for a moment and review the scheme. Section 704(c) taxes built-in gains and losses to the contributing partner (P) when the partnership sells or exchanges the property. Section 707(a)(2)(B) taxes P if she engages in a disguised sale or exchange of the property with the partnership or another partner. It looks for related transactions. Section 704(c)(1)(B) taxes P if the partnership distributes the property to another partner within 7 years. Section 737 taxes P if the partnership distributes other property to P within 7 years. Does this make a coherent system? A wise or necessary one?

PROBLEM 4-6

Please explain the outcome of the following transactions: Z and X agree to form the equal ZX Partnership. Z contributes land, with an adjusted basis of $80 and worth $100, plus cash of $100 in exchange for her interest in the ZX Partnership. X contributes cash of $200.

a) If the partnership subsequently sells the land when it is worth $150, what is the tax impact to Z and X?

b) Same facts as above, except that instead of selling the land, pursuant to their prearranged plan, the ZX partnership distributes $100 in cash to Z and the land to X? What is the tax impact to Z and X? *See* Reg. § 1.707-3(b)(2) for a list of factors that might apply (to find "sales or exchanges").

c) Same as "(b)," but there is no prearranged plan, although the distributions occur 18 months after the contributions.

d) Instead of undertaking any of the transactions in "(a)" thru "(c)" above, the only notable event is that six years after the contributions the ZX partnership distributes the land to X, at a time when the land is still worth $100. Which partner, if either, is taxed? What is X's basis in the property?

e) Same as "(a)," except that, instead of contributing $200, X originally contributed a painting with a value and basis of $100, plus cash of $100. Four years later, the partnership distributes that painting to Z. There is no tax avoidance intent in the partners' dealings. Is either partner taxed as a result of the transactions, and if so, what is the amount of the income or gain? Remember: Z contributed land with an adjusted basis of $80 and value of $100.

F. FRINGE BENEFITS

The Code grants a number of nontaxable benefits to *employees*. Examples include premiums on up to $50,000 of group-term life insurance coverage under § 79 and certain meals and lodging under § 119. Because partners are not employees, such benefits are unavailable to partners. Thus, even though some benefits, such as daycare assistance plans, are available to partners because such plans' tax benefits can extend to non-employees, no one will choose the partnership form of doing business for its fringe benefit advantage.

Chapter 5

PARTNERSHIP ALLOCATIONS

A. ALLOCATION OF PROFITS AND LOSSES GENERALLY
Read § 704(b).

Tax lawyers involved in structuring a partnership often have to address the validity of the allocations among the partners of overall profits and losses or of specific items. To the extent an allocation is invalid, the tax law requires that it be adjusted to take account of the real economics of the partnership. If that occurs as a result of an IRS audit, the remedial adjustments may cause major additional taxes as well as interest and possible penalties.

Section 704(a) declares that each partner's distributive share of the partnership's income, gain, loss, deduction, and credit is generally determined by the partnership agreement unless the allocation of those items in the agreement lacks "substantial economic effect." "The agreement" includes amendments made up to the filing date for the partnership's tax return. § 761(c). Subchapter K's unique flexibility invites manipulation by structuring the partnership agreement to allocate a disproportionate amount of tax-exempt income or depreciation deductions to high-bracket partners while allocating the taxable income to low-bracket partners. The government's previous approach to such abuses was to invalidate allocations that were designed to avoid taxes. The core idea under the current regulations is that the partners' agreement as to how income or deductions are allocated must be accompanied by real economic impacts, or be disregarded. *See* Reg. § 1.704-1(b)(2)(ii)(a). Taxpayer motivations no longer count.

This chapter concentrates heavily on the concept of the partner's capital account to measure the viability of allocations of gains and losses, or of particular items, to the partners. The capital account is an accounting concept, not a tax concept. Its purpose is to compute what the partner would be entitled to as a matter of state law on the liquidation of the partnership. The Code never refers to capital accounts, but the partnership tax Regulations rely on them heavily. If one wanted to define the term loosely, one might say the capital account is the account that values the partner's interest in the partnership. One notable result is that if the partnership has significant losses, capital accounts can become negative because the losses are often based on money that the partnership borrowed.

If the partners adhere to the capital account rules now found in the Regulations, they will use fair market values (not basis) net of liabilities to report contributions (and distributions) in order to compute capital accounts. This is because the allocation provisions in the § 704(b) regulations dictate that in order to ensure that allocations are viable, the capital accounts must be maintained using fair-market values. Many commentators now assume that all partnership capital accounts use fair market values. However, this does not call for constantly revaluating the accounts, rather, the regulations call for using fair market values (net of associated liabilities) for property contributed to the partnership and distributed from the partnership, and the Regulations countenance the idea of revaluing partnership property when a service partner is admitted for a profits interest. This assures the service partner is really getting a share of profits, as opposed to a share of unrealized appreciation, when she is admitted. *See* Rev. Proc. 93-27. 1933-1 CB 32. Valuing property net of associated liabilities is referred to as using "book value." The other nontax role of the capital account is to record income and losses attributable to each partner.

It also makes business sense to use fair market values to value capital accounts because partnership agreements commonly provide that a partner's claim on the partnership's assets when the partnership liquidates (or when the partner withdraws) turns on the dollar amount of the partner's capital account.

To illustrate: Scientist contributes a patent worth $200 and having a basis of $10 to a 50:50 partnership with J.P. Bigley, a venture capitalist, who contributes $200 in cash, and who takes a special allocation of all operating losses. The partnership agreement requires the maintenance of capital accounts, using fair market values for contributions and distributions. If the venture loses $200 in cash and goes out of business, the only remaining asset is the patent. Under their partnership agreement, Bigley has a $0 capital account and Scientist has a $200 capital account, which entitles him to $200 in cash or kind when the partnership winds up its affairs and distributes its assets. As a practical matter, the partnership can either sell the patent (for $200) or distribute $200 in cash to him, or scientist may take back the patent.

Now, back to allocations. If an allocation does fail under the tax law, then one must determine the "real" allocation by evaluating what the Regulations refer to as the "partner's interest in the partnership," essentially meaning the real economics that underlie the partnership agreement.

You need to know about so-called "gain charge backs." These are special allocations of gain on the sale of partnership assets, the primary purpose of which is to attribute gains based on prior depreciation deductions back to partners who disproportionately enjoyed such deductions. In the typical real estate partnership, wealthier partners find such charge backs economically acceptable because the tax benefit of current depreciation deductions is not truly offset by the burden of subsequent identical gains because of the time value of money, and the gentle top rate of 25% at which real estate recapture gain is taxed. A simple example goes like this. We are partners in a realty business. You are rich. We buy a building for investment for $100. You claim all the depreciation. When the building has a $0 basis, the partnership sells it for $160. If there is a gain chargeback, you are allocated the first $100 of gain, which will be taxed at not over 25%, with the balance taxed at not over 15%.

The following case was decided under the old motives-based Regulations, but read it carefully and try to understand it, because its ghost rides again and again through the materials that follow.

ORRISCH v. COMMISSIONER
55 T.C. 395 (1970), *aff'd per curiam in unpublished opinion* (9th Cir. 1973)

FEATHERSTON, JUDGE:

[The Orrisches and the Crisafis were partners in a partnership that owned depreciable real estate. They orally agreed to allocate all the depreciation to the Orrisches, provided that when the property was sold the Orrisches would be allocated an amount of gain on sale equal to their extra measure of depreciation (a form of gain charge back). There was no evidence as to how the parties would share an economic loss on the disposition of the properties. The special allocation of losses offered the parties an overall tax benefit, as the court explains herein.]

Opinion

The only issue presented for decision is whether tax effect can be given the agreement between petitioners and the Crisafis that, beginning with 1966, all the partnership's depreciation deductions were to be allocated to petitioners for their use in computing their individual income tax liabilities. In our view, the answer must be in the negative, and the amounts of each of the partners' deductions for the depreciation of partnership property must be determined in accordance with the ratio used generally in computing their distributive shares of the partnership's profits and losses.

Among the important innovations of the 1954 Code are limited provisions for flexibility in arrangements for the sharing of income, losses, and deductions arising from business activities conducted through partnerships. The authority for special allocations of such items appears in section 704(a), which provides that a partner's share of any item of income, gain, loss, deduction, or credit shall be determined by the partnership agreement. That rule is coupled with a limitation in section 704(b), however, which states that a special allocation of an item will be disregarded if its "principal purpose" is the avoidance or evasion of Federal income tax. *See Smith v. Commissioner,* 331 F.2d 298 (C.A. 7, 1964), affirming a Memorandum Opinion of this Court; *Jean v. Kresser,* 54 T.C, 1621 (1970). In case a special allocation is disregarded, the partner's share of the item is to be determined in accordance with the ratio by which the partners divide the general profits or losses of the partnership. Sec. 1.704-1(b)(2), Income Tax Regs.

The report of the Senate Committee on Finance accompanying the bill … explained the tax-avoidance restriction prescribed by section 704(b) as follows:

> "Subsection (b) . . . provides that if the principal purpose of any provision in the partnership agreement dealing with a partner's distributive share of a particular item is to avoid or evade the Federal income tax, the partner's distributive share of that item shall be redetermined in accordance with his distributive share of partnership income or loss described in section 702(a)(9) [i.e., the ratio used by the partners for dividing general profits or losses]. . . ."

Where, however, a provision in a partnership agreement for a special allocation of certain items has substantial economic effect and is not merely a device for reducing the taxes of certain partners without actually affecting their shares of partnership income, then such a provision will be recognized for tax purposes. . . .

This reference to "substantial economic effect" did not appear in the House Ways and Means Committee report … discussing section 704(b), and was apparently added in the Senate Finance Committee to allay fears that special allocations of income or deductions would be denied effect in every case where the allocation resulted in a reduction in the income tax liabilities of one or more of the partners. The statement is an affirmation that special allocations are ordinarily to be recognized if they have business validity apart from their tax consequences. …

In resolving the question whether the principal purpose of a provision in a partnership agreement is the avoidance or evasion of Federal income tax, all the facts and circumstances in relation to the provision must be taken into account. Section 1.704-1(b)(2), Income Tax Regs., lists the following as relevant circumstances to be considered:

> "Whether the partnership or a partner individually has a business purpose for the allocation; whether the allocation has "substantial economic effect," that is, whether the allocation may actually affect the dollar amount of the partners' shares of the total partnership income or loss independently of tax consequences; whether related items of income, gain, loss, deduction, or credit from the same source are subject to the same

allocation; whether the allocation was made without recognition of normal business factors and only after the amount of the specially allocated item could reasonably be estimated; the duration of the allocation; and the overall tax consequences of the allocation. . . ."

Applying these standards, we do not think the special allocation of depreciation in the present case can be given effect.

The evidence is persuasive that the special allocation of depreciation was adopted for a tax-avoidance rather than a business purpose. Depreciation was the only item which was adjusted by the parties; both the income from the buildings and the expenses incurred in their operation, maintenance, and repair were allocated to the partners equally. Since the deduction for depreciation does not vary from year to year with the fortunes of the business, the parties obviously knew what the tax effect of the special allocation would be at the time they adopted it. Furthermore, as shown by our Findings, petitioners had large amounts of income which would be offset by the additional deduction for depreciation; the Crisafis, in contrast, had no taxable income from which to subtract the partnership depreciation deductions, and, due to depreciation deductions which they were obtaining with respect to other housing projects, could expect to have no taxable income in the near future. On the other hand, the insulation of the Crisafis from at least part of a potential capital gains tax was an obvious tax advantage. The inference is unmistakably clear that the agreement did not reflect normal business considerations but was designed primarily to minimize the overall tax liabilities of the partners.

Petitioners urge that the special allocation of the depreciation deduction was adopted in order to equalize the capital accounts of the partners, correcting a disparity ($14,000) in the amounts initially contributed to the partnership by them ($26,500) and the Crisafis ($12,500). But the evidence does not support this contention. Under the special allocation agreement, petitioners were to be entitled, in computing their individual income tax liabilities, to deduct the full amount of the depreciation realized on the partnership property. For 1966, as an example, petitioners were allocated a sum ($18,904) equal to the depreciation on the partnership property ($18,412) plus one-half of the net loss computed without regard to depreciation ($492). The other one-half of the net loss was, of course, allocated to the Crisafis. Petitioners' allocation ($18,904) was then applied to reduce their capital account. The depreciation specially allocated to petitioners ($18,412) in 1966 alone exceeded the amount of the disparity in the contributions. Indeed, at the end of 1967, petitioners' capital account showed a deficit of $25,187.11 compared with a positive balance of $405.65 in the Crisafis' account. By the time the partnership's properties are fully depreciated, the amount of the reduction in petitioners' capital account will approximate the remaining basis for the buildings as of the end of 1967. The Crisafis' capital account will be adjusted only for contributions, withdrawals, gain or loss, without regard to depreciation, and similar adjustments for these factors will also be made in petitioners' capital account. Thus, rather than correcting an imbalance in the capital accounts of the partners, the special allocation of depreciation will create a vastly greater imbalance than existed at the end of 1966. In the light of these facts, we find it incredible that equalization of the capital accounts was the objective of the special allocation.

This case is to be distinguished from situations where one partner contributed property and the other cash; in such cases sec. 704(c) may allow a special allocation of income and expenses in order to reflect the tax consequences inherent in the original contributions.

Petitioners rely primarily on the argument that the allocation has "substantial economic effect" in that it is reflected in the capital accounts of the partners. Referring to the material quoted above from the report of the Senate Committee on Finance, they contend that this alone is sufficient to show that the special allocation served a business rather than a tax-avoidance purpose.

According to the regulations, an allocation has economic effect if it "may actually affect the dollar amount of the partners' shares of the total partnership income or loss independently of tax consequences." The agreement in this case provided not only for the allocation of depreciation to petitioners but also for gain on the sale of the partnership property to be "charged back" to them. The charge back would cause the gain, for tax purposes, to be allocated on the books entirely to petitioners to the extent of the special allocation of depreciation, and their capital account would be correspondingly increased. The remainder of the gain, if any, would be shared equally by the partners. If the gain on the sale were to equal or exceed the depreciation specially allocated to petitioners, the increase in their capital account caused by the charge back would exactly equal the depreciation deductions previously allowed to them and the proceeds of the sale of the property would be divided equally. In such circumstances, the only effect of the allocation would be a trade of tax consequences, i.e., the Crisafis would relinquish a current depreciation deduction in exchange for exoneration from all or part of the capital gains tax when the property is sold, and petitioners would enjoy a larger current depreciation deduction but would assume a larger ultimate capital gains tax liability. Quite clearly, if the property is sold at a gain, the special allocation will affect only the tax liabilities of the partners and will have no other economic effect.

To find any economic effect of the special allocation agreement aside from its tax consequences, we must, therefore, look to see who is to bear the economic burden of the depreciation if the buildings should be sold for a sum less than their original cost. There is not one syllable of evidence bearing directly on this crucial point. We have noted, however, that when the buildings are fully depreciated, petitioners' capital account will have a deficit, or there will be a disparity in the capital accounts, approximately equal to the undepreciated basis of the buildings as of the beginning of 1966. Under normal accounting procedures, if the building were sold at a gain less than the amount of such disparity petitioners would either be required to contribute to the partnership a sum equal to the remaining deficit in their capital account after the gain on the sale had been added back or would be entitled to receive a proportionately smaller share of the partnership assets on liquidation. Based on the record as a whole, we do not think the partners ever agreed to such an arrangement. On dissolution, we think the partners contemplated an equal division of the partnership assets which would be adjusted only for disparities in cash contributions or withdrawals. Certainly there is no evidence to show otherwise. That being true, the special allocation does not "actually affect the dollar amount of the partners' share of the total partnership income or loss independently of tax consequences" within the meaning of the regulation referred to above.

In the light of all the evidence we have found as an ultimate fact that the "principal purpose" of the special allocation agreement was tax avoidance within the meaning of section 704(b). Accordingly, the deduction for depreciation for 1966 and 1967 must be allocated between the parties in the same manner as other deductions.

Decision will be entered for the respondent.

NOTE

Here is a simplified model of the capital account analysis that the Orrisch court was struggling with:

To illustrate: The Orrisches and the Crisafis contribute $10 each and the partnership borrows $80 on a nonrecourse basis from the Friendly Bank to buy a building for $100. The building is written off to $0, with the Orrisches taking all the depreciation. If it is sold for $0, the $80 loan still encumbers the property, so there is an $80 *Tufts* gain, which is charged back in full to the Orrisches.

Capital Accounts:

	Orrisches	Crisafis
Contribution	$10.00	$10.00
Deductions	($100.00)	-0-
Capital account	($90.00)	$10.00
Gain on sale	$80.00	-0-
Balance	($10.00)	$10.00

If the partnership agreement had obligated the Orrisches to contribute $10 to eliminate their deficit and thereby pay the Crisafis their capital account, the court might have been satisfied with the result, but there was no such duty. There was only a charge back of the $80 gain, with any cash liquidating distributions made without reference to the post-charge back capital accounts. Another way to put it is that the special allocation of depreciation was not felt in cash, so the special allocation was meaningless.

1. SPECIAL ALLOCATIONS VERSUS "BOTTOM-LINE" ALLOCATIONS

A "bottom-line allocation" is an allocation of a partner's share of a partnership's profit or loss, exclusive of partnership items that have to be separately stated under § 702(a). Reg. § 1.704-1(b)(1)(vii). By contrast, a "special allocation" is an allocation of some particular item, such as tax-exempt interests the partnership earns or spends and which differs from the division of profits and losses generally.

What you are about to read is novel and intricate. You must keep your sense of perspective about this topic. The subject matter is whether a particular allocation – whether special or "bottom-line" – to a partner reported on a Form K-1 for a particular year is valid in the sense of deserving enough respect on economic grounds to let the partner report the allocation on her personal tax return. If it is not, then one must divine and retrofit the "true" allocation based on the economic realities of partnership. There is almost no authority on how to go about this, except a statement in Reg. § 1.704-1(b)(3) to the effect that one uses "the partner's interest in the partnership," based on all the facts and circumstances, and a virtually useless presumption that everyone is an equal partner. The overarching idea is that tax allocations are good only if they follow economic reality; that generally calls for matching the tax allocation with an actual flow of cash and other property by value into and out of the partnership.

2. POST-1985 APPROACH TO PARTNERSHIP ALLOCATIONS

The Treasury Department greatly modified the § 704(b) regulations for post-1985 years, moving away from a search for motives and substituting a complicated economic analysis. The essential effect of the new rules is to disregard either special or "bottom-line" allocations if they lack "substantial economic effect." In such cases, the partners' distributive shares are instead allocated in accordance with their "interests in the partnership."

The approach of the new regulations is to apply a dual test at the end of each partnership taxable year. The first test requires that the allocation have "economic effect." Reg. 1.704-1(b)(2)(i). The second test requires the economic effect to be "substantial." *Id.* If the allocation satisfies the rigorous standards imposed by the regulations by both having economic effect *and* being substantial, it is definitely validated. Hence, the new regulations in effect offer a safe harbor. If an allocation cannot find its way into the safe harbor, it may still be valid on the theory that it reflects the partner's interest in the partnership.

a. Economic Effect

The fundamental concept is that any allocation must reflect the economic arrangement of the partners, i.e., generally have a realistic chance of being felt in cash, the value of property, or both combined. To do so, Reg. § 1.704-1(b)(2)(ii)(b) applies a cumulative three-step test, which is commonly referred to as the three-part mechanical test.

Three-part mechanical test: This powerful test grants an allocation "economic effect" if, throughout the life of the partnership, the partnership agreement (including all side agreements) assures that:

1. The partners' capital accounts are determined and maintained under the usual rules for determining outside basis, except that one uses fair-market values (minus associated liabilities) in connection with computing contributions and distributions of property; *and*

2. On the liquidation of the partnership (or of a partner's interest in the partnership) distributions are made exclusively in accordance with the positive capital account balances of each partner; *and*

3. If a partner has a deficit capital account balance after all adjustments for the year of the liquidation, he or she must contribute enough cash to the partnership to restore the deficit in order to pay partnership creditors or partners with positive capital account balances. This requirement is often referred to as a "deficit make-up" or "deficit restoration" provision. To the extent the partner has a limited duty to restore the deficit, this test is met to the extent of the duty to restore. State law may impose such an obligation. One affirmative way to generate a limited duty is to contribute one's own promissory note. Reg. § 1.704-1(b)(2)(iv)(d)(2).

Think back to how the taxpayer's agreement in *Orrisch* failed to meet these tests.

Alternative economic effect test: If a partnership allocation fails only the third part of the three-part mechanical test, the allocation may still have economic effect if it satisfies the "alternate economic effect test." Reg. § 1.704-1(b)(2)(ii)(d). This requires that the partnership agreement contain a "qualified income offset" (QIO). A QIO is an allocation of items of income and gain in an amount sufficient to eliminate, as quickly as possible, any deficit balance caused by *unexpected* adjustments, allocations, or distributions. (An example of an expected adjustment would be a depreciation deduction; an easy example of an unexpected adjustment would be a casualty loss.) This dictates that every partnership agreement without a deficit restoration clause contain a QIO. Note that the QIO is a highly legalistic concept. It only works as long as there are no deficits in excess of the partner's deficit make up obligation. A QIO does not validate an allocation that produces a deficit. The following QIO language was extracted from an actual partnership agreement:

> "(v) Prior to any allocations for a fiscal year under [a prior section of the agreement], in the event any partner unexpectedly receives any adjustments, allocations or distributions described in Treasury Regulations – Section 1.704-1(b)(2)(ii)(d)(4), (5) or (6) and such adjustment, allocation or distribution results in any partner having a deficit in his or her capital account, then items of income and gain shall be specially allocated to each such partner in an amount and manner sufficient to eliminate, as quickly as possible, to the extent required by Treasury Regulations, the deficit of such

partner. This provision is intended to comply with the qualified income offset requirement in Treasury Regulations Section 1.704-1(b)(2)(ii)(d)(3), and shall be interpreted consistently therewith."

If there is a QIO, limited obligations of a partner to restore his deficit will be respected. Reg. § 1.704-1(b)(2)(ii)(f).

To illustrate: X is an equal member of the XYZ partnership, which lost $60 this year. His capital account at year-end is $15, before allocating $20 of loss to him. The partnership agreement fails the deficit restoration part of the three-part economic effect test, but it does have a QIO. The allocation of $15 of losses to him has economic effect, but the allocation of the last $5 does not. Instead, the remaining $5 will generally be allocated to the partners who have a deficit restoration duty or who have positive capital accounts. Reg. §§ 1.704-1(b)(3)(iii) and 1.704-1(b)(5), examples (1)(iv)-(vi) and (15)(ii) and (iii).

Economic effect equivalency test: If the partnership agreement fails both the three-part mechanical test *and* the alternate test for economic effect, allocations made to partners pursuant to the partnership agreement may nevertheless be treated as having economic effect if the partnership agreement ensures that a liquidation of the partnership as of the end of each partnership taxable year will produce the same economic results to the partners as would occur if the Three Part Mechanical Test had been in operation.

This back-up protection is likely to be important if there is no deficit make-up provision in the partnership agreement, but state law in effect supplies such a provision. *See* Reg. § 1.704-1(b)(2)(ii)(i). This is the only reference you will see to the economic effect equivalency test in this book.

b. Substantial

(1) General Rule

If an allocation is found to have economic effect, the next step is to determine whether that effect is also "substantial." If not, the allocation fails and must be retrofitted in light of the partner's interest in the partnership. Generally, the economic effect of an allocation is substantial if there is a reasonable possibility that the allocation will significantly affect the dollar amounts or value of property to be received by partners from the partnership independent of tax consequences. Reg. § 1.704-1(b)(2)(iii)(a). Conversely, the Regulations contain a general rule that stabs tax arbitrage in the heart; specifically, an allocation cannot be substantial if at the time the allocation becomes part of the partnership agreement:

1. The after-tax economic consequences of at least one partner may, in present value terms, be enhanced by the allocation; and

2. There is a "strong likelihood" that the after-tax economic consequences of no partner will, in present value terms, be substantially diminished by the allocation.

"In present value terms" means that one uses discounting techniques to take account of "futurity," simply meaning the fact that a dollar received tomorrow is worth less than one received today. The Regulations do not tell one what interest rate to use when discounting future receipts or disbursements. The Regulations tell one to apply this test in light of each partner's tax situation outside the partnership. In the real world this is hard to do and is perhaps largely an *in terrorem* clause which prevents marketing structures which are based on tax arbitrage.

(2) Shifting and Transitory Allocations

The regulations attack specific types of allocations for lack of substantiality, namely "shifting allocations" and "transitory allocations." These specific rules are in addition to the general rule.

a) Shifting Allocations

A shifting allocation is one which, when inserted in the partnership agreement, creates a strong likelihood that (1) the net increases and decreases in the partners' capital accounts within a single tax year will not differ substantially from the net increases and decreases if the allocation were not part of the partnership agreement, *and* (2) the total tax liability of the partners will decline as a result of the allocation. For this purpose, one again takes into account the impact of the partners' non-partnership tax items. Reg. § 1.704-1(b)(2)(iii)(b) and (c).

PROBLEM 5-1

A and B are equal members of the AB partnership.

1) Each contributes cash of $100,000. The Partnership buys business equipment that it writes off on the straight line method at a rate of $20,000/year over an anticipated 10-year life. A claims the entire depreciation deduction every year. Assume the partnership otherwise runs at a break even level. Three years later, the partnership sells the business assets for $140,000 (at no gain or loss) and goes out of business. How must the partners distribute the cash proceeds in order to be in compliance with the Big Three requirements?

2) How would the answer to "(1)" differ if the business assets were instead sold for $200,000?

3) Assume A and B are equal members of the AB partnership. Assume the AB partnership is expected to report a $100 ordinary income and $80 of tax-exempt income. A is in the 40% tax bracket and B has a $100 net operating loss carryover this year. Knowing this, the partners amend the agreement for the year to provide that A will get all the tax-exempt income and B will get the $100 of operating income. Assume the partnership agreement satisfies the economic effect requirements.

    a. Is this year's allocation valid?

    b. Would it matter if A and B were unaware of each other's tax situations?

b) Transitory Allocations

These are multi-year variants of the shifting allocation. The sin here is creating an allocation this year that will likely be offset by a countervailing allocation within five years, plus a net tax saving to the partners. More precisely, the Regulations find a transitory allocation if there is a strong likelihood, at the time the allocations became part of the partnership agreement, that the net increases and decreases in the partners' capital accounts as a result of allocations over several years will not differ substantially from the net increases and decreases that would have occurred had the allocations not been made, *and* the partners' collective tax liability declines. If these two conditions are met, the Regulations rebuttably presume the likelihood that these events would occur. Reg. § 1.704-1(b)(2)(iii)(c).

Although the "likelihood" is often within the subjective control of the partners (such as a decision to sell property in the future), the Regulations avoid the search for intentions by providing that if the two conditions (no big capital account change plus tax saving) are met, the likelihood is rebuttably presumed to have existed from the outset. Conversely, offsetting allocations that are separated by over five years are presumed innocent.

An example of a transitory allocation would be a two-person partnership which specially allocated all its income in one year to a partner with a net operating loss deduction, with an agreement that in the following year(s) the other partner would be allocated an offsetting amount of income; the effect is to stabilize the capital account balances over time while reducing aggregate tax liability of the collaborating partners. Because the allocation is "transitory," it is disregarded and restructured in accordance with the partner's interest in the partnership.

The "transitory allocation" rules create the possibility that any extra claim to depreciation deductions will be invalidated if the partnership agreement contains a "gain chargeback" under which the partner who claimed an extra measure of depreciation is allocated a gain equal to the extra depreciation previously claimed when the property is sold. Reg. § 1.704-1(b)(2)(iii)(c)(2) comes to the partners' rescue by conclusively (and unrealistically) presuming that cost recovery deductions are matched by an equal decrease in the property's value, thereby obliterating the risk that the initial allocation of gain will be invalidated because it creates a fiction that the gain charge back will never apply. That, by administrative magic, renders the special allocation of depreciation "permanent" rather than transitory. This can be boon for the real estate industry, where tax depreciation is an all-important factor and investors generally assume that the property will not really decline in market value.

PROBLEM 5-2

Scientist has invented a new industrial process that is in need of development. Scientist thinks $200,000 is needed to bring it to market. The partnership agreement satisfies the mechanical three-part test. Money is willing to invest $200,000 in cash to become a 50:50 partner. Money insists that all losses be allocated to him, and that once the partnership becomes profitable, he be allocated enough profit to restore his capital account up to $200,000 after which profits will be shared 50:50. Because the three-part test is met, Scientist could have been allocated a disproportionate share of the losses because they would be covered by his deficit make-up obligation. As expected, the partnership spends $200,000 and then, four years later, begins making money. Is the allocation invalid by virtue of being "transitory"? *See* Reg. §§ 1.704-1(b)(2)(iii)(c)(2) and 1.704-1(b)(5), Example (3).

c) Amendment of the Partnership Agreement

The Regulations assume that one is dealing with "the" partnership agreement, but we have already seen that § 761 generously allows amendments to the agreement, as long as they are made before the original due date of the partnership's tax return. This flexibility means there is always a risk that the partners have an unwritten agreement to change the partnership document at a crucial moment and in a way that subverts the allocation provisions. For example, the partners may presently have a viable allocation of depreciation with the correct gain charge backs on sale of the property in anticipation of liquidation, but they may secretly agree that at that future date they will amend the partnership agreement to eliminate the deficit make-up provision. Reg. § 1.704-1(b)(4)(vi) contains a menacing statement that the prior allocations will be modified retroactively in such cases.

c. Partner's Interest in the Partnership

If an allocation does not pass the substantial economic effect test, it will be reallocated in accordance with the partner's interest in the partnership. One determines a partner's interest in the partnership by reference to the real economics dictated by the partnership agreement. Reg. § 1.704-1(b)(3)(i). This generally calls for evaluating the partner's contributions to the partnership, his or her share of current cash flow, and claims to distributions of cash and property (by value) during the partnership's entire life. Think back to how empty the *Orrisch* deal was in this respect, i.e., how the Tax Court realized in truth that the Orrisches and the Crisafis really split all cash income and losses, causing the attempted special allocation of depreciation to fail.

The following elaborate problem poses an allocation that does not smell right and asks you to determine for yourself what the partners' interest in the partnership really is. The problem is challenging. Do not despair if you cannot solve it, but do appreciate how even a fairly basic issue in this area calls for intensive analysis.

PROBLEM 5-3

Money Partner (MP), skeptical of Development Partner's (DP) grandiose claims with respect to the marketability of a building which DP proposes to build with MP's funds, negotiates the following agreement:

Profits and losses will be allocated equally, although MP will contribute $100 and DP only $1. MP's claim to cash distributions will grow at a rate of 10% simple interest for each year that any part of his capital remains unrecovered. They agree that the preferential distributions to MP will not reduce MP's capital account. No cash distribution will be made to DP until MP's claim to preferential distributions is satisfied, after which, cash will be shared in accordance with the partners' relative capital accounts, and provided that in all events MP will be paid in full before DP shares in cash flow. The unpaid accumulated claims against future cash flow, which grow at interest, are to be recorded in a memorandum account off the formal tax or financial records. What this means is that, if DP's claims about the building are true, he will get a lot of cash; if not, MP will have a preferential position with respect to whatever cash may grow out of the investment, with compensation for delay. There is no deficit make-up provision in the agreement (nor does state law impose one).

At the beginning of Year 1, the partners' capital accounts are as follows:

Money Partner   *Development Partner*

$100.00 $1.00

During Year 1, the partnership loses $2. The loss is shared equally, and the capital accounts will appear as follows:

Money	*Partner*	*Development Partner*
Opening	$100.00	$1.00
Loss	*($1.00)*	*($1.00)*
Year-end	$99.00	$0.00

For the next decade, the partnership is inexplicably inert, as a consequence of which MP's memorandum account shows a preferential claim to distributions of $109, based on $100 outstanding for one year and $99 for ten years at 10% simple interest.

At the beginning of Year 12, the partnership sells the property for $399 cash. Assume that the adjusted basis of the property sold by the partnership is $99. Accordingly, the partnership has a recognized gain of $300, and $399 in cash to be shared. The partners' capital accounts appear as follows:

Money	*Partner*	*Development Partner*
Opening	$99.00	$ 0.00
Gain	$150.00	$150.00
Year-end	$249.00	$150.00

Because of their agreement as to cash distributions, MP will get the lion's share of the $399. First, he gets a $109 preferential distribution, which is *not* viewed as reducing his claims against his capital account balance for purposes of the agreement; accordingly, he is entitled to a further $249, which in combination leaves $41 for DP, punishing DP for delay. Thus, MP will have netted $259 in cash as a consequence of participating in the venture ($358 *less* his $99 investment, treating the $1 loss as reducing his investment) and will report a capital gain on termination of the partnership of $109 (his cash receipts of $249 plus $109 *less* his $249 capital account). §§ 731(a)(1) and 741.

DP will net $41 in cash (termination proceeds, ignoring his $1 investment because of the offsetting $1 loss) and will claim a $109 capital loss, the difference between his closing outside basis of $150 and the $41 he actually received on termination.

QUESTION

What is your analysis of this complicated transaction? Specifically, does MP have:

1) A generous distribution,

2) A guaranteed payment,

3) Interest income, or

4) An allocation of profits as a result of the "preferential distribution" of cash?

Consider Reg. § 1.707-4(a)(2).

94

B. APPORTIONING PARTNERSHIP LIABILITIES

Attribution of partnership debt to particular partners is crucial to any taxpayer who plans to invest in a partnership that may operate at a loss. This is because § 704(d) limits the pass-through effect of each partner's share of the losses to his or her outside basis, with any excess carried forward to future years. To the extent a partner is attributed a share of partnership debt, her outside basis increases as if she had contributed cash to the partnership. §§ 722 and 752.

As you will see, apportioning partnership liabilities among the partners is an involved process. Section 752 purports to apportion liabilities among the partners, but the real authority in the area is found in the Regulations under § 752 and companion provisions in the § 704 Regulations. Note that one must work simultaneously with the § 704 and § 752 Regulations, because they are interdependent.

1. THE MEANING OF "PARTNERSHIP LIABILITIES"

Most of the examples that follow involve real estate partnerships that borrow money to buy a building, which might leave the reader with the impression that "partnership liabilities" are limited to mortgages. That is not the case. Partnership liabilities are defined to mean a limited list of obligations incurred by the partnership, namely any obligation that:

- Creates or increases the partnership's basis in its assets (even cash); or

- Results in an immediate deduction when it is incurred, or

- Is attributable to an expenditure that is neither deductible nor qualifies as a capital expenditure. Rev. Rul. 88-77, 1988-2 C.B. 128, and Reg. § 1.752-1(a)(4).

2. DETERMINING WHETHER A PARTNERSHIP LIABILITY IS RECOURSE OR NONRECOURSE

A recourse liability is one as to which there is personal liability. A nonrecourse liability is one as to which the borrower has no personal responsibility; the only thing at risk is the property used as collateral. The most common example is the nonrecourse debt incurred to acquire real estate. If the obligor defaults on the mortgage, the bank can take back the encumbered property, but the borrower has no other exposure. The duty to make payments out of one's own pocket can arise under the debt agreement, state law, or a guarantee of a debt. If the borrower is a general partnership, recourse makes all the partners personally liable. If a limited partnership borrows, only the general partners are personally liable, and if an LLC borrows, none of the members (owners) are personally liable with respect to the recourse debt.

The Regulations put these basic business concepts in more formal terms. They provide that a debt is recourse for purposes of § 752 if a partner, or someone who is related to a partner, bears the economic risk of loss with respect to the liability, Reg. § 1.752-1(a)(1). If no one has such a risk, then it is nonrecourse. The search for the result depends on a "doomsday" analysis, described below, which essentially asks, "if the partnership were liquidated and its properties were worthless, who would bear exactly how much of the loss?" The analysis depends on a capital account analysis, and looks for who, if anyone, who would have to make capital contributions to pay off the creditor, and how much.

Note that a nonrecourse loan is treated as a recourse loan if the partner or a related person is the creditor. Reg. §1.752-2(c)(1). It only applies to greater than 10% partners. § 1.752-2(d)(1).

3. APPORTIONING RECOURSE LIABILITIES

The core idea of the Regulations is to apportion recourse liabilities to partners who bear the economic risk of loss associated with each particular liability. The Regulations consider that a partner bears the economic risk of loss for a partnership liability to the extent the partner (or someone related to the partner) would bear the economic burden of discharging the obligation created by the liability if the partnership were financially unable to discharge it. This forces an evaluation of how the parties agreed to share economic losses arising out of partnership liabilities. A partner's contribution of his own note is considered part of his net capital contribution which is exposed to loss for § 752 purposes. Reg. § 1.752-2(h)(4).

To determine how the partners bear the economic risk of loss, one applies a hypothetical liquidation test in which one evaluates the effect of a sudden end of the partnership. In running through this imaginary "doomsday" liquidation of the partnership, one presumes that all four of the following events will occur:

- The partnership's assets become worthless.

- All liabilities fall due, and the partnership surrenders its assets to its creditors.

- The partnership allocates all of its operating results as of that moment among the partners in accordance with the partnership agreement and then liquidates. Reg. § 1.752-2(a), (b)(1). Each partner is generally presumed to pay any liability he or she is attributed, unless the facts indicate a plan to avoid liability. Reg. § 1.752-1(b)(6). This is a simplifying assumption, to put it mildly. A key factor is that each encumbered property's disposition will produce a loss because there will be no amount realized.

- The losses are then allocated according to the directives in the partnership agreement. Reg. § 1.752-2(b)(1)(ii), (iv). For example, if the partners are equal members of a general partnership, they share partnership recourse liabilities equally, absent some other agreement. Generally, limited partners are never liable for recourse debt, unless they somehow manufacture personal liability by such acts as signing guarantees or other side agreements. *See* R.U.L.P.A. § 303. A limited partner's guaranty is effective only if she waives her right of subrogation. *See* Reg. § 1.752-2(T), Examples 10 and 11.

PROBLEM 5-4

1. Which of the following is a "partnership liability" of a cash method partnership?

    a) A $100 debt owed to a business lawyer for his services collecting on an overdue account?

    b) Would the answer to "(a)" differ if the partnership were on the accrual method?

    c) $100 that a finance company lends the partnership?

    d) $100 owed to a lender for business equipment the partnership bought?

2. M and D organize the MD general partnership. The initial contributions will be $20 from M and $20 from D. The MD partnership will then borrow $60 from an unrelated lender, with recourse, to buy a property for $100. The allocation provisions will satisfy the § 704(b) Regulations, including an obligation to restore capital account deficits. M, your client, wants to be allocated 90% of the losses. D agrees to this. M wants to know his basis in the MD partnership. What is your opinion? *See* Reg. § 1.752-2(f), Example 1.

4. APPORTIONING NONRECOURSE LIABILITIES

Nonrecourse liabilities are those as to which no partner has personal liability. Reg. § 1.752-1(a)(2). One cannot use a risk of loss analysis with respect to such liabilities because no partner bears any such risk; only the creditor bears the risk.[1] Still, such liabilities exist and Reg. § 1.752-3 tells one how they are apportioned to each partner. The basic general rule is intact, namely, nonrecourse liabilities are apportioned among the partners in accordance with how the partners share profits, the theory apparently being that the debt will only be paid off out of partnership's profits.

Using the general profit-sharing ratio as the guiding principle has its shortcomings. There may in fact be no general profit-sharing ratio because the partnership agreement is nothing but a mass of special allocations; or there may be a general profit-sharing ratio, but it may be subject to change if and when some specified level of profitability occurs. The Regulations acknowledge this problem and attempt to adapt to it by declaring that special allocations of profit for purposes of allocating excess nonrecourse liabilities are valid if, *inter alia,* they are consistent with some significant items of partnership income or gain. Reg. § 1.752-3(a)(3).

The Regulations state that a partner's share of partnership nonrecourse liabilities are the sum of:

- The partner's share of "minimum gain;" plus

- The gain the partner would have to report under § 704(c) to account for built-in gains and losses; plus

- The partner's share of "excess nonrecourse liabilities" – meaning those left over after allocating minimum gains plus § 704(c) gain.

Now, let's look at these three items in detail:

1. **Minimum gain**. Initially, there will be no minimum gain because such gain does not arise until nonrecourse liabilities exceed the basis of a encumbered property, but once it arises, it is the first tier of debt to be allocated among the partners. Partnership minimum gain means the smallest amount of book gain that the partnership would recognize if it abandoned the property. Reg. § 1.704-2(g). This is a most interesting provision. It means, for example, that if a partner is allocated depreciation deductions based on a bank's money, the partner gets a share of the debt sufficient to cover such deductions. It is not often that the partnership allocation provisions are so generous. Perhaps it is attributable to the lobbying power of the real estate industry.

---

[1] A non-recourse liability is deemed recourse if a partner or related person is the creditor. Reg. § 1.752-2(c)(1).

To illustrate: A is a limited partner with an 80% profit-sharing ratio and B is the general partner with the remaining 20% interest in the cash method AB limited partnership. The AB partnership borrows $1,000 on a nonrecourse basis in order to buy a building, which it depreciates at the rate of $100 per year for book and tax purposes. The $1,000 was the sole consideration for the purchase. The building and the partnership generate no other receipts or disbursements. At the end of the partnership's first taxable year it has claimed $100 of depreciation and, therefore, has a $900 basis in the building. *Commissioner v. Tufts*, 461 U.S. 300, 307, *reh'g denied*, 463 U.S. 215 (1983). If the partnership abandoned the building, it would have a gain of $100, the excess of the $1,000 loan over the partnership's $900 basis in the building. This is the minimum gain. Because A claimed an $80 depreciation deduction, A has an $80 minimum gain and is apportioned $80 of the "first" $100 of partnership debt; B has a $20 minimum gain. Notice how this dollar amount rises over time.

2. **Section 704(c) gain**. One next apportions nonrecourse debt in accordance with the partner's share of § 704(c) gain. This is the share of gain that the contributing partner must report on the sale of property that he contributed with a value in excess of basis. Reg. § 1.752-3(a)(2). This coordinates the general rule of § 704(c) with the debt apportionment rules. Because of the exceptional complications associated with § 704(c) allocations, the details of this tier are too complex for a survey course and are not further discussed, except to say that it is helpful to partners who contribute assets subject to built in gains because it minimizes the risk of incurring a taxable gain on contributing such property, and the amount of nonrecourse allocations attributed this tier generally remains static.

3. **Excess nonrecourse liabilities**. Finally, liabilities that are not attributed to partners under rules "1" and "2", known as "excess nonrecourse liabilities," are shared in accordance with:

- Profit-sharing ratios (theoretically the only source of repayment); or

- At the partnership's election,

  - In accordance with a special allocation of profits for this purpose, provided the arrangement is reasonably consistent with the allocation of some other item that has substantial economic effect; or

  - The same way as they reasonably expect to share nonrecourse deductions attributable to the nonrecourse liability. Reg. § 1.752-3(a)(3). This is an open sesame for the real estate industry, justifying investor limited partners' claims to hefty shares of depreciation deductions. This is a better choice than the one immediately above because other elections in more complex annual calculations.

5. ALLOCATING DEDUCTIONS ATTRIBUTABLE TO NONRECOURSE DEBT

The partners will not in fact bargain over how to allocate nonrecourse debt. The lawyers and accountants will do that. The partners will bargain over allocating deductions founded on nonrecourse debt, especially depreciation deductions, and refinancing proceeds that are founded on nonrecourse debt; they will call on their lawyers for the right documents, drafted with a careful eye to taxes.

a. Background

The Regulations validate the apportionment of nonrecourse deductions any way the partners agree, provided the allocation meets a four-part test, a key aspect of which is that there must be a so-called "minimum-gain charge back." Reg. § 1.704-2(e)(3)(f). The basic problem in this area is that, in reality, no allocation of a deduction based on nonrecourse debt is borne by the partner claiming the deduction. It is borne by the lender.

The Treasury Department, therefore, could have written Regulations requiring the partners to share such deductions in accordance with their relative capital accounts, or just equally. Either would be equally lacking in economic substance. At the opposite extreme, the Treasury Department might have permitted deductions of such items willy nilly, on the theory that the entire area lacked substance. In fact, it chose a middle ground which does not require strong economic substance (by dropping a firm deficit make-up requirement from the partnership agreement), but does require that, when the property is sold, any gains based on deductions founded on the lender's nonrecourse debt be allocated to the partners who got those deductions. This pattern creates "tax substance," in the sense that the tax benefit of the prior deductions will be reversed in the form of an extra measure of gain when the property is disposed of, but only to the extent that the gain was based on depreciation deductions that, in a more normal world, would have been deducted by the lender, because it bears the real economic risk of loss of value of the property.

The amount of gain that is charged back to the partners collectively at the time of disposition is referred to as the "minimum gain." *See* Reg. § 1.704-1(b)(4)(iv)(c). It is the same as the minimum gain you just read about. For example, as you saw before, if the partnership received contributions of $100 and borrowed $900 to buy a depreciable building, the first $100 of depreciation deductions would be seen as coming out of the partners' capital. Any further depreciation will produce minimum gain, and that minimum gain will grow in amount as the years pass. Henceforth, in the interest of economy of language this book refers only to depreciation deductions; in fact the analysis incorporates other deductions based on nonrecourse debt, such as operating expenses.

b. The Four-Part Test

Nonrecourse deductions are deductions attributable to nonrecourse liabilities. The Regulations allow the partnership to allocate depreciation (or other deductions) attributable to nonrecourse liabilities any way the partners care to, but only if four rigorous tests are met. If they are not all met, then the deductions (and any other nonrecourse deductions) are shared in accordance with the partners' overall interests in the partnership, which calls for an *ad hoc* analysis. Reg. § 1.704-2(b)(1).

- First, the allocation agreement on all material tax items *other than* the nonrecourse deductions must have substantial economic effect, under either the three-part mechanical test or the alternative economic effect test. Reg. § 1.704-2(e)(4). This is just an extra barrier erected by the Treasury Department.

- Second, the allocation of nonrecourse deductions must be "reasonably consistent" with some other significant partnership item attributable to the property securing the nonrecourse liabilities of the partnership. Reg. § 1.704-2(e)(2). This is not quite as difficult as it sounds, partly because the "other significant items" can be realized by the partnership in future years. Reg. § 1.704-2(m), Ex.(1)(ii). This means, for example, that as long as depreciation deductions founded on nonrecourse debt are within the partner's range of overall profit and loss-sharing over the years, the requirement is met.[2] This requirement fits hand in glove with real estate deals in which the investor partners get hefty overall distributive shares in early years (90% is common) and lower shares (often 50%) when the property has proven its worth.[3]

- Third, the partnership agreement must satisfy the three-part mechanical test or the alternative economic effect test. This requires inclusion in the partnership agreement of either a deficit make-up provision or a QIO. Reg. § 1.704-2(b). In *Orrisch,* there was neither. Requiring only a QIO seems the equivalent of twenty lashes with a wet noodle, because in substance a QIO is just legal "boilerplate" language grafted onto the partnership agreement. Amazingly, for this purpose a QIO is deemed to have economic effect. Reg. § 1704-2(g)(1).

- Fourth, starting when there are nonrecourse deductions (or distributions of the proceeds of nonrecourse liabilities) there must be a minimum gain charge-back in the partnership agreement, so as to allocate to each partner an amount of income or gain equal to his share of the decrease. It must apply when a partner's share of partnership minimum gain for the year declines. The following language addresses the need for a minimum gain charge back. The language was excerpted from the same partnership agreement quoted before:

> "(vi) After the application of (v) above [the QIO], but prior to the application for such fiscal year of any other provision of this section, if there is a net decrease in partnership minimum gain attributable to a partner nonrecourse debt during a fiscal year, then any partner with a share of the partnership minimum gain attributable to such debt at the beginning of such year shall be allocated items of income and gain for such year (and, if necessary, subsequent years) in the amount and proportions necessary to satisfy the provisions of Treasury Regulation Sections 1.704-2(b)(2) and related provisions."

A reduction in minimum gain will typically occur when the partnership pays down principal on the nonrecourse debt or when the secured property is sold. The following is an example of a nonrecourse allocation that works:

To illustrate: A is a general partner with a 10% profit share and B is a limited partner with a 90% share of profits. They agree that once B recoups his investment, they will share profits 60:40. Assuming there is a "reasonable likelihood" that 90:10 and 60:40 provisions will in fact apply to "significant amounts of income, any allocation of nonrecourse items (such as depreciation) to B from 9:1 to 6:4 will be valid, provided the 9:1 and 6:4 allocations themselves have substantial economic effect. *See* Reg. § 1.704-2(m), Example (1)(ii).

PROBLEM 5-5

---

[2] Reg. § 1.704-2(m).

[3] This suggests that as the proportionate payment of recourse interest expense obligations on the debt track the special allocation of depreciation, this test is met. However, the Regulations do not clarify the "reasonably consistent" test and instead approve of special allocations that lie within the range of overall allocations. The commentators in turn focus on the latter, leaving the prior analysis up in the air.

1) Several partners form an equal limited partnership, which borrows $1,000 (nonrecourse) to buy a building for $1,000. How will each of the following affect partnership minimum gain (treat each alternative as separate)?:

    a. The partners repay $200 to the lender.

    b. The partnership's encumbered property is subject to $100 of depreciation.

    c. The partnership borrows $500 against an unencumbered property with a basis of $200 and a value of $800. Reg. §§ 1.704-2(d)(1) and 1.704-2(g)(1). Will the borrowing alone be part of the partners' shares of partnership minimum gain for debt allocation purposes, or must there also be a distribution of the refinancing proceeds?

2) Will there be a nonrecourse deduction in year one of the above limited partnership?

3) X and Y become partners, X as the general partner and Y as the limited partner. X contributes $10, and Y contributes $90. XY then buys a building for $1,000, encumbered by $900 of nonrecourse debt, which calls for no principal payments until maturity. Assume that the allocation provisions are valid and that they call for allocating 90% of the profits and losses in favor of Y, but a special 50:50 allocation of the excess nonrecourse liabilities and depreciation deductions. Some years later, there is a $50 minimum gain because the property has a basis of $750 but is subject to a debt of $800. The allocations other than the nonrecourse deductions have substantial economic effect (except there is a QIO instead of a deficit restoration requirement) and there is a minimum gain chargeback. Also, all other material allocations and capital account adjustments are valid under the § 704(b) Regulations. According to their understanding, X and Y have a $5/$45 share of the minimum gain, respectively. The partners believe this means the debt is apportioned as follows:

	X	Y
Minimum Gain	$5.00	$45.00
§ 704(c) allocation	$0.00	$0.00
Excess nonrecourse liabilities	$375.00	$375.00
TOTAL:	$380.00	$420.00

Do you agree with their analysis? *See* Reg. § 1.752-3.

Specifically:

    a) Is the 50:50 allocation of depreciation valid?

    b) Is the calculation of the shares of nonrecourse liabilities valid?

C. VARYING CAPITAL INTERESTS THROUGHOUT THE YEAR

Read §706 (d) and Treas. Reg. §1.706-4

Before 2015, partnerships used one set of rules for determining a partner's distributive share of partnership income when a partner's interest varied throughout the year and another set of rules when a partner left the partnership entirely.

When the partner left the partnership entirely, the partnership year closed as to that partner and the partnership assigned the departing partner his or her share of partnership items from the beginning of the partnership tax year until the date of the partner's departure.

When the partner's interest in the partnership varied throughout the year, the partnership assigned one portion of partnership items for one period and another portion for the second period.

Example of pre 2015 allocations:

The ABC partnership is a calendar year, cash partnership. The partnership earns $100,000 for the first six months of the year. During the rest of the year, the ABC partnership has a $200,000 loss. Result: The partnership has a ($100,000) loss for the year.

A is a 40% partner in the ABC partnership. B is a 40% partner in the same ABC partnership.

On July 1, A becomes a 10% partner in the partnership for the rest of the year. On June 30 of the same year, B sells his entire interest.

Allocations for the year under the pre 2015 rules:

Computation for A who remains a partner for the entire year although his percentage of ownership changed during the year.

A's share of the ABC partnership's ($100,000 loss) for the year is 40 % of $50,000 for the first six months of the year plus 10% of $50,000 for the last six months. The computation is ($20,000) for the first half of the year plus ($5,000) for the second half of the year or a ($25,000) share of partnership loss.

Computation for B who leaves the partnership in the middle of the year. For B, the partnership year closes before the partnership realized any loss. The partnership allocates 40% of its $100,000 income from the first six months and no loss to B. B reports $40,000 of partnership income for the year.

The results explained above have changed for allocations for 2015 and beyond.

Since 2015, Treas. Reg. § 1.706-4 requires that partnerships follow ten steps in allocating partnership items to partners whose interests either vary or end. Treas. Reg. § 1.706-4(a)(3).

1.   First, the partnership must determine whether the allocations fall under two exceptions contained in Treas. Reg. § 1.706-4 (b). Treas. Reg. § 1.706-4(a)(3)(i)

The first exception is for allocations of separately stated items among contemporaneous partners where the partners are contemporaneous for the entire partnership year or for the entire segment of the year if the item is entirely attributable to a segment. Treas. Reg. § 1.706-4(b)(1). These two exceptions are described in 1.706-4(b)(1) and (2):

The first exception is described in 1.706-4(b)(1). The exception only applies if:

(1) the partnership's proposed allocations have substantial economic effect, and
(2) any variation in a partner's interest is not attributable to either:
      (a) a contribution of money or property by a partner to the partnership, or
      (b) a distribution of money or property by the partnership to a partner.

The second exception is where capital is not a material income-producing factor for the partnership, in which case, the partnership may determine the partner's distributive share using any reasonable method to account for the varying interests of the partners during the taxable year so long as the allocations otherwise comport with §704(b). Treas. Reg. § 1.706-4(b)(2)

2.	Second, the partnership must determine if its Form 1065 reflects extraordinary items as defined in Reg. § 1.706-4(e)(1) and must allocate those items among the partners in proportion to their interests in the partnership item on the day that the extraordinary item occurred, regardless of the method (interim closing or proration method) and convention (daily, semi-monthly, or monthly) that the partnership otherwise uses. Thus, for example, the rules make extraordinary items an exception to the proration method that would otherwise ratably allocate the extraordinary items across the segment, and the conventions, which could otherwise inappropriately shift extraordinary items between a transferor and transferee.

3.	Third, the partnership must determine whether it will apply the interim closing method or the proration method for each variation in a partner's interest in the partnership. Reg. § 1.706-4(a)(3)(iii) and (f). However, the partnership must use the interim closing of the books method to determine the partner's share of partnership items unless the partnership agreement adopts the proration method. The partnership may generally use different methods (interim closing or proration) for different variations within each partnership taxable year. Reg. § 1.706-4(a)(3)(iii)

Interim Closing Method.
	Under the interim closing method, the partnership takes into account any variations in a partner's interest during the tax year by determining the distributive share of partnership items for each segment of the year using an interim closing of the books method and by then allocating those items among the partners in accordance with their respective interests during that segment; segments are specific periods of the partnership's tax year. Reg. § 1.706-4(c)(1). The partnership can use either a calendar-day convention, a monthly convention, or the semi-monthly convention to establish segments. Id.
	Absent an agreement of the partners to perform regular monthly or semi-monthly interim closings, the only interim closings during the partnership's taxable year is at the deemed time of the occurrence of variations for which the partnership uses the interim closing method. Reg. § 1.706-4(a)(3)(v)

Proration Method.
	A partnership agreement may adopt the proration method under which the partnership allocates the distributive share of partnership items among the partners according to their pro rata shares of those items for the entire year, using the calendar-day convention. Reg. § 1.706-4(d)(2)(ii)

4.	Fourth, the partnership determines when each variation has occurred under the partnership's selected convention. Reg. § 1.706-4(a)(3)(iv) and (c)

5.	Fifth, the partnership determines whether the partnership agreement calls for regular monthly or semi-monthly interim closings. Reg. § 1.706-4(a)(3)(v) and (c) and (f)

A partnership has a choice. The partnership can decide that it wants to perform regular closings of the partnership's books. In that case, the partnership has to further decide if it will perform monthly or semi-monthly closings. If the partnership agreement calls for montly closings, then the partnership performs an interim closing of its books at the end of each month. If the partnership performs semi-monthly closings, then it has to decide whether to perform the closings at the end or the middle of each month, regardless of whether any variation occurred in the period. Absent an agreement of the partners to perform regular montly or semi-monthly interim closings, the only interim closings during the partnership's taxable year are at the time of the occurrence of variations for which the partnership uses the interim closing method.

6. Sixth, determine the partnership's segments, which are specific periods of the partnership's taxable year created by interim closings of the partnership's books. Reg. § 1.706-4(a)(3)(vi)

The first segment starts with the beginning of the partnership's tax year and ends at the time of the first interim closing. Any additional segments start immediately after the prior segment closes and ends when the next interim closing occurs. However, the last segment of the partnership's taxable year cannot end later than the very end of the partnership's taxable year.

If there are no interim closings, the partnership has one segment, which is its entire taxable year.

7. Seventh, apportion the partnership's items for the year among its segments. Reg. § 1.706-4(a)(3)(vii)

The partnership determines the items of income, gain, loss, deduction, and credit of the partnership for each segment. In general, a partnership treats each segment as though the segment were a separate distributive share period. For example, a partnership may compute a capital loss for a segment of a taxable year even though the partnership has a net capital gain for the entire taxable year.

8. Eighth, determine the partnership's proration periods. Reg. §1.706-4(a)(3)(viii)

Proration periods are specific portions of a segment created by a variation for which the partnership chooses to apply the proration method.
The first proration period in each segment begins at the beginning of the segment and ends the first time of the first variation within the segment for which the partnership selects the proration method. The next proration period begins immediately after the close of the prior proration period and ends at the time of the next variation for which the partnership selects the proration method. However, each proration period must end no later than the close of the segment.

9. Ninth, prorate the items of income, gain, loss, deduction, and credit in each segment among the proration periods within the segment. §1.706-4(a)(3)(ix)

10. Tenth, determine the partners' distributive shares of partnership items under § 702(a) by taking into account the partners' interests in such items during each segment and proration period. §1.706-4(a)(3)(x)

PROBLEM 5-6

ABC is a calendar year partnership with three equal partners. None of the partnership's items fall under the definition of extraordinary items in Treas. Reg. §1.706-4(e)(2) and capital is a material income-producing factor for the partnership.

104

- On April 16, Partner A sells 50% of her interest to new partner D.

- On August 6, Partner B sells 50% of his interest to new partner E.

- During all of the year, the partnership earned $75,000 of ordinary income, incurred $33,000 of ordinary deductions, earned $12,000 of capital gain in the ordinary course of its business, and sustained $9,000 of capital loss in the ordinary course of its business.

- Between January 1 and July 31, the partnership:

  Earned $60,000 of ordinary income and incurred $24,000 of ordinary deductions.

  Earned $12,000 of capital gain and sustained $6,000 of capital loss.

- Between August 1 and December 31 the partnership:

  Earned $15,000 of gross ordinary income and incurred $9,000 of gross ordinary deductions.

  Earned no capital gains and sustained $3,000 of capital loss.

- The partnership agreement applies the proration method to the April 16 variation and the default application of the interim closing method to the August 6 variation.

Determine each partner's distributive share of partnership items for partners A, B, C, D, and E.

D. SPECIAL ALLOCATIONS AND THE CEILING RULE

The partnership allocation rules under Reg. §1.704-1(b) are meant to strike a balance between the partnership's right to allocate partnership items of income, deduction and loss between partners under §704(a) and the government's command that partnership allocations reflect the partners' economic relationship under §704(b). In the case of contributed property, §704(c) and Reg. §1.704-3 force the partnership to make special allocations in order to reduce the difference between fair market value and basis on contribution. The regulations give the partnership three choices of how to handle the special allocations: (1) the traditional method, (2) the traditional method with "curative allocations" and (3) the "remedial allocation" method. A partnership may use different methods with respect to different items of contributed property, provided that the partnership and the partners consistently apply a single reasonable method for each item of contributed property and that the overall method or combination of methods are reasonable based on the facts and circumstances and consistent with the purpose.

THE TRADITIONAL METHOD: Regs. § 1.704-3(b)

Under the traditional method, the "ceiling rule" forbids the partnership from allocating any more tax items than the contributed property generates. Accordingly, where the "ceiling rule" applies, special allocations under §704(c) might not fully account for the difference between the contributed property's outside basis and capital account. Regs. § 1.704-3(b)(1)

Example:

Contributing partner (CP) buys an asset for $50, contributes the asset to the partnership when the asset is worth $100 and the Partnership sells the asset for $125.

Result:

The partnership has a gain of $75 which is the difference between CP's basis ($50) which transferred to the partnership and the partnership's amount realized of $125.

The first $50 of gain is pre-contribution gain under §704(c) because CP would have been taxed on $50 had he sold the property rather than contributing it to the partnership. The $50 of pre-contribution gain must be allocated to the contributing partner.

The remaining $25 of the partnership's $75 gain is allocated among all of the partners in the same manner that this gain would have been allocated if the partnership had purchased the asset for $100.

If instead the asset declined in value to $75 after it was contributed to the partnership, the partnership would have taxable gain of only $25 to allocate: an amount realized of $75 minus the tax basis of $50. The partnership's total gain would be smaller than the unrealized increase in value at the time CP contributed the asset. Now the amount of gain that can be allocated to the contributing partner has traditionally been limited by the "ceiling rule" to the partnership's total realized gain, leaving no gain or loss for allocation to the noncontributing partners. See Treas. Reg. § 1.704-3(b)(2), Ex. (1)(iii). The ceiling rule can also apply to depreciation. Under the traditional method, the noncontributing partners do not get the tax benefit of any of the $25 of economic loss that the partnership has sustained.

In order to allow noncontributing partners an opportunity to receive their fair share of partnership tax items associated with contributed property, the Treasury issued regulations that permit partnerships to use curative or remedial allocations to correct for these distortions.

In this example, a curative allocation would take $25 of unrelated gain that otherwise would have been allocated to all the partners, and would allocate that gain instead to the contributing partner, so that the contributing partner is allocated a full $50 of gain, and all the partners enjoy the tax benefit of the $25 post-contribution loss by the curative allocation of $25 of gain away from them.

Curative allocations are effective only when there is sufficient unrelated gain or loss available to offset the effects of the ceiling rule. To deal with this shortcoming, the regulations also permit partnerships to use a remedial method, under which the partnership creates notional items of gain or loss in equal amounts, and specially allocates these notional items to offset the effects of the ceiling rule.

E.   FAMILY PARTNERSHIPS
Read § 704(e)(1).

In principle, there is no reason why family members should not be able to form partnerships to conduct business or to make investments. In fact, there is good reason for the IRS to be leery of them, because family partnerships invite shifting income to members who are in relatively low tax brackets, thereby minimizing the family's overall federal income tax.

1.   RECOGNITION OF THE FAMILY PARTNERSHIP

106

If capital is a material income-producing factor, the safe harbor rule of § 704(e)(1) recognizes the partnership as long as the transfer of partnership interest is genuine. This will call for adequate protection of a particularly young or malleable donee, by such means as a guardianship or a trust for the donee. Reg. § 1.704-1(e)(2)(viii). In the case of a service partnership, however, there is no such safe harbor and the partnership will be validated only if it is a bona fide venture. *See Commissioner v. Culbertson,* 337 U.S. 733 (1949).

Under Reg. § 1.704-1(e)(1)(iv) "substantial inventories" or a "substantial investment in plant, machinery and equipment" qualify as capital. The courts have been more liberal, even going so far as to hold that a partnership's goodwill can qualify as capital as long as goodwill is a substantial source of the partnership's revenues. *Bateman v. United States,* 490 F.2d 549 (9th Cir. 1973). *But see* I.R.S. AOD-1975-244 (Aug. 4, 1975), in which the IRS expressed non-acquiescence to this case.

Minors can be partners for federal income tax purposes if they are competent to fend for themselves. Reg. § 1.704-1(e)(2)(viii). If they cannot fend for themselves, their partnership interests will have to be held by trustees, custodians, or guardians. If a trust distributes appreciated assets to a beneficiary, there is generally no tax to the trust unless the distribution satisfies a specific pecuniary amount (say $10,000). . Rev. Rul. 55-117, 1955-1 C.B. 233. *Id.* As a result, a trust can hold a partnership interest, which it can generally distribute tax-free to the beneficiary or beneficiaries. The price paid is that the beneficiary will take the trust's basis in the partnership interest.

2. LIMITS ON ALLOCATIONS
Read § 704(e)(2).

Assuming that the family partnership is viable, the donee or family buyer is taxed on his or her distributive share of partnership income, but § 704(e)(2) imposes two important limits:

1. The donor or family member seller must be reasonably compensated *before* partnership profits can be allocated; and

2. The donee's or related buyer's distributive share of partnership profits cannot be proportionately greater, by reference to capital interests, than the distributive share allocated to the donor or related seller.

PROBLEM 5-7

1) Mary, an unmarried woman, runs a general store. She gave a one-third interest in the capital worth $30,000 to her boyfriend on January 1 of the present year. They agree to share profits and losses 50:50. The store is a cash method, calendar-year partnership. Mary's services are worth $40,000 per year. The store earned a net profit of $100,000 this year, before compensation to Mary. Mary took no compensation for services this year.

a) What is Mary's boyfriend's distributive share of partnership profits this year?

b) What would be the difference, if any, if Mary is married and sold the interest to her husband?

Chapter 6

SALES AND EXCHANGES OF PARTNERSHIP INTERESTS
Read §§ 741 and 751(a)-(d).

If one were building a partnership tax system from scratch, one would almost surely be puzzled as to how one ought to treat the sale of a partnership interest. If one believed that the aggregate concept should predominate over the entity concept, one would prefer to treat the sale of the partnership interest as *a de facto* sale of a share of each partnership asset. This is how sole proprietorships are taxed when they are sold. *See Williams v. McGowan,* 152 F.2d 570 (2d Cir. 1945). At the opposite extreme, one might prefer to use the entity model, taxing the sale of the interest as if it were a share of corporate stock. This is the view reflected in RULPA at §§ 701 and 702 for transfers of limited partnership interests.

Early judicial decisions echoed the entity concept embodied in state law and treated the sale of a partnership interest much like the sale of common stock. *See, e.g., CIR v. Smith,* 173 F.2d 470 (1949). This effectively lets partners convert unrealized ordinary income into long-term capital gains. Even the income the partnership earned during the year in which the interest was sold was converted into capital gain. *Swiren v. Commissioner,* 183 F.2d 656 (7th Cir. 1950).

In enacting § 741, the 1954 Congress continued the basic analogy to the sale of common stock. Once Congress established that the sale of a partnership interest involved the transfer of a single asset rather than of a ratable share of each portion of the "mixed grill" of partnership assets, the transaction fitted neatly into the usual rules of § 1001 involving sales of property of any sort. However, Congress also attempted to plug the loopholes of prior law. It did so by means of § 751, which selectively converts gain based on unrealized ordinary income in the hands of the partnership into ordinary income in the hands of the partner, and § 706, which requires a sharing of the income for the year of sale between the buyer and the seller.

This chapter assumes that the sale is aboveboard, and not a matched liquidation of one partner's interest combined with the admission of a new partner.

A. TAXATION OF THE SELLER: THE GENERAL RULE
Read §§ 751(c)-(d).

The vital Code provision here is § 741, which at heart declares that a partner who transfers a partnership interest must recognize a gain or loss on the transaction. More significantly, the section goes on to say that the transaction is deemed a sale or exchange of a capital asset – a unique provision, but probably not much of a loophole, since there are few dealers in partnership interests.

Section 741 has a broad sway. It covers sales to strangers, sales to fellow partners, sales by the partners as a group to a third person, and even the sale of one partner's interest to the one remaining partner. Reg. § 1.741-1(b). It does not cover acquisitions of partnership interests under §§ 721- 723. Those are acquisitions by means of a contribution to the partnership.

One uses familiar principles to determine the partner's gain or loss. The amount realized includes the cash or fair market value of other consideration received by the selling partner plus the selling partner's share of partnership liabilities, as defined by § 752(d). The seller's adjusted basis in the partnership interest is outside basis, adjusted to reflect the seller's pro rata share of partnership income or loss from the start of the current taxable year up to the date of sale. *See* § 705(a).

To illustrate: C is a one-third member of the ABC partnership, which uses the cash method and is on the calendar year. C is a calendar year, cash method taxpayer and has a prior-year-end basis of $100 in her partnership interest. C sells her interest to D for $150 on June 30. ABC earns $300 in the January 1-June 30 period. C will report $100 as her interim distributive share of partnership income and will, therefore, increase her basis to $200. Ignoring any § 751 issues, C will report a $50 capital loss on the sale to D. Whether it is a long or short-term loss generally depends on how long C held the interest.

Because one must adjust the seller's outside basis to reflect the seller's share of partnership income or loss up to the date of sale, one must know how to do the proration. As you saw in the previous chapter, the applicable rule here is that the partnership's taxable year closes as to the partner who sells her entire interest. § 706. If the partner sells only part of her interest, the year does not close as to her, but instead the share of partnership's income or loss for the whole year attributable to the portion of the interest she sold is prorated to her on a daily basis. *Id.*

PROBLEM 6-1

1) X and Y are individuals who form the equal XY general partnership. X, Y and the partnership use the cash method and calendar year. XY has recourse liabilities of $40. X sells his interest to Z for $30 in cash when X has an outside basis of $40 (excluding the pro rata share of the partnership profit as of that date). Z assumes X's share of the partnership's liabilities. The partnership earned a profit of $20 in the year of sale, earning an equal amount every day.

    a) If X sold on June 30 (mid-year), what is X's basis in his partnership interest on the date of the sale?

    b) What is the amount of X's gain or loss on selling his interest to Z?

    c) What is the character of X's gain or loss?

    d) What tax form will X receive to report the partnership income in "(b)?"

B. EXCEPTION FOR SECTION 751

If taxpayers could simply sell their partnership interests like a share of stock in a C corporation, there would be a potential tax loophole. Partners could sell their interests after the partnership had developed ordinary-income producing assets such as inventories, service contracts, or unrealized receivables. (The latter would be of concern in the case of cash method partnerships. Accrual method partnerships would already have reported income from receivables and service contracts after the services were performed.) Although the gain realized by a selling partner under such circumstances would be based on ordinary-income producing assets, the profit would stand to be taxed at favorable long-term capital gains rates. Enter § 751, which is designed to interdict these potential conversions of ordinary income into capital gain.

Section 751 works by selectively recharacterizing the elements on the disposition of the partnership interest by in effect imagining that the partner made two sales – one of the § 751 properties and another sale of the balance of the partnership. The first group attracts ordinary gain (or possibly loss, in the case of inventory items) and the other attracts capital gain or loss treatment.

The exceptions under § 751 apply only if and to the extent the consideration received in the sale reflects *unrealized receivables* or *inventory items,* or both combined, as those terms are specially defined in § 751(c) and (d). Unrealized receivables and inventory items are often referred to a "section 751 property" or "hot assets." This has the effect of allocating sale proceeds to particular items of partnership property as if they had been sold separately in the marketplace. Thus, § 751, when applicable, results in taxing proceeds from the sale of a partnership interest in much the same way that the sale of a proprietorship would be addressed, but with one major difference; thanks to § 741, there is a capital asset backdrop for all the sale proceeds not captured by § 751.

1. CONTRACT INTERESTS AS UNREALIZED RECEIVABLES

Reread § 751(c) and (d) and then decide for yourself if the following case reaches a reasonable result. Do not concern yourself about the dollar figures stated in the case or the discussion of goodwill. The goodwill issue is handled later in the text and the law has changed so pay minor attention to that issue.

LEDOUX v. COMMISSIONER
77 T.C. 293 (1981), *aff 'd,* 695 F.2d 1320 (11th Cir. 1983)

Sterrett, Judge:

After concessions, the sole issue remaining for our decision is whether any portion of the amount received by petitioner John W. Ledoux pursuant to an agreement for the sale of a partnership interest was attributable to an unrealized receivable of the partnership and thus was required to be characterized as ordinary income under section 751, I.R.C. 1954.

Findings of Fact

[The petitioner was partner in the Collins-Ledoux partnership, the purpose of which was to manage and operate a dog racing track in Florida. The track itself, was the property of an unrelated taxpayer, the Sanford-Orlando Kennel Club, Inc. The Collins-Ledoux partnership was obligated to pay the first $200,000 of annual net profits to Sanford-Orlando. The track was highly profitable.]

After the 1972 racing season two of the partners, Jerry Collins and Jack Collins, decided to purchase petitioner's 25-percent partnership interest. They agreed to allow Ledoux to propose a fair selling price for his interest. Ledoux set a price based on a price-earnings multiple of 5 times his share of the Partnership's 1972 earnings. This resulted in a total value for his 25-percent interest of $800,000. There was no valuation or appraisal of specific assets at the time, and the sales price included his interest in all of the assets of the Partnership. . . .

On his 1972 Federal income tax return, petitioner properly elected to report the gain from the sale of his partnership interest under the installment method as prescribed in section 453. Petitioner calculated the total gain on such sale to be as follows:

Sales price	$800,000.00
Basis in partnership interest	$62,658.70
Total gain on sale	$737,341.30

During 1972, 1973 and 1974 petitioner received payments in accordance with the October 17, 1972 Agreement of Sale. In each of those years, he characterized the reported gain, calculated pursuant to the installment sales method, as capital gain.

110

After consummation of the sale of petitioner's interest in the Collins-Ledoux Partnership, the remaining partners continued to operate the dog track under the Agreement of July 9, 1955 as amended.

Respondent, in his notice of deficiency, did not disagree with petitioner's calculation of the total gain. However, he determined that $575,392.50 of the gain was related to petitioner's interest in the Dog Track Agreement and should be subject to ordinary income treatment pursuant to section 751.[1]

Opinion

The sole issue presented is whether a portion of the amount received by petitioner on the sale of his 25-percent partnership interest is taxable as ordinary income and not as capital gain. More specifically, we must decide whether any portion of the sales price is attributable to "unrealized receivables" of the Partnership.

Generally, gain or loss on the sale or exchange of a partnership interest is treated as capital gain or loss. Sec. 741. Prior to 1954, a partner could escape ordinary income tax treatment on his portion of the partnership's unrealized receivables by selling or exchanging his interest in the partnership and treating the gain or loss therefrom as capital gain or loss. To curb such abuses, section 751 was enacted to deal with the problem of the so-called "collapsible partnership." *See S*. Rept. 1622, 83d Cong., 2d Sess. 98 (1954). . . .

Petitioner contends that the Dog Track Agreement gave the Collins-Ledoux Partnership the right to manage and operate the dog track. According to petitioner, the Agreement did not give the Partnership any contractual rights to receive future payments and did not impose any obligation on the Partnership to perform services. Rather, the Agreement merely gave the Partnership the right to occupy and use all of the Corporation's properties (including the racetrack facilities and the racing permit) in operating its dog track business; if the Partnership exercised such right, it would be obligated to make annual payments to the Corporation based upon specified percentages of the annual mutual handle. Thus, because the Dog Track Agreement was in the nature of a leasehold agreement rather than an employment contract, it did not create the type of "unrealized receivables" referred to in section 751.

Respondent, on the other hand, contends that the Partnership operated the racetrack for the Corporation and was paid a portion of the profits for its efforts. As such, the Agreement was in the nature of a management employment contract. When petitioner sold his partnership interest to the Collinses in 1972, the main right that he sold was a contract right to receive income in the future for yet-to-be-rendered personal services. This, respondent asserts, is supported by the fact that petitioner determined the sales price for his partnership interest by capitalizing his 1972 annual income (approximately $160,000) by a factor of 5. Therefore, respondent contends that the portion of the gain realized by petitioner that is attributable to the management contract should be characterized as an amount received for unrealized receivables

---

[1] Respondent determined that the value of petitioner's proportionate share of partnership assets other than the Dog Track Agreement was as follows:

Asset	Value
Escrow deposit	$12,500.00
Sanford-Seminole Development Company stock	$1,000.00
Fixed Assets	$211,107.50
	$224,607.50

The difference between this value and the total purchase price ($800,000) was treated by respondent as having been received by petitioner in exchange for his rights in the Dog Track Agreement.

of the Partnership. Consequently, such gain should be characterized as ordinary income under section 751.

The legislative history is not wholly clear with respect to the type of assets that Congress intended to place under the umbrella of "unrealized receivables." The House Report states:

> The term "unrealized receivables or fees" is used to apply to any rights to income which have not been included in gross income under the method of accounting employed by the partnership. The provision is applicable mainly to cash basis partnerships which have acquired a contractual or other legal right to income for goods or services. . . [H. Rept. 1337, 83d Cong., 2d Sess. 71 (1954).]

Essentially the same language appears in the report of the Senate Committee. S. Rept. 1622, 83d Cong., 2d Sess. 98 (1954). In addition, the Regulations elaborate on the meaning of "unrealized receivables" as used in section 751. Section 1.751-1(c), Income Tax Regs., provides:

> (c) Unrealized receivables. (1) The term "unrealized receivables," means any rights (contractual or otherwise) to payment for –
>
> (i) Goods delivered or to be delivered (to the extent that such payment would be treated as received for property other than a capital asset), or
>
> (ii) Services rendered or to be rendered, to the extent that income arising from such rights to payment was not previously includable in income under the method of accounting employed by the partnership. Such rights must have arisen under contracts or agreements in existence at the time of sale or distribution, although the partnership may not be able to enforce payment until a later time. For example, the term includes trade accounts receivable of a cash method taxpayer, and rights to payment for work or goods begun but incomplete at the time of the sale or distribution.

In determining the amount of the sale price attributable to such unrealized receivables, or their value in a distribution treated as a sale or exchange, any arm's length agreement between the buyer and the seller, or between the partnership and the distributee partner, will generally establish the amount or value. In the absence of such an agreement, full account shall be taken not only of the estimated cost of completing performance of the contract or agreement, but also of the time between the sale or distribution and the time of payment.

The language of the legislative history and the Regulations indicates that the term "unrealized receivables" includes any contractual or other right to payment for goods delivered or to be delivered or services rendered or to be rendered. Therefore, an analysis of the nature of the rights under the Dog Track Agreement, in the context of the aforementioned legal framework, becomes appropriate. A number of cases have dealt with the meaning of "unrealized receivables" and thereby have helped to define the scope of the term. Courts that have considered the term "unrealized receivables" generally have said that it should be given a broad interpretation. Cf. *Corn Products Co. v. Commissioner,* 350 U.S. 46, 52 (1955) (the term "capital asset" is to be construed narrowly, but exclusions from the definition thereof are to be broadly and liberally construed). For instance, in *Logan v. Commissioner,* 51 T.C. 482, 486 (1968), we held that a partnership's right in *quantum meruit* to payment for work in progress constituted an unrealized receivable even though there was no express agreement between the partnership and its clients requiring payment.

112

In *Roth v. Commissioner,* 321 F.2d 607 (9th Cir. 1963), *aff'g.* 38 T.C. 171 (1962), the Ninth Circuit dealt with the sale of an interest in a partnership which produced a movie and then gave a 10-year distribution right to Paramount Pictures Corporation in return for a percentage of the gross receipts. The selling partner claimed that his right to a portion of the payments expected under the partnership's contract with Paramount did not constitute an unrealized receivable. The court rejected this view, however, reasoning that Congress "meant to exclude from capital gains treatment any receipts which would have been treated as ordinary income to the partner if no transfer of the partnership interest had occurred." 321 F. 2d at 611. Therefore, the partnership's right to payments under the distribution contract was in the nature of an unrealized receivable.

A third example of the broad interpretation given to the term "unrealized receivable" is *United States v. Eidson, 3* 10 F.2d 111 (5th Cir. 1962), *revg. an unreported opinion* (W.D. Tex. 1961). The court there considered the nature of a management contract which was similar to the one at issue in the instant case. The case arose in the context of a sale by a partnership of all of its rights to operate and manage a mutual insurance company. The selling partnership received $170,000 for the rights it held under the management contract, and the government asserted that the total amount should be treated as ordinary income. The Court of Appeals agreed with the government's view on the ground that what was being assigned was not a capital asset whose value had accrued over a period of years; rather, the right to operate the company and receive profits therefrom during the remaining life of the contract was the real subject of the assignment. 310 F.2d at 116. The Fifth Circuit found the Supreme Court's holding in *Commissioner v. P. G. Lake, Inc.,* 356 U.S. 260 (1958), to be conclusive:

> The substance of what was assigned was the right to receive future income. The substance of what was received was the present value of income which the recipient would otherwise obtain in the future. In short, consideration was paid for the right to receive future income, not for an increase in the value of the income-producing property. [356 U.S. at 266, cited in 310 F.2d at 115.]

In *United States v. Woolsey,* 326 F.2d 287 (5th Cir. 1963), *rev 'g.* 208 F. Supp. 325 (S.D. Texas 1962), the Fifth Circuit again faced a situation similar to the one that we face herein. The Fifth Circuit considered whether proceeds received by taxpayers on the sale of their partnership interests were to be treated as ordinary income or capital gain. There, the court was faced with the sale of interests in a partnership which held, as one of its assets, a 25-year contract to manage a mutual insurance company. As in the instant case, the contract gave the partners the right to render services for the term of the contract and to earn ordinary income in the future. In holding that the partnership's management contract constituted an unrealized receivable, the court stated:

> When we look at the underlying right assigned in this case, we cannot escape the conclusion that so much of the consideration which relates to the right to earn ordinary income in the future under the "management contract," taxable to the assignee as ordinary income, is likewise taxable to the assignor as ordinary income although such income must be earned. Section 751 has defined "unrealized receivables" to include any rights, contractual or otherwise, to ordinary income from "services rendered, or to be rendered," (emphasis added) to the extent that the same were not previously includable in income by the partnership, with the result that capital gains rates cannot be applied to the rights to income under the facts of this case, which would constitute ordinary income had the same been received in due course by the partnership. . . It is our conclusion that such portion of the consideration received by the taxpayers in this case as properly should be allocated to

the present value of their right to earn ordinary income in the future under the "management contract" is subject to taxation as ordinary income. . . . [326 F.2d at 291.]

Petitioner attempts to distinguish *United States v. Woolsey, supra,* and *United States v. Eidson, supra,* from the instant case by arguing that those cases involved a sale or termination of contracts to manage mutual insurance companies in Texas and that the management contracts therein were in the nature of employment agreements. After closely scrutinizing the facts in those cases, we conclude that petitioner's position has no merit. The fact that the *Woolsey* case, involved sale of 100, percent of the partnership interests, as opposed to a sale of only a 25-percent partnership interest herein, is of no consequence. In addition, the fact that *Eidson* involved the surrender of the partnership's contract right to manage the insurance company, as opposed to the continued partnership operation in the instant case, also is not a material factual distinction.

The Dog Track Agreement at issue in the instant case is similar to the management contract considered by the Fifth Circuit in *Woolsey.* Each gives the respective partnership the right to operate a business for a period of years and to earn ordinary income in return for payments of specified amounts to the corporation that holds the state charter. Therefore, based on our analysis of the statutory language, the legislative history and the Regulations and relevant case law, we are compelled to find that the Dog Track Agreement gave the petitioner an interest that amounted to an "unrealized receivable" within the meaning of section 754(c).

Petitioner further contends that the Dog Track Agreement does not represent an unrealized receivable because it does not require or obligate the Partnership to perform personal services in the future. The Agreement only gives, the argument continues, the Collins-Ledoux Partnership the right to engage in a business.

We find this argument to be unpersuasive. The words of section 751(c), providing that the term "unrealized receivable" includes the right to payment for "services rendered, or to be rendered," do not preclude that section's application to a situation where, as here, the performance of services is not required by the Agreement. As the Fifth Circuit said in *United States v. Eidson, supra*:

> The fact that . . . income would not be received by the [partnership] unless they performed the services which the contract required of them, that is, actively managed the affairs of the insurance company in a manner that would produce a profit after all of the necessary expenditures, does not, it seems clear, affect the nature of this payment. It affects only the amount. This is, the fact that the taxpayers would have to spend their time and energies in performing services for which the compensation would be received merely affects the price at which they would be willing to assign or transfer the contract. . . . [310 F.2d at 115.]

Consequently, a portion of the consideration received by Ledoux on the sale of his partnership interest is subject to taxation as ordinary income.

* * *

Having established that the Dog Track Agreement qualifies as an unrealized receivable, we next consider whether all or only part of petitioner's gain in excess of the amount attributable to his share of tangible partnership assets should be treated as ordinary income. Petitioner argues that this excess gain was attributable to goodwill or the value of a going concern.

With respect to goodwill, we note that petitioner's attorney drafted, and petitioner signed, the Agreement for Sale of Partnership Interest, dated October 17, 1972 which contains the following statement in paragraph 7:

7. In the determination of the purchase price set forth in this agreement, the parties acknowledge no consideration has been given to any item of goodwill.

The meaning of the words "no consideration" is not entirely free from doubt. They could mean that no thought was given to an allocation of any of the sales price to goodwill, or they could indicate that the parties agreed that no part of the purchase price was allocated to goodwill. The testimony of the attorney who prepared the document indicates, however, that he did consider the implications of the sale of goodwill and even did research on the subject. He testified that he believed, albeit incorrectly, that, if goodwill were part of the purchase price, his client would not be entitled to capital gains treatment.

Petitioner attempts to justify this misstatement of the tax implications of an allocation to goodwill not by asserting mistake, but by pointing out that his attorney "is not a tax lawyer but is primarily involved with commercial law and real estate." We find as a fact that petitioner agreed at arm's length with the purchasers of his partnership interest that no part of the purchase price should be attributable to goodwill. The Tax Court long has adhered to the view that, absent "strong proof," a taxpayer cannot challenge an express allocation in an arm's-length sales contract to which he had agreed. *See, e.g., Major v. Commissioner,* 76 T.C. 239, 249 (1981), *appeal pending* (7th Cir. July 7, 1981); *Lucas v. Commissioner,* 58 T.C. 1022, 1032 (1972). In *Spector v. Commissioner,* 641 F.2d 376 (5th Cir. 1981), *rev'g.* 71 T.C. 1017 (1979), the Fifth Circuit, to which an appeal in this case will lie, appeared to step away from its prior adherence to the "strong proof" standard and move toward the stricter standard enunciated in *Commissioner v. Danielson,* 378 F.2d 771, 775 (3d Cir. 1967), *remanding* 44 T.C. 549 (1965), *cert. denied* 389 U.S. 858 (1967). However, in this case, we need not measure the length of the step since we hold that petitioner has failed to introduce sufficient evidence to satisfy even the more lenient "strong proof" standard.

We next turn to petitioner's contention that part or all of the purchase price received in excess of the value of tangible assets is attributable to value of a going concern. In *VGS Corp. v. Commissioner,* 68 T.C. 563 (1977), we stated that –

Going-concern value is, in essence, the additional element of value which attaches to property by reason of its existence as an integral part of a going concern. . . [T]he ability of a business to continue to function and generate income without interruption as a consequence of the change in ownership, is a vital part of the value of a going concern. . . [Cites omitted; 68 T.C. at 591-592]

However, in the instant case, the ability of the dog-racing track to continue to function after the sale of Ledoux's partnership interest was due to the remaining partners' retention of rights to operate under the Dog Track Agreement. Without such Agreement, there would have been no continuing right to operate a business and no right to continue to earn income. Thus, the amount paid in excess of the value of Ledoux's share of the tangible assets was not for the intangible value of the business as a going concern but rather for Ledoux's rights under the Dog Track Agreement.

Finally, we turn to petitioner's claim that a determination of the value of rights arising from the Dog Track Agreement has never been made and no evidence of the value of such rights was submitted in this case. We note that the $800,000 purchase price was proposed by petitioner and was accepted by Jack Collins and Jerry Collins in an arm's-length agreement of sale evidenced in the Memorandum of Agreement of July 19, 1972 and the Agreement for Sale of Partnership interest of October 17, 1972. In addition, the October 17, 1972 sales agreement, written by petitioner's attorney, provided in paragraph 1 that the "[s]eller [Ledoux] sells to buyer [Jerry Collins and Jack Collins] all of his interest in [the partnership] . . . including but not limited to, the seller's right to income and to acquire the capital stock of The Sanford-Orlando

Kennel Club, Inc." . . . Section 1.751-1(c)(3), Income Tax Regs., provides that an arm's-length agreement between the buyer and the seller generally will establish the value attributable to unrealized receivables.

Based on the provision in the Agreement that no part of the consideration was attributable to goodwill, it is clear to us that the parties were aware that they could, if they so desired, have provided that no part of the consideration was attributable to the Dog Track Agreement. No such provision was made? Furthermore, the Agreement clearly stated that one of the assets purchased was Ledoux's rights to future income. Considering that petitioner calculated the purchase price by capitalizing future earnings expected under the Dog Track Agreement, we conclude that the portion of Ledoux's gain in excess of the amount attributable to tangible assets was attributable to an unrealized receivable as reflected by the Dog Track Agreement.

Decision will be entered for the respondent.

2. TRADITIONAL RECAPTURE ITEMS

The second type of "unrealized receivable" involves traditional recapture items that would have produced ordinary income when the associated property is sold. Referring to these as unrealized receivables is obviously a misnomer, but the theory for including them under § 751 is sound because a partner could otherwise convert her ordinary gain into capital gain. Examples include depreciation of personal property (§ 1245) and intangible drilling and development costs (§ 1254). *See* § 751(c).

3. INVENTORY ITEMS

Inventory items are defined more broadly than inventory, and include such things as dealer property, and noncapital or non-section 1231 assets in the partnership's hands. § 751(d). The portion of the sales price of the partnership interest attributable to sales of these items is also weeded out and given ordinary gain or loss treatment.

PROBLEM 6-2

1) Which of the following items are unrealized receivables or inventory items?

   a) Grain held by a cash method grain dealer?

   b) Accounts receivable of a cash method grain dealer?

   c) Accounts receivable of an accrual method grain dealer?

   d) The dealer's right to be paid for services rendered in repairing a silo?

   e) Depreciation the dealer claimed on a railroad car? The partnership bought the car for $100, wrote it off to $40 and it is now worth $50.

   f) An artwork produced by the partnership in a moment of inspiration, not in the course of its business.

2. Can partnership interests be exchanged tax-free? *See* § 1031.

4. CALCULATING GAINS AND LOSSES FROM SALE OR EXCHANGE OF PARTNERSHIP INTERESTS
Read Reg. § 1.751-1(a), (b).

When § 751 does apply, there usually will be a mix of capital and ordinary gain or loss results. But how much of each? The partnership is treated as if it sold its hot assets attributable to the selling partner, who in turn recognizes the gains on those hypothetical sales.

There is a further twist involving sales of interests in partnerships that hold "collectibles" (top rate is 28%) and real estate that is subject to recapture on its sale (top rate 25%). These are sometimes referred to as "lukewarm assets." Section 1(h)(5) and the Regulations thereunder call for using largely the same process as with "hot assets" to cull out such gains in order to assure that the partner reports a share of her gain – to the extent founded on collectibles or real estate recapture gain – subject to those higher top rates, rather than subject to the general top rate of 15%. So, once again, these transactions are handled as if the partnership sold all these assets and allocated the results to the selling or deceased partner before the partner sold her interest.

Once those steps are completed, one deals with the residue, which is the regular capital gain component of the sale. The result of this calculation can be surprising. For example, it may produce a gain whereas the hot assets calculations produced a loss.

PROBLEM 6-3

1) X is a one-third member of the AXZ partnership. Her outside basis is $60 and her share of the inside basis of the partnership's assets is $46.67. The partnership's only property is land held for investment. What is the amount and character of her gain if she sells her one-third interest for $100?

2) The equal ABC partnership is on the cash method and has the following assets on its balance sheet (assume the partnership bought the equipment for $10 and wrote it all off):

Asset	Adjusted Basis	FMV
Accounts Receivable	$0.00	$20.00
Equipment	$0.00	$10.00
Inventory	$20.00	$20.00
Land	$50.00	$60.00
Cash	$70.00	$70.00
	$140.00	$180.00

a) Assuming A's basis in her partnership interest is $46.67 (*i.e.*, the same as her share of inside basis of $140/3). What is the amount and character of the gain on the sale of her partnership interest for $60? Assume that the ABC partnership uses the cash method of accounting and assume that A is not a real estate dealer.

b) How, if at all, would your answer to "(a)" change if the ABC partnership were on the accrual method?

c) How, if at all, would your answer to "(a)" change if A were a real estate dealer? *See* § 751(d).

117

d) How, if at all, would your answer to "(a)" change if the accounts receivable were collectibles held for over a year. *See* Reg. § 1.1(h)-(b)(2)(ii).

C. TAXATION OF THE BUYER
Read §§ 754 and 743(b), (c).

1. INTRODUCTION

The buyer of the partnership interest will take a cost basis in the interest. §§ 742, 1011, and 1012. The incoming partner will include his or her allocable share of partnership liabilities under § 752(d), and will generally inherit the transferor's capital account. Reg. § 1.704-1(b)(2)(iv)(1).

2. SECTION 743(b) OPTIONAL BASIS ADJUSTMENT

Sales and exchanges of partnership interests tend to obliterate the symmetry between inside and outside basis. The reason is that a partner will rarely sell the partnership interest for an amount equal to his or her share of inside basis because as time passes, inside basis ceases to reflect market value.

To illustrate: C has a $100 basis in her 33% share of the ABC partnership, which is on the calendar year and uses the cash method. ABC's total inside basis is $300. The sole asset is a tract of unencumbered raw land, worth $330. She sells her interest to D on December 31 for $110, as a result of which D has a $110 outside basis. If ABD sells the land for $330 soon after D buys, D will be taxed on $10, his share of the $30 gain. This seems unfair to D. However, when the partnership is liquidated and the remaining cash is distributed, D will show a $10 loss because his liquidation proceeds ($110) will be $10 less than his outside basis. § 731(a)(2). If the transactions all occur in the same year, D will likely not care, but if the proceeds from the sale of the land are not distributed, D may become distraught.

Enter § 754 (a procedural provision granting powers of election to the partnership) and § 743 (the operative provision). The so-called section 754 election must be made on a timely tax return for the partnership, and can be revoked only with IRS consent. If the facts involve a multi-tiered partnership pattern, selling an interest in an upper-tier partnership causes an adjustment to the basis of lower-tier partnership property only if both partnerships elect. Rev. Rul. 87-115, 19872 C.B. 163 If the partnership makes the § 754 election, it can adjust its basis in assets allocable to the incoming partner. The result is equivalent to what would have happened if the partner had bought the assets directly, rather than buying a partnership interest.

A sale of a partnership interest is not the only event that triggers § 754, but it is the most obvious. For example, § 743 also applies to the death of a partner. In essence, § 754 is an imprecise effort to equate a partner's outside basis with his share of inside values. If a § 754 election is in effect, the relationship between aggregate inside basis and outside basis remains intact transfer-by-transfer.

As applied to the ABC partnership example, ABD would increase its basis in the raw land by $10 but only as to D. As a result, ABD will report only a $20 gain on the sale of the land, and the $20 will be allocated to A and B alone. If the partnership immediately liquidates, D will report no gain or loss, because the cash she receives will exactly equal her outside basis. Thanks to the election, D will be in the same overall position, in that she will not ultimately be taxed on the $10 but, thanks to § 743, freedom from taxation will occur by preventing the gain in the first instance rather than by combining an exaggerated gain with a later exaggerated loss.

118

The § 754 election is formidable. It ties up all subsequent partners who got their interests by purchase or inheritance, and it also forces the partnership to apply a companion provision (§ 734) to distributions from the partnership. Moreover, the adjustment implicates the new partner's share of depreciation, amortization, and depletion, as well as its gains and losses. Electing under § 754 means that partners who buy (or inherit) partnership interests at a discount must watch with displeasure as their allocable shares of inside basis are reduced.

The section 754 election is especially important when one sells an interest in a cash method service partnership holding large amounts of receivables. Absent the election, the buying partner will be taxed when the receivables are paid. Also, note that the single section 754 election causes basis adjustments under both § 743 and its companion provision, § 734, which is discussed in Chapter 7. One must accept neither or both, and once made the election is irrevocable, unless the government consents to a revocation. There is another option; the partnership can be put through a technical termination under § 708, thereby creating a "new" partnership that can make "new" elections. That subject is discussed in a later chapter.

Section 743 is mandatory if the partnership has a "substantial built-in loss" after the transfer of a partnership interest, meaning that the partnership's assets' collective basis is more than $250,000 higher than their collective value. § 743(d)(1). The practical effect is that a partner who buys an interest in a partnership with a big inherent loss will watch with dismay as his share of inside basis drops to its value. The obvious purpose of the reform is to take the pleasure out of buying losses owned by partnerships. It is a one-way street. People who buy interests in partnerships with big built-in gains do not get the benefit of an automatic § 754 election. There is an elective exception for a narrow range of investment partnerships (but this exception is eroded by a loss limitation rule) and a mandatory exception for securitization partnerships. § 743(e), (f).

Under the Tax Cuts and Jobs Act the definition of a "substantial built-in loss" is modified so that a substantial built-in loss also exists if the transferee would be allocated a net loss in excess of $250,000 upon a hypothetical disposition at fair market value by the partnership of all partnership assets immediately after the transfer of the partnership interest.

Example

Partnership XYZ does not have a section 754 election in place. The partnership has two assets, M and P. Asset M has a built-in gain of $5 million; Asset P has a built-in loss of $3,000,000. Under the partnership agreement, any gain on the sale of Asset M is specially allocated to Partner X. Partners X, Y and Z share equally in all other partnership items, including the built-in loss in Asset P.

Partner Y and Z each have a net built-in loss of $1,000,000 (one third of $3,000,000) allocable to their partnership interests.

But the partnership itself does not have an overall built-in loss. Rather, it has a net built-in gain of $2,000,000 ($5 million minus $3,000,000).

Partner Z sells her partnership interest to D for $666,666.

The test for a substantial built-in loss applies both at the partnership level and at the transferee partner level. If the partnership were to sell all of its assets for cash at their fair market value immediately after the transfer to D, D would be allocated a loss of $1,000,000 (one third of the built-in loss of $3,000,000 in Asset P).

There is a substantial built-in loss under the partner-level test. The partnership must adjust the basis of its assets accordingly with respect to D.

Rev. Rul. 87-115

Issues

Under section 743(b) of the Internal Revenue Code, does a sale of an interest in an upper-tier partnership (UTP) result in an adjustment to the basis of the property of a lower-tier partnership (LTP) in which UTP has an interest if:

(1) Both UTP and LTP have made an election under section 754?

(2) Only UTP has made the election under section 754?

(3) Only LTP has made the election under section 754?

Facts

UTP is a partnership in which A, B, C, and D are equal partners. UTP is a partnership in which A, B, C, and D each contributed 30x dollar of cash to UTP upon its formation, and they each have a 30x interest in partnership capital and surplus. A's share of the adjusted basis of partnership property is 30x dollars, the sum of A's interest as a partner in partnership capital and surplus, plus A's share of partnership liabilities (neither UTP nor LTP have any liabilities). UTP is an equal partner in LTP, along with X and Y. LTP was formed by X, Y, and Z, who each contributed 110x dollars of cash to LTP upon its formation. UTP purchased its interest in LTP from Z for 80x dollars in a taxable year for which LTP did not have an election under section 754 in effect. UTP, X, and Y each have a 110x dollar interest in partnership capital and surplus.

UTP has an adjusted basis of 120x dollars in its property as follows: an adjusted basis of 80 dollars in its partnership interest in LTP and an adjusted basis of 40x dollars in inventory. UTP's partnership interest in LTP has a fair market value of 120x dollars, and UTP's inventory has a fair market value of 80x dollars. LTP has only one asset, a capital asset that is not a section 751 asset. LTP's asset has an adjusted basis of 330x dollars and a fair market value of 360x dollars.

In 1985, A sold A's entire interest in UTP to E for 50x dollars.

Situation 1: Both UTP and LTP have valid section 754 elections in effect.

Situation 2: UTP has a section 754 election in effect, but LTP does not.

Situation 3: UTP does not have a section 754 election in effect, but LTP does.

Law and Analysis

Section 742 of the Code provides that the basis of an interest in a partnership acquired other than by contribution shall be determined under part II of subchapter O of chapter 1 (sections 1011 through 1015).

Section 1012 of the Code provides, with certain exceptions, that the basis of property shall be the cost of such property.

120

Section 754 of the Code provides that if a partnership files an election, in accordance with Regulations prescribed by the Secretary, the basis of partnership property shall be adjusted, in the case of a transfer of a partnership interest, in the manner provided in section 743(b). Such election shall apply with respect to all transfers of interests in the partnership during the taxable year with respect to which such election was filed and all subsequent years.   Section 743(a) of the Code provides the general rule that the basis of partnership property shall not be adjusted as the result of a transfer of an interest in a partnership by sale or exchange or on the death of a partner unless the election provided by section 754 is in effect with respect to such partnership.

Section 743(b) of the Code provides that, in the case of a transfer of an interest in a partnership by sale or exchange or upon the death of a partner, a partnership with respect to which the election provided in section 754 is in effect shall (1) increase the adjusted basis of partnership property by the excess of the basis to the transferee partner of such partner's interest in the partnership over the partner's proportionate share of the adjusted basis of partnership property; or (2) decrease the adjusted basis of partnership property by the excess of the transferee partner's proportionate share of the adjusted basis of partnership property over the basis of such partner's interest in the partnership. Section 743(b) further provides that the increase or decrease shall be an adjustment to the basis of partnership property with respect to the transferee partner only.

Section 1.743-1(b)(1) of the Income Tax Regulations provides that, in general, a partner's share of the adjusted basis of partnership property is equal to the sum of that partner's interest as a partner in partnership capital and surplus, plus that partner's share of partnership liabilities.

Section 755(a) of the Code requires that, in general, the amount of the basis adjustment be allocated among partnership assets in a manner which has the effect of reducing the difference between the fair market value and the adjusted basis of those assets, or in any other manner permitted by the Regulations prescribed by the Secretary.

Section 755(b) of the Code provides that in applying the allocation rules provided in section 755(a), increases or decreases in the adjusted basis of partnership property arising from the transfer of an interest attributable to (1) capital assets and property described in section 1231(b)("capital assets"), or (2) any other property of the partnership, shall in general be allocated to partnership property of like character.

Section 1.755-1(b)(2) of the Income Tax Regulations provides that to the extent an amount paid by a purchaser of a partnership interest is attributable to the value of capital assets, any difference between the amount so attributable and the transferee partner's share of the partnership basis of such property shall constitute a special basis adjustment with respect to partnership capital assets. Similarly, any such difference attributable to any other property of the partnership shall constitute a special basis adjustment with respect to such property.

Section 741 of the Code provides that, except as provided in section 751, the gain or loss on the exchange of an interest in a partnership shall be considered as a gain or loss from the sale of a capital asset.

Rev. Rul. 78-2, 1978-1 C.B. 202, concerns the transfer of an interest in an investment partnership, X, which is a partner of an operating partnership, Y. The ruling concludes that if elections under section 754 of the Code are in effect for X and Y, the adjustment to the basis of partnership property under section 743(b) includes (a) an adjustment to X's partnership interest in Y and (b) a corresponding basis adjustment to Y's property with respect to X and the transferee partner of X only.

In essence, if an election under section 754 is not in effect, the partnership is treated as an independent entity, separate from its partners. Thus, absent a section 754 election, even though the transferee receives a cost basis for the acquired partnership interest, the partnership does not adjust the transferee's share of the adjusted basis of partnership property. If, however, an election under section 754 is in effect, the partnership is treated more like an aggregate of its partners, and the transferee's overall basis in the assets of the partnership is generally the same as it would have been had the transferee acquired a direct interest in its share of those assets. Nevertheless, the transferee's adjusted basis for specific partnership assets will not necessarily equal the basis the assets would have had if the transferee had acquired a direct interest in the assets. The difference is due to the fact that the transferee's basis in specific partnership assets is controlled by section 755, which does not adopt a pure aggregate approach. See section 1.755-1(c) of the Regulations.

Situation 1

E purchased A's interest for 50x dollars. Thus, under section 742, E's basis in E's partnership interest is 50x dollars. Because UTP made a valid section 754 election, under section 743(b) UTP must increase the adjusted basis of its property by 20x dollars, the excess of the transferee partner's basis in the partnership interest (50x dollars) over that partner's share of the adjusted basis of such property. Under section 1.743-1(b)(1), E's share of the adjusted basis of partnership property is 30x dollars, because E succeeds to A's interest in partnership capital and surplus. See, e.g., section 1.743-1(b)(1) Example (2). The 20x dollar special basis adjustment raises UTP's adjusted basis in its partnership property to 140x dollars, but the additional 20x dollars must be segregated and allocated solely to E. Under section 755, the 20x dollars must be allocated between capital assets (UTP's interest in\ LTP) and other assets (UTP's inventory).

Under section 1.755-1(b)(2) of the Regulations, to the extent that an amount paid by a purchaser of a partnership interest (here, 50x dollars) is attributable to the value of capital assets (here, 120x dollars, the value of UTP's interest in LTP), any difference between the amount so attributable and the transferee partner's share of the partnership basis of such property constitutes a special basis adjustment with respect to such capital assets. In the instant case, 30x dollars (60 percent of 50x dollars) of E's purchase price is attributable to the value of UTP's interest in LTP, because 120x dollars, the value of UTP's interest in LTP, is 60 percent of 200x dollars, the total value of UTP's property. Thus, 10x dollars, the difference between the 30x dollars attributable to the value of UTP's interest in LTP and 20x dollars, E's proportionate share of UTP's basis in LTP, is a special basis adjustment to UTP's interest in LTP. This adjustment gives E an adjusted basis of 30x dollars in UTP's interest in LTP. The remaining 10x dollars of the 20x dollar special basis adjustment is allocated to the adjusted basis of UTP's inventory. This gives E a 20x dollar adjusted basis in UTP's inventory.

Because UTP made a section 754 election manifesting an intent to be treated as an aggregate for purposes of sections 754 and 743, it is appropriate, for purposes of section 743 and 754, to treat the sale of A's partnership interest in UTP as a deemed sale of an interest in LTP. The selling price of E's share of UTP's interest in LTP is deemed to equal E's share of UTP's adjusted basis in LTP, 30x dollars (1/4 of 80x dollars plus 10x dollars, E's special basis adjustment). Further, this deemed sale of an interest in LTP triggers the application of section 743(b) to LTP. Because LTP made a valid section 754 election, under section 743(b) LTP must increase the adjusted basis of its partnership property by 2.5x dollars, the excess of E's share of UTP's adjusted basis in LTP (30x dollars) over E's share of the adjusted basis of LTP's property (1/4 of 110x dollars, or 27.5x dollars). Section 755 applies to LTP to allocate this basis adjustment, but because LTP has only one asset, no allocation is necessary. The 2.5x dollar adjustment must be segregated and allocated solely to UTP and E, the transferee partner of UTP.

Situation 2

UTP has made a valid section 754 election. Thus, as in Situation 1, E gets an adjusted basis of 30x dollars in UTP's interest in LTP and an adjusted basis of 20x dollars in UTP's inventory. Also, as in Situation 1, because UTP made a section 754 election, it is appropriate, for purposes of sections 754 and 743, to treat the sale of A's interest in UTP as the sale of an interest in LTP. However, in this situation, LTP does not have a section 754 election in effect. That is, under section 743(a), LTP chose not to have the basis of its property adjusted as the result of the transfer of an interest in it. Thus, E's purchase of a partnership interest in UTP has no affect on LTP's adjusted basis in its property.

Situation 3

LTP has made a valid election under section 754, but UTP does not make a section 754 election. On the sale by A of an interest in UTP, E succeeds to A's 20x dollar adjusted basis in UTP's interest in LTP and to A's 10x dollar adjusted basis in UTP's inventory. E succeeds to these bases because, by not making a section 754 election, UTP chose not to have the basis of its property adjusted as the result of the transfer of an interest in UTP. In addition, by not making a section 754 election, UTP manifested an intent to be treated as an entity for purposes of sections 754 and 743. Thus, it is inappropriate, for purposes of sections 754 and 743, to treat A's sale of an interest in UTP as the sale of an interest in LTP. Consequently, UTP cannot increase E's share of the basis of LTP's property. Nevertheless, LTP's section 754 election is not meaningless. If UTP were to sell its partnership interest in LTP, the purchaser's share of the adjusted basis of LTP's assets would be adjusted.

Holdings

Situation 1

Upon the sale of A's partnership interest in UTP, the transferee's (E's) share of UTP's adjusted basis in its assets is adjusted by the amount by which the basis in E's partnership interest differs from E's share of UTP's adjusted basis in its assets. In addition, E's share of LTP's adjusted basis in its assets is adjusted by the amount by which E's share of UTP's adjusted basis in LTP differs from E's share of the adjusted basis of LTP's property.

Situation 2

Upon the sale of A's partnership interest in UTP, E's share of UTP's adjusted basis in its assets is adjusted by the amount by which the basis in E's partnership interest differs from E's share of UTP's adjusted basis in its assets. However, because LTP did not make a section 754 election, the transfer does not affect LTP's adjusted basis in its property.

Situation 3

The sale of A's partnership interest in UTP does not affect either UTP's adjusted basis in its property or LTP's adjusted basis in its property.

PROBLEM 6-4

1) A and B are equal members of the AB general partnership. The partnership's sole asset is a building with basis of $200 and a value of $500. A sells his interest to C for $250.

    1) If no § 754 election is in force, what is the most depreciation C will be able to claim with respect to the building?

    2) What if there is a § 754 election in force?

    3) Will the election have any impact on B's depreciation deductions?

    4) If, instead, the inside basis were $600, would the election be desirable to C?

    5) Can C make the § 754 election? If not, who makes it?

    6) Can the election be made during the tax year following the sale to C? Reg. § 1.754-1(b)(1).

    g) Many years later, partner C sells his partnership interest to D for its value of $2 million at a time when the partnership's assets are worth $4 million and have a basis of $8 million. There is no § 754 election in force. Must the partnership reduce the basis of its assets to $4 million? Why or why not?

3. SECTION 755: ALLOCATING SECTION 743 BASIS ADJUSTMENT
Read Reg. §1.755-1(a)(1), § 1.755-1(a)(4)(i)(A) and § 1.755-1(b)(1)-(3).

Section 755 tells one how to allocate the disparity between inside and outside basis. These adjustments apply even where the net amount of the basis adjustment is zero. Similarly, the portion of the basis adjustment allocated to property within a class increases the basis, while the portion allocated to another property within the class decreases the basis, even where the net basis adjustment allocated to the class is zero. Reg. § 1.755-1(b)(1)(i). The system creates outcomes that one definitely would not expect. For convenience, call a built-in gain that has to be allocated a "positive adjustment." If the subject is a built-in loss, refer to it as a "negative adjustment."

The allocation process works in four basic stages and is performed solely with respect to the partner who is affected by § 743, namely the buyer or heir. The following summary is highly simplified.

- *First,* divide the affected partner's share of all the assets into two classes: (1) § 1231 and capital assets; (2) all other assets.

- *Second,* determine the net appreciation or depreciation in each asset in the class as if the assets had been sold for their fair market values.

- *Third,* allocate the adjustments within a class among the assets in the class in proportion to the net appreciation or depreciation in value of *each asset* in the class.

- *Fourth*: if the buyer paid more than the proportionate share of the value of the assets, treat the excess as a purchase of goodwill under § 197.

PROBLEM 6-5

1) Assume an equal three-person cash method partnership consisting of A, B and C. The ABC partnerships owns the following assets:

Partnership Asset	Value	Basis
Building	$1,200.00	$3,000.00
Accounts Receivable	$400.00	($0.00)

C sells her interest (which has a basis of $1,000) to D for $533.33 (one third of the total value of $1,600)

   a) What is the amount and character of C's gain or loss? *See* §§ 741 and 751.

   b) What is D's basis in each share of the partnership's assets if the § 754 election is in force? *See* Reg. § 1.755-1(a), (b).

   c) How would your answer to b) differ if the accounts receivable had an inside basis greater than $400?

   d) How would your answer to b) differ if the buyer paid $700?

   e) If shortly after the purchase, and with a § 754 election in force, D receives an undivided one-third interest in the building in an operating distribution, what should D's basis be in that one-third interest? *See* Reg. § 1.743-1(g)(1).

Chapter 7

OPERATING DISTRIBUTIONS

A. EFFECT ON THE PARTNER
Read §§ 705, 731(a)-(c)(2)(A), 732(a) and 733.

1. INTRODUCTION

The subject of this disagreeably arithmetical chapter is the treatment of *operating (*or *"current")* distributions of cash and property, meaning distributions that neither eliminate the partner's interest in the partnership, nor eliminate the partnership itself. Because the distribution received from a partnership generally emanates from either capital contributed by the partner or from previously-taxed profits, it is normally granted tax-deferred treatment.

The Code generally ensures that a current distribution is tax-free to the distributee partner because the partner takes the partnership's basis in the distributed property, so long as the partnership's basis in the property does not exceed the partner's outside basis. § 732(a)(2). If the partner lacks outside basis, the general result is to reduce the basis of the property the partner received. In effect, the distribution just depletes the partnership's pool of assets to the extent of the partnership's basis in the distributed asset. Inasmuch as the distributee partner remains a partner, the distribution does not close out the investment relationship. Consequently, operating distributions reduce the partner's outside basis, but *never* produce losses to the distributee partner. They produce gains to the partner only if and to the extent more money is distributed than the partner has outside basis. § 731(a).

Distributions are usually easy to spot. When the partners, or at very least the managing partners, periodically review the partnership's finances and agree to distribute money or property to the partners, there is an obvious distribution. Some distributions may be less obvious: for example, when a partner's share of partnership liabilities declines, there is a "constructive" distribution. *See* § 752(b). In other instances, while there is a transfer of money or property from the partnership to a partner, the transfer is not a distribution in substance. Disguised sales provide typical examples of such non-distributions. That subject is discussed in Chapter 4 in connection with mixing bowl transactions.

2. DISTRIBUTIONS OF CASH

A partner has a taxable gain if and to the extent she receives cash in excess of her basis in her partnership interest *immediately before the distribution.* § 731(a); Reg. § 1.731-1(a)(1)(i). This means one has to compare the amount of the cash distribution to the partner's basis when the distribution is made, and not at the partner's year-end basis. However, Reg. §1.705-1(a) provides a general rule favoring year-end computations of basis. The special rule of § 731 requiring one to compare basis immediately before the transaction trumps the general rule and makes it important to check the partners' outside bases before making distributions of cash les the distributions produce taxable gains.

A distribution of cash includes a reduction in a partner's share of partnership liabilities and can create a gain. *See* § 752(b). Section 731 deems the gain to be from the sale of the partnership interest, so it will almost always be a capital gain. The special rule for distributions of cash is virtually inevitable, because, to avoid absurd results, cash always takes basis equal to its face amount. The legislative choices were to reduce the basis of cash (absurd), grant the partner a negative basis in his partnership interest (unacceptable to Congress as an unwritten rule of tax policy), or require the partner to report a gain. You might want to review § 733 for the refusal to allow negative basis.

PROBLEM 7-1

(1) A is a member of the ABC partnership. A has a $20 basis in her partnership interest at the end of the year, at which time the following events occur:

a) The partnership distributes cash of $10 to A. What are the income and basis effects to A? Consider only A's basis in her partnership interest.

b) Same as "(a)," but the distribution is of $40 in cash.

c) Same as "(a)," but some time later after the distribution described in "(a)," her share of the ABC partnership's liabilities declines by $70. What are the income and basis effects to A?

d) Is there any income tax impact to the partnership from "(a)," "(b)" or "(c)" or the three events, combined?

Cancellations of Partnership Debt Distinguished. A creditor's cancellation of a partnership's debt is not a distribution. It is a form of gross income to the partnership, which is allocable to the partners in accordance with their partnership distributive shares. *See Gershkowitz v. Commissioner,* 88 T.C. 984 (1987), *supra.* It is up to each partner to find a justification outside Subchapter K for excluding the cancellation of indebtedness income from gross income. *See* § 108.

Treatment of Partnership Draws. Partners in professional firms can rarely wait until year-end to take their profits out in cash, yet they will not know until year-end how prosperous the partnership is for that year. The Regulations have provided a solution for the treatment of midstream withdrawals. The solution works as follows: a "draw" against a distributive share of partnership income is treated as an interim loan followed by a year-end distribution to the partner which the partner uses to repay the loan. This model applies only if the partner is obligated to restore amounts taken out during the year that exceed the partner's distributive share for the partnership's taxable year. Reg. § 1.731-1(a)(1)(ii), (c)(2). This is the traditional "draw." If there is no duty to repay, then the draw is a current distribution.

PROBLEM 7-2

(1) Murray is an equal one-third partner in the equal cash method calendar year MM&J Junkyard partnership, which uses the cash method and calendar year. At the beginning of the year, Murray had an outside basis of $15. Each month he received a traditional $10 "draw" in an envelope from the company's bookkeeper, Ms. Fish. Murray is obligated to restore amounts received during the year that exceed his distributive share for the year. At the end of the year, Ms. Fish correctly calculated the partnership's profits at $400. The $400 was earned at year-end, when the firm's major client paid its bill in full.

a) Are the draws taxable? Reg. §§ 1.731-1 and 1.705-1(a).

b) Is it clear from the regulations that outside basis is determined at year-end?

c) What form will Ms. Fish use when preparing the partnership's federal income tax return?

d) How, if at all, would your answer differ if Murray had no duty to repay his draws? Just consider the first three months' results.

e) Assuming the original facts, when Ms. Fish prepares the MM&J partnership's federal income tax return, what will she show as each partner's share of partnership income?

f) In light of the treatment of the draws as traditional ones, when she prepares the Form K-1 for Murray, how much will she report as his increase in his outside basis? Assume that nothing is distributed to Murray that year other than his $10 monthly draws.

3. DISTRIBUTIONS OF PROPERTY

One of the striking features of partnership taxation is that distributions of property are generally tax-free both to the partner and the partnership. § 731(a), (b). By contrast, a corporation is taxed when it distributes appreciated assets. §§ 311 and 336. The shareholder also will generally be taxable. *See* § 301. One of the rationales for this favorable treatment of partnerships is that good economics dictate that there be no tax impediment to moving assets in and out of business enterprises. The same rationale should apply with equal force to corporations, but does not for questionable reasons.

A distribution requires the partner to allocate outside basis between the distributed property and his interest in the partnership. § 732 and § 733. In extreme cases distributions will reduce outside basis to zero, but – as always – never below zero. § 733. By contrast, a distribution reduces the capital account without limit, and can quickly produce a negative number, especially if the partnership is leveraged and loaded with depreciable property. §1.704-1(b)(2)(iv)(e)(1).

a. Distributee's Basis in Distributed Property and Partnership Interest

In the usual operating distribution one simply reduces the partner's basis in her partnership interest by the sum of the cash distributed and the partnership's basis in the distributed property. § 732(a). This has the practical effect of splitting the partner's outside basis between the property received and her remaining outside basis in her partnership interest. If the partnership distributes cash and property at the same time, one calculates the tax implications of the cash distribution first. Reg. § 1.732-1(a). This rule favors taxpayers by minimizing the taxability of distributions.

Because the distributee takes the partnership's basis in the distributed property, the result is only a deferral of gain or loss until the partner disposes of the property. However, § 732(a)(2) imperiously limits the basis of distributed property to the partner's basis in his partnership interest.

To illustrate: A is an equal partner in the AB partnership. She has an outside basis of $10. The partnership distributes $5 in cash plus an asset with a basis (to the partnership) of $10. Section 732(a)(2) ensures that her basis in the asset will be $5, namely, her original outside basis minus the $5 of cash. Section 733 will reduce her outside basis to $0.

If there were no § 732(a)(2) limit and no tax on the distribution of property, there would have to be negative basis in the partnership interest. Negative basis is apostasy throughout the Code, so § 732(a)(2) is not so imperious after all. Notice how distributions *generally* maintain the equality between inside and outside basis. Each distribution reduces each account equally. The exception occurs if the distributee partner's outside basis is insufficient to absorb the partnership's basis in the property (cash or noncash) which it distributes. If the surfeit is caused by cash, the result is a gain. If it is caused by property, the result is a reduction in the basis of the distributed property.

PROBLEM 7-3

(1) The equal ABC partnership has decided to distribute $100 in cash plus a tract of land with a value and an inside basis of $100 to partner A. A's pre-distribution basis in her partnership interest is $180.

a) What is the income tax effect to A? Would the result be the same if what was distributed was not cash but instead an interest in a common trust fund?

b) What is her basis in the land?

c) What is A's basis in her partnership interest after the distribution?

d) Does the partnership report any gain or loss as a result of the distribution?

e) In your view, has basis been expropriated with no corresponding current or future tax deduction?

Operating distributions of multiple classes of property: Usually, current distributions are of cash, but because nothing prevents other kinds of distributions, §§ 731 and 732 cover:

(1) Money and near money items,

(2) Receivables and inventory, and

(3) All other property.

One can think of the simultaneous distributions as occurring in "rounds" in the sense that if the taxpayer gets all three kinds in a single distribution, (1) the first round is money and near money, then (2) receivables and inventory, then (3) all other property, in that order.

Round one: money and near money. Distributions of money in excess of outside basis give rise to a gain to the distributee partner under § 731. To avoid such gain, taxpayers in the past manipulated the concept of "money" by arranging for the partnership to buy near cash items (like shares of a money market mutual fund) and have the partnership distribute the mutual fund shares. The partner would take the tax position that the mutual fund shares were "property," not "money," and so there was no taxable gain on the distribution. Congress discovered the trick and enacted § 731(c), which retaliates by turning "marketable securities" (including mutual fund stock) into "money."

To illustrate: C has a $200 basis in the ABC partnership, of which he is a 33% partner. He receives marketable securities worth $60. His basis in the securities is $60, and his outside basis declines to $140. If the marketable securities were instead worth $600, his gain would be $400.

There are exceptions to what constitutes "marketable securities," most importantly the following:

- Securities that the distributee originally contributed to the partnership; Treas. Reg. §1.731-2(d)(1)(i)

- Securities that are not marketable when acquired; Treas. Reg. §1.731-2(d)(1)(iii) and

- Securities distributed by an investment partnership that has never engaged in business and is rich with investment-type assets. *See* § 731(a)(1), (c). Treas. Reg. §1.731-2(e).

These exceptions do not interfere with the Congressional intention to prevent the use of money market funds to avoid gains. Once distributed, money will obviously take a basis equal to its face amount; marketable securities near money will receive a basis equal to their fair market values at the time of their distribution. § 731(c)(1). Strangely, marketable securities do not count as money for purposes of reporting a loss under § 731(a). § 731(c)(1), (a)(2).

Round two: receivables and inventory. This analysis starts after the impact of cash and marketable securities has been worked out. The logic here is that there ought be a way to ensure that the partner will recognize the same amount of gain as the partnership would have if the partnership itself had sold receivables and inventory. Section 732(c)(1) saves the day by providing that if the inside basis of such distributed property exceeds the partner's outside basis, remaining outside basis is allocated first to unrealized receivables and inventory items in proportion to the partnership's basis in such assets. This humane rule helps prevent the distributee partners from getting a step-down in the basis of these "hot assets," while at the same time preventing a windfall in the form of giving distributees an artificially high basis, which could trigger unrealistic ordinary losses if the partner later sells inventory or merchandise. Again, § 732(c)(l) strains to ensure that the partner will recognize the same amount of ordinary income as the partnership would have recognized on its sale of receivables and inventory items.

Round three: other property. Now comes the end of the story. If the partner *still* has basis after the first two rounds of allocations, that remaining outside basis is allocated to the residual properties. § 732(a)(1). The illustration involving the land and inventory (above) is a good example.

To illustrate: (Continuing the example) C has an outside basis of $140 after round one. The partnership has inventory items (as defined in § 751(d)) with an inside basis of $100, which it distributes to C. C gets a basis of $100 in the inventory. Section 732(c)(1). Now assume that partnership also distributes to C land with an inside basis of $100. Section 732(c)(1)(A)(i) says that the inventory is considered first. C will take a $100 basis in the inventory. The tract will, by necessity, take a basis of $40 (i.e., $140 minus the $100 basis in the inventory). C will have an outside basis of $0.

There can be a complication. What if the partner does not have enough basis to absorb the basis of partnership properties? Section 732(c)(3) steps in and directs that the reduction in basis of such properties be allocated first to properties with unrealized depreciation (meaning basis in excess of value), in proportion to their respective amounts of unrealized depreciation (but only to the extent of each property's unrealized depreciation), and then in proportion to their respective adjusted bases (taking into account the adjustments already made). *See* § 732(c)(3). This process of reduction even applies to unrealized receivables and inventory if there is not enough outside basis to cover "round two." § 732(c)(3)(B); Reg. § 1.732-1(c)(2)(i).

The following example shows a straightforward case where the partner's outside basis is greater than the inside basis of the properties, and one of the properties has declined in value.

To illustrate: (Continuing the example) Assume C did not get any inventory or receivables, and that he has an outside basis of $140 after round one. ABC partnership next distributes a tract of land and a barn. The tract has a basis to the partnership of $90 and a value of $70, and the barn has a basis to the partnership of $70 and a fair market value of $70. Basis is first allocated under § 732(b) as follows: $70 to the tract (because of its unrealized depreciation) and then $70 to the barn (its adjusted basis to the partnership). By contrast, if the barn and tract both had an inside basis of $90, § 732(c)(2)(B) would cause each asset to get a basis of $70, based on their proportionate inside bases.

b. Character and Holding Period of Distributed Property

Potential depreciation recapture under § 1245 or § 1250 inherent in distributed property carries over into the distributee partner's hands and converts part of any later gain on its sale into ordinary income. §§ 1245(b)(3) and 1250(d)(b)(3). The partner tacks the partnership's holding period to her own holding period. § 735. If the asset is an *unrealized receivable,* the property retains its ordinary income character forever. § 735(a)(1). If it is an *inventory item,* it only retains its ordinary character for five subsequent years, after which it loses its taint unless the taxpayer in fact holds it in inventory. § 735(a)(2). These rules ensure that the character of so-called "hot assets" (especially receivables and inventory) is generally preserved after their distribution. The term *inventory item* is defined in § 751(d) to include seemingly any property that would be taxed as ordinary income if sold by the partnership.

c. Section 732(d) Election
Read § 732(d).

Recall that a § 754 election triggers § 743, and that under § 743 a person who purchases a partnership interest takes "look through" basis in his or her share of the partnership's assets. Section 732(d) lets the taxpayer elect to make a "mini" § 754 election as to himself alone with respect to property that the partnership distributes. The effect of the election is to hypothesize that a § 754/743 election was in force when the taxpayer acquired the partnership interest. The § 732(d) election is available only if the distribution took place within two years of the time a partner acquired his interest and there was in fact no § 754 election in force when the taxpayer acquired the interest. The IRS reserves the right to impose the "election" on people who receive distributions of appreciated assets. §732(d).

There is great practical significance in making the election; taxes can be deferred via stepping up the bases of assets.

To illustrate: A year and a half ago, D paid $200 to buy out B's 33% interest in the ABC partnership. D's one-third of the ABC partnership's assets at the time of their purchase consisted of inventory worth $50, with a basis of $20, and a tract of investment land worth $150, with a basis of only $100. There was no § 754 election in force when D bought in, but if there

131

had been, D's allocable share of inside basis would have risen from $120 to $200 as to D. Assuming the partnership will distribute those assets pro rata in the very near future and that D makes the § 732(d) election, he will have a $50 basis in inventory and a $150 basis in the land, whatever their value when he gets them. Assuming his share of the tract is worth $155 when he receives it from the partnership, he can sell it immediately for a gain of $5 as opposed to $55.

PROBLEM 7-4

(1) Alice is an equal member of the ABC partnership, which consists of three individuals. Alice has an outside basis of $100. At year-end, she receives cash of $50, a tract of raw land with an inside basis of $40, inventory with a basis of $20, and unrealized receivables with a basis of $10. (Later you will see that § 751 may complicate your answer, but it is ignored here.) The partnership has held all the properties for six months.

    a)   What is the income tax impact to Alice of the distributions?

    b)   What is Alice's basis in the properties she receives in the distribution?

    c)   What is the holding period of the properties in Alice's hands?

    d)   How long will Alice have to hold the properties in order to recognize a capital gain or capital loss on their later sale?

(2)   Now vary the facts considerably. ABC has cash of $30 and land with an adjusted basis of $150 and a value of $210. C sells her partnership interest to D for $80 when a § 754 election is not in effect. At the time of the sale, C's outside basis is $60.

    (a)   Does the purchase by D have any effect on the "inside basis" of the partnership's assets?

    (b)   If the partnership then distributes one-third of the land to D in a non-liquidating distribution, will D recognize gain or loss on the distribution?

    (c)   Absent a basis adjustment under § 732(d), what basis will D take in the distributed property?

    (d)   What will be D's outside basis after the distribution?

    (e)   If D elects the optional basis adjustment under § 732(d), what is D's basis in the land and what is her outside basis?

    (f)   How much time can elapse before the distribution and still have the § 732 election occur?

d. Distributions of Encumbered Property

The distribution rules and the debt rules are not properly coordinated in the Code. The IRS has helped out with an important ruling in which the Service provided the necessary supplemental rules.

Rev. Rul. 79-205
1979-2 C.B. 255 amplified by Rev. Rul. 87-120

* * *

Issues

When a partnership makes a nonliquidating distribution of property, (1) is a partner permitted to offset the increase in the partner's liabilities against the decrease in the partner's liabilities in determining the extent of recognition of gain or loss, and (2) is partnership basis adjusted before or after the property distribution?

Facts

A and B are general partners in M, a general partnership, which was formed for the purposes of owning and operating shopping centers.

On December 31, 1977, M made nonliquidating distributions in a single transaction of a portion of its property to A and B. A and B are equal partners in M. M, A and B are calendar year taxpayers. No assets of the type described in § 751(a) of the Internal Revenue Code of 1954 were distributed by M to either A or B.

Immediately prior to the distribution A had an adjusted basis for A's interest in M of 1,000x dollars, and B had an adjusted basis for B's interest in M of 1,500x dollars. The property distributed to A had an adjusted basis to M of 2,000x dollars, and was subject to liabilities of 1,600x dollars. The property distributed to B had an adjusted basis to M of 3,200x dollars and was subject to liabilities of 2,800x dollars. A's individual liabilities increased by 1,600x dollars by reason of the distribution to A. B's individual liabilities increased by 2,800x dollars by reason of the distribution to B. A's share and B's share of the liabilities of M each decreased by 2,200x dollars (1/2 of 1,600x + 1/2 of 2,800x dollars) by reason of the distributions. The basis and fair market value of the properties distributed were greater than the liabilities to which they were subject.

Law

Section 705(a) of the Code provides, in part, that the adjusted basis of a partner's interest in a partnership shall be the basis of such interest determined under § 722 decreased (but not below zero) by partnership distributions as provided in § 733.

Section 722 of the Code provides, in part, that the basis of a partnership interest acquired by a contribution of money shall be the amount of such money.

Section 731(a)(1) of the Code provides that in the case of a distribution by a partnership to a partner gain shall not be recognized to such partner, except to the extent that any money distributed exceeds the adjusted basis of such partner's interest in the partnership immediately before the distribution.

Section 732(a)(1) of the Code provides that the basis of property (other than money) distributed by a partnership to a partner other than in liquidation of the partner's interest shall,

133

except as provided in § 732(a)(2), be its adjusted basis to the partnership immediately before such distribution.

Section 732(a)(2) of the Code provides that the basis to the distributee partner of property to which § 732(a)(1) is applicable shall not exceed the adjusted basis of such partner's interest in the partnership reduced by any money distributed in the same transaction.

Section 733 of the Code provides that in the case of a distribution by a partnership to a partner other than in liquidation of a partner's interest, the adjusted basis to such partner of the interest in the partnership shall be reduced (but not below zero) by the amount of any money distributed to such partner and the amount of the basis to such partner of distributed property other than money, as determined under § 732.

Section 752(a) of the Code provides that any increase in a partner's share of the liabilities of a partnership, or any increase in a partner's individual liabilities by reason of the assumption by such partner of partnership liabilities, shall be considered as a contribution of money by such partner to the partnership.

Section 752(b) of the Code provides that any decrease in a partner's share of the liabilities of a partnership, or any decrease in a partner's individual liabilities by reason of the assumption by the partnership of such individual liabilities, shall be considered as a distribution of money to the partner by the partnership.

Section 752(c) of the Code provides that for purposes of § 752 a liability to which property is subject shall, to the extent of the fair market value of such property, be considered as a liability of the owner of the property.

Analysis & Holding

In general, partnership distributions are taxable under § 731(a)(1) of the Code only to the extent that the amount of money distributed exceeds the distributee partner's basis for the partner's partnership interest. This rule reflects the Congressional intent to limit narrowly the area in which gain or loss is recognized upon a distribution so as to remove deterrents to property being moved in and out of partnerships as business reasons dictate. *See* S. Rep. No. 1622, 83rd Cong., 2nd Sess., page 96 (1954). Here, since partner liabilities are both increasing and decreasing in the same transaction offsetting the increases and decreases tends to limit recognition of gain, thereby giving effect to the Congressional intent. Consequently, in a distribution of encumbered property, the resulting liability adjustments will be treated as occurring simultaneously, rather than occurring in a particular order. Therefore, on a distribution of encumbered property, the amount of money considered distributed to a partner for purposes of § 731(a)(1) is the amount (if any) by which the decrease in the partner's share of the liabilities of the partnership under § 752(b) exceeds the increase in the partner's individual liabilities under § 752(a). The amount of money considered contributed by a partner for purposes of § 722 is the amount (if any) by which the increase in the partner's individual liabilities under § 752(a) exceeds the decrease in the partner's share of the liabilities of the partnership under § 752(b). The increase in the partner's individual liabilities occurs by reason of the assumption by the partner of partnership liabilities, or by reason of a distribution of property subject to a liability, to the extent of the fair market value of such property.

Because the distribution was part of a single transaction, the two properties are treated as having been distributed simultaneously to A and B. Therefore, all resulting liability adjustments relating to the distribution of the two properties will be treated as occurring simultaneously, rather than occurring in a particular order.

Treatment of Partner A

134

A will be deemed to have received a net distribution of 600x dollars in money, that is, the amount by which the amount of money considered distributed to A (2,200x dollars) exceeds the amount of money considered contributed by A (1,600x dollars). Since 600x dollars does not exceed A's basis for A's interest in M immediately before the distribution (1,000x dollars), no gain is recognized to A.

Under § 732(a) of the Code, the basis to A of the property distributed to A is the lesser of (i) the adjusted basis of the property to the partnership (2,000x dollars), or (ii) the adjusted basis of A's partnership interest (I,000x dollars) reduced by the amount of money deemed distributed to A (600x dollars). Therefore, the basis of the property in A's hands is 400x dollars. Under § 733, the adjusted basis of As partnership interest (1,000x dollars) is reduced by the amount of money deemed distributed to A (600x dollars) and by the basis to A of the distributed property (400x dollars). The adjusted basis of A's partnership interest is therefore reduced to zero.

Treatment of Partner B

B will be deemed to have made a net contribution of 600x dollars, that is, the amount by which the amount of money considered contributed by B (2,800x dollars) exceeds the amount of money considered distributed to B (2,200x dollars). In applying §732(a) and 733 of the Code to B, the adjustment to B's basis in B's partnership interest attributable to the liability adjustments resulting from the distributions will be treated as occurring first, and the distribution of property to B as occurring second. By so doing, B's basis for the distributed property is increased and B's basis in B's partnership interest is decreased. This allocation gives greater effect to the general rule of § 732(a)(1), which provides for the partner to have the same basis in distributed property as the partnership had for that property.

Therefore, the first step is that B's basis for B's partnership interest (1,500x dollars) is increased under §§ 722 and 705(a) by the amount of the net contribution deemed made by B (600x dollars), and is equal to 2,100x dollars. Next, under § 732(a) of the Code, the basis to B of the property distributed to B is the lesser of (i) the adjusted basis of the property to the partnership (3,200x dollars), or (ii) the adjusted basis of B's partnership interest (2,100x dollars) reduced by the amount of money deemed distributed to B (zero). Therefore, the basis of the property in B's hands is 2,100x dollars. Under § 733, the adjusted basis of B's partnership interest (2,100x dollars) is reduced by the amount of money deemed distributed to B (zero) and by the basis to B of the distributed property (2,100x dollars). The adjusted basis of B's partnership interest is therefore zero.

Rev. Rul. 87-120 applies the same reasoning to liquidations and contributions of property with liabilities.

PROBLEM 7-5

(1) A and B agree to form the equal AB general partnership. A owns a boat worth $20, with a basis of $5 and subject to a recourse debt of $12, which he will contribute to the partnership, if the partnership will agree to assume the debt, which it does, thereby relieving him of half the debt. B agrees to contribute equal value, namely cash of $8. See Reg. §1.752-1(f).

a) What is A's gain or loss, if anything, as a result of the contribution of the boat, and A's sharing of the debt?

b) What is B's basis in his partnership interest?

c) What difference, if any, is there if the debt were nonrecourse?

d) What difference, if any, is there from "(a)" if the partnership is a limited partnership and A is the limited partner?

B. EFFECT ON PARTNERSHIP
Read § 731(b).

The partnership is not taxed when it distributes appreciated property, nor can it claim a loss deduction when it distributes property that has lost value. § 731(b). Nor is there depreciation recapture when it distributes property. §§ 1245(b)(3) and 1250(d)(6).

The view, in simple terms, is that "nothing happened." Income and loss are deferred via frozen basis of property in the partner's hands. Things are equally straightforward for the partnership. The partnership simply reduces its inside basis by its predistribution basis in the property, not because of some special Code provision, but because it no longer owns the property. Again, the only exception to the rule against taxation of the partnership involves disproportionate distributions of "hot assets," which is discussed later in this Chapter.

1. SECTION 734 ELECTION
Read §§ 754 and 734(a) and (b).

Distributions of partnership property implicate the partnership's right to make a section 734(b) election, enabling the partnership to modify its basis in its *retained* assets. The adjustment comes in two forms; one merely affects timing. The other prevents the apostasy of disappearing basis or multiplicative basis.

Because the following rules are sometimes difficult to keep sorted out, here is a summary of how they work, assuming there is a § 754 election in force:

- To the extent the basis of distributed property increased, or the partner recognized a loss, increase the inside basis of like property the partnership holds.

- To the extent the basis of distributed property declined, or the partner recognized a gain, decrease the basis of like property the partnership holds.

a. Ameliorating timing problems: Section 734(b)(1)(A) and (b)(2)(A)

Section 734(b)(1)(A). This provision allows the partnership to increase its basis in its retained assets by the § 731 gain a distributee partner recognized as a result of a partnership distribution. The adjustment reflects the fact that the distributee has indirectly recognized some of the gain inherent in partnership assets caused by the appreciation of partnership assets.

To illustrate: A is an equal member of the ABC partnership. Like her partners, she has a $30 outside basis, but the partnership's major asset, a tract of raw land held for investment, has appreciated in value from $30 to $120. It is a capital asset. The partnership also has $60 in cash and no liabilities, so the total value of its assets is $180. The partners agree that A will receive her share of the partnership's assets and will stay on as a partner, but her interest will be so small that henceforth it is disregarded. The partnership appropriately distributes $60 cash (a third of the partnership's value), leaving the same raw land, with the same inherent $90 gain as ever, in the partnership's hands. Partner A has a $30 taxable gain under § 731(a)(1) because she got cash that was $30 more than her outside basis. That taxable gain reflected the untaxed appreciation in the value of the land.

Here is the problem. If the partnership sells the land for $120, it will have a $90 gain ($120 less $30 basis). B and C will each be taxed on $45, increasing their outside bases to $75 each. If the partnership folds up at this point, the partners will in fact only get $60 each (*i.e.*, half of the $120 sales proceeds). Section 731(a)(2) allows them to report a $30 loss ($150 aggregate outside basis less $120 sales proceeds).

A recognized a $30 gain based on a distribution of $60 that was partly based on her share of the appreciation in value of the land, but if the partnership later sells that land, we know there is still a $90 gain. This is seemingly multiple taxation. In fact, when the partnership liquidates, there will admittedly be an offsetting $30 capital loss under § 731(a)(2) that B and C will share, so the over-taxation will eventually come out in the wash. There are two policy choices. The first is to forget the issue because it is just a timing problem; the other is to complicate the Code by accelerating the correction. Congress opted for the latter.

The Congressional solution – found in § 734(b)(1)(A) – is to increase the basis in remaining partnership assets by gains recognized by the distributee (A in the example). Going back to the example, the partnership would increase its basis in the land by $30. This will reduce the later gain when the tract is sold to $30 each to B and C, and will prevent a § 731(a)(2) loss to the partners on liquidation of the partnership. This opportunity is available only if the partnership makes the section 754 election. If it does, then § 755 supplies the mechanical rules for making the adjustments to the bases of the properties that the partnership retained.

Section 734(b)(2)(A). This provision is the converse of §734(b)(1)(A). It reduces inside basis when a distributee partner recognizes a loss on the distribution. This can only occur in a liquidating distribution. That is not true of a gain. That can occur in liquidation or as a result of a current distribution. The taxation of liquidating distributions is reserved for a later chapter.

b. Basis: Section 734(b)(1)(B) and (b)(2)(B)

This set of rules has a more serious purpose. It prevents the permanent disappearance of basis or proliferation of basis. Section 734(b)(1)(B) takes effect when a partnership distributes property to a partner and § 732(a)(2) limits the partner's basis in the distributed property to the partner's predistribution outside basis. The election causes an increase in the partnership's inside basis in its remaining assets by the reduction in the basis of the distributed assets.

To illustrate: A is an equal member of the AB partnership. Like B, she has a $75 outside basis. The partnership has cash and two capital assets:

Asset	Inside Basis	Fair Market Value
Cash	$30.00	$30.00
Capital Asset X	$90.00	$30.00
Capital Asset Y	$30.00	$90.00
Total	$150.00	$150.00

If the partnership distributes $30 in cash to B and capital asset X to A, § 732(a)(2) crimps A's basis in capital asset X down to $75. If she later sells asset X for its $30 fair market, value of $30, she will correctly report a $45 loss (*i.e.*, $75 basis – $30 amount realized). The remaining $15 loss ($90- $75) disappears forever, and the full potential gain on a later sale of capital asset Y remains intact. This evaporation of basis will not do.

The solution is to increase the basis of the partnership's remaining assets by the $15 of disappearing basis. In this case, it means increasing the basis of capital asset Y from $30 to $45. This adjustment is available only if the partnership makes the section 754 election. Again, § 755 supplies the mechanical rules for attributing the otherwise lost basis to the remaining assets. The key principle is to attach the increase to the same type of assets as generated the problem, treating capital assets and § 1231 assets as a single class and all other assets as another class.

Things are not quite as nifty as they seem. Now that the adjustment has been made, namely increasing the basis of capital asset Y to $45, should there be a special allocation in favor of the remaining partner? The answer should be "yes." A has already gotten the benefit of one-third of the appreciation inherent in the assets via a step-up in basis; the balance of the loss should go B, as a matter of common sense.

Section 734(b)(2)(B) is the converse. It reduces the inside basis of property when the distribution increases the basis of distributed property. This only occurs in a complete liquidation and is reserved for a later chapter.

Section 734(d), a lopsided reform provision, requires that the partnership reduce its inside basis, even though there is no § 754 election in force, if the distribution causes a substantial reduction in inside basis. When § 734(d) applies, the same adjustments to the partnership's assets are made as if there were a § 754 election in force. A basis reduction is substantial for these purposes if the sum of the following exceeds $250,000:

1. The amount of the partner's loss on the distribution, plus

2. The increase in the basis of the distributed properties

This is the same basis reduction that § 734 would have imposed were a § 754 election in effect. There is a complex exception for securitization partnerships that is beyond the scope of this book. § 734(e).

PROBLEM 7-6

(1) X's adjusted basis in her partnership interest was $150 before she recently received the following properties in an operating distribution:

Assets		Inside Basis	Fair Market Value
Cash		$100.00	$100.00
Inventory		$25.00	$27.00
Tract A		$20.00	$18.00
Tract B		$21.00	$26.00
	Total	$166.00	$171.00

For purposes of this problem, ignore § 751(b). Also, assume that X remains a partner after the distribution.

a) Will the partnership recognize any gain or loss on the distribution of these properties?

b) Knowing that the tax impact of the distribution demands that one first consider the impact of cash, what is X's basis in her partnership interest after the distribution of the cash?

c) Knowing that the tax impact of the distribution demands that one next consider the impact of inventory and unrealized receivables, what is X's basis in her partnership interest after the distribution of the inventory?

138

d) What is X's basis in the inventory?

e) How long will the inventory retain its character as inventory in X's hands, assuming it would not otherwise be inventory to her?

f) Assume instead the partnership simply distributed $171 in cash to X, i.e., the value of her interest. How much gain, if any, would X report?

g) What would be the effect of § 734 in "(f)"? Do not determine how the adjustment applies to, but state the amount of the adjustment and to whom it applies.

h) Now assume instead she received cash, the inventory and the two tracts of land. What is her basis in Tract A? Consider § 732(c)(3)(A).

(2) Continuing with the facts of Problem 7-6(1)(h), what is X's basis in Tract B?

a) Now, continuing the facts in 7-6(1)(h) assume the partnership made a § 754 election, thereby implicating § 734. What impact does that provision have on X's basis in the tracts she receives?

b) How much will the basis of the remaining partnership assets change as a result of § 734?

c) Same as "(b)." What kind of assets will have their bases adjusted?

C. DISPROPORTIONATE DISTRIBUTIONS INVOLVING "HOT ASSETS"

If there were an election for worst section of the Code, no list of candidates would be complete without § 751(b). Its purpose is to prevent wicked partners from using partnership distributions to reshuffle proportionate interests in "hot assets." Section 751(b) applies both to current distributions and to those which terminate the partner's interest in the partnership.

Section 751 and Reg. § 1.751-1(b) and (c) employ a reconstructive model, which works as follows. Once it is clear that §751(b) applies to a distribution, one uses a three-step process to recharacterize the distribution.

First, one constructs a hypothetical distribution of the property that was not actually distributed, but proportionately should have been. This hypothetical distribution is subject to the usual §§ 731, 732 and 733 distribution rules.

Second, this hypothetically distributed property is treated as if sold back to the partnership for the excess property that was actually distributed, but proportionately should not have been.

Third, the rest of the property actually distributed is taxed under the usual distribution rules of §§ 731-733. Reg. §§1.751-1(b)(2)-(3).

1. To the extent a partner gets a disproportionately small interest in "hot assets," the partner is deemed to have received a distribution of a proportionate interest in each class of partnership assets, and to have exchanged some of his "hot assets" with the partnership in order to obtain extra regular assets from the partnership. (This rationalizes how he came to hold so few hot assets.) If the partnership has a gain or loss on the imaginary disposition of the additional regular assets, it is allocated only to the other partners. This reconstruction is supposed to prevent partnerships from cleverly shifting capital assets to higher bracket taxpayers.

2.   *To the extent a partner gets a disproportionately large interest in "hot assets,"* the model again starts by assuming that the distributee partner got his pro-rata share of all the assets not distributed, but that he then exchanged a share of his regular assets for the extra share of "hot assets" with the partnership. This means the partner is likely to have a capital gain on the imaginary disposition of the regular assets and that the partnership will commonly have ordinary gain on its disposition to him of the "hot assets"; the ordinary gain is allocated only to the other partners. The basis rules track the reconstruction. For example, the distributee partner's basis in the "hot assets" will be partly founded on the carryover rules and partly on cost. This reconstruction is supposed to discourage partnerships from shifting ordinary income to partners in low tax brackets.

Substantially appreciated inventory items. "Inventory items" are also subject to the disproportionate distribution rules, but (mercifully) only if they are substantially appreciated. Notice the difference from § 751(a) involving sales of partnership assets, which reaches all "inventory items," whereas § 751(b) only reaches substantially appreciated inventory items.

- "Substantially appreciated" means the inventory item's value (which transitorily includes receivables) exceeds its basis by at least 20%. Notice that in determining whether a partnership's inventory is substantially appreciated, one must look at the inventory items as a whole. If aggregate inventory meets the definition of substantial appreciation, then every item of inventory is treated as substantially appreciated. One disregards inventory purchased in order to fail the greater-than-20% test.

- Section 751(b) has a major weakness. It is triggered by the relative disproportion in the value of § 751(b) assets, not the amount of ordinary income inherent in those assets. This still makes it possible to distribute such assets equally by value, but to shift the lion's share of the ordinary income to lower-bracket taxpayers.

PROBLEM 7-7

(1) The equal XYZ partnership has three assets and three partners, as follows. The partners each have an outside basis of $110, and the value of each of their partnership interests is $160. The following shows how the assets appear on the partnership's books.

Assets	Basis	Value
Cash	$210.00	$210.00
Inventory	$90.00	$180.00
Capital asset	$30.00	$90.00
Total	$330.00	$480.00

At a time when no § 754 election is in force, X receives $160 of cash from the partnership, but remains a partner.

a) Is this a disproportionate distribution of the kind to which § 751(b) applies?

b) What would a proportionate distribution look like?

c) How much gain or loss, if any, does X report?

140

d) How much gain or loss, if any, does the partnership report?

e) How, in general, will the partnership's basis in the inventory and capital asset be affected?

f) Would § 751(b) apply if the distribution were in connection with X's retirement from the partnership?

Chapter 8

LIQUIDATION OF A PARTNERSHIP INTEREST

A. INTRODUCTION

Read §§ 731(a) and (b), 761(d), 736, and Reg. § 1.761-1(d).

In life or after death, there are only three ways for a partner (or the partner's estate) to get out of an ongoing partnership. One is by a transfer to a third party. The second is by a sale to one or more of the other partners. The final way is for the partnership to buy out his entire interest, known as liquidating the partner's interest. The buyout may be immediate or in a series of redemptions. As far as the partner is concerned, sales to remaining partners have the same economic results as liquidations. Either way, the retiring or deceased partner gets paid for his interest, and the remaining partners use their money, directly out of their pockets or out of their share of partnership assets, to buy out the exiting partner. However, the tax results can differ sharply. As a result, tax considerations dominate this field.

Congress has deliberately made the tax results elective. From a policy perspective that is a good idea, because it means the elections are transparent, rather than accessible only to wealthy people who alone can afford to pay for the tax skills to find implicit elections. It is also efficient from a purely economic standpoint. Another good thing is that the retirement of a majority partner does not result in a termination of the partnership under § 708. Reg. § 1.736-1(a)(6). Partnership terminations are discussed in a later chapter.

For the time being, the important point is that we are now beginning the study of liquidations as opposed to sales of partnership interests. Do not underrate this section. Liquidations of partnership interests occur all the time, are complicated, and call for skillful representation. They also tend to be emotionally charged events.

Note the quirky rule that a distribution that retires one partnership interest (e.g., as a limited partner) but leaves the partner holding another interest (*e.g.*, as a general partner) is not a liquidating distribution. Chase v. Commissioner, 92 TC 874, 884 (1989).

B. SALE VERSUS LIQUIDATION

PROBLEM 8-1

F is an equal member of the ABF partnership. F's outside basis is $300.

1) F receives a liquidating distribution that consists solely of a share of stock with an inside basis of $50 and a value of $100. Does F have taxable income or gain as a result of the distribution?

2) Same as "(1)". What is F's basis in the stock?

3) Same as "(1)", but now assume that there is a § 754 election in force. What is the impact of § 734(b)?

4) Same as "(1)", but the transaction is instead a current distribution. What is F's basis in the stock?

5) Same as "(1)", but the transaction is a liquidating distribution of inventory with an "inside basis" of $150? What is F's basis in the inventory? Can she claim a loss and if so, how much?

6) Same as "(5)", but F also receives some investment real estate with an inside basis and value of $50. Can F now claim a loss? What is F's basis in the real estate?

7) Same as "(1)", but F receives only inventory with a basis and value of $400.

    a)   Does F have taxable income or gain?

    b)   What is F's basis in the inventory?

8) Would § 732(b) alone apply to "(7)" or must one also consult § 732(c) to determine the basis of the distributed inventory in "(7)"?

9) Same as "(5)". What is the impact of § 734(b)?

10) Same as ("1"), but F got marketable shares with a value of $400 and a basis of $300. Does F report a taxable gain, and if so, how much?

11) Does § 751(b) apply to liquidating distributions?

FOXMAN v. COMMISSIONER
352 F.2d 466 (3d Cir. 1965), *aff'g* 41 T.C. 535 (1964), *acq.* 1966-2 C.B. 4, 5

SMITH, CIRCUIT JUDGE.

This matter is before the Court on petitions to review decisions of the Tax Court, 41 T.C. 535, in three related cases consolidated for the purpose of hearing. The petitions of Foxman and Grenell challenge the decision as erroneous only as it relates to them. The petition of the Commissioner seeks a review of the decision as it relates to Jacobowitz only if it is determined by us that the Tax Court erred in the other two cases. . . .

As the result of agreements reached in February of 1955, and January of 1956, Foxman, Grenell, and Jacobowitz became equal partners in a commercial enterprise which was then trading under the name of Abbey Record Manufacturing Company. hereinafter identified as the Company. They also became equal shareholders in a corporation known as Sound Plastics, Inc. When differences of opinion arose in the spring of 1956, efforts were made to persuade Jacobowitz to withdraw from the partnership. These efforts failed at that time but were resumed in March of 1957. Thereafter the parties entered into negotiations which, on May 21, 1957 culminated in a contract for the acquisition of Jacobowitz's interest in the partnership of Foxman and Grenell. The terms and conditions, except one not here material, were substantially in accord with an option to purchase offered earlier to Foxman and Grenell. The relevant portions of the final contract are set forth in the Tax Court's opinion.

The contract, prepared by an attorney representing Foxman and Grenell, referred to them as the "Second Party," and to Jacobowitz as the "First Party." We regard as particularly pertinent to the issue before us the following clauses:

"WHEREAS, the parties hereto are equal owners and the sole partners of ABBEY RECORD MFG. Co., a partnership, . . . , and are also the sole stockholders. officers and directors of SOUND PLASTICS, INC., a corporation organized under the laws of the State of New York; and

"WHEREAS, the first party is desirous of selling, conveying, transferring and assigning all of his right, title and interest in and to his one-third share and interest in the said ABBEY to the second parties; and

"WHEREAS, the second parties are desirous of conveying, transferring and assigning all of their right, title and interest in and to their combined two-thirds shares and interest in SOUND PLASTICS, INC., to the first party;

"NOW, THEREFORE, IT IS MUTUALLY AGREED AS FOLLOWS:

"First: The second parties hereby purchase all the right, title, share and interest of the first party in ABBEY and the first party does hereby sell, transfer, convey and assign all of his right, title, interest and share in ABBEY and in the moneys in banks, trade names, accounts due, or to become due, and in all other assets of any kind whatsoever, belonging to said ABBEY, for and in consideration of the following. . . "

The stated consideration was cash in the sum of $242,500; the assignment by Foxman and Grenell of their stock in Sound Plastics; and the transfer of an automobile, title to which was held by the Company. The agreement provided for the payment of $67,500 upon consummation of the contract and payment of the balance as follows: $67,500 on January 2, 1958, and $90,000 in equal monthly installments, payable on the first of each month after January 30, 1958. This balance was evidenced by a series of promissory notes, payment of which was secured by a chattel mortgage on the assets of the Company. This mortgage, like the contract, referred to a sale by Jacobowitz of his partnership interest to Foxman and Grenell. The notes were executed in the name of the Company as the purported maker and were signed by Foxman and Grenell, who also endorsed them under a guarantee of payment.

The down payment of $67,500 was by a cashier's check which was issued in exchange for a check drawn on the account of the Company. The first note, in the amount of $67,500, which became due on January 2, 1958, was timely paid by a check drawn on the Company's account. Pursuant to the terms of an option reserved to Foxman and Grenell, they elected to prepay the balance of $90,000 on January 28, 1958, thereby relieving themselves of an obligation to pay Jacobowitz a further $17,550, designated in the contract as a consultant's fee. They delivered to Jacobowitz a cashier's check which was charged against the account of the Company.

In its partnership return for the fiscal year ending February 28, 1958, the Company treated the sum of $159,656.09, the consideration received by Jacobowitz less the value of his interest in partnership property, as a guaranteed payment made in liquidation of a retiring partner's interest under § 736(a)(2). . . . This treatment resulted in a substantial reduction of the distributive shares of Foxman and Grenell and consequently a proportionate decrease in their possible tax liability. In his income tax return, Jacobowitz treated the sum of $164,356.09, the consideration less the value of his partnership interest, as a long term capital gain realized upon the sale of his interest. This, of course, resulted in a tax advantage favorable to him. The Commissioner determined deficiencies against each of the taxpayers in amounts not relevant to the issue before us and each filed separate petitions for redetermination.

The critical issue before the Tax Court was raised by the antithetical positions maintained by Foxman and Grenell on one side and Jacobowitz on the other. The former, relying on § 736(a)(2), *supra,* contended that the transaction, evidenced by the contract, constituted a liquidation of a retiring partner's interest and that the consideration paid was accorded correct treatment in the partnership return. The latter contended that the transaction constituted a sale of his partnership interest and, under § 741 of the Code, 26 U.S.C.A., the profit realized was correctly treated in his return as a capital gain. The Tax Court rejected the position of Foxman and Grenell and held that the deficiency determinations as to them were not erroneous; it sustained the position of Jacobowitz and held that the deficiency determination as to him was erroneous. The petitioners Foxman and Grenell challenge that decision as erroneous and not in accord with the law.

It appears from the evidence, which the Tax Court apparently found credible, that the negotiations which led to the consummation of the contract of May 21, 1957, related to a contemplated sale of Jacobowitz's partnership interest to Foxman and Grenell. The option offered to Foxman and Grenell early in May of 1957, referred to a sale and the execution of "a bill of sale" upon completion of the agreement. The relevant provisions of the contract were couched in terms of "purchase" and "sale." The contract was signed by Foxman and Grenell, individually, and by them on behalf of the Company, although the Company assumed no liability there under. The obligation to purchase Jacobowitz's interest was solely that of Foxman and Grenell. The chattel mortgage on the partnership assets was given to secure payment.

Notwithstanding these facts and the lack of any ambiguity in the contract, Foxman and Grenell argue that the factors unequivocally determinative of the substance of the transaction were: the initial payment of $67,500 by a cashier's check issued in exchange for a check drawn on the account of the Company; the second payment in a similar amount by check drawn on the Company's account; the execution of notes in the name of the Company as maker; and the prepayment of the notes by cashier's check charged against the Company's account.

This argument unduly emphasizes form in preference to substance. While form may be relevant "[the] incidence of taxation depends upon the substance of a transaction." *Commissioner of Internal Revenue v. Court Holding Co.,* 324 U.S. 331, 334, 65 S. Ct. 707, 708, 89 L. Ed. 981 (1945); *United States v. Cumberland Pub. Serv. Co.,* 338 U.S. 451, 455, 70 S. Ct. 280, 94 L. Ed. 251 (1950). The "transaction must be viewed as a whole, and each step, from the commencement of negotiations" to consummation, is relevant. *Ibid.* Where, as here, there has been a transfer and an acquisition of property pursuant to a contract, the nature of 'the transaction does not depend solely on the means employed to effect payment. *Ibid.*

It is apparent from the opinion of the Tax Court that careful consideration was given to the factors relied upon by Foxman and Grenell. It is therein stated, 41 T.C. at page 553:

"These notes were endorsed by Foxman and Grenell individually, and the liability of [the Company] thereon was merely in the nature of security for their primary obligation under the agreement of May 21, 1957. The fact that they utilized partnership resources to discharge their own individual liability in such manner can hardly convert into a section 736 'liquidation' what would otherwise qualify as a section 741 'sale.'"

". . .the payments received by Jacobowitz were in discharge of their [Foxman's and Grenell's] obligation under the agreement, and not that of [the Company.] It was they who procured those payments in their own behalf from the assets of the partnership which they controlled. The use of [the Company] to make payment was wholly within their discretion and of no concern to Jacobowitz; his only interest was payment."

We are of the opinion that the quoted statements represent a fair appraisal of the true significance of the notes and the means employed to effect payment.

When the members of the partnership decided that Jacobowitz would withdraw in the interest of harmony they had a choice of means by which his withdrawal could be effected. They could have agreed *inter se* on either liquidation or sale. On a consideration of the plain language of the contract, the negotiations which preceded its consummation, the intent of the parties as reflected by their conduct, and the circumstances surrounding the transaction, the Tax Court found that the transaction was in substance a sale and not a liquidation of a retiring partner's interest. This finding is amply supported by the evidence in the record. The partners having employed the sale method to achieve their objective, Foxman and Grenell cannot avoid the tax consequences by a hindsight application of principles they now find advantageous to them and disadvantageous to Jacobowitz.

The issue before the Tax Court was essentially one of fact and its decision thereon may not be reversed in the absence of a showing that its findings were not supported by substantial evidence or that its decision was not in accord with the law. . . There has been no such showing in this case.

The decisions of the Tax Court will be affirmed.

NOTES

1. **Economic equivalence and tax disparity.** Imagine that A wants to withdraw from a real estate partnership in exchange for cash and then put the money to some other use. In a world without taxes A would not care if the money came from a stranger, or from her partners as buyers of her interest, or from the partnership itself. However, as *Foxman* shows, it can make a big difference in a world with taxes. Despite the identity of *economic* results, the *tax* implications of a liquidation are more subtle and complex than a sale.

2. *Step transaction and substance over form principles remain important.* Basic tax principles are not entirely banished. For example, if the "liquidating" partner, A, sells the distributed assets to D, who in turn contributes them to the partnership, thereby becoming a partner in the BCD partnership, the step transaction analysis will prevail and the transaction will rightly be classified as a sale of the distributee partner's interest for tax purposes. *Crenshaw v. United States,* 450 F.2d 472 (5th Cir. 1971). Likewise, a sale of a partnership interest for a share of future partnership profits may result in the selling partner being taxed on partnership income under assignment of income theories. *Collins v. Commissioner,* 14 T.C. 301, 306 (1950), *acq.*

1. MODIFIED DISTRIBUTION RULES FOR PARTNERSHIP LIQUIDATIONS
Read §§ 732(b), (c) and 731(a)(2).

The taxation of liquidating distributions differs sharply from the treatment of current distributions. Because the ex-partner will, by definition, have a $0 basis in her interest after a liquidating distribution, § 732(b) requires the partner to allocate her entire *outside* basis to the money and property distributed to her in connection with the distribution. Money – US money, that is – always takes a basis equal to its face amount.

Liquidating distributions of receivables and inventory are singled out for a special restriction that you saw before with current distributions where the partner's basis was less than the inside basis of the distributed property. In the case of liquidating distributions, Congress was concerned that a partner might achieve a step-up in the basis of such property from the partnership's inside basis to the partner's outside basis. For example, if a partner had an outside basis of $3,000 and the partner received $1,000 in cash plus inventory with a value and inside basis of $100, the $1,000 of cash would first reduce the partner's basis to $2,000 and the remaining $2,000 might be carried over to the inventory, which sets the stage for a $1,900 ordinary loss on selling the inventory. To block the step-up, § 732(c)(1) declares that in the context of a liquidation, the basis of distributed properties is allocated first to any unrealized receivables and inventory in an amount equal to the basis of each such property to the partnership, with the result that the inventory takes a $100 basis, and the rest of the taxpayer's outside basis will be allocated to whatever further property he got. For example, if in addition, the partner received any other property, even a pencil, that asset would take a $1,900 basis, and the partner would wind up with what may be the pencil with the highest basis in the history of the world. Reg. § 1.732-1(a)(4) example (1).

2. LOSSES ON DISTRIBUTION

Section 731(a)(2) prevents the partner from recognizing loss on the liquidation of his interest, unless the distribution consists solely of money, unrealized receivables or inventory items (or some combination thereof), in which event a loss is recognized to the extent that his outside basis exceeds the money plus his basis in the receivables and inventory items. This is an important issue from both planning and conceptual perspectives. The loss is a capital loss unless the partner is a dealer in partnership interests.

The reasoning behind § 731(a)(2) is fairly straightforward. Congress generally defers gains and losses when a partner receives a distribution of property, even though he may have withdrawn as a partner, because the partner continues his investment via his ownership of the property he received. To carry out the thought, § 731(a) generally refuses to allow a loss, and § 732(b) gives the partner a basis in the property equal to his former outside basis. This is a plain example of a nonrecognition transaction. The nonrecognition approach collapses, however, if the partner got money alone, because there is no conceivable way to assign money a basis other than its face amount, so there is no escape from recognizing gains and losses when money alone is distributed, and there is no reason to wait any longer; the partner has truly "cashed out." Section 731(a)(1) and (2) reflect that reality.

The nonrecognition approach is unavailable for inventory and receivables because of congressional anxiety that the distributee might receive such assets with a basis higher than their inside basis, thereby causing an ordinary loss. Section 732(c)(l) stops that by limiting the basis in distributed inventory and unrealized receivables to their inside bases. The trouble is that the partner's outside basis may be higher than the property's inside basis. In such a case, the distributee can recognize a loss, assuming there are no non-§ 751 assets to be allocated basis under § 732(c)(2). § 731(a)(2). Note again that the loss will be a capital loss. §§ 731(a) and 741. If the loss was triggered by depreciated inventory, it may be better to have the partnership sell it, allocate the resulting ordinary loss among the partners, and distribute the cash proceeds.

Finally, observe again that if the partnership distributes only cash (and perhaps unrealized receivables as well) and throws in any other asset (aside from receivables and inventory items), there is no loss. Instead, there is a lonely asset with what may have a preposterously high basis.

To summarize the loss rules, partners can recognize losses only on liquidating distributions, but only if the distribution consists solely of cash and selected ordinary income property and the inside basis of the distributed property plus the distributed cash is less than the partner's outside basis.

PROBLEM 8-2

F has been squeezed out of the former ABF general partnership of which he used to be an equal one-third member. Assuming he had an outside basis of $100, and he received the following liquidating distributions, how would he be taxed on each?

1) Cash of $160?

2) Cash of $80?

3) Investment assets with a basis of $10 and a fair market value of $160?

4) Cash of $80 and property with an inside basis and value of $1.00?

5) Cash of $10 plus relief from partnership liabilities of $150?

6) Inventory with a basis of $100 and a value of $160?

7) Inventory with an inside basis of $80 and a value of $160? Read § 732(c)(1) carefully and compare it to § 732(b).

C. TAXING THE PARTNER: SECTION 736

Imagine you have been a partner in a prosperous law firm for a few years and for whatever reason you decide it is time to move on. The firm has done well over the years, and your partners realize you are entitled to be paid well for the departure and have clauses in the partnership agreement that provide for payments in the event of a partner's withdrawal, retirement or expulsion.

What might you be paid for? First, the firm probably has cash on hand, receivables, furniture and equipment that your efforts helped buy, and a reputation for good work. Imagine you felt you should be paid $100 in cash as follows for your share of the following items. The dollar amounts are for your share, not the firm's total value:

Value of the receivables	$10.00
Value of furniture and fixtures	$40.00
Goodwill value of the firm	$45.00
"Premium value" over goodwill	$5.00

As you will come to see, § 736 will characterize the cash you receive for each of these items.

The final thing you might want from your partners is a flow of income from future operations. You could structure that flow either as a fixed amount – say $20 per year for five years – that does not vary with the partnership's income or as a percentage of the firm's future profits – say 10% – over some given number of years. The former would be a guaranteed payment if you were still a partner; the latter would be a distributive share.

What you have just read describes the kinds of cash payments that § 736, below, sorts into either of two categories – a cash distribution or a stream of income.

1. ROLE OF § 736

Section 736 has a monopoly on characterizing cash payments to withdrawing and deceased partners. Exactly how it might apply to distributions of property is unclear, and from now on we will work with the usual assumption that the distributions are strictly in the form of cash or reductions of liability, which § 752 treats as if they were distributions of cash. Note that § 736 does not apply when the partnership itself liquidates.

Section 736 is a procedural section whose function is to sort payments that the partner receives from the partnership into either of two pigeonholes. Other Code sections of a general character then come into play to determine the federal income tax implications of the sorting process.

The two pigeonholes are the following:

1. Payments for the partner's interest in partnership "property." These are commonly referred to as "section 736(b)" payments, and they are taxed as liquidating distributions. § 736(b)(1). Solely in the case of a general partner in a service partnership this excludes (i) most unrealized receivables and (ii) goodwill *(unless the partnership agreement provides to the contrary)*. They go into the next pigeonhole.

2. All other payments. These are known as "section 736(a) payments" and are treated as income – either a guaranteed payment or a distributive share, depending on their characteristics. Notice that this is the residual category. For example, the $5 premium in the example of your imaginary retirement belongs here.

The second class is either a § 707(c) guaranteed payment if *not* geared to partnership income, or as a distributive share of partnership income if geared to partnership income. § 736(a)(1). These characterizations stick whether the payments are made in a lump sum or over time. These classes of payments can occur simultaneously with respect to the same partner.

2. PAYMENTS FOR PARTNER'S SHARE OF PROPERTY: § 736(b)

These payments are considered cash distributions in complete liquidation of the partner's interest, and can generate a capital gain or loss to the partner. *See* § 731. The gain or loss is measured by the difference between the partner's outside basis and the amount paid to the partner (or the partner's estate or successor in interest), and should generally be reported in the year paid. Reg. § 1.731-1(a)(2). As usual, one includes reductions in partnership liabilities as constructive distributions of money. § 752(d). Also, if there is a § 754 election in force, § 734(b) adjustments will occur.

To illustrate: The ABC partnership has three equal members, and has as its sole asset a parcel of raw land with a basis and value of $300. If equal partner A retired in exchange for a $100 cash payment from the partnership, it would be obvious that the payment would be for property and that under § 731(a) A would have a gain or loss on the distribution, depending on whether the $100 he received was more or less than his outside basis in his partnership interest.

Normally there will be a written agreement between the retiring partner and the partnership which states exactly how much the partner was paid for the particular properties of the partnership, in which case the agreement will generally be respected if it was the result of arm's-length bargaining. Reg. § 1.736-1(b)(1).

3. TREATMENT OF PAYMENTS FOR PARTNER'S SHARE OF UNREALIZED RECEIVABLES AND GOODWILL

Payments for *a general partner's* share of unstated goodwill and unrealized receivables are *not* for property if the payee is a general partner in a service partnership. § 736(b). This can be most painful for retiring doctors and lawyers, because their share of these items (especially receivables) can produce significant amounts of ordinary income. In all other cases, payments for stated goodwill, unstated goodwill, and even receivables are considered to be for property.

To illustrate: Assume that A is a one-third general partner of the equal ABC service partnership, which has no assets other than goodwill worth $300. Assume that ABC buys out A's interest in cash for 33% of the next three years' worth of partnership income and that there is no provision in the partnership agreement for making payments to retiring partners to account for their share of goodwill. Assuming that A has an outside basis of $0, the proceeds A receives have to be treated as a § 736(a)(1) distributive share, taxable to A. Its composition will depend on the character of the income earned by ABC and may, for example, include tax-exempt income and capital gains. The chance to buy the remaining partner out for a share of the partnership's income may appeal greatly to the remaining partners, because it reduces their future income taxes, compared to having the partner sell his interest to the remaining partners, which produces no tax reductions for the buyers. The taxation of § 736(a) payments is discussed below. By contrast, if the partnership agreement provided for fixed payments to be made for goodwill, the tax result would be a deemed payment for property. As a result, if A received $20 for five years he would be deemed to receive distributions staggered over five years. In this simple case, every dollar received would be taxed as a capital gain, because A has an outside basis of $0. §§ 736(b), 731(a), and 741.

Section 736 literally says the full amount of a payment for an unrealized receivable or unstated goodwill is a § 736(a) payment, but this cannot be right if either has a basis. For example, if a retiring partner is paid $100 for a receivable which has a basis of $60, the income component should be $40, not $100. The Regulations agree, in effect treating the $60 as a § 736(b) payment. Reg. §§ 1.736-1(b)(2) and (3) and 1.736-1(b)(3).

4. TREATMENT OF § 736(a) PAYMENTS

Again, § 736(a) payments are those for unrealized receivables and unstated goodwill of general partners in service businesses, and those otherwise not in exchange for the withdrawing partner's interest in partnership property. Reg. § 1.736-1(a)(3). Section 736(a) payments are treated as distributive shares of partnership income if they vary with partnership income, and § 707(c) guaranteed payments if they do not. Either way, the remaining partners avoid taxes because the money paid out will either reduce part of their distributive shares of income or produce a § 162(a) deduction for the partnership, which the remaining partners will enjoy.

Think about a prosperous "name" partner who retires from a big law firm. He probably has only a relatively small amount of his money tied up in the firm, but his partners are willing to pay him well to retain his name and to keep him friendly. The Code provides great bargaining flexibility. The major alternatives are:

1. Amend the partnership agreement to provide for a payment for stated goodwill to the "name" partner. Treat the cash paid for it as a payment of a distribution in exchange for goodwill and thereby let A report a capital gain.

2. Do not provide for payments for goodwill in the partnership agreement. Treat the payments as being for unstated goodwill. The retiring partner will report the payout as income but in exchange will bargain for more cash than under (1) because he will be taxed on the ordinary income at rates that are currently higher than capital gains tax rates.

The latter is a reasonable result, in the sense that the essence of the deal may be that the retiring partner is being paid a continuing "quasi-salary" taxed under § 707(c) or a cut of the firm's profits, taxable as if he were still a partner. This can be viewed as the retirement plan the partners expect.

150

A, B and F are equal members of the ABF service partnership and the partnership has no unrealized receivables, inventory items or unstated goodwill. The partnership has been in business for several years. Assume F is a general partner and has an outside basis of $0 and that his partnership interest is worth $100.

1) What is the tax impact to F if F sells the partnership to his partners for $50 each?

2) What is the sale's impact to A and B?

3) Now assume that F retires and receives a $100 liquidating distribution from the partnership. What is the impact to F?

4) Same as 3). What is the tax impact to A and B?

5) Same as 4), but there is a § 754 election in force?

6) Now assume that the $100 is properly characterized as a guaranteed payment to F. What is the tax impact to F and how does it differ, if at all, from the result in 3)?

7) Assume the same facts as in 6). What would be the impact the guaranteed payment on A and B?

8) Does a liquidation of a majority partner's interest cause a technical termination? *See* § 708(b)(1)(B) and Reg. § 1.708-1(b)(2).

5. INTERACTION OF § 751(b) WITH § 736 PAYMENTS

Recall that § 751(b) works to rectify the situation where there are disproportionate distributions of "hot assets." It therefore cannot apply to a § 736(a) payment because such a payment is a form of income and not a distribution. One has to apply § 736 first to determine if a payment is a distribution. If so, § 751 may step in.

To illustrate: F is an equal member of the ABF partnership, which is not a service partnership. Its assets consist of a receivable with a basis of $0 and a value of $300 and cash of $300. It distributes $200 to F. This is not a § 736(a) payment, but is instead a distribution because the partnership is not a service partnership. However, there has still been a disproportionate distribution, so one must go through the retrofitting required by § 751(b) and hypothesize that the partnership distributed $100 of receivables to F, who then sold them back to the partnership, with all the collateral implications of that model.

6. TIMING OF A § 731(a) GAIN

If there are § 736(b) payments only, the withdrawing partner recognizes gains only after cash distributed exceeds the retiring partner's outside basis. § 731(a)(1). This is a rare application of the open transaction doctrine described in *Burnet v. Logan,* 283 U.S. 404, 413 (1931). However, Reg. § 1.736-1(b)(6) permits an optional proration of the gain, such that a portion of each payment is taxable. Presumably, most retiring partners will select the general rule, thereby deferring their tax bills, rather than prorating the gain. Losses are deferred until the last payment is made, unless the partner elects to prorate the loss. *Id.*

If there are both § 736(a) and §736(b) components, each payment is apportioned between § 736(a) and § 736(b) in accordance with the partner's retirement agreement. For example, all payments could by contract first be attributed to property until exhausted, which might achieve a major tax deferral. (Reg. § 1.736-1(b)(5)(iii) provides that the total amount allocated to § 736(b) cannot exceed the value of the partner's interest in partnership property when he died or retired).

If there is no apportionment provision in the retirement agreement and the payments are *not fixed,* then unless the partners agree to a different pattern the payments are deemed to be 100% for property until the property interest is fully paid for. The rest is a guaranteed payment or distributive share. Reg. § 1.736-1(b)(5)(ii). If they do agree to a different pattern it can be structured "in any manner to which the remaining partners and the withdrawing partner . . . agree. . ." subject to the same caveat as above concerning the value of the interest. Reg. §1.736-1(b)(5)(iii). If there is no agreement and there are § 736(a) and (b) payments that are *fixed* then the default result is to allocate the payments between (a) and (b) payments in proportion to their relative values.

To illustrate: C is leaving the ABC partnership. It is agreed that her interest in property is worth $100. The retirement agreement also contains a bare bones statement that, "The ABC partnership agrees to buy out C in exchange for 35% of partnership profits for three years, starting this year." Assume her resulting share turns out to be $50 per year for each of the three years. The Regulations treat the first two payments as being for property alone. The last $50 is a distributive share because it is tied to profits, taxable as ordinary income to C. It correspondingly reduces the distributive shares of A and B.

By contrast, if the payments are *fixed,* the default result is that each payment is prorated between § 736(a) and § 736(b) payments by relative value.

To illustrate: C is retiring from the ABC partnership and did not enter into any special agreement as to how to handle the timing and composition of the payments for tax purposes. This year she retired and agreed to be paid a total of $150, of which $100 is for her interest in partnership property, by value. She will receive the $150 in the form of $50 per year for the next three years. Each $50 has to be divided into two elements – $33.33 as a payment for property and $16.67 as a guaranteed payment. C can report the gain (if any) on the $33.33 installments under the open-transaction method, or she can elect to prorate the gain under Reg. § 1.736-1(b)(6) as if the transaction were an installment sale. The former method defers gain until C has recovered her basis in the property, after which all § 736(b) receipts are fully taxed. § 731(a)(1) and Reg. §§ 1.731-1(a)(1), 1.736-1(b)(6)-(7), Example (1).

The difference between these two treatments was a large feature of the following case.

ESTATE OF THOMAS P. QUIRK v. COMMISSIONER
55 T.C.M. 1188 (1988)

Clapp, Judge

[Quirk was a member of the QLM engineering partnership until his withdrawal. There was no written partnership agreement, even though the partnership was a large enterprise. The business thereafter continued as the LMS partnership. Quirk's share of the partnership at the time of his withdrawal consisted of a share of the receivables, a share of the cash, and a share of the liabilities owed to a bank. No agreement was reached about his retirement compensation. The partnership reported cash distributions to Quirk plus reductions of his share of partnership liabilities as guaranteed payments of about $119,000 in 1974 and $185,000 in 1975. Quirk reported about $112,000 in 1974 and none in 1975 (the correct numbers turned out to be much higher, as shown in the last paragraph of the decision. The court accepted the outside accountants' (Peat, Marwick) analysis of the value of Quirk's capital account, given the confused record.]

Opinion

At the outset, it must be noted that Quirk presented no evidence to controvert the figures contained in the Peat, Marwick financial statements. No independent evaluation or financial statement prepared by qualified accountants was entered into evidence on behalf of Quirk, and no witnesses testified on behalf of Quirk as to an alternative valuation. . .

Where parties fail to agree as to the value of a retired partner's interest in partnership property, we will value the property based on a review of the facts and circumstances before us. Based on a review of the uncontroverted evidence before us, we will adopt Peat Marwick's financial statement as the basis for our conclusions of the issues of this case. Peat Marwick had been QLM's accountants from 1971 through 1974, and prior to the instant controversy, Quirk took no issue with their tax conclusions on partnership matters. Moreover, the testimony of Michael Manus, a partner at Peat Marwick and a certified public accountant, confirmed to our satisfaction that the statements were prepared in a professional manner and in accordance with generally accepted accounting principles. Finally, and foremost, Quirk presented no alternative financial statements for us to review, and accordingly, has not sustained his burden of proof with respect to the unreliability of the statements on which respondent bases his deficiencies. With this determined, we turn to the issues at hand.

Quirk and the remaining partners disagree as to the character and treatment of the distributions. We will discuss each in turn.

Section 736 applies to payments made to a `retiring partner' by the partnership in liquidation of the partner's entire interest in the partnership . . . , and provides the framework to determine the nature and character of such distributions.

Section 736 and the Regulations there under state that payments made in liquidation of the entire interest of a retiring partner are considered as a distribution, and not as a distributive share or as a guaranteed payment, to the extent that the payments are made in exchange for the partner's entire interest in the partnership property, except unrealized receivables (and good will, not at issue here). . . [S]ection 736 payments include items treated as distributions of money under section 752.

Unrealized receivables as defined by section 751(c), include any rights to payments for goods, which are not considered capital assets, or for services to the extent that the payments have not been taken into income by the taxpayer under his method of accounting. If the payments are made for unrealized receivables of the partnership, then they are taken into account in the income of the withdrawing partner as a distributive share under section 702 if

153

they are determined with regard to the income of the partnership, or under section 61(a) as a guaranteed payment if they are determined without regard to the income of the partnership. . . If a guaranteed payment is involved, the relevant amount would be deductible by the partnership if the requirements of section 162(a) have been satisfied.

If the payments are not made for partnership unrealized receivables, then the amounts are treated as made for the partner's interest in assets and as a distribution in complete liquidation under section 731. The remaining partners are not allowed any deduction for those payments since they represent either a distribution or a purchase of the withdrawing partner's capital interest by the partnership and the remaining partners. . . The withdrawing partner does not recognize any gain except to the extent that any money distributed exceeds the adjusted basis of the partner's interest in the partnership. Section 731(a)(1). The gain to be recognized would be capital in nature. . . [The Regulations provide] that the distributions to a withdrawing partner must be allocated between section 736(a) and 736(b) payments. The Regulations, after requiring the above allocations, then discuss how the allocation should be made when the amount to be paid is a 'fixed amount' or is not a fixed amount. We will address each of these. . . .

In addition to the stipulated distributions, the parties agree that Quirk received a distribution in liquidation of his partnership interest by virtue of his release from the Chemical Bank note in 1974 and 1975, but disagree over whether Quirk's release from the Chemical Bank debt by the partnership's payment of Quirk's share of the Chemical Bank note liability constituted a deemed distribution of cash to him for his interest in unrealized receivables or rather for his interest in other partnership assets.

Respondent determined, and the remaining partners maintain, that the special rules under section 736(b)(2) are applicable to the distributions to Quirk to the extent the partnership's assets consisted of unrealized receivables, 89.45989 percent according to the stipulation among the parties. Therefore, they contend, 89.45989 percent of the distributions to Quirk are to be treated as guaranteed payments since the amounts were determined without regard to the income of the partnership. As guaranteed payments, they are ordinary income to Quirk and deductible by the partnership under section 162 by virtue of section 707(c). The balance of each distribution or 10.5401 percent is a nontaxable return of basis to Quirk to the extent of his basis and not deductible by the remaining partners. Finally, they contend that the overall distributions to Quirk include the $184,002 release of liability of the Chemical Bank note pursuant to sections 752 and 736.

Quirk, on the other hand, disputes this analysis, and characterizes the distributions to him by the partnership as payments in exchange for his partnership interest under section 736(b)(1). Quirk maintains that with respect to each disputed item of the state lawsuit there was a reasonable prospect that the asset valuation could be changed. Those areas included the value of Quirk's overall partnership interest, the method by which QLM computed and valued accounts receivable, doubtful accounts, and the omission from the QLM financial statement of computer tapes and programs. That being the case, distributions might very well be deemed as made for assets other than unrealized receivables, and, if the payments are not for partnership unrealized receivables, then the amounts paid are treated as made for the partner's interest in assets and as a distribution under section 731.

We find for respondent and the remaining partners on these issues despite Quirk's arguments. Quirk provided no evidence to support his contentions that the distributions made to him for his interest in the partnership represented for the most part partnership assets other than unrealized receivables, and for purposes of this analysis, we will adopt the amounts and figures in the Peat Marwick statements. To the extent the payments were made for unrealized receivables, 89.45989 percent, Quirk must take the payments into income as guaranteed payments because the payments to him were made according to percentage interest in the assets of the partnership. Moreover, as the $184,002 decrease in Quirk's individual liability on the

Chemical Bank note is considered as a distribution of cash to him by the partnership under section 752(b), and 89.45989 percent of that distribution is accordingly treated as attributable to unrealized receivables, this amount must also be found to be a guaranteed payment.

Having determined the nature of the payments, we must now determine the proper allocation of the distributions and whether or not the distributions received by Quirk were fixed or contingent within the meaning of the Regulations and section 736, to decide their proper tax treatment.

As previously stated, [the Regulations provide] that when a partnership makes payments to retire a withdrawing partner's entire interest, the payments must be allocated between payments under section 736(a) and payments under section 736(b). Payments made to a retiring partner for the value of his interest in partnership property other than unrealized receivables are classified as 'section 736(b) payments, whereas payments to the retiring partner for unrealized receivables are classified as 'section 736(a) payments'. Depending upon the circumstances, payments for goodwill may be section 736(a) or section 736(b) payments.

The Regulations, after requiring the above allocation, which was determined to be 89.45989 percent/10.5401 percent, based on the Peat Marwick financial statement, discuss how the allocation should be made when the amount to be paid to the retiring partner (1) is a fixed amount and (2) is not a fixed amount.

Payments which are fixed in amount – The discussion in the Regulations regarding the payment of a fixed amount assumes that the fixed amount will be paid over a specific period of time and provides that if the fixed amount *(whether or not supplemented by any additional amounts)* is to be received over a fixed number of years, a portion of each payment is treated as a distribution in exchange for partnership property under section 736(b). The portion of each payment so treated is equal to the ratio of the total fixed agreed payments under section 736(b) to the total fixed agreed payments under sections 736(a) and (b). The balance of each payment is treated as a payment under section 736(a)(1) or (2). . . .

Payments which are not fixed in amount – When the retiring partner receives payments which are not fixed in amount, 'such payments shall first be treated as payments in exchange for his interest in partnership property under section 736(b) to the extent of the value of that interest and, thereafter, as payments under section 736(a).' . . . Payments which are not fixed in amount are payments such as those based on a percentage of partnership income earned over a period of future years. . . .

It is respondent's and the remaining partner's position that the determination of the character of each distribution to Quirk (of cash, or of a release of liability under section 752) is to be determined pursuant to section 1.736-1(b)(5)(i), Income Tax Regs., because the payments are of a fixed amount. They contend that while there is a dispute over the value of the assets, there is no dispute that Quirk is entitled to his percentage of the partnership assets as of October 31, 1974. It is submitted that Quirk's share of these assets represents a fixed amount as that term is used in the Regulations, and the fact that Quirk could receive more as a result of the litigation would merely represent the 'supplemental' amounts contemplated by the Regulations.

Petitioner Quirk argues to the contrary. He contends these distributions can not be characterized as fixed amounts because they were contingent pursuant to section 1.736-1(b)(5)(ii), Income Tax Regs., and that any payments to him in 1974 and 1975 must be treated as payments under section 736(b)(1) to the extent of his partnership basis, and that no part of the payments would be treated as attributable to unrealized receivables until Quirk had received payment for his interest in partnership property. Quirk provides two reasons for classifying his distribution payments as contingent and, therefore, as payments for his interest in partnership property under section 736(b)(1).

155

First, Quirk argues that the Regulations describe the requisite fixed amount in conjunction with its receipt over a fixed number of years because the language explicitly requires both the existence of a fixed sum and a certain pay out period before a fixed sum can qualify as a payment to which the allocation ratio should be applied. In the present case, he points out that even if it might be said that a fixed amount is present, there are no facts from which it can be determined the period of time payments were to be made. . .

The second reason why Quirk believes that the distribution payments should be treated as made pursuant to section 736(b)(1) is that the language of the Regulations requires the existence of an agreement between the parties with respect to the total of the fixed payments, which he reads as stemming from the phrase `total fixed agreed payments' in section 1.736-1(b)(5)(i), Income Tax Regs. In this case, he continues, the parties have not agreed in any respect on the issue of the totality of the payments Quirk will receive. Furthermore, it is incorrect to suggest that because minimum total payments, pursuant to the Peat Marwick financial statement, may eventually be paid to Quirk, the regulatory requirements needed to establish the existence of fixed payments have been met. The regulation does not specify or call for the existence of such a minimum amount.

Once again, we cannot agree with Quirk's interpretation of the Regulations . . . and find that the distribution payments to Quirk in the instant case were of a `fixed amount.'

First, we do not read the Regulations as necessarily requiring payments of a fixed amount *and* over a fixed period of time. The legislative history of section 736 illustrates this point:

Section 736. Payments to a retiring partner or a deceased partner's successor in interest. This section provides rules for the treatment of payments made to a retiring partner or to the estate, heir, or any other successor in interest of a deceased partner. The provisions are applicable only if the payments are in exchange for the liquidation of the partnership interest of the recipient. *It is immaterial whether such payments are based on a percentage of partnership income, or are fixed in amount and payable either in a lump sum or periodically over an interval of time.* Emphasis added.

If we were to adopt petitioner's interpretation, a lump-sum payment could never be deemed a `fixed amount' because by its terms it would not be payable over a fixed period. A lump-sum payment could not, therefore, ever be allocated between section 736(a) and 736(b) payments. This is in contradiction to the legislative history, and clearly not what the Regulations intended. Moreover, in section 1.736-1(b)(5)(ii), Income Tax Regs., which discusses contingent payments, contingent payments are described as not fixed in amount. There is no mention of the `not received over a fixed number of years' aspect, the emphasis of Quirk's argument. The Regulations and the legislative history highlight the fixed `amount' and not the fixed number of payments. . .

Second, nowhere in the Regulations is an agreement required between the parties with respect to a set number of payments in order to have a `fixed amount.' Section 1.736-1(b)(5)(iii), Income Tax Regs., specifically states that:

"In lieu of the rules provided in subdivisions (i) and (ii) of this subparagraph, the allocation of each annual payment between section 736(a) and (b) may be made in any manner to which all the remaining partners and the withdrawing partner . . . agree. Thus, in the *absence* of an agreement, subdivisions (i) and (ii) apply." [Emphasis added]

Finally, Quirk makes the argument that the possibility he might receive an amount in excess of the Peat Marwick valuation of his share of the partnership assets means that all distributions made to him must be treated as contingent payments and not as a fixed amount. We do not agree with this contention. Any excess would be an additional amount within the meaning of section 1.736-I(b)(5)(i), Income Tax Regs., and would not disrupt his entitlement to

30.667 percent of the partnership assets. To interpret otherwise would allow any withdrawing partner to have the ability to create contingent payments merely by initiating litigation, thereby circumventing the Regulations and allocation sanctioned therein. Moreover, this specified minimum amount based on a fixed percentage of partnership assets is due Quirk without regard to partnership income and would satisfy the definition of fixed amount pursuant to section 736 Regulations.

Because we find a fixed amount is due Quirk, the applicable regulation is section 1.736-1(b)(5)(i), Income Tax Regs., and Quirk's payments must be allocated according to its provisions. Thus, the payment must be allocated between unrealized receivables and other assets. Of each payment received, 89.45989 percent is to be treated as guaranteed payments and reportable as ordinary income to Quirk and deductible by the partnership. The balance, or 10.5401 percent of each distribution, is a recovery of basis and then capital gain.

The total payments to Quirk after October 31, 1974, in liquidation of his partnership interest amounted to $151,945 in 1974 and $207,372 in 1975 and 89.45989 percent of each payment represented a guaranteed payment deductible by the partnership in 1974 to the extent of $135,929.83 ($151,945 x 89.45989 percent) and $185,514.76 in 1975 ($207,372 x 89.45989 percent). The balance of the distributions, $16,015 in 1974 ($151,945 x 10.5401 percent) in 1974 and $21,857 in 1975 ($207,372 x 10.5401 percent) are to be applied against Quirk's adjusted basis of his interest in the partnership under sections 736(b) and 731(a)(I). Quirk must report capital gain only to the extent his distributions exceed his adjusted basis in the partnership. Section 736(b).

Decisions will be entered under Rule 155.

QUESTION

Is it clear to you what was at stake to each party in this case?

D. LIQUIDATING THE TWO-PERSON PARTNERSHIP

Section 736 ensures that, as long as payouts are being made to the withdrawing partner (or her estate), the partnership continues for federal income tax purposes, even if it was originally just a two-person partnership that disappeared at local law. *See* Reg. §§ 1.708-1(b)(1)(i)(b) and 1.736-1(a)(6). This means the partnership is deemed to continue even though the remaining partner may sell the assets and retire from the business during the § 736 payment period. Except for this special case, § 736 does not apply when the partnership liquidates, because § 736 contemplates a continuing partnership.

E. TAXATION OF THE PARTNERSHIP

The partnership is not taxed on the distribution of appreciated or depreciated assets to a withdrawing partner. § 731(b). This stands in stark distinction to corporate distributions.

F. SELECTING BETWEEN A SALE OR A LIQUIDATION OF THE PARTNERSHIP INTEREST

If there are only two partners, one of whom plans to sell out to the other, it does not matter from an economic point of view whether the transaction is structured as a sale of a partnership interest or a liquidation of the selling partner's interest, followed by the liquidated partner's sale of the distributed assets to his former partner. It can, however, matter for federal income tax purposes. The dollar figures cited by the court do not seem entirely correct; try to understand the tax strategy the taxpayers were trying to use and why it did or did not work.

KINNEY v. UNITED STATES
228 F. Supp. 656 (1964), *aff'd,* 358 F.2d 738 (5th Cir. 1966)

HUNTER, DISTRICT JUDGE.

This is an action for the recovery of $10,679.37, plus interest, paid as income tax for the year 1958. . .

In the early part of 1958 disagreements arose between the two men and they began discussing the termination of their partnership association. Stine, who wanted to operate the mill as an individual, made an offer to buy out Kinney's interest and further proposed that they divide various land holdings in kind. Kinney wanted to get out of the mill and discussed selling his interest to Stine. The men negotiated for some time and ultimately each placed the matter in the hands of their respective attorneys for resolution. The taxpayer was represented by Norman F. Anderson and Stine was represented by Richard A. Anderson. Since the taxpayer wanted to get out of the mill, his attorney approached the negotiations with the view to sell out or liquidate the business. Conversely, since Mr. Stine wanted to acquire the mill and continue to operate it individually, he instructed his attorney to negotiate to purchase Mr. Kinney's interest. . . .

Finally, on June 14, 1958, Richard Anderson, on behalf of Mr. Stine, proposed to buy Mr. Kinney's interest in the partnership in the following terms: The fixed assets were to be transferred to a Texas corporation, which would be formed, in exchange for all of the stock of the corporation which would be distributed equally to Messrs. Stine and Kinney; Mr. Stine was to have an option to purchase Mr. Kinney's stock for $110,000 on terms, or $85,000 in cash; Mr. Stine was to acquire Mr. Kinney's remaining interest in the business by canceling certain obligations owed to it by the partners, assuming all of the liabilities, and paying Mr. Kinney an additional $172,000. In his capacity as the taxpayer's representative, Norman Anderson made a counter-proposal pertaining to a change in the form of security for the notes Mr. Stine was to give to the taxpayer, and further proposed that the purchase price for the taxpayer's interest in the partnership which would remain after the transfer to the corporation be allocated to the individual assets at book value with the loss being absorbed in the inventory.

This proposal was acceptable to both parties and the respective attorneys began drafting the various instruments for signature. Finally, on July 7, 1958, the parties executed five documents reciting:

1) That the land and improvements owned by the partnership were transferred to the newly formed corporation, Orange Rice Milling Company, Inc., in exchange for its stock, said stock divided equally between Stine and Kinney.

2) That the depreciable, movable property owned by the partnership was transferred to the newly formed corporation, Orange Rice Milling Company, Inc., in exchange for its stock, said stock divided equally between Stine and Kinney.

3) That the Orange Rice Milling Company partnership be dissolved as of June 30, 1958.

4) That Mr. Stine was granted an option to purchase the taxpayer's stock in the new corporation.

5) That the taxpayer conveyed his interest in all of the other assets of the partnership to Mr. Stine, for $172,000, plus the assumption by Mr. Stine of all of the liabilities of the partnership and the cancellation of certain debts owed by the partners.

The document reciting the sale of the taxpayer's remaining interest in the partnership after the transfer to the corporation allocated the purchase price to the individual assets on this basis:

Asset	Consideration
A. Cash, receivables, claims, securities:	Book value
B. Sublease, trade names, patents, goodwill:	Zero
C. Inventory:	Remaining selling price in excess of items denoted in A

On July 31, 1958, Mr. Stine exercised the option and discount feature by purchasing the taxpayer's stock in the newly formed corporation for $85,000. In their income tax return for 1958 the taxpayers reported a long-term capital loss on the sale of the stock in the amount of $61,233.85 computed as follows:

Cost or other basis in stock determined by basis in assets:	$171,233.85
Selling price:	-$110,000.00
Loss:	$ 61,233.85

They also reported an ordinary loss of $18,033.12 and claimed that it was sustained on the sale of inventory to Mr. Stine. This loss was computed as follows:

Sale of inventory received upon dissolution of Orange Rice Milling Co. (Partnership):

Acquired 6-30-58 at a cost of	$922,132.05
Sold 7-7-58 for	-$904,098.93
Loss	$ 18,033.12

Upon audit of the return, the Internal Revenue Service contended that several errors had been made in reporting the items listed above. The taxpayer's basis in the stock was found to be $152,290.16, rather than $171,233.85, and the selling price was discovered to be $85,000, rather than $110,000. The result of these adjustments was to allow a capital loss of $67,290.16, rather than $61,233.85 as had been reported. The determination was also made that the taxpayers did not sustain an ordinary loss of $18,033.12 on the sale of inventory, as had been reported, but that instead, a long-term capital loss of $36,976.81 was sustained on the sale of his remaining partnership interest computed as follows:

Basis of Mr. Kinney's one-half interest in partnership	$208,976.81
Selling price	$ 172,000.00
Long-term Capital Loss	$ 36,976.81

The Law

The issue to be decided by the Court is whether the loss of $36,976.81 claimed by the taxpayers in the transaction hereinabove described should be treated as an ordinary loss, as they contend, or as a capital loss, as the Government contends. We are not concerned with that part of the partnership assets (land and depreciable items) which were transferred to the Texas corporation. The loss here in controversy only stems from the sale covering the miscellaneous assets (principally receivables and inventories). Also, it is not the amount, but the character of this loss which is in controversy.

The economic consequences, apart from income taxes, would be the same to the parties irrespective of whether the sale was a partnership interest or of property received as a distribution from the partnership.

The taxpayers' argument is that Congress has provided for different tax consequences dependent upon which procedure and form is followed. Where a partnership interest is sold, Section 741 specifies capital gain or loss treatment with exceptions not here involved; but, says the taxpayer, under Section [735], the sale by a distributee of property received as a distribution from a partnership keeps its character as either a capital item, or ordinary income or loss items, as if the distribution had been made by the partnership itself.

It is the substance of a transaction rather than the form in which it is cast that governs the tax consequences. *(Weiner's Estate v. Commissioner,* 294 F.2d 750, 755, C.A.5th). The record here reveals that the substance of the transaction which gave rise to this lawsuit is far more than the sale of items of inventory. The essence of the transaction was a sale by the taxpayer of his interest in a partnership to his partner who continued to carry on the business. All the testimony on the subject, including that of the taxpayer and his attorney, leads us to that conclusion. We consider this transaction in its entirety, for to fragment or otherwise isolate a minute segment of the transaction is diametrically opposed to the entire philosophy of our tax laws. The Court of Appeals for the Sixth Circuit made this plain in very cogent language *(Mather v. Commissioner,* 149 F.2d 393, 397, *certiorari denied,* 326 U.S. 767):

> "It has been said too often to warrant citation, that taxation is an intensely practical matter, and that the substance of the thing done and not the form it took, must govern, and the courts have recognized that where the essential nature of a transaction is the acquisition of property, it will be viewed as a whole, and closely related steps will not be separated either at the instance of the taxpayer or the taxing authority. *Commr. v. Ashland Oil & Refining Co.,* 99 F.2d 588, 591 (C.C. A.6). . . "

An examination of this transaction in its entirety leaves no doubt but that the taxpayer sold his interest in the partnership to Mr. Stine and that the latter continued to operate the business formerly conducted by the partnership. It is, of course, an elementary principle that the sale or exchange of a partnership interest in a going concern is a capital transaction resulting in either a capital gain or a capital loss. It can in no way give rise to an ordinary loss as claimed by the taxpayer. Section 741 of the Internal Revenue Code of 1954. . . .

Here, Stine acquired more than a group of assets. He acquired the right to continue operating the business formerly conducted by the partnership using the same assets, owing the same creditors, and using the same brand names. The business operation did not cease even during the negotiations and was continued by Mr. Stine after the transaction was closed just as the parties always contemplated.

We conclude that in this case Mr. Stine purchased the going business of the partnership "lock, stock and barrel." In fact, the contract reciting the sale of the assets even recites that he bought the taxpayer's half-interest in the cash owned by the partnership.

160

The significance of the total sale of a partner's total interest in a partnership has been noted by the Court of Appeals for the Sixth Circuit in *Commissioner v. Shapiro, supra (p.* 535):

It is fundamental in applying tax statutes that matters of substance are of first importance: The price paid for the property in question may have been based partly on assets excluded under the act from the phrase "capital assets" such as inventories of property held by the partnership primarily for sale to customers in the ordinary course of its trade or business, but the sale made by respondent was not a sale of those assets. It is a well settled rule of law that the joint effects of a partnership belong to the firm and not the partners and that a partner has no individual property in any specific assets of the firm, instead the interest of each partner in the partnership property is his share in the surplus, after the partnership debts are paid and after the partnership accounts are settled. *Blodgett v. Silberman,* 277 U.S. 1, 10. Respondent sold all of his interest in the partnership, tangible and intangible, as a going concern, which in all essentials is different from the ordinary assets of the partnership used in the usual course of its business.

It was made clear in this decision that whether or not the selling price was based on property other than capital assets is of no significance since the sale was the sale of the partner's total interest in the partnership. Coincidentally, the Court of Appeals for the Eighth Circuit had the same question before it in a case involving a taxpayer with the same name. *United States v. Shapiro,* 178 F.2d 459.

The critical question here is whether in fact and in substance the petitioners actually sold their respective interests in the partnership, and the facts show that the substance of what occurred was a sale by the taxpayer of his entire interest in the partnership to his partner.

In arguing that the transaction requires ordinary loss treatment, taxpayer is arguing that the execution on July 7, 1958, of a document reciting the dissolution of the partnership and distribution of the assets actually accomplished both of these things on June 30, 1958, or seven days earlier. In truth and in fact neither occurred. The business did not terminate on June 30, 1958, for its operations were in progress through July 7, 1958, and there was no real distribution of assets. What really happened is that on July 7, 1958, the taxpayer sold his entire one-half partnership interest to Edward J. Stine. That the transaction was divided into two parts, one being the creation of a corporation, is of no consequence. The creation of the corporation and transfer to it of the fixed and depreciable assets in exchange for stock amounts to a partial distribution to the partners and was not a taxable transaction. Section 731 of the Internal Revenue Code of 1954. . . Although the taxpayer refers to it as the sale of "miscellaneous assets" the second part of the transaction was a sale by him of what remained of his partnership interest. These same circumstances existed in *Long v. Commissioner,* 173 F.2d 471. In holding that there had been a capital transaction, the Court noted that there had been no cessation of business or complete liquidation and that there had merely been a sale of the partnership interest that remained after the distribution of some assets.

Moreover, the taxpayer erroneously states that the sale of the miscellaneous assets was preceded by the termination of the business on July 7, 1958, as of June 30, 1958. Section 708(b) of the Internal Revenue Code of 1954 . . . sets forth the only two circumstances under which a partnership shall be considered terminated for tax purposes. . . .

Conclusion

Judgment is entered in favor of the Government. Taxpayers' complaint is dismissed with prejudice.

1. **Which is the controlling cliché?** The most popular bromide of the tax avoider is Learned Hand's famous quotation, "Any one may so arrange his affairs that his taxes shall be as low as possible; he is not bound to choose that pattern which will best pay the Treasury; there is not even a patriotic duty to increase one's taxes." *Helvering v. Gregory,* 69 F. 2d 809, 810 (2d Cir. 1934), *aff'd,* 293 U.S. 465 (1935). Conversely, every law student who has had even one tax course knows that the courts love to lecture the parties in tax litigation that substance must prevail over mere forms. Did Hunter, J. get it right in the *Kinney* decision, or did he merely pick the more attractive cliché and recklessly apply it to the facts?

2. **The tax stakes in Kinney.** The tax stakes apparently were that if the partnership interest were sold, even though it was rich in inventory, it would not generate any ordinary loss, because (as far as inventory goes) § 751 only reached ordinary gains on inventory. Thus, the parties (we presume) decided on a distribution (with carryover basis) followed by a sale at a loss by the distributee. If the taxpayers had won, § 735(a) would have assured a continuance of the character of the distributed properties, especially inventory, without regard to whether it was substantially appreciated. We assume there were no other "hot assets." This issue can take a more common form. Nowadays, § 751(a) reaches gains and losses.

   To illustrate: A is an equal member of the ABC partnership, whose primary asset has a basis of $0 and a value of $90. A proposes to buy the asset from the partnership. Would you advise that the partnership first distribute the asset? The answer is "almost surely yes," because if A buys the asset from the partnership, A will be taxed on the $30 gain attributable to her share. If A buys the asset (after it is distributed to the partners) from B and C, only they will pay a tax. Is this an example of a trap for the unwary? How ignorant do you have to be to be "unwary," as opposed to dull-witted?

3. **The "basis strip."** This is a good point to introduce the "basis strip" concept, which is used in advance of a sale of an asset. The idea is to use the § 734(b) election aggressively to increase the basis of undistributed assets, thereby reducing the gain (or increasing the loss) on the sale of the distributed asset. For example, if the ABC partnership planned to sell asset M, which had a basis of $1,000, it might distribute asset N, which also has a $1,000 basis, to a partner with a zero basis in his partnership interest. This could increase ABC's basis in M to $2,000, and could even produce a loss on its sale. Should this be denounced as a mere manipulation of forms, or does it stand up? This leads us to the next topic, but first a problem.

PROBLEM 8-4

A, B and F are equal members of the ABF general partnership, which uses the calendar year. It is not a service partnership. Each partner has an outside basis of $10. The partnership has no unrealized receivables or inventory items. F wants to retire. The following table describes the ABF partnership's assets in dollars. The transactions all occur in year one, unless otherwise stated. The partnership agreement makes no reference to payments for goodwill.

Asset	Inside Basis	Value
Cash	$0.00	$0.00
Capital asset (land)	$30.00	$60.00

Goodwill		$0.00	$30.00

1) What result to F if the partnership sells the land and distributes cash of $30 to F, who remains an equal partner?

2) Assume the same basic transaction as in 1), but that F is distributed the $30 (which A and C contributed in cash for this purpose) in cash in liquidation of his partnership interest. Does the distribution include any § 736(a) payments?

3) Does the distribution in "(2)" include any § 736(b) payments?

4) Same as "(1)." What is the result to A and B?

5) The ABF partnership is a law partnership, and the partnership agreement provides for an appropriate payment to retiring partners to reflect the partnership's goodwill. Does this change the result in "(2)?"

6) Same as "(5)," but there is no provision of the type described in "(5)" in the partnership agreement, but the partners are considering inserting one. Should they?

7) Could the partners retroactively amend the partnership agreement in the following year to insert such a provision? If so, when, at the latest? Does this present a trap of some sort?

8) Could the partners value the land at $90 and then make no payment with respect to goodwill? *See* Reg. § 1.736-1(b)(3).

9) Same as "(1)," but the partners agree that F will get $20 on account of his interest in the capital asset, plus 10% of the next year's profits, which turns out to be the usual $10. How is F taxed on the $10?

10) Why might A and B prefer the result in "(9)" to the result in "(1)?"

11) Now assume the capital asset is instead a zero basis unrealized receivable and the ABF partnership is not a service partnership.

   a)   Will the $20 cash payment in respect of the unrealized receivable be treated as a distribution or as a § 736(a) payment?

   b)   Will §751(b) apply to the cash payment? If so, what are the effects?

   c)   Same as a) but the partnership is a law firm. Will the $20 payment with respect to the receivable be subject to § 751(b) or § 736(a), and what is the result?

12) Same as "(1)" but instead of paying $30 outright to redeem his interest in the partnership, the partnership pays $35 outright to F. What is the character of the extra $5?

163

G. THE PARTNERSHIP ANTI-ABUSE RULE REGULATIONS

In 1994, the IRS issued final Regulations establishing a broad anti-abuse rule for partnerships. Reg. § 1.701-2. These *in terrorem* Regulations permit the IRS to take virtually any action, including overriding the literal words of a particular statutory or regulatory provision, if it deems any partnership-related transaction to be abusive. The breadth and subjectivity of the Regulations and the lack of any safe harbors may mean that transactions the parties considered innocent may easily be abusive under the Regulations.

1. General Anti-abuse Rule

The Regulations consider a partnership transaction abusive if:

"a partnership is formed or availed of in connection with a transaction a principal purpose of which is to reduce substantially the present value of the partners' aggregate federal income tax liability in a manner that is inconsistent with the intent of subchapter K."

According to the Regulations, the intent of Subchapter K is to let taxpayers conduct joint business and investment activities through a flexible economic arrangement without incurring an entity level tax. The Regulations set forth certain requirements for a partnership transaction or series of related transactions to be treated as being within the intent of Subchapter K.

- First, the partnership must be bona fide, and the transaction (or series of related transactions) must be entered into for a substantial business purpose.

- Second, the form of the transaction (or series of related transactions) must be respected under substance-over-form principles.

- Third, the tax consequences to each partner from partnership operations and transactions must accurately reflect the partners' economic agreement and clearly reflect the partners' income. However, the Regulations provide an exception to the last requirement where such tax consequences result from certain provisions of Subchapter K that were adopted to promote administrative convenience and other policy objectives. Such tax consequences, taking into account all the relevant facts and circumstances, are clearly contemplated by such provisions.

If the IRS determines that a partnership transaction is abusive under the above-described rule, it is empowered to recast the transaction in almost any manner in order to achieve tax results that are consistent with Subchapter K. For example, the IRS may disregard the partnership, treat one or more of the purported partners as not being a partner, adjust the partnership's or a partner's method of accounting, reallocate the partnership's items of income, deductions, losses, and credits, or otherwise adjust or modify the claimed tax treatment.

In determining whether a partnership was formed or availed of for an abusive purpose, the IRS will look to all the surrounding facts and circumstances. In addition, the Regulations list the following factors, the existence of which *may* indicate the presence of an abusive purpose:

- The present value of the partners' aggregate tax liability is substantially less than if the partnership did not exist and the partners conducted the partnership's activities directly;

- The present value of the partners' aggregate tax liability is substantially less than if a series of purportedly separate transactions designed to achieve an end result were integrated and treated as steps in a single transaction;

- One or more partners who are necessary to achieve the claimed tax treatment have nominal interests, are substantially protected from any risks of loss or have little or no participation in profits in excess of a preferred return for the use of their capital;

- Substantially all of the partners are related;

- Partnership tax items are allocated in accordance with the literal language of the allocation rules but the allocations result in consequences inconsistent with the purpose of such rules – thereby rendering compliance with the (formidable) substantial economic effect Regulations inadequate;

- The benefits and burdens of property nominally contributed to the partnership are retained in substantial part by the contributing party; and

- The benefits and burdens of partnership property are shifted to or from the distributee before or after the distribution of such property is made to the distributee partners.

A transaction may be abusive if merely "a" principal purpose of the transaction, as opposed to "the" principal purpose of the transaction, is to reduce the partners' federal income tax liabilities in a proscribed manner. This means that even if the form of the partnership transaction is driven by business considerations, it may be deemed abusive if there is also a principal purpose to reduce the partners' tax liabilities.

Similarly, in order to determine whether a transaction causes a proscribed reduction of the partners' aggregate tax liability, it is necessary to identify the partners' baseline tax liability for purposes of comparison. The Regulations provide no guidance in this regard. Thus, for example, the baseline may be the tax liability that would have resulted if a party was not a partner, if the partnership did not engage in the transaction or if a corporation was used instead of a partnership.

The anti-abuse Regulations do not displace the other more specific anti-abuse provisions of Subchapter K, such as the "disguised sale" provisions, nor do they displace general tax law doctrines, such as the concept that substance must prevail over form in tax matters. *See* Reg. § 1.701-2(h).

In issuing the Regulations, the Treasury strained to assure taxpayers that the Regulations are "expected primarily to affect a relatively small number of partnership transactions that make inappropriate use of subchapter K." T.D. 8588, at 5, 1995-1 C.B. 190. A key theme is that if the economic transaction would have occurred anyway, the choice of the partnership form to minimize taxes is not an abuse; rather, it is consistent with the flexibility subchapter K is supposed to afford taxpayers. *See, e.g.,* Reg. § 1.701-2(d), Examples 3 and 4.

2. Abuse of Entity Treatment

The Regulations provide in general that the IRS can treat a partnership for tax purposes as an aggregate of its partners, and not as an entity, in order to carry out the purposes of any provision of the Code or Regulations. For example, if a joint venture that includes corporate partners issues a high-yield discount obligation, under the Regulations, the corporate partners will be subject to the same restrictions on the deductibility of their allocable shares of interest deductions on such obligation as would apply to a corporate issuer of such an obligation, notwithstanding that the partnership issued the obligation and not the corporate partners.

The Regulations provide an exception to this rule to the extent a statutory or regulatory provision treats a partnership as an entity and that treatment and the ultimate tax results, taking into account all the relevant facts and circumstances, are "clearly contemplated" by the provision. The trouble is it may often be difficult to determine whether the particular tax consequences resulting from treating a partnership as an entity are clearly contemplated by a particular statutory or regulatory provision.

Now, how do you think the "basis strip" stands up under the new Regulations?

Chapter 9

TERMINATIONS

A. INTRODUCTION

In this short chapter the focus swings from the termination of a partner's interest in the partnership to the termination of the partnership itself. From the partner's perspective, the tax implications are generally the same as if the partner had liquidated his interest, except that § 736 is inapplicable. Thus, once again when property is distributed in complete liquidation, there is generally no taxable gain or loss to the partners or to the partnership. Instead, the tax deferral is reflected in an adjustment to the basis of the distributed property. However, the distribution of cash alone can produce a taxable gain. § 731(a)(1). In contrast, the partner may recognize a loss if she receives only money, unrealized receivables, inventory, or some combination. § 731(a)(2). The loss is easy to compute if cash alone is distributed. One just subtracts the cash from predistribution outside basis; the shortfall is deemed a loss on the sale of the partnership interest. Moreover, no other result is plausible. One cannot defer gains and losses by tinkering with the basis of cash, because cash must take a basis equal to its face amount. Any other result would be absurd. Given that, there must be a recognized loss where cash alone is distributed. If, instead, only unrealized receivables or inventory items are distributed, there is a capital loss to the extent that inside basis of the distributed property is less than the distributee partner's outside basis. This arises because § 732(b) insists that the partner take a basis in receivables and inventory equal to their inside bases less any distributed cash. § 732(b). These tax outcomes are exactly the same as for the liquidation of a partner's interest, except that all the partners must perform these calculations. Note that in many instances the partnership first sells its assets, reports its gain or loss, and then distributes cash to the partners, greatly simplifying the calculations.

The first step is to read § 708(a) and (b), observing that § 708 tells one nothing about the effect of a termination. Instead, one must look to other Code sections, primarily §§ 706, 731 and 732, concerning the taxable year of, and distributions from the partnership, respectively.

B. TERMINATION BY CESSATION OF BUSINESS

As you read the following case, make sure to understand what Mr. Neubecker was after from a federal income tax perspective.

NEUBECKER v. COMMISSIONER
65 T.C. 577 (1975)

Drennen, Judge:

Findings of Fact

Some of the facts have been stipulated and are accordingly so found.

Petitioners were husband and wife during 1969, and at all times material hereto resided in Milwaukee, Wis. Petitioners' joint Federal income tax return for the taxable year 1969 was filed with the Director, Internal Revenue Service Center, Kansas City, Mo., on June 22, 1970.

Edward F. Neubecker (hereinafter referred to as Neubecker or petitioner) is an attorney-at-law who engaged in the practice of law in Milwaukee, Wis. From December 1, 1964, to

February or March of 1969, petitioner practiced law as a partner in the firm of Frinzi, Catania, and Neubecker (hereinafter sometimes referred to as the partnership), of which Messrs. Frinzi, Catania, and Neubecker were the sole members. No formal written partnership agreement existed among the three partners although there was an informal understanding as to the partners' respective duties and the division of partnership profits. The partnership maintained a bank account on which each of the partners was authorized to draw.

At some time in either February or March of 1969, the partnership was dissolved upon oral agreement of all the partners, whereupon petitioner and Catania left the location of the partnership, acquired office facilities elsewhere in Milwaukee, and immediately thereafter formed a new partnership under the name of Catania and Neubecker. Petitioner and Catania did not execute a written agreement evidencing the new arrangement.

No formal accounting occurred among the three partners incident to the dissolution of Frinzi, Catania, and Neubecker. The partnership bank account, as well as whatever accounts receivable were then outstanding, were left with Frinzi who continued to occupy the offices previously maintained by the partnership. To the extent some fees had at the time of dissolution been received from clients, no attempt was made to allocate these payments among the partners. Although no formal division or assignment of clients and pending cases took place petitioner and Catania, as partners in Catania and Neubecker, retained certain clients and cases for which they had responsibility when practicing as partners in Frinzi, Catania, and Neubecker.

Upon the dissolution of Frinzi, Catania, and Neubecker, petitioner actually received the following:

Item on dissolution	Fair market value
Cash Accounts Receivable	$0.00
Inventory	$0.00
1 typewriter	$100.00
1 secretary chair	$50.00
2 file cabinets	$100.00
Miscellaneous books and pamphlets	$100.00
1 waiting room chair	$50.00
Office supplies	$15.00
Total value	$415.00

The bulk of the equipment and property used in the conduct of the business of the partnership remained with Frinzi.

As of the date of dissolution of the partnership, petitioner's capital account had a balance of $2,425.57.

* * *

Under Part 111 of Schedule E attached to their return for 1969, petitioners reported as income from partnerships the amount of $13,258.49 from Catania and Neubecker and $3.521.01 from Frinzi, Catania, and Neubecker. The employer identification number listed thereon was the same for both partnerships.

On Schedule D, "Sales or Exchanges of Property," under Part 1, "Short-term capital gains and losses," petitioners reflected a $2,425.57 loss on the partnership interest in Frinzi, Catania, and Neubecker. Of this amount, petitioners claimed a deduction of $1,000, which respondent has disallowed in its entirety.

Opinion

The principal issue remaining for decision is whether, incident to the dissolution of the partnership of Frinzi, Catania, and Neubecker, petitioners sustained a recognizable loss on Edward F. Neubecker's interest in the partnership. We must also determine whether petitioners are liable for the addition to tax asserted by respondent pursuant to section 6651(a).

With regard to the partnership loss issue, petitioners' position is predicated on the dissolution of the Frinzi, Catania, and Neubecker partnership. Since Neubecker had, at the time of dissolution, a capital account in the amount of $2,425.57, and in view of the fact that the items taken by Neubecker and Catania for use in their new office were of minimal value, petitioners concluded they sustained a deductible loss on said partnership interest. On brief, petitioners shift the thrust of their argument and characterize the value of Neubecker's share of the assets which remained with Frinzi as an abandonment or forfeiture loss, which theory is premised on petitioner's contention that the Code sections specifically relating to the taxation of partners and partnerships (subchapter K) fail to deal with the treatment to which petitioners are entitled.

Respondent, on the other hand, argues that petitioners sustained no deductible loss on the partnership interest because the Frinzi, Catania, and Neubecker partnership, albeit dissolved, did not terminate within the meaning of section 708, and thus, there was no event occasioning realization of loss. Further, if under section 708, Neubecker's interest remained in partnership solution and therefore not completely liquidated, section 731(a)(2) would operate to deny recognition of the loss. In the alternative, even if a termination and complete liquidation of Neubecker's interest did occur, respondent contends that petitioners nevertheless failed to satisfy the requirement of section 731(a)(2) as to the nature of the property distributed and are thereby precluded from recognizing any realized loss.

While it can be argued that the provisions of subchapter K did not envision such an informal splitting up of a partnership as occurred here, we must agree with respondent's analysis that the provisions of subchapter K do prevent the recognition of any loss to petitioners under the circumstances here present.

We note as a threshold matter that in the context of section 708 there is an implicit distinction drawn between dissolution and termination, which dispels the dispositive significance which petitioners would accord the dissolution of Frinzi, Catania, and Neubecker. *See Elaine Yagoda,* 39 T.C. 170, 183 (1962), *aff'd.* 331 F.2d 485, 591 n.5 (2d Cir. 1964), *cert. denied* 379 U.S. 842 (1964). Under the law there would appear to be no termination of Frinzi, Catania, and Neubecker but rather a continuation of that partnership in Catania and Neubecker with Frinzi being the withdrawing partner.

Section 708(a) provides that an existing partnership shall be considered as continuing if it is not terminated, and subsection (b)(I)A provides that a partnership shall be considered as terminated only if "(A) no part of any business, financial operation, or venture of the partnership continues to be carried on by any of its partners in a partnership, or. . . " Section 708(b)(2)(B) provides that:

In the case of a division of a partnership into two or more partnerships, the resulting partnerships (other than any resulting partnership the members of which had an interest of 50 percent or less in the capital and profits of the prior partnership) shall, for purposes of this section, be considered a continuation of the prior partnership. . .

We believe that the extant facts warrant no other conclusion than that a sufficient part of the business conducted by Frinzi, Catania, and Neubecker continued to be carried on by the Catania and Neubecker partnership such that the former cannot be considered as terminated. Sec. 708(b)(1)(A). . . Immediately upon dissolution of the partnership, Catania and Neubecker formed the Catania and Neubecker partnership. To the extent that petitioner and Catania, as partners in Catania and Neubecker, retained certain clients and cases for which they had responsibility when practicing as partners in Frinzi, Catania, and Neubecker, the continuity of operation contemplated in section 708(b)(I)(A) is clearly established. Although petitioners have not argued, nor does the record demonstrate, that these cases and clients were taken by Neubecker and Catania incident to winding down and arriving at a final accounting in respect of Frinzi, Catania, and Neubecker, that partnership would nevertheless be considered as continuing while in the process of winding down since section 708(b)(1)(A) requires complete cessation of business in order to effect a termination. . .

The fact that the Catania and Neubecker partnership kept the same employer identification number further supports our determination as to the continuation of Frinzi, Catania, and Neubecker. Contrary to the emphasis placed by petitioners on the fact that Neubecker and Catania vacated the old premises and relocated in other office facilities, we attribute little significance to such fact which, although indicative of some physical interruption of operation, is irrelevant in terms of the criteria set forth in section 708.

If, then, Frinzi, Catania, and Neubecker continued by virtue of the fact that its business was in part carried on by its partners, Neubecker and Catania, in a partnership, it follows that the receipt of the few items of office equipment and supplies, to the extent characterized as a distribution to Neubecker, nevertheless did not constitute a distribution in liquidation of his partnership interest, which is the threshold requirement for recognition of loss pursuant to section 731(a)(2) and the Regulations thereunder.

Section 731(a)(2) provides that in the case of a distribution to a partner loss shall not be recognized to such partner unless the distribution is in liquidation of his interest in the partnership and then only if the property distributed to him consists only of money, unrealized receivables, and inventory. Here the assets received by Catania and Neubecker were not received in liquidation of their interests in the partnership; they retained their interests in the continuing partnership. But even if the partnership did terminate within the meaning of section 708 and Neubecker's interest in the firm was completely liquidated, section 731(a)(2) would still operate to preclude recognition of a loss at that time. While we need not decide precisely what property comprised the liquidating distribution to Neubecker, clearly such distribution did not consist solely of money, unrealized receivables, or inventory as specified in section 731(a)(2)(A) and (B).

The record is devoid of any evidence indicating receipt of any of the prescribed items of property. Petitioner received no cash. Presumably the business of Frinzi, Catania, and Neubecker involved no inventory. Neubecker himself testified that no allocation of receivables, if any existed, occurred. And further, petitioners have presented no evidence that Neubecker was relieved of any partnership liabilities so as to constitute a distribution of money under section 752(b). Furthermore, even if we might infer from Neubecker's retention of certain cases and clients that he in fact acquired accounts receivable or money, petitioners fail to qualify for recognition of loss under section 731(a)(2) by virtue of Neubecker's receipt of the aforementioned proscribed property.

Thus, under either approach, section 731(a)(2) dictates nonrecognition of petitioners' claimed loss. Moreover, we find that the applicability of section 731(a)(2) renders petitioners' characterization of the loss as a forfeiture or an abandonment loss, deductible under section 165, unavailing. In respect of the relation of subchapter K to the more general provisions of the Code, "the specific language of Section 731 prevails over the general language of Section 165(a) as to a fact situation falling within the ambit of Section 731." *Estate of Dupree v. United States,* 391, F.2d 753, 757-758 (5th Cir. 1968).

Not only does section 731 itself operate to deny petitioners recourse under section 165, but our findings and analysis necessary to determine the applicability of section 731 also preclude, as a factual matter, characterization of the loss in issue as an abandonment or forfeiture loss, both of which characterizations must be predicated on the contention that Neubecker received nothing in respect of his partnership interest. The record, however, clearly disproves this premise in view of the fact that Neubecker did receive some property upon dissolution of the partnership.

Further, we do not find support for either characterization in *Gaius G. Gannon,* 16 T.C. 1134 (1951), *acq.* 1951-2 C.B. 2, and *Palmer Hutcheson,* 17 T.C. 14 (1951), upon which petitioners primarily rely. In these cases, the respective petitioners, who were partners in the same law firm, voluntarily withdrew from the partnership and, by application of explicit forfeiture provisions in the partnership agreement, were thereby denied any compensation for their respective interests in the firm. We held in both cases that the petitioner was entitled to a deductible loss by virtue of the forfeiture of the partnership interest.

Unlike the facts in *Gaius G. Gannon, supra,* and *Palmer Hutcheson, supra,* the Frinzi, Catania, and Neubecker partnership agreement contained no forfeiture provision or restriction on Neubecker's right to receive a return of his investment upon withdrawal from, or the dissolution or termination, of the partnership. And, as we have emphasized, Neubecker did in fact receive property upon dissolution of the partnership. . . .

On the basis of the foregoing, we hold that petitioners did not sustain a deductible loss in 1969 in respect of Neubecker's interest in the Frinzi, Catania, and Neubecker partnership.

Decision will be entered under Rule 155.

PROBLEM 9-1

a. A, B and C are calendar year cash method individuals and equal members of the profitable calendar year ABC partnership. The partnership owns and manages a ranch. The partners recently had a major falling out, as a result of which they agreed to dissolve the partnership. Their agreement was signed on June 30, but they continued in business until September 30 when all of the partnership's remaining assets were distributed to A, B and C.

   a) When did the partnership terminate? *See* Reg. § 1.708-1(b)(1).

   b) Same as "(a)", except that the partnership distributes the ranch assets to the partners who operate them in the name of a tenancy in common and share the net profits from the real estate. When did the partnership terminate, if at all?

   c) Same as "(a)". How many months of partnership income would the partners report on the returns they file for the calendar year of the liquidation?

   d) Assume the same facts as "(a)" except that the partnership consists of A and B only, and that A's interest is liquidated over 8 years, a transaction that falls under § 736. Does this mean that § 736 cannot apply to the payments? *See* Reg. §§ 1.708-1(b)(1)(B)(ii) and 1.736-1(a)(6).

C. TECHNICAL TERMINATIONS — PRIOR LAW

Former section 708(b) provided that a termination occurred when there was a sale of exchange of 50% of more of the total interest in partnership capital and profits within a twelve-month period. The technical termation rules were repleased as of tax year 2018.

Chapter 10

MERGER AND DIVISION OF PARTNERSHIPS

A. MERGER OF PARTNERSHIPS
Read § 708(b) and Reg. 1.708-1(a)-(c)(3).

Section 708(b)(2)(A) provides an economical statement of what happens when partnerships merge. Read it. Congress obviously expected the subject to be a particularly simple one, and on the whole, they were right. The ruling that follows is the first major administrative pronouncement (aside from the Regulations) and is consistent with the theme of simplicity and indifference to form.

REV. RUL. 68-289
1968-1 C.B.314

Where three partnerships merged, the terminating partnerships are treated as having contributed all of their assets and transferred their liabilities to the continuing partnership in exchange for interests in such partnership that are distributed to the respective partners of the terminating partnerships in liquidation of heir interests.

Basis of the partnership interests acquired in the resulting partnership is determined under section 732(b) of the Internal Revenue Code of 1954.

Advice has been requested whether, under the circumstances described below, assets and liabilities of terminating partnerships, P1 and P2, are treated as having been distributed to the respective partners in liquidation and such assets and liabilities considered as subsequently recontributed by the respective partners to P3, the resulting partnership.

As of December 31, 1965, P1, P2, and P3 were limited partnerships engaged in the oil and gas business.

A and B, the only general partners, each owns a 20 percent interest in capital and profits of the three partnerships. The limited partners in P1 and P2 are also the limited partners in P3.

On January 1, 1966, in accordance with a written agreement, the three existing partnerships merged into one partnership with P3 contributing the greatest dollar value of assets.

In accordance with section 708(b)(2)(A) of the Internal Revenue Code of 1954 and section 1.708-1(b)(2)(i) of the Income Tax Regulations, P3 is the resulting partnership and P1 and P2 are considered terminated.

Accordingly, P3 is the resulting partnership and PI and P2 are treated as having contributed all of their respective assets and transferred their liabilities to P3 in exchange for a partnership interest. P1 and P2 are thereafter considered terminated and their respective partners are considered to have received in liquidation partnership interests in P3 with a basis to them as determined under section 732(b) of the Code.

NOTES

1. **Basis effects**. Thereafter, in Rev. Rul. 77-458, 1977-2 C.B. 220, the government in effect announced, unsurprisingly, that the continuing partnership takes a carryover basis in the disappearing partnerships' assets. Thus inside basis continues unchanged, consistent with the general theme that nothing happened except for a change of form.

2. **Is there always a surviving partnership?** Not necessarily. For example, if three law firms of identical size combined and there were no overlapping partners, there would be no surviving partnership, merely a new, resulting one. *See* Reg. § 1.708-1(b)(2)(i).

REV. RUL. 90-17
1990-1 C.B. 119

Issue

If a partnership resulting from a partnership merger is considered a continuation of one of the merging partnerships under section 708(b)(2)(A) of the Internal Revenue Code, do liquidating distributions by the other merging partnerships of 50 percent or more of the capital and profits interests in the resulting partnership cause the resulting partnership to terminate under section 708(b)(1)(B) because of the application of section 761(e)?

Facts

A and B each owned a 50 percent interest in RP, a partnership having assets worth $500x. B and C each owned a 50 percent interest in MP1, a partnership having assets worth $400x. D and E each owned a 50 percent interest in MP2, a partnership having assets worth $100x. For business reasons independent of federal income tax consequences, the parties agreed to merge RP, MP1, and MP2. The merger was effected by each merging partnership contributing its assets to the resulting partnership in exchange for an interest in the resulting partnership. With respect to the interests in the resulting partnership RP received 50 percent, MP1 received 40 percent, and MP2 received 10 percent. The interests in the resulting partnership were then distributed proportionately to the respective partners of RP, MP1 and MP2. After the merger transaction, the interests in the resulting partnership were held, 25 percent by A, 45 percent by B, 20 percent by C, and 5 percent each by D and by E.

Law and Analysis

Section 708(a) of the Code provides that an existing partnership shall be considered as continuing until such time as it is deemed terminated under section 708(b).

Section 708(b)(1) of the Code provides rules of general application governing the termination of partnerships. Section 708(b)(1)(B) provides that a partnership shall be considered terminated if, within a 12-month period, there is a sale or exchange of 50 percent or more of the total interest in partnership capital and profits.

Section 708(b)(2) of the Code provides rules of special application governing the termination of partnerships involved in mergers, consolidations, and divisions. Section 708(b)(2)(A) provides that, in the case of a merger or consolidation of two or more partnerships, the resulting partnership shall be a continuation of any merging or consolidating partnership whose members own an interest of more than 50 percent in the capital and profits of the resulting partnership.

Section 1.708-1(b)(2)(i) of the Income Tax Regulations provides that, if a resulting partnership can, under section 708(b)(2)(A) of the Code, be considered a continuation of more than one of the merging or consolidating partnerships, it shall be considered the continuation of the partnership that is credited with the contribution of the greatest dollar value of assets to the resulting partnership. Any other merging or consolidating partnership shall be considered as terminated.

Section 761(e) of the Code, which was added by the Tax Reform Act of 1984, section 75(b), 1984-3 C.B. (Vol. 1) 1, 102, provides that, except as otherwise provided in Regulations, for purposes of section 708, any distribution of an interest in a partnership (not otherwise treated as an exchange) shall be treated as an exchange.

In Rev. Rul. 68-289, 1968-1 C.B. 314, three partnerships, P1, P2, and P3 are merged. All three partnerships have the same partners and, therefore, under section 708(b)(2)(A) of the Code, the partnership resulting from the merger could be treated as the continuations of either P1, P2 or P3. However, because P3 contributes the greatest dollar value of assets, the resulting partnership is considered the continuation of P3, P1 and P2 are treated as having first transferred their assets and liabilities to P3 in exchange for partnership interests and then as having distributed the P3 interests in liquidation.

Rev. Rul. 77-458, 1977-2 C.B. 220, considers the proposed merger of ten partnerships, P1-P10. These partnerships all have the same equal partners, A and B. Under the plan of merger P2-P10 will transfer all of their assets and liabilities to P1 (the largest partnership by dollar value of assets) in exchange for partnership interests in P1. P2-P10 will then distribute their interests in P1 to A and B. Rev. Rul. 77-458 concludes that the partnership resulting from the merger of P1-P10 will be considered the continuation of P1 because P1 will contribute the greatest dollar value of assets to the resulting partnership.

Under section 708(b)(2)(A) of the Code, the partnership resulting from the merger of RP, MP1, and MP2 can be considered the continuation of either RP or MP1. This is because both the members of RP (A and B) and the members of MP1 (B and C) become the owners of more than 50 percent of the capital and profits interests in the resulting partnership. In accordance with section 1.708-1(b)(2)(i) of the Regulations, however, the resulting partnership is the continuation of RP, the partnership that contributes the greatest dollar value of assets ($500x).

Consistent with the analysis in Rev. Rul. 68-289, MP1 and MP2 are considered to have contributed their assets to RP in exchange for ownership interests in RP. MP1 and MP2 then liquidate and distribute their assets, the RP interests, to their partners. Because the RP partnership interests are received 40 percent by MP1 and 10 percent by MP2, a total of 50 percent of the RP interests is distributed in the course of the merger. If section 761(e) of the Code causes the distributions to be treated as exchanges to which section 708(b)(1)(B) applies, RP will terminate.

The question thus presented is whether sections 761(e) and 708(b)(1)(B) of the Code have the effect of adding an additional requirement to section 708(b)(2)(A), namely, that fewer than 50 percent of the interests in the resulting partnership are distributed in the merger.

Section 708(b)(2)(A) of the Code applies only to mergers and consolidations. Together with section 1.708-1(b)(2)(i) of the Regulations, it provides the exclusive means for deciding whether a partnership involved in a merger will terminate. Section 708(b)(2)(A) does not define the term "merger." However, as illustrated in Rev. Rul. 68-289 and Rev. Rul. 77-458, a merger includes the distribution by the terminating partnerships of interests in the resulting partnership. Thus, section 708(b)(2)(A) is a statute that creates a specific rule for a particular transaction, a merger, and that transaction includes the distribution of resulting partnership interests.

Paragraphs (1) and (2) of section 708(b) set forth, respectively, a general rule on the termination of partnerships and specific rules on partnership terminations where a partnership merger, consolidation, or division is involved. The specific rules are clearly exceptions to the general rule and intended to override the general rule in the limited circumstances to which they apply. Even if this relationship were not clear from the provisions themselves, a basic principle of statutory construction is that a specific statutory provision, like section 708(b)(2), is not controlled or nullified by a more general one, like section 708(b)(1), unless that result is clearly intended. *Bulova Watch Co. v. United States,* 365 U.S. 753 (1961).

The legislative history of section 708(b)(1)(B) neither states nor implies a congressional intent that the provisions of section 708(b)(1)(B) take precedence over the partnership merger rules under section 708(b)(2)(A). *See S.* Rep. No. 1622, 83d Cong., 2d Sess. 388 (1954), and

H.R. Rep. No. 2543, 83d Cong., 2d Sess. 61 (1954). Nor does the legislative history of section 761(e) state or imply a congressional intent to change the relationship between the provisions of sections 708(b)(1)(B) and 708(b)(2)(A). . .

In other words, the purpose of the exception contained in section 708(b)(2)(A) of the Code and section 1.708-1(b)(2)(i) of the Regulations is to provide for the continuation of one of the merging partnerships as the resulting partnership if the 50 percent test of those provisions is met, notwithstanding the provisions of the general rule of section 708(b)(1). Consistent with this purpose, a resulting (continuing) partnership in a merger to which section 708(b)(2)(A) applies is, as to the elements of the merger itself, excepted from the application of the terminal ion provisions of section 708(b)(1).

Since section 761(e) of the Code cannot cause a termination of a partnership except through its effect on the term "exchange" in section 708(b)(1)(B), and since a resulting partnership in a merger to which section 708(b)(2)(A) applies is excepted from the application of section 708(b)(1) as to the elements of the merger itself, section 761(e) cannot cause the termination of the resulting partnership merely by virtue of its section 708(b)(2) merger.

Thus, the distribution of a total of 50 percent of the RP interests by MP1 and MP2 during the course of the merger will not cause a termination of RP under section 708(b)(I)(B) of the Code.

Holding

In a partnership merger, if the resulting partnership is considered a continuation of one of the merging partnerships under section 708(b)(2)(A), liquidating distributions by the other merging partnerships of 50 percent or more of the capital and profits interest in the resulting partnership do not cause the resulting partnership to terminate under section 708(b)(1)(B).

NOTES

1. **Impact on Taxable Year.** Observe how the taxable year of the terminating partnership ends on its termination, thereby dumping the income or loss of the disappearing firm into the partners' laps on the spot. Reg. § 1.708-1(b)(1)(iii). By contrast, the continuing partnership (if there is one) just steams along using its normal tax period. *Id.* This could result in bunching a good deal of income if the terminating partnership had a fiscal year such as January 31 and it terminated, say, on December 1 of the prior year.

2. **Form of Merger or consolidation.** The default treatment of any merger or consolidation is the so-called "assets-over" method under which the terminated partnership is deemed to have contributed its assets to the resulting partnership in exchange for interests in the resulting partnership in liquidation of the terminated partnership. However, this can be avoided if the partners of the terminated partnership in fact receive their partnership's assets and then contribute them to the resulting partnership. This is known as the "assets-up" method. Reg. §1.708-1(c)(3). It is the only form that will not be treated as "assets over."

PROBLEM 10-1

What would be the proper tax accounting result when a cash method partnership merges into an accrual-method partnership at a time when the cash method partnership had substantial accounts receivable? If this creates a problem, how might it be solved?

PROBLEM 10-2

The equal XY partnership is owned by X and Y. C and D are equal members of the CD partnership. All parties are on the calendar year. The partnerships merge on September 30, year 1, and form the XYCD partnership After the merger, the partners have capital and profits interests as follows: X, 30 percent; Y, 30 percent; C, 20 percent; and D, 20 percent.

1) Which, if any, partnership is the survivor?

2) Does the taxable year of either party close, and if so which one and when?

3) Must either partnership file a short year return? If so, which one?

4) Can the members of either partnership elect the assets-up method to account for any termination that might have taken place?

5) What would be the difference in a) if X, Y, C and D each owned 25% of the capital and profits of XYCD?

6) Would it matter if in "(5)" X and Y contributed most of the property that XYCD got?

7) When value of property is determined for purposes of determining contributions, how does one handle liabilities? Are assets determined using book or market values?

B. DIVISION OF A PARTNERSHIP

Reg. § 1.708-1(d) provides the road map. The basic rule is that upon the division of a partnership (the "divided partnership") into two or more partnerships, the greater resulting partnership (the "resulting partnership") is treated as the continuation of the divided partnership and is saddled with the elections the predecessor may have made as well as with the predecessor's inside basis in its remaining assets.

The partners who are considered to have moved to the resulting partnership are deemed to have received their interests via a liquidating distribution from the divided partnership of interests in the resulting partnership. This is known as the "assets-over" model.

The "assets-over" model applies absent a decision to use the "assets-up" model. In the "assets-up" model, the divided partnership actually distributes assets to the departing former partners, which partners in turn contribute the assets into the resulting partnership. Reg. § 1.708-1(d)(3).

Note that this is just a broad brush description.

PROBLEM 10-3

Architecture Partners is a 100 member architecture firm, each of whom has precisely a 1% interest in the capital and profits of the firm. There has been recent dissatisfaction among the members of the firm. What are the implications of the following proposals?

1) All the partners go off their own. How will each partner be taxed? The partnership sells all its assets and distributes the cash proceeds to the partners.

b) 51 of the partners form a new partnership and 49 of them form a different new partnership.

176

c) Same as b) and the form of the transaction is that the original ("divided") partnership distributes assets to the 49 partners who form their own partnership. Will the form of the distribution be respected, or is there some other tax model that is superimposed on the transaction? *See* Reg. § 1.708-1(d)(3)(ii)(A).

d) The firm breaks into two partnership, each of which has 50 partners, but one has more assets by value than the other. Which, if either, is the survivor? *See* Reg. § 1.708-1(d)(4)(i).

Chapter 11

DEATH OF A PARTNER

One of several things can happen to a partnership interest when one of the partners dies: the interest can pass automatically to a successor in interest, such as a joint tenant; the interest can pass to the estate; or, it can pass automatically to another person or persons under a buy-sell contract of some sort. In default of an affirmative act, it will pass to the decedent's estate by law, and the estate will step into the decedent's shoes. Thereafter, the estate may distribute the interest to an heir, sell the interest, or liquidate the interest in exchange for distributions from the partnership. Recall from your introductory tax course that a decedent's spouse can file a joint return with the decedent's executor or administrator for the year of death. § 6013(a)(3).

A. PARTNERSHIP INCOME

1. GENERALLY
Read § 706(c).

As a matter of state law, the death of a general partner dissolves a general partnership, but does not necessarily mean that it is obligated to wind up its affairs and go out of business. UPA § 31. The remaining partners can immediately reinstate the partnership, and in any event the technical dissolution will not cause a § 708 termination. The state law rules are more generous for limited partnerships. *See* RULPA § 801. Thus, in a partnership consisting of more than two partners, whether it is a general or limited partnership, the entity typically continues along, despite the funeral.

Section 706(c)(2)(A) provides that the taxable year of a partnership will close with respect to a partner whose entire interest in the partnership terminates, whether by death, liquidation, or otherwise. This means that a deceased partner's share of partnership items actually earned up to the date of death are taxed to the decedent on his final return, and any items allocated to the period after death will be taxed to the decedent's estate or to a successor in interest. For example, if a calendar year partner to dies on August 5, year 1, and her partnership's year ended on June 30, year 1, her final return will include the partnership's income through June 30, year 1, as well as the short period results for June 30 through August 5, year 1. The rest of the partner's distributive share will be reported by her estate or successor in interest, because the estate or successor is the owner of the partnership interest on the last day of the partnership's taxable year. Reg. § 1.706-1(c)(3)(ii). Returning to the example, the deceased partner's successor, administrator, or executor will report the remaining (post-August 5) income in its return.

To illustrate: A, who is unmarried, is a member of the ABC accounting partnership, which uses the cash method. She and the partnership are both calendar year taxpayers. A died on October 9 of year 1. Although her estate succeeds to her interest (there being no provision for a buyout of her interest), A's own final return will include the partnership's income up to her death in October. A's estate will report the partnership's year 1 income from the date of death on October 9 to the end of year 1 (and as long as the estate remains a partner).

Absent an automatic successor, the estate will succeed to the partnership interest, and, therefore, it is the estate that will report the post-death short year's income, and if the estate is probated quickly enough, such that the heir gets the interest by the end of the partnership's tax year, the heir will report the income earned after inheriting the interest.

PROBLEM 11-1

A was a calendar year member of the cash method ABC partnership, which is also on the calendar year. A was married to Dee. A died on March 31, year one. The estate was wound up on November 30, year one, at which time Dee inherited A's partnership interest. The partnership was reinstated under local law on A's death.

1) For what period of year one is A attributed partnership income? *See* § 443(a)(2) and Reg. § 1.706-1(c)(3)(ii).

2) Does the partnership's tax year close as a result of A's death?

3) Will the apportionment of income to A be by a closing of the books method or a daily proration method?

4) For what period is the estate attributed partnership income?

5) For what period, if any, does Dee report income from the partnership?

6) Same as e) but what if she were an automatic taker?

7) How would result as to Dee differ if she did not receive her partnership interest until the middle of year two?

2. PROBLEM OF LOST DEDUCTIONS

If there is no advance planning, all of the partnership's post-death period income appears on the estate's income tax return. If the partnership had a major loss, the loss is likely to be worthless on the estate's return because estates rarely have large amounts of income. With a little advance planning, these losses can be salvaged by, for example, making the spouse the automatic successor to the interest (for example, by a designation in the partnership agreement shifting the interest to the spouse at the date of death) and having the interim loss reported on the spouse's joint return filed with the decedent partner, or by having an automatic buy-sell arrangement so that at death the interest passes instantly to the other partners. *See* Reg. § 1.706-1(c)(3)(iii). There might also be a termination of the entire partnership by prearrangement. The following example is a synopsis of *Hesse v. Commissioner*, 74 T.C. 1307 (1980).

To illustrate: Mr. A, who is married, is an equal member of the ABC real estate partnership. A and ABC are calendar year taxpayers. A dies on July 16, year one. The partnership has a $300,000 loss for the year. Because the estate cannot file a joint return with Mrs. A, the estate alone, not A or his widow, gets the portion of A's post-death share of the $100.000 loss from ABC. Had A's interest been immediately sold to B and C the loss would have been reported on the returns of B and C. Relief with respect to losses that an estate cannot use is available under § 642(h), which provides that if, on the termination of an estate (or trust) there is an unused NOL carryover under § 172 or, for the last taxable year of the estate (or trust) deductions exceed gross income, the carryover or excess deduction will be allowed to the beneficiary who succeeds to the property of the estate or trust. However, the NOL or excess deduction cannot be carried back.

B. ESTATE TAXES

The partnership interest is appraised and assigned a fair market value, not reduced by liabilities, as of the date of death for federal estate tax purposes. § 1014 (basis). Estate taxes are imposed net of liabilities, including partnership liabilities, for otherwise the estate tax would be exaggerated. § 2053(a)(4). The gross estate includes income in respect of a decedent (IRD), but IRD items are subtracted from basis to the extent they were previously included in valuing the partnership interest, consistent with the general principle that IRD items do not get a new basis at the date of death, even though they are included in the decedent's gross estate. § 1014(c). For income tax purposes, IRD items have a zero basis. Items of income in respect of a decedent are taxed to their actual payee, which may be the estate or some other distributee. Recognizing that estate and income taxation of the same dollars is too harsh, § 691(c) grants the recipient of the IRD an income tax deduction for the increase in estate taxes attributable to the inclusion of the IRD items in the gross estate.

To illustrate: If the cash method ABC partnership accrued $99 of unpaid income in the year during which A's death occurred, so that A died with a right to $33 of IRD, the estate tax value of A's partnership interest would be augmented by that $33, and that value would be subject to federal estate taxation. However, as noted above, IRD items always have a zero basis, and § 1014 does not apply to them. It is therefore necessary to reduce the estate taxed appraised value of A's partnership interest by $33 when determining the basis of the partnership interest after A's death. Section 691(c) lets A deduct the estate taxes on the $33.

Section 753 assures that § 736(a) payments to a decedent's successor in interest are always IRD. That seems entirely reasonable, as they are clearly income when held by the decedent.

QUICK'S TRUST v. COMMISSIONER
54 T.C. 1336 (1971), *aff'd per curiam.* 444 F.2d 90 (8th Cir. 1971)

Opinion

When Quick died he was an equal partner in a partnership which had been in the business of providing architectural and engineering services. In 1957, the partnership had ceased all business activity except the collection of outstanding accounts receivable. These receivables, and some cash, were the only assets of the partnership. Since partnership income was reported on the cash basis, the receivables had a zero basis.

Upon Quick's death in 1960, the estate became a partner with Maguolo and remained a partner until 1965 when it was succeeded as a partner by petitioner herein [*i.e.*, the trust. Ed.]. The outstanding accounts receivable were substantial in amount at that time. In its 1960 return, the partnership elected under section 754 to make the adjustment in the basis of the partnership property provided for in section 743(b) and to allocate that adjustment in accordance with section 755. On the facts of this case, the net result of this adjustment was to increase the basis of the accounts receivable to the partnership from zero to an amount slightly less than one-half of their face value. if such treatment was correct, it substantially reduced the amount of the taxable income to the partnership from the collection of the accounts receivable under section 743(b) and the estate and the petitioner herein were entitled to the benefit of that reduction.

The issue before us is whether the foregoing adjustment to basis was correctly made. Its resolution depends upon the determination of the basis to the estate of its interest in the partnership, since section 743(b)(1) allows only an "increase [in] the adjusted basis of the partnership property by the excess of the basis to the transferee partner of his interest in the partnership over his proportionate share of the adjusted basis of the partnership property." This in turn depends upon whether, to the extent that "the basis to the transferee partner" reflects an interest in underlying accounts receivable arising out of personal services of the deceased partner, such interest constitutes income in respect of a decedent under section 691(a)(1) and (3). In such event, section 1014(c) comes into play and prohibits equating the basis of Quick's partnership interest with the fair market value of that interest at the time of his death under section 1014(a).

Petitioner argues that the partnership provisions of the Internal Revenue Code of 1954 adopted the entity theory of partnership, that the plain meaning of those provisions, insofar as they relate to the question of basis, requires the conclusion that the inherited partnership interest is separate and distinct from the underlying assets of the partnership, and that, therefore, section 691, and consequently section 1014(c), has no application herein.

Respondent counters with the assertion that the basis of a partnership interest is determined under section 742 by reference to other sections of the Code. He claims that, by virtue of section 1014(c), section 1014(a) does not apply to property which is classified as a right to receive income in respect of a decedent under section 691 and that the interest of the estate and of petitioner in the proceeds of the accounts receivable of the partnership falls within this classification. He emphasizes that, since the accounts receivable represent money earned by the performance of personal services, the collections thereon would have been taxable to the decedent, if the partnership had been on the accrual basis, or to the estate and to petitioner if the decedent had been a cash basis sole proprietor. Similarly, he points out that if the business had been conducted by a corporation, the collections on the accounts receivable would have been fully taxable, regardless of Quick's death.

Respondent concludes that no different result should occur simply because a cash basis partnership is interposed.

The share of a general partner's successor in interest upon his death in the collections by a partnership on accounts receivable arising out of the rendition of personal services constituted income in respect of a decedent under the 1939 Code. *United States v. Ellis*, 264 F.2d 325 (C.A. 2, 1959); *Riegelman's Estate v. Commissioner*, 253 F.2d 315 (C.A. 2, 1958), *affirming* 27 T.C 833 (1957). Petitioner ignores these decisions, apparently on the ground that the enactment of comprehensive provisions dealing with the taxation of partnerships in the 1954 Code and what it asserts is "the plain meaning" of those provisions render such decisions inapplicable in the instant case. We disagree.

The partnership provisions of the 1954 Code are comprehensive in the sense that they are detailed. But this does not mean that they are exclusive, especially where those provisions themselves recognize the interplay with other provisions of the Code. Section 742 specifies:

> "The basis of an interest in a partnership acquired other than by contribution shall be determined under part II of subchapter O (sec. 1011 and following)." With the exception of section 722, which deals with the basis of a contributing partner's interest and which has no applicability herein, this is the only section directed toward the question of the initial determination of the basis of a partnership interest. From the specification of section 742, one is thus led directly to section 1014 and by subsection (c) thereof directly to section 691. Since, insofar as this case is concerned, section 691 incorporates the provisions and legal underpinning of its predecessor (sec. 126 of the 1939 Code) we are directed back to a recognition, under the 1954 Code, of the decisional effect of *United States v. Ellis*, supra, and *Riegelman's Estate v. Commissioner*, supra.

Thus, to the extent that a "plain meaning" can be distilled from the partnership provisions of the 1954 Code, we think that it is contrary to petitioner's position. In point of fact, however, we hesitate to rest our decision in an area such as is involved herein exclusively on such linguistic clarity and purity. See *David A. Foxman*, 41 T.C. 535, 551 fn. 9 (1964), *aff'd.* 352 F.2d 466 (C.A. 3, 1965). However, an examination of the legislative purpose reinforces our reading of the statute. Section 751, dealing with unrealized receivables and inventory items, is included in subpart D of subchapter K, and is labeled "Provisions Common to Other Subparts." Both the House and Senate committee reports specifically state that income rights relating to unrealized receivables or fees are regarded "as severable from the partnership interest and as subject to the same tax consequences which would be accorded an individual entrepreneur." See H. Rept. No. 1337, 83d Cong., 2d Sess., p. 71 (1954); S. Rept. No. 1622, 83d Cong., 2d Sess., p. 99 (1954). And the Senate committee report adds the following significant language:

> THE HOUSE BILL PROVIDES THAT A DECEDENT PARTNER'S SHARE OF UNREALIZED RECEIVABLES ARE [sic] TO BE TREATED AS INCOME IN RESPECT OF A DECEDENT. Such rights to income are to be taxed to the estate or heirs when collected, with an appropriate adjustment for estate taxes. * * * YOUR COMMITTEE'S BILL AGREES SUBSTANTIALLY WITH THE HOUSE IN THE TREATMENT DESCRIBED ABOVE but also provides that other income apart from unrealized receivables is to be treated as income in respect of a decedent.

In light of the foregoing, the deletion of a provision in section 743 of the House bill Which specifically provided that the optional adjustment to basis of partnership property should not be made with respect to unrealized receivables is of little, if any, significance. H.R. 8300, 83d Cong., 2d Sess., sec. 743(e) (1954) (introduced print). The fact that such deletion was made without comment either in the Senate or Conference Committee reports indicates that the problem was covered by other sections and that such a provision was therefore unnecessary. Similarly, the specific reference in section 753 to income in respect of a decedent cannot be given an exclusive characterization. That section merely states that certain distributions in liquidation under section 736(a) shall be treated as income in respect of a decedent. It does not state that no other amounts can be so treated.

Many of the assertions of the parties have dealt with the superstructure of the partnership provisions-assertions based upon a technical and involuted analysis of those provisions dealing with various adjustments and the treatment to be accorded to distributions after the basis of the partnership has been determined. But, as we have previously indicated (see pp. 1340-1341, *supra*), the question herein involves the foundation, not the Superstructure, i.e., what is the basis of petitioner's partnership interest?

Petitioner asserts that a partnership interest is an "asset separate and apart from the individual assets of the partnership" and that the character of the accounts receivable disappears into the character of the partnership interest, With the result that such interest cannot, in whole or in part, represent a right to receive income in respect of a decedent.

In making such an argument, petitioner has erroneously transmuted the so-called partnership "entity" approach into a rule of law which allegedly precludes fragmentation of a partnership interest. But it is clear that even the "entity" approach should not be inexorably applied under all circumstances. *See* H. Rept. No. 2543, 83d Cong., 2d Sess., p. 59 (1954). Similarly, the fact that a rule of nonfragmentation of a partnership interest (except to the extent that the statute otherwise expressly provides) may govern sales of such an interest to third parties (*cf. Donald L. Evans*, 54 T.C. 40 (1970)) does not compel its application in all situations where such an interest is transferred. In short, a partnership interest is not, as petitioner suggests, a unitary res, incapable of further analysis.

A partnership interest is a property interest, and an intangible one at that. A property interest can often be appropriately viewed as a bundle of rights. Indeed, petitioner suggests this viewpoint by pointing out that the partnership interest herein is "merely a right to share in the profits and surplus of the Partnership." That partnership interest had value only insofar as it represented a right to receive the cash or other property of the partnership. Viewed as a bundle of rights, a major constituent element of that interest was the right to share in the proceeds of the accounts receivable as they were collected. This right was admittedly not the same as the right to collect the accounts receivable; only the partnership had the latter right. But it does not follow from this dichotomy that the right of the estate to share in the collections merged into the partnership interest. Nothing in the statute compels such a merger. Indeed, an analysis of the applicable statutory provisions points to the opposite conclusion. Accordingly, we hold that section 691(a)(1) and (3) applies and that the right to share in the collections from the accounts receivable must be considered a right to receive income in respect of a decedent. Consequently, section 1014(c) also applies and the basis of the partnership interest must be reduced from the fair market value thereof at Quick's death. The measure of that reduction under section 1014 is the extent to which that value includes the fair market value of a one-half interest in the proceeds of the zero basis partnership accounts receivable. *See* sec. 1.742-1, Income Tax Regs. It follows that the optional adjustment to basis made by the partnership under section 743(b) must be modified accordingly and that respondent's determination as to the amount of additional income subject to the tax should be sustained.

Petitioner would have us equate the absence of statutory language specifically dealing with the problem herein and purported inferences from tangential provisions with an intention on the part of Congress entirely to relieve from taxation an item that had previously been held subject to tax. We would normally be reluctant to find that Congress indirectly legislated so eccentrically. *See* separate opinion in *Henry McK. Haserot*, 46 T.C. 864, 877 (1966), *affirmed sub nom. Commissioner v. Stickney*, 399 F.2d 828 (C.A. 6, 1968). In any event, as we have previously indicated, we think the enacted provisions prevent us from so doing herein. [The portion of the opinion concerning the taxability of the estate is omitted. Ed.] Decisions will be entered under Rule 50.

NOTE

Assuming the election was in force at the date of death, § 754 will cause a § 743(b) adjustment of the partnership's assets to reflect the § 1014 set-up or step-down in outside basis at death. However, this process becomes curious in a community property state if the surviving spouse already owns half the partnership interest under the local community property laws. In such cases, § 1014(b)(6) will automatically adjust the survivor's interest to a fair market value at death (or optional valuation date) basis. Will the survivor also share in the § 743(b) adjustment?

REV. RUL. 79-124
1979-1 C.B. 224

Issue

What is the effect of section 743(b) of the Internal Revenue Code of 1954 under the circumstances described below?

Facts

A, a domiciliary of a community property state, was a member of a partnership at the time of A's death. Under state law the interest in the partnership was community property of A and A's spouse, B, but B was not a member of the partnership under state law. The election provided by section 754 of the Code was in effect with respect to the partnership for 1976, the year in which A's death occurred.

One-half of the partnership interest that was owned by A and B as community property was transferred to A's estate at A's death and was included in A's gross estate for federal estate tax purposes. A's estate was substituted by the partnership as a successor partner for purposes of administering the estate. B was not substituted as a successor partner but continued to own one-half of the partnership [as] a member of the partnership under state law.

Law and Analysis

Section 754 of the Code provides, in part, that if a partnership files an election in accordance with Regulations prescribed by the Secretary of Treasury, the basis of partnership property shall be adjusted in the case of a transfer of a partnership interest in the manner provided in section 743. Such election shall apply with respect to all transfers of interest in the partnership during the taxable year with respect to which such election was filed and for all subsequent years.

Section 743(b) of the Code provides that if the election under section 754 is in effect, in the case of a transfer of an interest in a partnership by sale or exchange or upon the death of a partner, the partnership shall (1) increase the adjusted basis of its property by the excess of the basis to the transferee partner of the partner's interest in the partnership over the partner's proportionate share of the adjusted basis of the partnership property, or (2) decrease the adjusted basis of its property by the excess of the transferee partner's proportionate share of the adjusted basis of partnership property over the basis of the partner's interest in the partnership. Such increase or decrease is an adjustment to the basis of partnership property with respect to the transferee partner only.

Section 1014(a) of the Code provides, in part, that the basis of property in the hands of a person acquiring the property from a decedent or to whom the property passed from a decedent shall, if not sold, exchanged, or otherwise disposed of before the decedent's death by such person, be the fair market value of the property at the date of the decedent's death.

Section 1014(b)(6) of the Code provides that property which represents the surviving spouse's one-half share of property held by the decedent and the surviving spouse under the community property laws of any state, or possession of the United States or of any foreign country, shall be considered to have been acquired from or to have passed from the decedent if at least one-half of the whole of the community interest in such property was includable in determining the value of the decedent's gross estate for purposes of the federal estate tax.

Because one-half of the partnership interest owned by A and B as community property was included in A's gross estate for federal estate tax purposes, B's share of the partnership interest is considered, under section 1014(b)(6) of the Code, to have been acquired from A upon A's death. A's half of the partnership interest was actually transferred to A's estate at A's death. Therefore, the basis of the entire partnership interest in the hands of A's estate and B is to be determined in accordance with section 1014(a). In addition, for purposes of section 743(b), both A's community interest and B's community interest in the partnership interest are considered to have been transferred, upon the death of A, to A's estate and to B respectively.

Holding

Adjustments to the basis of partnership properties under section 743(b) of the Code are to be made in respect of the portion of such properties that is allocable to the entire interest in the partnership that was owned by A and B as community property immediately preceding the death of A. Furthermore, the same result would apply if B predeceased A.

PROBLEM 11-2

D was an equal member of the cash-method ABCD partnership, which has no § 754 election in force. His capital account and outside basis were $100. His share of ABCD's value was $200. The share includes accounts receivable with a basis of $0 and a value of $40.

1) Is the basis of his capital account adjusted as the result of his death? *See* Reg. § 1.704-1(b)(2)(iv)(f)(5).

2) What is the estate tax value of his interest?

3) What is the estate's outside basis after he dies?

4) What tax benefit will the person who collects the cash payments from the receivables get?

5) Would a § 754 election cause an increase the in estate's basis in the receivables?

6) Should depreciation recapture potentially be entitled to a basis step-up?

C. OTHER ESTATE TAX ISSUES

1. ESTATE FREEZE

The federal estate tax basically falls on the value of a deceased taxpayer's property held at death. § 2001. The estate tax is buttressed by a federal gift tax which falls on inter vivos transfers. § 2501. (If there were no gift tax, people would avoid the estate tax by the simple expedient of making lavish gifts during their lives.) The taxes are integrated, and the rates of both taxes are now as high as 45%, so avoiding federal transfer taxes on interests in family businesses is a matter of great concern to business owners. An older partner's financial planners are likely to worry about the estate tax burdens that could arise if the partnership becomes lucrative. One instinctive reaction will be to try to devise ways to shift future appreciation in value to members of a younger generation.

The simplest planning idea has been to give away a volatile partnership interest while retaining a partnership interest which offers a preferred return. Recently, it has become popular for wealthy people to transfer assets to a family limited partnership, taking back a limited partnership interest and claiming a large (30-40%) discount on the value of the interest received. The IRS has had mixed success in court fighting these cases, and the Treasury Department has not amended the partnership anti-abuse Regulations to cover these tax-driven deals.

The primary tax planning problem nowadays will be § 2701, which, as applied to partnerships, disregards retained interests in partnerships when a partner transfers property to a spouse, a lineal descendent, or a spouse of a lineal descendent, in effect treating the retained interest as also having been given away, triggering an immediate gift tax liability. Section 2701 does not reach transfers to other people, such as nieces and nephews, nor does it reach cases where the retained interest's value is supported by "qualified payment rights," meaning payments at a fixed rate or tied to a market index of some sort, much like dividends on preferred stock. A transfer in which the transferor retains such rights is fairly easy to achieve in a corporate setting using preferred stock. It is not so easy in a partnership setting. Moreover, to use the qualified payments route, the recapitalization transactions must be sufficiently disclosed to the IRS, and the consent of other senior members must be obtained. §§ 2701(a)(3), 2701(c)(3), and 6051(c)(9), and Reg. § 25.2701-2(2)(4).

Another alternative is to wait until death and give a preferred interest to the surviving spouse and the regular interest to the beneficiaries to whom the decedent wants to shift appreciation. However, this is poor planning in the case of a large estate; the real trick is to shift value *before* death.

2. BUY-SELL AGREEMENT

When a partner dies and her interest cannot realistically be shifted to an heir, say in the case of a law partnership, there has to be a mechanism to compensate the deceased partner's estate. The Uniform Partnership Act generally grants the estate of a deceased partner a right to the net value of the partner's interest at death, plus interest. UPA § 42. The estate of a deceased limited partner generally steps into the partner's shoes and can withdraw as a member and demand a similar distribution of its share of the partnership's properties. RULPA §§ 603, 604, and 705. The partners can trump this general rule with a specified agreement as to how the estate will be paid, e.g., net asset value plus the appraised value of goodwill, an arbitrated figure, or perhaps a fixed figure. The buyer can be either the other partner(s) or the partnership itself.

Because the federal estate tax falls on the value of the decedent's estate, family business owners are motivated to minimize the fair market value of their business interests. One obvious way to do so is by obligating the business to buy up the decedent's interest at a low price. The rest of the family will be indifferent to the bargain price, because they will not share the discount with outsiders. However, if the price is low enough, it is clear that the decedent indirectly transferred value to surviving owners, who may all be family members.

Once again, the Congress, the courts, and the IRS have been forced to draw practical lines to resolve an essentially impossible question. Nevertheless, if there is a buy-sell agreement, the value it fixes generally determines the value of the interest for estate taxes as well. The following case indicates the state of the law concerning the use of buy-sell agreements to limit the value of partnership interests for federal estate tax purposes. Before reading the case, review Reg. § 20.2031-2(h). This requirement continues in force if a purchase price determined under a buy-sell agreement is to fix the value of an interest in a closely-held business.

ST. LOUIS COUNTY BANK, EXECUTOR v. UNITED STATES OF AMERICA
674 F.2d 1207 (8th Cir. 982),*rev' g and rem 'g* 511 F. Supp. 653 (E.D. Mo. 1981)

Before LAY, CHIEF JUDGE, ARNOLD, CIRCUIT JUDGE, and WOODS, DISTRICT JUDGE.

ARNOLD, JUDGE.

The government appeals the District Court's entry of summary judgment in favor of St. Louis County Bank, executor of the estate of Lee J. Sloan, in a suit brought to recover an alleged overpayment of estate taxes. . . The central question on the merits is the proper valuation of certain stock in L.J.S. Investment Company held by Mr. Sloan at the time of his death. . . .

I.

As of December 24, 1956, Lee J. Sloan owned all but one of the 466 shares of Sloan's Moving & Storage Company. The one share not owned by him belonged to his wife. On that day he made five gifts of 38 shares each (190 shares in all) to the following persons: Nina Roth (his daughter); Karl Roth (his son-in-law); and in trust for the benefit of Nancy Lee, Judy Ann, and Joy Anita Roth (his granddaughters).

Sometime after the gifts were made Sloan became concerned about the possibility that the stock might pass to persons outside the family. Sloan asked Woodside to prepare an agreement restricting the transfer of the stock. In 1964 all the shareholders entered into such an agreement, restricting inter vivos transfers of the stock to persons outside of Lee Sloan's immediate family. Under the agreement, at the death of any shareholder or at any time a shareholder wished to transfer his or her stock to someone outside the family, the company and the other shareholders had the option to purchase the shares at a price determined by a formula set out in the agreement. If the company or other family members failed to exercise their option, the shares could then be sold to someone outside the family. The formula price provided for in the agreement was ten times the average annual net earnings per share for the five years preceding the offer, adjusted to eliminate gains or losses on real estate and the income tax consequences of such gains or losses.

Until 1972 the company continued to engage in the moving, storage, and parcel-delivery business. In that year the company sold virtually all of its operating assets and changed its name to L.J.S. Investment Company. Thereafter it engaged primarily in the rental of real estate. This change in the nature of the business had a significant, adverse impact on the "value" of the stock of the company. While engaged in the moving business the company generated substantial yearly income as defined by the formula in the stock-purchase agreement. From the years 1964 to 1970 the value per share of the stock, as measured by the formula embodied in the agreement, fluctuated from a high of $1,061.15 in 1968 to a low of $597.00 in 1970. As a company engaged in the rental of real estate, however, the "value" of each share of L.J.S. Investment Company as determined by the formula went down to $0 per share in 1971, and remained at that level through 1975. This was so because L.J.S. began to show substantial net losses as defined in the stock-purchase agreement. The years after 1975 are not relevant to our discussion here.

During this time there was one death among the parties to the stock-purchase agreement, that of Karl Roth. Karl left his entire estate, including his stock, to his wife, Nina Roth, who also served as his executrix. She did not offer the shares to either the corporation or the surviving shareholders as called for in the agreement, and apparently there was no objection. At that time Karl Roth's shares could have been purchased pursuant to the agreement for $0 per share. For federal estate tax purposes his estate reported the shares at $850 per share, reflecting their adjusted book value.

At the date of Lee J. Sloan's death, May 8, 1976, he held 265 shares of L.J.S. Investment Company, a controlling interest in the company. Shortly after Sloan's death his estate offered his 265 shares to the company under the terms of the stock-purchase agreement at $0 per share. The company accepted. As a result, Sloan's daughter and granddaughters became the beneficial owners of all the stock.

Sloan's estate filed an estate tax return in February of 1977 and paid the sum of $36,383.06. On the return the 265 shares of stock were valued at $0 per share. On March 26, 1979, the Internal Revenue Service assessed deficiency of $23,179.35 based on a valuation of L.J.S. stock at $544.60 per share, their book value. At the time the total assets of L.J.S. were valued at approximately $256,000, of which $201,000 was in cash. The estate paid the deficiency, and this action followed.

The government's principal argument for reversal is that the District Court erred in granting summary judgment because there were genuine issues of fact left unresolved. When considering a motion for summary judgment a court must view the facts in the light most favorable to the party opposing the motion, and it must afford that party the benefit of all favorable inferences which may be derived from the facts contained in the pleadings, depositions. and affidavits. . . The granting of the motion is appropriate only where there is no genuine issue of material fact and where the moving party is entitled to a judgment as a matter of law. Fed. R. Civ. P. 56(c). . . . With these standards in mind we now look to the decision of the District Court.

The law of the tax consequences of restrictive agreements to purchase stock is, for the most part, well settled. Several courts of appeals have held that such agreements, if enforceable both at death and during a person's lifetime, establish the value of the stock for estate tax purposes. See *Brodrick v. Gore*, 224 F.2d 892 (10th Cir. 1955). . . . Embodied in these decisions is the rule stated in Treas. Reg. 20.2031-2(h) (1958), that (e)ven if the decedent is not free to dispose of the underlying securities at other than the option or contract price, such price will be disregarded in determining the value of the securities unless it is determined under the circumstances of the particular case that the agreement represents a bona fide business arrangement and not a device to pass the decedent's shares to the natural objects of his bounty for less than an adequate and full consideration in money or money's worth. . . .

In sum, the law is that a restrictive agreement may fix the value of property for estate tax purposes if the agreement has a bona fide business purpose and if it was not used as a tax-avoidance testamentary device.

We have no problem with the District Court's findings that the stock-purchase agreement provided for a reasonable price at the time of its adoption, and that the agreement had a bona fide business purpose – the maintenance of family ownership and control of the business. Courts have recognized the validity of such a purpose. *See Estate of Bischoff v. Commissioner,* 69 T.C. 32 (1977). . . . Here the District Court concluded that the existence of a valid business purpose necessarily excluded the possibility that the agreement was a tax-avoidance testamentary device. . . . We disagree. The fact of a valid business purpose could, in some circumstances, completely negate the alleged existence of a tax-avoidance testamentary device as a matter of law, but those circumstances are not necessarily presented here.

At the time of the agreement Lee J. Sloan had a heart condition and had previously suffered two heart attacks in the early 1960's. . . Given this fact and the fact of the family relationship between the parties to the agreement, a reasonable inference could be drawn that the agreement was testamentary in nature and a device for the avoidance of estate taxes. Similar facts were before the court in *Slocum v. United States, supra.* The court there recognized that varying inferences could be drawn from the facts surrounding the agreement, and thus left the drawing of those inferences to the trier of fact at trial. . .

We are also bothered by the fact that decedent's stock was valued by his estate for estate tax purposes at $0 when its total book value was admittedly in excess of $200,000. Appellee argues that courts should look only to the adequacy of the consideration at the time the agreement was entered into, rather than the date of decedent's death, when considering whether the agreement is a testamentary device to avoid estate taxes. *Estate of Bischoff v. Commissioner, supra,* 69 T.C. at 41 n.9. This may well be the best rule of general applicability (although appellees cite no appellate authority, and we have found none), but we think it has no application in the case at bar.

In 1964 the parties to the stock-purchase agreement adopted a formula for valuation of the stock that was admittedly reasonable at the time. However, some seven years later the assets of the moving and storage business, which was generating substantial net income as defined by the formula, were liquidated, and the proceeds transferred to an investment company, which engaged primarily in the rental of real estate. As a result of this transformation in the nature of the business, the value of the stock as determined by the formula was reduced to zero. Moreover, from all indications the decision to sell the assets of Sloan's Moving and Storage was Lee J. Sloan's and his alone. He held a majority of the stock, and there is no evidence that any of the minority shareholders took an active part in the management of the company. In light of these facts it would be unreasonable to restrict the court's inquiry to the adequacy of consideration and the conduct of the parties at the time of the agreement. The contrary rule, urged by taxpayers, may have some appeal in a situation where a wide disparity in formula price and other valuation methods, such as book value, is a result of failure of the business to generate a profit or other economic conditions outside the control of the parties to the agreement. Presumably such events would be within the contemplation of the parties to the agreement. The same cannot be said here where the nature of the business was completely transformed several years down the line.

Finally, the record reveals that at the time of Karl Roth's death the provisions of the agreement were not invoked. Under the agreement, at his death, his stock was to be offered first to the company at the formula price, and if refused, then to the other shareholders. Instead, his interest in the company passed under his will to his wife, Nina. At this point Karl Roth's shares (then numbering 43) could have been purchased at the formula price of $0 per share, though their book value was $850 per share. These events could be the basis for an inference that the agreement was being used for the purpose of passing property to members of the family other than Lee J. Sloan, and thus ultimately accomplishing a tax-avoidance purpose benefiting the estate of Lee J. Sloan.[1]

At this stage of the case we must afford the government the benefit of all favorable inferences which could have been derived from the underlying facts. The historical facts themselves were left unchallenged by the government, to be sure, but they are subject to more than one interpretation. The trier of fact at trial should decide which interpretation is more persuasive. The judgment of the District Court is reversed, and the cause is remanded for further proceedings consistent with this opinion.

It is so ordered.

NOTES

1) If continuing family control is so important to the decedent, could he not have taken care of the problem directly by bequeathing the business interest to his heirs?

2) The suppression of values has risen to a virtual art form. For a fascinating article on the subject, *see* Cooper, *A Voluntary Tax? New Perspectives on Sophisticated Estate Tax Avoidance,* 77 Colum. L. Rev. 161 (1977). Some favorite taxpayer theories for claiming low estate tax values are that: (i) the decedent held a minority interest, which has to be discounted because the interest was subject to being dominated by others in important voting matters affecting the firm; (ii) if the decedent held a large interest and it were sold, it would suffer a price discount because it would flood the market (known as the "blockage rule").

If the parties decide on a cross-purchase funded by insurance, the benefit is that the insurance proceeds will not be taxable to the policy owner or the decedent. § 101(a). Rev. Rul. 56-397,1956-2 C.B. 599. If the partnership owns the policy, the proceeds are not directly includable in the insured's estate, but they do increase the value of the decedent's partnership interest by the decedent's ratable share of the insurance proceeds unless the proceeds are explicitly excluded from the buy-sell calculation and the agreement is effective in setting values for estate tax purposes. Any such proviso should appear in the buy-sell agreement. *See Newell v. Commissioner,* 66 F.2d 102 (7th Cir. 1933).

---

[1] The adverse inference here is not that the agreement was used to benefit Karl Roth's estate. Indeed, on his estate-tax return his holdings were valued at $850 per share, their book value. Had the formula been used, his interest in the company would have been valued at $0. Dennis K. Woodside, attorney for Roth's estate as well as Lee J. Sloan and the company, stated that "it did not occur to (him) that the Stock Purchase Agreement might be used in that fashion...." Of course, the trier of fact might think that the parties' conduct at the time of Roth's death shows there was no tax-avoidance purpose. Our point is that a contrary inference may reasonably be drawn.

PROBLEM 11-3

Review Reg. § 25.2703-1 and determine whether the restrictions in the *St. Louis Bank* case would be followed under present law for purposes of suppressing estate tax values.

Chapter 12

INTRODUCTION TO THE CORPORATE INCOME TAX

The Code taxes a corporation as a separate taxpayer. It has not always been so. The first national income taxes were enacted during the Civil War by both the Union and the Confederacy. The 1864 Union version taxed corporate profits only once, either to the corporation or to its shareholders, but not both. The act imposed a flat 5% tax on the profits of certain kinds of corporations (mainly financial and transportation companies) but dividends from those companies were excludable by shareholders to the extent that the dividends came from previously taxed earnings. Most corporations paid no taxes. Instead, corporate profits were taxed to shareholders at once, even if the profits were not distributed; essentially, the income of the corporation was treated as the income of its shareholders. This would now be called a pass-through or partnership approach. The tax was held constitutional in *Collector v. Hubbard,* 79 U.S. (12 Wall) 1 (1870), though later repudiated in *Eisner v. Macomber,* 252 U.S. 189 (1920).

This first income tax was repealed after the Civil War, and in 1894 another national corporate tax was enacted, taking a different approach. It was also fully integrated with the personal income tax, which had been enacted at the same time. A small flat tax was imposed upon all individuals and corporations, and integration was achieved by simply exempting from tax all dividends paid to individual shareholders. These taxes never went into effect because the Supreme Court held the 1894 act unconstitutional as an unapportioned "direct tax" in *Pollack v. Farmers' Loan & Trust Co.,* 157 U.S. 429 (1895). Because the 1894 act was held unconstitutional in its entirety, the corporate tax was annulled as well.

In 1909, Congress enacted a tax of 1% of net earnings and imposed it solely upon corporations as an excise tax, for the privilege of conducting business in corporate form, measured by income. This time the tax was upheld in *Flint v. Stone Tracy Co.,* 220 U.S. 107 (1911), in which the Supreme Court held that the tax was an excise tax rather than an unconstitutional direct tax. Thereafter, the Sixteenth Amendment was passed in order to ensure the validity of the individual income tax. It became effective on February 25, 1913. *See Doyle v. Mitchell Bros.,* 247 U.S. 179 (1918). The 1909 tax, treating the corporation as a taxpayer taxed on its own income, set the pattern for future developments.

There was no problem of "integration" of the corporate and individual income taxes under the 1909 act because there was no individual income tax in effect at the time. After enactment of the individual tax in 1913, however, corporate income was in effect taxed twice, unlike the 1864 and 1894 acts, because individuals were taxed on corporate dividends that represented profits on which the corporation was already taxed. The problem may have arisen because the two taxes were enacted at different times and Congress simply failed to consider how the two taxes would interact.

It is certainly the case that two levels of taxation on corporate profits means that shareholders investing in corporate stock are put at a disadvantage compared to more direct investmentsbject to one level of tax, all other things being equal. The problem remains with us today, although nowadays dividends from domestic corporations are generally taxed at a maximum rate of not over 23.8% when received by individuals thanks to § 1(h). The recipient must have held the stock for more than 60 days during the 121-day period that begins 60 days before the ex-dividend date in order for the dividend to qualify for the 23.8% top rate. For middle income taxpayers the rate is 15%. §1(h)(11).

As we have seen earlier in the book, there is no problem of double taxation with partnerships, nor S corporations or limited liability companies, the last of which are considered later in this book. The integrated "double tax" on distributed corporate profits in the U.S.

probably misallocates resources, induces overuse of debt and undercapitalization with equity (stock), causes excessive and inefficient retention of corporate profits, discourages the use of the incorporated form of doing business and contributes to arguable over-taxation of income from capital.

Another anomaly concerns the taxation of capital gains. Shareholders are entitled under § 1(h) to the benefit of a limit of 20% on the top rate of tax on net capital gains plus a potential 3.8% investment tax to support health coverage, versus a top rate of 37% on ordinary income. By contrast, corporations pay the same rate on capital gain and ordinary income. Corporations that incur large capital losses can only offset them against capital gains for the same taxable year and after that, indefinitely into the future. By contrast, individual taxpayers can deduct up to $3,000 of capital losses against their other income for the year and then can carry their losses forward indefinitely under § 1212(b).

A. INCIDENCE OF THE CORPORATE INCOME TAX

Assume a world in which there is no corporate income tax. If the legislature suddenly imposed such a tax there would be a number of possible outcomes in terms of who actually bears the burden of the tax. Under one scenario, the corporation might be able to pass the tax on to consumers by marking up the price of the products or services it sells. In such a case, the incidence of the tax would be said to be on the consumer. Alternatively, the corporation might be able to cut its employees' wages. In that case, the incidence of the tax would be on the employees. Finally, if it could not make up the cost by either of these techniques, then the incidence of the tax falls on the shareholders and the burden takes the form of reduced value of the company's stock. In most cases, the incidence of the tax probably will be on some mix of consumers, shareholders and employees.

The problem is actually more complex. First, even if the corporation can mark up the price of its output to cover the tax, it may wind up selling fewer goods or services, with the adverse result that the drop in demand will be felt by either the shareholders, the employees, the consumers, or some combination of them. Also, there may be a considerable difference between the incidence of the tax in the short run as opposed to the long run. In general, it seems unlikely that the tax can be shifted in the short run to persons other than the shareholders, at least in a competitive industry, but in the long run the burden can be pushed off shareholders and onto consumers and employees in some proportion, which depends on the circumstances of the particular corporation. It may be, as Harberger contends, that in the long run, the corporate income tax is shifted to all owners of capital in the economy. There is extensive economic literature on this subject, but a shortage of firm conclusions. *See, e.g.,* C. McLure, *Must Corporate Income Be Taxed Twice? (1979);* J.G. Ballentine, *Equity, Efficiency and the United States Corporation Income Tax, AEI (1980).*

B. INTEGRATION OF CORPORATE AND SHAREHOLDER LEVEL TAXES

Business corporations and their owners, as well as economists and tax theorists, have long complained about the corporate *double tax,* on fairness and efficiency grounds. The objection is that the corporation itself pays a federal income tax on its earnings, leaving a diminished amount for distribution to its owners. When the entity does distribute its profits, those profits are taxed a second time at the shareholder level. The problem is easy.

To illustrate: Mr. Big owns 100% of the stock of the Big Book Corporation. Last year Big Book Corporation earned net profits of $1,000. Assuming for convenience that it paid a tax of $210, that would leave over $790 for distribution to Mr. Big. Assuming Mr. Big pays capital gains taxes at 20% and that Big Corporation distributed all of the profits, Mr. Big would receive

$790 and would pay a tax of $158. The total tax bill would be $368. To put it another way, the tax burden would be 36.8% of net profits. By contrast, if Mr. Big were instead a proprietor or partner, the total tax bill could reach $~~790.~~ *40.8 %* [handwritten]

Over many years, a number of proposals to remove or ameliorate this unintegrated double taxation have emerged. The reduced rate on corporate income combined with the reduced rate on qualified dividends is the 2017 tax act's remedy.

C. CORPORATE TAX BASE AND TAX RATES
Read § 11, § 55(a), (b)(1)(B), and (c), and § 59A.

Business corporations are subject to a flat rate of 21%. Corporations file an annual federal income tax return on Form 1120, reporting taxable income. Often one corporation is the parent of a constellation of subsidiary corporations, in which case it may file a so-called consolidated return, which has the practical effect of treating the affiliated group as one big corporation.

The taxable income of a corporation is determined in much the same way as for individuals, with obvious exceptions, such as the lack of deductions for personal exemptions or medical expenses. Section 291(a) imposes some special reductions, known as corporate preference items. This provision is hard to explain except as a revenue measure.

Sections 61 and 63 provide the base on which the tax is imposed. A corporation does not employ the § 62 "adjusted gross income" calculation used by individuals, nor is it subject to the Alternative Minimum Tax.

D. OPERATING VIA OVERSEAS SUBSIDIARIES

U.S. corporations that operate overseas are said to operate via "branches." Income or losses from branches are included in the corporation's U.S. income tax base just as if the branch were in another state; that is, the operating results are included currently. By contrast, operating via a foreign subsidiary that retains its business profits can result in major deferral of U.S. tax.

In order to encourage U.S. corporations to repatriot their reduced profits in foreign subsidiaries Congress passed Section 245A, which provides up to a 100% deduction for dividends received by a United States corporate shareholder from a 10 percent or greater owned foreign corporation.

COMPARISON OF THE TAX SYSTEMS OF THE UNITED STATES, THE UNITED KINGDOM, GERMANY, AND JAPAN, July 20, 1992 Joint Committee Print; JCS-13-92

Description of the United States Tax System

U.S. Taxation of Income Earned Through Foreign Corporations

U.S. persons that conduct foreign operations through a foreign corporation generally pay no U.S. tax on the income from those operations until the foreign corporation repatriates or is deemed to have repatriated its earnings to the United States. The income appears on the U.S. owner's tax return for the year that the repatriation or deemed repatriation occurs, and the United States imposes tax on it then, subject to allowance of a foreign tax credit.

Several existing regimes provide exceptions to the general rule under which U.S. tax on income earned indirectly through a foreign corporation is deferred. The primary anti-deferral regime involves rules applicable to controlled foreign corporations and their shareholders . . . Anti-deferral regimes not discussed in this pamphlet include, among others, foreign personal holding company rules, passive foreign investment company rules, and rules applicable to foreign investment companies.

Chapter 13

RECOGNITION OF THE CORPORATE FORM

A. BACKGROUND

The corporation has been a convenient rabbit in the hat of the business lawyer for many decades. As one can imagine, perhaps, not every entity that is a properly organized corporation for state law purposes will pass muster for federal income tax purposes. Corporations have often been used in artificial arrangements whose sole purpose was tax minimization, and as the following chapters will show, corporate taxation is in some measure the study of substance versus form. In cases they consider abusive, the courts have been known to characterize the corporation as a sham and to disregard its existence. On the other hand, according to the Supreme Court in *Moline Props., Inc., v. Commissioner*, 319 U.S. 436 (1943), if the formation of the corporation has a business purpose or if the corporation engages in more than insignificant business activities, it will not be treated as a sham and its separate taxable identity will be respected.

This has led to a number of close cases in which title-holding companies that were organized to avoid local usury laws were respected or disregarded on the basis of narrowly different fact patterns involving the extent to which the corporation engaged in financial transactions. It is difficult to predict exactly how such cases will come out without a careful evaluation of the facts, but in general, as long as the corporate formalities are respected and the corporation is not completely inert, the likelihood is that it will be respected as a separate entity for income tax purposes.

For many years, it was generally conceded that if a corporation could not be disregarded as a sham, then it also could not be treated as a nominee or agent. That theory was inherently illogical, because individuals often act as agents for other persons to perform such functions as collecting rent, managing property, and executing leases. When these operations are performed by individuals, there has not been any difficulty respecting their status as agents; hence it is illogical to say that a corporation cannot occupy the same status.

Note that an agent and a nominee are not the same thing. Agency is a contractual relationship under which one party, the agent, acts as a sort of delegate of another person – the principal. By contrast, a nominee is a person that holds bare legal title to property for the exclusive benefit of another party. The other party is the real party in interest, if a struggle over ownership were ever to break out, the nominee's effort to retain the property would fail. For an excellent article on this subject, *see* Miller, *The Nominee Conundrum: The Live Dummy Is Dead but the Dead Dummy Should Live!*, 34 Tax L. Rev. 213 (1979).

COMMISSIONER v. BOLLINGER
485 U.S. 340, 108 S. Ct. 1173 (1988)

[The following is a modified version of the Supreme Court syllabus. Because Kentucky's usury law limited the annual interest rate for non-corporate borrowers, lenders willing to provide money only at higher rates required borrowers to use a corporate nominee as the nominal debtor and the record titleholder of mortgaged property. Accordingly, the taxpayers, who formed a series of partnerships to develop Kentucky apartment complexes, in each instance entered into an agreement with a corporation wholly owned by respondent Bollinger, which provided that the corporation would hold title to the property as the partnership's nominee and agent solely to secure financing, that the partnership would have sole control of and responsibility for the complex, and that the partnership was the principal and owner of the property during financing, construction, and operation. All parties who had contact with the complexes, including lenders, contractors, managers, employees, and tenants, regarded the partnerships as the real owners and knew that each corporation was merely the partnerships' agent, if they were aware of the corporation at all. Income and losses from the complexes were reported on the partnerships' tax returns, and respondents reported their distributive share of the income and losses on their individual returns. Although the IRS disallowed respondents deductions for losses on the ground that they were attributable to the corporation as the owner of the property, the Tax Court held that the corporation was the partnerships' agent and should therefore be disregarded for tax purposes, and the Court of Appeals affirmed. The case then was taken to the Supreme Court.]

Justice Scalia delivered the opinion of the Court.

Petitioner, the Commissioner of Internal Revenue, challenges a decision by the United States Court of Appeals for the Sixth Circuit holding that a corporation which held record title to real property as agent for the corporation's shareholders, was not the owner of the property for purposes of federal income taxation . . . We granted certiorari . . . to resolve a conflict in the Courts of Appeals over the tax treatment of corporations purporting to be agents for their shareholders. . . .

II

For federal income tax purposes, gain or loss from the sale or use of property is attributable to the owner of the property . . . The problem we face here is that two different taxpayers can plausibly be regarded as the owner. Neither the Internal Revenue Code nor the Regulations promulgated by the Secretary of the Treasury provide significant guidance as to which should be selected. It is common ground between the parties, however, that if a corporation holds title to property as agent for a partnership, then for tax purposes the partnership and not the corporation is the owner. Given agreement on that premise, one would suppose that there would be agreement upon the conclusion as well. For each of respondents' apartment complexes, an agency agreement expressly provided that the corporation would hold such property as nominee and agent for "the partnership," App. to Pet. for Cert. 21a, n.4, and that the partnership would have sole control of and responsibility for the apartment complex. The partnership in each instance was identified as the principal and owner of the property during financing, construction, and operation. The lenders, contractors, managers, employees, and tenants – all who had contact with the development – knew that the corporation was merely the agent of the partnership, if they knew of the existence of the corporation at all. In each instance the relationship between the corporation and the partnership was, in both form and substance, an agency with the partnership as principal.

The Commissioner contends, however, that the normal indicia of agency cannot apply for tax purposes when, as here, the alleged principals are the controlling shareholders of the alleged agent corporation. That, it asserts, would undermine the principle of *Moline Properties v. Commissioner,* 319 U.S. 436, (1943), which held that a corporation is a separate taxable entity even if it has only one shareholder who exercises total control over its affairs. Obviously, *Moline's* separate-entity principle would be significantly compromised if shareholders of closely held corporations could, by clothing the corporation with some attributes of agency with respect to particular assets, leave themselves free at the end of the tax year to make a claim – perhaps even a good-faith claim – of either agent or owner status, depending upon which choice turns out to minimize their tax liability. The Commissioner does not have the resources to audit and litigate the many cases in which agency status could be thought debatable. Hence, the Commissioner argues, in this shareholder context he can reasonably demand that the taxpayer meet a prophylactically clear test of agency.

We agree with that principle, but the question remains whether the test the Commissioner proposes is appropriate. The parties have debated at length the significance of our opinion in *National Carbide Corp. v. Commissioner, supra.* In that case, three corporations that were wholly owned subsidiaries of another corporation agreed to operate their production plants as "agents" for the parent, transferring to it all profits except for a nominal sum. The subsidiaries reported as gross income only this sum, but the Commissioner concluded that they should be taxed on the entirety of the profits because they were not really agents. We agreed, reasoning first, that the mere fact of the parent's control over the subsidiaries did not establish the existence of an agency, since such control is typical of all shareholder-corporation relationships . . . and second, that the agreements to pay the parent all profits above a nominal amount were not determinative since income must be taxed to those who actually earn it without regard to anticipatory assignment, *id.,* at 435-436, 69 S. Ct., at 733-734. We acknowledged, however, that there was such a thing as "a true corporate agent . . . of [an] owner-principal," *id.,* at 437, 69 S. Ct., at 734, and proceeded to set forth four indicia and two requirements of such status, the sum of which has become known in the lore of federal income tax law as the "six National Carbide factors": "[1] Whether the corporation operates in the name and for the account of the principal, [2] binds the principal by its actions, [3] transmits money received to the principal, and [4] whether receipt of income is attributable to the services of employees of the principal and to assets belonging to the principal are some of the relevant considerations in determining whether a true agency exists. [5] If the corporation is a true agent, its relations with its principal must not be dependent upon the fact that it is owned by the principal, if such is the case. [6] Its business purpose must be the carrying on of the normal duties of an agent." *Ibid.* (footnotes omitted).

We readily discerned that these factors led to a conclusion of nonagency in National Carbide itself. There each subsidiary had represented to its customers that it (not the parent) was the company manufacturing and selling its products each had sought to shield the parent from service of legal process; and the operations had used thousands of the subsidiaries' employees and nearly $20 million worth of property and equipment listed as assets on the subsidiaries' books . . . .

The Commissioner contends that the last two National Carbide factors are not satisfied in the present case. To take the last first: The Commissioner argues that here the corporation's business purpose with respect to the property at issue was not "the carrying on of the normal duties of an agent," since it was acting not as the agent but rather as the owner of the property for purposes of Kentucky's usury law. We do not agree. It assuredly was not acting as the owner in fact, since respondents represented themselves as the principals to all parties concerned with the loans. Indeed, it was the lenders themselves who required the use of a corporate nominee. Nor does it make any sense to adopt a contrary-to-fact legal presumption that the corporation was the principal, imposing a federal tax sanction for the apparent evasion of Kentucky's usury law. To begin with, the Commissioner has not established that these transactions were an evasion. Respondents assert without contradiction that use of agency arrangements in order to permit higher interest was common practice, and it is by no means clear that the practice violated the spirit of the Kentucky law, much less its letter. It might well be thought that the borrower does not generally require usury protection in a transaction sophisticated enough to employ a corporate agent – assuredly not the normal modus operandi of the loan shark. That the statute positively envisioned corporate nominees is suggested by a provision which forbids charging the higher corporate interest rates "to a corporation, the principal asset of which shall be the ownership of a one (1) or two (2) family dwelling," Ky. Rev. Stat. § 360.025(2) (1987) – which would seem to prevent use of the nominee device for ordinary home-mortgage loans. In any event, even if the transaction did run afoul of the usury law, Kentucky, like most States, regards only the lender as the usurer, and the borrower as the victim. *See* Ky. Rev. Stat. § 360.020 (1987) (lender liable to borrower for civil penalty), § 360.990 (lender guilty of misdemeanor). Since the Kentucky statute imposed no penalties upon the borrower for allowing himself to be victimized, nor treated him as in pari delicto, but to the contrary enabled him to pay back the principal without any interest, and to sue for double the amount of interest already paid (plus attorney's fees), *see* Ky. Rev. Stat. § 360.020 (1972), the United States would hardly be vindicating Kentucky law by depriving the usury victim of tax advantages he would otherwise enjoy. In sum, we see no basis in either fact or policy for holding that the corporation was the principal because of the nature of its participation in the loans.

Of more general importance is the Commissioner's contention that the arrangements here violate the fifth *National Carbide* factor – that the corporate agent's "relations with its principal must not be dependent upon the fact that it is owned by the principal." The Commissioner asserts that this cannot be satisfied unless the corporate agent and its shareholder principal have an "arm's-length relationship" that includes the payment of a fee for agency services. The meaning of *National Carbide's* fifth factor is, at the risk of understatement, not entirely clear. Ultimately, the relations between a corporate agent and its owner-principal are always dependent upon the fact of ownership, in that the owner can cause the relations to be altered or terminated at any time. Plainly that is not what was meant, since on that interpretation all subsidiary-parent agencies would be invalid for tax purposes, a position which the *National Carbide* opinion specifically disavowed. We think the fifth *National Carbide* factor – so much more abstract than the others – was no more and no less than a generalized statement of the concern, expressed earlier in our own discussion, that the separate-entity doctrine *of Moline* not be subverted.

In any case, we decline to parse the text of *National Carbide* as though that were itself the governing statute. As noted earlier, it is uncontested that the law attributes tax consequences of property held by a genuine agent to the principal; and we agree that it is reasonable for the Commissioner to demand unequivocal evidence of genuineness in the corporation-shareholder context, in order to prevent evasion of *Moline*. We see no basis, however, for holding that unequivocal evidence can only consist of the rigid requirements (arm's-length dealing plus agency fee) that the Commissioner suggests. Neither of those is demanded by the law of agency, which permits agents to be unpaid family members, friends, or associates. *See* Restatement (Second) of Agency §§ 16, 21, 22 (1958). It seems to us that the genuineness of the agency relationship is adequately assured, and tax-avoiding manipulation adequately avoided, when the fact that the corporation is acting as agent for its shareholders with respect to a particular asset is set forth in a written agreement at the time the asset is acquired, the corporation functions as agent and not principal with respect to the asset for all purposes, and the corporation is held out as the agent and not principal in all dealings with third parties relating to the asset. Since these requirements were met here, the judgment of the Court of Appeals is

Affirmed

NOTES AND QUESTIONS

1. **What is the Court saying**? Has the Supreme Court managed to sort out the distinction between an agent and a nominee? If not, does it matter?

2. **Applying the theory**. The Bollinger decision opens the door to the use of nominees and agents. If you represented an investor who planned to use a corporation to hold title to property as a nominee or agent, what steps would you take to ensure that the agency or nominee relationship would be respected?

3. **De facto corporations.** A corporation that was defectively formed under state law can nevertheless achieve corporate status for federal income tax purposes. The tax law tracks this concept. *See, e.g., Van Heusden v. Commissioner*, 44 T.C. 491 (1965).

B. OTHER BASES FOR ATTACKING THE CORPORATION FORM

Sham corporation theory takes the relatively primitive position that there is no corporation. It rarely works. The government has an extensive arsenal of other theories for attacking transactions in which it believes that the corporation is being manipulated for tax avoidance purposes. The following case illustrates these weapons in their most common setting, the closely held corporation dominated by family members. Before reading the next case, read §§ 482 and 269(a). Also, skim § 269A, which was enacted after the tax years involved in the following case.

ACHIRO v. COMMISSIONER
77 T.C. 881 (1981)

HALL, JUDGE:

[Achiro and Rossi each owned 50% of the stock of Tahoe City Disposal, and each owned 25% of the stock of Kings Beach Disposal. In 1974, Achiro and Rossi incorporated A & R for the purpose of providing management services to Tahoe City Disposal and Kings Beach Disposal. Achiro and Rossi each owned 24% of A & R's stock, and Renato Achiro, who happened to be Achiro's brother and Rossi's brother-in-law, held the remaining 52%. A & R contracted to provide management services to Tahoe City Disposal and Kings Beach Disposal in exchange for management fees. Achiro and Rossi entered into exclusive employment contracts with A & R, and, acting in their capacities as A & R's employees, rendered management services to Tahoe City Disposal and Kings Beach Disposal. A & R's books and records consisted of a bank statement, a checkbook, and a bankbook. In addition, A & R's accountants kept a record of receipts and disbursements, payroll records, a summary general ledger, work papers, and tax information. A & R had no separate office, its name did not appear on any office door or building, it had no separate telephone number or listing, and it had no printed business cards bearing its name, but it did have stationery bearing its name on the letterhead. All three companies had profit-sharing plans, and A & R had a pension plan.]

Opinion

[Part A, involving the burden of proof, is omitted.]

B. Respondent's Reallocation of Income and Deductions

Next, we turn to the substantive issues raised by respondent. His reliance on sections 482, 269, and 61 to reallocate all of A & R's income and deductions to Tahoe City Disposal and Kings Beach Disposal represents a frontal attack on a taxpayer's use of a personal service corporation. The impetus behind respondent's all-out attack on A & R stems from his apparent concern about the use of corporations for the principal purpose of obtaining the benefits associated with corporate retirement plans.

It is well known that operating a business in corporate form provides advantages not available to self-employed individuals. In recent years, however, the driving force behind an ever increasing use (particularly by professionals) of corporations is the advantage of the richer

199

tax deferral obtained through establishment of a corporate retirement plan. For example, for taxable years beginning before 1982, an employee not otherwise covered by a retirement plan is limited to the use of an individual retirement account which permits qualified contributions not in excess of 15 percent of compensation or $1,500, whichever is less. Sec. 219. Also for taxable years beginning before 1982, the tax deferred contribution available to a self-employed individual under a Keogh Plan (also known as H.R. 10 plan) is limited to the lesser of $7,500 per year or 15 percent of earned income. Sec. 404(e)(1). For taxable years beginning after 1981, however, even active participants in employer-sponsored plans may contribute to an individual retirement account. Additionally, the maximum amount of a qualified contribution to an individual retirement account is increased to the lesser of $2,000 or 100 percent of compensation. The Economic Recovery Act of 1981. Pub. L. 97-34, sec. 311, 95 Stat. 274-283 (1981). Similarly, for taxable years beginning after 1981, the maximum contribution to a Keogh Plan is increased to the lesser of $15,000 or 15 percent of income, and the amount of income that can be taken into account when computing the deduction is increased from $100,000 to $200,000 . . . In contrast, under a qualified pension or profit-sharing plan, a corporate employee-shareholder can enjoy annual contributions on his behalf to defined contribution plans in an amount not exceeding $41,500. Sec. 415(c)(1)(A); IRS News Release 81-16, Feb. 4, 1981. Alternatively, under a qualified defined benefit pension plan, the maximum contribution is an amount that will provide him with an annuity of $124,500 or an annuity equal to his average compensation for his most remunerative 3 consecutive years. Sec. 415(b)(1); IRS News Release 81-16, Feb. 4, 1981. The corporate employee can also have a combination of benefits through contributions to both defined contribution plans and defined benefit plans subject to the rule of 1.4. Sec. 415(e).

Respondent's distaste for this use of the corporate form is not new. However, respondent has significantly altered his mode of attacking personal service corporations. Prior to August 8, 1969, respondent relied primarily on the so-called Kintner Regulations[1] to attack professional service corporations. As a result of numerous successful taxpayer challenges to the Regulations, respondent announced on August 8, 1969, that he would no longer litigate the tax classification of professional service corporations formed under State professional corporations laws.

Since that time, the Service has accepted professional service corporations that have respected their corporate form in conducting their businesses. As a result, the use of professional service corporations and other personal service corporations has spiraled without any significant legislation from Congress intended to halt such use of the corporate form. In recognition of these facts, the Seventh Circuit recently stated: "We think that our approach in this case of recognizing some vitality in personal service corporations accords with congressional intent. A history of legislation targeted at personal service corporations, the absence of any special exclusion of such corporations from corporate taxation and the personal holding company tax provisions indicate that to some extent Congress has sanctioned the incorporation of service businesses for tax purposes."

The keynote in respondent's present position under sections 482, 269, and 61 is his contention that incorporation for the principal purpose of taking advantage of corporate pension and profit-sharing plans amounts to an evasion or avoidance of income taxes, an unclear reflection of income, and/or an assignment of income. We disagree. Of course, a mere corporate skeleton, standing alone and without any flesh on its bones, will not suffice to provide its shareholder-employees with corporate retirement benefits. See Roubik v. Commissioner, 53 T.C. 365, 382 (1969) (Tannenwald, J., concurring). Once incorporated, the personal service business

---

[1] See §§ 301.7701-2(a)(5) and (h), Proced. & Admin. Regs., as they read prior to their revocation in 1977 by T.D. 7515, 1977-2 C.B. 482. The name attached to these regulations derives from the case United States v. Kinter, 216 F.2d 418 (9th Cir. 1954).

must be run as a corporation. Its shareholder-employees must recognize, respect, and treat their personal service corporation as a corporation. The corporation must accept the disadvantages as well as advantages of incorporation. Once a corporation is formed and all organizational and operational requirements are met, it should be recognized for tax purposes regardless of the fact that it was formed to take advantage of the richer corporate retirement plans. In light of this general discussion, the following discussion of respondent's sections 482, 269, and 61 assertions will be directed at determining the existence of any specific or extenuating circumstances compelling the use of one of those sections.

1. Section 482

The first substantive issue is whether respondent's allocations are justified under Section 482. Section 482 states: In any case of two or more organizations, trades, or businesses (whether or not incorporated, whether or not organized in the United States, and whether or not affiliated) owned or controlled directly or indirectly by the same interests, the Secretary or his delegate may distribute, apportion, or allocate gross income, deductions, credits, or allowances between or among such organizations, trades, or businesses, if he determines that such distribution, apportionment, or allocation is necessary in order to prevent evasion of taxes or clearly to reflect the income of any such organizations, trades, or businesses.

Relying on this statute, respondent allocated all of A & R's income and deductions to Tahoe City Disposal and Kings Beach Disposal. In essence, respondent is attempting to utilize section 482 to ignore the corporate existence of A & R.

The purpose of Section 482 is set forth in the Regulations: (b) *Scope and purpose.* (1) The purpose of Section 482 is to place a controlled taxpayer on a tax parity with an uncontrolled taxpayer, by determining according to the standard of an uncontrolled taxpayer, the true taxable income from the property and business of a controlled taxpayer. The interests controlling a group of controlled taxpayers are assumed to have complete power to cause each controlled taxpayer so to conduct its affairs that its transactions and accounting records truly reflect the taxable income from the property and business of each of the controlled taxpayers. If, however, this has not been done and the taxable incomes are thereby understated, the district director shall intervene, and, by making such distributions, apportionments, or allocation as he may deem necessary of gross income, deductions, credits, or allowances, or of any item or element affecting taxable income, between or among the controlled taxpayers constituting the group, shall determine the true taxable income of each controlled taxpayer. *The standard to be applied in every case is that of an uncontrolled taxpayer dealing at arm's length with another uncontrolled taxpayer* . . . 1.482-1(b)(1), Income Tax Regs. [Emphasis added]

Reg. § 1.482-2(b)(1) deals specifically with circumstances involving the performance of services by one corporation for the benefit of another similarly controlled corporation: Where one member of a group of controlled entities performs marketing, managerial, administrative, technical, or other services for the benefit of, or on behalf of another member of the group without charge, or at a charge which is not equal to an arm's length charge as defined in subparagraph (3) of this paragraph, the district director may make appropriate allocations to reflect an arm's length charge for such services. Reg. § 1.482-2(b)(3) defines an arm's-length charge: For the purpose of this paragraph an arm's length charge for services rendered shall be the amount which was charged or would have been charged for the same or similar services in independent transactions with or between unrelated parties under similar circumstances considering all relevant facts . . .

In the context of the present case, respondent may utilize Section 482 to insure that the charges among the controlled entities represent arm's-length amounts. Instead of making such an allocation, respondent chose to allocate all of A & R's income and deductions to Tahoe City Disposal and Kings Beach Disposal. The evidence in the present case indicates that A & R received the arm's-length value of the services it rendered to Tahoe City Disposal and Kings Beach Disposal. In addition, respondent has essentially conceded that the payments reflect arm's-length charges by agreeing that if the payments are not allowed as deductible management fees to A & R, they will be allowed almost in their entirety to Tahoe City Disposal and Kings Beach Disposal as deductible salary payments.

Moreover, the cases respondent relies on do not support his position that without showing an arm's-length price for the services rendered, he may reallocate the entire price of such services from one corporation to another. In *Ach v. Commissioner, supra*, the taxpayer transferred her profitable sole proprietorship to her son's defunct corporation in exchange for the corporation's non-interest-bearing note. As a result of this transfer, the taxpayer was able to offset the income of her dress business against the net operating loss carry-overs from her son's corporation. In sustaining most of respondent's allocations under Section 482 we stated: Plainly, this was not an arm's length transaction. The corporation was hopelessly insolvent, and it is utterly beyond belief that any unrelated third party would have sold a prosperous business for a non-interest bearing $30,705.57 note of such an insolvent maker where the level of earnings of that business was about $30,000 a year and rising, and where the seller contemplated continued full-time management of the business without compensation . . .

In *Borge v. Commissioner*, 405 F.2d 673 (2d Cir. 1968), . . . entertainer Victor Borge formed a corporation to which he transferred the assets of an unprofitable poultry business. In addition, Borge entered into an employment agreement with the corporation pursuant to which he agreed to perform entertainment services for the corporation in exchange for an annual salary of $50,000. The $50,000 salary was far less than the amount Borge's entertainment activities produced each year, and it was found that Borge would not have made a similar agreement in an arm's-length transaction. Accordingly, respondent properly allocated a larger amount of Borge's entertainment earnings directly to him.

In *Rubin v. Commissioner*, 56 T.C. 1155 (1971), . . . the taxpayer and his brothers owned during the relevant tax years all the stock of Park, a corporation which, pursuant to management contracts, provided management services to Dorman Mills and its subsidiaries, also corporations controlled by the taxpayer. The taxpayer's efforts accounted for all of Park's income from management services. The taxpayer apparently never entered into an employment contract with Park and during the time he performed services for Dorman Mills as an employee of Park, he also received salaries from other corporations to which he rendered services. The taxpayer received from Park a substantially lower salary for his services than the amount received by Park from Dorman Mills. In light of these facts, we held that respondent properly allocated a greater portion of Park's income directly to the taxpayer. Although we did not specifically mention the lack of arm's-length dealing between the taxpayer and Park, it is clear that the result reached was intended to reflect an arm's length approach to the transactions between them. The circumstances clearly indicated that the employment relationship between the taxpayer and Park did not resemble the type of relationship that would have resulted had the taxpayer been dealing at arm's length with an unrelated third party.

In *Jones v. Commissioner*, 64 T.C. 1066 (1975), the taxpayer was an official court reporter for a Federal District Court. He formed a personal service corporation to loan out his services despite the legal requirement that an official court reporter be an individual and not a corporation. Furthermore, the taxpayer never entered into an employment agreement with his corporation, remained under the control of the judge to whom he was assigned, and personally certified the transcripts. Holding that the transactions between the taxpayer and his corporation were not at arm's-length, we stated (p. 1078):

> "In the situation here, an uncontrolled taxpayer could not have dealt with another uncontrolled taxpayer as Mr. Jones dealt with the corporation because the functions of Mr. Jones in reporting the proceedings by stenographic note taking and the functions

of the corporation in producing, selling, and certifying the transcripts must, by statute, be performed by the official court reporter, who must be an individual."

The fact that petitioners in the present case chose to incorporate A & R for the primary purpose of obtaining the benefits of its retirement plans does not justify respondent's Section 482 allocations. In addition, none of the cases relied on by respondent support his sweeping reallocation of all service income from A & R to Tahoe City Disposal and Kings Beach Disposal. Accordingly, Section 482 is inapplicable. This is true regardless of where the burden of proof lies. Respondent's 100 percent reallocation in the present case is arbitrary, capricious, and unreasonable. To utilize Section 482 in the present context respondent's allocations must, at the least, be reasonable attempts to reflect arm's-length transactions among the related entities. We see no reasonableness in respondent's present allocations and find that the transactions, as structured, reflected arm's-length charges for the services performed.

2. Section 269

The second issue is whether respondent properly utilized his authority under Section 269 to allocate A & R's income and deductions to Tahoe City Disposal and Kings Beach Disposal.

The "principal purpose" for the acquisition of control of the corporation must have been the evasion or avoidance of Federal income tax by securing the benefit of a deduction, credit, or other allowance not otherwise available. In the present case, the principal purpose for the formation of A & R was to secure the tax benefits of its retirement plans. We have already held that as a general proposition, the formation of a corporation for the principal purpose of securing the tax benefits of retirement plans is not an evasion or avoidance of taxes. Accordingly, Section 269 does not apply.

Furthermore, even if the formation of a corporation for such a purpose were an evasion or avoidance of taxes, it would not be so in the present case because the benefits expected from A & R's plans are not available. (*See* the sec. 414(b) discussion, *infra*.)

3. Section 61

The third issue is whether section 61 applies to shift A & R's income and deductions. Respondent stated his position as follows: "[A & R] is a sham for tax purposes; it did not actually earn the management fees which it reported. Section 61. Without citing *Moline Properties v. Commissioner*, respondent apparently is asking us to disregard the corporate existence of A & R. This we decline to do. *Moline Properties v. Commissioner*, requires the recognition of a corporation as a separate entity if either (1) the purpose for the formation of the corporation is the equivalent of a business activity or (2) the incorporation is followed by the carrying on of business. In the present case, A & R carried on a business subsequent to its incorporation. It hired employees and entered into employment contracts with them. It entered into management service contracts with Tahoe City Disposal and Kings Beach Disposal. Its employees respected its separate identity. It filed separate tax returns, paid taxes, kept separate books, formed pension and profit-sharing plans, etc. It rendered services through its two employees to the disposal companies. These subsequent acts amount to the carrying on of the business of a management company. Accordingly, A & R must be recognized as a viable entity for tax purposes . . .

Under his Section 61 approach, respondent further asks us to attribute the employees of A & R (namely, Achiro and Rossi) to Tahoe City Disposal and Kings Beach Disposal on the basis that their actions as employees were controlled by those companies instead of A & R. To do this we must, among other things, disregard their employment contracts with A & R and A

& R's management contracts with Tahoe City Disposal and Kings Beach Disposal. Respondent relies on *Jones v. Commissioner, supra,* and *Roubik v. Commissioner,* 53 T.C. 365 (1969).

In *Jones (see discussion, supra)*, this Court found that the taxpayer's personal service corporation was not a sham and that it engaged in substantial business activity. We also found, however, that the taxpayer performed services in his individual capacity because by law his corporation could not perform such services. Accordingly, we held that he assigned his income to the corporation. The present case is distinguishable. Here, we have found that Achiro and Rossi functioned as employees of A & R under valid exclusive employment agreements. In their capacities as employees, they rendered services to Tahoe City Disposal and Kings Beach Disposal pursuant to management contracts between A & R on the one hand and Tahoe City Disposal and Kings Beach Disposal on the other hand. Furthermore, the parties were not precluded by law from operating in corporate form as in *Jones.*

In *Roubik v. Commissioner,* 53 T.C. 365 (1969), four radiologists who had separate practices formed a personal service corporation ostensibly to carry on their practices. We found as a fact that the radiologists continued to carry on their prior separate practices and merely assigned their income to their corporation. *Lucas v. Earl,* 281 U.S. 111 (1930). Although they entered into employment agreements with their corporation, the corporation never entered into loan-out agreements with the hospitals or others for whom the radiologists performed their services. The doctors did not respect the corporate form after the personal service corporation was formed. That is not our situation here. Respondent, on whom the burden of proof rests, has not proved that A & R is not a viable corporation, or that the petitioners did not respect its separate existence and the contracts into which it entered with them and with others . . .

4. Section 414(b)

The final issue is whether the employees of A & R and the employees of Tahoe City Disposal should be aggregated pursuant to Section 414(b). Respondent asserts that once so aggregated, A & R's pension and profit-sharing plans (which cover only petitioners) discriminate in favor of officers, shareholders, and highly compensated persons because those plans do not include Tahoe City Disposal's employees and because the North Tahoe P-S Plan's contributions and benefits are not commensurate with A & R's plans. Accordingly, respondent contends that A & R's pension and profit-sharing plans are not qualified trusts under Section 401, and the contributions made to such plans should be treated as income to petitioners under the provisions of Sections 402(b) and 83(a). Petitioners agree that if the employees of A & R are aggregated with the employees of Tahoe City Disposal, then A & R's pension and profit-sharing plans are not qualified trusts, and the contributions to those plans should be income to petitioners. Petitioners contend, however, that Section 414(b) does not require the aggregation of the employees of A & R with the employees of Tahoe City Disposal.

Section 414(b) requires aggregation of the employees of all corporations which are members of a controlled group of corporations as defined in Section 1563(a). Section 1563(a) applies to both parent-subsidiary and brother-sister controlled groups. The brother-sister controlled group determination consists of two tests. Sec. 1563(a)(2). The 80 percent test requires that five or fewer persons alone or in combination have at least an 80 percent interest in each of two or more organizations. The 50 percent test requires that the same five or fewer persons have more than a 50 percent interest in each organization, taking into account the interests of each person only to the extent that such interests are identical with regard to each organization.

Reg. § 1.1563-1(a)(6), Income Tax Regs. defines voting powers for purposes of section 1563(a) as follows: in determining whether the stock owned by a person (or persons) possesses a certain percentage of the total combined voting power of all classes of stock entitled to vote of a corporation, consideration will be given to all the facts and circumstances of each case. A share of stock will generally be considered as possessing the voting power accorded to such share by the corporate charter, bylaws, or share certificate. (On the other hand, if there is any agreement, whether express or implied, that a shareholder will not vote his stock in a corporation, the formal voting rights possessed by his stock may be disregarded in determining the percentage of the total combined voting power possessed by the stock owned by other shareholders in the corporation, if the result is that the corporation becomes a component member of a controlled group of corporations. Moreover, if a shareholder agrees to vote his stock in a corporation in the manner specified by another shareholder in the corporation, the voting rights possessed by the stock owned by the first shareholder may be considered to be possessed by the stock owned by such other shareholder if the result is that the corporation becomes a component member of a controlled group of corporations.)

Achiro and Rossi each owned 50 percent of the voting stock of Tahoe City Disposal and each held record title to 24 percent of the stock of A & R. Renato Achiro, Achiro's brother and Rossi's brother-in-law, held record title to the remaining 52 percent of the voting stock of A & R. Considering only record title, Tahoe City Disposal and A & R were not a brother-sister controlled group under Section 1563(a)(2). However, we have found that Renato implicitly agreed that he would either not vote his stock in A & R or vote his stock in the manner specified by Achiro. Under the Regulations, the validity of which has not been challenged by the parties, Renato's voting rights may be disregarded or attributed to Achiro. Therefore, Achiro and Rossi are deemed each to have 50 percent interests in Tahoe City Disposal and A & R (or Achiro is deemed to have a 76 percent interest in A & R), and the corporations constitute a brother-sister controlled group.

Since the corporations form a controlled group, the employees of A & R and the employees of Tahoe City Disposal must be aggregated under Section 414(b) for purposes of Section 401. Such a holding complies with the intent of Congress in enacting Section 414(b) as expressed in H. Rept. 93-779, at 49 (1974), 1974-3 C.B. 292:

> "The committee, by this provision, intends to make it clear that the coverage and anti-discrimination provisions cannot be avoided by operating through separate corporations instead of separate branches of one corporation. For example, if managerial functions were performed through one corporation employing highly compensated personnel, which has a generous pension plan, and assembly-line functions were performed through one or more other corporations employing lower-paid employees, which have less generous plans or no plans at all, this would generally constitute an impermissible discrimination. . . ."

A & R was formed for the express purpose of rendering managerial services to Tahoe City Disposal and Kings Beach Disposal. In 1975 and 1976, A & R's employees, Achiro and Rossi, were officers, shareholders, and highly compensated. Sec. 1.401-4(a)(1), Income Tax Regs. The "assembly-line functions" of the day-to-day waste disposal and dump operations were carried on by the employees of Tahoe City Disposal and Kings Beach Disposal. This is the very kind of situation Congress had in mind when it enacted Section 414(b).

Accordingly, for the years 1975 and 1976, A & R's pension and profit-sharing plans were not qualified because they discriminated in favor of Achiro and Rossi who were officers, shareholders, and highly compensated. Sec. 401. Contributions made to such plans must be included in the gross income of Achiro and Rossi under Sections 402(b) and 83(a).

Petitioners contend that the prescribed relationship between the stockholders of A & R and the stockholders of Tahoe City Disposal did not exist in 1975 or 1976. Petitioners' contention rests squarely on their assertion that Renato's 52% interest in A & R is not attributable to them and must be considered as owned by an unrelated and uncontrolled party when determining whether A & R and Tahoe City Disposal are members of a controlled group of corporations. In support of this contention, petitioners list numerous reasons for the acquisition of a controlling interest in A & R by Renato and cite two recent decisions of this Court, *Garland v. Commissioner*, 73 T.C. 5 (1979). and *Kiddie v. Commissioner*, 69 T.C. 1055 (1978).

Petitioner's factual arguments are without merit. Renato testified that it was his brother's wish that he acquire a controlling interest in A & R and that was the only reason for his acquisition of A & R's stock. Achiro believed that benefits from increased contributions to A & R's pension and profit-sharing plans were possible if Renato owned 52 percent of A & R's voting stock. We have found as a fact that Renato implicitly agreed not to vote his stock or to vote as Achiro instructed him.

Petitioner's reliance on *Garland v. Commissioner, supra, and Kiddie v. Commissioner, supra,* is similarly misplaced. The Kiddie decision states that attribution of partnership characteristics to a partner does not occur unless the partner controls the partnership. In that case, we held that a corporate partner, who never owned more than a 50 percent interest in a partnership, is not attributed [to] the employees of the partnership when determining whether the corporate partner's pension and profit-sharing plans are discriminatory. In Garland, the parties agreed that neither Section 414(b) nor Section 414(c) applied. Accordingly, our decision here, which rests on the applicability of Section 414(b), does not conflict with our *Kiddie* and *Garland* decisions.

Decisions will be entered under Rule 155.

NOTE

The problem with assignment of income. If a taxpayer is found to have engaged in a defective attempt to assign income, it is possible that the results will be asymmetrical as between the taxpayer/assignor and the assignee of the income. This can arise because the assignee may have reported the income already and the statute of limitations may have closed on the assignee's ability to file an amended return correcting the "error" of reporting the income. By contrast, § 482 presupposes that both parties are under a joint audit and calls for the IRS to make "correlative adjustments," so the outcome should be symmetrical to both taxpayers. *See Rubin v. Commissioner,* 429 F.2d 650 (2d Cir. 1970).

PROBLEM 13-1

1) Bob and Ray are plumbers. They formed X Co. some years ago with a view to perhaps using it for some future business they might get into. They funded it with $150, but have not kept up with the paperwork in that they have never held any directors' meetings and the by-laws were never formally adopted. They did establish a bank account for the company. Recently, they used the name of the corporation in dealing with one of their customers, including a clause in their service contract calling for the customer to make payments to X Co., not themselves, for work they will perform.

   a) Is X Co. a sham corporation?

   b) Is their arrangement instead a mere defective attempt to assign income to X Co.?

   c) If, instead, Bob and Ray formed X Co. to take title to rental real estate as a nominee for themselves and if all paperwork regarding the rental real estate made it clear that X Co.

was their nominee, would the IRS be successful in arguing that no deductions should pass through to Bob and Ray?

d) Under "(c)," Who would be taxed on the income from the real estate?

e) Would the result be the same as "(d)" if X Co. were nominated an agent instead of a nominee?

f) What business corporations by industry can use the cash method of accounting?

g) For corporations that are not exempted from the accrual method by virtue of what they do, explain how much money the corporation can earn before it must use the accrual method.

2) Bob and Ray are in the wholesale computer components business, operating as equal shareholders of Overbyte, Inc., whose office is located in Flyneck, N.J., convenient to the port. Recently, they have expanded their activities to selling overseas, and Overbyte, Inc. has formed a 100%-owned Bahamas corporation, Overbyte International, to undertake foreign sales. The pattern is for Overbyte, Inc. to locate the overseas customer and then direct the customer to Overbyte International to close the deal. Overbyte International buys the product from Overbyte, Inc. at lower prices than Overbyte, Inc. charges its customers. Title to the goods passes at sea on the way to the foreign port. The customer calls a number in the Bahamas, which rings through on a different phone in the United States, which is invariably answered by Bob, Ray, or one of their staff in Flyneck. Overbyte International has a name on an office door in the Bahamas and has a part-time employee who completes the paperwork on these transactions and makes sure that Overbyte International is in compliance with Bahamian law. Income taxes are trivial in the Bahamas.

If you were an IRS agent auditing Overbyte, Inc. and you believed that the Bahamas corporation was formed for tax avoidance purposes, what theories might you use to increase Overbyte, Inc.'s taxes? How do you appraise the likelihood of success of each theory?

3) Dr. Good recently formed Dr. Good, PC, a professional corporation (the "PC"), which in turn contracted with the Friendly Hospital Clinic to provide Dr. Good's services on a full-time basis to the Clinic. He formed the corporation partly to avoid personal liability and partly to optimize his pension arrangements. He owns all the stock of the PC.

a) Is the PC automatically in the 35% federal income tax bracket? Could he solve the problem by giving away some stock to family members?

b) Could the IRS apply § 269A to allocate the PC's income to Dr. Good?

Chapter 14

ORGANIZATION OF A CORPORATION

A. INTRODUCTION

The legal requirements for forming a corporation vary from state to state. Even in the most relaxed state, some money or property must be contributed to the corporation in return for stock in connection with its organization. State laws vary as to the acceptability and appraisal of stock that is issued for property or services. From a practical point of view, the formation of a corporation will require the establishment of a bank account to accept the minimum required contribution. The account will be in the name of the corporation and will be drawn upon by one or more individuals identified in the corporation's organizational documents. In all events, stock will have to be issued to the founders and in addition the corporation may issue debt (longer-term debt is known as "securities" in tax law parlance) and possibly hybrid instruments such as stock options or stock warrants.

These transactions require a determination of whether the corporation will pay income taxes on what it receives in return for issuing its shares, whether the shareholders will pay taxes when they exchange property or money for stock, and a determination of the basis of the properties received by the corporation and the basis of the stock or securities issued to the shareholders. As will become apparent, decisions at the dawn of the enterprise about how its capital structure is arranged are a matter of great importance for purposes of planning for its future tax liabilities.

B. TAXATION OF THE CORPORATION
Read § 1032.

The corporation will recognize neither gain nor loss when it issues stock for money or other property, even though it may have realized a gain or loss. That is true even if the stock is treasury stock, i.e., stock that was previously issued by the corporation but which the corporation bought back. Curiously, this means that even if the corporation actively trades in its own stock and makes a healthy profit doing so, there is no taxable income. There is also no tax if the corporation transfers its own stock as compensation for services. Reg. § 1.1032-1(a).

As a consequence of not recognizing gain or loss on issuance of its stock to contributors of property or money, at least if the exchange satisfies § 351 or amounts to a contribution to capital not in exchange for stock under §118, the general rule is that the corporation will take a basis in property it receives equal to the basis the property had in the hands of each transferor, increased by the amount of any gain the transferor recognized. *See* § 362(a). The variations in § 362(b) and (c) are for later. In thinking about the nonrecognition and basis rules in this context, recall the similar rules applicable in § 721 (partnership formations). Be sure always to determine first gain or loss *realized* and then move to the question of the amount, if any, that is *recognized.*

C. TAXATION OF THE SHAREHOLDER
Read § 351(a), (b), (d).

In the absence of § 351, the exchange of property by contributors for stock of the issuing corporation would constitute a sale or other disposition that would result in taxable gains or losses to the shareholder, subject to the risk that § 267(a) might disallow any loss if the shareholder (directly and by attribution) owned more than half of the corporation's outstanding stock by value. *See* § 267(b)(2). Section 351 grants nonrecognition treatment to contributing shareholders who receive back stock if, and only if, the conditions specified in § 351 are met.

The basic rationale of § 351 is that incorporation or capital infusion into an ongoing corporation, is a mere change in form of an ongoing business. In fact, that is only sometimes true, because if there are transferors who were not previously in business together, the result is a diversification of the shareholders' investments.

Section 351(e) removes the nonrecognition benefits of § 351 if there is a transfer of property to an *investment company*, but this is only true if the transfer is to a mutual fund, real estate investment trust or to a corporation more than 80% of whose assets, aside from cash and certain debt securities, are held for investment and consist of readily marketable stock or securities, as well as precious metals, foreign currencies, interests in entities that hold securities, and a variety of other financial investments. On the other hand, if each transferor transfers a diversified portfolio of stocks and securities then there is no diversification and §351 is available to protect the transfers from a current tax. Reg. §1.351-1(c)(6).

The time has now come to learn the definitional elements of § 351.

D. TRANSFER OF PROPERTY IN EXCHANGE FOR STOCK

Section 351 applies only if "property" is exchanged for stock. For this purpose, "property" includes money. *See* § 317. For § 351 purposes, § 351(d) makes it clear that "property" does not include services, or some specified indebtedness or interest. What else does or does not constitute "property"?

This issue is addressed in the *Stafford* decision in the partnership section of the book, and it is clear from that decision that the term "property" under § 351 is generally consistent with its meaning under § 721 and that property is broadly defined and includes such things as technical know-how and contractual rights.

The question of whether there has been an exchange of property for stock should also be familiar. The most common problem is determining whether a transfer of intangible property such as a patent to a controlled corporation qualifies as an exchange. If the transferor retains a significant economic interest in the transferred property, the retained interest may be so extensive as to constitute the transfer of a "license" rather than an exchange.

Section 1032 provides that the corporation is not taxed on the receipt of money or property in exchange for stock. The hard part for tax advisors is determining whether the transaction fits §351 so as to protect the contributing shareholders.

E. STOCK
Read Reg. §§ 1.351-1(a), and §118(a), (b).

There is not much turmoil as to the meaning of the term "stock"; for example, it is clear that the term does not include stock rights, stock warrants or convertible debt. Other terms in § 351 have required interpretation and have entailed controversy. Until recently, all preferred stock invariably qualified as stock, but that is no longer true. This issue is taken up later in the book.

For many years and until fairly recently, §351 granted nonrecognition to a transfer solely in exchange for stock or securities (longer-term debt instruments) in the corporation, so some cases or rulings you read may involve both or either; however, § 351 now applies only to a transfer solely in exchange for stock.

HAMRICK v. COMMISSIONER
43 T.C. 21 (1964)

BRUCE, JUDGE:

[Hamrick and another inventor, Hensley, patented a device which they transferred to a corporation (Jet), receiving as consideration over half of the issued stock plus the right to receive additional shares if the future earnings reached certain agreed goals, until the stock they received amounted to two-thirds of the total shares issued. One inventor withdrew and sold his stock and rights to another stockholder. The stockholders formed a new agreement to allow Hamrick to receive up to 44 percent of the stock. After the three years had elapsed Hamrick duly received his 44 percent.]

Opinion

The principal issue involves the taxable status of shares of capital stock issued by Jet to Hamrick in 1958, 1959, and 1960 pursuant to the assignment of November 6, 1957, and the memorandum of agreement of November 24, 1958. The petitioner contends that the provisions of section 351(a) of the Internal Revenue Code of 1954 apply, that all the stock he received was received in exchange for property, and that no gain or loss is to be recognized upon such receipt.

It will facilitate discussion if we treat all the stock involved as having a par value of $1. On this basis, Hamrick received the following amounts at the time stated:

Year	*Shares*	*Year*	*Shares*
1957	19,000	1959	9,824
1958	4,070	1960	14,249

Of the stock received in 1960, 8,106 shares brought the total issued to Hamrick up to one-third of the total issued by Jet, and the additional 6,143 brought his total up to 44 percent of the issued stock. . . .

The respondent concedes that the shares petitioner received in 1957 were received in a nontaxable exchange, but takes the position that the next 22,000 shares, received in 1958, 1959, and 1960, bringing the petitioner's total to one-third of the issued stock, represented long-term capital gains under section 1235 of the Internal Revenue Code of 1954, to the extent of the fair market value of the stock, and that the last 6,143 shares received in 1960 are taxable as ordinary income.

The respondent contends that section 351(a) is not applicable because (1) the right to receive the additional shares was neither "stock" nor "securities," (2) the time limitation of "immediately after the exchange" is not satisfied, (3) part of the stock was issued for services to be rendered, and (4) application of section 351 to certain of the shares would result in a tax-free distribution of earnings.

The respondent's first argument is that the right of the petitioner to receive additional stock in Jet was neither stock nor securities within the meaning of section 351(a) but was "other property," which is to be recognized as gain to the extent of its fair market value. Respondent cites *Helvering v. Southwest Corp.*, 315 U.S. 194 (1942), in which assets were acquired in a reorganization for voting stock and warrants which allowed the holder to acquire shares of stock upon payment of specified sums. The issue was whether the assets were acquired in a reorganization within the definition in section 112(g)(1) of the Internal Revenue Code of 1939, solely for voting stock. The Court said that "solely" leaves no leeway and that voting stock plus some other consideration does not meet the requirements, and held that the warrants were not voting stock nor did they carry the rights of a shareholder. The respondent says that the petitioner's contract right to acquire Jet stock was not the equivalent of stock but had more of the characteristics of the warrants in the cited case.

The petitioner cites *Carlberg v. United States*, 281 F.2d 507 (C.A. 8, 1960), which involved an exchange of stock for stock and certificates of contingent interest. The issue was whether such certificates were "stock" within the meaning of section 354(a)(1) of the 1954 Code or "other property," within the meaning of section 356(a)(1). The case arose from the merger of two lumber companies, referred to as Maryland and Missouri, into International Paper Co. At the time, Missouri had pending substantial unsettled liabilities. To protect International, certain shares were reserved and certificates of contingent interest issued with respect to them. The stockholders of Maryland and Missouri received shares of International plus certificates. When the liabilities were settled, the reserved shares would be distributed in accordance with the certificates if settlement were made within 10 years. The purpose of the device was to place the ultimate burden of the liabilities on the Missouri stockholders. The court referred to the Southwest case, and observed that there were obvious differences between the warrants in that case and the certificates in *Carlberg*, as the warrants provided rights to purchase at stated prices during a stated time, the holders having only an option to purchase, while the certificate holders were immediately entitled to all the reserved shares to be distributed and need take no positive action nor provide further consideration. The court said that the certificates could produce nothing but stock, that the arrangement for reserved shares seemed an ideal and logical solution of the problem of the contingent liabilities and that what the holder possessed was either stock or nothing. The court held that the property interest represented by the certificates was "stock" within the meaning of section 354(a)(1) rather than "other property" or "boot."

The contract here was a solution of a problem, as in *Carlberg*. The cash investors were willing to allow Hamrick and Hensley voting control of the corporation to be formed but were unwilling to put up $35,000 for only one-third of the shares in an untried invention. The inventors wanted one-third of the stock each. The arrangement for additional shares to be issued to them in the event the invention proved salable was a compromise and a good faith solution of their differences. There was a valid business purpose in the arrangement. If earnings were meager, the investors would receive in dividends nearly half of them. If the business was successful, they would be content with one-third of satisfactory earnings. The inventors were willing to take the hazard of the sale ability of their invention which, if successful, would result in their receiving eventually the interests they wanted.

The respondent concedes that the stock issued in 1957 was received in exchange for the transfer of property. The contract right to receive additional stock was also a part of the consideration for the transfer. The right, as in *Carlberg*, can produce nothing other than stock to the petitioner. While the exact number of shares is not specified, what the petitioner can receive is nothing other than stock. Applying the rule of substance over form, we must conclude that the substance of the contract provides for only a stockholder's interest. It does not represent current gain, but additional equity ownership.

In *Carlberg*, the certificates authorized the issue of additional stock if certain conditions were met within 10 years. Here the contract authorized the issue of additional stock if certain conditions were met within 7 years. The stock was authorized and available for issuance if the conditions were met. The principle of the *Carlberg* case is applicable here, and Hamrick's right under the agreement was the equivalent of stock. *See* also *Philip W. McAbee*, 5 T.C. 1130 (1945), acq. 1946-2 C.B. 4, in which certificates were issued for stock placed in escrow in a reorganization and we held that the stock was received pursuant to a plan of reorganization and at the time of the escrow.

The respondent next contends that the time limitation of section 351 is not met under that section gain is not to be recognized if "immediately after" the exchange the transferors are in control of the corporation. The respondent contends that if the transaction is prolonged and spread out over several years it becomes impossible to determine the fact of control within the time limitation of the statute, and that an interval of 7 years within which the petitioner's rights are in abeyance would make the tax effect indeterminable within a reasonable time after the exchange.

The required control is 80 percent of the voting stock. Sec. 368(c). In this case Hamrick and Hensley exchanged their patent rights for 38,000 shares ($1 par value), plus the right to receive additional shares; the cash investors exchanged money for 35,000 shares; and 2,000 shares were issued to others for services. Stock issued for services is not considered as issued in return for property. Sec. 351(a). "Property," for the purpose of section 351, includes "money." *George M Holstein III*, 23 T.C. 923 (1955). "Immediately after the exchange" the persons who transferred the rights to the patent and the cash, both of which are property, to the corporation were in control of it to the required extent. Hamrick and Hensley and the cash investors held 73,000 shares and the rights to additional shares, while other persons who rendered services, that is, Newcombe and the attorneys, held 2,000 shares, or less than 3 percent. Momentary control is sufficient. *American Bantam Car Co.*, 11 T. C. 397 (1948), *aff'd.* 177 F. 2d 513 (C. A. 3, 1949), certiorari denied, 339 U.S. 920. The tax effect is determinable immediately. The conclusion is not affected by subsequent issues, even where such issues result in reducing the transferors' control to less than 80 percent, *Lodi Iron Works, Inc.*, 29 T.C. 696 (1958), and we may observe that the right of Hamrick and Hensley to receive additional shares in the future could not possibly reduce the degree of control of the transferors here.

The respondent next contends that at least a part of the additional shares was issued for services rendered or to be rendered by the petitioner, referring to the covenant by Hamrick and Hensley in the original assignment that they would disclose to the corporation and assign to it any and all improvements made by either of them in the invention and all rights under any patents pertaining to such improvements or inventions. The respondent says that this contemplates services by petitioner in working toward improving the invention and that this is a service to be rendered Jet in exchange for the consideration passing from it. Stock issued for services is not considered as issued in return for property, and gain on such stock is not entitled to nonrecognition under section 351(a).

It is an established practice in patent assignments to provide for the assignment of future improvements and similar inventions by the assignor in order to protect the assignee from having his acquisition made worthless by reason of such improvements. *Aspinwall Manuf'g Co. v. Gill*, 32 F.2d 697 (1887). This is not construed as a contract for services. Hamrick was separately employed by Jet as an engineer and was separately compensated for services as such. No part of the stock to be issued to him was intended or may be regarded as compensation for services. He was not hired to invent, as in *Arthur N Blum*, 11 T.C. 101 (1948), of 'd. 183 F.2d 281 (C.A. 3, 1950). Nor was there a provision in the agreement for separate compensation for inventing or promoting and developing inventions, as in *Arthur C. Ruge*, 26 T.C. 138 (1956); nor for a provision reasonably to be interpreted as providing was such compensation as in *Spence v. United States,* 156 F. Supp. 556 (Ct. Cl. 1957). The agreement to assign a subsequent improvement does not have the effect of an assignment. See *Roland Chilton*, 40 T.C. 552 (1963). There is no indication that any such transfer was in fact made here.

[The court went on to conclude that the stock was received pursuant to an amendment of the original agreement, not a new contract, and that the stock was worth somewhat over $14. Certain other issues are also omitted.]

Decision will be entered under Rule 50.

F. THE SPECIAL PROBLEM OF NON-QUALIFIED PREFERRED STOCK

Read: §351(g).

The benefits of tax deferral under § 351 used to be available to people who took back "stock," including any preferred stock. Financially conservative taxpayers found it was possible to design preferred stock that was comfortably similar to debt. Preferred stock is stock (as opposed to debt) that has debt-like features. There is no single definition, but a common example would be stock with a face amount of $100/share that pays a fixed dividend of 6%, but only if the directors determine there is enough cash to allow the corporation to make the payment.

For example, the recipients could bargain for a dividend rate tied to an external index, such as the rate of interest charged on loans to prime customers over a given time period, or they could bargain for a redemption feature forcing the corporation to buy back their preferred stock. Congress felt that stock with such features was too close to debt, and withdrew the protection of § 351 from its receipt. In effect, preferred stock is now treated as no better than debt. § 351(g).

Under § 351(g) preferred stock becomes non-qualified preferred stock (NQP) in any one of four situations:

- The issuer or a related person (*e.g.*, a subsidiary) must redeem the stock;

- The holder has the right to require such a redemption or purchase;

- The issuer or related person has a right to redeem or purchase, and as of the issue date the right is likely to be exercised; or

- The dividend rate on the stock varies at least in part with reference to interest rates, commodity prices, or other similar indices.

The first three requirements apply only if the right or obligation may be exercised in the 20-year period beginning on the issue date of the stock and the repurchase right or obligation is not subject to a contingency which, as of the issue date, makes the likelihood of the redemption or purchase remote. § 351(g)(2)(B).

Congress understandably felt that NQP is closer to debt than to stock because it is either likely to be turned into cash or is insulated from the trends in the value of the equity in the corporation. The blow of getting NQP is softened in that even though it is taxable as boot, it remains "stock" for purposes of the "control" requirement under § 351. (Control under § 368 requires 80% control of voting stock and of each class of nonvoting stock. NQP becomes a class of nonvoting stock for this purpose. H.R. Rep. No. 105-35, 105th Cong., 2d Sess. 2 (1997). The control requirement is discussed below.)

The NQP rules also apply to tax-deferred acquisitive and divisive corporate reorganizations, which are explored in later chapters.

G. THE CONTROL REQUIREMENT
Read § 368(c).

Unlike its partnership analog (§ 721), the corporate tax provisions require that the transferors of property to a corporation be "in control" as defined in § 368(c) immediately after the exchange. It is important to note that control need not arise as a result of the exchange itself. Section 351 also applies where the transferor or transferors were already in control of the corporation, so that § 351 applies to transfers to both pre-existing and newly created corporations. This allows further tax-free infusions of property in exchange for stock.

The term "control" as defined in section 368(c) of the Internal Revenue Code of 1954 requires the ownership of stock possessing at least 80 percent of the total combined voting power of all classes of voting stock and the ownership of at least 80 percent of the total number of shares of each class of outstanding non-voting stock.

Advice has been requested whether "control" as defined in section 368(c) of the Internal Revenue Code of 1954 requires ownership of at least 80 percent of the total number of shares of each class of nonvoting stock for the purposes of section 351 of the Code.

Certain persons transferred property to a corporation in exchange for voting and non-voting stock, *i.e.*, 83 percent of the Class A voting common stock, 83 percent of the Class A non-voting common stock, and 22 percent of the non-voting preferred stock. However, due to the relative number of non-voting common and preferred shares outstanding, these persons owned more than 80 percent of the total number of shares of the outstanding non-voting stock.

Section 351 of the Code provides, in effect, that no gain or loss shall be recognized to the transferors of property to a corporation if immediately after the transfer, the transferors are in "control" of the corporation as defined by section 368(c) of the Code.

Section 368(c) of such Code in defining "control" states, in part, as follows: . . . the term "control" means the ownership of stock possessing at least 80 percent of the total combined voting power of all classes of stock entitled to vote and at least 80 percent of the total number of shares of all other classes of stock of the corporation.

The legislative history of section 368(c) of the Code indicates a congressional intent that ownership of each class of non-voting stock is required. The provisions of what is now section 368(c) of the Code were first enacted into law as section 202(c)(3) of the Revenue Act of 1921. That section as originally passed by the House of Representatives (H.R. 8245, 67th Cong., (1921)), defined "control" as the ownership of:

[A]t least 80 per centum of the voting stock and 80 per centum of all other classes of stock of the corporation . . . .

The section was reported out of the Senate and enacted into law in a form substantially identical to its present form, retaining the reference to classes of non-voting stock. It is apparent, therefore, that the words "classes of stock" as used in section 368(c) of the Code refers to ownership of 80 percent of the total number of shares of each class of non-voting stock, as there is no other logical reason for retaining the words "classes of stock" in section 202(c)(3) of the Revenue Act of 1921.

Moreover, percentage ownership of the number of non-voting shares outstanding, as contrasted to percentage ownership of each class of non-voting shares, is ordinarily of no significance and can lead to results which are inconsistent with the statutory scheme and clear congressional purpose. Ownership of large numbers of non-voting shares in a multi-class stock structure would not necessarily assure, in itself, the continuation of substantial proprietary interests in modified corporate forms as contemplated by the statute. See section 1.368-1 of the Income Tax Regulations.

In view of the foregoing, it is held that "control" as defined by section 368(c) requires ownership of stock possessing at least 80 percent of the total combined voting power of all classes of voting stock and the ownership of at least 80 percent of the total number of shares of each class of outstanding non-voting stock. Therefore, a transfer of property under the above circumstances does not constitute a transfer to a controlled corporation within the purview of section 351 of the Code.

Classes of Stock. A problem may arise when some transferors provide "hard" assets, such as cash or appreciated property that is easily valued and convertible to cash, and others provide "softer" assets, such as goodwill of a going business, intellectual property, or services. The contributors of "hard" assets will often desire some guarantee of the safety of their capital in the form of a privileged return from earnings and or first rights to the corporate property upon liquidation of the new corporation if it fails. The provider of soft assets, on the other hand, will often want an equal voice in management and equal enjoyment of future growth of the business. These competing goals cannot easily be met by issuing a single class of common stock to all transferors.

The problem could be solved by issuing corporate debt to providers of hard assets in addition to stock, thus giving them a preferred claim to the extent of the debt, but debt "securities" do not qualify for tax-free treatment to the recipient under § 351. One solution is to issue more than one class of stock. All stock, including preferred stock (other than nonqualified preferred stock), may be received tax-free under § 351, and all classes of stock count toward the control requirement. Also, securities do not count toward the "control" requirement of § 351.

To illustrate: Money, Brains, and Land wish to form a computer corporation by contributing their respective assets in exchange for stock. Brains will contribute sufficient cash to meet the 10% requirement as a transferor (a requirement discussed a few pages later), but will also contribute 90% by value in services and goodwill from his former computer business. Money and Land will contribute property of equal value, but want a guaranteed return before any profits are paid to Brains, and want a first call on the corporate assets in liquidation. Brains, on the other hand, wants a full third of the stock, which, implies an equal share in profits and assets in liquidation. Both Brains and Land want the transfers to qualify under § 351. A solution: issue voting preferred stock to Money and Land that pays a guaranteed return before any dividend can be paid on the common, and that also enjoys a preference in liquidation, and issue common stock to Brains, equal to half the value of the preferred stock. Money and Land need make sure theirs is not nonqualified preferred stock to the extent appreciated property will be used to pay for the preferred stock.

PROBLEM 14-1

Tom, not a shareholder, transfers a computer in which he has a basis of $900 to X Corp. in exchange for a $500 face value debenture. At the time of the exchange, the computer has a fair market value of $500. Assume Bill holds all the shares of X Corp.

1) Does the transaction qualify under the provisions of §351?

2) What are the income tax consequences of "(1)" to Tom and X Corp.? What if instead Tom were the 100% shareholder?

3) What basis does X Corp. take in the computer in "(1)"?

4) Would it make a difference if, instead of the debt instrument, X Corp. issued Tom 85 shares of its 100 authorized common stock, assuming Bill held 15 shares at the time?

H. CONTROL IMMEDIATELY AFTER THE TRANSACTION

The statute says that the transferors must be in control "immediately after the transaction." What does the "control requirement" of § 351 really mean? Who exactly must be in such "control"? When you read the following case, you can ignore the dollar figures and just focus on the fact that the corporation claimed a loss on the sale of certain land.

FAHS v. FLORIDA MACHINE & FOUNDRY CO.
168 F.2d 957 (5th Cir. 1948.)

MCCORD, CIRCUIT JUDGE.

Appellee, Florida Machine and Foundry Company, filed suit to recover additional income and excess profits taxes, aggregating $19,089.44, paid for the years 1941 and 1942 under protest. From a judgment for appellee taxpayer, the Collector takes this appeal.

The only question presented is the proper cost basis to be used by taxpayer in computing gain or loss on the sale of certain land it owned in 1941, and in determining taxpayer's equity invested capital for the years 1941 and 1942. [§ 351 provides]

Recognition of gain or loss:

(b) Exchanges solely in kind

Transfer to corporation controlled by transferor. No gain or loss shall be recognized if property is transferred to a corporation by one or more persons solely in exchange for stock or securities in such corporation, and immediately after the exchange such person or persons are in control of the corporation; . . . .

Section 368(c) defines the term "control," as used in the above quoted provision, as follows:

Definition of control. As used in this section the term "control" means the ownership of stock possessing at least 80 per centum of the total combined voting power of all classes of stock entitled to vote and at least 80 per centum of the total number of shares of all other classes of stock of the corporation. . . . The basis to be used for property acquired by a corporation after December 1, 1920, through the issuance of its stock for property in accordance with [Section 351], above, is the same as it would be in the hands of the transferor . . . If, however, the issuance of the stock for property is not governed by [Section 351], the taxpayer's basis is the cost to it of such property, or the fair market value of the property on the date of acquisition . . . .

The evidence reveals that for some years prior to 1912, Franklin G. Russell, senior, as sole owner, operated a business known as Florida Machine Works on Riverside Avenue in Jacksonville, Florida. On May 31, 1912, he purchased a tract of land bordering on West Church Street in Jacksonville, to which location the plant was later moved.

About the year 1920, it was shown that the Senior Mr. Russell, who had little technical education for foundry and machine shop work, discussed with his son, Franklin G. Russell, Junior, the possibility of the son eventually succeeding him in the business. The son had graduated from college in 1916 with a degree in mechanical engineering and, with the exception of about two years spent as a soldier in World War 1, had served since that time as an apprentice in the various departments of his father's plant, later becoming assistant manager. When the location of the business was changed from Riverside Avenue to West Church Street, the son himself had planned and laid out the new plant installations. In 1921 the father and son entered

216

into an agreement whereby the son would eventually receive a one-half interest in the business, if he remained with it and continued to operate the plant. In pursuance of this agreement, the Florida Machine and Foundry Company, taxpayer, was organized and incorporated on July 16, 1924. At the organization meeting on that date, the Senior Russell conveyed to the corporation all of the assets of the business which he then owned individually, including the tract of land in question, for stock in the corporation, with the shares thereof to be issued directly to himself, his son, and one share each to three other persons. The father received 1,181 shares and his son 1,176 shares, the father thereby retaining only a bare majority of the stock issued.

In 1941, the corporation sold a parcel of the land on West Church Street for $15,000. The March 1, 1913, value of this tract was $7,522.60. On July 16, 1924, the date taxpayer corporation was organized, the fair market value of the tract sold was $13,164.55.

In its 1941 return, the taxpayer claimed a loss on the above sale in the sum of $11,270, using as its basis of value for the land sold, the amount $26,270, which was the proportionate fair market value of the land sold as compared with the fair market value of the entire tract as of July 16, 1924, the date of organization of the corporation and acquisition of the land by taxpayer. The Commissioner denied the validity of the basis used, on the ground that the transfer to the corporation on July 16, 1924, was really a non-taxable exchange of property for stock, as described in [Section 351] of the Code, and ruled that, for the purpose of computing taxpayer's gain or loss under Sec. 113(a)(8), the proper basis of value was the March 1, 1913 value in the hands of the transferor, Franklin G. Russell, Senior, or $7,824.53, so that instead of a loss of $11,270, as claimed by taxpayer, there was a taxable gain of $7,175.47; he further required the use of the same basis in computing taxpayer's equity invested capital under Sec. 718(a)(2), for the years 1941 and 1942.

We are of opinion the district court's finding that Franklin Russell, Senior, was not in "control" of taxpayer corporation "immediately after the transfer" on July 16, 1924, and therefore, that [Section 351] did not apply, is abundantly supported by the evidence . . .

Appellant's contention that the son, Franklin Russell, Junior, by virtue of the agreement with his father in 1921, acquired an equitable one-half interest in the land involved, which thereafter placed him and his father, as joint transferors, in "control" of taxpayer immediately after the transfer, is not borne out by the evidence. We further find no merit in the argument that taxpayer should be required to use the basis of its transferor, Franklin G. Russell, Senior, because of the latter's failure to report the transfer in 1924. There can be no estoppel against taxpayer for the act of its transferor, who was not in control of taxpayer corporation immediately after the transfer, and who was shown to have acted in good faith. *Cf. Portland Oil Co. v. Commissioner,* 1 Cir., 109 F.2d 479. . . .

It follows that the proper basis for the land in question is its fair market value when acquired by taxpayer corporation on July 16, 1924.

We find no reversible error in the record, and the judgment is therefore affirmed.

NOTES

1. **Contractual v. noncontractual transactions**. The courts seem more willing to tolerate intentional post-incorporation abandonment of control where the actions are based on estate planning or other personal motives as opposed to commercial purposes. It is therefore generally possible to have the transferors receive all of the stock from the corporation and then reduce ownership to under 80% by giving away stock to family members and still have a tax-free incorporation without violating the control requirement. *See,* e.g., *Wilgard Realty Co. v. Commissioner,* 127 F.2d 514 (2d. Cir.), cert. denied, 317 U.S. 655 (1942). If the transferors are contractually bound by a commercial arrangement at the time of incorporation to dispose of stock, thereby divesting themselves of control, however, or there is a preconceived plan to do so without which the incorporation would not have taken place,

the control test is not met. *See*, e.g., *Intermountain Lumber Co.,* 65 T.C. 1025, 1031-32 (1976). and *See* B. Bittker & J. Eustice, Federal Income Taxation of Corporations and Shareholders ¶¶3.09 and 91.5.

2. **What about options?** In *American Bantam Car Co. v. Commissioner,* 11 T. C. 397 (1948), *aff'd per curiam,* 177 F.2d 513 (3rd Cir. 1949), cert. denied, 339 U.S. 920 (1950), the Tax Court held that a loss of control due to the later exercise by non-transferors of a contractual right, such as an option, to acquire shares did not remove the protection of § 351, by reasoning that the incorporators retained the right to cancel the option contract at any time, and that the incorporation itself would have taken place with or without the subsequent transfers.

I. ACCOMMODATION TRANSFERORS
Read Reg. § 1.351-1(a).

In order for § 351 to apply, the *transferor* person or persons must be in "control" of the corporation. So who is the *transferor*? Take the example of the corporation that already exists and which has invited in a new shareholder who wants to contribute some high-value, low-basis real estate in exchange for stock. The new shareholder wants to make sure that there is no tax on her exchange, but she will wind up with only 25% of the stock after the proposed transfer. Assume that the only other shareholder, whose ownership will be reduced to 75% by the exchange, says, "Okay, I'll transfer in $1 and I will get one share of stock and you can transfer in your real estate which is worth $100,000, for 100,000 shares of stock and that way § 351 will apply because we are both *transferors*." Wrong. That transaction is a sham. So how much is enough? According to the IRS, the existing shareholder who accommodates the transaction (in the example, the 100%-75% shareholder) must transfer property or cash worth at least 10% of her original stock ownership. Rev. Proc. 77-37, 1977-2 C.B. 568. Rev. Proc. 2018-12, 2018-6 IRB 349 amplifies Rev. Proc. 77-37.

There are more complicated variants of this situation. Imagine a corporation that is about to be formed by two shareholders, one contributing property with a value of $100 and a basis of zero, and the other contributing only services which are worth $80. This transaction will not satisfy § 351 because there is only one transferor of property and he is not in control after the transaction. Now imagine that the service provider proposes to contribute cash of $20. Does this make the service provider a transferor? According to Rev. Proc. 77-37, *supra*, it does. The reasoning is that as long as the service provider transfers property that is not of "relatively small value," the service provider will be viewed as a transferor. The property is of relatively small value if it does not equal at least 10% of the value of the stock received for services. In our example, the stock received for services is worth $80 and the $20 cash transferred equals 25% of the value of the stock received for services, so the service provider is a transferor. The key is that we now have two transferors. Together they are in control, hence their property exchanges are protected by § 351.

Keep in mind that even though this reasoning prevents the transfers of property from being taxable, the service provider will always be taxed on stock issued for services. Thus, in the example, the service provider will have $80 of ordinary income on receipt of the stock, unless the service provider's stock is restricted in such a way that it is not taxable until the restrictions lapse. *See* § 83(a).

Section 351 is laconic in its description of how the exchange is expected to take place. The Regulations make it clear that the exchanges by several persons need not be simultaneous, as long as all the transfers are pursuant to a prearranged plan. This is an important relaxation of what otherwise might be a rigid set of rules and prevents panic over precise closing dates. Also, it has the benefit of protecting punctual taxpayers from their indolent colleagues. For example, if two shareholders plan to take over an existing company by making large contributions to it so that together they wind up with at least 80% control, the first shareholder can diligently make her contribution while waiting, at least for a little while, for her colleague to get around to it.

PROBLEM 14-2

Mrs. Vernon and her son, Edgar, transferred the following properties to a recently-organized corporation, VE Corp. for its common stock. Edgar became a 30% shareholder and she got 70% of the stock, of which there is only one class.

1) If she transferred a large quantity of valuable inventory in return for 70% of VE Corp.'s common stock, and Edgar transfers a truck worth $30,000 for his 30% are the transfers nontaxable?

2) If instead Edgar sells the truck to VE Corp., can Edgar recognize a loss? *See* § 267(a), (b)(1) and (c)(2). If §351 applies, can he recognize a loss?

3) Would your answer to "(2)" differ if Mrs. Vernon were his aunt? *See* § 267(b)(4)-(5).

4) Suppose the facts are: Mrs. Vernon, now his aunt, got all of the voting common stock for inventory and Edgar got solely preferred stock for the truck. The stock gives Edgar the power to force VE Corp. to buy back the stock at his command. How is he taxed?

5) If in addition to stock, Mrs. Vernon received options to buy more VE Corp. stock, would the receipt of the options be nontaxable under § 351?

6) In what is an otherwise tax-free incorporation of VE Corp., Edgar exchanges a truck with a basis of $600 and a value of $1,000 for a VE Corp. bond with a face amount of $1,000. What result?

7) Would your answer to "(1)" change if, pursuant to a contract entered into before VE Corp.'s formation, Mrs. Vernon agreed to sell all her VE stock to an unrelated corporation at a hefty profit?

8) What if Mrs. Vernon got half the stock, worth $50,000, but $15,000 worth of it was in consideration for her services?

9) Same as "(1)" but the transfers are separated by six months because Edgar had trouble registering the stock. *See* Reg. § 1.351-1(a)(1).

10) Same as "(1)" but each only contributes a handful of publicly traded stocks.

11) Same as "(1)" but Edgar transfers two valuable patents the corporation will use. *See* § 482, last sentence. Does this suggest the royalty rates (not just amounts) the corporation owes Edgar will fluctuate?

J. THE IMPACT OF "BOOT"
Read § 351(b).

If the transferor receives not only shares of stock but also other property, such as bonds or notes, § 351(b) requires the recognition of any realized gain to the extent of the value of such

219

nonqualifying property. If you review the partnership analog, namely § 721, you will notice that it does not contain similar words, but the result may well be the same because only an interest in the partnership can be received tax-free under § 721. Note that § 351(b)(2) prevents the recognition of realized losses, which makes § 351(b) a one-way street. At the time of the ruling below, the long-term capital gain holding period was 6 months and a day.

REV. RUL. 68-55
1968-1 C.B. 140 amplified by Rev. Rul. 85-164

In determining the amount of gain recognized under section 351(b) of the Internal Revenue Code of 1954 where several assets were transferred to a corporation, each asset must be considered transferred separately in exchange for a portion of each category of consideration received. The fair market value of each category of consideration received is separately allocated to the transferred assets in proportion to the relative fair market values of the transferred assets. Where as a result of such allocation there is a realized loss with respect to any asset, such loss is not recognized under section 351(b)(2) of the Code.

Advice has been requested as to the correct method of determining the amount and character of the gain to be recognized by Corporation X under section 351(b) of the Internal Revenue Code of 1954 under the circumstances described below.

Corporation Y was organized by X and A, an individual who owned no stock in X. A transferred 20x dollars to Y in exchange for stock of Y having a fair market value of 20x dollars and X transferred to Y three separate assets and received in exchange stock of Y having a fair market value of 100x dollars plus cash of 10x dollars.

In accordance with the facts set forth in the table below if X had sold at fair market value each of the three assets it transferred to Y, the result would have been as follows:

	Asset I	*Asset II*	*Asset III*
Character of asset:	Capital asset held more than 6 months	Capital asset held not more than 6 months	Section 1245
Fair market value:	$22x	$33x	$55x
Adjusted basis	$40x	$20x	$25x
Gain (loss)	($18x)	$13x	$30x
Character of gain/loss	Long-term capital loss	Short-term capital gain	Ordinary income

The facts in the instant case disclose that with respect to the section 1245 property the depreciation subject to recapture exceeds the amount of gain that would be recognized on a sale at fair market value. Therefore, all of such gain would be treated as ordinary income under section 1245(a)(1) of the Code.

Under section 351(a) of the Code, no gain or loss is recognized if property is transferred to a corporation solely in exchange for its stock and immediately after the exchange the transferor is in control of the corporation. If section 351(a) of the Code would apply to an exchange but for the fact that there is received, in addition to the property permitted to be received without recognition of gain, other property or money, then under section 351(b) of the Code gain (if any) to the recipient will be recognized, but in an amount not in excess of the sum of such money and the fair market value of such other property received, and no loss to the recipient will be recognized.

The first question presented is how to determine the amount of gain to be recognized under section 351(b) of the Code. The general rule is that each asset transferred must be considered to have been separately exchanged. See the authorities cited in Revenue Ruling 67-

192, C.B. 1967-2, 140, and in Revenue Ruling 68-23, page 144, this Bulletin, which hold that there is no netting of gains and losses for purposes of applying sections 367 and 356(c) of the Code. Thus, for purposes of making computations under section 351(b) of the Code, it is not proper to total the bases of the various assets transferred and to subtract this total from the fair market value of the total consideration received in the exchange. Moreover, any treatment other than an asset-by-asset approach would have the effect of allowing losses that are specifically disallowed by section 351(b)(2) of the Code.

The second question presented is how, for purposes of making computations, under section 351(b) of the Code, to allocate the cash and stock received to the amount realized as to each asset transferred in the exchange. The asset-by-assets approach for computing the amount of gain realized in the exchange requires that for this purpose the fair market value of each category of consideration received must be separately allocated to the transferred assets in proportion to the relative, fair market values of the transferred assets. *See* section 1.1245-4(c)(1) of the Income Tax Regulations which, for the same reasons, requires that for purpose of computing the amount of gain to which section 1245 of the Code applies each category of consideration received must be allocated to the properties transferred in proportion to their relative fair market values.

Accordingly, the amount and character of the gain recognized in the exchange should be computed as follows:

Total	Asset I	Asset II	Asset III
Fair-market value of asset transferred $110x	$22x	$33x	$55x
Percent of total fair market value	20%	30%	50%
Fair market value of Y stock received in exchange $100	$20x	$30x	$50x
Cash received in exchange $10x	$2x	$3x	$5x
Amount realized $110x	$22x	$33x	$55x
Adjusted basis	$40x	$20x	$25x
Gain (loss) realized	$40x/($18x)	$20x/$13x	$25x/$30x

Under section 351(b)(2) of the Code the loss of 18x dollars realized on the exchange of Asset Number 1 is not recognized. Such loss may not be used to offset the gains realized on the exchanges of the other assets. Under section 351(b)(1) of the Code, the gain of 13x dollars realized on the exchange of Asset Number II will be recognized as short-term capital gain in the amount 3x dollars, the amount of cash received. Under sections 351(b)(1) and 1245(b)(3) of the Code, the gain of 30x dollars realized on the exchange of Asset Number III will be recognized as ordinary income in the amount of 5x dollars, the amount of cash received.

K. ASSUMPTION OF LIABILITIES
Read § 357(a)-(c).

As a general rule, a transfer of encumbered property to a corporation under § 351 will not result in any tax liability to the transferor, even though the transferee corporation assumes the liability or takes the property subject to it. This is in contrast to the usual result under Reg. § 1.1001-2(a). This general rule and the exception found in § 357(b) (for tax-avoidance purposes) have been the law since 1939. Another important exception was added in 1954; that exception is § 357(c).

To illustrate*:* A shareholder in the course of forming a new corporation contributes property with a basis of $50,000 and a value of $100,000. The property is subject to a long-standing mortgage of $30,000. The shareholder will receive stock worth $70,000 (the difference between the value of the property and the mortgage debt). The shareholder will have a realized gain of $50,000 (i.e., the amount realized is $70,000 worth of stock plus $30,000 of debt relief or $100,000, minus the $50,000 basis), but the recognized gain is zero because of § 351 and § 357(a), which prevent the assumed liability from being treated as boot under § 351(b). The shareholder's basis in the stock will equal the basis of the property, $50,000, minus the assumed liability of $30,000, for a net figure of $20,000. See § 358(d). If he sells the stock, he will get cash of $70,000 and report a $50,000 gain, exactly the same as if he had simply sold the encumbered property. This result indicates that the basis rules are appropriate and properly makes §351 a mere deferral rule, as Congress intended.

Section 357(b) treats as money received (*i.e.*, as boot) any liabilities that are assumed with a principal purpose to avoid tax or, if not for that purpose, without a bona fide business purpose. The Regulations suggest that there must be a business purpose for both the transferor and the corporation even though the statute speaks only of the transferor.

On top of that, if there is an improper purpose for any assumption of liability, all the liabilities assumed from that transferor must be treated as money received. If challenged by the IRS, the taxpayer is required to demonstrate her purity of motive "by the clear preponderance of the evidence," which is an abnormally high burden of proof.

The usual case to which § 357(b) is directed arises where the taxpayer seeks to wring out some tax-free cash by encumbering an asset just before transferring it to the corporation. Section 357(b) would also apply to more remote situations where the transferee corporation assumes a personal liability of the transferor, such as alimony, and there is no business reason for doing so. In order to obtain a ruling for a § 351 transaction, the taxpayer must represent (among a myriad of other things) that any liabilities to be assumed were incurred in the ordinary course of business, or if not, must state the business reason for such assumption. Rev. Proc. 83-59, 1983-2 C.B. 575, at 03.b.(2).

Section 357(c) is the more common problem. Where the amount of liabilities transferred exceeds the aggregate bases of the assets transferred, the excess is treated as immediately taxable gain. Note that as in the case of § 357(b), this inquiry is posed shareholder-by-shareholder and not by considering the transferor group as a whole. Although § 357(c) may look harmless, it can be a painful trap because the taxpayer has received no cash or other property with which to pay the tax. The constitutionality of § 357(c) was upheld in *Wiebusch v. Commissioner*, 59 T.C. 777, *aff'd per curiam*, 487 F.2d 515 (8th Cir. 1973). Note also that § 357(c) does not apply to liabilities that would be deductible if they were paid, in other words, to most current account payables such as business rent, wages, insurance and the like. § 357(c)(3)(A)(i).

According to the Treasury Department, contingent liabilities do not count for purposes of § 357. Rev Rul 95-74, 1995-2 CB 36. If and when the liabilities mature, the liabilities are deducted or capitalized, as appropriate, as if the transferee corporation had owned the property for the same time as the transferor. In other words, the transferee corporation treats the liabilities as if it were just a continuing corporation that always had the liability.

Recall how much simpler partnerships are where debt is concerned. The transferor's debt is treated like a simultaneous contribution and distribution of cash, deferring the day of reckoning to when the property is disposed of or the debt is released. That favorable tax result is one of the reasons why corporations are relatively unpopular from a tax perspective, and illustrates the unfortunate fact that tax considerations often inappropriately shape economic decisions.

PERACCHI v. COMMISSIONER
143 F.3d 487 (9th Cir. 1998)

Kozinski, Circuit Judge:

We must unscramble a Rubik's Cube of corporate tax law to determine the basis of a note contributed by a taxpayer to his wholly-owned corporation.

The Transaction

The taxpayer, Donald Peracchi, needed to contribute additional capital to his closely-held corporation (NAC) to comply with Nevada's minimum premium-to-asset ratio for insurance companies. Peracchi contributed two parcels of real estate. The parcels were encumbered with liabilities which together exceeded Peracchi's total basis in the properties by more than half a million dollars. As we discuss in detail below, under section 357(c), contributing property with liabilities in excess of basis can trigger immediate recognition of gain in the amount of the excess. In an effort to avoid this, Peracchi also executed a promissory note, promising to pay NAC $1,060,000 over a term of ten years at 11% interest. Peracchi maintains that the note has a basis equal to its face amount, thereby making his total basis in the property contributed greater than the total liabilities. If this is so, he will have extracted himself from the quicksand of section 357(c) and owe no immediate tax on the transfer of property to NAC. The IRS, though, maintains that (1) the note is not genuine indebtedness and should be treated as an unenforceable gift; and (2) even if the note is genuine, it does not increase Peracchi's basis in the property contributed.

The parties are not splitting hairs: Peracchi claims the basis of the note is $1,060,000, its face value, while the IRS argues that the note has a basis of zero. If Peracchi is right, he pays no immediate tax on the half a million dollars by which the debts on the land he contributed exceed his basis in the land; if the IRS is right, the note becomes irrelevant for tax purposes and Peracchi must recognize an immediate gain on the half million. The fact that the IRS and Peracchi are so far apart suggests they are looking at the transaction through different colored lenses. To figure out whether Peracchi's lens is rose-tinted or clear, it is useful to take a guided tour of sections 351 and 357 and the tax law principles undergirding them.

Into the Lobster Pot: Section 351

The Code tries to make organizing a corporation pain-free from a tax point of view. A capital contribution is, in tax lingo, a "nonrecognition" event: A shareholder can generally contribute capital without recognizing gain on the exchange. It's merely a change in the form of ownership. like moving a billfold from one pocket to another. See I.R.C. § 351. So long as the shareholders contributing the property remain in control of the corporation after the exchange, section 351 applies: It doesn't matter if the capital contribution occurs at the creation of the corporation or if – as here – the company is already up and running. The baseline is that Peracchi may contribute property to NAC without recognizing gain on the exchange.

Gain Deferral: Section 358(a)

Peracchi contributed capital to NAC in the form of real property and a promissory note. Corporations may be funded with any kind of asset, such as equipment, real estate, intellectual property, contracts, leaseholds securities or Collectibles and unrecaptured section 1250 gain are sometimes referred to as "lukewarm assets" in tax lingo. The tax consequences can get a little complicated because a shareholder's basis in the property contributed often differs from its fair market value. The general rule is that an asset's basis is equal to its "cost." See I.R.C. § 1012. But when a shareholder like Peracchi contributes property to a corporation in a nonrecognition transaction, a cost basis does not preserve the unrecognized gain. Rather than take a basis equal to the fair market value of the property exchanged, the shareholder must substitute the basis of that property for what would otherwise be the cost basis of the stock. This preserves the gain for recognition at a later day: The gain is built into the shareholder's new basis in the stock, and he will recognize income when he disposes of the stock.

The fact that gain is deferred rather than extinguished doesn't diminish the importance of questions relating to basis and the timing of recognition. In tax, as in comedy, timing matters. Most taxpayers would much prefer to pay tax on contributed property years later – when they sell their stock – rather than when they contribute the property. Thus what Peracchi is seeking here is gain deferral. He wants the gain to be recognized only when he disposes of some or all of his stock.

Continuity of Investment: Boot and section 351(b)

Continuity of investment is the cornerstone of nonrecognition under section 351. Nonrecognition assumes that a capital contribution amounts to nothing more than a nominal change in the form of ownership; in substance the shareholder's investment in the property continues. But a capital contribution can sometimes allow a shareholder to partially terminate his investment in an asset or group of assets. For example, when a shareholder receives cash or other property in addition to stock, receipt of that property reflects a partial termination of investment in the business. The shareholder may invest that money in a wholly unrelated business, or spend it just like any other form of personal income. To the extent a section 351 transaction resembles an ordinary sale, the nonrecognition rationale falls apart.

Thus the central exception to nonrecognition for section 351 transactions comes into play when the taxpayer receives "boot" – money or property other than stock in the corporation – in exchange for the property contributed. See I.R.C. §351(b). Boot is recognized as taxable income because it represents a partial cashing out. It's as if the taxpayer contributed part of the property to the corporation in exchange for stock, and sold part of the property for cash. Only the part exchanged for stock represents a continuation of investment; the part sold for cash is properly recognized as yielding income, just as if the taxpayer had sold the property to a third party.

Peracchi did not receive boot in return for the property he contributed. But that doesn't end the inquiry: We must consider whether Peracchi has cashed out in some other way which would warrant treating part of the transaction as taxable boot.

The property Peracchi contributed to NAC was encumbered by liabilities. Contribution of leveraged property makes things trickier from a tax perspective. When a shareholder contributes property encumbered by debt, the corporation usually assumes the debt. And the Code normally treats discharging a liability the same as receiving money: The taxpayer improves his economic position by the same amount either way. *See* I.R.C. § 61(a)(12). NAC's assumption of the liabilities attached to Peracchi's property therefore could theoretically be viewed as the receipt of money, which would be taxable boot. *See United States v. Hendler*, 303 U.S. 564, 82 L. Ed. 1018, 58 S. Ct. 655 (1938).

The Code takes a different tack. Requiring shareholders like Peracchi to recognize gain any time a corporation assumes a liability in connection with a capital contribution would greatly diminish the nonrecognition benefit section 351 is meant to confer. Section 357(a) thus takes a lenient view of the assumption of liability: A shareholder engaging in a section 351 transaction does not have to treat the assumption of liability as boot, even if the corporation assumes his obligation to pay. See I.R.C. § 357(a).

This nonrecognition does not mean that the potential gain disappears. Once again, the basis provisions kick in to reflect the transfer of gain from the shareholder to the corporation: The shareholder's substitute basis in the stock received is decreased by the amount of the liability assumed by the corporation. See I.R.C. §358(d), (a). The adjustment preserves the gain for recognition when the shareholder sells his stock in the company, since his taxable gain will be the difference between the (new lower) basis and the sale price of the stock.

Sasquatch and The Negative Basis Problem: Section 357(c)

Highly leveraged property presents a peculiar problem in the section 351 context. Suppose a shareholder organizes a corporation and contributes as its only asset a building with a basis of $50, a fair market value of $100, and mortgage debt of $90. Section 351 says that the shareholder does not recognize any gain on the transaction. Under section 358, the shareholder takes a substitute basis of $50 in the stock, then adjusts it downward under section 357 by $90 to reflect the assumption of liability. This leaves him with a basis of minus $40. A negative basis properly preserves the gain built into the property: if the shareholder turns around and sells the stock the next day for $10 (the difference between the fair market value and the debt), he would face $50 in gain, the same amount as if he sold the property without first encasing it in a corporate shell.

But skeptics say that negative basis, like Bigfoot, doesn't exist. Compare *Easson v. Commissioner*, 33 T.C. 963, 970 (1960) (there's no such thing as a negative basis) with *Easson v. Commissioner*, 294 F.2d 653, 657-58 (9th Cir. 1961). (Yes, Virginia, there is a negative basis). Basis normally operates as a cost recovery system: Depreciation deductions reduce basis, and when basis hits zero, the property cannot be depreciated farther. At a more basic level, it seems incongruous to attribute a negative value to a figure that normally represents one's investment in an asset. Some commentators nevertheless argue that when basis operates merely to measure potential gain (as it does here), allowing negative basis may be perfectly appropriate and consistent with the tax policy underlying nonrecognition transactions. See, e.g., J. Clifton Fleming, Jr., The Highly Avoidable Section 357(c): A Case Study in Traps for the Unwary and Some Positive Thoughts About Negative Basis, 16 J. Corp. L. 1, 27-30 (1990). Whatever the merits of this debate, it seems that section 357(c) was enacted to eliminate the possibility of negative basis. See George Cooper, Negative Basis, 75 Harv. L. Rev. 1352, 1360 (1962).

Section 357(c) prevents negative basis by forcing a shareholder to recognize gain to the extent liabilities exceed basis. Thus, if a shareholder contributes a building with a basis of $50 and liabilities of $90, he does not receive stock with a basis of minus $40. Instead, he takes a basis of zero and must recognize a $40 gain.

Peracchi sought to contribute two parcels of real property to NAC in a section 351 transaction. Standing alone the contribution would have run afoul of section 357(c). The property he wanted to contribute had liabilities in excess of basis and Peracchi would have had to recognize gain to the extent of the excess, or $566,807:

	Liabilities	Basis
Property # 1	$1,386,655.00	$349,774.00
Property # 2	$161,558.00	$631,632.00
	$1,548,213.00	$981,406.00

Liabilities:	$1,548,213.00
Basis:	$981,406.00
Excess (357(c)):	$566,807.00

The Grift: Boosting Basis with a Promissory Note

Peracchi tried to dig himself out of this tax hole by contributing a personal note with a face amount of $1,060,000 along with the real property. Peracchi maintains that the note has a basis in his hands equal to its face value. If he's right, we must add the basis of the note to the basis of the real property. Taken together, the aggregate basis in the property contributed would exceed the aggregate liabilities:

	Liabilities	Basis
Property # 1	$1,386,655.00	$349,774.00
Property # 2	$161,558.00	$631,632.00
Note	$0.00	$1,060,000.00
	$1,548,213.00	$2,041,406.00

Under Peracchi's theory, then, the aggregate liabilities no longer exceed the aggregate basis, and section 357(c) no longer triggers any gain. The government argues, however, that the note has a zero basis. If so, the note would not affect the tax consequences of the transaction, and Peracchi's $566,807 in gain would be taxable immediately.

Are Promises Truly Free?

Which brings us (phew!) to the issue before us: Does Peracchi's note have a basis in Peracchi's hands for purposes of section 357(c)? The language of the Code gives us little to work with. The logical place to start is with the definition of basis. Section 1012 provides that "the basis of property shall be the cost of such property - - - -." But "cost" is nowhere defined. What does it cost Peracchi to write the note and contribute it to his corporation? The IRS argues tersely that the "taxpayers in the instant case incurred no cost in issuing their own note to NAC, so their basis in the note was zero." Brief for Appellee at 41. See *Alderman v. Commissioner*, 55 T.C. 662, 665 (1971); Rev. Rul. 68-629, 1968-2 C.B. 154, 155n13 Building on this premise, the IRS makes Peracchi out to be a grifter: He holds an unenforceable promise to pay himself money, since the corporation will not collect on it unless he says so.

Peracchi owned all the voting stock of NAC both before and after the exchange, so the control requirement of section 351 is satisfied. Peracchi received no boot (such as cash or securities) which would qualify as "money or other property" and trigger recognition under 351(b) alone. Peracchi did not receive any stock in return for the property contributed, so it could be argued that the exchange was not "solely in exchange for stock" as required by section 351. Courts have consistently recognized, however, that issuing stock in this situation would be a meaningless gesture: Because Peracchi is the sole shareholder of NAC, issuing additional stock would not affect his economic position relative to shareholders. *See, e.g., Jackson v. Commissioner*, 708 F.2d 1402, 1405 (9th Cir. 1983).

It's true that all Peracchi did was make out a promise to pay on a piece of paper, mark it in the corporate minutes and enter it on the corporate books. It is also true that nothing will cause the corporation to enforce the note against Peracchi so long as Peracchi remains in control. But the IRS ignores the possibility that NAC may go bankrupt, an event that would suddenly make the note highly significant. Peracchi and NAC are separated by the corporate form, and this gossamer curtain makes a difference in the shell game of C Corp organization and reorganization. Contributing the note puts a million dollar nut within the corporate shell, exposing Peracchi to the cruel nutcracker of corporate creditors in the event NAC goes bankrupt. And it does so to the tune of $1,060,000, the full face amount of the note. Without the note, no matter how deeply the corporation went into debt, creditors could not reach Peracchi's personal assets. With the note on the books, however, creditors can reach into Peracchi's pocket by enforcing the note as an unliquidated asset of the corporation.

The key to solving this puzzle, then, is to ask whether bankruptcy is significant enough a contingency to confer substantial economic effect on this transaction. If the risk of bankruptcy is important enough to be recognized, Peracchi should get basis in the note: He will have increased his exposure to the risks of the business – and thus his economic investment in NAC – by $1,060,000. If bankruptcy is so remote that there is no realistic possibility it will ever occur, we can ignore the potential economic effect of the note as speculative and treat it as merely an unenforceable promise to contribute capital in the future.

When the question is posed this way, the answer is clear. Peracchi's obligation on the note was not conditioned on NAC's remaining solvent. It represents a new and substantial increase in Peracchi's investment in the corporation. The Code seems to recognize that economic exposure of the shareholder is the ultimate measuring rod of a shareholder's investment. Cf. I.R.C. § 465 (at-risk rules for partnership investments). Peracchi therefore is entitled to a step-up in basis to the extent he will be subjected to economic loss if the underlying investment turns unprofitable. Cf. *HGA Cinema Trust v. Commissioner*, 950 F.2d 1357, 1363 (7th Cir. 1991) (examining effect of bankruptcy to determine whether long-term note contributed by partner could be included in basis). See also Treas. Reg. § 1.704-1(b)(2)(ii)(c)(1) (recognizing economic effect of promissory note contributed by partner for purposes of partner's obligation to restore deficit capital account).

The economics of the transaction also support Peracchi's view of the matter. The transaction here does not differ substantively from others that would certainly give Peracchi a boost in basis. For example, Peracchi could have borrowed $1 million from a bank and contributed the cash to NAC along with the properties. Because cash has a basis equal to face value, Peracchi would not have faced any section 357(c) gain. NAC could then have purchased the note from the bank for $1 million which, assuming the bank's original assessment of Peracchi, creditworthiness was accurate, would be the fair market value of the note. In the end the corporation would hold a million dollar note from Peracchi – just like it does now – and Peracchi would face no section 357(c) gain. The only economic difference between the transaction just described and the transaction Peracchi actually engaged in is the additional costs that would accompany getting a loan from the bank. Peracchi incurs a "cost" of $1 million when he promises to pay the note to the bank; the cost is not diminished here by the fact that the transferor controls the initial transferee. The experts seem to agree: "Section 357(c) can be avoided by a transfer of enough cash to eliminate any excess of liabilities over basis; and since a note given by a solvent obligor in purchasing property is routinely treated as the equivalent of cash in determining the basis of the property, it seems reasonable to give it the same treatment in determining the basis of the property transferred in a § 351 exchange." Bittker & Eustice Par. 3.06[4][b].

We are aware of the mischief that can result when taxpayers are permitted to calculate basis in excess of their true economic investment. See *Commissioner v. Tufts*, 461 U.S. 300, 75 L. Ed. 2d 863, 103 S. Ct. 1826 (1983). For two reasons, however, we do not believe our holding will have such pernicious effects. First, and most significantly, by increasing the taxpayer's personal exposure, the contribution of a valid, unconditional promissory note has substantial economic effects which reflect his true economic investment in the enterprise. The main problem with attributing basis to nonrecourse debt financing is that the tax benefits enjoyed as a result of increased basis do not reflect the true economic risk. Here Peracchi will have to pay the full amount of the note with after-tax dollars if NAC's economic situation heads south. Second, the tax treatment of nonrecourse debt primarily creates problems in the partnership context, where the entity's loss deductions (resulting from depreciation based on basis inflated above and beyond the taxpayer's true economic investment) can be passed through to the taxpayer. It is the pass-through of losses that makes artificial increases in equity interests of particular concern. See, e.g., *Levy v. Commissioner*, 732 F.2d 1435, 1437 (9th Cir. 1984). We don't have to tread quite so lightly in the C Corp context, since a C Corp doesn't funnel losses to the shareholder.

We find further support for Peracchi's view by looking at the alternative: What would happen if the note had a zero basis? The IRS points out that the basis of the note in the hands of the corporation is the same as it was in the hands of the taxpayer. Accordingly, if the note has a zero basis for Peracchi, so too for NAC. *See* I.R.C. § 362(a).[1] but what happens if NAC – perhaps facing the threat of an involuntary petition for bankruptcy – turns around and sells Peracchi's note to a third party for its fair market value? According to the IRS's theory, NAC would take a carryover basis of zero in the note and would have to recognize $1,060,000 in phantom gain on the subsequent exchange even though the note did not appreciate in value one bit. That can't be the right result.

Accordingly, we hold that Peracchi has a basis of $1,060,000 in the note he wrote to NAC. The aggregate basis exceeds the liabilities of the properties transferred to NAC under section 351, and Peracchi need not recognize any section 357(c) gain.

Fernandez. Circuit Judge, Dissenting:

Is there something that a taxpayer, who has borrowed hundreds of thousands of dollars more than his basis in his property, can do to avoid taxation when he transfers the property? Yes, says Peracchi, because by using a very clever argument he can avoid the strictures of 26 U.S.C. § 357(c). He need only make a promise to pay by giving a "good," though unsecured,

---

[1] *But see Lessinger v. Commissioner*, 872 F.2d 519 (2d Cir. 1989). In *Lessinger*, the Second Circuit analyzed a similar transaction. It agreed with the IRS's (faulty) premise that the note had a zero basis in the taxpayer's hands. But then, brushing aside the language of section 362(a), the court concluded that the note had a basis in the corporation's hands equal to its face value. The court held that this was enough to dispel any section 357(c) gain to the taxpayer, proving that two wrongs sometimes do add up to a right. We agree with the IRS that *Lessinger*'s approach is untenable. Section 357(c) contemplates measuring basis of the property contributed in the hands of the taxpayer, not the corporation. Section 357 appears in the midst of the Code sections dealing with the effect of capital contributions on the shareholder: sections 361 et seq., on the other hand, deal with the effect on a corporation, and section 362 defines the basis of property contributed in the hands of the corporation. Because we hold that the note has a face value basis to the shareholder for purposes of section 357(c). However, we reach the same result as *Lessinger*.

228

promissory note to his corporation when he transfers the property to it. That is true even though the property remains subject to the encumbrances. How can that be? Well, by preparing a promissory note the taxpayer simply creates basis without cost to himself. But see 26 U.S.C. § 1012; Rev. Rul. 68-629, 1968-2 C.B. 154; *Alderman v. Commissioner*, 55 T.C. 662, 665 (1971). Thus he can extract a large part of the value of the property, pocket the funds, use them, divest himself of the property, and pay the tax another day, if ever at all.

But as with all magical solutions, the taxpayer must know the proper incantations and make the correct movements. He cannot just transfer the property to the corporation and promise, or be obligated, to pay off the encumbrances. That would not change the fact that the property was still subject to those encumbrances. According to Peracchi, the thaumaturgy that will save him from taxes proceeds in two simple steps. He must first prepare a ritualistic writing – an unsecured promissory note in an amount equal to or more than the excess of the encumbrances over the basis. He must then give that writing to his corporation. That is all. But is not that just a "promise to pay," which "does not represent the paying out or reduction of assets?" *Don E. Williams Co. v. Commissioner*, 421) U.S. 569, 583, 97 S. Ct. 850, 858, 51 L. Ed. 2d 48 (1977). Never mind, he says. He has nonetheless increased the total basis of the property transferred and avoided the tax. I understand the temptation to embrace that argument, but I see no real support for it in the law.

Peracchi says a lot about economic realities. I see nothing real about that maneuver. I see, rather, a bit of sortilege that would have made Merlin envious. The taxpayer has created something – basis – out of nothing.

Thus, I respectfully dissent.

PROBLEM 14-3

Landlord owns a piece of real estate that may be subject to a disputed Comprehensive Environmental Response Compensation and Liability Act (CERCLA) liability. The liability would attach to the land, not the landlord. Landlord's basis in the real estate is $100,000, and its fair market value is $500,000. He decides to contribute the property to his newly-formed, wholly-owned corporation, Shell, Inc.

1) If, before Landlord contributed the real estate, it had attracted a $400,000 fixed CERCLA liability, will he be taxed at all on the contribution, and if so, what will be his taxable income or gain? *See* § 357(c).

2) If the disputed liability was merely contingent at the time of the contribution, would Landlord be taxed on the liability transferred to Shell, Inc. under § 357(c)?

3) If Shell, Inc. pays the disputed liability, can it claim a deduction (if any) for the disputed CERCLA liability? Skim § 198 for a special opportunity.

4) If Shell, Inc. instead spends $200,000 to clean up a CERCLA problem that was contingent at the time of transfer, should Shell be entitled to deduct the expense?

L. PROPERTY TRANSFERRED IN EXCHANGE

JAMES v. COMMISSIONER
53 T.C. 63 (1969)

SIMPSON, JUDGE.

The issue for decision is whether the transaction by which Mr. James and Mr. Talbot acquired stock in a corporation was taxable or whether such transaction was tax-free under section 351 of the Internal Revenue Code of 1954. The answer to the question thus posed with respect to each person depends on the determination of whether Mr. James received his stock in exchange for a transfer of property or as compensation for services.

Findings of Fact

For many years, Mr. James was a builder, real estate promoter, and developer with offices in Myrtle Beach, S.C. He has held the office of vice president of the National Association of Home Builders and was chairman of the association's Senior Citizens Housing Committee. During 1963, the James Construction Co. was licensed by the State of South Carolina to engage in the business of general contracting.

On January 12, 1963, Mr. and Mrs. Talbot entered into an agreement with Mr. James for the promotion and construction of a rental apartment project. The agreement provided that on completion of the project the parties would form a corporation to take title to the project. The voting stock in such corporation was to be distributed one-half to the Talbots and one-half to Mr. James . . . The Talbots agreed to transfer to the corporation the land on which the apartment project was to be built, such land to be the only asset contributed by the Talbots to the venture. Mr. James agreed "to promote the project . . . and . . . [to] be responsible for the planning, architectural work, construction, landscaping, legal fees, and loan processing of the entire project." The agreement gave him until January 1. 1964, to promote the project . . .

After the execution of the January 12 agreement, Mr. James began negotiations to fulfill his part of the contract. He made arrangements with an attorney and an architectural firm to perform the work necessary to meet FHA requirements – development of legal documents, preparation of architectural plans, and the like: and he obtained from United Mortgagee Service Corp. (United Mortgagee), a lender, its agreement to finance the project and a commitment by FHA to insure the financing. The attorney's and architect's fees were not paid by Mr. James but were paid out of the proceeds of the construction loan by the corporation subsequently established. . .

On November 5, 1963, Chicora Apartments, Inc. (Chicora), was granted, upon application of Messrs. Talbot and James, a corporate charter, stating its authorized capital stock to consist of 20 no-par common shares. On the same date, the land on which the apartment project was to be constructed was conveyed to Chicora by Mrs. Talbot in consideration for 10 shares of stock . . . Chicora's board of directors determined that on the date of this conveyance the value of the real property so transferred was $44,000. Also on November 5, 1963, 10 shares of stock were issued to Mr. James. The minutes of a meeting of Chicora's board of directors held on that date state that those 10 shares were issued to Mr. James in consideration of his "transfer" to the corporation of the "following described property":

1. FHA Commitment issued pursuant to Title 2, Section 207 of the National Housing Act, whereby the FHA agrees to insure a mortgage loan in the amount of $850,700.00, on a parcel of land in Myrtle Beach, South Carolina, more particularly described in Schedule "A" hereto attached, provided 66 apartment units are constructed thereon in accordance with plans and specifications as prepared by Lyles, Bissett, Carlisle & Wolff, Architects-Engineers, of Columbia, South Carolina.

2. Commitment from United Mortgagee Servicing Corp., agreeing to make a mortgage loan on said property in the amount of $850,700.00 and also commitment from said mortgagee to make an interim construction loan in an identical amount.

3. Certain contracts and agreements which W. A. James over the past two years have [sic] worked out and developed in connection with the architectural and construction services required for said project.

4. The use of the finances and credit of W. A. James during the past two years (and including the construction period) in order to make it possible to proceed with the project.

Thus, as a result of these transactions, Chicora had outstanding all 20 of its authorized shares of stock . . . Both Mr. and Mrs. James and Mr. and Mrs. Talbot deemed their receipt of Chicora common stock to be in return for a transfer of property to a controlled corporation under section 351. Accordingly, neither family reported any income from such receipt on their respective income tax returns for 1963. In his statutory notice of deficiency, the respondent determined that Mr. James received such stock, with a value of $22,000, for services rendered and not in exchange for property, and thus received taxable income in that amount. He further determined that the Talbot's transfer of property to Chicora did not meet the requirements of section 351, with the result that they should have recognized a long-term capital gain of $14,675 – the difference between $7,325, the basis of the land transferred and $22,000, the value of the stock received.

Opinion

The first, and critical, issue for our determination is whether Mr. James received his Chicora stock in exchange for the transfer of property or as compensation for services. The petitioners argue that he received such stock in consideration of his transfer to Chicora of the FHA and United Mortgagee commitments and that such commitments constituted "property" within the meaning of section 351. The respondent does not appear to challenge the petitioners' implicit assertion that Mr. James was not expected to render future services to the corporation in exchange for the issuance of stock to him. Although the accuracy of this assertion is subject to some question, the state of the record is such that we must decide the issues as the parties have presented them. Thus, the sole question on this issue is whether Mr. James' personal services, which the petitioners freely admit were rendered, resulted in the development of a property right which was transferred to Chicora, within the meaning of section 351.

. . . According to the petitioners' argument, Mr. James, as a result of the services performed by him, acquired certain contract rights which constituted property and which he transferred to Chicora. The fact that such rights resulted from the performance of personal services does not, in their view, disqualify them from being treated as property for purposes of section 351. In support of this position, the petitioners refer to situations involving the transfer of patents and secret processes. *James C. Hamrick*, 43 T.C. 21 (1964); *Lanova Corporation*, 17 T.C. 1178 (1952); *Ralph L. Evans*, 8 B.T.A. 543 (1927); Rev. Rul. 64-56, 1964-1 C.B. (Part I) 133. *Cf. Roberts Co.*, 5 T.C. 1 (1945).

It is altogether clear that for purposes of section 351, not every right is to be treated as property. The second sentence of such section indicates that, whatever may be considered as property for purposes of local law, the performance of services, or the agreement to perform services, is not to be treated as a transfer of property for purposes of section 351. Thus, if in this case we have merely an agreement to perform services in exchange for stock of the corporation to be created, the performance of such services does not constitute the transfer of property within the meaning of section 351.

Although patents and secret processes – the product of services – are treated as property for purposes of section 351, we have carefully analyzed the arrangement in this case and have concluded that Mr. James did not transfer any property essentially like a patent or secret process;

he merely performed services to Chicora. In January of 1963, he entered into an agreement to perform services for the corporation to be created. He was to secure the necessary legal and architectural work and to arrange for the financing of the project, and these were the services performed by him. Although he secured the services of the lawyer and the architect, they were paid for by the corporation. He put in motion the wheels that led to the FHA commitment, but it was not a commitment to him – it was a commitment to United Mortgagee to insure a loan to Chicora, a project sponsored by Mr. James. It was stipulated that under the FHA Regulations, a commitment would not be issued to an individual, but only to a corporation. Throughout these arrangements, it was contemplated that a corporation would be created and that the commitment would run to the corporation. . . .

The facts of this case are substantially similar to those in *United States v. Frazell*, 335 F.2d 487 (C.A. 5, 1964), *rehearing denied*, 339 F.2d 885 (C.A. 5. 1964), *certiorari denied*, 380 U.S. 961 (1965). In that case, the taxpayer, a geologist investigated certain oil and gas properties to be acquired by a joint venture, and he was to receive an interest in the joint venture. However, before any transfer was made to him, a corporation was formed to take over the assets of the joint venture, and part of the stock was transferred to the taxpayer. It was not clear whether the taxpayer acquired an interest in the joint venture which was then exchanged for his share of the stock or whether he acquired the stock directly in exchange for the services performed by him. The court found that, in either event, the taxpayer received compensation for his services. If he received the stock in return for the services performed by him, such stock was taxable as compensation, and he did not transfer any property to the corporation within the meaning of section 351. See also *Mailloux v. Commissioner*, 320 F.2d 60 (C.A. 5, 1963), affirming on this issue a Memorandum Opinion of this Court.

The next question is whether the Talbots are taxable on the gain realized from the exchange of their land for Chicora stock. Section 351(a) applies only if immediately after the transfer those who transferred property in exchange for stock owned at least 80 percent of Chicora's stock. Sec. 368(c). Since Mr. James is not to be treated as a transferor of property, he cannot be included among those in control for purposes of this test. *Fahs v. Florida Machine & Foundry Co.*, 168 F.2d 957 (C.A. 5, 1948); *Mojonnier & Sons, Inc.*, 12 T.C. 837 (1949). The transferors of property, the Talbots, did not have the required 80-percent control of Chicora immediately after the transfer, and, therefore, their gain must be recognized. This result is inconsistent with the apparent meaning of the second sentence from the committee report, but the statutory scheme does not permit any other conclusion. . . .

Decision will be entered for the respondent.

PROBLEM 14-4

So what? What were the tax implications to both incorporators as a result of the lack of control in *James*?

M. BASIS OF TRANSFEROR'S STOCK
Read § 358(a), (b).

In general, the basis of stock in the transferor's hands will be the same as the basis of the property now in the corporation's hands. The result, as with partnerships, is that the amount of basis in the world has doubled through legal magic, with the possibility for gain or loss also doubling. For instance, if the property had a basis in excess of its value, the corporation could sell the property at a loss and the shareholder could sell his stock at a loss. The potential for proliferation of gains and losses is serious. For example, if the corporate recipient just described promptly formed its own subsidiary using the very same property, that would triple the amount of potential loss.

232

If the shareholder also receives boot, § 358(a)(2) gives the boot a basis equal to its value. American money (but not foreign currency) obviously has to take a basis exactly equal to its face amount. The general result of boot is that it causes recognition of gain which is taxed at its fair market value and converted into basis in the boot. Any remaining unrecognized gain in the contributed property is deferred in the form of built-in gain in the stock received. The distributing corporation is taxed on any gain inherent in boot it distributes as if it sold the boot. §§ 311 and 1001(c).

Boot also requires adjusting the transferor's basis in the stock received. § 358(a)(1). Starting with the same basis as the transferred property, the stock basis is then decreased by the amount of boot received (because boot is a disinvestment from the continuing business) and increased by the amount of gain recognized (to prevent double taxation of the same gain to the same person).

To illustrate: Mr. Small transfers property with a basis of $30 and a value of $50 to Newco in exchange for $40 worth of Newco stock plus $10 cash. The cash is boot and is fully taxed. The stock has a basis of $30 ($30 substituted basis less $10 boot plus $10 gain recognized). The adjustments will not always be equal. If Mr. Small had received $25 worth of stock plus $25 cash, only $20 of the $25 boot would be taxable, because Mr. Small's realized gain is only $20 (i.e., the $50 amount realized less $30 basis). But under § 358(a)(1) the full amount of boot must be subtracted from basis, which therefore equals $25 ($30 substituted basis less $25 boot plus $20 gain recognized). This gives the correct result because the stock is presumably worth $25 (i.e., the $50 property less $25 boot paid for it), and if sold, it should not trigger any additional gain, because the original $20 of built-in gain has already been fully taxed through Mr. Small's receipt of boot.

Section 358(d) provides a logical way to handle liabilities of the transferors or encumbrances on the property transferred to the corporation. It requires the transferor to reduce basis in the stock she receives as if she had received cash boot in the amount of the liabilities. If this did not happen, the basis of the stock would be exaggerated and an opportunity for artificial losses would arise. Remember, however, that this transferred-liability-as-boot treatment is limited to basis calculations under § 358; receipt of the deemed boot is generally not taxed thanks to § 357(a).

To illustrate: Mr. Small transfers property with a basis of $30 to Newco. In exchange, he gets back stock and the assumption of a $10 debt which is associated with the property. Section 358(d) makes Mr. Small's basis in the stock $20. Assuming that the property has a fair market value of $50, ignoring the mortgage, we know that the unrealized gain on the property is $20 (i.e., $50 value minus $30 basis). We have just seen that the basis of the stock will be $20. We know that if the corporation sells the land, and the land is the only asset, it will get a net cash amount of $40. That means that the stock must also be worth $40. Now, if Mr. Small sells the stock he will receive $40 but will have a basis of only $20. This means that he will report a $20 gain on his tax return in the year he sells the stock, and this is correct; it is identical to the gain that he would have reported had he sold the land directly. But for § 358(d), his basis in the stock would have been too high, and a loophole would have been created.

Stock basis is not reduced for the assumption of liabilities which would have been deductible by the transferor, such as accounts payable. § 358(d)(2). This exception parallels the exception of § 357(c)(3), under which deductible liabilities do not count in determining whether the aggregate liabilities transferred exceed the aggregate basis of the assets transferred.

Holding period for stock. The holding period for stock received tax-free consists of its actual holding period from the date of the exchange plus the transferor's holding period for the transferred property which is "tacked" on, but only if and to the extent that the property was a capital asset or § 1231 property. § 1223(1). If the transferred property consisted of a mix of capital assets, 1231 assets, and noncapital assets, which is usually the case when a proprietorship or partnership is incorporated, each share will have a divided holding period which is allocated according to the relative fair market value of the transferred property. Rev. Rul. 85-164, 1985-2 C.B. 117.

To illustrate: Return to Rev. Rul. 68-55, *supra* Section 1, and observe that three different assets were exchanged for one class of stock (plus cash). Two of the assets were capital, of which only one had already been held long-term, and the third asset was noncapital. Each share of stock will have a split holding period in proportion to the fair market value of the assets, respectively 20%, 30%, and 50%. Thus, if the transferor-shareholder sells a share of stock the day after the exchange, 20% of the proceeds will be long-term and 80% will be short-term, taxable at ordinary income rates if those are the taxpayer's only capital transactions for the year.

PROBLEM 14-5

Mr. Big forms Big Co. by transferring land worth $150 and having a basis of $90, plus equipment worth $50 and having a basis of $80. In exchange, Big Co. issued stock worth $160 and cash of $40.

1)   How much gain or loss does Mr. Big realize?

2)   How much gain or loss does he recognize?

3)   What is the basis of his stock of Big Co.? See §358.

4)   If he immediately sells the stock of Big Co., how much gain or loss will he recognize?

N. CORPORATION'S BASIS IN PROPERTY IT RECEIVES
Read § 362(a).

The corporation will generally take the shareholder's basis in contributed property, increased by the amount of gain that the shareholder recognizes on the transfer. If the corporation receives property subject to a liability or assumes liabilities, this will have no impact on the basis of the transferred property, except to the extent that the transferor recognizes gain under § 357.

PROBLEM 14-6

Two individuals, A and B, decide to form X Corporation. A transfers land worth $100,000 (basis $120,000) for 50 shares of stock in X Corp. worth $100,000. B transfers a building worth $60,000 (basis $30,000) and cash of $40,000 for 50 shares of stock in X Corp. worth $100,000. The land and building had both been held for 3 years and used in A's and B's business. *See* § 351(a) and Reg. § 1.351-1.

1) How much gain or loss do A and B recognize under §§ 351 and 1001?

2) What is the basis of the shares held by A? By B?

3) How much gain or loss does X Corp. recognize as a result of the transfer?

4) What is X Corp.'s basis in the property it received?

5) What is X Corp.'s holding period in the assets it received?

PROBLEM 14-7

C, an accrual method taxpayer, transfers equipment worth $65,000 in which she has a basis of $35,000. C used the equipment for many years in her sole proprietorship before she incorporated. She originally paid $100,000 for the equipment. C also contributes $25,000 (by basis and value) of accounts receivable, to her wholly-owned corporation. In return, C receives stock in the corporation worth $50,000 and a note receivable from the corporation with a face amount and value of $40,000.

1) How much and of what character gain or loss does C *realize* on the transaction?

2) What fraction of the properties C received (*i.e.*, the note) is allocable to the equipment she transferred to the corporation?

3) Should any portion of the note C received be treated as boot, and if so, in what amount?

4) What is the amount of gain *recognized* by C allocable to the equipment and allocable to the accounts receivable respectively?

5) What is C's subsequent basis in the stock and note received from the corporation?

6) Does the corporation recognize any gain or loss on the transaction?

7) Is C's holding period in the equipment and accounts receivable tacked to the corporation's holding period?

PROBLEM 14-8

Eric owns a rental building held for investment worth $200, in which he has a basis of $110. The building, which he had held for six months, is subject to a nonrecourse mortgage which has a balance of $150. Eric transfers the building to his wholly-owned corporation in return for 500 shares of stock worth $50.

1) How much gain or loss does Eric realize as a result of the transfer?

2) How much gain or loss does Eric recognize as a result of the transfer?

3) What is the character of any gain recognized?

4) What basis and holding period does Eric take in the stock?

5) Does the corporation recognize any gain or loss on the transaction?

235

6) What basis does the corporation take in the building?

O. SPECIAL PROBLEMS OF MIDSTREAM INCORPORATION

Corporations may be formed to begin a new business, but they also may be used to incorporate an existing business that was carried on as a proprietorship or partnership. In such cases, there would typically be unpaid accounts payable and receivable and a variety of other bookkeeping entries that have a potential for tax mischief.

HEMPT BROS., INC. v. UNITED STATES
490 F.2d 1172 (3d Cir. 1974), cert. denied (1974)

Aldisert, Circuit Judge.

In this appeal by a corporate taxpayer from a grant of summary judgment in favor of the government in a claim for refund, we are called upon to decide the proper treatment of accounts receivable and of inventory transferred from a cash basis partnership to a corporation organized to continue the business under Section 351(a). This appeal illustrates the conflict between the statutory purpose of Section 351, postponement of recognition of gain or loss, and the assignment of income and tax benefit doctrines.

The facts were wholly stipulated; therefore, they may be summarized as set forth by the government in its brief:

The taxpayer is a Pennsylvania Corporation with its principal place of business with its principal place of business in Camp Hill, Pennsylvania. From 1942 until February 28, 1957, a partnership comprised of Loy T. Hempt, J. F. Hempt, Max C. Hempt, and the George L. Hempt Estate was engaged in the business of quarrying and selling stone, sand, gravel, and slag; manufacturing and selling, ready-mix concrete and bituminous material; constructing roads, highways, and streets, primarily for the Pennsylvania Department of Highways and various political subdivisions of Pennsylvania, and constructing driveways, parking lots, street and water lines, and related accessories.

The partnership maintained its books and records, and filed its partnership income tax returns. on the basis of a calendar year and on the cash method of accounting so that no income was reported until actually received in cash. Accordingly in computing its income for federal income tax purposes the partnership did not take uncollected receivables into income, and inventories were not used in the calculation of its taxable income although both accounts receivable reflecting sales already made and physical inventories existed to a substantial extent at the end of each of the partnership's taxable years. Rather than using the inventory method of accounting. the partnership deducted the costs of its physical inventories of sand, gravel, and stone as incurred . . . On March 1, 1957 the partnership business and most of its assets were transferred to the taxpayer solely in exchange for taxpayer's capital stock, the 12,000 shares of which were issued to the four members of the partnership. These shares constituted 100% of the issued and outstanding shares of the taxpayer. This transfer was made pursuant to Section 351(a) of the Internal Revenue Code of 1954.

Thereafter the taxpayer conducted the business formerly conducted by the partnership.

Among the assets transferred by the partnership to the taxpayer for taxpayer's shares of stock were accounts receivable in the amount of $662,824.40 arising from performance of construction projects, sales of stone, sand, gravel, etc., and rental of equipment prior to March 1, 1957. Also among the assets transferred were physical inventories of sand, gravel, and stone, with respect to which the partnership had deducted costs of $351,266.05 and the value of which was no less than $351.266.05.

Commencing with its initial fiscal year (which) ended February 28, 1958, taxpayer maintained its books and filed its corporation income tax returns on the cash method of accounting and, accordingly, did not take uncollected receivables into income and did not use inventories in the calculation of its taxable income. In its taxable years ending in 1958, 1959, and 1960, taxpayer collected the respective amounts of $533,247.87, $125,326.71 and $4,249.72 of the accounts receivable in the aggregate amount of $662,824.40 [sic] that had been transferred to it, and included those amounts in income in computing its income for its federal income tax returns for those years, respectively . . .

The Commissioner of Internal Revenue assessed deficiencies in taxpayer's federal income taxes for its fiscal years ending February 28, 1958, and 1959. The taxpayer paid the amounts in 1964, and in 1965 filed claims for refund of $621,218.09 plus assessed interest. The claims were disallowed in full on September 24, 1968, and the district court action was timely instituted on December 5, 1968.

The district court held (1) taxpayer was properly taxable upon collections made with respect to accounts receivable which were transferred to it in conjunction with the Section 351 incorporation . . .

Taxpayer argues here, as it did in the district court, that because the term "property" as used in Section 351 does not embrace accounts receivable, the Commissioner lacked statutory authority to apply principles associated with Section 351. The district court properly rejected the legal interpretation urged by the taxpayer.

The definition of Section 351 "property" has been extensively treated by the Court of Claims in *E.I. Du Pont de Nemouri and Co. v. United States*, 471 F.2d 1211, 1218-1219 (Ct. Cl. 1973), describing the transfer of a non-exclusive license to make, use and sell area herbicides under French patents:

Unless there is some special reason intrinsic to . . . [Section 351], . . . the general word "property" has a broad reach in tax law. . . . For section 351, in particular, courts have advocated a generous definition of "property". . . , and it has been suggested in one capital gains case that nonexclusive licenses can be viewed as property though not as capital assets. . . . We see no adequate reason for refusing to follow these leads.

We fail to perceive any special reason why a restrictive meaning should be applied to accounts receivables so as to exclude them from the general meaning of "property." Receivables possess the usual capabilities and attributes associated with jurisprudential concepts of property law. They may be identified, valued, and transferred. Moreover, their role in an ongoing business must be viewed in the context of Section 351 application. The presence of accounts receivable is a normal, rather than an exceptional accouterment of the type of business included by Congress in the transfer to a corporate form. They are "commonly thought of in the commercial world as a positive business asset." *Du Pont v. United States. supra*, at 1218. As aptly put by the district court: "There is a compelling reason to construe `property' to include . . . (accounts receivable): a new corporation needs working capital, and accounts receivable can be an important source of liquidity." *Hempt Bros., Inc. v. United States, supra*, at 1176. In any event, this court had no difficulty in characterizing a sale of receivables as "property" within the purview of the "no gain or loss" provision of Section 337 as a "qualified sale of property within a 12-month period." *Citizens Acceptance Corp. v. United States,* 462 F.2d 751, 756 (3d Cir. 1972).

The taxpayer next makes a strenuous argument that "the government is seeking to tax the wrong person." It contends that the assignment of income doctrine as developed by the Supreme Court applies to a Section 351 transfer of accounts receivable so that the transferor, not the transferee-corporation, bears the corresponding tax liability. It argues that the assignment of income doctrine dictates that where the right to receive income is transferred to another person in a transaction not giving rise to tax at the time of transfer, the transferor is taxed on the income when it is collected by the transferee; that the only requirement for its application is a transfer of a right to receive ordinary income; and that since the transferred accounts receivable are a present right to future income, the sole requirement for the application of the doctrine is squarely met. In essence, this is a contention that the nonrecognition provision of Section 351 is in conflict with the assignment of income doctrine and that Section 351 should be subordinated thereto. Taxpayer relies on the seminal case of Lucas v. Earl, 281 U.S. 111, 74 L. Ed. 731, 50 S. Ct. 241 (1930), and its progeny for support of its proposition that the application of the doctrine is mandated whenever one transfers a right to receive ordinary income.

On its part the government concedes that a taxpayer may sell for value a claim to income otherwise his own and he will be taxable upon the proceeds of the sale. Such was the case in *Commissioner v. P. G. Lake, Inc.*, 356 U.S. 260, 2 L. Ed. 2d 743, 78 S. Ct. 691 (1958). in which the taxpayer-corporation assigned its oil payment right to its president in consideration for his cancellation of a $600,000 loan. Viewing the oil payment right as a right to receive future income, the Court applied the reasoning of the assignment of income doctrine, normally applicable to a gratuitous assignment and held that the consideration received by the taxpayer-corporation was taxable as ordinary income since it essentially was a substitute for that which would otherwise be received at a future time as ordinary income.

Turning to the facts of this case, we note that here there was the transfer of accounts receivable from the partnership to the corporation pursuant to Section 351. We view these accounts receivable as a present right to receive future income. In consideration of the transfer of this right, the members of the partnership received stock – a valid consideration. The consideration, therefore, was essentially a substitute for that which would otherwise be received at a future time as ordinary income to the cash basis partnership. Consequently, the holding in Lake would normally apply, and income would ordinarily be realized, and thereby taxable, by the cash basis partnership-transferor at the time of receipt of the stock.

But the terms and purpose of Section 351 have to be reckoned with. By its explicit terms Section 351 expresses the Congressional intent that transfers of property for stock or securities will not result in recognition. It therefore becomes apparent that this case vividly illustrates how Section 351 sometimes comes into conflict with another provision of the Internal Revenue Code or a judicial doctrine, and requires a determination of which of two conflicting doctrines will control.

As we must, when we try to reconcile conflicting doctrines in the revenue law, we endeavor to ascertain a controlling Congressional mandate. Section 351 has been described as a deliberate attempt by Congress to facilitate the incorporation of ongoing businesses and to eliminate any technical constructions which are economically unsound.[2] Appellant-taxpayer seems to recognize this and argues that application of the Lake rationale when accounts

---

[2] "One of the purposes of this section (Section 202(c)(3) of the Revenue Act of 1921) was to permit changes in form (of business) involving no change in substance to be made without undue restriction from the tax laws." Note, *Section 351 of the Internal Revenue Code and "Mid-Stream" Incorporations*, 38 U. Cin. L. Rev. 96 (1969). *See* S. Rep. No. 275, 67th Cong. 1st Sess. 11 (1921). This intention is also reflected in the report of the House of Representatives accompanying 351 of the Internal Revenue Code of 1954. H.R. Rep. No. 1337, 83rd Cong. 2d Sess. 34 (1954). The House Ways and Means Committee recommended that nonrecognition treatment be granted for incorporation, reorganization and certain other types of exchanges to "permit business to go forward with the readjustments required by existing conditions" and to prevent "taxpayers from taking colorable losses in wash sales and other fictitious exchanges." *See* H.R. Rep. 350 67th Cong., 1st Sess. 10 (1921). The Senate Finance Committee added that such treatment would eliminate "many technical constructions which are economically unsound." *See* S. Rep. 275, 67th Cong. 1st Sess. 12 (1921). Weiss, *supra* 41 Ind. L.J. 666 n.4 (1966).

receivable are transferred would not create any undue hardship to an incorporating taxpayer. "All a taxpayer (transferor) need do is withhold the earned income items and collect them, transferring the net proceeds to the Corporation. Indeed . . . the transferor should retain both accounts receivable and accounts payable to avoid income recognition at the time of transfer and to have sufficient funds with which to pay accounts payable. Where the taxpayer (transferor) is on the cash method of accounting (as here), the deduction of the accounts payable would be applied against the income generated by the accounts receivable . . . " (Appellants' Brief at 32.)

While we cannot fault the general principle "that income be taxed to him who earns it," to adopt taxpayer's argument would be to hamper the incorporation of ongoing businesses; additionally it would impose technical constructions which are economically and practically unsound. None of the cases cited by taxpayer, including *Lake* itself, persuades us otherwise. In *Lake* the Court was required to decide whether the proceeds from the assignment of the oil payment right were taxable as ordinary income or as long term capital gains. Observing that the provision for long term capital gains treatment "has always been narrowly construed so as to protect the revenue against artful devices," 356 U.S. at 265, 78 S. Ct. at 694, the Court predicated its holding upon an emphatic distinction between a conversion of a capital investment "income-producing property" – and an assignment of income per se. "The substance of what was assigned was the right to receive future income. The substance of what was received was the present value of income which the recipient would otherwise obtain in the future." *Ibid.,* at 266, 78 S. Ct. at 695. A Section 351 issue was not presented in Lake. Therefore the case does not control in weighing the conflict between the general rule of assignment of income and the Congressional purpose of nonrecognition upon the incorporation of an ongoing business.

We are persuaded that, on balance, the teachings of *Lake* must give way in this case to the broad Congressional interest in facilitating the incorporation of on-going businesses. As desirable as it is to afford symmetry in revenue law, we do not intend to promulgate a hard and fast rule. We believe that the problems posed by the clash of conflicting internal revenue doctrines are more properly determined by the circumstances of each case. Here we are influenced by the fact that the subject of the assignment was accounts receivable for partnership's goods and services sold in the regular course of business, that the change of business form from partnership to corporation had a basic business purpose and was not designed for the purpose of deliberate tax avoidance, and by the conviction that the totality of circumstances here presented fit the mold of the Congressional intent to give nonrecognition to a transfer of a total business from a non-corporate to a corporate form.

But this too must be said. Even though Section 351(a) immunizes the transferor from immediate tax consequences, Section 358 retains for the transferors a potential income tax liability to be realized and recognized upon a subsequent sale or exchange of the stock certificates received. As to the transferee-corporation, the tax basis of the receivables will be governed by Section 362.

[The other issues are omitted.]

We have carefully considered each of appellant's contentions and have concluded that the judgment of the district court will be affirmed.

NOTES

1. **Tax benefit rule**. In *Nash v. United States*, 398 U.S. 1 (1970), the Supreme Court resolved a long-standing uncertainty about how previously deducted reserves for bad debts should be treated when a business is transferred from a proprietorship to a corporation. The Supreme Court held that the taxpayer did not have to take his bad-debt reserves into income when he transferred his receivables. Instead he was treated as having transferred only the

net value of his receivables. For example, if a proprietor who has a $10 reserve for bad debts transfers $100 of receivables, the *Nash* case would allow him to treat the transfer as if he contributed $90 worth of receivables to the corporation rather than forcing him to report $10 of tax benefit income and a $100 transfer to the corporation.

2. **Some tax planning implications**. One should not assume that tax advisors simply suggest their clients dump *all* of their business assets into a corporation. For example, they may suggest that the contributor engage in any one of the following planning devices:

   a) Retention of property that can be sold at a loss, or retention of nondepreciable real estate that can be leased to the corporation. This can permit the owners to drain off corporate income in a deductible manner and shift it to owners of the land, which might be a benefit to the founders' children if they are in a low tax bracket.

   b) Sale (rather than contribution for stock) of property to the corporation at a loss, provided § 267(a) can be avoided.

   c) Sale of property to the corporation in exchange for a long-term debt obligation in order to drain off corporate income as interest and to allow the debt holder to withdraw her investment in the corporation as a nontaxable return of capital.

   d) Sale of appreciated land to a corporation in exchange for an installment obligation, if the corporation then subdivides the land and generates ordinary income from sales. This may ensure the transferor a long-term capital gain for the pre-existing appreciation while shifting future ordinary income to the corporation, which may be taxed at a lower rate.

   e) Avoiding § 351 on the entire transaction, so as to be able to report losses, say by issuing too much stock in exchange for services or the stock of a single small class to a service provider.

3. **Is a business purpose required for a § 351 transaction?** The government's position is not surprising: "yes." See Rev. Rul.70-140 1970-1 C.B. 73. The Tax Court agrees. *See West Coast Mktg. Corp. v. Commissioner*, 46 T.C. 32 (1966), in which a purported § 351 transaction was ignored for tax purposes and treated as a taxable sale because the transferors immediately disposed of the stock and because the acquirer promptly liquidated the controlled corporation, indicating that its sole purpose was to avoid taxation of the transferors' gain. There is older authority to the contrary, but it seems suspect. *See, e.g., W&K Holding Co. v. Commissioner,* 38 B.T.A. 830 (1938).

4. **Assignments of income**. Consider a lawyer who is about to get lucky. He is a plaintiff's lawyer who works on a contingent fee basis. The biggest case of his life has just gone to trial and he expects to collect a million dollar contingent fee. He incorporates his practice, assigns all his right to payment and all his receivables to a newly-formed corporation in anticipation of a favorable decision by the jury. Will he be taxed on the contingent fee on an assignment of income theory, even though it has been legally transferred to the corporation? The answer is "yes," according to *Brown v. Commissioner*, 40 B.T.A. 565 (1939), *aff'd* 1 15 F.2d 337 (2d Cir. 1940). He might also lose on the theory that there was no business purpose for the incorporation.

5. **Section 482**. Consider a farmer who deducts lots of money for seed and planting in the spring, incorporates the farm in the summer, and harvests and sells the crop in the fall. The corporation's income tax return shows the crop income and the farmer's shows the big deductions for seeds and planting. Can the IRS successfully make a § 482 assertion that there was a tax-driven mismatch of income and expenses, and add the deductions to the corporation's tax return, on the theory that the transaction was between commonly controlled entities (the farm proprietorship and the corporation) and distorted their incomes? Yes, according to *Rooney v. Commissioner*, 305 F.2d 681 (9th Cir. 1962).

REV. RUL. 84-111
1984-2 C.B. 88

Issue

Does Rev. Rul. 70-239. 1970-1 C.B. 74, still represent the Service's position with respect to the three situations described therein?

Facts

The three situations described in Rev. Rul. 70-239, 180-1 C.B. 74 involve partnerships X, Y. and Z. respectively. Each partnership used the accrual method of accounting and had assets and liabilities consisting of cash, equipment, and accounts payable. The liabilities of each partnership did not exceed the adjusted basis of its assets. The three situations are as follows:

Situation 1

X transferred all of its assets to newly-formed corporation R in exchange for all the outstanding stock of R and the assumption by R of X's liabilities. X then terminated by distributing all the stock of R to X's partners in proportion to their partnership interests.

Situation 2

Y distributed all of its assets and liabilities to its partners in proportion to their partnership interests in a transaction that constituted a termination of Y under section 708(b)(1)(A) of the Code. The partners then transferred all the assets received from Y to newly-formed corporations in exchange for all the outstanding stock of S and the assumption by S of Y's liabilities that had been assumed by the partners.

Situation 3

The partners of Z transferred their partnership interests in Z to newly-formed corporation T in exchange for all the outstanding stock of T. This exchange terminated Z and all of its assets and liabilities became assets and liabilities of T.

In each situation, the steps taken by X, Y, and Z, and the partners of X, Y, and Z, were parts of a plan to transfer the partnership operations to a corporation organized for valid business reasons in exchange for its stock and were not devices to avoid or evade recognition of gain. Rev. Rul. 70-239, 1970-1 C.B. 74 holds that because the federal income tax consequences of the three situations are the same, each partnership is considered to have transferred its assets and liabilities to a corporation in exchange for its stock under section 351 of the Internal Revenue Code, followed by a distribution of the stock to the partners in liquidation of the partnership.

Law and Analysis

Section 351(a) of the Code provides that no gain or loss will be recognized if property is transferred to a corporation by one or more persons solely in exchange for stock or securities in such corporation and immediately after the exchange such person or persons are in control (as defined in section 368(c)) of the corporation.

Section 1.351-1(a)(1) of the Income Tax Regulations provides that, as used in section 351 of the Code, the phrase "one or more persons" includes individuals, trusts, estates, partnerships, associations, companies, or corporations. To be in control of the transferee corporation, such person or persons must own immediately after the transfer stock possessing at least 80 percent of the total combined voting power of all classes of stock entitled to vote and at least 80 percent of the total number of shares of all other classes of stock of such corporation.

Section 358(a) of the Code provides that in the case of an exchange to which section 351 applies, the basis of the property permitted to be received under such section without the recognition of gain or loss will be the same as that of the property exchanged, decreased by the amount of any money received by the taxpayer.

Section 358(d) of the Code provides that where, as part of the consideration to the taxpayer, another party to the exchange assumed a liability of the taxpayer or acquired from the taxpayer property subject to a liability, such assumption or acquisition (in the amount of, the liability) will, for purposes of section 358, be treated as money received by the taxpayer on the exchange.

Section 362(a) of the Code provides that a corporation's basis in property acquired in a transaction to which section 351 applies will be the same as it would be in the hands of the transferor.

Under section 708(b)(1)(A) of the Code, a partnership is terminated if no part of any business, financial operation, or venture of the partnership continues to be carried on by any of its partners in a partnership. Under section 708(b)(1)(B), a partnership terminates if within a 12-month period there is a sale or exchange of 50 percent or more of the total interest in partnership capital and profits.

Section 732(b) of the Code provides that the basis of property other than money distributed by a partnership in a liquidation of a partner's interest shall be an amount equal to the adjusted basis of the partner's interest in the partnership reduced by any money distributed. Section 732(c) of the Code provides rules for the allocation of a partner's basis in a partnership interest among the assets received in a liquidating distribution.

Section 735(b) of the Code provides that a partner's holding period for property received in a distribution from a partnership (other than with respect to certain inventory items defined in section 751(d)(2)) includes the partnership's holding period, as determined under section 1223, with respect to such property.

Section 1223(1) of the Code provides that where property received in an exchange acquires the same basis, in whole or in part, as the property surrendered in the exchange, the holding period of the property received includes the holding period of the property surrendered to the extent such surrendered property was a capital asset or property described in section 1231. Under section 1223(2), the holding period of a taxpayer's property, however acquired, includes the period during which the property was held by any other person if that property has the same basis, in whole or in part, in the taxpayer's hands as it would have in the hands of such other person.

Section 741 of the Code provides that in the case of a sale or exchange of an interest in a partnership, gain or loss shall be recognized to the transferor partner. Such gain or loss shall be considered as a gain or loss from the sale or exchange of a capital asset, except as otherwise provided in section 751.

242

Section 751(a) of the Code provides that the amount of money or the fair value of property received by a transferor partner in exchange for all or part of such partner's interest in the partnership attributable to unrealized receivables of the partnership, or to inventory items of the partnership that have appreciated substantially in value, shall be considered as an amount realized from the sale or exchange of property other than a capital asset.

Section 752(a) of the Code provides that any increase in a partner's share of the liabilities of a partnership, or any increase in a partner's individual liabilities by reason of the assumption by the partner of partnership liabilities, will be considered as a contribution of money by such partner to the partnership.

Section 752(b) of the Code provides that any decrease in a partner's share of the liabilities of a partnership, or any decrease in a partner's individual liabilities by reason of the assumption by the partnership of such individual liabilities, will be considered as a distribution of money to the partner by the partnership. Under section 733(1) of the Code, the basis of a partner's interest in the partnership is reduced by the amount of money received in a distribution that is not in liquidation of the partnership.

Section 752(d) of the Code provides that in the case of a sale or exchange of an interest in a partnership, liabilities shall be treated in the same manner as liabilities in connection with the sale or exchange of property not associated with partnerships.

The premise in Rev. Rul. 70-239, 180-1 C.B. 74 that the federal income tax consequences of the three situations described therein would be the same, without regard to which of the three transactions was entered into, is incorrect. As described below, depending on the format chosen for the transfer to a controlled corporation, the basis and holding periods of the various assets received by the corporation and the basis and holding periods of the stock received by the former partners can vary.

Additionally, Rev. Rul. 70-239 raises questions about potential adverse tax consequences to taxpayers in certain cases involving collapsible corporations defined in section 341 of the Code, personal holding companies described in section 542, small business corporations defined in section 1244, and electing small business corporations defined in section 1371. Recognition of the three possible methods to incorporate a partnership will enable taxpayers to avoid the above potential pitfalls and will facilitate flexibility with respect to the basis and holding periods of the assets received in the exchange.

Holding

Rev. Rul. 70-239. 180-1 C.B. 74 no longer represents the Service's position. The Service's current position is set forth below, and for each situation, the methods described and the underlying assumptions and purposes must be satisfied for the conclusions of this revenue ruling to be applicable.

Situation 1

Under section 351 of the Code, gain or loss is not recognized by X on the transfer by X of all of its assets to R in exchange for R's stock and the assumption by R of X's liabilities.

Under section 362(a) of the Code, R's basis in the assets received from X equals their basis' to X immediately before their transfer to R. Under section 358(a) the basis to X of the stock received from R is the same as the basis to X of the assets transferred to R, reduced by the liabilities assumed by R which assumption is treated as a payment of money to X under section 358(d). In addition, the assumption by R of X's liabilities decreased each partner's share of the partnership liabilities, thus, decreasing the basis of each partner's partnership interest pursuant to sections 752 and 733.

On distribution of the stock to X's partners, X terminated under section 708(b)(1)(A) of the Code. Pursuant to section 732(b), the basis of the stock distributed to the partners in liquidation of their partnership interests is, with respect to each partner, equal to the adjusted basis of the partner's interest in the partnership.

Under section 1223(1) of the Code, X's holding period for the stock received in the exchange includes its holding period in the capital assets and section 1231 assets transferred (to the extent that the stock was received in exchange for such assets). To the extent the stock was received in exchange for neither capital nor section 1231 assets, X's holding period for such stock begins on the day following the date of the exchange. See Rev. Rul. 70-598, 1970-2 C.B. 168. Under section 1223(2), R's holding period in the assets transferred to it includes X's holding period. When X distributed the R stock to its partners, under sections 735(b) and 1223, the partners' holding periods included X's holding period of the stock. Furthermore, such distribution will not violate the control requirement of section 368 (c) of the Code.

Situation 2

On the transfer of all of Y's assets to its partners, Y terminated under section 708(b)(1)(A) of the Code and, pursuant to section 732(b), the basis of the assets (other than money) distributed to the partners in liquidation of their partnership interests in Y was with respect to each partner, equal to the adjusted basis of the partner's interest in Y, reduced by the money distributed. Under section 752, the decrease in Y's liabilities resulting from the transfer to Y's partners was offset by the partners' corresponding assumption of such liabilities so that the net effect on the basis of each partner's interest in Y with respect to the liabilities transferred was zero.

Under section 351 of the Code, gain or loss is not recognized by Y's former partners on the transfer to S in exchange for its stock and the assumption of Y's liabilities, of the assets of Y received by Y's partners in liquidation of Y.

Under section 358(a) of the Code, the basis to the former partners of Y in the stock received from S is the same as the section 732(b) basis to the former partners of Y in the assets received in liquidation of Y and transferred to S, reduced by the liabilities assumed by S, which assumption is treated as a payment of money to the partners under section 358(d).

Under section 362(a) of the Code, S's basis in the assets received from Y's former partners equals their basis to the former partners as determined under the section 732(c) immediately before the transfer to S.

Under section 735(b) of the Code, the partners' holding periods for the assets distributed to them by Y includes Y's holding period. Under section 1223(1), the partners' holding periods for the stock received in the exchange includes the partners' holding periods in the capital assets and section 1231 assets transferred to S (to the extent that the stock was received in exchange for such assets). However, to the extent that the stock received was in exchange for neither capital nor section 1231 assets, the holding period of the stock began on the day following the date of the exchange. Under section 1223(2), S's holding period of the Y assets received in the exchange includes the partner's holding periods.

Situation 3

Under section 351 of the Code, gain or loss is not recognized by Z's partners on the transfer of the partnership interests to T in exchange for T's stock. On the transfer of the partnership interests to the corporation, Z terminated under section 708(b)(1)(A) of the Code.

Under section 358(a) of the Code, the basis to the partners of Z of the stock received from T in exchange for their partnership interests equals the basis of their partnership interests transferred to T, reduced by Z's liabilities assumed by T, the release from which is treated as a payment of money to Z's partners under sections 752(d) and 358(d).

T's basis for the assets received in the exchange equals the basis of the partners in their partnership interests allocated in accordance with section 732(c). T's holding period includes Z's holding period in the assets.

Under section 1223(1) of the Code, the holding period of the T stock received by the former partners of Z includes each respective partner's holding period for the partnership interest transferred, except that the holding period of the T stock that was received by the partners of Z in exchange for their interests in section 751 assets of Z that are neither capital assets nor section 1231 assets begins on the day following the date of the exchange . . .

[Thus, although all three types of transaction may be tax-free under § 351, they will differ as to the basis and holding period of both stock received and properly transferred depending upon the transactional form chosen.]

P. CONTRIBUTIONS TO CAPITAL DISTINGUISHED
Read § 118.

Recall that the difference between a § 351 transaction and one described in § 118 is that the contributor does not get stock or anything else back in exchange for his contribution to the corporation.

SENATE REPORT NO. 1622
83d Congress, 2d Session; H.R. 8300

Part III. – Items Specifically Excluded from Gross Income

Section 118. Contributions to the capital of a corporation

This section (except for a change in a cross-reference) is identical with section 118 of the bill as passed by the House. It has no counterpart in the 1939 Code: however, the rule of this section, that contributions to the capital of a corporation are excluded from income, merely restates the existing law as developed through administration and court decisions. Determination of the basis of property contributed to the capital of a corporation is to be made under section 362.

NOTES

1. **What is a "contribution to capital"?** First of all, consider that there may be either shareholder or non-shareholder contributions to capital. The Regulations identify contributions by government units or civic groups that are designed to encourage the corporation to locate its business in a particular community or to expand its facilities, which do qualify under § 118, as opposed to payments for goods or services rendered or subsidies that are designed to limit its production, which do not qualify. *See* Reg. § 1.118-1. Section 118(b) covers the ambiguous case of contributions by customers to regulated utilities. The approach to that subsection is to exempt the payments from the recipient corporation's tax base but also to prevent the corporation from claiming such tax benefits as investment credits and increases in basis.

2. **Significance.** The practical difference between § 118 and § 351 is that § 118 permits a non-taxable transfer to occur at the shareholder level even though no stock was issued and in

spite of the fact that the transferor or group of transferors are not in control of the corporation. Although the language of the Regulations could be clearer, Reg. § 1.118-1 means that shareholders can only increase the basis in their stock to the extent that they contribute additional assets to the corporation. If the contributor is an outsider who never had any stock in the corporation and does not yet have any stock, § 118 guarantees that the corporation will not be taxed at the time of contribution, but the property takes a zero basis under § 362(c)(1).

PROBLEM 14-9

1) From the contributing shareholder's point of view, what fact(s) distinguish a § 118 from a § 351 transaction?

2) Landlord contributes appreciated inventory to Shell, Inc., in which he has owned all the stock for ten years. Shell, Inc. issues no stock in connection with the transfer.

   (a) What Code section, § 118 or § 351, applies to the transfer, taking into account the discussion in the *Peracchi* case of the "meaningless gesture" concept?

   (b) What impact should the transfer have on the holding period of the stock in Shell, Inc. that Landlord already owns, assuming half the value of the company is attributable to the inventory?

3) If "(2)" poses a tax problem for Landlord with respect to the holding period of the Shell, Inc. stock after contributing the inventory, could the situation be improved for Landlord if he first gave some stock of Shell, Inc. to his adult children?

Q. ORGANIZATIONAL AND SYNDICATION EXPENDITURES
Read § 248; § 1.248-1(a) & (b).

These expenditures are treated the same way as for partnerships, and so they are given only passing reference here. Section 248 authorizes the elective amortization of organizational expenditures over a 180-month period beginning with the month in which the corporation begins business. The deductible amount in the year business begins is the lesser of:

(A) Actual organizational expenses; or

(B) $5,000 reduced (not below $0) by the amount by which the organizational expenditures with respect to the taxpayer exceed $50,000.

The rest of the organizational expenditures can be deducted ratably over 180 months (*i.e.*, 15 years). § 248(a). Reg. § 1.248-1(b)(3) excludes expenditures in connection with issuing or selling stock. These include such items as commissions, professional fees, and printing costs for prospectuses. A corporation can also deduct up to $5,000 of start-up expenditures (under § 195) in the year that its business begins.

Chapter 15

PLANNING THE CORPORATION'S CAPITAL STRUCTURE

In one sense, capitalizing a corporation means funding it with the assets and resources it will need. Alternatively, it means arranging its capital structure in the sense of determining what claims against the corporation (stock, debt, etc.) will be exchanged with providers of actual assets, financial or otherwise. Will the corporation issue only common stock (or other proprietary claims) or will it also issue debt instruments that are creditors' claims?

Even in a world free of income taxes, the decision about how to capitalize the corporation can be a difficult one. At one extreme, the corporation might be in such a risky business that virtually no one will lend to it. In such a case, it will have no choice but to issue stock alone. On the other end, if the corporation has stable prospects, it may be able to raise money from lenders. Such loans will range all the way from long-term bonds – which are heavily ornamented promissory instruments running many pages and ordinarily held by institutional lenders – to short-term advances from trade creditors, notes from shareholders and others and bank loans that may or may not be secured by the corporation's property.

Sometimes debt may be subordinated to other claims. On top of that, the corporation may issue preferred stock, which is a kind of a hybrid equity lying between a bond and common stock. The usual features of preferred stock are that it has a preferred claim on the corporation's available cash flow, usually in the form of a right to some minimum dividend level, and a priority for distributions in liquidation. The dividend level is commonly a rate similar to the market rate of interest and it may include a "kicker" that would allow the holder of the preferred stock to participate in further cash flow if the company does particularly well (known as "participating preferred stock"). On the other hand, if the company collapses, holders of preferred stock must wait in line until the creditors are first paid in full. Then the preferred stock shareholders will be paid their accumulated dividends and the face or par value of their stock according to the terms of their liquidation preference, and only thereafter will the common shareholders get anything. It is often the case that, if the company defaults on its dividends on nonvoting preferred stock, then the holders of preferred stock will become entitled to vote and may obtain a position on the board of directors as a result.

Even common stock may be broken down into several classes. For example, there may be a Class A that is entitled to one vote per share. There may be a Class B stock that does not vote but has the same claim on dividends and to assets in the event the corporation liquidates. The typical Class B shareholder in a small corporation is a child of the founder of the corporation who cannot yet be trusted to vote the stock, but to whom the founder wishes to pass dividend income. Beyond that, there may be options and warrants, a subject not taken up here.

Finally, there may be convertible preferred stock or convertible securities. For example, the holders of some of the corporation's debt may have the right to convert the debt into a certain number of shares of common stock. Even more common is the feature found in many issues of preferred stock that allows the holders to convert one share of preferred stock into a given number of shares of common stock. Such an arrangement can give the holders of preferred stock much greater "upside potential" (participation in future profits) than does regular preferred stock.

In short, this is a complex issue that requires keeping an eye on the tax laws, state law restrictions and the interests of the various stakeholders in the corporation. Failure to appreciate the many risks and opportunities inherent in structuring the corporation's capital can be a basis for mortification.

A. THE DEBT-EQUITY PROBLEM
Read § 385.

One of the most unstable areas of corporate tax law is whether a particular debt instrument constitutes equity rather than debt for federal income tax purposes. The distinction is crucial for several reasons, most especially: (1) the corporation can deduct interest expenses under § 163, but not dividends; and, (2) if the company buys back stock from a shareholder, the shareholder may have a taxable dividend or capital gain, whereas if it buys back or repays debt, that is generally treated as a nontaxable return of capital to the lender. Thus, often debt furnishes a way for an investor to get back cash from the corporation with more favorable tax treatment than does equity.

Sometimes "hybrid" instruments bear characteristics of both debt and equity; they wander near or over the line between the two. The most common issue is whether an instrument that the corporation claims to be debt is really stock, such that there can be no tax deduction for the alleged interest payments because they really are dividends. There is an endless stream of cases on the subject and a rich literature from the commentators. The following discussion of the subject is from a document prepared by the Congress' Joint Committee on Taxation in 1989:

JOINT COMMITTEE ON TAXATION
"DISTINGUISHING DEBT FROM EQUITY"

The characterization of an investment in a corporation as debt or equity for Federal income tax purposes is generally determined by the economic substance of the investor's interest in the corporation. The form of the instrument representing the investment and the taxpayer's characterization of the interest as debt or equity is not necessarily controlling. However, taxpayers have considerable latitude in structuring the terms of an instrument so that an interest in a corporation will be considered to be debt or equity, as so desired.

There is presently no definition in the Code or the Regulations which can be used to determine whether an interest in a corporation constitutes debt or equity for tax purposes. Such a determination must be made under principles developed in case law. Courts have approached the issue of distinguishing debt and equity by trying to determine whether the particular investment at issue in each case more closely resembles a pure debt interest or a pure equity interest. It is generally understood that a pure debt instrument is ordinarily represented by a written, unconditional promise to pay a principal sum certain, on demand or before a fixed maturity date not unreasonably far in the future, with interest payable in all events and not later than maturity. *See, e.g., Farley Realty Corp. v. Comm 'r*, 279 F.2d 701 (2d Cir. 1960), and B. Bittker & J. Eustice, Federal Income Taxation of Corporations and Shareholders, para. 4.03 (1979).

Conversely, a pure equity interest is generally understood as an investment which places the funds contributed by the investor at the risk of the enterprise, provides for a share of any future profits, and carries with it rights to control or manage the enterprise.

The determination of whether an interest constitutes debt or equity is generally made by analyzing and weighing the relevant facts and circumstances of each case. Some interests in a corporation can clearly be characterized, on their face, as either debt or equity. However, other interests may have features common to both debt and equity ("hybrid securities"), or underlying facts and circumstances may indicate that an interest has been inappropriately characterized as debt or equity (such as when purported debt is held by the corporation's shareholders on a pro rata basis or when "debt" is held in a thinly capitalized corporation).

Courts have determined that these features, among others, are characteristic of debt:

1. A written unconditional promise to pay on demand or on a specific date a sum certain in money in return for an adequate consideration in money or money's worth, and to pay a fixed rate of interest;

2. A preference over, or lack of subordination to, other interests in the corporation;

3. A relatively low corporate debt to equity ratio;

4. The lack of convertibility into the stock of the corporation;

5. Independence between the holdings of the stock of the corporation and the holdings of the putative debt;

6. An intent of the parties to create a creditor-debtor relationship;

7. Principal and interest payments that are not subject to the risks of the corporation's business;

8. The existence of security to ensure the payment of interest and principal, including sinking fund arrangements, if appropriate;

9. The existence of rights of enforcement and default remedies;

10. An expectation of repayment;

11. The holder's lack of voting and management rights (except in the case of default or similar circumstances);

12. The availability of other credit sources on similar terms;

13. The ability to freely transfer the interest;

14. Interest payments that are not contingent on or subject to management or board of directors' discretion;

15. The labeling and financial statement classification of the instrument as debt; and

16. Pro-rata stock/debt holdings.

In 1969, in response to the increased level of corporate merger activity and the increased use of debt for corporate acquisition purposes, Congress enacted Code § 279 (disallowance of interest deductions incurred to acquire certain stock or assets) and § 385 (treatment of certain interests in corporations as stock or indebtedness). Section 385 granted the Secretary of the Treasury the authority to prescribe such Regulations as may be necessary or appropriate to determine whether an interest in a corporation is to be treated as stock or as indebtedness for Federal income tax purposes. The Regulations were to prescribe factors to be taken into account in determining, with respect to particular factual situations, whether a debtor-creditor relationship or a corporation-shareholder relationship existed. In addition, § 385 provided that the factors set forth in the Regulations could include, among others, the first five of the fifteen factors listed above.

Proposed Regulations under § 385 were issued on March 20, 1980, and became final on December 29 of that year. The final Regulations originally had an effective date of May 1, 1981, but this date was subsequently postponed to January 1, 1982, and then to July 1, 1982. New proposed Regulations were issued on December 30, 1981. However, these Regulations never became effective and on July 6, 1983, all § 385 Regulations were withdrawn and to date no additional Regulations have been issued.

The § 385 Regulations did not succeed in the attempt to develop objective standards for distinguishing debt from equity. For example, one feature of the Regulations was the development of objective safe harbor tests which, if met, would classify an interest as debt. The use of such mechanical tests would have allowed corporations to create instruments which would be considered to be debt for Federal income tax purposes, but economically had many of the characteristics of equity. Federal Income Tax Aspects of Corporate Financial Structures, January 18, 1989, Joint Committee Print; JCS-1-89; corrected by JCX-1-89, pp. 35-37.

PLANTATION PATTERNS, INC. v. COMMISSIONER
462 F.2d 712 (5th Cir. 1972)

[Plantation Patterns was a closely held corporation that made various types of metal chairs. For convenience, it was referred to as "Old Plantation." A tycoon investment banker by the name of Mr. Jemison acting through his corporation, Jemison Investment Co. ("JIC"), agreed to form a new company ("New Plantation," for convenience). He promised that JIC would contribute $155,000 in cash to New Plantation. of which $150,000 would be in return for 6½% subordinated notes and $5,000 for common stock. The $5,000 was contributed for stock, but a third party – Bradford and Company. Inc. – lent the $150,000 on a subordinated basis at an interest rate of 6.2%. Soon thereafter, New Plantation agreed to buy the stock of Old Plantation for about $701,000 consisting of $100,000 cash at the closing and the rest in installment payments (evidenced by interest-bearing subordinated notes) in the total amount of $609,878.33 over about 10 years. JIC and the tycoon guaranteed the purchase obligations. This total amount consisted of two parts: $100,000 of 52% guaranteed notes and $509,878.33 of partially subordinated notes. The IRS asserted that the substance of these deals was a hypothetical loan from an outsider to New Plantation, followed by a contribution from New to Old Plantation. If the IRS won, the alleged interest payments would be nondeductible distributions by New Plantation.]

SIMPSON. CIRCUIT JUDGE:

The Tax Court held that all steps taken by Mr. Jemison and the shareholders of Old Plantation were parts of a single transaction for the purchase by New Plantation of the wrought iron furniture business of Old Plantation, and, applying the relevant factors with respect to debt-equity situations to the facts here, one of which was found to be thin capitalization, that the guaranteed debt must be treated as an indirect contribution to New Plantation's capital by Mr. Jemison. Therefore, it held that New Plantation was not entitled to deductions claimed under Code Section 163 for interest on the 5 1/2% serial notes in its taxable years ended September 30, 1963 to September 30, 1966 and that the Jemisons were taxable in 1963 under Code Sections 301 and 316 with the principal and interest payments on these guaranteed notes in that year.[7]

II. The Issues on Appeal

---

[7] The Tax Court allowed the Jemisons a deduction for interest paid the sellers by New Plantation.

The issues presented for our consideration are these:

1) Whether $100,000 of guaranteed 5 1/2% serial debentures issued by New Plantation to the sellers of Old Plantation are to be treated as debt for income tax purposes where the notes were not subordinated and were paid when due by New Plantation without recourse to other financing?

2) Whether $509,878.33 of guaranteed 5½ % notes issued by New Plantation to the sellers of Old Plantation are to be treated as debt for income tax purposes where the notes were subordinated to general creditors but were senior to $150,000 of other debentures which the Tax Court did treat as debt for income tax purposes?

3) Whether Jemison Investment Company, a co-guarantor, rather than John S. Jemison Jr., a co-guarantor, should be deemed to have made the contribution to the equity capital of New Plantation in the event that any of the $609,878.33 principal amount of 5 1/2% notes is deemed to represent a contribution to the equity capital of New Plantation?

III. The Relevant Law

The criteria for adjudicating debt-equity cases were set forth most clearly by Judge Jones for this Court in 1963 in Montclair, Inc. v. C.I.R, 5 Cir., 1963, 318 F.2d 38. At page 40 of Volume 318 F.2d the factors which bear most strongly on the determination of the label to be applied to the transaction are enunciated: "(1) the names given to the certificates evidencing the indebtedness; (2) the presence or absence of a maturity date; (3) the source of the payments; (4) the right to enforce the payment of principal and interest; (5) participation in management; (6) a status equal to or inferior to that of regular corporate creditors; (7) the intent of the parties; (8) "thin" or adequate capitalization; (9) identity of interest between creditor and stockholder; (10) payment of interest only out of "dividend" money; (11) the ability of the corporation to obtain loans from outside lending institutions."

Since *Montclair Inc.* consideration of debt-equity cases has frequently demanded the attention of this Court. . . . In applying these factors, each case must be decided on its own facts, and no one standard is controlling. See generally the cases just cited, supra. The tests are not "talismans of magical power," and the most that can he said is that they are a source of helpful guidance. *Tyler v. Tomlinson, supra.* Thus we decide debt-equity issues by a case by case analysis, applying the Montclair rubrics as best we can to the facts at hand.

IV. Treatment of the $100,000 Unsubordinated 5 1/2% Debentures and the $509,878.33 Partially Subordinated 5½% Notes

With regard to the $100,000 unsubordinated debentures, the taxpayers urge us to reverse the Tax Court for the following reasons: (1) There was a reasonable prospect of payment when due, (2) the notes were not subordinated to any other indebtedness of New Plantation, (3) the holders, along with general creditors, had first claim on more than $1,000,000 in assets of New Plantation, (4) the notes matured within two years, (5) the notes could have been paid by New Plantation's cash flow, and (6) the notes were paid when due without recourse to additional financing.

Of these factors, taxpayers point first and foremost to the fact that the debentures were totally unsubordinated, and thus conferred on the holders the right to participate with general creditors. They further call to our attention that under the Code of Alabama had the creditors paid the notes, their subrogation rights would have permitted them to participate in any insolvency proceeding as a general creditor. Section 87, Title 9, Code of Alabama of 1940 as amended.

Taxpayers also vigorously assert that the assets of the corporation were more than adequate to support the $100,000 unsubordinated notes because on September 30, 1962, New Plantation's assets had a fair market value of $1,261,327.81 . . . Central to this appeal is the taxpayers' contention that the Tax Court erroneously concluded that New Plantation was thinly capitalized.

Additionally, with regard to the $100,000 of unsubordinated 5½% debentures taxpayers emphasize that they were to mature within two years, a factor militating strongly against a conclusion that the money was put "at the risk" of the business. Bolstering this point taxpayers state that the cash flow from depreciation in 1963 and 1964 the years of payment of the $100,000 notes, exceeded the principal payments of $50,000 due on the notes. They say that in view of the fact that the interest on the notes is deducted in determining net income, it was not necessary for New Plantation to have net income to pay these notes, and thus their repayment was not contingent on the profitability of the business.

Finally, the taxpayers criticize the Tax Court for not giving greater weight in assessing the economic realities of the situation to the fact that the notes were paid on time. Taxpayers claim that giving this development its proper weight will lead us to the conclusion that the Tax Court was clearly erroneous in its holding that when the notes were issued there was no reasonable expectation that New Plantation could pay the notes. In this regard taxpayers also insist that the Tax Court gave undue emphasis to the overall debt-equity ratio, which they assert bears slight relevance to the determination of the treatment given unsubordinated notes. Taxpayers argue that whether a corporation can pay *all* of its debts is irrelevant to the question whether it can pay its priority debts.

Turning to the remaining $509,878.33 of partially subordinated 5 1/2% serial debentures, the taxpayers argue five points in support of their proposition that the Tax Court erred: (1) There was reasonable prospect of payment when due, (2) the notes, though partially subordinated, were senior to $150,000 of 6½% debentures and $5,000 of common stock, (3) the assets of New Plantation were sufficient to support the debt, (4) the cash flow was sufficient to pay the debt, and (5) the notes were paid when due without recourse to additional financing.

Many of the arguments made by the taxpayers in favor of debt treatment for the $100,000 unsubordinated debentures are equally applicable for the remaining $509,878.33 of partially subordinated notes, and the taxpayers have urged us to accord them equal vitality here. New arguments also are raised at this juncture, however. Taxpayers contend that it is anomalous and inconsistent for the Tax Court to characterize the $509,878.33 partially subordinated debentures as equity while at the same time characterizing inferior fully subordinated debentures held by Bradford and Company as debt, arguing that if the fully subordinated 6 1/2% notes held by Bradford and Company are equity, surely the $509,878.33 debentures are entitled to the same treatment. Here the taxpayers protest vigorously against the Tax Court's determination of the proper debt-equity ratio to apply in assessing the nature of the transaction. The principal dispute with the Tax Court revolves about that Court's valuation of the intangible assets of New Plantation with particular emphasis on the personal business skills of Mr. Jemison. The Tax Court did recognize that intangible assets not carried on the balance sheet might have a bearing on the ability of the corporation to pay its debts. *Murphy Logging Company v. United States,* 9 Cir. 1967, 378 F.2d 222. But the Tax Court held that the relationship of Mr. Jemison's business skills to the well-being of New Plantation was not demonstrated with the specificity requisite to alter the picture of the overall debt-paying potential of New Plantation. Relying heavily on *Murphy Logging, supra,* the taxpayers contend that the record amply demonstrates that Mr. Jemison was a veritable financial genius, commanding Jemison Investment Company, a company with control of assets valued at more than $11,000,000 and with annual gross receipts of over $10,000,000. They point to the record as reflecting that Mr. Jemison was successfully engaged in a broad variety of business ventures. He was a director of several successful corporations, a bank, and two insurance companies. More important, however, taxpayers assert, is Mr. Jemison's demonstrated close contact with several large department store chains which provided ideal outlets for New Plantation's products. Taxpayer on this account urges that a proper debt-equity ratio should take into account the financial skills of Mr. Jemison.

Without receding from their strong stand that the 5 1/2% debentures constitute debt, the taxpayers alternatively argue that if the court should hold that such notes do not constitute debt, the same equity treatment should be given to the 6 1/2% subordinated debentures held by Bradford and Company. Stated otherwise, they argue that if the 5 1/2% partially subordinated debentures are to be regarded as equity, then the 6 1/2% totally subordinated debentures should logically be deemed to constitute preferred stock in New Plantation. Taxpayers point out that long-term debt held by non-stockholders has been held to be an equity interest in the nature of preferred stock. *Foresun, Inc. v. Commissioner of Internal Revenue*, 6 Cir. 1965, 348 F.2d 1006, affirming 41 T.C. 706 (1964). Taxpayers claim that they were denied the right to further trial on this point in the Tax Court, and they contend that at the very least this Court should remand the case to the Tax Court to permit development of further evidence as to the treatment to be given the $150,000 in Bradford and Company notes. If these notes are regarded as equity, taxpayers argue that the debt-equity ratio of New Plantation would be approximately 4 to 1 ($609,878.33 to $155,000), and not the plus 125 to 1 ratio which the government asserts is the proper debt-equity ratio ($759,878.33 to $5,000). This would effectively demolish the Tax Court finding of thin capitalization . . .

More specifically the Commissioner places primary emphasis on the Tax Court's findings that the assets of the new corporation vis-a-vis its debts were insufficient to give New Plantation viable independence as a corporation. The Tax Court found that the corporate assets of New Plantation were "wholly inadequate to sustain a debt of $609,878.33." The Commissioner suggests that *Murphy Logging, supra*, the keystone in appellants' argument, is distinguishable. The Commissioner argues that in *Murphy Logging*, the guarantee of a guarantor-stockholder was held not significant because the corporation had substantial ability to meet its debts without the aid of a guarantor, a factor absent in this case. Further distinction is noted in that in *Murphy Logging* the Ninth Circuit was not dealing with a thinly capitalized corporation, as is the case here. The Commissioner discounts the tact that New Plantation was in actuality able to pay its obligations without resort to its guarantors, pointing out that we must view the transaction on the basis of the economic realities as they existed at New Plantation's inception and not in the light of later developments. As matters stood September 28, 1962, asserts the Commissioner the deal had not set up a bona fide corporation reasonably to be expected to manage to go it alone, and later developments do not alter the nature of the transaction for tax purposes.

Making further use of the debt vs. equity criteria established by *Montclair* and later cases, the Commissioner notes particularly that the sellers took the unusual step of agreeing to subordinate all but $100,000 of the purchase money notes. The Commissioner asserts that this action was taken because the sellers looked first and foremost to the guarantee of Mr. Jemison, an obligation which was primary in nature.

The Commissioner also claims that no third party arm's-length creditors, because of New Plantation's paper thin capitalization, would have loaned the amount of money by which the corporation became indebted. Establishment of any indebtedness, argues the respondent, would have required Mr. Jemison's guarantee, and therefore for tax purposes the indebtedness should be regarded as that of the Jemisons.

Resolving these two conflicting views of this amorphous transaction is no easy task, but we are not persuaded that the taxpayers have successfully demonstrated the incorrectness of the position taken by the Tax Court. Certainly we recognize that this transaction was initially cast to have all of the outward appearances of a debt transaction, complete with instruments styled "debentures" which had fixed maturity dates. But these surface considerations do not end our examination. Closer scrutiny establishes that the other factors which would give the transaction the aura of debt are noticeable by their absence.

Of critical importance in determining whether financial input is debt or equity is whether or not the money is expended for capital assets. In the instant case the substantial portion of the $609,878.33 was directed to the purchase of capital assets and to finance initial operations. In contrast, only $5,000.00 was set up as equity to finance launching of the corporate venture.

Other equity factors exist. While the sellers were ostensibly to look to the corporation for payment of the debt, it is apparent from the meager capital position of the company that Mr. Jemison's guarantee was regarded as the real understanding for the deal. Our conclusion is reinforced by noting that the sellers apparently considered financially acceptable the agreement to subordinate the great majority of the 5 1/2% debentures to almost all other corporate indebtedness so long as the debentures were guaranteed by Mr. Jemison. Mr. Jemison's guarantee was, of course, an obligation primary in nature.

Further, while Mrs. Jemison was the stockholder of record, and Mr. Jemison on the surface was only a guarantor, surrounding circumstances clearly demonstrate that Mr. Jemison completely controlled the shares held by Mrs. Jemison. Mrs. Jemison seldom attended the meetings of the corporation, and took little active interest in it. In contrast, Mr. Jemison was intimately and continuously involved in the operations of New Plantation. Regarding Mr. Jemison as the "constructive" owner of the stock, we have an identity of interest between the stockholder and the guarantor – a factor which points strongly toward equity treatment.

The record cannot support a determination by us that the Tax Court's finding that New Plantation was thinly capitalized is "clearly erroneous." The balance sheet of the corporation showed that its quick assets (cash and accounts receivables) of $317,000 could not cover its current liabilities of approximately $490,000. This ratio is one of the acid test indicators used by businessmen to determine the health of a business. After the dissolution of Old Plantation the new corporation had tangible assets, at fair market value, of approximately $1,064,000 securing debts of approximately $1,078,000. We regard this as thin capitalization, as did the Tax Court.

The guarantee enabled Mr. Jemison to put a minimum amount of cash into New Plantation immediately, and to avoid any further cash investment in the corporation unless and until it should fall on hard times. At the same time he exercised total control over its management. Adding together the personal guarantee of Mr. Jemison to the guarantee of Jemison Investment Company, which was wholly owned by him and Mr. Jemison's control of New Plantation, we think that the result is that Mr. Jemison's guarantee simply amounted to a covert way of putting his money "at the risk of the business." Stated differently, the guarantee enabled Mr. Jemison to create borrowing power for the corporation which normally would have existed only through the presence of more adequate capitalization of New Plantation.

We do not regard as significant the fact that ultimately things progressed smoothly for New Plantation and that its debts were paid without additional financing. The question is not whether, looking back in time, the transaction was ultimately successful or not, but rather whether at its inception there was a reasonable expectation that the business would succeed on its own. The transaction must be judged on the conditions that existed when the deal was consummated, and not on conditions as they developed with the passage of time. When New Plantation was incorporated its prospects of business success were questionable indeed without the Jemison guarantees.

We hold also that the Tax Court was correct in refusing to give value to the intangible financial skills of Mr. Jemison for purposes of computing the corporation's debt-equity ratio. . . .

We decide only this case. We do not assert that intangible assets are never another consideration in assessing debt-equity ratio . . .

Our holding does not require that we find the notes held by Bradford and company to be equity interests. While the Bradford and Company notes were subordinated, subordination is far from the sole criterion for determining whether an interest is debt or equity. It is not controlling. Aside from this single factor this record is productive of nothing to indicate that this was not a bona fide loan made by Bradford with the primary motive of inducing New Plantation to employ young Bradford. We agree with the Tax Court that this was a legitimate loan.

V. Should the Equity Contribution Be Deemed to Have Been Made by Jemison Investment Company Rather Than by Mr. Jemison?

The Tax Court found that the equity contribution was to be attributed to Mr. Jemison and not to Jemison Investment Company. Although acknowledging that Jemison Investment Company received a fee of $15,000.00 for its guarantee on the notes, the Tax Court reasoned that inasmuch as Mr. Jemison controlled both Jemison Investment and New Plantation, the fee for the guarantee was either a matter of internal accounting or for cosmetic effect, and not an indication that the sellers of Old Plantation realistically looked to Jemison Investment Company for any security. It is uncontested that practically all of Mr. Jemison's assets consisted of stock in Jemison Investment Company. It owned the house he lived in and the automobile he drove, but he owned it in its entirety. Furthermore, the Tax Court found that the sellers of Old Plantation only investigated the credit of Mr. Jemison, and that the Messrs. Jernigans as sellers looked at all times to Mr. Jemison's guarantee as the real insurance for the notes.

Although the appellants cast some doubt on the Tax Court's finding that the sellers did not investigate the financial statements of the Jemison Investment Company, in no other respect have they demonstrated error in the Tax Court's conclusion that through all of the haze of corporate red tape, the real financial keystone supporting the entire deal, the person to whom the sellers ultimately looked for their protection in the event of the failure of New Plantation was Mr. John S. Jemison, Jr . . .

NOTES

1. **Is there a way out of this mess**? Maybe. Perhaps the most sensible proposal is the "objective" analysis proposed in *Scriptomatic, Inc. v. Commissioner*, 555 F.2d 364, 367-68 (3d Cir. 1977). In essence the case casts the debt versus equity question along the following lines: "If this instrument had been proposed to an independent outside lender, would that lender consider it was making a loan?" Although this will not solve all cases, it is an excellent first cut. As a lawyer planning a transaction, it is especially useful because it forces the parties away from being entranced by their cleverness and into looking objectively into what they are doing. It tends to elicit the inevitable proposal, "Well, let's talk to our banker and see what the banker thinks." If the banker can be induced to go on the record that the character of the obligation is debt, that will produce useful documentation in the event of a future IRS audit.

2. **Once classified, always classified**? No. It is clear that the character of the corporation and its capital may change. For example, a corporation may issue a reasonable amount of subordinated debt at the outset, but later on may issue so much further debt or run into such financial difficulties that what in an earlier day was unquestionably debt for tax purposes may become equity.

3. **Why doesn't the Treasury do something about it?** The answer, as you read above, is that the Treasury did write extensive Regulations pursuant to § 385 to try to sort out the debt-equity tangle, but the Regulations were hooted down by practitioners and the Treasury Department reluctantly withdrew them.

4. **MIPS.** Aggressive taxpayers have noticed that the debt-equity issue can be a two-way street, and have designed preferred stock (for state law purposes) that produces "interest expenses" for income tax purposes. Wall Street has even given this kind of stock a fancy name – "monthly income preferred securities." The idea is to design the assurances of payment of the dividends to be so strong that the shareholder feels more like a creditor. The outcome is ideal from the issuer's point of view because the preferred stock does not show up as a liability on the issuer's balance sheet. Should the IRS be concerned about MIPS, or just leave the issue alone as an inevitability?

5. **Reconstruction of the facts.** It is extremely important to recognize the difference between the nominal facts of a transaction, as opposed to the judicially reconstructed facts that form the basis of the application of the tax law. The ability to predict judicial reconstruction is one of the characteristics of a skilled tax lawyer. It sets tax lawyers apart from accountants and others.

6. **Leveraged buy-outs.** The case you just read provides an insight into the fashionable "leveraged buy-out." In the simplest situation, officers of a subsidiary of a larger corporation want to buy the stock of the subsidiary. They agree on a price, and cause the subsidiary to borrow heavily (for the ultimate benefit of the selling corporation) so that the subsidiary offsets its taxable income with interest payments to the lender. The subsidiary will typically trim its expenses and do the things the managers believe will save or make money. If they are right, then the company in effect pays for itself out of its own profits. If it works out, the debts get paid off and managers wind up rich. *Plantation Patterns* differs from this simple model in that it included the use of a new corporation formed to undertake the acquisition, but the basic tax strategy of using deductible interest to offset earnings remains.

7. **What is equity for the capitalization purposes?** Equity means the excess of assets over liabilities, but it is not clear whether one uses the value of assets or their basis.

PROBLEM 15-1

The founders of L&B Corporation each own half of its common stock. There is no other stock. Presently, the corporation has the following assets and liabilities. Assume the basis and value of each item is the same, except that the building may be worth $200,000.

Assets		Liabilities	
Cash	$22,000.00	Note due directors	$100,000.00
Building	$0.00	Mortgage on land	$50,000.00
Land	$39,000.00	Working capital loan	$50,000.00
Office Equip.	$14,000.00		
Total:	$75,000.00	Total:	$200,000.00
Assets - Liabilities = ($125,000.00) in Equity by Basis			

The founders think they have access to an exciting business opportunity, and their accountant has advised them to raise the money by having L&B sell convertible debentures with a total face amount of $200,000 and a total value of $100,000, bearing simple interest of 5%. They do not want to go through the complications of offering the debentures to the public, and they instead propose to buy half of the debentures each, and in any case, they doubt a bank would lend money on these terms. The debentures are unsecured, and are convertible into 100 shares of stock. The value of the stock is speculative.

1) What characteristics of the proposed transaction point toward classification of the debentures as debt instruments?

2) What characteristics make the proposed debentures likely to be classified as equity instruments?

3) Does it seem more likely that a court would characterize these as debt or equity instruments?

4) Now assume the shareholders characterized the securities as preferred stock. Is there the possibility these securities might be modified so as to be characterized as debt for tax purposes?

5) What would be the advantage of the securities being characterized as preferred stock as opposed to debt for federal income tax or financial accounting purposes?

B. THE SECTION 1244 STOCK OPPORTUNITY
Read § 1244.

If corporate stock becomes worthless, the investor normally is forced to report a capital loss. See § 165(g). Because of the severe restrictions imposed on capital losses, the result can be an unhappy one. *See* § 1211(b). This unhappy outcome also applies if the investor owns "securities," which for federal income tax purposes generally means corporate debt obligations with a maturity of at least five years.

If you have already read the partnership materials, you will probably think that the right solution is for the company to operate in partnership form during the early, risky years of its existence so that the losses can be passed through directly to its shareholders. That is a reasonable reaction. However, § 1244 opens another door in that it allows individual investors to treat what would otherwise be capital losses on "section 1244 stock" as ordinary losses. (Section 1244 stock includes preferred and common stock.) The difficulty with § 1244 is that it is ringed with restrictions on its availability, including an annual limitation of $100,000 for spouses filing a joint return, or $50,000 for other taxpayers. § 1244(b). The excess loss cannot be carried forward. Instead the taxpayer is stuck with trying carefully to recognize exactly $100,000 or $50,000 per year, as the case may be, in the event of a major loss. One difficulty is if the corporation becomes worthless and the shareholder has a particularly large block of stock, only the first $100,000 stock loss on a joint return will be treated as an ordinary loss. Presumably, the remainder must be treated as a capital loss.

PROBLEM 15-2

Gyro Klopman invented the Klopman Spiromometer several years ago and it was sure to be a tremendous success. Gyro invested no money at all to invent the device, and so his stock has a $0 basis. Later, the company went public and the investment bankers raised $2 million. Harold and Maude, married individuals who file a joint return, invested $200,000 in the public issue of Klopman Spiromometer, Inc. stock. Sure enough, two years later the company's fortunes collapsed when a 14-year old boy invented a superior spiromometer. The stock now trades for 1 cent per share, down from $10/share when Harold and Maude bought their stock. The unhappy couple is in your office and is peppering with you with questions.

1) Is their stock § 1244 stock? How can they tell?

2) Does § 1244 require any active elections?

3) Assuming it is otherwise § 1244 stock, does the fact that they bought the stock from investment bankers (who held the stock temporarily in the course of underwriting the new issue) declassify it?

4) Harold suspects some of the stock is held by his personal service corporation. Could it claim a § 1244 loss?

5) Assuming it is § 1244 stock, do they have to wait for the company to go broke, or can they sell the stock now and claim § 1244 treatment?

6) If the answer to "(5)" is "yes," how much can they write off this year? Can they carry forward any unused loss?

C. SECTION 1202 AND 1045 OPPORTUNITIES
Read § 1202(a), (b)(1)-(2) and (c)(1).

The following description of the then-new provision is from the House-Senate Conference Report in 1994:

"The conference agreement generally follows the House bill, which generally permits a noncorporate taxpayer who holds qualified small business stock for more than five years to exclude from income 50 percent of any gain on the sale or exchange of the stock. The amount of gain eligible for the 50-percent exclusion is limited to the greater of (1) 10 times the taxpayer's basis in the stock or (2) $10 million of gain from stock in that corporation. [Part] of any exclusion claimed is treated as an alternative minimum tax preference item. The conference agreement modifies the House bill by basing the $50 million qualified small business size limitation applied at the date of issuance on the issuer's gross assets (*i.e.*, the sum of the cash and the adjusted bases of other assets held by the small business) without subtracting short-term indebtedness.
In addition, for purposes of the size limitation, the conference agreement provides that corporations that are part of a parent-subsidiary controlled group are treated as a single corporation. Under the conference agreement, the provision applies to stock issued after the date of enactment."

The exclusion can reach 100% for stock purchased after 2010. §1244(a)(4)(A).
There are some drawbacks. Seven percent of the exclusion amount is a tax preference item. § 57(a)(7). Also, the special benefits of § 1202 generally do not apply to S corporations. *See* § 1202(c)(2)(A). S corporations are covered in later chapters.

There is a chance to defer taxation of gain by investing in qualified small business stock under § 1045. Section 1045 lets individuals roll over tax-free gain from the sale of qualified small business stock held for more than six months if the taxpayer uses the proceeds to buy other qualified small business stock within sixty days. The replacement stock must meet the active business requirement of § 1202(c) for the six-month period following the purchase. § 1045(b)(4). For this purpose "qualified small business stock" has the same meaning as under § 1202(c), relating to the sale of stock that qualifies for the 50% or 100% exclusions discussed above. One feature of the replacement stock is that it must be acquired by the taxpayer at its original issue. §§ 1045(b)(1) and 1202(c)(1)(B). This is a dream deal for investment bankers and venture capitalists, who can roll over the proceeds from selling qualified small business stock of a company they incubated.

PROBLEM 15-3

P Corp., a Texas entity, has net assets (assets by basis minus liabilities) totaling $29 million and its wholly-owned subsidiary, S Corp., has net assets totaling $15 million. So, in effect, P has $44 million in net asset value. George has owned all 1,000 shares of P Corp. stock, now worth $101 million, since the corporation's inception 8 years ago. His basis is $1 million. P Corp's initial asset base was $1 million from George's cash. George decides to sell all of his P Corp. stock at fair market value.

1) Is this a sale of stock falling under § 1202?

2) Assuming this is a § 1202 sale of small business stock, what is the amount and character of gain George will *recognize*?

3) Would it make a difference if P Corp. had assets totaling $43 million in value and in addition, S Corp had assets totaling $12 million in value as of the date P and S were formed? *See* § 1202(d)(1)(A).

4) Under what circumstances can P Corp. be formed using assets other than cash and still qualify its stock for § 1202's benefits. *See* § 1202(d)(2)(A) for a clue.

5) Same as "(1)." George sold his 1,000 shares and a week later reinvested the proceeds in stock of another qualified small business ("QSB"), how would his gain be treated? Assume P Corp. is a QSB.

D. LIMITS ON BUSINESS INTEREST: §163(j)

Starting in 2018, all types of taxpayers are subject to limits on their business interest deductions. Under §163(j) the business interest deduction is limited to the sum of the taxpayer's: (1) business interest income, plus (2) 30 percent of "adjusted taxable income," plus (3) "floor plan financing interest". §163(j)(1). Taxpayers carry any interest disallowed under § 163(j)(1) forward and treat that business interest as paid or accrued in the next tax year. § 163(j)(2).

"Business interest" is interest paid or accrued on indebtedness properly allocable to a trade or business. "Business interest" does not include investment interest just as "business interest income" does not include investment income. § 163(j)(5) & (6).

Small businesses (generally, those with less than average annual gross receipts of not more than $25 million) escape the §163(j) limitation as do farms or public utilities. § 163(j)(3).

PROBLEM 15-4

1) For 2018, Corporation X has $100,000 of adjusted taxable income, $2,000 of business interest income, and $12,000 of business interest expense. It has no floor plan financing interest. How much business interest can Corporation X deduct this year? Next year?

2) In 2019, Corporation X in "(1)" has only $10,000 of adjusted taxable income and again has $2,000 of business interest income and $12,000 of business interest expense. How much business interest can Corporation X deduct this year? Next year?

3) Assume that in 2019, Corporation X in "(1)" had adjusted taxable income of ($20,000), $2,000 of business interest income, and $12,000 of business interest expense. How much business interest can Corporation X deduct this year? Next year?

Chapter 16

DISTRIBUTIONS FROM CORPORATIONS TO SHAREHOLDERS "WITH RESPECT TO THEIR SHARES"

A. INTRODUCTION

The subject of this chapter is current distributions of money or property from corporations to their shareholders in their capacity as shareholders. The topic is sometimes intricate, but reasonably logical. There are a number of legislative alternatives to the present regime. If one were sitting down to work out the taxation of corporate distributions from scratch one might choose from any number of alternatives but the primary ones seem to be the following:

1. Tax all distributions to shareholders on a presumption that the corporation makes distributions to its shareholders only out of profits;

2. Do not tax distributions to shareholders at all, on the ground that corporate profits have already been taxed to the corporation, but instead require shareholders to reduce basis in their shares by each distribution's fair market value;

3. Tax distributions only after the shareholder has recovered his basis in his stock (*i.e.*, capital recovery first);

4. Tax distributions to shareholders only to the extent that the distributions actually do come out of corporate profits.

What we have in substance is a combination of the first, second, and third alternatives. The general rule is that distributions are taxed to shareholders on the assumption that all distributions come out of profits first. To the extent that distributions exceed profits, they are not taxable, but shareholders must then reduce stock basis, and to the extent distributions exceed basis, the shareholder is treated as if she had sold her stock for a gain equal to the excess.

While the structure is reasonably coherent, it necessarily involves two levels of taxation, which is a feature of our tax system that many economists and commentators consider excessive. On the other hand, it is true that both corporate and individual tax rates have dropped substantially since their high points after World War II, so that the combined burden is much reduced. In fact, dividends are now generally taxed at rates not over 20%.

Distributions by a corporation to a corporate shareholder are subject to the same basic system but with a special deduction (acting like an exclusion) to remove or soften what could be a triple (or higher) tax on distributed corporate profits. Treatment of individual shareholders will be taken up first. The subject of the remainder of this Chapter will be distributions out of current operations as distinct from distributions resulting from a partial or total liquidation of the enterprise, which are discussed in Chapters 17 and 18, respectively.

B. BASIC STRUCTURE
Read §§ 301(a), 301(c) and 316 and Reg. § 1.316-1(a).

In case there was any doubt about it, § 61(a)(7) specifically includes "dividends" distributed to shareholders as a form of gross income to the shareholders. However, a distribution is only a dividend to the extent it is covered by current or post-1913 "earnings and profits" ("E & P") as provided in § 316. To the extent that a distribution exceeds the corporation's E & P, § 301(c)(2) treats the excess as a return of capital to the shareholder which reduces the adjusted basis of his stock. Distributions in excess of basis are taxed as proceeds from an imaginary sale of the stock. §301(c)(3).

First, observe that the term "dividend" for federal income tax purposes does not mean the same thing as a dividend for state corporate law purposes. For example, a distribution from a corporation may be a dividend for federal income tax purposes even though it unlawfully impairs capital for state law purposes. To make things even more confusing to people who may have an accounting background, what the corporation shows as its "earned surplus" – which is generally thought of as the measure of the corporation's historical profitability – is not the same as E & P, although it is similar.

Section 316 defines and identifies two sources of taxable dividends:

1. Distributions out of E & P accumulated after February 28, 1913, and

2. Distributions out of E & P for the current taxable year.

The second source, E & P for the current taxable year, probably ought to be repealed as having outlived its usefulness. It was enacted in 1936 in order to limit the sting of a special tax on undistributed profits by permitting corporations to deduct dividends that came out of current earnings. The special tax itself was later repealed, but the rule that E & P for the current year are always a source of taxable dividends was not, despite the fact that it no longer had any rationale.

Be this as it may, § 316(a) plays a central role by dictating that, if a distribution is made to shareholders, the first source is presumptively considered to be current E & P. If current E & P is at least as large as the distribution, then one need not look at the accumulated E & P account. Most surprisingly, even if the corporation has a huge cumulative loss that dwarfs the current year's E & P, any current E & P nevertheless converts an equal amount of the distribution into a dividend. This is the tax law variant of so-called "nimble dividend" rule under state corporate law.

Assuming that distributions for the year exceed current E & P, then one must look next at the cumulative undistributed E & P since 1913 as the second source of potential dividends. The 1913 date was commendably designed to forgive earnings and profits accumulated before enactment of the first income tax act after the passage of the Sixteenth Amendment so that the new tax would not apply retroactively.

Most large corporations have cautious dividend-paying practices because there is so much adverse publicity associated with being forced to cut a dividend. As a result, there is almost always more than enough current or accumulated E & P to cover any distribution. However, while this is true for most publicly-held corporations, it is not nearly so true for smaller closely-held corporations that are frequently viewed by their owners as private pocketbooks.

One important tax rule is that E & P are calculated as of the close of the taxable year, undiminished by actual distributions during that year. As a result, it is often not until well after the end of the taxable year that the accountants can finally determine how much of the distributions made in the prior year are dividends and how much are mere returns of capital. It also makes the payment of distributions early in the year risky because a corporation that expected a nontaxable distribution might discover that the distribution was taxable after all due to a surge in profits late in the year.

C. CHRONOLOGICAL ASPECTS OF DIVIDENDS
Read Reg. § 1.316-2(a).

One needs to master four basic rules in order to handle complicated dividend patterns. First, current E & P is drained off first (before accumulated E & P) and in proportion to the amount of the distributions paid over the year.

To illustrate: Corporation has $3 of current E & P, but it distributes a total of $9 over the course of the year, of which $6 is paid on June 30 and $3 is paid on December 30. $2 of the current E & P would be deemed distributed on June 30, and the remaining $1 would be deemed distributed on December 30. That is how the $3 of current E & P out of the $9 of distributions is handled.

Second, accumulated E & P is deemed paid out in chronological order.

To illustrate: In the above example, if in addition the corporation had $4 of accumulated E & P as of the beginning of the current year, all $4 would be deemed distributed as a dividend on June 30. Thus, the entire June 30 distribution was a dividend, and $1 of the December 30 distribution was a dividend.

Third, the accumulated E & P account and the current E & P accounts are combined at the very end of the year *after* giving effect to all distributions for the year

To illustrate: If a corporation had a large accumulated deficit in its E & P account over the years since 1913 but had a profitable year this year, it would first reduce its current E & P account by any distributions made during the current year and only then combine whatever E & P is left over with the deficit in its accumulated E & P account at the end of the year, leaving over a diminished deficit for the following year.

Fourth, a distribution cannot produce a deficit in the accumulated E & P account. § 312(a). A loss can produce a deficit in E & P. §1.312-7(b).

D. "EARNINGS AND PROFITS" EXPLAINED
Read §§ 312(a), (b), (k)(1), (n)(2)-(3), (5), and (6).

Roughly speaking, the E & P concept is designed to provide a measure of the corporation's ability to make cash distributions to shareholders without invading the corporation's capital. It is similar to the accounting concept of "earned surplus" insofar as paid-in capital is ignored, but it also differs in some fundamental ways. For example, distributions of stock of the distributing corporation do not reduce E & P. The crucial term "earnings and profits" is not defined in the Code. Instead, § 312 works backwards by prescribing adjustments to the corporation's taxable income to arrive at its E & P.

One can conveniently divide the adjustments to taxable income into two main categories. The first category consists of a number of rules that reflect the corporation's actual cash flow more accurately than does taxable income. For example, many nondeductible items are subtracted from E & P to reflect the cash outlay, such as fines and penalties, capital losses in excess of capital gains, and federal income tax liabilities. Similarly, a number of items that are excludible or deductible for tax purposes must be included in E & P to reflect the cash inflow. These include, for example, tax-free municipal-bond interest, life-insurance proceeds, and intercorporate dividends received.

The second main category of adjustments involves changes in accounting rules to conform more nearly to financial accounting and forbids the use of certain favorable rules that are allowed only for tax purposes. For example, installment sale reporting is not permitted for purposes of calculating E & P. Instead, the profit must be included in full in the year of sale. Inventory profits must be reported on the first-in-first-out (FIFO) method rather than the often more favorable last-in-first-out (LIFO) method. Also, depreciation methods are slower than for purposes of calculating taxable income.

PROBLEM 16-1

Suzy, a high-bracket taxpayer has held all 1,000 shares of stock in X Corp., a Delaware corporation, for two years. At the beginning of the taxable year, she had a basis of $10,000 in her X Corp. stock and X Corp. had no accumulated earnings and profits. That year, X Corp. makes $25,000 in profits and distributes $5,000 to Suzy.

1) How is is Suzy taxed on the distribution? *See* §§ 61(a)(7) and 316.

2) What tax rate (if any) presumably applies to the $5,000?

3) How long must she have held preferred stock to qualify for 20% treatment for the dividend?

4) Suppose X Corp. decides before the year's end to distribute another $10,000 to Suzy. What is her tax treatment on the additional distribution? *See* §§ 61(a)(7) and 316.

5) X Corp. decides to be extremely generous around Christmas time that same taxable year and, after making the above two payments, X Corp. distributes to Suzy another $25,000 for an annual total of $40,000. What is the tax treatment of the entire $40,000? *See* §§ 61(a)(7), 301(c)(2) and 316.

6) In "(5)" what is Suzy's basis in her stock at the year's end?

7) Would the 20% rate be available if Suzy were a corporation?

8) Could there be any difference in result if X Corp. were a North Korean corporation?

PROBLEM 16-2

Newton Steel Corporation's recent financial statements reported the following items from its profit and loss statement:

Income from operations:	$120,000.00
Administrative and sales expenses:	$75,000.00
Interest income from U.S. Treasury bonds:	$15,000.00
Dividends from 70%-owned corporation:	$5,000.00
Tax-exempt interest income from Montana public school obligations:	$5,000.00
Gain recognizable in future years from current installment sale:	$1,000.00
Accelerated depreciation allowed:	$17,500.00[*]
Life insurance proceeds paid on death of president of the company:	$20,000.00
Net operating loss carried over from prior year and currently deducted:	$5,000.00
Federal income taxes paid:	$8,940.00
Capital gains:	$500.00
Capital losses:	$1,000.00
Penalty paid to city:	$250.00
Interest expense on working capital:	$10,000.00
Interest expense for production of income from Montana public school obligations:	$500.00

Determine the effect each of these items has on the corporation's taxable income for the year and on its current E & P. *See* Reg. §§ 1.312-6 and 1.312-7.

PROBLEM 16-3

Angry Kennels, Inc. has $57,000 of accumulated earnings and profits at the beginning of the year and has current earnings and profits of $28,000. This year Angry Kennels, Inc. distributed $45,000 on April 15th and again on September 15th equally to each of its two equal

---

[*]Straight-line depreciation would have been $12,000.

shareholders, Danny and Gertrude (*i.e.*, it distributed $22,500 ~~$27,500~~ to each of them on April 15 and ~~$27,500~~ $22,500 to each of them again on September 15). As of the beginning of this year, Danny's basis in his stock was $3,000, and Gertrude's basis was $1,000.

1) Describe how current E & P is apportioned to distributions, as opposed to how accumulated E & P is apportioned.

2) What portion of each distribution is deemed to come out of current E & P?

3) What portion of each distribution is then deemed to have been paid out of accumulated E & P?

4) Is there any portion of either distribution payment unaccounted for by current or accumulated E & P?

5) If so, what is its effect on Gertrude's and Danny's bases in their stock?

6) Does either Danny or Gertrude recognize a gain?

E. DISGUISED AND CONSTRUCTIVE DISTRIBUTIONS

We have already seen that corporations and their shareholders suffer from a problem of double taxation, creating pressure on shareholders to devise ways to extract cash, property, or other value from the corporation without triggering the double tax. Shareholders have shown great ingenuity in beating the system. Common devices include leasing property to the corporation at exorbitant rates, selling property to the corporation at unreasonably high prices, paying excessive compensation, or making loans to shareholders (directly or indirectly) that lack the usual features of genuine debtor-creditor relationships. These transactions are risky because they may be reconstructed as distributions taxable as dividends. Further, as you will see in a later case, overly clever intercorporate transfers can create unintended dividends to shareholders who own stock in both corporations. Nowadays, the 20% rate cap on dividends paid to noncorporate shareholders and the dividends-received deduction for corporate recipients have reduced the pressure for this kind of planning.

In the real world, what tends to happen if the corporation prospers is that its tax advisers struggle to find ways to bleed income out of the corporation through deductions. One popular idea is to pay a "bonus" for past services. Will it work? Compensation for past services has been held deductible, but only if the corporation intended all along to pay more generous compensations in later years, as opposed to making a spontaneous decision with the benefit of hindsight that the employee had been under-compensated in previous years. *See, e.g.*, *Acme Construction Company v. Commissioner*, 69 TCM 1596 (1995). Another general strategy is to get the corporation a deduction and the payee a tax-exempt fringe benefit. For example, § 79 allows employers to provide up to $50,000 of nontaxable annual life insurance coverage, and § 162 allows the corporation to deduct the premiums.

STINNETT'S PONTIAC SERVICE, INC. v. COMMISSIONER
730 F.2d 634 (11th Cir. 1984)

HATCHETT, CIRCUIT JUDGE:

In this case, we review the Tax Court's holdings regarding the tax consequences of transactions involving two corporations and their common shareholder, the taxpayer. We affirm.

266

Facts

Richard W. Stinnett is president of Pontiac, an automobile dealership, and he owns 74% of the stock in the company. . . .

On or about July 2, 1973, Stinnett, Danford L. Sawyer (Sawyer), and Albert L. Bundy (Bundy) purchased the entire stock of Cargo Construction Company, Ltd. (Cargo), a Bahamian corporation. Cargo's principal business activity was commercial fishing, and its only asset was the lobster boat, RN Victory. Stinnett owned 43%; Sawyer owned 35%; and Bundy owned 22% of Cargo's stock. Stinnett, Sawyer, and Bundy also purchased the RJV Victory for approximately $55,000. The three shareholders realized that Cargo would need additional capital to satisfy certain unforeseen initial costs and, therefore, agreed to contribute additional capital, in proportion to each shareholder's stock ownership in Cargo, to Cargo to meet its needs.

From 1973 to 1975, Sawyer and Bundy contributed funds to Cargo as required by the shareholders' agreement. Stinnett, however, failed to contribute to Cargo pursuant to the shareholders' agreement. Pontiac, the corporation which Stinnett controlled, contributed funds and boat parts to Cargo. In 1973, Pontiac transferred $12,969.86 to Cargo, and, in return, Cargo issued interest bearing unsecured demand notes to Pontiac. During this same period, Pontiac also purchased marine parts for Cargo. Although Pontiac usually sold marine parts at 100% markup, it sold the marine parts to Cargo at only a 10% markup. Pontiac also made additional payments of $12,000 to Cargo. Cargo failed to issue any notes to Pontiac for any part of this amount.

From 1974 to 1975, Pontiac transferred an additional $45,000 to Cargo. Pontiac did not obtain any financial statements from Cargo prior to making any of the transfers, nor were the amounts of the transfers secured. After realizing that Cargo's lobster venture was unsuccessful, the shareholders decided to sell the RN Victory and recoup their investment. On February 23, 1976, therefore, they agreed to sell the boat for $80,000 with Pontiac receiving $20,000 from the sale. That sale never materialized, but the RN Victory was eventually sold for $42,000, and Cargo paid Richard Stinnett $6,000 for the sale of the boat.

On its 1974 federal income tax return, pursuant to § 166(a), Pontiac deducted $56,388.63 as a partially worthless debt for its advances to Cargo. It computed this amount by subtracting $20,000, the anticipated amount Pontiac would have received from the sale of the R/V Victory, from $76,388.63, the total amount Pontiac claimed it had advanced Cargo. The Commissioner disallowed the partially worthless debt deduction, and determined that the contributions from Pontiac to Cargo constituted constructive dividends to Stinnett in 1973 and 1974. Therefore, these dividends were taxable to Stinnett pursuant to §§ 301, 316. . . .

B. Were Pontiac's Advances to Cargo Constructive Dividends to Stinnett?

A corporate distribution to a shareholder is a dividend which the shareholder must include in his gross income if the distribution comes out of current and accumulated earnings and profits. §§ 61(a)(7); 301(c)(1). "[A] transfer of property from one corporation to another corporation may constitute a [constructive] dividend to an individual who has an ownership interest in both corporations." *Sammons v. Commissioner of Internal Revenue*, 472 F.2d 449, 451 (5th Cir. 1972).

In Sammons, the Fifth Circuit delineated the standard to determine whether a transfer of funds from one corporation to another corporation constitutes a dividend to an individual who owns shares in both corporations:

> In every case, the transfer must be measured by an objective test [the distribution test]: did the transfer cause funds or other property to leave the control of the

transferor corporation and did it allow the stockholder to exercise control over such funds or property either directly or indirectly through some instrumentality other than the transferor corporation. If this first assay is satisfied by a transfer of funds from one corporation to another rather than by a transfer to the controlling shareholder, a second, subjective test of purpose must also be satisfied before dividend characterization results. Though a search for intent or purpose is not ordinarily prerequisite to discovery of a dividend, such a subjective test must necessarily be utilized to differentiate between the normal business transactions of related corporations and those transactions designed primarily to benefit the stockowner. *Id.* at 451.

The advances from Pontiac to Cargo satisfy the distribution test. Stinnett, the common owner of shares in Cargo and Pontiac, received the funds from Pontiac and transferred them to Cargo as a capital contribution. *Sammons*, 472 F.2d at 453. Such a distribution is effected on the theory "that the funds pass from the transferor to the common stockholder as a dividend and then to the transferee as a capital contribution." *Id.* The only question, therefore, is whether the purpose test has been met in this case.

In determining whether the primary purpose test has been met, we must determine not only whether a subjective intent to primarily benefit the shareholders exists, but also whether an actual primary economic benefit exists for the shareholders. *Kuper v. Commissioner of Internal Revenue,* 533 F.2d 152, 160 (5th Cir. 1976). The Tax Court's finding of the primary purposes for the transfers is a question of fact and may not be disturbed unless clearly erroneous. *Kuper*, 533 F.2d at 161; *Sammons*, 472 F.2d at 452. In this case, the tax court concluded that the transfers were motivated to primarily benefit Stinnett and not Pontiac. This finding is not clearly erroneous.

If Pontiac had not made the advances to Cargo on Stinnett's behalf, Stinnett would have forfeited his interest in Cargo. Moreover, when Cargo was liquidated, Stinnett received $6,000 in the distribution. If the advances had not been made, Stinnett would have been unable to recoup any of his investment. Additionally, Stinnett's ownership interest in Cargo increased from 43% to 55% because of these advances. The evidence indicates that the advances from Pontiac to Cargo benefited Stinnett. We, therefore, must affirm the Tax Court's ruling. Since the contributions from Pontiac to Cargo satisfy the Sammons test, they constitute constructive dividends to Stinnett; and therefore, the tax court properly included the amount of the advances in Stinnett's income. . . .   *Affirmed.*

PROBLEM 16-4

Consider the following fact pattern and how you would reconstruct it, if at all:

Jr. and Sis own J & S, Inc., an accrual method, calendar year corporation in the newspaper business. Sis is prim and proper and has grown up to be a powerful business executive. Junior is a slob and an alcoholic. Sis has no children but Junior has two, both of whom are minors and are beneficiaries of a trust fund established for them with a modest contribution by their grandparents five years ago. The grandparents have since died. J & S is owned equally by Jr. and Sis, and it pays both a salary. Junior received a salary of $80,000 a year, which is lavish, and Sis received a salary of $120,000 a year, which is almost surely not enough for a woman of her extraordinary talents. Every year the siblings, acting as directors of J & S, have caused J & S, Inc. to contribute $20,000 to the trust fund for the children. Things have gone on like this for years, and it is unlikely that they are going to change for quite some time. J & S recently hired you to enter the scene and make an honest appraisal of the situation from a federal income tax perspective. What do you think?

F. DISTRIBUTIONS OF PROPERTY
Read § 311 (a) and (b)(1)-(2).

The amount of a distribution of property in kind is its value. § 301(b)(1). That means the shareholder takes a fair market value basis in the property. § 301(d). If the property is encumbered, then the amount of the distribution, but not the basis of the property, is correspondingly reduced. § 301(c).

If a corporation distributes property, other than its own stock or rights to acquire its own stock, to a shareholder and the value of the property exceeds the corporation's adjusted basis in the property, the corporation is treated as if it had sold the property at the time of the distribution. § 311(b). The corporation will recognize gain on the excess of the fair market value over the adjusted basis of the property. Moreover, the corporation's earnings and profits increase, thereby enhancing the likelihood that the distribution will produce a taxable dividend to the recipient(s) of the property. § 312(a), (b).

To illustrate: Midwest Freight Lines, Inc. distributes appreciated property to its sole shareholder. The corporation's basis in the distributed property is $200. The fair market value of the property is $500. The debt on the property is $370. That debt is assumed by the shareholder as part of the distribution. The Corporation's accumulated earnings and profits exceed the amount of the distribution.

A. Treatment of Corporation

Step 1: The Corporation has realized $300 of gain. The amount realized is the $500 FMV minus the $200 adjusted basis. The liability is not the basis of the amount realized. See §§ 311(b)(2) & 336(b) That $300 gain is recognized under §311(b)(1)

Step 2: The Corporation's current earnings and profits are increased by the $300 gain. §312(b)(2)

Step 3: The Corporation's earning and profits are decreased by $130.

Under §312(a)(3) as amplified by §312(b)(2) the Corporation's current earnings and profits are decreased by the distributed property's $500 FMV. However, because of the $370 liability,

§312(c) and Treas. Reg. §1.312-3 reduce the $500 decrease in earnings and profits by the debt so that the decrease in earnings and profits is only $130 ($500 "tentative" reduction less the $370 liability).

Under §312(a) a distribution cannot reduce earnings and profits below zero. That is not a problem in this illustration because the corporation has sufficient earnings and profits to cover the distribution.

B. Treatment of the shareholder

Step 4: The amount of the distribution to the shareholder is $130 calculated as the property's $500 FMV less the $370 debt. §301(b)

Step 5: The shareholder has a dividend to the extent that the Corporation has earnings and profits that equal or exceed the amount of the distribution. Here, the current earnings and profits, presumed to be $170 ($300 increase - $130 decrease, assuming no other events) as well as accumulated earnings and profits in excess of the amount of the distribution, means that all $130 will be treated as a dividend. §316 .

If for some reason the corporation has no accumulated earnings and profits and current earning and profits of less than $130, then the distribution may not be treated entirely as a dividend. If a portion of the distribution is not a dividend, then the shareholder reduces its basis in the stock until all that basis is depleted.

If a portion of the distributions exceeds the corporation's earnings and profits and the shareholder's basis in the stock, then the shareholder has gain from the sale or exchange of the stock and thus likely a capital gain. § 301(c)

Step 6: The shareholder's basis in the distributed property is its $500 FMV. § 301(d).

If shareholders think they can receive nontaxable dividends and safely avoid adjusting their stock basis under § 301(c), they are wrong. The corporation must file Form 5452 reporting nontaxable dividends paid to stockholders, thereby tipping off the IRS. The information called for by the form is extensive.

NOTES AND PROBLEMS

1. **How about losses?** Review § 311(a)&(b). Does it allow the corporation to report a loss on distributed property? If not, what should a corporation do instead of distributing loss property?

2. **Effect on earnings and profits**. A distribution of property in kind at a gain increases the corporation's earnings and profits, as noted above. The distribution also reduces earnings and profits by the fair market value of appreciated property, just like a cash distribution. § 312(a)(3), (b)(2). In the case of a distribution of loss property, the corporation reduces earnings and profits by the property's basis. Thus, the corporation enjoys the full value of the loss for purposes of its earnings and profits account. § 312(a)(3).

3. **Tax planning**. The problem with § 311 is that if the corporation holds rapidly appreciating property that it plans to dispose of, it will pay a major tax whether it distributes the property or sells it. One popular proposal is to have the corporation contribute the property to a partnership it forms with its shareholders and continue to have access to the property via a lease. The partnership is structured to shift a hefty portion of the subsequent gain to the

shareholders when the property is sold. Section 704(c) will prevent allocating away pre-contribution gain, but not post-contribution gain. The Service has attacked these freezes in *Boca Investerings Partnerships*, 314 F.3d 625; *Asa Investerings Partnership*, 201 F.3d 505.

4. **Valuation.** Assigning a value to property is not easy if there is no ready market for the item. Can a corporation minimize its own and its shareholders' tax liabilities by declaring that the property is not even worth the amount of the liabilities? *See* §§ 311(b)(2) and 336(b).

5. **Assignment of income**. In *Commissioner v. The First State Bank of Stratford,* 168 F.2d 1004 (5th Cir.), cert. denied, 335 U.S. 867 (1948), a bank distributed third-party promissory notes to its shareholders. The notes had been written off as worthless in the past, but the bank thought they might be collectible at some time. The notes turned out to have some value and later were collected on. The Fifth Circuit held that the collections were taxable to the bank rather than the shareholders on the theory that the distribution was an anticipatory assignment of income which should be taxed to the transferor corporation. What tax consequences does this holding imply for the shareholders?

PROBLEM 16-5

X Corp. wants to decrease its corporate assets account. It has no E & P. To do so, it distributes a bulldozer worth $2 million in which it has an adjusted basis of $1 million to one of its shareholders, George. It also distributes a set of carpentry tools worth $110,000 in which it has a basis of $120,000 to another shareholder, Mark.

1) Is the corporation taxed on either of these distributions? Can it claim any losses?

2) Does either of the distributions increase the corporation's earnings and profits account?

3) What effect, if any, does "(2)" have on the shareholders' likely taxation on the distributions?

4) What is X Corp's E & P after these transactions?

G. DISTRIBUTION OF CORPORATE OBLIGATIONS

A corporation may decide that it is cheaper to distribute its own promissory obligations instead of cash. In such cases, it seems clear that an individual shareholder would have to report the value of each obligation as income under § 301 to the extent of available earnings and profits. It is also clear that the distributing corporation will not be taxed on the distribution under §§ 311(b) and 317. Importantly, the amount of earnings and profits that are eliminated as a result of the distribution is limited to the obligation's value instead of its principal amount. § 312(a)(2). Based on the concept of original issue discount, principal amount is limited to value. If it were not for the limit, a gaping loophole would open. A corporation could distribute an obligation worth far less than its face amount, say because it bore a low or zero rate of interest, and still reduce its earnings and profits by the full face amount. This would permit earnings and profits to be artificially eliminated, thereby tending to make later distributions tax-free returns of capital.

To illustrate: X Corp. distributes a ten-year bond with a value of $60 and a face amount of $100. The $40 difference is original issue discount, which will be reported as income to the holder and as a deduction to X Corp., over the life of the bond. *See* §§ 1272-1273 (income) and

§ 163(e) (deduction). The corporation reduces its E & P by $60, not $100 at the time of the distribution.

H. DIVIDENDS-RECEIVED DEDUCTION
Read § 243.

Each time a corporation pays a dividend to a higher-tier corporation that owns stock in the payor, yet another layer of corporate income taxes is imposed on the distribution. As the number of tiers increases, the amount of tax on the original profit might approach 100%. The result is hard to justify.

To address this problem, the Code grants a special deduction for corporate shareholders that receive dividends from corporations. The general deduction is equal to 50% of the dividends. A close reading of § 243 shows that there is a spectrum of rates applicable to the deduction that increases with the degree to which the distributing corporation owns the distributing corporation:

Recipient's Ownership of Distributing Corporation	Deductible Percentage of Dividend
Less than 20%-owned	50% § 243(a)(1)
At least 20%-owned	65% § 243(c)(1)
Small business investment corporation	100% § 243(a)(2)
Qualifying dividends	100% § 243(a)(3)

I. MINIMUM HOLDING PERIOD TO GET DIVIDENDS-RECEIVED DEDUCTION
Read § 246(c).

Section 246(c) is designed to take the fun out of claiming the dividends-received deduction if the recipient corporation really just planned to pop in and out of the stock market long enough to (1) receive a dividend, (2) claim a dividends-received deduction with respect to the dividend, and then (3) sell the stock at a loss that reflects the fact that the dividend was paid. The loss would not be a true economic loss because ordinarily it would be equal to the dividend paid out.

Under § 246(c), in order to enjoy a dividends-received deduction with respect to common stock, the corporate recipient must hold the stock for more than 45 days during the 90-day period that begins 45 days before the date the stock goes ex-dividend. That forces the corporation to take an economic risk that the dividend "play" will be accompanied by a real economic risk of a market fluctuation in the stock. Because preferred stock prices are generally less volatile than common stock, the sanitary period is doubled to 180 days for preferred stock. A backstop rule extends the sanitary period to the extent that the taxpayer works out a way to offset the market risk. § 246(c)(1)(B).

J. MANDATORY STOCK BASIS REDUCTION FOR EXTRAORDINARY DIVIDENDS
Read § 1059(a),(c),(e).

This provision captures corporations that held stock long enough under § 246(c)(1)(B) but not long enough to make Congress happy due to the exceptionally large size of the dividend.

In order to prevent tax arbitrage by means of receiving large dividends and then selling the stock in order to claim a loss deduction solely due to payment of the dividend, § 1059 requires a reduction in the basis of stock held by corporate shareholders when they receive such dividends. (There can even be a taxable gain if the nontaxed portion of the extraordinary dividend exceeds the distributee's basis in the stock.) True to its purpose of preventing short-term tax planning, this rule does not apply if the stock with respect to which the dividend is paid was held for at least two years before announcement of the dividend.

Basis in the stock with respect to which the dividend was paid is reduced by the non-taxed portion of the dividend (*i.e.*, the dividend-received deduction). This effectively eliminates the possibility of duplicating the benefit of the dividends-received deduction. To be "extraordinary," the dividend must exceed a threshold level of 5% of the shareholder's adjusted basis in preferred stock or 10% of its adjusted basis in common stock.

Congress felt certain kinds of dividend-creating transactions were too easily staged and that § 1059 had to be fortified to deal with them. The response was § 1059(e), a provision that can come as a nasty surprise to a corporate shareholder that had no evil in mind. That is because § 1059(e) mechanically drops both the protective two-year limitation and the threshold ownership percentage standards for identifying an extraordinary dividend in the context of certain stock redemptions (*i.e.*, cases where the corporation buys stock from its shareholder), namely:

1) A redemption in partial liquidation under § 302(e);

2) A non-pro-rata redemption; or

3) A redemption treated as a dividend because of option attribution rules (§ 318(a)(4)), or a related-party redemption under § 304(a).

If one of these events occurs, then the non-taxed portion of the dividend reduces the basis of the recipient's stock, thereby increasing the gain on ultimate disposition of the stock, no matter how small the dividend, no matter how long the stock was held, and no matter how small a share of the distributing corporation the recipient corporation owned. There is a special exception for the presumably harmless case where the corporate shareholder held the stock during the entire life of the corporation whose stock is being redeemed.

To illustrate: Big Corp. has for many years been the 70% owner of the 100 shares of common stock of Mini Corp. The 70 shares have an adjusted basis of $20 per share. Big Corp. bought the stock 10 years after Mini Corp. was organized. Mini Corp. has E & P of $10,000. Mini Corp. engages in a non-pro rata redemption of its stock in partial liquidation of Mini Corp. by redeeming 20 of its shares for $30 per share, paying Big Corp. a total of $600. Assume the redemption is taxable as a distribution because Big Corp. remains the controlling shareholder. This means the $600 that Big Corp. received is a § 301(c)(1) dividend in its entirety because of Mini Corp's large E & P pool. As a result, Big Corp.'s basis in the Mini Corp. stock must be reduced, but not below zero, by the "non-taxed portion" of the $600. Section 243(c) allows a 65% dividends-received deduction on these facts (*i.e.*, a dividend to a more than 20% shareholder). That means the non-taxed portion of the dividend is 65% of $600 (*i.e.*, $390). As a result, Big Corp. must reduce its basis in its remaining Mini Corp. stock by $390 under § 1059(e). If the untaxed portion of the extraordinary dividend is greater than Big Corp.'s basis in the stock, then Big Corp. has to recognize the excess as a gain, immediately. § 1059(a)(2). If Big Corp. always owned the Mini Corp. stock, § 1059 would not apply. § 1059(d)(6).

Some affiliated corporations, such as a parent and subsidiary or subsidiaries, can qualify to file a consolidated income tax return under §§ 1501-1504. The effect is to eliminate tax on intercorporate transactions within the consolidated group, including dividends paid by a subsidiary to its parent. The Regulations under these sections are renowned for their length and complexity. A later Chapter offers an overview of the consolidated return Regulations.

PROBLEM 16-6

1) X Corp. owns 5% of Y Corp.'s common stock. Both are domestic corporations. X Corp. has held the Y stock over a year. If Y Corp. pays a dividend of $10,000 to X Corp., how much of it will be taxable to X Corp.?

2) What tax rate will apply to "(1)" to the taxable portion of the dividend? Assume both corporations are highly prosperous.

3) What if Y Corp. is a Danish corporation?

4) Suppose X Corp. owned 40% of Y Corp.'s common stock, and Y Corp. paid a dividend of $10,000 to X Corp. What portion is taxable to X Corp.?

5) Same as "(4)". What if X Corp. sold all of its stock in Y Corp. 30 days after the dividend payment. What portion of the $10,000 dividend would now be taxable to X Corp.?

6) What portion of the dividend would be taxable if X Corp. owned all of Y Corp. and X Corp. got a dividend from Y Corp?

7) Smart Corp. discovered that Zell Computer plans to pay a big dividend, so it buys a share (1%) of Zellco for $100 before the record date for the dividend and gets a $40 dividend two days later. A week later, Smart Corp. sells its Zell stock for $60. What is Smart Corp.'s taxable income from these dealings?

8) Same as "(7)", but Smart Corp. holds the stock for 18 months ?

K. LEVERAGED DIVIDENDS
Read § 246A.

A crafty corporate taxpayer might conclude that it could borrow money at 10% and use the borrowed money to purchase stock that produce dividends at a rate of 10% (highly unlikely, but useful for illustrative purposes). If so, then each time the corporation received $100 in dividends it could claim a deduction of $50% and would report only $50 of income because of the 50% dividends-received deduction. At a 21% tax rate, this would cost the corporation $10.50 in taxes. At the same time the corporation is entitled to claim an interest expense deduction of $100, which at a 21% tax rate is worth $21. As a result, the taxpayer would have manufactured a financial gain entirely due to tax arbitrage.

The economic transaction is a complete wash of $100 income and outgo. This is obviously a preposterous outcome and must be blocked. Section 246A does so by limiting the dividends-received deduction in proportion to the extent to which that deduction is leveraged. For example, if half the stock were acquired with debt, then half the deduction is denied.

On January 10th of last year, corporation Buyer buys 1,000 shares of the common stock of Portfolio Corporation for a total cost of $100,000. Buyer finances 60% of the purchase by borrowing $60,000. On April 14th of the same year, while the full amount of the debt is still outstanding, Buyer becomes entitled to a $1,000 dividend on the Portfolio Corporation stock (payable May 1). Buyer owns less than 20% by value of the outstanding Portfolio stock. Is Buyer's dividends-received deduction limited, and if so, to what extent, assuming allocable interest expense deductions for carrying the Portfolio stock were $500?

L. DIVIDENDS-RECEIVED DEDUCTIONS AND SALE OF A SUBSIDIARY

A parent company is entitled to a dividends-received deduction of up to 100 percent, but it cannot get the benefit of a capital gains preference, in sharp contrast to individuals. Now, imagine a large corporation that wants $100 million for selling the stock of its wholly owned unconsolidated subsidiary ("the sub"), in which it has a basis of $10 million. Assume the sub has a lot of extra cash, say $30 million. Assume, to keep things very tidy, that the buyer can only afford to pay $70 million. How about having the sub pay a $30 million dividend before the sale, allowing the corporate parent to claim a $30 million dividends-received deduction? If it works, the parent has $60 million of gain ($70 million amount realized minus $10 million basis) on the sale, and no taxable income from the dividend, instead of $90 million of taxable gain.

It sounds good, but first a word of warning in the form of a review of *Waterman Steamship Corp. v. Commissioner,* 430 F.2d 1185 (5th Cir. 1970), cert. denied (1971). The facts involved a subsidiary, Pan-Atlantic Steamship Corporation, which drafted and distributed a large note as a dividend to its parent, Waterman Steamship Corporation, in anticipation of Waterman's selling the stock of Pan American (and another sub) and in order to minimize its overall taxes on selling the Pan American stock. Pan American issued a note, as a dividend, to Waterman. Waterman had a low basis in the Pan American stock. The buyer, McLean, paid Waterman correspondingly less cash, but shortly after the purchase of the stock was completed, Pan American paid off the note with money provided by McLean. The entire life cycle of the note was 90 minutes.

This arrangement raised a basic question of form over substance: was the real deal a dividend paid with a note plus a reduced purchase price (ideal for Waterman) or a full purchase price paid to Waterman, combined with a lot of hocus-pocus over an alleged dividend? The Tax Court concluded that it was the latter and disallowed the intercorporate dividends exclusion and correspondingly increased the gain on the sale of the stock of Pan American.

Wait a minute – what if the sellers in *Waterman Steamship* had been individuals? Well, they would settle for the court's conclusion; a capital gain *used to* beat a dividend any day of the week, but not any more thanks to the 20% rate cap on dividends. Now that you appreciate how the chance to obtain a dividends-received deduction (or intercorporate dividend exclusion) might be bungled, consider the following case.

LITTON INDUSTRIES, INC. v. COMMISSIONER
89 T.C. 1086 (1987)

CLAPP, JUDGE.

After concessions, the issue for decision is whether Litton Industries received a $30 million dividend from Stouffer Corp., its wholly owned subsidiary, or whether that sum represented proceeds from the sale of Stouffer stock to Nestle Corp.

Findings of Fact

Litton Industries, Inc. (petitioner), and its subsidiaries manufactured and sold, inter alia, business systems and equipment, defense and marine systems, industrial systems and equipment, and microwave cooking equipment. It maintained its principal office in Beverly Hills, California, at the time it filed its petition in this case.

On October 4, 1967, petitioner acquired all the outstanding stock of Stouffer Corp. (Stouffer), a corporation whose common stock was listed and traded on the New York stock exchange. Stouffer manufactured and sold frozen prepared food, and operated hotels and food management services and restaurants . . .

In early 1972, Charles B. Thornton (Thornton), the chairman of Litton's board of directors; Joseph Imirie, president of Stouffer; and James Biggar, an executive of Stouffer, discussed project "T.I.B.," i.e., the sale of Stouffer. In July 1972, Litton's board of directors discussed the mechanics and problems of selling Stouffer. As of August 1, 1972, Stouffer's accumulated earnings and profits exceeded $30 million. On August 23, 1972, Stouffer declared a $30 million dividend which it paid to Litton in the form of a $30 million negotiable promissory note, and at that time, Thornton believed that Litton would have no difficulty in receiving an adequate offer for Stouffer. Two weeks later, on September 7, 1972, petitioner announced publicly its interest in disposing of Stouffer. Subsequent to said announcement, Litton received inquiries from a number of interested sources, including TWA, Green Giant, investment banking houses, and business brokers about the possible purchase of all or part of the Stouffer business.

Beginning in mid-September 1972, Litton and several underwriters discussed the feasibility of a public offering of Stouffer Stock. In early September 1972, Litton negotiated with Lehman Bros. for a public offering of Stouffer stock, but Lehman Bros. decided not to participate in the offering. During October 1972, Litton, Stouffer, and Merrill Lynch, a brokerage firm that thought Stouffer had an excellent outlook, prepared a public offering of Stouffer stock. During November 1972, petitioner, Stouffer, and Hornblower and Weeks prepared a partial public offering of Stouffer stock. Merrill Lynch had a policy of not effecting partial distributions of corporate subsidiaries and thus did not participate in the negotiations with Hornblower and Weeks. In mid-December 1972, Litton decided that a complete public offering was preferable and abandoned the idea of a partial public offering. The S-1 Registration Statement, which Stouffer filed with the Securities and Exchange Commission, stated that $30 million of the proceeds would be used to pay the promissory note which Litton received as a dividend.

On March 1, 1973, Nestle Alimentana S.A. Corp. (Nestle), a Swiss corporation, offered to buy all of Stouffer's stock for $105 million. On March 5, 1973, Nestle paid Litton $74,962,518 in cash for all the outstanding stock of Stouffer and $30 million in cash for the promissory note. Because Litton sold Stouffer to Nestle, the underwriters stopped work on the scheduled public offering.

Opinion

The issue for decision is whether the $30 million dividend declared by Stouffer on August 23, 1972, and paid to its parent, Litton, by means of a negotiable promissory note was truly a dividend for tax purposes or whether it should be considered part of the proceeds received by Litton from the sale of all of Stouffer's stock on March 1, 1973. If, as petitioner contends, the $30 million constitutes a dividend, petitioner may deduct 85 percent of that amount as a dividend-received credit pursuant to section 243(a), as that section read during the year at issue. However, if the $30 million represents part of the selling price of the Stouffer stock, as contended by respondent, the entire amount will be added to the proceeds of the sale and taxed

276

to Litton as additional capital gain. Respondent's approach, of course produces the larger amount of tax dollars.

The instant case is substantially governed by *Waterman Steamship Corp. v. Commissioner*, 50 T.C. 650 (1968), rev'd. 430 F.2d 1185 (5th Cir. 1970), cert. denied 401 U.S. 939 (1971). Respondent urges us to follow the opinion of the Fifth Circuit, which in substance adopted the position of judge Tannenwald's dissent (concurred in by three other judges) [charts omitted here.eds] from our Court-reviewed opinion. If we hold for respondent, we must overrule our majority opinion in *Waterman Steamship*. Petitioner contends that the reasoning of the Fifth Circuit in *Waterman Steamship* should not apply since the facts here are more favorable to petitioner. Additionally, petitioner points out that several business purposes were served by the distribution here which provide additional support for recognition of the distribution as a dividend. For the reasons set forth below, we conclude that the $30 million distribution constituted a dividend which should be recognized as such for tax purposes. We believe that the facts in the instant case lead even more strongly than did the facts in *Waterman Steamship* to the conclusion that the $30 million was a dividend. Accordingly, we hold that the Stouffer distribution to Litton was a dividend within the meaning of section 243(a).

In many respects, the facts of this case and those of *Waterman Steamship* are parallel. The principal difference, and the one which we find to be most significant, is the timing of the dividend action. In *Waterman Steamship*, the taxpayer corporation received an offer to purchase the stock of two of its wholly owned subsidiary corporations, Pan-Atlantic and Gulf Florida, for $3,500,000 cash. The board of directors of Waterman Steamship rejected that offer but countered with an offer to sell the two subsidiaries for $700,000 after the subsidiaries declared and arranged for payments of dividends to Waterman Steamship amounting in the aggregate to $2,800,000. Negotiations between the parties ensued, and the agreements which resulted there from included, in specific detail, provisions for the declaration of a dividend by Pan-Atlantic to Waterman Steamship prior to the signing of the sales agreement and the closing of that transaction. Furthermore, the agreements called for the purchaser to loan or otherwise advance funds to Pan-Atlantic promptly in order to pay off the promissory note by which the dividend had been paid. Once the agreement was reached, the entire transaction was carried out by a series of meetings commencing at 12 noon on January 21, 1955, and ending at 1:30 p.m. the same day. At the first meeting, the board of directors of Pan-Atlantic met and declared a dividend in the form of a promissory note in the amount of $2,799,820. The dividend was paid by execution and delivery of the promissory note. At 12:30 p.m., the board of directors of the purchaser's nominee corporation (Securities) met and authorized the purchase and financing of Pan-Atlantic and Gulf Florida. At 1 p.m., the directors of Waterman authorized the sale of all outstanding stock of Pan-Atlantic and Gulf Florida to Securities. Immediately following that meeting, the sales agreement was executed by the parties. The agreement provided that the purchaser guaranteed prompt payment of the liabilities of Pan-Atlantic and Gulf Florida including payment of any notes given by either corporation as a dividend.

Finally, at 1:30 p.m., the new board of directors of Pan-Atlantic authorized the borrowing of sufficient funds from the purchaser personally and from his nominee corporation to pay off the promissory note to Waterman Steamship, which was done forthwith. As the Fifth Circuit pointed out, "By the end of the day and within a ninety minute period, the financial cycle had been completed. Waterman had $3,500,000, hopefully tax-free, all of which came from Securities and McLean, the buyers of the stock." 430 F.2d at 1190. This Court concluded that the distribution from Pan-Atlantic to Waterman was a dividend. The Fifth Circuit reversed, concluding that the dividend and sale were one transaction. 430 F.2d at 1192.

The timing in the instant case was markedly different. The dividend was declared by Stouffer on August 23, 1972, at which time the promissory note in payment of the dividend was issued to Litton. There had been some general preliminary discussions about the sale of Stouffer, and it was expected that Stouffer would be a very marketable company which would sell quickly. However, at the time the dividend was declared, no formal action had been taken to initiate the sale of Stouffer. It was not until 2 weeks later that Litton publicly announced that Stouffer was for sale. There ensued over the next 6 months many discussions with various corporations, investment banking houses, business brokers, and underwriters regarding Litton's disposition of Stouffer through sale of all or part of the business to a particular buyer, or through full or partial public offerings of the Stouffer stock. All of this culminated on March 1, 1973, over 6 months after the dividend was declared, with the purchase by Nestle of all of Stouffer's stock. Nestle also purchased the outstanding promissory note for $30 million in cash.

In the instant case, the declaration of the dividend and the sale of the stock were substantially separated in time in contrast to *Waterman Steamship* where the different transactions occurred essentially simultaneously. In *Waterman Steamship*, it seems quite clear that no dividend would have been declared if all of the remaining steps in the transaction had not been lined up in order on the closing table and did not in fact take place. Here, however, Stouffer declared the dividend, issued the promissory note, and definitely committed itself to the dividend before even making a public announcement that Stouffer was for sale. Respondent argues that the only way petitioner could ever receive the dividend was by raising revenue through a sale of Stouffer. Therefore, respondent asserts the two events (the declaration of the dividend and then the sale of the company) were inextricably tied together and should be treated as one transaction for tax purposes. In our view, respondent ignores the fact that Stouffer could have raised sufficient revenue for the dividend from other avenues, such as a partial public offering or borrowing. Admittedly, there had been discussions at Litton about the sale of Stouffer which was considered to be a very salable company. However, there are many slips between the cup and the lip, and it does not take much of a stretch of the imagination to picture a variety of circumstances under which Stouffer might have been taken off the market and no sale consummated. Under these circumstances, it is unlikely that respondent would have considered the dividend to be a nullity. On the contrary, it would seem quite clear that petitioner would be charged with a dividend on which it would have to pay a substantial tax. Petitioner committed itself to the dividend and, thereby, accepted the consequences regardless of the outcome of the proposed sale of Stouffer stock . . .

Since the facts here are distinguishable in important respects and are so much stronger in petitioner's favor, we do not consider it necessary to consider further the opinion of the Fifth Circuit in *Waterman Steamship*.

The term "dividend" is defined in section 316(a) as a distribution by a corporation to its shareholders out of earnings and profits. The parties have stipulated that Stouffer had earnings and profits exceeding $30 million at the time the dividend was declared. This Court has recognized that a dividend may be paid by a note. *T.R. Miller Mill Co. v. Commissioner*, 37 B.T.A. 43, 49 (1938), aff'd., 102.2d 599 (5th Cir. 1939). Based on these criteria, the $30 million distribution by, Stouffer would clearly constitute a dividend if the sale of Stouffer had not occurred. We are not persuaded that the subsequent sale of Stouffer to Nestle changes that result merely because it was more advantageous to Litton from a tax perspective.

It is well established that a taxpayer is entitled to structure his affairs and transactions in order to minimize his taxes. This proposition does not give a taxpayer carte blanche to set up a transaction in any form which will avoid tax consequences, regardless of whether the transaction has substance. *Gregory v. Helvering,* 293 U.S. 465 (1935). A variety of factors present here preclude a finding of sham or subterfuge. Although the record in this case clearly shows that Litton intended at the time the dividend was declared to sell Stouffer, no formal action had been taken and no announcement had been made. There was no definite purchaser waiting in the wings with the terms and conditions of sale already agreed upon. At that time, Litton had not even decided upon the form of sale of Stouffer. Nothing in the record here suggests that there was any prearranged sale agreement, formal or informal, at the time the dividend was declared.

278

Petitioner further supports its argument that the transaction was not a sham by pointing out Litton's legitimate business purposes in declaring the dividend. Although the code and case law do not require a dividend to have a business purpose, it is a factor to be considered in determining whether the overall transaction was a sham. *T.S.N. Liquidating Corp. v. United States*, 624 F.2d 1328 (5th Cir. 1980). Petitioner argues that the distribution allowed Litton to maximize the gross after-tax amount it could receive from its investment in Stouffer. From the viewpoint of a private purchaser of Stouffer, it is difficult to see how the declaration of a dividend would improve the value of the stock since creating a liability in the form of a promissory note for $30 million would reduce the value of Stouffer by approximately that amount. However, since Litton was considering disposing of all or part of Stouffer through a public or private offering, the payment of a dividend by a promissory note prior to any sale had two advantages. First, Litton hoped to avoid materially diminishing the market value of the Stouffer stock. At that time, one of the factors considered in valuing a stock, and in determining the market value of a stock was the "multiple of earnings" criterion. Payment of the dividend by issuance of a promissory note would not substantially alter Stouffer's earnings. Since many investors were relatively unsophisticated, Litton may have been quite right that it could increase its investment in Stouffer by at least some portion of the $30 million dividend. Second, by declaring a dividend and paying it by a promissory note prior to an anticipated public offering, Litton could avoid sharing the earnings with future additional shareholders while not diminishing to the full extent of the pro rata dividend, the amount received for the stock. Whether Litton could have come out ahead after Stouffer paid the promissory note is at this point merely speculation about a public offering which never occurred. The point, however, is that Litton hoped to achieve some business purpose, and not just tax benefits, in structuring the transaction as it did.

Under these facts, where the dividend was declared 6 months prior to the sale of Stouffer, where the sale was not prearranged, and since Stouffer had earnings and profits exceeding $30 million at the time the dividend was declared, we cannot conclude that the distribution was merely a device designed to give the appearance of a dividend to a part of the sales proceeds. In this case, the form and substance of the transaction coincide; it was not a transaction entered into solely for tax reasons, and it should be recognized as structured by petitioner.

On this record, we hold that for Federal tax purposes Stouffer declared a dividend to petitioner on August 23, 1972, and, subsequently, petitioner sold all of its stock in Stouffer to Nestle for $75 million.

Decision will be entered under Rule 155.

PROBLEM 16-8

If you were a director of Stouffer and you knew that half the stock of Stouffer was held by Litton and half was held by shareholders who were members of the public, would you still do the same deal as transpired in the Litton case? How would you decide, whether to accept a larger sale price for all sellers or a dividend plus a smaller sale price?

M. STOCK DIVIDENDS
Read § 305(a).

Common stock of a corporation represents the owner's equity in the corporation, meaning the value of the corporation less the amount of its liabilities. As far as the owners are concerned, it makes no economic difference whether additional shares of stock are issued to the same owners in proportion to their predistribution ownership, because the additional stock will have no effect on their proportionate share of the equity. In fact, companies often declare stock dividends in order to keep the price per share of the stock low so that it will be more attractive to the public and to stimulate excitement about the company. Stock dividends were held to be tax-free in the early Supreme Court decision *Eisner v. Macomber*, 252 U.S. 189 (1920). Complications later arose in situations other than the simple common-on-common-shares distribution in *Macomber*, and it was not until 1969 that the tax law in this area was stabilized in the form of what is now § 305 of the Code. Stock "splits," in which the shareholder receives say one, two, or three shares for each share currently held are rightly treated in exactly the same way for tax purposes as stock "dividends" in which one typically receives fewer shares, say one for each ten shares currently held, and in connection with which state corporation law generally requires that surplus be capitalized.

The structure of § 305 is exceptionally tidy by Code standards. It opens with the general statement in § 305(a) that gross income does not include stock distributions (or distributions of stock rights), except as otherwise provided in § 305(b). Section 305(b) in turn describes five situations in which a stock distribution is taxable to the distributee by exception to the general rule, and § 305(c) contains a subtle definitional provision that embellishes § 305(b)(2). The remainder of this section is given over to a study of § 305, largely using the problem method.

PROBLEM 16-9

Mrs. A bought 1,000 shares of common stock in XYZ Corp. at $24 per share on September 1, three years ago. On September 1, this year, XYZ Corp. distributed a stock dividend of one share of common stock on every five shares of its common stock issued and outstanding. The fair market value of XYZ Corp.'s common stock on September 1, this year, was $50 per share, before the stock dividend.

1) How much taxable income does Mrs. A recognize as a result of the stock dividend?

2) What is A's total cost basis and basis per share in her XYZ common stock after the stock distribution? *See* § 307(a) and Reg. § 1.307-1.

3) What is A's holding period for the stock? *See* § 1223.

4) What if the number of shares held by each taxpayer was not evenly divisible by 5, and so it was provided that rights to fractional shares would be paid in cash? *See* Reg. § 1.305-3(c).

1. OPTIONAL DISTRIBUTIONS TO SHAREHOLDERS
Read § 305(b)(1).

This is a draconian section because if even one shareholder has the right to get a distribution of cash or property, all the other shareholders who received stock are deemed to have received cash distributions instead.

To illustrate*:* The Friendly Corporation has 15,000 shareholders and is registered on the American Stock Exchange. It has decided to issue a stock dividend in which shareholders of common stock are entitled to receive one additional share of common stock for each two they currently hold, subject to one proviso, namely that Mrs. Thelma Klotz, a long-time employee of the company, is entitled to take the value of the stock dividend ($1 in her case because she only had one share) in cash instead of in the form of an additional share of stock. The company has accumulated earnings and profits of three million dollars. What is the tax impact of the stock distribution on Mrs. Klotz? On the other shareholders? If your conclusion is that everybody has taxable income from the stock distribution, how are they expected to pay the tax without any additional cash?

The answer is that all the shareholders will collectively recognize up to $3 million of dividend income pursuant to § 305(b)(1)(A) and Reg. § 1.305-2 because one stock dividend could be paid in cash in lieu of stock at Mrs. Klotz's election, even if she elects to take the stock! Cash in lieu of fractional stock does not create a taxable result to all shareholders, just the recipient. *See, e.g.,* Rev. Rul. 69-15, 1969-1 C.B. 95.

2. DISTRIBUTIONS OF COMMON AND PREFERRED STOCK
Read § 305(b)(3).

PROBLEM 16-10

Polluting Enterprises, Inc. has 1,000 public shareholders and two classes of common stock, Class A and Class B. Its board of directors decides to issue a dividend on the Class A shares payable in preferred stock and a dividend on the B shares payable in additional shares of Class B common stock.

1) Is this a taxable distribution under § 305?

2) Who is taxed? You need to read the Code closely.

3. DISTRIBUTIONS ON PREFERRED STOCK
Read § 305(b)(4).

PROBLEM 16-11

Some years after the distribution discussed in Problem 15-10, in an unrelated transaction, the preferred shareholders of Polluting Enterprises, Inc. receive one share of newly issued preferred stock with respect to each share of preferred stock that they held as of a certain date. The fair market value of each share of the newly issued preferred stock is $100.

1) Do the shareholders who receive the preferred stock have income and if so in what amount?

2) Do the common shareholders have the right to claim a deduction for the diminution in their share of the equity of the corporation?

3) As to "(2)," if not, is that an unfair result?

4. DISTRIBUTIONS OF CONVERTIBLE PREFERRED STOCK
Read § 305(b)(5).

PROBLEM 16-12

The Friendly Corporation has three million shares of common stock outstanding at a time when it has an enormous amount of earnings and profits. The Corporation issues one share of convertible preferred stock as a stock dividend on each share of common stock presently outstanding, which means that it has issued three million shares of the new preferred stock. The convertible preferred stock has a face amount and value of $10 per share when it is issued, and each share is convertible into one share of common stock. At present, the common stock trades at $5 per share on a national stock market. The preferred stock is convertible for the next 10 years, after which the conversion feature lapses. Is this distribution taxable? *See* Reg. § 1.305-6(a).

5. DISPROPORTIONATE DISTRIBUTIONS
Read § 305(b)(2).

This is the most difficult aspect of § 305(b). The basic concept is that a distribution of stock or rights is taxable if the distribution (or series of distributions) has the effect of receipt of cash or property by some shareholders and an increase in the proportionate equity interest held by the other shareholders. This calls for testing for disproportionality within each class and among all of the classes of stock. If there is a series of distributions, it will be treated as a single transaction if the steps indicate an overall plan.

The Regulations provide a presumption that there is no such plan only if the time between the distribution of stock and the distribution of cash or property is at least thirty-six months. Reg. § 1.305-3(b)(4). That is small comfort. Also, notice how if, after a stock distribution to shareholders, one shareholder is redeemed out for cash by a § 304 related-corporation in a prearranged plan and the others stand pat, then the others enjoy an increased share of the equity while the distributee gets cash. Does that mean § 305(b)(2) applies? Yes, unless it is an "isolated redemption." Reg. § 1.305-3(b)(3). This is a trap that is easily overlooked.

PROBLEM 16-13

Dual Corp. has two classes of common stock outstanding. Class A common and Class B common. On August 31, Dual Corp. declared a cash dividend on its Class A stock of $2 per share and declared a stock dividend of one share of Class B common on every share of its Class B common issued and outstanding. Will the shareholders of Dual Corp.'s Class B stock recognize taxable income? *See* § 305(b)(2) and Reg. § 1.305-3(b)(2).

6. CONSTRUCTIVE DISTRIBUTIONS

Section 305(c) authorizes the Treasury Department to issue Regulations that cause various corporate transactions to be treated as constructive distributions with respect to any shareholder whose proportionate interest in the corporation's earnings and profits or assets increases as a result of the transaction. This buttresses § 305(b)(2) by creating an array of imaginary distributions that one must consider in the search for changes in proportionate interest in order to determine whether § 305(b)(2) applies. For example, the Regulations indicate that a forbidden disproportionate distribution can be accomplished by a plan for periodic stock redemptions as well as through stock dividends. Notice how the Regulations insist that both the redeemed and nonredeemed shareholders can be taxed, even though the nonredeemed shareholders have received no actual distribution at all. For an example, *see* Rev. Rul. 78-60, 1978-1 C.B. 80 (periodic redemption plan involving three of five shareholders; ruled: the nonredeemed shareholders have § 305(b)(2) stock dividends because of their proportionately increased positions in the company, citing Reg. § 1.305-3(e), examples (8) and (9)).

PROBLEM 16-14

Small Corporation, Inc. has ten shareholders, one of whom is tired of the business and wants to sell. The board of directors agrees to redeem her stock – that is, buy back all her stock – in order to facilitate her retirement. Is this transaction a distribution within the meaning of § 305(b)(2)? *See* Reg. § 1.305-3(e), Example 10.

Section 305 and the Regulations go very far. The statute authorizes Regulations under which, even *without any distribution of stock by the corporation,* the following transactions or events are treated as a distribution to which § 301 applies (viz., a potentially taxable dividend) with respect to any shareholder whose proportionate interest in the earnings and profits or assets of the corporation is increased by such event: (a) a change in conversion ratio; (b) a change in redemption price; (c) a difference between redemption price and issue price; (d) a redemption that is treated as a distribution to which § 301 applies; or (e) any transaction, including a recapitalization, having a similar effect on the interest of any shareholder. The Regulations also are broad and scary. A "deemed" distribution under § 305(c) is taxable if it has a result described in § 305(b)(2)-(5). Read § 1.305-7(a).

PROBLEM 16-15

National Arm Chair Corp. is equally owned by ten shareholders, each of whom owns 10% of the stock in the company. Curiously, the names of the shareholders are A, B, C, D, E, F, G, H, I, and J. The Board of Directors of the company agrees to redeem half of the stock of A, B, and C this year, half of the stock of C, D, and E next year and all of the stock of I the following year. Who, if anyone, has enjoyed a distribution within the meaning of § 305? Assume the redemptions are otherwise properly treated as distributions.

N. BASIS AND HOLDING PERIOD OF STOCK
Read § 307(a) and Reg. § 1.307-1.

You already considered this in a prior problem, but here is an expanded discussion. If a shareholder receives new stock tax-free under § 305(a), then the shareholder's basis must be reallocated from the old stock to the new stock by reference to the relative values of the old and new stock. § 307. For example, if the old stock has a basis of $20 and was worth $40 after the distribution, and the new stock was worth $10 after the distribution, then one-fifth of the basis ($10/$50 of total value), or $4, would be allocated to the new stock, and the old stock would have a basis of $16 ($40/$50 x $20). In addition, the holding period of the new stock will include the period during which the shareholder held the old stock. § 1223(5).

The practical effect is to split the basis between the old and the new stock and to assign the new stock a "tacked" holding period. The corporation will not reduce its earnings and profits in connection with a nontaxable distribution of stock. *See* § 312(d)(1). This is logical because the distribution is not viewed as a dividend, it is viewed as a non-event, the only impact of which is to require a reallocation of basis and holding period at the shareholder level.

By contrast, if the distribution is taxable, § 301 will apply. The amount of the distribution will, as usual, be its fair market value. Reg. § 1.305-2(b), Example 1 and Reg. § 1.301-1(d). This is consistent with the usual rule for distributions of property. The corporation will reduce its earnings and profits by the fair market value of the stock or rights distributed. Reg. § 1.312-1(d). There is no § 307 reallocation of basis and no tacking of the holding period. This is the standard result whenever one receives property in a fully taxable transaction. Distributions of stock rights are generally taxed the same way as distributions of stock.

O. SECTION 306 STOCK

The background of § 306 is a single case, namely the Sixth Circuit's decision in *Chamberlin v. Commissioner*, 207 F.2d 462 (6th Cir. 1953*), cert. denied*, 347 U.S. 918 (1954). The steps in *Chamberlin* were as follows:

1. The Corporation distributed nonvoting preferred stock pro-rata to the shareholders of the common stock, allocating part of the basis of the common stock to the newly issued preferred stock, as directed by § 307;

2. The common shareholders sold their preferred stock to a life insurance company by prearranged plan, reporting a capital gain; and

3. Some years later, the insurance company has its preferred stock redeemed by the corporation.

    The result when the dust clears was that the original shareholders had not surrendered any control and they had cash in their pockets from the sale of the stock to the insurance company, which is taxed at favorable capital gains rates with an offset for the allocated basis as well.

A less generous court might have concluded that the overall transaction was really a dividend and the insurance company little more than a well-paid puppet. Be that as it may, rather than risk further losses in litigation, the Treasury got its way in Congress instead when § 306 was enacted in 1954. Section 306 created a new type of stock known as "Section 306 stock."

The magic of Section 306 stock is that at least some of the "amount realized" is taxable as ordinary income when it is sold or otherwise disposed of. Section 306 has its complications, and some important exceptions, but if you keep the *Chamberlin* pattern in mind, it is not difficult to see why § 306 operates as it does.

Section 306 stock arises only if "stock other than common stock" is issued at a time when the corporation has earnings and profits. For this purpose, "common stock" is stock that has no dividend or liquidation limit. Rev. Rul. 82-191, 1982-2 C.B. 78.

PROBLEM 16-16

L and M are the two sole shareholders of X Corp.; each owns 50% of X Corp.'s issued and outstanding common stock. This year, L and M each received preferred stock from X Corp. in a § 305 stock dividend. Each block of stock they received had an allocable basis of $15,000 under § 307(a). The value of the stock when distributed to both L and M was $30,000 ($15,000 each). The accumulated and current earnings and profits of X Corp. totaled $40,000 at the time of the distribution.

In the next year, X Corp. redeemed L's preferred stock for $35,000. X Corp.'s accumulated and current E & P at the time of the redemption was $25,000. In the following year, M sold his preferred stock to D for $20,000. X Corp.'s accumulated and current E & P at the time of the sale was $5,000.

1) Is the stock received by L and M "Section 306 stock" ? *See* § 306(c)(1) and Reg. § 1.306-3.

2) What are the tax consequences to L on his redemption of his preferred stock? *See* § 306(a)(2) and Reg. § 1.306-1.

3) What are the tax consequences to M resulting from the sale of his preferred stock? *See* § 306(a)(1) and Reg. § 1.306-1.

4) Identify two ways that a shareholder can purge her Section 306 stock problem.

5) What prior planning do these rules invite?

P. FOREIGN DIVIDENDS: DIVIDENDS RECEIVED DEDUCTION

Read: §§ 245 and 245A

Discussion of Code Sections 245 and 245A requires some understanding of the taxation of foreigners and foreign income under subchapter F.

Generally, federal income tax is imposed on U.S. taxpayers on their worldwide income. Therefore, whether an individual U.S. citizen has compensation for work performed in Iowa or India is of no concern. The individual U.S. citizen includes the compensation in income for purposes of the federal income tax. At the same time, a corporation's income is not taxed to a shareholder until the corporation makes a distribution to the shareholder.

For example, even though Iowa Corporation might own all the stock of California Corporation, Iowa Corporation is not taxed on California Corporation's income until California Corporation makes a distribution to Iowa Corporation. Instead, California Corporation is taxed on its income as accrued. Further, if Iowa Corporation's subsidiary India Corporation earns income, , Iowa Corporation is not taxed on India Corporation's income until India Corporation distributes the income. Additionally, India Corporation is not subject to federal income tax on its own income because there is no federal income tax on foreign taxpayers who have no contact with the United States.

An exception to the rule that foreign corporations that do no business in the U.S. escape federal income tax is the taxation of "controlled foreign corporations." Even absent a distribution, certain offending classes of income ("Subpart F income") that a controlled foreign corporation's income may be taxed to its major U.S. shareholders.

More particularly, before 2017, U.S. shareholders escaped tax on genuine business profits of a controlled foreign corporation, absent a distribution. However, a U.S. person who owned at least ten percent of the value or voting control of a controlled foreign corporation was required to include its pro rata share of the corporation's subpart F income even without a distribution. In other words, the consequence of Congress' scheme for taxing controlled foreign corporations was that certain foreign income held overseas in a corporate subsidiary was offensive enough that U.S. taxation of this income trumped the non-taxation of undistributed income.

Now, Code Section 245 allows a Dividend Received Deduction to a corporate shareholder for dividends with a U.S. source base from certain foreign corporations, Section 245A allows a dividends received deduction to a domestic corporation on the receipt of dividends from certain foreign corporations out of foreign source earnings of that foreign corporation.

Section 245A was added to give certain U.S. shareholders of foreign corporations a 100 percent dividends received deduction for the foreign source portion of a dividend. In other words, Congress has now adopted a "territorial" approach to foreign tax, at least with respect to qualifying foreign corporate income. Now U.S. shareholders of foreign corporations can avoid U.S. income tax on dividends that the foreign distributing corporation pays to its U.S. corporate shareholders.

Section 245 governs the dividend received deduction for payments from a foreign corporation. Section 245(a) permits a shareholder of a "qualified 10-percent owned foreign corporation" to deduct an amount equal to the § 243 percentage specified on the *U.S. source portion* of the dividend. A qualified 10 percent owned foreign corporation is any foreign corporation at least 10 percent of whose stock, measured by vote and value, is owned by the U.S. taxpayer. If the foreign subsidiary is wholly owned by a domestic corporation, then § 245(b) permits the domestic corporation to deduct all of the dividends received from the foreign subsidiary but if all the sub's income is from American sources, § 245A allows a domestic corporation that is a U.S. shareholder of a "specified 10-percent owned foreign corporation" to deduct "an amount equal to the foreign-source portion" of the dividend that the U.S. Corporation receives from the foreign corporation. Not all dividends paid by the foreign corporation are deductible, only those which have a foreign source. This represents a major opportunity to locate foreign businesses, e.g., factories, in jurisdictions with very low income tax rates.

If the foreign subsidiary is wholly owned by a domestic corporation, then § 245(b) permits the domestic corporation to deduct all of the dividends received from the foreign subsidiary.

Code § 245(c) permits a domestic corporation to deduct amounts ranging from 100 percent down to 50 percent of dividends from foreign corporations if they are foreign sales corporations.

Chapter 17

REDEMPTIONS OF CORPORATE STOCK

State law generally permits corporations to repurchase (redeem) their own stock for cash or other property. For example, it is common for publicly-held corporations that have excess cash to buy back their own stock on the open market if they have no better use for the money. This is generally welcomed by investors, because it tends to support the price of the stock. The picture looks different for several reasons when it comes to redemptions of stock of closely-held corporations. For one thing, redemptions may tip the balance of power among the shareholders. For another, the redemption is likely to implicate some serious tax questions.

To understand the tax problem, consider the following two extreme cases. In one case, Mr. A owns all the stock of X Corp., 100 shares. If he causes X Corp. to buy back some of his stock (50 shares) in exchange for cash, it is obvious that the end result is no different from a distribution of cash with respect to his 100 shares, and deserves to be treated as such because his level of 100% ownership is completely unchanged by the redemption. Conversely, if Mr. B, who owns 1% of the stock of X Corp., sells three-fourths of that stock to X Corp. in exchange for cash, it looks much more like a true sale, so that Mr. B should be entitled to sale or exchange treatment ensuring gain or loss on the transaction, as if he had sold to an unrelated buyer; the Code will generally ensure that result. The picture is further confused if Mr. B is Mr. A's son and is fond of Mr. A. In that case, if one views A and B as a group, the transaction looks more like a distribution than an exchange. A redemption is never exactly the same as a distribution, because the amount of stock outstanding does change.

A. CONSTRUCTIVE OWNERSHIP
Read § 318(a).

The reform-minded attribution rules "consider" stock to be owned by certain related parties by virtue of their relationship to the actual owner. The rules are simple in concept, but tricky to apply. The key provisions attribute constructive ownership of stock from some family members to others, from some entities to their owners, and from some owners to entities. You might think of it as the Theory of Relatives. For this purpose, the term "owners" is used loosely to include beneficiaries of estates and trusts.

A few general comments about the constructive ownership rules are in order. First, they are somewhat arbitrary. For example, a grandchild is never deemed to own her grandparent's stock, but the grandparents are deemed to own her stock, presumably on the theory that a grandparent always controls the grandchildren. § 318(a)(l)(A)(ii). That usually makes sense, but not always. The rules do not apply to some family relationships for reasons difficult to discern. For example, siblings are not deemed to own each others' stock, nor does one count aunts, uncles, nieces and nephews. The rule against double family attribution in § 318(a)(5)(B) keeps it that way. For example, stock which is first attributed from a son to his father under § 318(a)(I)(A)(ii) cannot be attributed a second time from the father to his daughter under the same Code section. If the father holds an option to buy his son's shares, however, the shares can be double-deemed to the daughter because of a special rule giving priority to constructive ownership through options over family attribution in the event that both rules apply. § 318(a)(5)(D).

To illustrate: The family consists of Mom, Dad, Sis and Junior (who are siblings). Mom has an option to buy 1,000 shares of stock held by Sis. Mom is deemed to own the 1,000 shares of stock under either of two theories, namely that she is Sis's family member and that she holds an option over someone else's stock. The stock Mom holds constructively because of the option can be attributed to Junior, because § 318(a)(5)(D) says the option rule displaces the family ownership rule when they overlap.

Another interesting feature is that there is no "sideways" attribution. § 318(a)(5)(C). This means that stock attributed from an owner to an entity cannot be attributed again from the entity to another owner. By contrast, stock actually held by the entity is attributed proportionately to the owners of the entity.

To illustrate: Partner A, who is an equal partner of the ABC Partnership, owns as an individual 300 shares of X Corp. All 300 shares of X Corp. are constructively owned by the ABC Partnership under§ 318(a)(3)(A). Now assume the ABC Partnership actually owns 300 shares of Y Corp. Each of the partners is deemed to own 100 shares of Y Corp. under § 318(a)(2)(A), but partners B and C are not deemed to own 100 shares of X Corp., because that would violate the anti-sidewise attribution rule of § 318(a)(5)(C).

Apart from the above two prohibitions against double-attribution, multiple-attribution is *required*. For example, if father A is a beneficiary of Estate E which owns stock in X Corp., the X Corp. stock must be attributed to A in proportion to his percentage interest in E; then A's constructively owned stock in X Corp. must be attributed to his son B, and again from son B to Partnership BC of which B is a partner. Note that each of these persons is deemed an owner of X Corp. stock not just Y Corp. The result can be an extraordinary proliferation of ownership. You will return to the constructive ownership rules frequently in this chapter in connection with analyzing the various Code sections that permit redemptions to be treated like sales, which is the principal subject of the remainder of this chapter.

The basic theme henceforth is that if the shareholder's percentage interest in the corporation is contracted sufficiently as a result of the redemption, then the result will be an *exchange* for federal income tax purposes. If not, then the exchange is a *distribution*. In general, the contraction is measured at the shareholder level. Measuring contraction of activity at the corporate level is important only for determining whether a distribution qualifies as a "partial liquidation" under § 302(b)(4) and (e). Partial liquidations are considered later in this chapter.

Notice the stakes here. Shareholders that are corporations ("corporate shareholders") generally are taxed on only 0%-50% of the "dividends" they receive, whereas shareholders that are individuals ("individual shareholders") are generally taxed at a 20% rate. To potentially qualify as a "dividend," the redemption first must be treated as a *distribution*. Only then do we ask if there is sufficient E & P to qualify the distribution as a dividend.

Redemptions treated as *exchanges* produce capital gains and losses to *corporate* shareholders. Capital gains are taxable to corporations at the full 21% tax rate. Capital losses are useless to corporations unless they have capital gains to offset the losses.

Redemptions taxable as *exchanges* generally produce capital gains and losses to *individual* shareholders as well. These are capped at 20% (except for short-term capital gains, which are taxable as ordinary income). As with corporations, capital losses generally are useless to individuals unless there are capital gains to offset the losses.

The rest of the chapter covers stock redemptions described in §§ 302 and 303, which can generate an "exchange," namely those which are:

1. Not essentially equivalent to a dividend; § 302(b)(1)

2. Substantially disproportionate in terms of shareholder ownership; § 302(b)(2)

3. In complete termination of a shareholder's interest; §302(b)(3)

4. In partial liquidation to a noncorporate shareholder; § 302(b)(4)

5. Redemptions by certain regulated investment companies; or §302(b)(5)

6. To pay a shareholder's estate taxes, funeral expenses, and costs of administering the estate. § 303

B. REDEMPTION NOT ESSENTIALLY EQUIVALENT TO A DIVIDEND
Read § 302(a) and (b) and Reg. § 1.302-2.

The following case is the fountainhead of learning for interpreting § 302(b)(1):

UNITED STATES v. DAVIS ET UX.
397 U.S. 301 (1970), reh'g denied 397 U.S. 1071 (1970)

MARSHALL, J.

In 1945, taxpayer and E. B. Bradley organized a corporation. In exchange for property transferred to the new company, Bradley received 500 shares of common stock, and taxpayer and his wife similarly each received 250 such shares. Shortly thereafter, taxpayer made an additional contribution to the corporation, purchasing 1,000 shares of preferred stock at a par value of $25 per share.

The purpose of this latter transaction was to increase the company's working capital and thereby to qualify for a loan previously negotiated through the Reconstruction Finance Corporation. It was understood that the corporation would redeem the preferred stock when the RFC loan had been repaid. Although in the interim taxpayer bought Bradley's 500 shares and divided them between his son and daughter, the total capitalization of the company remained the same until 1963. That year, after the loan was fully repaid and in accordance with the original understanding, the company redeemed taxpayer's preferred stock.

In his 1963 personal income tax return taxpayer did not report the $25,000 received by him upon the redemption of his preferred stock as income. Rather, taxpayer considered the redemption as a sale of his preferred stock to the company a capital gains transaction under § 302 of the Internal Revenue Code of 1954 resulting in no tax since taxpayer's basis in the stock equaled the amount he received for it. The Commissioner of Internal Revenue, however, did not approve this tax treatment. According to the Commissioner, the redemption of taxpayer's stock was essentially equivalent to a dividend and was thus taxable as ordinary income under §§ 301 and 316 of the Code. Taxpayer paid the resulting deficiency and brought this suit for a refund. The District Court ruled in his favor, 274 F. Supp. 466 (D.C.M.D. Tenn. 1967), and on appeal the Court of Appeals affirmed. 408 F.2d 1139 (C.A. 6th Cir. 1969).

The Court of Appeals held that the $25,000 received by taxpayer was "not essentially equivalent to a dividend" within the meaning of that phrase in § 302(b)(1) of the Code because the redemption was the final step in a course of action that had a legitimate business (as opposed to a tax avoidance) purpose. That holding represents only one of a variety of treatments accorded similar transactions under § 302(b)(1) in the circuit courts of appeals. We granted certiorari, 396 U.S. 815 (1969), in order to resolve this recurring tax question involving stock redemptions by closely held corporations. We reverse.

The Internal Revenue Code of 1954 provides generally in §§ 301 and 316 for the tax treatment of distributions by a corporation to its shareholders; under those provisions, a distribution is includable in a taxpayer's gross income as a dividend out of earnings and profits to the extent such earnings exist. There are exceptions to the application of these general provisions, however, and among them are those found in § 302 involving certain distributions for redeemed stock. The basic question in this case is whether the $25,000 distribution by the corporation to taxpayer falls under that section – more specifically, whether its legitimate business motivation qualifies the distribution under § 302(b)(1) of the Code. Preliminarily, however, we must consider the relationship between § 302(b)(1) and the rules regarding the attribution of stock ownership found in § 318(a) of the Code.

Under subsection (a) of § 302, a distribution is treated as "payment in exchange for the stock," thus qualifying for capital gains rather than ordinary income treatment, if the conditions contained in any one of the four paragraphs of subsection (b) are met. In addition to paragraph (1)'s "not essentially equivalent to a dividend" test, capital gains treatment is available where (2) the taxpayer's voting strength is substantially diminished,[or]](3) his interest in the company is completely terminated . . . Taxpayer admits that paragraphs (2) and (3) do not apply. Moreover, taxpayer agrees that for the purposes of §§ 302(b)(2) and (3) the attribution rules of § 318(a) apply and he is considered to own the 750 outstanding shares of common stock held by his wife and children in addition to the 250 shares in his own name.

Taxpayer, however, argues that the attribution rules do not apply in considering whether a distribution is essentially equivalent to a dividend under 302(b)(1). According to taxpayer, he should thus be considered to own only 25 percent of the corporation's common stock, and the distribution would then qualify under § 302(b)(1) since it was not pro rata or proportionate to his stock interest, the fundamental test of dividend equivalency. See Treas. Reg. 1.302-2(b). However, the plain language of the statute compels rejection of the argument. In subsection (c) of § 302, the attribution rules are made specifically applicable "in determining the ownership of stock for purposes of this section." Applying this language, both courts below held that § 318(a) applies to all of § 302, including 302(b)(1) – a view in accord with the decisions of the other courts of appeals, a longstanding treasury regulation, and the opinion of the leading commentators.

Against this weight of authority, taxpayer argues that the result under paragraph (1) should be different because there is no explicit reference to stock ownership as there is in paragraphs (2) and (3). Neither that fact, however, nor the purpose and history of § 302(b)(1) support taxpayer's argument. The attribution rules – designed to provide a clear answer to what would otherwise be a difficult tax question – formed part of the tax bill that was subsequently enacted as the 1954 Code. As is discussed further, *infra,* the bill as passed by the House of Representatives contained no provision comparable to § 302(b)(1). When that provision was added in the Senate, no purpose was evidenced to restrict the applicability of § 318(a). Rather, the attribution rules continued to be made specifically applicable to the entire section, and we believe that Congress intended that they be taken into account wherever ownership of stock was relevant.

Indeed, it was necessary that the attribution rules apply to § 302(b)(1) unless they were to be effectively eliminated from consideration with regard to §§ 302(b)(2) and (3) also. For if a transaction failed to qualify under one of those sections solely because of the attribution rules, it would according to taxpayer's argument nonetheless qualify under § 302(b)(l). We cannot agree that Congress intended so to nullify its explicit directive. We conclude, therefore, that the attribution rules of § 318(a) do apply; and, for the purposes of deciding whether a distribution is "not essentially equivalent to a dividend" under § 302(b)(1), taxpayer must be deemed the owner of all 1,000 shares of the company's common stock.

II

After application of the stock ownership attribution rules, this case viewed most simply involves a sole stockholder who causes part of his shares to be redeemed by the corporation. We conclude that such a redemption is always "essentially equivalent to a dividend" within the meaning of that phrase in § 302(b)(1) and therefore do not reach the Government's alternative argument that in any event the distribution should not on the facts of this case qualify for capital gains treatment.

The predecessor of § 302(b)(1) came into the tax law as § 201(d) of the Revenue Act of 1921, 42 Stat. 228:

> "A stock dividend shall not be subject to tax but if after the distribution of any such dividend the corporation proceeds to cancel or redeem its stock at such time and in such manner as to make the distribution and cancellation or redemption essentially equivalent to the distribution of a taxable dividend, the amount received in redemption or cancellation of the stock shall be treated as a taxable dividend . . . Enacted in response to this Court's decision that pro rata stock dividends do not constitute taxable income, *Eisner v. Macomber*, 252 U.S. 189 (1920), the provision had the obvious purpose of preventing a corporation from avoiding dividend tax treatment by distributing earnings to its shareholders in two transactions – a pro rata stock dividend followed by a pro rata redemption that would have the same economic consequences as a simple dividend. Congress, however, soon recognized that even without a prior stock dividend essentially the same result could be effected whereby any corporation, "especially one which has only a few stockholders, might be able to make a distribution to its stockholders which would have the same effect as a taxable dividend." H.R. Rep. No. 1, 69th Cong., 1st Sess., 5. In order to cover this situation, the law was amended to apply "(whether or not such stock was issued as a stock dividend)" whenever a distribution in redemption of stock was made "at such time and in such manner" that it was essentially equivalent to a taxable dividend. Revenue Act of 1926, § 201(g), 44 Stat. 11.

This provision of the 1926 Act was carried forward in each subsequent revenue act and finally became § 115(g)(1) of the Internal Revenue Code of 1939. Unfortunately, however, the policies encompassed within the general language of § 115(g)(1) and its predecessors were not clear, and there resulted much confusion in the tax law. At first, courts assumed that the provision was aimed at tax avoidance schemes and sought only to determine whether such a scheme existed. *See*, e.g., *Commissioner v. Quackenbos*, 78 F.2d 156 (C.A. 2d Cir. 1935). Although later the emphasis changed and the focus was more on the effect of the distribution, many courts continued to find that distributions otherwise like a dividend were not "essentially equivalent" if, for example, they were motivated by a sufficiently strong nontax business purpose. . . . There was general disagreement, however, about what would qualify as such a purpose, and the result was a case-by-case determination with each case decided "on the basis of the particular facts of the transaction in question." *Bains v. United States,* 153 Ct. Cl. 599, 603, 289 F.2d 644, 646 (1961).

By the time of the general revision resulting in the Internal Revenue Code of 1954, the draftsmen were faced with what has aptly been described as "the morass created by the decisions." *Ballenger v. United States*, 301 F.2d 192, 196 (C.A. 4th Cir. 1962). In an effort to eliminate "the considerable confusion which exists in this area" and thereby to facilitate tax planning, H.R. Rep. No. 1337, 83d Cong., 2d Sess. 35, the authors of the new Code sought to provide objective tests to govern the tax consequences of stock redemptions. Thus the tax bill passed by the House of Representatives contained no "essentially equivalent" language. Rather, it provided for "safe harbors" where capital gains treatment would be accorded to corporate redemptions that met the conditions now found in §§ 302(b)(2) and (3) of the Code.

It was in the Senate Finance Committee's consideration of the tax bill that § 302(b)(1) was added, and Congress thereby provided that capital gains treatment should be available "if the redemption is not essentially equivalent to a dividend." Taxpayer argues that the purpose was to continue "existing law" and there is support in the legislative history that § 302(b)(1) reverted "in part" or "in general" to the "essentially equivalent' provision of § 115(g)(1) of the 1939 Code. According to the Government, even under the old law it would have been improper for the Court of Appeals to rely on "a business purpose for the redemption" and "an absence of the proscribed tax avoidance purpose to bail out dividends at favorable tax rates." *See Northup v. United States*, 240 F.2d 304, 307 (C.A. 2d Cir. 1957); *Smith v. United States,* 121 F.2d 692, 695 (C.A. 3d Cir. 1941); cf. *Commissioner v. Estate of Bedford*, 325 U.S. 283 (1945). However, we need not decide that question, for we find from the history of the 1954 revisions and the purpose of § 302(b)(1) that Congress intended more than merely to re-enact the prior law.

In explaining the reason for adding the "essentially equivalent" test, the Senate Committee stated that the House provisions "appeared unnecessarily restrictive, particularly, in the case of redemptions of preferred stock which might be called by the corporation without the shareholder having any control over when the redemption may take place." S. Rep. No. 1622, 83d Cong., 2d Sess., 44. This explanation gives no indication that the purpose behind the redemption should affect the result. Rather, in its more detailed technical evaluation of § 302(b)(1), the Senate Committee reported as follows:

> "The test intended to be incorporated in the interpretation of paragraph (1) is in general that currently employed under section 115(g)(1) of the 1939 Code. Your committee further intends that in applying this test for the future . . . the inquiry will be devoted solely to the question of whether or not the transaction by its nature may properly be characterized as a sale of stock by the redeeming shareholder to the corporation. For this purpose the presence or absence of earnings and profits of the corporation is not material. Example: X, the sole shareholder of a corporation having no earnings or profits causes the corporation to redeem half of its stock. Paragraph (1) does not apply to such redemption notwithstanding the absence of earnings and profits." S. Rep. No. 1622, *supra*, at 234."

The intended scope of § 302(b)(1) as revealed by this legislative history is certainly not free from doubt. However, we agree with the Government that by making the sole inquiry relevant for the future the narrow one whether the redemption could be characterized as a sale, Congress was apparently rejecting past court decisions that had also considered factors indicating the presence or absence of a tax-avoidance motive. At least that is the implication of the example given: Congress clearly mandated that pro rata distributions be treated under the general rules laid down in §§ 301 and 316 rather than under § 302, and nothing suggests that there should be a different result if there were a "business purpose" for the redemption. Indeed, just the opposite inference must be drawn since there would not likely be a tax-avoidance purpose in a situation where there were no earnings or profits. We conclude that the Court of Appeals was therefore wrong in looking for a business purpose and considering it in deciding whether the redemption was equivalent to a dividend. Rather, we agree with the Court of Appeals for the Second Circuit that "the business purpose of a transaction is irrelevant in determining dividend equivalence" under § 302(b)(1). *Hasbrook v. United States*, 343 F.2d 811, 814 (1965).

Taxpayer strongly argues that to treat the redemption involved here as essentially equivalent to a dividend is to elevate form over substance. Thus, taxpayer argues, had he not bought Bradley's shares or had he made a subordinated loan to the company instead of buying preferred stock, he could have gotten back his $25,000 with favorable tax treatment. However, the difference between form and substance in the tax law is largely problematical, and taxpayer's complaints have little to do with whether a business purpose is relevant under

292

§ 302(b)(1). It was clearly proper for Congress to treat distributions generally as taxable dividends when made out of earnings and profits and then to prevent avoidance of that result without regard to motivation where the distribution is in exchange for redeemed stock.

We conclude that that is what Congress did when enacting § 302(b)(1). If a corporation distributes property as a simple dividend, the effect is to transfer the property from the company to its shareholders without a change in the relative economic interests or rights of the stockholders. Where a redemption has that same effect, it cannot be said to have satisfied the "not essentially equivalent to a dividend" requirement of § 302(b)(1). Rather, to qualify for preferred treatment under that section, a redemption must result in a meaningful reduction of the shareholder's proportionate interest in the corporation. Clearly, taxpayer here, who (after application of the attribution rules) was the sole shareholder of the corporation both before and after the redemption, did not qualify under this test. The decision of the Court of Appeals must therefore be reversed and the case remanded to the District Court for dismissal of the complaint.

It is so ordered.

MR. JUSTICE DOUGLAS, with whom the CHIEF JUSTICE and MR. JUSTICE BRENNAN concur, dissenting.

I agree with the District Court . . . and with the Court of Appeals . . . that respondent's contribution of working capital in the amount of $25,000 in exchange for 1,000 shares of preferred stock with a par value of $25 was made in order for the corporation to obtain a loan from the RFC and that the preferred stock was to be redeemed when the loan was repaid. For the reasons stated by the two lower courts, this redemption was not "essentially equivalent to a dividend," for the bona fide business purpose of the redemption belies the payment of a dividend. As stated by the Court of Appeals:

> "Although closely-held corporations call for close scrutiny under the tax law, we will not, under the facts and circumstances of this case, allow mechanical attribution rules to transform a legitimate corporate transaction into a tax avoidance scheme . . . "

When the Court holds it was a dividend, it effectively cancels § 302(b)(1) from the Code. This result is not a matter of conjecture, for the Court says that in the case of closely held or one-man corporations a redemption of stock is "always" equivalent to a dividend. I would leave such revision to the Congress.

NOTES AND QUESTIONS

1. **Attribution of stock ownership**. Do you agree with the Court that, as a matter of statutory construction, it is clear that one must apply the attribution rules in a § 302(b)(1) case? See § 302(c). If so, does that inject an excessive rigidity into the rules?

2. **Family hostility**. There is some room for eliminating family attribution if one can show "family hostility," but the authorities are in conflict. See *Robin Haft Trust v. Commissioner*, 510 F.2d 43 (1st Cir. 1975) (mitigation of § 318 allowed); Rev. Rul. 80-26, 1980-1 C.B. 66 (contra); *Metzger Trust v. Commissioner*, 76 T.C. 42 (1981), aff'd, 693 F.2d 459 (5th Cir. 1982), *cert. denied*, 463 U.S. 1207 (1983) (attribution principles must be applied in assessing a shareholder's post-redemption proportionate interest, but if a reduction has

occurred, hostility will then be a factor in determining whether such reduction was meaningful). This is useless for a taxpayer who owns 100% by attribution before and after the redemption, as in *Davis,* but may be helpful in other situations.

3. **What factors count?** It is rarely easy to tell whether a particular redemption meets the standards of § 302(b)(1). The IRS and the courts have developed a fairly large body of authorities on the subject, but as the authorities increase in number they come to look more and more like a vipers' tangle than an aid to navigation. The primary reason for the confusion is that while a variety of factors have emerged as important, they are unranked. Before looking at the vipers' tangle, one needs to know that a shareholder has three different interests in a corporation, namely: the right to vote and thereby exercise control; the right to participate in current earnings and accumulated surplus; and the right to share in net assets on liquidation. Of these interests, voting power appears to be the most important one, in part at least because minority (or nonvoting) shareholders who lack control of the corporation are rarely in a position to engineer schemes to disguise dividends as redemptions. Consider the following examples:

a) A redemption causing loss of super-majority voting control when a shareholder's interest dropped from 85% to 61.7% was held to be an exchange, not a distribution, in *Wright v. United States,* 482 F.2d 600 (8th Cir. 1973). *See also Rickey v. United States,* 427 F. Supp. 484 (D.C. La. 1976), affirmed (CA5 1979). *But see* Rev. Rul. 78-401, 1978-2 C.B. 127 (contra).

b) Reduction of a shareholder's voting power from over 50% to under 50% indicates the redemption should be treated as an exchange, not a distribution. *Estate of Squier v. Commissioner*, 35 T.C. 950 (1961). There are few cases on point, which may mean the IRS simply agrees and has decided not to fight the issue.

c) The smaller the shareholder's original interest, the greater the likelihood that the redemption will be considered meaningful because a small shareholder can rarely influence corporate policy. For example, in Rev. Rul. 75-512, 1975-2 C.B. 112, a decline from 30% ownership to 24.3% was meaningful.

d) A related issue is whether the shareholder can easily gang up with other major shareholders to exercise control. In Rev. Rul. 76-364, 1976-2 C.B. 91, the redeemed shareholder owned 27% of the outstanding stock, and each of three other shareholders owned 23.33%. The redemption reduced the redeemed shareholder's interest to 22.27% and the percentage of stock owned by each of the other shareholders increased to 25.91%. In ruling that the reduction was meaningful, the IRS observed that the redemption caused the redeemed shareholder to go from a position where he could control the corporation by acting in concert with only one other shareholder to a position where that would not be possible.

e) Reduction of a shareholder's voting power from 57% to exactly 50% was held sufficient to qualify for exchange treatment in Rev. Rul. 75-502, 1975-2 C.B. 111.

f) A particularly small interest before the redemption is a strongly favorable factor. For example, where the redeemed shareholder owned 0.0001118% of the shares of a public corporation's only class of stock before the redemption and 0.0001081% after the redemption, the reduction was meaningful, largely because the shareholder exercised no control over the corporation's affairs. Rev. Rul. 76-385, 1976-2 C.B. 92.

4. **Impact of redemptions of other shareholders.** Meaningfulness of any alleged reduction in the redeemed shareholder's proportionate interest must be evaluated with respect to each redeemed shareholder separately. Rev. Rul. 81-289, 1981-2 C.B. 82. If several shareholders' stock is redeemed at the same time or pursuant to a plan, one looks at each shareholder after the redemption plan has been completed.

5. **Reporting to the IRS.** If a shareholder sells stock to the corporation that issued the stock, the facts of the exchange must be reported on the shareholder's return. Reg. §§ 1.302-2(b), 1.331-1(d). Query: If a shareholder of IBM sells some of the shares on the New York Stock Exchange, and unbeknownst to him the buyer is IBM, do the Regulations apply, and if so, how?

6. **The problem of disappearing basis.** If a stock redemption is treated as an exchange, then the basis of the redeemed stock is offset against the proceeds of the redemption when calculating the shareholder's gain or loss. However, if the redemption is taxed as a distribution, then the basis of the redeemed shares could disappear. If the basis did disappear, then the shareholder would not only incur a tax on a dividend, but would also suffer an unfairly enlarged gain or diminished loss when the remaining stock is sold. To prevent this anomaly, Reg. § 1. 302-2(c) provides that basis of the redeemed stock is allocated to the shareholder's unredeemed stock, and to the extent there is no unredeemed stock, it is allocated to the stock owned by those from whom it was attributed under the § 318 rules for constructive ownership. The problem can only arise if the shareholder owns stock constructively because, if the corporaton redeemed all of the shareholder's actual and constructive holdings, exchange treatment is guaranteed under § 302(b)(3).

PROBLEM 17-1

The Heyburn family consists of Mom, Dad, Daughter, and Son. Mom and Son each own 50 shares in HB Corp. Additionally, Mom and Dad are equal partners in Heyburn, Ltd., a partnership which owns 75 shares of HB Corp. Daughter owns no shares. HB Corp. has 200 outstanding shares. An unrelated person owns 25 shares. How many shares of stock is each individual and entity deemed to own directly and constructively?

1) Mom:

2) Dad:

3) Daughter:

4) Son:

5) Heyburn, Ltd.:

6) HB Corp.:

PROBLEM 17-2

Bob holds 95 shares of X Corp.'s 100 outstanding common stock. In anticipation of his selling all the stock of X Corp., X Corp. redeems 15 shares of Bob's stock for $5,000 in cash at a time when X Corp. has a lot of E & P but the stock's value equals its basis.

1) Will Bob likely incur ordinary income or capital gains treatment in the redemption? *See* §§ 301, 316, 302.

2) All things being equal, would Bob likely prefer to see the transaction treated as a distribution?

3) Would your answer change if you knew that Bob owned 50 shares and Bob's uncle owned the other 50 shares of X Corp. common stock prior to and after the redemption? What if it was Bob's son who owned the other shares?

PROBLEM 17-3

A, B, and C are otherwise unrelated equal partners in the ABC partnership. The partnership holds half of the stock of X Corp., and each partner separately owns 1/6th of the stock of X Corp. Assume that all of the stock held by the shareholders directly is redeemed by X Corp. so that the partnership emerges as the sole shareholder of X Corp.

1) Should the redemption be treated as an exchange or a distribution?

2) What becomes of the shareholders' basis in the X Corp. stock that was redeemed?

3) Change the facts to assume that A is only a 2% partner and that B and C are each 49% partners. Will the result to A differ this time?

C. SUBSTANTIALLY DISPROPORTIONATE REDEMPTIONS
Read § 302(b)(2) and Reg. § 1.302-3.

Section 302(b)(2) contains a safe harbor provision that provides a three-part bright line rule that guarantees exchange treatment provided that the requirements of all three parts are met. After the redemption, (1) the taxpayer must own less than 50% of the voting stock, (2) the shareholder's ownership of voting stock must fall to less than 80% of the percentage of the shareholder's pre-redemption holdings, and (3) the shareholder's ownership of all classes of common stock must fall by the same 80%, computed by aggregate value. The 50% rule refers to ownership of the corporation's outstanding stock, but both the 80% rules refer only to the degree of the shareholder's reduction of ownership, no matter whether it was large or small at the outset. In making calculations, be sure to adjust for the fact that after the redemption there will be fewer shares outstanding.

To illustrate: Shareholder A owns 55% and unrelated shareholder B owns the remaining 45% of the outstanding shares of X Corp.'s common stock. If a redemption of A's shares brings Shareholder A's percentage ownership down to 49% of the shares outstanding after the redemption, he has met the first test by owning less than 50% of the voting stock. His ownership has not dropped to below 80% of the percentage of his former holdings, however, because 49% is 89% of his former 55% holdings (49/55 = 89%). To meet the 80% test, A must go below 44% ownership (80% of 55% equals 44%). If A had owned 5% of the stock before the redemption, he would automatically meet the first test, but would still have to reduce his holdings to below 4% of the new, smaller number of shares outstanding in order to meet the second (80% of 5% is 4%).

If the taxpayer fails the bright line tests of § 302(b)(2), then he may still qualify for exchange treatment under § 302(b)(1) if the redemption is not essentially equivalent to a dividend. Thus if A has 5 of his 30 shares redeemed in the above example, he would very likely qualify for exchange treatment as a small minority shareholder despite failing the 80% test. Nevertheless, after the *Davis* case, and under the constructive ownership rules of § 302(c), it may be difficult to fit within § 302(b)(1)'s safe haven. See the next case.

PATTERSON TRUST v. UNITED STATES
729 F.2d 1089 (6th Cir. 1984)

KRUPANSKY, CIRCUIT JUDGE.

The United States of America appeals the decision of the United States District Court for the Northern District of Ohio, Eastern Division, in favor of plaintiff-appellee Henry T. Patterson Trust (Trust) in this action for a refund of federal income taxes with interest. The Trust, by its Trustee, the Reeves Banking & Trust Company (Reeves), instituted this action for a refund of $115,747.98 in federal income taxes paid by the Trust in 1979 for the year 1976, plus interest of $15,805.94 which had accrued as of 1979. The Internal Revenue Service had assessed such taxes on the basis that the amount paid to the Trust for the redemption of all of the Trust's shares in the Puritan Laundry and Dry Cleaning Company (Puritan) should be taxed as a dividend, and not as a sale of stock. The record reveals the following facts.

Prior to 1969, Henry Patterson, Sr. was the sole shareholder and chief executive officer of Puritan. In 1969, he gave forty shares of Puritan stock to each of his children – John, Hank and Ellen. At the time, Ellen was married to Bill Hicks (Hicks), who, along with Hank, was employed by Puritan. Henry Patterson retained 200 shares of Puritan stock.

Bill Hicks was apparently a skilled business manager, while Hank Patterson (Hank) lacked effectiveness. Through the years, a bitter tension between Hicks and Hank developed, resulting in numerous altercations, one of which ended with Hank's hospitalization. At one point, John Patterson (John) participated in the management of the business but, because of the Hank-Hicks rivalry, John resigned and pursued a teaching career.

At trial, there was testimony that Henry Patterson desired that Hicks operate the company after Patterson's retirement. In early 1970, Patterson suffered a broken hip which forced him to remain away from the company. He designated Hicks to act as Puritan's president and general manager in his absence. Patterson's health continued to deteriorate and he died in November 1971.

In June 1971, Hicks presented the Puritan directors with a demand for an increase in salary and a proposal that they place all of the Puritan shares in a voting trust which Hicks would then control. The directors demurred and Hicks resigned. He immediately staged a slowdown of Puritan employees and persuaded the company's most substantial commercial accounts to demand that Puritan rehire him. Within ten days of Hicks' resignation, Puritan was on the verge of collapse. John, who had since returned to the business, contacted Hicks and negotiated a five-year employment contract with him.

Hicks' contract provided an increased salary, a profit sharing arrangement, and a five-year option to acquire eighty shares of Puritan stock. Hicks acquired five of those shares and his option on the remaining seventy-five shares remained open. At the same time, Hank also received a five-year contract.

During the ensuing five years, Puritan performed well but problems between Hank and Hicks became increasingly aggravated; Hank, John, and Ella Patterson their mother, often were at odds with Hicks and his wife, Ellen.

In the spring of 1976, the Patterson estate was closed. Henry Patterson had placed his 200 shares of Puritan stock in the Henry T. Patterson Trust (Trust) with his widow, Ella, as the beneficiary with the power to appoint the corpus at her death. Following the closing of the estate, the Puritan stock was thus distributed:

Henry T. Patterson Trust	200 shares
Ella Patterson	25 shares
Hank Patterson	40 shares
John Patterson	40 shares
Ellen (Patterson) Hicks	40 shares
Bill Hicks	5 shares
Lester Winkler	6 shares

Hicks devised a two-step plan whereby he and his wife could obtain control of Puritan. First, Puritan would redeem the Trust shares and, following the redemption, Hicks would exercise his option and acquire an additional seventy-five shares. As a result, Hicks and his spouse would own 120 shares and the remaining shareholders would control only 111 shares, thus Hicks would acquire a controlling interest in Puritan.

The Reeves Bank, as Trustee, determined that if it refused to redeem the shares, Hicks would leave the company and eventually the Trust corpus would be worthless. Thus, acting in what it perceived as the best interests of the Trust and the beneficiary, the Reeves Bank determined to accept the proposed redemption. On April 2, 1976, the directors were presented with the proposal. The Trustee reported that it would be in Ella's best interest to redeem the shares and invest the proceeds. The minutes report:

After detailed discussion, it was moved by Wm. Hicks and seconded by [Hank] F. Patterson, that the company purchase the outstanding 200 shares held by the Reeves Banking and Trust Company, in trust for Mrs. Patterson upon the following terms:

Price:	One Hundred Ninety Thousand and no/100 dollars (200 shares $950.00), $47,500 Down
Balance:	$47,500 Due January 15, 1977 $47,500 Due January 15, 1978 $47,500 Due January 15, 1979

Following the redemption, on July 7, 1976 Hicks exercised his option and purchased seventy-five shares of Puritan stock from the company. Hicks thereafter forced a realignment of the Puritan Board of Directors. Prior to his attaining control, the Directors were:

Ella Patterson	Lester Winkler
Ellen Hicks	John Patterson
Hank Patterson	

Following the consummation of Hicks' plan, the Directors were:

Bill Hicks
Ellen Hicks
Lester Winkler

The Trust reported the transaction as a capital gains sale. Upon review, the Commissioner determined that the amount received by the Trust in the redemption, $190,000.00, was a dividend taxable as ordinary income under § 301 of the Internal Revenue Code of 1954. A deficiency of $115,747.98 plus interest of $15,805.94 was assessed. The Trust paid the deficiency, and as a result, netted $58,446.08 from the original transaction.

The Trust was denied a refund and instituted the within litigation. The district court rejected the Trust's argument that the transaction amounted to a termination of its interest in Puritan, but accepted the Trust's alternative argument that the transaction was not essentially equivalent to a dividend and was therefore entitled to capital gains treatment. This timely appeal by the United States followed.

The Internal Revenue Code of 1954, 26 U.S.C. § 301, as effective in 1976, provided that "a distribution of property . . . made by a corporation to a shareholder" would be taxed as the ordinary income of that shareholder. Section 302 of the Code 26 U.S.C. § 302, established, however, four exceptions to the general rule that proceeds from a redemption of stock by a corporation shall be treated, for tax purposes "as a distribution of property to which § 301 applies." . . .

In *United States v. Davis,* 397 U.S. 301, 90 S. Ct. 1041, 25 L. Ed. 2d 323 (1970) the Supreme Court evaluated the intended scope of § 302(b)(1). In that case. a sole shareholder caused part of his shares to be redeemed by the corporation; the Court concluded that such a redemption is always equivalent to a dividend and thus subject to ordinary income tax. However, the Court's examination of § 302(h)(1)'s history is germane to the analysis of this appeal:

> It was clearly proper for Congress to treat distributions generally as taxable dividends when made out of earnings and profits and then to prevent avoidance of that result without regard to motivation where the distribution is in exchange for redeemed stock.

> We conclude that is what Congress did when enacting § 302(b)(1). If a corporation distributes property as a simple dividend, the effect is to transfer the property from the company to its shareholders without a change in the relative economic interests or rights of the stockholders. Where a redemption has that same effect, it cannot be said to have satisfied the "not essentially equivalent to a dividend" requirement of § 302(b)(1). Rather, to qualify for preferred treatment under that section, a redemption must result in a meaningful reduction of the shareholder's proportionate interest in the corporation. Clearly, taxpayer here, who (after application of the attribution rules) was the sole shareholder both before and after the redemption did not qualify under this test. 397 U.S. at 313, 90 S. Ct. at 1048.

As explicated by the Supreme Court, § 302(b)(1) provides that corporate distributions which do not alter the shareholder's "relative economic interests or rights" will be taxed as a dividend, regardless of the form or nomenclature given the transactions. The test is to examine the change in the taxpayer's relationship to the corporation; § 302(b)(1) is satisfied, under this test, if the examination establishes a "meaningful reduction" of the taxpayer's relative interests or rights in the company.

Whether a distribution by redemption of stock was "essentially equivalent to a dividend" for the purposes of the 1954 Code is a question of fact. *Wright v. United States*, 482 F.2d 600 (8th Cir. 1973); *United States v. Fewell*, 255 F.2d 496 (5th Cir. 1958); 26 C.F.R. 1.302-2(b) (Treasury Regulations). The district court's factual determinations must be upheld on appeal if they are supported by substantial evidence within the record considered as a whole. Federal Rule of Civil Procedure 52(a).

To determine if the district court properly discerned a meaningful reduction in the Trust's interest and rights in Puritan, the starting point must be a comparison of the Trust's relative holdings prior to and after the redemption. As in *United States v. Davis, supra,* this comparison requires application of the attribution statutes.

Briefly stated, the 1954 Code provided that a trust constructively owned its shares plus the shares held by the beneficiary, including those shares which § 318 attributed to the beneficiary. 26 U.S.C. §§ 302(c), 318.

Applying this statute, it is readily apparent that prior to the redemption, the Trust constructively owned 345 shares of the Puritan company, computed from its own shares (200), Ella's holdings (25), and the shares owned by Ella's children (John- 40, Hank- 40, Ellen Hicks-40). Following the redemption, the Trust's constructive holdings were reduced to 145 shares (25 owned by Ella, 120 held by her children). Only 11 other shares remained actually outstanding (Hicks-5, Winkler- 6); therefore, the Trust held 345/356 shares, or 97%, before and 145/156 shares, or 93%, immediately after the redemption.

When the district court made this comparison it included the seventy-five option shares held by Hicks. Accordingly, the district court determined that the "trust held 80% of the company before redemption (345/431), and 62.8% after redemption (145/231). Because the Trust no longer controlled the company after the redemption (holding less than two-thirds of the stock), the district court concluded that the "meaningful reduction" test had been satisfied. The district court included the Hicks option in its calculations pursuant to the plain language of the attribution statute, 26 U.S.C. § 318 (a)(4), which stated [emphasis added]:

> If *any* person has an option to acquire stock, such stock shall be considered as owned by such person.

On appeal, the Government urges that § 318(a)(4) actually applies only to the taxpayer or to individuals whose shares are otherwise attributable to the taxpayer. The Government would therefore greatly narrow the scope of § 318(a)(4). Under the Government's view of the statute, the Trust's ownership interest in Puritan was reduced only 4% as a result of the redemption, from 97 to 93%, which, it contends, was not meaningful as a matter of law.

"In determining the scope of a statute, one is to look first at its language." *Dickerson v. New Banner Institute, Inc.*, 460 U.S. 103 . . . "Absent a clearly expressed legislative intention to the contrary, that language must ordinarily be regarded as conclusive." *Consumer Product Safety Comm'n v. GTE Sylvania, Inc.*, 447 U.S. 102 . . . Further, "it is axiomatic that where a statute is clear and unambiguous on its face, a court will not look to legislative history to alter the application of the statute except in rare and exceptional circumstances." *Pope v. Rollins Protective Services Co.*, 703 F.2d 197, 206 (5th Cir. 1983) . . . Finally, "Congress is presumed to use words in their ordinary sense unless it expressly indicates the contrary." *Davis Bros., Inc. v. Donovan*, 700 F.2d 1368, 1370 (11th Cir. 1983) *reh. and reh. en banc denied* (Eleventh Circuit refused to allow the Secretary of Labor to interpret "customarily furnished" meals as meaning "voluntarily accepted" meals for purposes of wage provisions in Fair Labor Standards Act) . . .

Nevertheless, the Government invites this court to examine the legislative history of § 318(a) (4) and conclude that "any person" actually means only those "parties in the line of attribution." *See* 26 U.S.C. §§ 318(a)(1)(A), 318 (a)(4). The Government relies on the

300

commentary in the "Detailed Discussion of Bill" portion of the Senate Report relative to § 318(a)(3) [currently effective as § 318(a)(4)]. The commentary describes the operation of the relevant portions of the attributive statute in the following manner:

§ 318. Constructive ownership of stock

This section describes the area in which although in fact transactions related to stock ownership are in connection with a specific individual, ownership of stock is deemed to be in the hands of persons other than the person directly involved. Thus, for the purpose of determining whether a redemption of stock qualifies as a disproportionate redemption, consideration is given not only to the stock held by such person but also to stock owned by members of his family . . .

The area of constructive ownership includes members of the family, persons having interests in . . . trusts, and stock held under an option.

In the family area (sec. 318(a) (1)) an individual is deemed to own stock owned by his parents, his children, and his grandchildren. . . . In the case of trusts, the beneficiary or grantor is deemed to own his proportionate interest in the stock owned by the trust or estate and the trust or estate is deemed to own all of the stock owned by its beneficiaries or grantors. *In any of the cases above described where stock, though not owned, is subject to an option, the holder of such option is deemed to own such stock* (sec. 318(a)(3)). S. Rep. No. 1622, 83d Cong., 2d Sess 45, *reprinted in* [1954] U.S. Code Cong. & Ad. News 4623, 4890-91. [Emphasis added.]

The Government urges that as a result of the commentary's apparent limitation of the option attribution rule to "the cases above described," the Senate indicated its intent that § 318(a)(3) (now § 318(a)(4)) should be limited to parties in the line of attribution. The Internal Revenue Service has consistently followed the reasoning herein argued by the Government (*see, e.g.,* Rev. Rul. 68-601), and the tax court has adopted the Service's view as well. *See Sorem v. Commissioner,* 40 T.C. 206 (1963); *Northwestern Steel and Supply Co., Inc. v. Commissioner,* 60 T.C. 356 (1973). However, only two appeals courts have addressed the issue and they, without analysis, adopted diverse positions.

In *Friend v. United States,* 345 F.2d 761 (1st Cir. 1965), the First Circuit's *dictum* indicated that court believed that "Congress intended that section to apply only where options are held by the person whose shares are being redeemed." 345 F. 2d at 764. In *Sorem v. C.I.R.,* 334 F.2d 275, 280 (10th Cir. 1964), the court, again without analysis, applied the plain language of the options attribution provision of § 318(a), and rejected the Government's view.

The Government argues that this court should defer to the Service's consistently-applied interpretation of the Code. However, while it is axiomatic that where statutory language remains vague even when illuminated by the legislative history, the construction offered by the agency charged with the enforcement of the statute will often be accorded dispositive weight, it is an equal principle that, the agency may not so interpret the statute as to controvert its plain and unambiguous language. Except in "rare and exceptional circumstances," *Rubin v. United States, supra,* such as where Congress "expressly indicates" its intent that the plain meaning of the statutory language be avoided, *Davis Bros., Inc. v. Donovan, supra,* unambiguous statutory language "is to be regarded as conclusive." *Dickerson v. New Banner Institute, supra.*

Instantly, the Government asserts only the commentary of the Senate Report, reprinted above, as support for its construction of "any person" in § 318(a)(4). The commentary falls short of a clear indication by Congress that the natural impact of the statutory language under review should be restrained. Accordingly, the district court appropriately included the option shares held by Hicks in determining the Trust's relative holdings prior to and following redemption.

It should be noted that, even if the Hicks shares were excluded, on the instant record the district court would have been entitled to enter the factual finding that the transaction under review was not essentially equivalent to a dividend and was therefore properly claimed as a capital gain. "The question whether a distribution in redemption of stock . . . is not essentially equivalent to a dividend . . . depends upon the facts and circumstances of each case." 26 C.F.R. § 1.302-3(b) (1983 Treasury Regulations); *United States v. Davis, supra.* Obviously, one of the pertinent facts would be the relative holdings of the taxpayer as computed under § 318's constructive stock ownership provisions, 26 C.F.R. [§ 1.302-3(b)], *United States v. Davis*, however, neither statutory enactment nor judicial construction would support the proposition that the resulting comparative calculation would become the exclusive and dispositive fact. In this case, the redemption effected "a change in the relative economic interests or rights" of all the stockholders of the Puritan company. Therefore, despite the fact that – excluding operation of § 318(a)(4) – the Trust's relative holdings fell only 4% after redemption, under the unique facts and circumstances of this case, such was a "meaningful reduction" and the distribution was therefore not a dividend.

Accordingly, because substantial evidence supports the district court's factual determination that the transaction was not essentially equivalent to a dividend, the judgment below is Affirmed.

NOTES

1. **Planning incomplete redemptions**. In light of *Patterson Trust,* what "real world" planning advice might you give to taxpayers in family-owned corporations in situations where the retiring shareholder cannot for some reason fully terminate her interest and the family wanted an "exchange" result?

2. **What about nonvoting stock and preferred stock**? Section 302(b)(2) says a redemption is substantially disproportionate only if the shareholder's reduction in ownership of all common stock (whether voting or nonvoting) meets the 80% requirement, but Reg. § 1.302-3(a) says that § 302(b)(2) does not apply to redemptions of nonvoting stock alone, whether common or preferred. However, if nonvoting stock is redeemed at the same time as voting stock, and the voting stock qualifies for exchange treatment under § 302(b)(2), the sale of the nonvoting stock can be combined with the voting stock and will qualify for exchange treatment as well. *See* Rev. Rul. 77-237, 1977-2 C.B. 88.

3. **What if the preferred stock is voting stock?** The votes of the preferred stock must be counted in applying the first test under § 302(b)(2)(C), because clauses (i) and (ii) refer to "the voting stock of the corporation owned by the shareholder." For purposes of the second, or 80%, test, the voting preferred is simply ignored, because it refers only to "the shareholder's ownership of the common stock of the corporation." If the stockholder has only voting preferred stock, § 302(b)(2) cannot be met by its literal terms.

PROBLEM 17-4

Big Corp. is a large publicly-traded corporation that has one class of voting common stock outstanding and has current and accumulated earnings and profits totaling $80,000,000. R owns 55% of Big Corp.'s 2,000,000 shares of outstanding voting common stock. R's basis in his Big Corp. stock is $11,000,000. R owns 1,100,000 shares with basis of $10 per share. R is not related (within the meaning of § 318) to any other shareholder of Big Corp. R decides to retire as president of Big Corp., and shortly thereafter Big Corp. redeems 225,000 shares of R's voting common stock for $2,250,000. What are the tax consequences to R as a result of the redemption?

D. COMPLETE TERMINATION OF THE SHAREHOLDER'S INTEREST
Read § 302(b)(3) and (c)(2) and Reg. § 1.302-4.

If a redemption completely terminates a shareholder's interest in the corporation, exchange treatment is assured under the safe harbor of § 302(b)(3). Even if all shares actually held are redeemed, however, the safe harbor does not apply if the shareholder still owns stock by attribution from related shareholders. However, exchange treatment is available thanks to § 302(c)(2), which permits the shareholder to break the chain of attribution, provided the shareholder renounces for ten years any and all interest in the corporation except that of a creditor.

This § 302(c)(2) safe harbor is useful in the common situation of a transfer of control of a family business from one generation to the next. For example, what if the founder and sole shareholder holds all the stock, and wishes to transfer the business to her daughter while redeeming the rest of her stock? If the founder transfers a few shares to daughter and has the corporation redeem the balance of the stock, the result is a distribution to the mother because by attribution the founder still owns 100% of the stock.

This is where the § 302(c)(2) waiver comes to the rescue. The founder can avoid attribution from her daughter and enjoy exchange treatment if she waives all connection with the business for the following ten years. She may remain a creditor, however, in order to permit redemption by means of a deferred payment sale to the corporation. Such sales are common because often the corporation does not have the cash to redeem the full value of the founder's stock, and so the value is often paid out of the corporation's future earnings. This in turn creates a serious risk. If the waiver is not fully complied with, and the founder remains a part-time paid consultant or derives other benefits from the corporation, the redemption may be treated as a dividend. This might be a disaster in the case of an installment sale, because § 453 only applies to sales and not to distributions, with the result that the entire fair market value of the installment note would be taxable immediately despite the lack of any actual cash from the sale to pay the tax.

Another frequently recurring problem in connection with decedents' estates is resolved by § 302(c)(2)(C). Suppose the founder dies leaving shares of the family business in his estate, and the beneficiaries of the estate are all family members who own the rest of the stock in the family corporation. If it is decided that the estate should have all its shares redeemed from the family corporation, the estate cannot waive attribution from its beneficiaries under § 302(c)(2) because that section applies by its terms only to family attribution under § 318(a)(1), not to attribution from beneficiaries to estates under § 318(a)(3). Accordingly, the estate continues to own 100% of the stock after redemption. Section 302(c)(2)(C) provides exchange treatment if both the estate and all of the shareholder-beneficiaries from whom stock is attributable to the estate jointly make the waiver and terminate their actual interests in the corporation. Note that this provision is of no use if one of the beneficiaries cannot divest himself of all his stock, say because he is the controlling shareholder. In such a case, he must terminate his beneficial interest in the estate instead if the waiver is to succeed. This can be done if the shareholder is a beneficiary of specific property or money as opposed to a beneficiary of the residue of the estate; if, for example, the taxpayer is entitled to a $100 bequest, he ceases to be a beneficiary of the estate when he gets the $100.

Here is an example of a simple situation:

To illustrate: Mom owns 80% of Family Corp. and Son owns 20%. Mom dies and Father is the sole beneficiary of her estate. If the estate redeems its stock, the redemption is incomplete because Son's stock is attributed to Father, then to the estate. The redemption can only be complete if family attribution is waived, which is possible here. If Father also were a shareholder, then the waiver could not work to permit a complete redemption because the incompleteness of the termination is not caused by family attribution.

The following Private Letter Ruling is a fairly complex example of §§ 302(b)(3) and 302(c)(2) at work in an estate planning context.

PRIV. LTR. RUL. 9041005
June 25, 1990

Company, a State X corporation operating as a personal holding company, has outstanding 758 shares of a single class of stock ("Company Stock"). Prior to taking step (i) below, Company Stock was held as follows:

Estate	=	237 shares
A	=	266 shares
B	=	123 shares
C	=	82 shares
Trust I	=	25 shares
Trust II	=	25 shares.

The Company Stock held by B, C, Trust I, and Trust II was received by these shareholders as a gift from D in 1983.

Estate is the estate of D, who was the husband of A. A and/or trusts for A's benefit are beneficiaries of Estate. B is the daughter of A and D. C is the son-in-law of A and D. Trusts I and II are trusts for the benefit of E and F, the grand-daughters of A and D. Thus, directly or indirectly (through constructive ownership under section 318(a) of the Internal Revenue Code), A owns all the outstanding Company Stock, except for the stock owned by C.

It is desired to terminate Estate, to give complete ownership of Company to B, C, and the Trusts, and to provide A with assets other than Company Stock. Accordingly, pursuant to a Stock Sales Agreement and a Stock Redemption Agreement, steps have been, or will be, taken as follows:

"(Step i) Estate sold all 237 shares of its Company Stock to A in exchange for a note ("Note I") in the amount of $418,345.23 ($1,765.17 per share). The note is due in 10 years and bears interest at approximately 8% per annum.

(Step ii) Estate will be terminated and will distribute all its assets to its beneficiaries. Note I is being distributed to Trust III, a trust for A's benefit.

(Step iii) Prior to the redemption in the last step, A will execute a disclaimer of all her interest (if any) in each of Trust I and Trust II.

(Step iv) Company will redeem all 503 shares of Company Stock held by A (the 266 shares held by A originally and the 237 shares purchased by A from Estate) for an amount equal to their fair market value at the time of redemption which will probably total approximately $900,000. Approximately two-thirds of the redemption price will be paid in cash, certificates of deposit, Treasury Bills, and securities in unrelated corporations or similar items. Approximately one-third of the redemption price will be paid with a Company note ("Note II")."

Note II will be a 10-year unsecured promissory note of Company bearing interest at the applicable rate provided by section 1274(d) of the Internal Revenue Code. Interest is payable monthly. Principal may be paid prior to maturity. The entire principal and any unpaid interest must be paid no later than 10 years from, the date of the note's issuance. In the event of default in any interest payment, the entire principal amount will become due and payable.

In connection with the proposed redemption, the following representations have been made:

a) There are no outstanding options or warrants to purchase Company Stock, nor are there any outstanding debentures or other obligations that are convertible into Company Stock or would be considered Company Stock.

b) At the time of the exchange, the fair market value of the consideration to be received by A will be approximately equal to the fair market value of the Company Stock to be surrendered in exchange therefore. The price to be paid for the Company Stock to be redeemed will not result in a loss with respect to those shares of stock.

c) No shareholder of Company has been or will be obligated to purchase any of the Company Stock that is to be redeemed.

d) In no event will the last payment on Note II (issued to A) be made more than 15 years after the date of issuance of the note.

e) None of the consideration being received by A from Company, including interest, consists entirely or partly of Company's promise to pay an amount that is based on, or contingent on, future earnings of Company, an amount that is contingent on working capital being maintained at a certain level, or any other similar contingency.

f) Note II will not be subordinated to the claims of general creditors of Company.

g) In the event of default on any note or other obligation, no shares of stock will revert to or be received by A nor will A be permitted to purchase the stock at a public or private sale.

h) The redemption described in this ruling request is an isolated transaction and is not related to any other past or future transaction.

i) There have been no redemptions, issuances, or exchanges by Company of its stock in the past 5 years. Company has no plan or intention to issue, redeem, or exchange additional shares of its stock.

j) On the date of the redemption, none of the stock redeemed will be entitled to declared but unpaid dividends.

k) The disclaimer by A of any interests in Trusts I and II (which will have been made prior to the redemption in Step (IV)) is irrevocable and is effective to divest: A of any interests in each of the trusts and is valid and binding under applicable local law. Therefore, after disclaimer by A of any interests in Trusts I and II, the Trustee of these trusts will not have authority to pay or distribute trust assets to or for the benefit of A.

l) Following the transaction, A will hold no stock in Company or its subsidiaries either directly, or indirectly (within the meaning of section 318(a)), except that the stock held by the Trusts is attributable to E and F and this stock plus the stock held by B would (absent a waiver of family attribution pursuant to section 302(c)(2)) be attributed to A under section 318(a)(1) (family attribution). In addition, following the transaction, A will have no interest (including an interest as officer, director, or employee) in Company or its subsidiaries, other than an interest as a creditor (as described in section 1.302-4(d) of the Income Tax Regulations).

m) A will execute and file the agreement described in section 302(c)(2)(A)(iii) of the Code in accordance with section 1.302-4(a) of the Regulations.

n) Except for the acquisition (in Step (i) of Company Stock from Estate, none of the Company Stock held by A will have been acquired from a related person within the meaning of section 318(a) of the Code in the 10-year period prior to Step (iv).

o) Estate will have been terminated prior to Step (iv).

p) Following the proposed transaction, no person who will own Company Stock will have directly or indirectly acquired any Company Stock from A."

Based solely upon the information submitted and the representations set forth above, and provided that the disclaimer in Step (iii) is executed prior to the redemption in Step (iv) and is effective under local law to permanently divest A of any interest she may have in either Trust 1 or Trust II, it is held as follows:

(1) The acquisition in Step (i) by A of Company Stock from Estate within the 10-year period prior to the proposed redemption in Step (IV) does not constitute an acquisition from a related person from whom stock ownership is attributable at the time of the proposed redemption (within the meaning of section 302(c)(2)(B)(i) of the Code) because Estate will have been terminated in Step (ii) prior to the redemption.

(2) Provided that A executes and files the agreement required by section 302(c)(2)(A)(iii) of the Code in accordance with section 1.302-4(a) of the Income Tax Regulations, section 318(a)(1) will be inapplicable in accord with section 302(c)(2) and the proposed redemption by Company of all its stock held by A will constitute a complete termination of A's interest in Company within the meaning of section 302(b)(3) of the Code. The redemption will be treated as in full payment in exchange for the stock redeemed, as provided in section 302(a). However, this ruling is subject to the conditions and limitations stated in section 302(c)(2)(A)(i) and (ii) and Rev. Rul. 71-211, 1971-1 C.B. 112.

(3) As provided by section 1001 of the Code, gain will be realized and recognized to A on the redemption of Company Stock, with this gain measured by the difference between the amount of cash and other consideration received by A for each share of Company Stock and the adjusted basis of the share of Company Stock surrendered as determined under section 1011. Provided section 341 (relating to collapsible corporations) is not applicable and the Company Stock is a, capital asset in the hands of A, the gain, if any, will constitute capital gain subject to the provisions and limitations of Subchapter P of Chapter 1. Pursuant to the provisions of section 267, no loss will be allowable.

(4) No gain or loss will be recognized to Company on the distribution of cash and Note II (its own note) to A in redemption of Company Stock (section 311(a) and (b)(1)(A)). Gain (but not loss) will be recognized to Company on the distributions of assets (other than cash and its own note) as provided by section 311 (b) of the Code. For purposes of this computation of gain under section 311(b), the term "cash" does not include any item, such as a Treasury Bill or certificate of deposit, where the fair market value of such property exceeds adjusted basis (section 311(b)(1)(13)).

(5) The remaining shareholders of Company will not receive a constructive dividend as a result of the redemption by Company of its stock held by A (Rev. Rul. 58-614, 1958-2 C.B. 920)."

The rulings in this letter will be considered void as to A, if Note II is subsequently determined to be equity and not debt. No opinion is expressed as to whether any note distributed is debt or equity because that determination is primarily one of fact (section 4.02(1) of Rev. Proc. 90-3, 1990-1 I.R.B. 54, 59). . . .

NOTES

1. **What about redemptions of preferred stock?** Section 302(b)(3) relating to a complete termination of a stockholder's interest in the corporation apparently must include preferred stock, because the statute finds a complete termination if the redemption is "in complete redemption of all of the stock of the corporation owned by the shareholder."

2. **What if the redeeming shareholder is a corporation?** A corporation will usually prefer a dividend over exchange treatment in order to enjoy the dividends-received deduction. That can be arranged by making relatively small redemptions, but a series of small redemptions spread over time, each of which is too small to qualify as a sale, may be lumped together as a single integrated transaction and treated as an exchange. *See Bleily Collishaw Inc. v. Commissioner*, 72 T.C. 751 (1979) (aff'd CA9 1982) (corporate shareholder whose interest was completely terminated via periodic redemptions over twenty-three weeks pursuant to a firm plan held to have engaged in an exchange, hence not entitled to dividends-received deduction).

3. **Bootstrap acquisitions.** Suppose that the taxpayer wishes to sell all the stock of a corporation but the buyer lacks the cash to pay its full value. If the corporation itself has enough cash, can the problem be solved by having the taxpayer first sell half of her stock to the buyer, and then subsequently cause the remaining half of the stock to be redeemed out of the corporation's cash? The answer is "yes" according to the seminal case of *Zenz v. Quinlivan*, 213 F.2d 914 (6th Cir. 1954), where the court found a meaningful reduction of interest under the predecessor of § 302(b)(1) on step-transaction principles. In *U.S. v. Carey*, 289 F.2d 531 (8th Cir. 1961), the steps were reversed but the conclusion was the same, namely a redemption treated as a sale under § 302(b)(3) where the shareholder first redeemed part of her stock and then sold the rest to the buyer as part of a single plan. The IRS agrees with the result. Rev. Rul. 75-447, 1975-2 C.B. 113.

4. **Effect on earnings and profits.** In *Zenz*, the buyer did have the cash to make an outright purchase. The bootstrap redemption method was designed to reduce the corporation's earnings and profits account at no cost to either buyer or seller. Under current § 312(n)(7), a redemption removes a ratable share of earnings and profits in proportion to the amount of stock redeemed, but not in excess of the amount of the redemption. Thus if a corporation has $500 of earnings and profits and redeems 50% of its stock for $800 in an exchange for tax purposes, this exchange reduces the earnings and profits account by $250. However, if the redemption proceeds were $100, then $100 of earnings and profits are removed because the reduction cannot exceed the redemption.

5. **Buy-sell agreements**. In order to prevent stock in a closely-held corporation from falling into the hands of strangers, it is common for the founders to agree that in the event of the death of either, the other may (or must) purchase the stock from the decedent's estate. Such agreements may be structured in many ways. One of the most convenient is redemption by the corporation itself of the stock from the decedent's estate. In the case of a two-shareholder corporation, the redemption leaves the survivor as sole owner. If the surviving shareholder in fact was under an unconditional obligation to purchase the decedent's stock but assigned the obligation to the corporation which then redeemed the estate's stock, the IRS will assert that the corporation paid the redemption proceeds to satisfy a debt of the surviving shareholder who will then be treated as having received a constructive distributions. *See* Rev. Rul. 69-608, 1969-2 C.B. 42. The moral here is that the survivor should not be

obligated to purchase the decedent's stock and should always have the right to assign the option or obligation to the corporation. Perhaps it is just safer to obligate the corporation to make the redemption and not the survivor.

6. **Redemption incident to divorce.** A further wrinkle is added when stock in a closely-held corporation must be divided between spouses pursuant to a divorce. If the corporation redeems out one spouse, there is a risk that the other will be treated as having received a constructive distribution if the divorce agreement places an unconditional obligation upon that spouse to personally buy the stock. Because the spouse's obligation to buy the stock was unconditional, the taxpayer lost in *Hayes v. Commissioner*, 101 T.C. 593 (1993). The opposite result was reached in *Ames v. Commissioner*, 102 T.C. 522 (1994), where the taxpayers-spouse's obligation was found not to be primary and unconditional. In a companion case, the wife who received the redemption proceeds was not taxed on the ground that the proceeds were excluded under § 1041 as an indirect payment from her husband incident to divorce. *See Ames v. Commissioner*, 981 F.2d 456 (9th Cir. 1992).

7. **Creditors**. Terminating one's investment in the company but staying on as a creditor exposes one to the risk that the debt one holds is "really" equity, and that one did not terminate one's stock interest. The Regulations allow one to have a debt position as long as it does not confer greater rights than necessary for enforcing the claim. Reg. § 1.302-4(d). A lot of people can be creditors. For example, a pensioner is technically a creditor. *See* Rev. Rul. 84-135, 1984-2 CB 80, permitting a redemption to be considered a complete termination even though a former shareholder is a pensioner.

8. **Impermissible intrafamily transfers in connection with a complete termination**. Clever taxpayers might try transferring stock to their spouses or children and then causing the corporation to redeem all the gifted stock or their own remaining stock. If the donee or donor could waive family attribution under § 302(c)(2), a loophole would open. Section 302(c)(2)(B) prevents this by denying the waiver where the redeeming party received stock from a related person, or gave stock to a related person, during the decade before the redemption, but only if the prior transfer was motivated by tax avoidance. The provision does not apply to legitimate intergenerational transfers of control, such as where a founder gives stock to his son as successor and has the balance redeemed because tax avoidance is not a principal purpose of such transactions.

GROVE v. COMMISSIONER
490 F.2d 241 (2d Cir. 1973)

KAUFMAN, CHIEF JUDGE:

[Mr. Grove, a wealthy engineer who graduated from Rensselaer Polytechnic Institute ("RPI") had a pattern of making gifts of stock in his closely-held corporation to RPI. The stock was held for a few years and then like clockwork redeemed by the corporation at RPI's request, pursuant to an agreement between the corporation and RPI which subjected the stock to a right of first refusal (i.e., before RPI could sell the stock, it had to offer the stock to Grove's Corporation at book value) which could be different from fair market value. Other minority shareholders of the corporation signed similar agreements. RPI invested the redemption proceeds in income-producing securities and made quarterly disbursements to Grove of any income received, which Grove reported as income. The IRS asserted that Grove had used RPI as a tax-free conduit for withdrawing funds from the Corporation and that redemption payments by the Corporation to RPI were constructive dividend payments to Grove.]

II

The Commissioner's view of this case is relatively simple. In essence, we are urged to disregard the actual form of the Grove-RPI-Corporation donations and redemptions and to rewrite the actual events so that Grove's tax liability is seen in a wholly different light. Support for this position, it is argued, flows from the Supreme Court's decision in *Commissioner v. Court Holding Co.*, 324 U.S. 331, 89 L. Ed. 981, 65 S. Ct. 707 (1945), which, in language familiar to law students, cautions that "the incidence of taxation depends upon the substance of a transaction . . . To permit the true nature of a transaction to be disguised by mere formalisms, which exist solely to alter tax liabilities, would seriously impair the effective administration of the tax policies of Congress." *Id.* at 334. In an effort to bring the instant case within this language, the Commissioner insists that whatever the appearance of the transactions here under consideration, their "true nature" is quite different. He maintains that Grove, with the cooperation of RPI, withdrew substantial funds from the Corporation and manipulated them in a manner designed to produce income for his benefit. In the Commissioner's view, the transaction is properly characterized as a redemption by the Corporation of Grove's, not RPI's, shares, followed by a cash gift to RPI by Grove. This result, it is said, more accurately reflects "economic reality."

The Commissioner's motives for insisting upon this formulation are easily understood once its tax consequences are examined. Although Grove reported taxable dividends and interest received from the Merrill Lynch account on his 1963 and 1964 tax returns, amounts paid by the Corporation to redeem the donated shares from RPI were not taxed upon distribution. If, however, the transactions are viewed in the manner suggested by the Commissioner, the redemption proceeds would be taxable as income to Grove. Moreover, because the redemptions did not in substance alter Grove's relationship to the Corporation – he continued throughout to control a majority of the outstanding shares – the entire proceeds would be taxed as a dividend payment at high, progressive ordinary-income rates, rather than as a sale of shares, at the fixed, and relatively low, capital gains rate. . . .

Clearly, then, the stakes involved are high. We do not quarrel with the maxim that substance must prevail over form, but this proposition marks the beginning, not the end, of our inquiry. The court in *Sheppard v. United States*, 361 F.2d 972, 176 Ct. Cl. 244 (1966), perceptively remarked that "all such 'maxims' should rather be called 'minims' since they convey a minimum of information with a maximum of pretense." *Id.* at 977 n. 9. Each case requires detailed consideration of its unique facts. Here, our aim is to determine whether Grove's gifts of the Corporation's shares to RPI prior to redemption should be given independent significance or whether they should be regarded as meaningless intervening steps in a single, integrated transaction designed to avoid tax liability by the use of mere formalisms.

The guideposts for our analysis are well marked by earlier judicial encounters with this problem. "The law with respect to gifts of appreciated property is well established. A gift of appreciated property does not result in income to the donor so long as he gives the property away absolutely and parts with title thereto before the property gives rise to income by way of sale." *Carrington v. Commissioner*, 476 F.2d 704, 708 (5th Cir. 1973), quoting *Humacid Co.*, 42 T.C. 894, 913 (1964). As noted below by the Tax Court, the Commissioner here "does not contend that the gifts of stock by [Grove] to RPI in 1961 and 1962 were sham transactions, or that they were not completed gifts when made." If Grove made a valid, binding, and irrevocable gift of the Corporation's shares to RPI, it would be the purest fiction to treat the redemption proceeds as having actually been received by Grove. The Tax Court concluded that the gift was complete and irrevocable when made. The Commissioner conceded as much and we so find.

It is argued, however, that notwithstanding the conceded validity of the gifts, other circumstances establish that Grove employed RPI merely as a convenient conduit for withdrawing funds from the Corporation for his personal use without incurring tax liability. The Commissioner would have us infer from the systematic nature of the gift-redemption cycle that Grove and RPI reached a mutually beneficial understanding: RPI would permit Grove to use its tax-exempt status to drain funds from the Corporation in return for a donation of a future interest in such funds.

We are not persuaded by this argument and the totality of the facts and circumstances lead us to a contrary conclusion. Grove testified before the Tax Court concerning the circumstances of these gifts. The Court, based on the evidence and the witnesses' credibility, specifically found that "there was no informal agreement between [Grove] and RPI that RPI would offer the stock in question to the corporation for redemption or that, if offered, the corporation would redeem it." Findings of fact by the Tax Court, like those of the district court, are binding upon us unless they are clearly erroneous, . . . and "the rule . . . applies also to factual inferences [drawn] from undisputed basic facts. . . . " It cannot seriously be contended that the Tax Court's findings here are "clearly erroneous" and no tax liability can be predicated upon a nonexistent agreement between Grove and RPI or by a fictional one created by the Commissioner.

Grove, of course, owned a substantial majority of the Corporation's shares. His vote alone was sufficient to insure redemption of any shares offered by RPI. But such considerations, without more, are insufficient to permit the Commissioner to ride roughshod over the actual understanding found by the Tax Court to exist between the donor and the donee. *Behrend v. United States*, (4th Cir. 1972), 73-1 USTC 9123, is particularly instructive. There, two brothers donated preferred shares of a corporation jointly controlled by them to a charitable foundation over which they also exercised control. The preferred shares were subsequently redeemed from the foundation by the corporation and the Commissioner sought to tax the redemption as a corporate dividend payment to the brothers. The court, in denying liability, concluded that although "it was understood that the corporation would at intervals take up the preferred according to its financial ability . . . this factor did not convert into a constructive dividend the proceeds of the redemption . . . [because] the gifts were absolutely perfected before the corporation redeemed the stock." Id.

Nothing in the December, 1954 minority shareholder agreement between the Corporation and RPI serves as a basis for disturbing the conclusion of the Tax Court. Although the Corporation desired a right of first refusal on minority shares – understandably so, in order to reduce the possibility of unrelated, outside ownership interests – it assumed no obligation to redeem any shares so offered. In the absence of such an obligation, the Commissioner's contention that Grove's initial donation was only the first step in a prearranged series of transactions is little more than wishful thinking grounded in a shaky foundation . . .

We are not so naive as to believe that tax considerations played no role in Grove's planning. But foresight and planning do not transform a non-taxable event into one that is taxable. Were we to adopt the Commissioner's view, we would be required to recast two actual transactions – a gift by Grove to RPI and a redemption from RPI by the Corporation – into two completely fictional transactions – a redemption from Grove by the Corporation and a gift by Grove to RPI. Based upon the facts as found by the Tax Court, we can discover no basis for elevating the Commissioner's "form" over that employed by the taxpayer in good faith. "Useful as the step transaction doctrine may be in the interpretation of equivocal contracts and ambiguous events, it cannot generate events which never took place just so an additional tax liability might be asserted." *Sheppard v. United States, supra,* at 978. In the absence of any supporting facts in the record we are unable to adopt the Commissioner's view; to do so would be to engage in a process of decision that is arbitrary, capricious and ultimately destructive of traditional notions of judicial review. We decline to embark on such a course.

Accordingly, the judgment of the Tax Court is affirmed.

[Judge Oakes dissented on the ground that the IRS's view of the substance of the transaction was correct.]

PROBLEM 17-5

Which of the following transactions qualifies as a redemption in complete termination of a shareholder's interest?

1) Jon has owned 100 shares of Deep Space Growth, Inc. for many years. There are 1,000 shares of such stock outstanding, all of which are owned by unrelated persons. This year Jon sold the stock back to the company for $500.

2) Same, but Jon's sister continues to hold 500 shares of Deep Space Growth.

3) Same as "(1)", but Jon's mother continues to own 500 shares of Deep Space Growth.

4) Same as "(3)", but Jon and his mother file the appropriate documentation under §302(c)(2)(A)(iii) needed to waive family attribution.

5) Same as "(4)", but Jon sold his stock using an installment note, which pays an appropriate rate of interest and is secured by the stock he sold. *See* Reg. § 1.302-4(d).

6) Same as "(5)", but 8 years after the sale, Jon takes a position as a director of Deep Space Growth.

7) Same as "(1)", but Jon got the stock from his mother as a gift nine years ago. Jon is not sure why he received the stock.

8) Mother is the sole beneficiary of Dad's estate. Jon, their son, owns 10 shares of Deep Space Growth, Inc. and Dad's estate owns 40 shares. Mother owns no shares. The estate plans to redeem its 40 shares.

    a) If the estate does redeem, will the result be a complete termination of the estate's interest?

    b) If not, what can be done to make the redemption a complete termination?

E. REDEMPTIONS IN PARTIAL LIQUIDATION OF THE CORPORATION
Read § 302(b)(4) and (e).

A redemption payment that results from a "corporate contraction" gets exchange treatment with respect to noncorporate shareholders if it meets the conditions of § 302(e). If it does meet those conditions, then no reduction in the shareholder's percentage ownership is required and even a pro rata distribution will be treated as an exchange. The distribution itself may be either in cash or in property. Note, however, that if the distribution consists of appreciated property, the corporation will be taxed under § 311(b) despite the privileged treatment at the shareholder level.

To qualify as a partial liquidation, the corporate contraction must meet one of two alternative tests. The first is the vague and uncertain language of § 302(e)(1)(A) that it must not be "essentially equivalent to a dividend (determined at the corporate level rather than at the shareholder level)." There is little authority as to what the essentially equivalent test means, but the leading examples of something not essentially equivalent to a dividend are: the sale of a line of business and a distribution of the sale's proceeds to shareholders; and, the destruction of two floors of a seven-story factory by fire, followed by a reduction in business and distribution of the insurance proceeds to shareholders. S. Rep. No. 1622, 83rd Cong., 2d Sess. 49 (1954). Another example of a legitimate partial liquidation is a corporation's decision to end a line of a business, sell the assets used in the line of business, and distribute the proceeds to shareholders. *See McCarthy v. Conley*, 229 F. Supp. 517, *aff'd*, 341 F.2d 948 (2d Cir.), *cert. denied*, 382 U.S. 838 (1965), citing Reg. § 1.346-1(a). In order to obtain a private letter ruling to guarantee exchange treatment, the IRS requires that the distribution result in a 20% or greater reduction in corporate gross revenues, net market value of assets, and number of employees. Rev. Proc. 82-40, 1982-2 C.B. 761. Nevertheless, the Service will not opine on the amount of working capital attributable to a business or portion of a business terminated that may be distributed in partial liquidation. Rev. Proc. 83-22 1983-1 CB 680, January 1, 1983, superseding Rev. Proc. 82-40. Regulation § 1.346-1 embellishes the concept of a partial liquidation.

The other test for partial liquidation status is a safe harbor under § 302(e)(2). It assures that a distribution qualifies for the safe harbor if it is attributable to the corporation's termination of a "qualified trade or business," if the distribution consists of the assets of that business, and if the corporation is engaged in a qualified trade or business immediately after the distribution. For these purposes a "qualified trade or business" is any trade or business that (1) was actively conducted throughout the 5-year period ending on the date of the redemption, and (2) was not acquired by the corporation within that 5-year period in a transaction in which gain or loss was recognized in whole or in part. The reason for the latter rule is that otherwise a corporation with excess cash could buy a trade or business with the intention of distributing it to shareholders in kind, or reselling it for cash to be distributed to shareholders as an alternative to paying a dividend, all without giving up any control of the business. This can still be done, but the corporation must age the purchased business for at least five years before the distribution. § 302(e)(3)(A). In addition, the corporation must continue to conduct at least one other suitably aged trade or business. § 302(e)(2)(B).

A subtle piece of drafting in § 302(b)(4) ensures that corporate shareholders are precluded from getting a partial liquidation result. That will generally be fine with them because they may get the benefit of the § 243 dividends-received deduction as a result.

PROBLEM 17-6

ZZ Corp. is a successful VCR manufacturing company that has been in operation for approximately twelve years. Because of ZZ Corp.'s success, the company in year 12 decided to incorporate the X division as "X Co.". X began manufacturing recordable compact disks in year 11. Because sales of recordable compact disks are weak, in year 17 ZZ Corp. sold X Corp. to Mega Corporation, which continued to operate the business.

The sales price for X Co. includes a large amount of cash in the company's bank accounts. ZZ Corp. has adopted a plan to distribute the sales proceeds from X Co. to the ZZ Corp.'s shareholders (all of whom are individuals) and thereby to redeem 10% of the ZZ Corp.'s stock, provided the shareholders will receive capital gains treatment. The chairman of ZZ Corp. has asked you to provide a legal opinion on the proposed distribution. Assume the year is year 17.

1) What is the analysis of the proposed transaction under § 302(b)(4) and § 302(e) with respect to ZZ Corp.'s shareholders?

2) Assume the same facts as in "(1)" except that instead ZZ Corp. acquired X Co. in year 11 in a tax-free merger under § 368(a)(1)(A) so that X Co. became a division of ZZ Corp. and its assets were sold off in year 13. Will the proposed distribution by ZZ Corp. of X Co.'s assets in partial redemption of its shares qualify under § 302(b)(4) and § 302(e)?

3) Assume the same facts as in "(1)," except that instead ZZ Corp. bought X Co. a year before the distribution.

PROBLEM 17-7

X Corp. is equally owned by the AB Partnership. AB Partnership is owned by Mr. A and Ms. B, and Big Corp. Big Corp. and AB Partnership each own 5,000 of the 10,000 X Corp. shares outstanding. AB Partnership's basis in its shares is $50,000 ($10 per share), and Big Corp's basis in its shares is $100,000 ($20 per share). Both Big Corp. and AB Partnership have held their shares for over five years. X Corp. has two lines of business that it has been engaged in for over five years, a publishing company and an amusement park company. X Corp. sold the amusement park company this year to Bubbly Brewing Co. As a result of the sale, X Corp. distributed cash from that sale to its shareholders in redemption of 10% of their stock in a transaction that qualified as a partial liquidation under §§302(b)(4) and 302(e). The total amount distributed was $200,000. X Corp. has more than $200,000 of current and accumulated earnings and profits. What is the result to AB Partnership and to Big Corp. on the distribution in exchange for their shares under § 302(b)?

F. REDEMPTIONS BY PUBLICLY OFFERED REGULATED INVESTMENT COMPANIES (MUTUAL FUNDS)

Read §§ 302(b)(5) and 67(c)(2)(B)

Under §302(b)(5), redemptions by a publicly offered regulated investment company — as defined in §67(c)(2)(B) — are given exchange treatment under §302(a) provided that the redemption is upon the demand of the stockholder and the publicly offered regulated investment company issues only stock that is redeemable upon the stockholder's demand.

G. REDEMPTIONS TO PAY DEATH TAXES
Read § 303(a) and (b).

When a taxpayer dies, the basis of his stock changes to fair market value at death (or as of the alternative valuation date six months following death) in the hands of the heirs. § 1014. That generally means that stock can be sold by the heirs (or the estate) to third parties with little or no subsequent gain or loss. However, sometimes, the stock cannot be sold to third parties if the estate holds a large block of stock that cannot be sold and the corporation is only willing to redeem a small amount of that stock, then the result to the estate is likely a taxable dividend. This is a harsh outcome if the cash is needed to pay funeral expenses, death taxes, or the costs of administering the estate. Section 303 addresses that concern.

The legislative history indicates that § 303 is oriented toward ensuring that family businesses are not destroyed by estate taxes, but § 303 does much more than that. Section 303 is literally a once in a lifetime opportunity to obtain a guaranteed "sale or exchange" (rather than "distribution") result for a redemption even if the estate owns 100% of the stock before and after the redemption.

To qualify under § 303, the stock need merely be a substantial part of the estate. However, the "sale or exchange" treatment extends only to an upper limit consisting of the sum of transfer taxes, funeral expenses, and administration expenses. The subject is generally a sideshow from the point of view of corporate tax planning (as opposed to estate planning), so it is covered here with a revenue ruling and one problem.

Section 303 redemptions entail a practical problem for some closely-held corporations because the redemption of a deceased shareholder's voting stock results in a proportionate increase in the voting power of the remaining shareholders. If the business is owned by a parent and children, this may not create a hardship, but if there are also outsiders, maintaining the desired balance of voting power is a problem that can often be solved, as the next ruling shows.

REV. RUL. 87-132
1987-2 C.B. 82

Issue

Whether the application of section 303 of the Internal Revenue Code to a stock redemption is precluded when the stock redeemed was newly distributed as part of the same transaction.

Facts

X corporation had outstanding 300 shares of voting common stock that were owned equally by an estate and by A, an individual, who had no interest in the estate under section 318 of the Code. The value of the X stock held by the estate exceeded the amount specified in section 303(b)(2)(A). The estate wanted to effect a redemption pursuant to section 303 to pay death taxes.

In order to maintain relative voting power and to preserve continuity of management, X undertook the following two steps. First, X issued 10 shares of a new class of nonvoting common stock on each share of common stock outstanding. Thus, the estate and A each received 1,500 shares of this stock. Immediately thereafter, 1,000 shares of the nonvoting common stock were redeemed by X from the estate in exchange for cash. The overall result of these two steps was that the estate obtained the cash it needed while giving up only nonvoting stock.

The redemption of the X nonvoting common stock occurred within the time limits prescribed by section 303(b)(1)(A) of the Code and did not exceed the amount permitted by section 303(a).

Law and Analysis

Section 303(a) of the Code provides that a distribution of property to a shareholder by a corporation in redemption of stock of the corporation, which (for federal estate tax purposes) is included in determining the gross estate of a decedent, is treated as a distribution in full payment in exchange for the stock redeemed to the extent of the sum of certain taxes and expenses. These taxes and expenses are the estate, inheritance, legacy and succession taxes plus the amount of funeral and administrative expenses allowable as deductions for federal estate tax purposes.

Section 303(c) of the Code provides that if a shareholder owns stock of a corporation (new stock) the basis of which is determined by reference to the basis of stock of a corporation (old stock) that was included in determining the gross estate of a decedent, and section 303(a) would apply to a distribution in redemption of the old stock, then section 303(a) applies to a distribution in redemption of the new stock. Section 1.303-2(d) of the Income Tax Regulations

314

specifically provides that section 303 applies to a distribution in redemption of stock received by an estate in a distribution to which section 305(a) applies.

Section 305(a) of the Code provides that, generally, gross income does not include the amount of any distribution of the stock of a corporation made by the corporation to its shareholders with respect to its stock. Section 305(b)(1), however, provides that if the distribution is, at the election of any of the shareholders (whether exercised before or after the declaration of the distribution), payable either in its stock or in property, then the distribution of stock is treated as a distribution to which section 301 applies. Section 305(b)(2) provides that if the distribution has the result of the receipt of property by some shareholders and an increase in the proportionate interest of other shareholders in the assets or earnings and profits of the corporation, then the distribution of stock is treated as a distribution to which section 301 applies.

Section 307(a) of the Code provides that if a shareholder already owning stock in a corporation ("old stock") receives additional stock ("new stock") in a distribution to which section 305(a) applies, then the basis of the old stock prior to the distribution is allocated between the old stock and new stock subsequent to the distribution.

Here, 3,000 shares of nonvoting common stock were distributed and 1,000 shares were subsequently redeemed by X as part of a plan designed to allow the estate to avail itself of the benefits of section 303 of the Code. The intent of Congress in enacting the statutory predecessor of section 303 was to provide an effective means whereby the estate of a decedent owning an interest in a family enterprise could finance the estate tax without being required to dispose of its entire interest in the family business in order to avoid the imposition of an ordinary dividend tax. H.R. Rep. No. 2319, 81st Cong., 2d Sess. 63-64 (1950). Given this intent, it follows that the estate should be able to obtain the benefits of section 303 without a substantially adverse effect on the estate's ownership of the family business.

Moreover, section 303(c) of the Code is a remedial provision that was added to expand the application of section 303 to the redemption of stock which, despite a technical change in the form of ownership, represents the same stock as that owned at death. S. Rep. No. 1622, 83rd Cong., 2nd Sess. 239 (1954). The sole requirement for application of section 303 to the redemption, under section 303(c), is that the basis of the stock redeemed ("new stock") be determined by reference to the basis of the "old stock" included in the estate. Section 1.303-2(d) of the Regulations provides that stock received by an estate in a section 305(a) distribution is entitled to section 303 treatment. Rev. Rul. 83-68, 1983-1 C.B. 75, holds that a distribution of stock that is immediately redeemable at the option of a shareholder gives the shareholder an election to receive either stock or property within the meaning of section 305(b)(1) and, therefore, is a distribution to which section 301 applies. See also Rev. Rul. 76-258, 1976-2 C.B. 95.

The nature of section 303 of the Code and the limited time period for redemption provided in section 303(b)(1) are generally indicative of a Congressional intent that section 303 be applicable to stock issued as part of the same plan as the redemption. Consequently, for purposes of section 303 only, section 305 should be applied prior to, and without reference to, the subsequent redemption.

Holding

The exclusion from gross income provision of section 305(a) of the Code, and the carryover of basis provisions of section 307(a), apply to X's distribution of its new nonvoting common stock to A and the estate. Section 303(a) applies to X's distribution of cash to the estate in redemption of the 1,000 shares of its new nonvoting common stock. For the tax consequences to A (the non-redeeming shareholder) as a result of this transaction, see section 305.

PROBLEM 17-8

A died with a gross estate of $20,000,000. The sum of death taxes and funeral and administration expenses was $3,000,000. Included in A's gross estate is A's 20% interest in Corp. X stock valued at $4,000,000 and A's 25% interest in Corp. Y stock valued at $5,000,000. One year after A's death, Corp. X and Corp. Y stock redeem the estate's stock for $9,000,000, paid over to A's son and sole legatee. What will be the tax treatment of the Corp. X and Corp. Y stock redemption under § 303?

H. REDEMPTIONS THROUGH RELATED CORPORATIONS
Read § 304(a) and (b)(1)-(2) and (c)(1).

Suppose that a taxpayer owns all the stock of two prosperous corporations. A redemption by either company of some of its shares will result in an (unacceptable) dividend to her as sole shareholder. Can the taxpayer obtain capital gain treatment simply by selling the stock of one company to the other? If so, then most of the barbed wire in § 302 is easily bypassed.

Section 304 prevents sale or exchange treatment by importing the rules of § 302 to apply to situations in which one or more shareholders have 50% or more control of both corporations. § 304(c)(1). Section 304 asks whether, following the sale, the taxpayer's direct and indirect interest in the "issuing" corporation was reduced enough to justify treating the transaction as an exchange rather than as a distribution. The change in indirect ownership is measured by looking through the acquiring corporation and attributing an amount of the issuing corporation's stock to the shareholder that is proportional to the amount of stock owned in the acquiring corporation for purposes of § 302. In the case of two 100%-owned corporations, the result is always a distribution.

To illustrate: A owns 80% of X Corp. and 60% of Y Corp., each of which has 100 shares outstanding. The minority shareholders are unrelated to A. A causes Y Corp. to purchase 20 shares of X Corp. stock from her for cash. As a result, A now owns 60 shares of X Corp. and Y Corp. owns 20 shares. A will get distribution treatment rather than exchange treatment, because her ownership in X Corp. has only declined from 80% to 72% computed as follows: A owns 60 shares outright, plus 12 shares attributed to her by looking through her 60% ownership of Y Corp.'s 20 shares (60% x 20 = 12 shares).

Another feature of § 304 is that it maximizes the likelihood of a taxable § 301 dividend because it combines the E & P of both companies for purposes of measuring the purchasing company's dividend-paying capacity. § 304(b)(2). This may be fine for corporate stockholders, but from the point of view of individual shareholders, it can be worse than the result of a direct redemption. That is because if there is a direct redemption, the corporation buying back its stock may not have enough E & P to cover the distribution, in which case there is a partial return of capital under § 301(c)(2).

So far this note has addressed transactions between commonly-owned corporations. The next subject is parent-subsidiary situations. An intuitively easy way to understand the problem § 304 deals with, and how it does so, is to consider an example under § 304(a)(2).

To illustrate: Individual B owns all the stock of X Corp., which has a wholly-owned subsidiary, Y Corp. Both corporations are awash in E & P. If X Corp. redeems any shares from B, the proceeds will be taxable to B as a dividend. What if Y Corp. purchases some of B's stock in X Corp. from B? How should the proceeds be taxable to B? Shouldn't this be a taxable dividend? *See* § 304(a)(2).

A § 304 transaction can be one whose facts also would fit, or nearly fit, § 351, and thus invoke the corollary rules of § 357 and § 358. Do you see how this could happen? Section 304(b)(3) coordinates § 304 with § 351 by specifying that § 304 will preempt § 351, and so it, not § 351, will apply to any property received in a distribution described in § 304(a).

PROBLEM 17-9

Harry owns 60 shares of T Corp.'s only class of common stock. There are 100 such shares altogether. He transfers all 60 shares to P Corp., of which he owns 80%, in exchange for cash.

1) Does § 304 apply to this transaction?

2) What Code section is used in conjunction with § 304 to determine if the result of the sale is a distribution or a sale?

3) What is the minimum ownership of T, P or both combined that Harry must have in order for § 304 to determine if the result of the sale is a distribution or a sale?

4) Assuming the result of the transaction in "(1)" is a distribution, what are the sources of earning and profits that produce the dividend?

5) Assume Harry has a moderate basis in the stock of T. Might Harry prefer a distribution result to the result of a sale of the stock?

6) If Harry were instead a corporation, and assuming the facts of "(2)", might the corporation prefer to see § 304 apply as compared to having an "exchange" for income tax purposes?

7) Now assume that Harry owns 100 percent of the stock of P Corp., which in turn owns 100 percent of the stock of S Corp. Harry sells some of his P stock to S for $50.

   a) Is this a sale or a distribution?

   b) Assuming the transaction is a distribution, whose earnings and profits are applied to measure the amount of the dividend?

   c) Assuming the result is a distribution, what is the impact on Harry's basis in P stock?

Chapter 18

LIQUIDATIONS

A. STATE LAW BACKGROUND

The legal terminations of a corporation results from a dissolution, which usually occurs via the voluntary filing of a certificate of dissolution with the state authority responsible for corporate documents, or involuntarily for failure to pay state income or franchise taxes. The process by which the corporation disgorges its assets, paying creditors and distributing assets to shareholders in exchange for their shares, is known as a liquidation. Because the federal income tax is concerned with economic realities rather than state law legalisms, the term "dissolution" does not rear its head in Subchapter C, and the question of whether a corporation has come to an end for federal income tax purposes depends on whether it has liquidated. It may liquidate "in kind" by distributing its assets to its shareholders or by selling some or all of its assets first and then distributing the proceeds or by a combination of the two.

The corporation is considered to have been liquidated for federal income tax purposes when it has ceased operating as a going concern and exists solely to wind up its affairs. *See* Reg. § 1.332-2(c). One implication of the contrast between dissolution for state law purposes and liquidation is that a corporation that has dissolved under state law but continues to limp along economically remains a corporation for federal income tax purposes.

Liquidations are not as ghoulish as they might first appear because in most cases the operating assets will continue to be used in someone else's business. In fact, they may even find their way into an affiliate of the liquidating corporation.

B. COMPLETE LIQUIDATIONS

Although entering corporate form is generally tax-free, exiting the corporate form is not and it can be expensive. Both the corporation and its shareholders are subject to federal income taxes as a result of a complete liquidation, except in the special case of liquidation of a controlled subsidiary into its corporate parent. That is treated in the last section of this Chapter.

1. SHAREHOLDER LEVEL EFFECTS
Read § 331.

In a complete liquidation, the shareholder-distributees are treated as if they sold their stock back to the corporation, which means that they report gain or loss, usually capital gain or loss (except for the unusual case of a dealer in stocks) under §§ 331 and 1001. Because the exchange is taxable, the shareholders take a fair-market value basis in the property they receive in liquidation, undiminished by associated liabilities. § 334(a). If one did reduce the basis of distributed assets by the liabilities, there would be a gain on the later sale by a shareholder of the distributed asset, which would mean double taxation of a single gain to the taxpayer, which is clearly inappropriate.

If the shareholder has several blocks of stock, the gain or loss calculations must be performed for each block. Reg. § 1.331-1(e). If the liquidation proceeds are distributed in two or more years, the shareholder can use an open-transaction approach, meaning no gain is reported until the liquidating distributions exceed stock basis after which all distributions are fully taxable. Rev. Rul. 85-48, 1985-1 C.B. 126. Similarly, if the shareholder receives a disputed claim, it apparently need not be treated as an amount realized until it is reduced to value. *See* Rev. Rul. 58-402. 1958-2 C.B. 15. Finally, if certain conditions are met, the shareholder can report installment proceeds of obligations that the corporation distributes to the shareholder on the installment method, as if the proceeds were paid for his stock. § 453(h)(1)(A) and (B).

To illustrate: Bob owns all the stock of Bobco. He originally contributed $100 to Bobco, which used the money to buy a factory. Some years later, Bobco undertook a liquidation in which it sold the factory on the installment method to one buyer for $200. It then distributed the installment note to Bob. The result is that Bob is taxed on a $100 gain (*i.e.*, the $200 sales proceeds under the note minus his $100 stock basis), but he reports the gain as the note is paid, rather than when he receives it. Bobco itself is also taxable on the distribution of the installment obligation. *See* § 453B, which you should have seen in your first federal income tax course. In other words, Bobco is taxable on the gain in its factory that it sold. Had it received cash, Bobco would have been taxable at once. Because it received an installment note, it will not be taxed until it collects or disposes of the note, which it did in the liquidation distribution to Bob. The taxation of distributed assets is discussed below.

Hold it! What if the final distribution in liquidation produced realization of a loss to the shareholder? Section 267 dictates that related persons usually cannot recognize losses when they sell or exchange property with each other. Can the shareholder recognize a loss on the liquidation even if he owns 100% of the stock of the corporation? The answer is "yes." *See* § 267(a)(1), second sentence. Otherwise, the loss would be permanently disallowed, not just deferred. However, the loss is deferred until the year in which the last and final liquidating distribution is made. Rev. Rul. 85-48, 1985-1 C.B. 126.

2. CORPORATE LEVEL EFFECTS
Read § 336(a)-(c).

The easiest way to understand the corporate-level effects of a complete liquidation and distribution of corporate assets in kind to shareholders is to imagine that the corporation sold each of its assets to strangers and then distributed the cash proceeds. The distributing corporation can, of course, recognize both gain and loss on the constructive sale of its various assets. Note that this rule is very different from that of current distributions in kind where the distributing corporation recognizes gain but not loss under § 311.

Under pre-1987 law, there was generally no tax on a corporation going through a complete liquidation when it distributed appreciated assets to its shareholders. *See* former § 337 and *General Util. & Oper. Co. v. Helvering*, 296 U.S. 200 (1935). (The *General Utilities* case actually involved a current distribution, but it gave its name to the general principle under former law that a corporation did not recognize gain or loss upon a distribution of property to its shareholders.) The *General Utilities* doctrine was legislatively reversed in 1986 via the introduction of §§ 311, 336.

One rationale for imposing a corporate level tax on the liquidating distribution is that the corporation realized the inherent gain or loss in each property when each property is distributed, and if the distributed property is not taxed at that point, it will never be taxed. (Remember that the shareholders take a fair market value basis in the property under § 334 and so the corporate level accrued gain will not later be taxed to the shareholders). Do you agree? Did the liquidating distribution really "cash in" the gain? If so, what consideration does the corporation receive in return? To look at another rationale, should the corporation be taxed just because it would have paid a tax if it had sold the assets to a third party?

Is it possible that the rule merely reflects a compulsive demand that the corporate double tax be completely unavoidable? In light of the spasmodic history of the double tax, is it a model we should honor? Might it be better to use the partnership model and give the shareholders a carryover basis in the distributed assets?

PROBLEM 18-1

ABC Corp. has been losing business over the past few years to a new giant in town, Wal Corp. ABC Corp. decides to call it quits and liquidates its assets, distributing them to individual shareholders, A, B, and C, as follows:

A, who owns stock with a basis of $100, receives equipment with a fair market value of $200;

B, who owns stock with a basis of $225, receives land with a fair market value of $450; and

C, who owns stock with a basis of $350, receives $700 cash.

1) How much and of what character of gain or loss will A, B, and C each recognize? *See* § 331.

2) What basis will each take in the assets received?

3) How would your answer to "(1) or "(2)" change if the equipment going to A was distributed subject to a $50 nonrecourse debt?

4) Suppose prior to the liquidation, ABC Corp. had a basis of $150 in the equipment and $300 in the land. Would ABC recognize any gain or loss on the distribution and, if so, what is the amount and character of that gain or loss? *See* § 336.

5) If you determine in "(4)" that there is gain, is that gain taxed at a capital gains rate, rather than the standard rate applicable to ordinary income?

PROBLEM 18-2

Harry and Sally each own 50 shares of the 100 shares of Movie, Inc. Harry's basis in his shares is $500,000, and Sally's basis in her shares is $200,000. Movie, Inc. has two assets, a completed motion picture, worth $1,000,000 and with a basis to the corporation of $500,000, and cash of $1,000,000. There is no creditor of the corporation.

1) What will be the tax consequences including basis, to a third party, to the corporation, and to each shareholder if: (a) Movie, Inc. sells its movie to a third party for its fair market value and (b) promptly distributes all its proceeds of sale and its cash (after payment of any corporate income tax) to its shareholders in a complete liquidation and repurchase of all their shares?

2) What will be the tax consequences, including asset basis, to the corporation and each shareholder if: (a) Movie, Inc. instead distributes all its assets in kind (after withholding for, or paying, any corporate tax) to its shareholders in complete liquidation, and (b) the shareholders sell the movie to an outsider for its fair market value?

3) Are the corporation's gains and losses computed asset by asset or in the aggregate?

NOTES

1. **Section 446(b) power**. The IRS often puts a liquidating corporation on the accrual method pursuant to an application of the § 446(b) power if its accounting method no longer clearly reflects income because of the liquidation. For example, the corporation may be denied further use of the completed contract method of accounting. This usually has the effect of accelerating corporate income. *See* Bittker & Eustice, Federal Income Taxation of Corporations and Shareholders ¶ 10.24[2] (2018).

2. **Tax returns**. A corporation going through liquidation must file federal income tax returns until the cessation of business and disposition of all its assets. Reg. § 1.6012-2(a)(2).

C. RECOGNITION OF LOSSES UNDER § 336
Read § 336(d)(1)-(2).

The repeal of the *General Utilities* doctrine might have offered opportunities to take advantage of deductible tax losses on liquidating distributions. For example, shareholders might contribute loss property to a corporation with the intent of liquidating the corporation and receiving the benefit of deductible losses realized at both the corporate and the shareholder levels. This possibility was anticipated by Congress and stymied in advance.

HOUSE OF REPRESENTATIVES REPORT NO. 841,
99th Congress, 2d Session, H.R. 3838 (September 18, 1986.)

RECOGNITION OF GAIN OR LOSS ON LIQUIDATING SALES AND DISTRIBUTIONS OF PROPERTY (GENERAL UTILITIES). P. L. 99-514

House Bill

In general

Under the House bill, gain or loss is recognized by a corporation on a liquidating distribution of its assets, as if the corporation had sold the assets to the distributee at fair market value, and on liquidating sales. In addition, the treatment of nonliquidating distributions is generally conformed to the treatment of liquidating distributions.

Conference Agreement

The conference agreement generally follows the House bill, with certain modifications and clarifications, thus repealing the *General Utilities* doctrine.

Thus, gain or loss is generally recognized by a corporation on a liquidating sale of its assets. Gain or loss is also generally recognized on a liquidating distribution of assets as if the corporation had sold the assets to the distributee at fair market value. Neither gain nor loss is recognized, however, with respect to any distribution of property by a corporation to the extent there is nonrecognition of gain or loss to the recipient under the tax-free reorganization provisions of the Code. . . .

Limitations on the recognition of losses

The conferees are concerned that taxpayers may utilize various means to avoid the repeal of the *General Utilities* doctrine, or otherwise take advantage of the new provisions, to recognize losses in inappropriate situations or inflate the amount of losses actually sustained. For example, under the general rule permitting recognition of losses on liquidating distributions, taxpayers may be able to create artificial losses at the corporate level or to duplicate shareholder losses in corporate solution through contribution of built-in loss property. Consequently, the conference agreement includes two provisions intended to prevent the recognition of such corporate level losses.

First, the conference agreement provides generally that no loss is recognized by a liquidating corporation with respect to any distribution of property to a related person (within the meaning of section 267), unless the property is distributed to all shareholders on a pro rata basis and the property was not acquired by the liquidating corporation in a section 351 transaction or as a contribution to capital during the five years preceding the distribution. Thus, for example, a liquidating corporation would not be permitted to recognize loss on a distribution of recently acquired property to a shareholder who, directly or indirectly, owns more than 50 percent in value of the stock of the corporation. Similarly, a liquidating corporation would not be permitted to recognize a loss on any property (regardless of when or how acquired) that is distributed to such a shareholder on a non-pro rata basis.

Second, the conference agreement generally provides that if a principal purpose of the contribution of property to a corporation in advance of its liquidation is to recognize a loss upon the sale or distribution of the property and thus eliminate or otherwise limit corporate level gain, then the basis (for purposes of determining loss) of any property acquired by such corporation in a section 351 transaction or as a contribution to capital will be reduced, but not below zero, by the excess of the basis of the property on the date of contribution over its fair market value on such date. For purposes of this rule, it is presumed, except to the extent provided in Regulations, that any section 351 transaction or contribution to capital within the two-year period prior to the adoption of a plan to complete liquidation (or thereafter) has such a principal purpose. Although a contribution more than two years before the adoption of a plan of liquidation might be made with a prohibited purpose, the conferees expect that those rules will apply only in the most rare and unusual cases under such circumstances.

If the adoption of a plan of complete liquidation occurs in a taxable year following the date on which the tax return including the loss disallowed by this provision is filed, the conferees intend that, in appropriate cases, the liquidating corporation may recapture the disallowed loss on the tax return for the taxable year in which such plan of liquidation is adopted. In the alternative, the corporation could file an amended return for the taxable year in which the loss was reported.

The conferees intend that the Treasury Department will issue Regulations generally providing that the presumed prohibited purpose for contributions of property two years in advance of the adoption of a plan of liquidation will be disregarded unless there is no clear and substantial relationship between the contributed property and the conduct of the corporation's current or future business enterprises. For example, assume that A owns Z Corporation which operates a widget business in New Jersey. That business operates exclusively in the northeastern region of the United States and there are no plans to expand those operations. In his individual capacity, A had acquired unimproved real estate in New Mexico that has declined in value. On March 22, 1988, A contributes such real estate to Z and six months later a plan of complete liquidation is adopted. Thereafter, all of Z's assets are sold to an unrelated party and the liquidation proceeds are distributed. A contributed no other property to Z during the two-year period prior to the adoption of the plan of liquidation. Because A contributed the property to Z less than two years prior to the adoption of the plan of liquidation, it is presumed to have been contributed with a prohibited purpose. Moreover, because there is no clear and substantial relationship between the contributed property and the conduct of Z's business, the conferees do not expect that any loss arising from the disposition of the New Mexico real estate would be allowed under the Treasury Regulations.

As another example, the conferees expect that such Regulations would permit the allowance of any resulting loss from the disposition of any of the assets of a trade or business (or a line of business) that are contributed to a corporation. In such circumstance, application of the loss disallowance rule is inappropriate assuming there is a meaningful relationship between the contribution and the utilization of the corporate form to conduct a business enterprise (*i.e.*, the contributed business, as distinguished from a portion of its assets, is not disposed of immediately after the contribution). The conferees also anticipate that the basis adjustment rules will generally not apply to a corporation's acquisition of property during its first two years of existence."

To illustrate: Assume that on June 1, 1987, a shareholder who owns a 10-percent interest in X corporation ("X") contributes nondepreciable property with a basis of $1,000 and a value of $100 to X in exchange for additional stock; X is a calendar year taxpayer. Assume further that on September 30, 1987, X sells the property to an unrelated third party for $200, and includes the resulting $800 loss on its 1987 tax return. Finally, assume that X adopts a plan of liquidation on December 31, 1988. Thereafter, X could file an amended return reflecting the fact that the $800 loss was disallowed because the property's basis would be reduced to $200. Alternatively, the conferees intend that X, under Regulations, may be permitted to recapture the loss on its 1988 tax return. The amount of loss recapture in such circumstances would be limited to the lesser of the built-in loss ($900, or $1,000, the transferred basis under section 362, less $100, the value of the property on that date it was contributed to X) or the loss actually recognized on the disposition of such property ($800, or the $1,000 transferred basis less the $200 amount realized). Thus, unless X files an amended return, X must recapture $800 on its return for its taxable year ending December 31, 1988.

Now read again the "anti-stuffing" rules of § 336(d)(1) and (d)(2).

PROBLEM 18-3

Terry owns all the stock of Atlas Corp. His basis in the stock is $100 and he has held the shares for several years. Atlas's only asset is a tract of land it paid $100 for seven years ago and which is now worth $90. Atlas adopts a plan of complete liquidation and distributes the land to Terry.

1) What are the income and basis consequences to Terry and Atlas? *See* §§ 331, 336 and Reg. § 1.331-1.

2) Same as "(1)," but Atlas received the land 19 months before the liquidation in a § 351 transaction. What impact, if any, does this change have on Terry and Atlas?

3) Assume instead that Terry contributed a different tract of land worth $20 with a basis of $30 to Atlas Corp. 19 months ago. As before, Atlas adopts a plan of liquidation and promptly liquidates and disposes of all its assets, which includes selling the land for $18 to an unrelated party.

4) Assume instead that Atlas uses the calendar year and has several shareholders. On June 1 of year 1, one of its shareholders contributed land worth $10, with a basis of $100. On September 30 of that same year, Atlas sold the property for $20 and reported a loss of $80 on its income tax return for year one. Atlas adopted a plan of complete liquidation on December 31 of year two. What impact, if any, does the liquidation have on the land sale?

PROBLEM 18-4

X Corp. received property with a fair market value of $20 and an adjusted basis of $30 as a contribution under § 118. Nineteen months later, X Corp. liquidates. In connection with the liquidation, X Corp. sells the property for $18.

1) How much loss is allowed on the liquidation? *See* § 336(d).

2) Same as "(1)" except that the corporation sells the property for $22. What is the result?

D. SECTION 332 LIQUIDATIONS
Read §§ 332 and 337.

Although liquidations are generally taxable to both the corporation and the shareholder, §§ 332 and 337 provide an exception for liquidations of 80%-owned subsidiaries into their parent corporations. Section § 332 protects the corporate parent from gain or loss on receipt of the assets from the controlled subsidiary, and § 337 protects the subsidiary against gain or loss on the distribution of its assets to its parent company.

The purpose of §§ 332 and 337 is to facilitate the simplification of complicated corporate financial structures by allowing the tax-free elimination of unnecessary subsidiaries. These liquidations may either involve dissolutions under state law or short-form mergers of subsidiaries into parent corporations under state law. In the latter case, § 332 is not the controlling tax provision. Use § 368(a)(1)(A) instead. That provision is discussed in Chapter 21. Assuming that such a restructuring is achieved – whether by merger or dissolution under state law – the parent corporation normally obtains the liquidated subsidiary's tax attributes, including its earnings and profits account. See § 381.

Section 337(a) ensures that the liquidated subsidiary is free of tax. Section § 334(b)(1) forces the recipient parent to take the assets with the bases that they had in the hands of the subsidiary. The result in effect is simply to ignore the corporate form of the subsidiary and treat its assets as if they had been owned by the controlling parent all along. This defers any gain or loss in those assets until the parent disposes of them. The curiosity of this arrangement is that the parent's basis in the stock of the subsidiary evaporates, which may be disadvantageous if the basis is particularly high compared to its value.

1. REQUIREMENTS IMPOSED BY § 332

The requirements of § 332 are not subtle or treacherous. First, the parent corporation must own 80% of the stock by vote and value of the corporation going through the liquidation, ignoring nonvoting, nonconvertible preferred stock. §§ 332(b)(1) and 1504(a)(2). The 80% level of ownership must be maintained at all times following the date on which the plan of the liquidation is adopted. § 332(b)(1).

Second, the subsidiary is supposed to engage in "a complete cancellation or redemption of all of its stock." § 332(b)(3). Although there is usually a state law dissolution, it is not mandatory and in fact the liquidating corporation can retain a few assets so as to continue its legal existence. Reg. § 1.332-2(c). This can save the parent corporation some legal fees and filing expenses in the event that it would like to have another corporation in storage for future use.

Third, the liquidating distributions must occur in one of the following two ways:

(1) The liquidation must occur in a single taxable year, which need not be specified in the plan of liquidation § 332(b)(2); or

(2) If the plan of liquidation contemplates a series of liquidations spread over more than a year, then the plan must provide that all the assets of the subsidiary will be distributed to the parent within three years after the end of the year in which the first distribution is made. § 332(b)(3).

Either way, § 332 allows the corporation time to "clean house" before the liquidation. If either the 80% requirement or the timing requirement is not satisfied, then the § 332 liquidation is retroactively disqualified, and the liquidation becomes fully taxable.

The protection of §§ 332 and 337 is available even if both the parent corporation and its controlled subsidiary liquidate, provided that the subsidiary is liquidated first so that the technical requirements of § 332 are met. *See Barkley Co. of Ariz v. Commissioner,* T.C. Memo 1988-324. This can be advantageous if the parent corporation has built-in gain in the subsidiary's stock because the liquidation eliminates that gain entirely.

There was some judicial confusion surrounding the *Fairfield Steamship Corp. v. Commissioner* decision, 157 F.2d 321 (2d Cir. 1946), cert. denied, 329 U.S. 774 (1946), which indicated that the parent corporation must continue the business of the subsidiaries. While this authority is shaky at best, it is reasonably clear that if both parent and subsidiary go out of business, § 332 does not apply if the parent liquidates first or is no longer the controlling shareholder when the subsidiary is liquidated. For an example where § 332 did not apply, *see Kamis Engineering Co. v. Commissioner*, 60 T.C. 763 (1973)(the parent distributed the stock of the subsidiary to the parent's shareholders).

To illustrate: Parent owns 100% of the stock of Sub, which is worth $500 and in which Parent has a basis of $200. Parent's operating assets are worth $100, and Parent's basis in them is $50. Sub's own assets are also worth $500 and have a basis of $75 in Sub's hands.

If Sub liquidates into Parent under §§ 332/337, there will be no tax to either corporation, and Parent simply inherits Sub's assets with Sub's $75 basis. If Parent then liquidates, it will have gain of $475 under §336 from the deemed sale of both its own and Sub's assets [(100-50) + (500-75)].

If Parent liquidates first, however, it must recognize its gain of $425 in the Sub stock under § 336 in addition to its gain of $50 with respect to its operating assets. When Sub liquidates outside the protection of §§ 332/337, its own inside gain of $475 is recognized.

If Parent has a built-in loss in its Sub stock, then the stakes are reversed and Parent has an incentive to flunk §§ 332/337 in order to deduct the loss that would otherwise evaporate.

2. MINORITY SHAREHOLDERS

Even if §§ 332 and 337 apply to the liquidation of a controlled subsidiary, the protection of § 332 is unavailable to minority shareholders, and, in addition, the liquidating subsidiary must recognize gain (but not loss) on any assets distributed to the minority shareholders. This is true even if the minority shareholder is itself a corporation. In effect, the minority shareholders and the liquidating subsidiary are treated as engaging in a separate §§ 331/336 taxable liquidation, except for the rule forbidding loss recognition under § 336(d). Section 336(d)(3) is designed to prevent "cherry-picking" of losses so that the liquidating subsidiary cannot distribute its gain assets tax-free to its parent and at the same time enjoy a deduction by targeting its loss assets to minority shareholders. The rules apply even if the pattern of the distributions is free of tax motives.

PROBLEM 18-5

Change the facts of Problem 18-2. Now, determine the tax consequences on the supposition that Movie, Inc. was 100% owned by a parent corporation that, in turn, was owned 50-50 by Harry and Sally. Also, assume that Movie, Inc. liquidated (both ways – under §§ 331 and 332) this year, and, soon afterwards, the parent liquidated. *See* §§ 332, 337, 381, 334(b)(1).

REV. RUL. 70-106
1970-I C.B. 70

Minority shareholders owned twenty-five percent of the capital stock of corporation X. The remaining seventy-five percent of the capital stock of X was owned by Corporation Y. Y desired to liquidate X in a transaction to which section 332 of the Internal Revenue Code of 1954 would apply in order that Y would recognize no gain on the transaction. The minority shareholders agreed to have their stock of X redeemed. Following the distribution to the minority shareholders, Y owned all the stock of X. Y then adopted a formal plan of complete liquidation of X and all of the remaining assets of X were distributed to Y.

Held

All of the shareholders of X received a distribution in liquidation under the provisions of section 331 of the Code, and the gain is recognized to Y and gain or loss is recognized to the minority shareholders under section 331 of the Code. The liquidation fails to meet the eighty percent stock ownership requirements of section 332(b)(1) of the Code since the plan of liquidation was adopted at the time Y reached the agreement with the minority shareholders and at such time, Y owned seventy-five percent of the stock of X.

NOTES

1. **Qualifying for § 332; is it quasi-elective?** Assume a corporation has two shareholders, an individual who owns 21 shares and an unrelated corporation that owns 79 shares. If the individual redeems her shares before a plan of liquidation is adopted, the result can be a good § 332 liquidation for the corporate shareholder. Does this make the system too elective? Despite Rev. Rul. 70-106, the courts have been generous in upholding taxpayers' efforts to "back into" 80% control by prior redemptions and stock sales, and have not found a "plan" of liquidation until its official corporate adoption. *See George L. Riggs, Inc. v. Commissioner*, 64 T.C. 474 (1975), in which the court goes so far as to say that § 332 is elective for those who know how to structure the transaction properly.

2. **What about deliberately avoiding § 332 by first dumping some stock in order to get under the 80% threshold?** Here it has been held that even a genuine sale after adoption of the plan of liquidation will disqualify the plan. *Commissioner v. Day & Zimmerman, Inc.*, 151 F.2d 517 (3d Cir. 1945). (The buyer was the corporation's treasurer who purchased at a public auction of stock.) Can you reconcile these results?

3. **What about debts of the subsidiary?** Parent corporations often lend generously to get their subsidiaries underway. If the subsidiary is a failure and is insolvent and the parent decides to liquidate the subsidiary, then there is no distribution with respect to stock (the stock having no value) and § 332 does not apply. As a result, the parent can claim a loss on the subsidiary's stock. If a liquidating subsidiary distributes property to its parent as repayment of its debt, the usual rule that gain or loss is recognized as if the property were sold to a stranger and the cash were used to pay the debt does not apply. Instead, § 337(b)(1) treats

the transfer as part of the §§ 332/337 liquidation with the result that the subsidiary recognizes no gain or loss. The rule is designed to prevent the subsidiary from creating loss deductions by paying off its debts with loss property while transferring its gain property tax-free. On the parent's side of the transaction, however, any gain or loss is recognized if it receives payments qua creditor, say because it bought the subsidiary's debt at a discount from a third party and was repaid the full face amount. Reg. § 1.332-7.

PROBLEM 18-6

Grabber International, Inc. buys 100% of the stock of Target, Inc. on day one and, three months later, liquidates it pursuant to § 332. Grabber paid $1 million for the stock. Target's assets have a basis of $100,000 and are worth $1 million. What gain or loss, if any, will Grabber and Target recognize? *See* §§ 332(a) and 337(a). What is Grabber's basis in Target's assets?

PROBLEM 18-7

Baby, Inc. is a corporation engaged in the business of manufacturing strollers. Dada Corp. has owned 85% of the only series of Baby stock for 9 years. Baby, Inc., however, hits an economic pothole when Consumer Reports declares that its strollers are unsafe for transporting children because they tend to tip over easily. As a result, Baby, Inc. halts business and liquidates immediately, distributing in the process $850 worth of its $1,000 in assets (by value) to Dada Corp. The remaining $150 worth of assets are distributed pro rata to Baby, Inc.'s only other shareholder, Mama, Ltd., which is a partnership consisting of individuals. Baby, Inc. had a basis of $100 in the assets prior to the distribution, Dada Corp. had a basis of $85 in its stock, and Mama, Ltd. had a basis of $15 in its stock. There are no other pertinent transactions

1) Will Baby, Inc. recognize a gain or loss on the distribution to Dada Corp.?

2) Would your answer to "(1)" change if, shortly before the liquidation, Dada bought 6% of Baby's stock from Mama Ltd. for tax reasons, namely to achieve 80% or more ownership of Baby?

3) Under the facts of "(1)," what is Dada Corp's basis in the assets it receives?

4) Under the facts of "(1)," will Dada Corp. be subject to any income tax as a result of the distribution?

5) Under the facts of "(1)," what portion of Baby, Inc.'s basis in its assets is logically attributable to the assets distributed to Mama, Ltd.?

6) Under the facts of "(1)," will Mama, Ltd. report a taxable gain or deductible loss on the liquidation?

7) Under the facts of "(1)," will Baby, Inc. recognize a gain or loss on the distribution to Mama, Ltd.?

8) Under the facts of "(1)," if Baby's assets were worth less than their bases, could Baby somehow report a loss on a transfer to Dada?

9) Under the facts of "(1)," assume Baby owes Dada $100, which it pays off with property with a basis of $80 and a value of $100. Does either Baby or Dada have a taxable gain?

10) Under the facts of "(1)," would the answer to "(9)" differ if Dada had bought the $100 debt from a bank that had lent to Baby, but paid only $90 for the debt? *See* Reg. § 1.332-7.

Chapter 19

TAXABLE ACQUISITIONS

A. INTRODUCTION

Business people and tax people think differently. The business person wants an acquisition that has business advantages, such as rounding out a product line. A tax person is brought in to optimize the tax results and may wind up suggesting transactions that are almost incomprehensible to the client, whose position is simply, "I want that business." Whether it is done as an acquisition of assets[1] – or as a stock acquisition[2] – may be of no direct concern. The tax advisor will then review the important tax features of the target and of the acquiror and their owners and will suggest an optimal way to shape the transaction, usually on the assumption that the seller is well advised in tax matters. The advisor will study such issues as the bases of the target's assets, the existence of net operating losses, and earnings and profits accounts.

Once the advisor has ascertained the facts and the tax stakes, the next step is to contemplate the various specific kinds of transactions contemplated in the Code with an eye to achieving the optimum tax result. The transactions can include partial liquidations, pre-acquisition distributions, spin-offs of businesses of the target company in advance of a nontaxable acquisitive reorganization of the target company, and so forth. These alternatives are not always explicit in the Code and can cost a lot of money to unearth. One of the deep issues in corporate taxation is whether the tax results of business acquisitions should be entirely elective, as opposed to relying on the manipulation of the "short list" of transactional forms meted out by the Code, which manipulation in effect produces elections visible only to the well-heeled.

In general, there are two basic ways for one corporation to acquire another. The simplest way is a taxable acquisition. Such an acquisition may be structured as a purchase of target assets or of target stock, for cash or for any other consideration. A purchase of assets often results in taxation at both the target and target shareholder levels. A taxable acquisition benefits the acquiror if it can get a stepped-up basis in the acquired assets equal to their fair market value, i.e. the purchase price, and also wipes out the target company's earnings and profits. If the acquiror buys the stock of the target, only the target shareholders are taxed on their capital gains and losses, but the price of avoiding a target-level tax is that the target's assets keep their historic basis and all of the target's tax history survives. The target has merely changed owners with no effect upon its internal tax affairs, except for problems of offsetting target loss carryforwards against future gains, which are treated in Chapter 23.

The other method is a tax-free corporate reorganization under § 368, in which the acquiror swaps its stock for stock or assets of the target company. There will generally be no shareholder-level tax, but there will also be no change in basis of the target corporation's former assets, much as under §§ 332/337 liquidations. Tax-free reorganizations are treated in Chapter 21. Here is a preliminary run-through of some major alternatives.

---

[1] This may be achieved as a taxable asset purchase, on a current basis, on a deferred sale basis under § 453, or nontaxably under § 1031 (like kind exchanges) or perhaps by means of a joint contribution by buyer and seller to a new corporation under § 351 or to a partnership under § 721.

[2] This can be a taxable stock purchase or a nontaxable acquisitive reorganization using stock as consideration, the latter being the subject of Chapter 20.

To illustrate: Suppose Grabber, Inc., a large, publicly-held corporation on the acquisition trail, wants to acquire the assets and business of Target Corp., a closely-held corporation owned by the Little family. Target's assets consist of real and personal property (some of it depreciable, some with low bases and some with high bases, but with an aggregate basis far below value), cash, accounts receivable, some advantageous contracts, leases and intangibles. Consider how Grabber might acquire Target's business and the tax results, in broad outline, of each method.

Grabber might buy all the stock of Target Corp., if everyone will sell; if not, Grabber may be stuck with a troublesome minority shareholder. After buying all or most of the stock, Grabber can: (1) continue Target as a subsidiary (with Target's internal tax characteristics unchanged); or (2) it can liquidate Target under §§ 332/337 and run its business as a division of Grabber; or (3) it could merge Target up and into Grabber; or (4) even merge Grabber into Target.

If Grabber buys all the assets and assumes all of Target's liabilities, it can: (1) run the business as a division; (2) "drop down" Target's assets and liabilities into a subsidiary; (3) distribute Target's assets to Grabber's shareholders, who could then incorporate the business.

These alternatives raise a myriad of questions, such as, how many levels of recognition of gain or loss would each method involve? Other considerations include whether the E & P account would be eliminated, whether Target's other tax attributes, such as taxable year and accounting method, would continue and whether Target's net operating losses might survive in the hands of Grabber.

B. TYPES OF TAXABLE ACQUISITIONS

A corporate business may be acquired taxably in one of two fundamental ways: by a purchase of the target corporation's stock from its shareholders, or by direct purchase of the assets from the target corporation itself. The differences between the two methods can be profound from both a business and a tax point of view.

Cautious buyers often prefer to buy assets because they wish to avoid the target corporation's hidden or contingent liabilities. The purchaser of stock buys the target's future lawsuits. On the other hand, a purchase of assets is often inconvenient or even impossible if the target corporation has valuable contracts or licenses to do business that might be difficult to replace. In that case, it might be essential to obtain the target corporation itself, which can only be done through a stock purchase.

If business factors do not compel a choice, say because the seller is highly solvent and willing to indemnify the buyer against all liabilities, tax law will influence whether an acquisition is structured as a purchase of assets or stock. To complicate matters, an acquisition of either stock or assets may be accomplished through a bewildering variety of tax-free reorganizations. That is the subject of Chapter 21. The tax stakes may be very high for both buyer and seller. As a result, structuring the sale of a business is many a tax lawyer's bread and butter.

In a taxable acquisition, the basic tax stakes are familiar ones: whether the seller is taxed at ordinary or capital gains rates, and whether the buyer will inherit the seller's tax history, including the basis and depreciation schedules of the seller's assets, net operating losses, and earnings and profits, or will the buyer begin anew with a cost basis and a fresh slate. In addition, after the repeal of *General Utilities*, the seller is taxed when it sells its assets or distributes them in liquidation. The picture becomes rapidly complicated where there are multiple parties to the transaction who may have conflicting interests, or where the buyer(s) wish to acquire some but not all of the seller's business, or both combined. Accommodating the business and tax needs of all the parties can become an extremely sophisticated and demanding task. Given the variety of possible tax structures of what may be essentially the same business deal, and the high stakes involved, it is not surprising that the craftiness and creativity of tax lawyers has produced an intricate body of law.

If a purchaser (P) buys all the target corporation's (T's) assets and T is left with cash or notes, T then has the option of liquidating under § 331 and creating a capital gain or loss result at the shareholder level. As was mentioned before, if T sold assets on the installment method in the course of the takeover, its shareholders can generally report their stock sale in exchange for the installment note on the same method, which provides some deferral of the double tax burden. *See* § 453(h). T is taxed on the distribution of the installment obligation, however, so it has nothing to gain by the strategy. § 453B(a). The shareholders get a modest timing benefit.

To illustrate: Corporation X is a wholly-owned C corporation. Its only asset is land with a basis of $70 and a value of $100. Its sole shareholder has a basis in its T Corporation stock of only $10. If T adopts a plan of liquidation and sells the land for a $10 down payment and an installment note having a face amount and value of $90, the corporation must recognize and pay tax on the entire remaining gain when it distributes the note. § 453B. The shareholder will take the note in liquidation, and will realize the $80 gain (i.e., $90 minus $10 stock basis). The shareholder can report the $80 gain on the installment method as payments are received on the $90 note. § 453(h).

A purchase of assets may be inconvenient for both parties because the cost of changing titles to property can be high. It is often easier to structure the transaction as a taxable merger. In a merger under state law, two corporations are legally combined and only the acquiring corporation survives. The target is automatically dissolved as a matter of state law and the surviving corporation becomes the owner of the target's assets as a matter of law. This does not solve the problem of avoiding the target's hidden or contingent liabilities, however. Under state law, the surviving corporation in a merger acquires all the target's assets and liabilities.

A merger may be "triangular" in the sense that the acquiring corporation forms a subsidiary to do the dirty work of taking over the target. A triangular merger can be made in two directions: either the target is merged into the new subsidiary, or the new subsidiary may merge into the target. For tax purposes, the former kind of merger is treated as an acquisition of the target's assets from the target followed by a liquidation of the target. The latter is known as a "reverse subsidiary merger" and is treated for tax purposes as an acquisition of the target's stock. Subsidiary mergers do not eliminate the target's liabilities, but they do at least quarantine them within the subsidiary and prevent them from becoming claims against the acquiror's other assets in the same way as a purchase of target stock.

Corporate lawyers tend to assume that all mergers are tax-free, but that is not the case. A merger can be taxable if the transaction fails to satisfy one of any number of conditions that the Code imposes, such as consideration paid to target shareholders consisting of too much cash in relation to stock in the acquiring corporation.

C. ASSET PURCHASES
Read § 1060(a) and (c).

A purchase of the assets of a business (as opposed to the acquisition of its stock) is treated for tax purposes as a separate purchase and sale of each and every asset of the business, including its intangible assets. This rule applies both to a sale of all of a corporation's assets and to a sale of any part, including the sale of a division that constitutes a separate line of business. However, do not assume that the buyer or seller is a corporation. That is plain from reading § 1060(c).

Thus, both the buyer and the seller of a business must assign part of the purchase price to each and every asset in the business in order to compare that part to the asset's basis to its value and to compute the resulting gain and loss, asset-by-asset. If the business is a substantial one, the burden of apportioning the sales proceeds can be daunting.

At this point, § 1060 enters the picture and imposes a number of important requirements. Section 1060 is triggered by the existence of an "applicable asset acquisition," meaning a direct or indirect transfer of assets that constitute a trade or business, if the transferee's (acquiror's) basis in the assets is determined by reference to what the buyer paid (the acquisition may be in part a like-kind exchange under § 1031). § 1060(c). Once § 1060 is swept in, there are a number of obligations:

1. The buyer and seller must generally use Form 8594, which they prepare jointly, to report the part of the sales price attributable to each asset. Unless there is a written allocation agreement, the parties are obligated to use the residual method (see below) of apportioning the purchase price to assets. Section 1060(b) makes this disclosure mandatory.

2. The basis of the acquired assets must be determined under the "residual method," the effect of which is to assign consideration sequentially, first to the most easily valued assets (*i.e.*, cash and certain bank deposits, known as "Class 1 assets") and last to the intangibles that are the most difficult to value, namely going concern value and goodwill (known as "Class VII assets"). Going concern value refers to the addition to value that arises from the fact that the business can be continued despite a change of ownership, whereas goodwill is supposed to reflect the above average earnings expectations for the enterprise. For historical reasons that are touched on later in the book, the mechanical rules are found in Reg. §§ 1.1060-1 and 1.338-6 and -7.

The Treasury Regulations break assets into seven classes. The groupings are:

Class I assets: cash and cash equivalents; § 1.338-6(b)(1)

Class II assets: actively traded personal property, certificates of deposit, and foreign currency; § 1.338-6(b)(2)(ii)

Class III assets: assets the taxpayer marks to market at least annually for federal income tax purposes, and debt instruments, other than debt instruments issued by related parties, contingent debt instruments, and certain convertible debt instrument; and, under earlier rules, accounts receivable, mortgages, and credit card receivables from customers that arise in the ordinary course of business; § 1.338-6(b)(2)(iii)

Class IV assets: generally includes stock in trade, inventory and dealer property; § 1.338-6(b)(2)(iv)

Class V assets: generally includes all assets other than those included in Class I, Class II, Class II, Class IV, Class VI, or Class VII (generally all furniture fixtures, land, buildings, equipment, and other tangible property); § 1.338-6(b)(2)(v)

Class VI assets: section 197 intangibles other than goodwill or going concern value; and, § 1.338-6(b)(2)(vi)

Class VII assets: goodwill or going concern value, whether or not it qualifies as a section 197 intangible. § 1.338-6(b)(2)(vii)

Ten percent owners of businesses must report contracts that are related to the acquisition. § 1060(e). This commonly forces disclosure of covenants not to compete, employment agreements, and other transactions. The administration of § 1060 is aggressive. Taxpayers who disregard the duty to disclose the allocation to the IRS face major penalties under §§ 6721(e) and 6724(d). Moreover, disclosing their agreement does not prevent the IRS from challenging the way the parties allocated the purchase price. Reg. § 1.1060-1(c)(4).

Under pre-1993 law, there was no amortization deduction for goodwill or going concern value. As a result, buyers of assets were tempted to allocate as little of the purchase price as possible to goodwill, and as much as possible to depreciable assets or amortizable intangibles such as noncompete agreements. This process led to frequent claims that hitherto unknown forms of intangibles were amortizable and distinguishable from goodwill.

Section 1060 and its accompanying Regulations were unable to cope with intangibles issues. For one thing, they failed to define goodwill, which allowed taxpayers to devise artful claims that new forms of intangibles had a limited useful life and a definitely ascertainable value.

Taxpayers have long strained to show that what might otherwise appear to be a large amount of undifferentiated goodwill can be broken down into particular elements, at least some of which have limited useful lives and so can be separately amortized. Taxpayers did fairly well with that argument. For example, in Revenue Ruling 74-456, 1974-2 C.B. 65, the IRS capitulated and accepted the *Houston Chronicle* decision, which no longer treated customer-related intangibles automatically as a mass asset that are "indistinguishable from goodwill." *Houston Chronicle Publ'g Co. v. United States*, 481 F.2d 1240 (5th Cir. 1973), *cert. denied*, 414 U.S. 1129 (1974).

The next major decision, which was overruled prospectively by the enactment of § 197 in the same year, shows the problem that §197 attempts to resolve.

NEWARK MORNING LEDGER CO. v. UNITED STATES
507 U.S. 546 (1993)

[The taxpayer was the successor to The Herald Company. When, in 1976, Herald bought the stock of Booth Newspapers, Inc., it allocated its adjusted income tax basis in the Booth shares among the assets it acquired in its merger with Booth. Among other things, it allocated $67.8 million to an intangible asset denominated "paid subscribers," a figure that was petitioner's estimate of future profits to be derived from identified subscribers to Booth's eight newspapers on the date of merger. On its federal income tax returns for 1977-1980, it claimed depreciation deductions based on the $67.8 million. The IRS asserted that the concept of "paid subscribers" was indistinguishable from goodwill and, therefore, was nondepreciable.]

JUSTICE BLACKMUN delivered the opinion of the Court.

Section 167(a) of the Code allows as a deduction for depreciation a reasonable allowance for the exhaustion and wear and tear, including obsolescence, of property used in a trade or business or of property held for the production of income . . . This Court has held that "the primary purpose" of an annual depreciation deduction is "to further the integrity of periodic income statements by making a meaningful allocation of the cost entailed in the use (excluding maintenance expense) of the asset to the periods to which it contributes."

The Revenue Act of 1918, § 234(a)(7), authorized a "reasonable allowance for the exhaustion, wear and tear of property used in the trade or business, including a reasonable allowance for obsolescence." 40 Stat., 1078 (1919). Treas. Regs. 45 (1919), promulgated under the 1918 Act, explicitly recognized that intangible assets "may be the subject of a depreciation allowance." Art. 163. Thereafter, the Regulations governing the depreciation of intangible assets have remained essentially unchanged.

Since 1927, the IRS consistently has taken the position that "goodwill is non-depreciable. One court has said specifically: "Indeed, this proposition is so well settled that the only question litigated in recent years regarding this area of the law is whether a particular asset is `goodwill.'" *Houston Chronicle Publishing Co. v. United States*, 481 F.2d 1240, 1247 (CA5 1973) . . .

"Goodwill" is not defined in the Code or in any Treasury Department Regulations. There have been attempts, however, to devise workable definitions of the term. In *Metropolitan Bank v. St. Louis Dispatch Co.*, 149 U.S. 436, 13 S. Ct. 944, 37 L. Ed. 799 (1893), for example, this Court considered whether a newspaper's goodwill survived after it was purchased and ceased publishing under its old name. It ruled that the goodwill did not survive, relying on Justice Story's notable description of "goodwill" as "the advantage or benefit, which is acquired by an establishment, beyond the mere value of the capital, stock, funds, or property employed therein, in consequence of the general public patronage and encouragement which it receives from constant or habitual customers, on account of its local position, or common celebrity, or reputation for skill or affluence, or punctuality, or from other accidental circumstances or necessities, or even from ancient partialities, or prejudices." *Id.*, at 446, 13 S. Ct., at 948, quoting J. Story, Partnerships § 99 (1841).

In *Des Moines Gas Co. v. Des Moines*, 238 U.S. 153 . . . (1915), the Court described goodwill as "that element of value which inheres in the fixed and favorable consideration of customers, arising from an established and well-known and well-conducted business."

Although the definition of goodwill has taken different forms over the years, the short-hand description of goodwill as "the expectancy of continued patronage," *Boe v. Commissioner*, 307 F.2d 339 . . . (CA 9 1962), provides a useful label with which to identify the total of all the imponderable qualities that attract customers to the business . . . This definition, however, is of little assistance to a taxpayer trying to evaluate which of its intangible assets is subject to a depreciation allowance. The value of every intangible asset is related, to a greater or lesser degree, to the expectation that customers will continue their patronage.[3] But since 1918, at least some intangible assets have been depreciable. Because intangible assets do not exhaust or waste away in the same manner as tangible assets, taxpayers must establish that public taste or other socioeconomic forces will cause the intangible asset to be retired from service, and they must estimate a reasonable date by which this event will occur. *See* B. Bittker &, M. McMahon, Federal Income Taxation of Individuals, p. 12.4 (1988). Intangibles such as patents and copyrights are depreciable over their "legal lives," which are specified by statute. Covenants not to compete, leaseholds, and life estates, for example, are depreciable over their useful lives that are expressly limited by contract.

The category of intangibles that has given the IRS and the courts difficulty is that group of assets sometimes denominated "customer-based intangibles." This group includes customer

---

[3] We emphasize that while the "expectancy of continued patronage" is a serviceable description of what we generally mean when we describe an intangible asset that has no useful life and no ascertainable value, this shibboleth tells us nothing about whether the asset in question is depreciable. The dissent concedes that "the law concerning the depreciation of intangible assets related to goodwill has developed on a case-by-case basis," yet, inexplicably, it suggests that "[s]uch matters are not at issue in this case, however, because the asset that Ledger seeks to depreciate is indistinguishable from goodwill." As we demonstrate below, an intangible asset with an ascertainable value and a limited useful life, the duration of which can be ascertained with reasonable accuracy, is depreciable under § 167 of the Code. The fact that it may also be described as the "expectancy of continued patronage" is entirely beside the point.

lists, insurance expirations, subscriber lists, bank deposits, cleaning-service accounts, drugstore-prescription files, and any other identifiable asset the value of which obviously depends on the continued and voluntary patronage of customers. The question has been whether these intangibles can be depreciated notwithstanding their relationship to "the expectancy of continued patronage."

When considering whether a particular customer-based intangible asset may be depreciated, courts often have turned to a "mass asset" or indivisible asset rule. The rule provides that certain kinds of intangible assets are properly grouped and considered as a single entity; even though the individual components of the asset may expire or terminate over time, they are replaced by new components, thereby causing only minimal fluctuations and no measurable loss in the value of the whole. The following is the usually accepted description of a mass asset:

> "[A] purchased terminable-at-will type of customer list is an indivisible business property_ with an indefinite, nondepreciable life, indistinguishable from – and the principal element of – goodwill, whose ultimate value lies in the expectancy of continued patronage through public acceptance. It is subject to temporary attrition as well as expansion through departure of some customers, acquisition of others, and increase or decrease in the requirements of individual customers. A normal turnover of customers represents merely the ebb and flow of a continuing property status in this species, and does not within ordinary limits give rise to the right to deduct for tax purposes the loss of individual customers. The whole is equal to the sum of its fluctuating parts at any given time, but each individual part enjoys no separate capital standing independent of the whole, for its disappearance affects but does not interrupt or destroy the continued existence of the whole." *Golden State Towel & Linen Service, Ltd. v. United States*, 179 Ct. Cl. 300 (1967).

The mass asset rule prohibits the depreciation of certain customer-based intangibles because they constitute self-regenerating assets that may change but never waste. Although there may have been some doubt prior to 1973 as to whether the mass asset rule required that any asset related to the expectancy of continued patronage always be treated as nondepreciable goodwill as a matter of law, that doubt was put to rest by the Fifth Circuit in the Houston Chronicle case. The court there considered whether subscription lists, acquired as part of the taxpayer's purchase of The Houston Press, were depreciable. The taxpayer had no intention of continuing publication of the purchased paper, so there was no question of the lists being self-regenerating; they had value only to the extent that they furnished names and addresses of prospective subscribers to the taxpayer's newspaper. After reviewing the history of the mass asset rule, the court concluded that there was no per se rule that an intangible asset is nondepreciable whenever it is related to goodwill. On the contrary, the rule does not prevent taking a depreciation allowance if the taxpayer properly carries his dual burden of proving that the intangible asset Involved (1) has an ascertainable value separate and distinct from goodwill, and (2) has a limited useful life, the duration of which can be ascertained with reasonable accuracy." *Id.* at 1250.

Following the decision in *Houston Chronicle*, the IRS issued a new ruling, modifying prior rulings "to remove any implication that customer and subscription lists, location contracts, insurance expirations, etc., are, as a matter of law, indistinguishable from goodwill possessing no determinable useful life." Rev. Rul. 74-456, 1974-2 C.B. 65, 66. The IRS continued to claim that customer-based intangibles generally are in the nature of goodwill, representing "the customer structure of a business, their value lasting until an indeterminate time in the future." Nonetheless, it acknowledged that, "in an unusual case," the taxpayer may prove that the "asset

335

or a portion thereof does not possess the characteristics of goodwill, is susceptible of valuation, and is of use to the taxpayer in its trade or business for only a limited period of time." *Ibid.* Under these circumstances, the IRS recognized the possibility that the customer-based intangible asset could be depreciated over its useful life.

Despite the suggestion by the Court of Appeals in this case that the mass asset rule is "now outdated," 945 F. 2d at 561, it continues to guide the decisions of the Tax Court with respect to certain intangible assets. In *Ithaca Industries, Inc. v. Commissioner,* 97 T.C. 253 (1991), for example, the Tax Court recently considered whether a taxpayer could depreciate the value allocated to the trained work force of a purchased going concern over the length of time each employee remained with the purchasing company. The court acknowledged that "whether the assembled work force is an intangible asset with an ascertainable value and a limited useful life separate from goodwill or going-concern value is a question of fact." *Id.* at 263-264. After reviewing the record, it concluded that the mass asset rule applied to prohibit the depreciation of the cost of acquiring the assembled work force:

> "Although the assembled work force is used to produce income, this record fails to show that its value diminishes as a result of the passing of time or through use. As an employee terminated his or her employment, another would be hired and trained to take his or her place. While the assembled work force might be subject to temporary attrition as well as expansion through departure of some employees and the hiring of others, it would not be depleted due to the passage of time or as a result of use. The turnover rate of employees represents merely the ebb and flow of a continuing work force. An employee's leaving does not interrupt or destroy the continued existence of the whole." *Id.* at 267.

As a factual matter, the Tax Court found that the taxpayer hired a new worker only so he could replace a worker "who resigned, retired, or was fired." *Id.,* at 268. The court found that the "assembled work force" was a nondiminishing asset; new employees were trained in order to keep the "assembled work force" unchanged, and the cost of the training was a deductible expense. *Id.* at 271.

Since 1973, when *Houston Chronicle* clarified that the availability of the depreciation allowance was primarily a question of fact, taxpayers have sought to depreciate a wide variety of customer-based intangibles. The courts that have found these assets depreciable have based their conclusions on carefully developed factual records. In *Richard S. Miller & Sons, Inc. v. United States,* 210 Ct. Cl. 431, 537 F.2d 446 (1976), for example, the court considered whether a taxpayer was entitled to a depreciation deduction for 1,383 insurance expirations that it had purchased from another insurer. The court concluded that the taxpayer had carried its heavy burden of proving that the expirations had an ascertainable value separate and distinct from goodwill and had a limited useful life, the duration of which could be ascertained with reasonable accuracy. The court acknowledged that the insurance expirations constituted a "mass asset" the useful life of which had to be "determined from facts relative to the whole, and not from experience with any particular policy or account involved." *Id.* at 443 . . . The court also noted, however, that the mass asset rule does not prevent a depreciation deduction "where the expirations as a single asset can be valued separately and, the requisite showing made that the useful life of the information contained in the intangible asset as a whole is of limited duration." *Id.* at 439, 537 F.2d at 452. All the policies were scheduled to expire within three years, but their continuing value lay in their being renewable. Based on statistics gathered over a 5-year period, the taxpayer was able to estimate that the mass asset had a useful life of not more than 10 years from the date of purchase. Any renewals after that time would be attributable to the skill, integrity, and reputation of the taxpayer rather than to the value of the original expirations. "The package of expirations demonstrably was a wasting asset." *Id.* at 444, 537 F.2d at 455. The court ruled that the taxpayer could depreciate the cost of the collection of insurance expirations over the useful life of the mass asset.

In *Citizens & Southern Corp. v. Commissioner*, 91 T.C. 463 (1988), aff 'd, 919 F.2d 1492 (CA 11 1990), the taxpayer argued that it was entitled to depreciate the bank-deposit base acquired in the purchase of nine separate banks.[4] The taxpayer sought to depreciate the present value of the income it expected to derive from the use of the balances of deposit accounts existing at the time of the bank purchases. The Commissioner argued that the value of the core deposits was inextricably related to the value of the overall customer relationship, that is, to goodwill. The Commissioner also argued that the deposit base consisted of purchased, terminable-at-will customer relationships that are equivalent to goodwill as a matter of law. The Tax Court rejected the Commissioner's position, concluding that the taxpayer had demonstrated with sufficient evidence that the economic value attributable to the opportunity to invest the core deposits could be (and, indeed, was) valued and that the fact that new accounts were opened as old accounts closed did not make the original purchased deposit base self-regenerating. *Id* at 499.

The court also concluded that, based on "lifing studies" estimating the percentage of accounts that would close over a given period of time, the taxpayer established that the deposit base had a limited useful life, the duration of which could be ascertained with reasonable accuracy. The taxpayer had established the value of the intangible asset using the cost-savings method, entitling it to depreciate that portion of the purchase price attributable to the present value of the difference between the ongoing costs associated with maintaining the core deposits and the cost of the market alternative for funding its loans and other investments. *Id.* at 510.

The Tax Court reached the same result in *Colorado National Bankshares, Inc. v. Commissioner,* 60 TCM (CCH) 771 (1990), aff'd 984 F.2d 383 (CA 10 1993). The Tax Court concluded that:

> "the value of the deposit base does not depend upon a vague hope that customers will patronize the bank for some unspecified length of time in the future. The value of the deposit base rests upon the ascertainable probability that inertia will cause depositors to leave their funds on deposit for predictable periods of time." *Id.* at 789.

The court specifically found, that the deposit accounts could be identified; that they had limited lives that could be estimated with reasonable accuracy; and that they could be valued with a fair degree of accuracy. They were also not self-regenerating. It is these characteristics which separate them from general goodwill and permits separate valuation." *Ibid.*

Although acknowledging the "analytic force" of cases, such as those discussed above, the Court of Appeals in the present case characterized them as "no more than a minority strand amid the phalanx of cases" that have adopted the Government's position on the meaning of goodwill. 945 F.2d at 565. "In any case, consistent with the prevailing case law, we believe that the [IRS] is correct in asserting that, for tax purposes, there are some intangible assets that, notwithstanding that they have wasting lives that can be estimated with reasonable accuracy and ascertainable values, are nonetheless goodwill and nondepreciable." *Id.* at 568. The Court of Appeals concluded further that in "the context of the sale of a going concern, it is simply often too difficult for the taxpayer and the court to separate the value of the list qua list from the

---

[4] The term "deposit base" describes "the intangible asset that arises in a purchase transaction representing the present value of the future stream of income to be derived from employing the purchased core deposits of a bank." *Citizens & Southern Corp. v. Commissioner*, 91 T.C., at 465.

goodwill value of the customer relationships/structure." *Ibid*. We agree with that general observation. It is often too difficult for taxpayers to separate depreciable intangible assets from goodwill. But sometimes they manage to do it. And whether or not they have been successful in any particular case is a question of fact.

The Government concedes: "The premise of the regulatory prohibition against the depreciation of goodwill is that, like stock in a corporation, a work of art, or raw land, goodwill has no determinate useful life of specific duration." Brief for United States 13. *See* also *Richard S. Miller & Sons, Inc. v. United States*, 210 Ct. Cl. at 437, 537 F.2d at 450 ("Goodwill is a concept that embraces many intangible elements and is presumed to have a useful life of indefinite duration").

The entire justification for refusing to permit the depreciation of goodwill evaporates, however, when the taxpayer demonstrates that the asset in question wastes over an ascertainable period of time. It is more faithful to the purposes of the Code to allow the depreciation deduction under these circumstances, for "the Code endeavors to match expenses with the revenues of the taxable period to which they are properly attributable, thereby resulting in a more accurate calculation of net income for tax purposes." *INDOPCO, Inc. v. Commissioner*, 503 U.S. [79], (1992).

In the case that first established the principle that goodwill was not depreciable, the Eighth Circuit recognized that the reason for treating goodwill differently was simple and direct: "As good will does not suffer wear and tear, does not become obsolescent, is not used up in the operation of the business, depreciation, as such, cannot be charged against it." *Red Wing Malting Co. v. Willcuts*, 15 F.2d 626, 633 (1926) . . . It must follow that if a taxpayer can prove with reasonable accuracy that an asset used in the trade or business or held for the production of income has a value that wastes over an ascertainable period of time, that asset is depreciable under § 167, regardless of the fact that its value is related to the expectancy of continued patronage. The significant question for purposes of depreciation is not whether the asset falls "within the core of the concept of goodwill," Brief for United States 19, but whether the asset is capable of being valued and whether that value diminishes over time. In a different context, the IRS itself succinctly articulated the relevant principle: "Whether or not an intangible asset, or a tangible asset, is depreciable for Federal income tax purposes depends upon the determination that the asset is actually exhausting, and that such exhaustion is susceptible of measurement." Rev. Rul. 68-483, 1968-2 Cum. Bul. 91-92. . . .

Petitioner has borne successfully its substantial burden of proving that "paid subscribers" constitutes an intangible asset with an ascertainable value and a limited useful life, the duration of which can be ascertained with reasonable accuracy. It has proved that the asset is not self-regenerating but rather wastes as the finite number of component subscriptions are canceled over a reasonably predictable period of time. The relationship this asset may have to the expectancy of continued patronage is irrelevant, for it satisfies all the necessary conditions to qualify for the depreciation allowance under § 167 of the Code.

The judgment of the Court of Appeals is reversed, and the case is remanded for further proceedings consistent with this opinion.

It is so ordered

[Judge Souter's dissent is omitted.]

D. OVERVIEW OF § 197
Read § 197(a)-(d).

The *Newark Morning Ledger* decision invited a potential flood of litigation that depended on exhaustive appraisals of fact. For example, assume you planned to buy a health club for a price well in excess of the cost of its hardware. The club enjoys a good reputation, has a well known name, reliable employees, and has a loyal customer base that the company regularly bombards with mailings. How would you go about sorting out how much of the premium in excess of the value of the hardware was paid for the intangibles and what each component consisted of? The only realistic solution was new legislation, which Congress delivered in the form of § 197, discussed below.

The 1993 Act prospectively changed the longstanding rule against writing off goodwill and going concern value by making purchased goodwill and going concern value amortizable on the straight-line method over fifteen years. § 197. That was a major change, likely for the better. *See* Reg. § 1.167(a)-3, which provided, "No deduction for depreciation is allowable with respect to goodwill." Now see § 1.197-2.

However, the 1993 Act went beyond that simple goal and, among other things, lengthened the amortization periods of many short-lived intangibles to fifteen years. The latter is obviously to taxpayers' disadvantage.

Section 197 divides intangible property into the following nine groups:

1. goodwill, §197(d)(1)(A)(A)

2. going concern value, §197(d)(1)(B)

3. any of the following intangible items:

    (i) workforce in place including its composition and terms and conditions (contractual or otherwise) of its employment, §197(d)(1)(C)(i)

    (ii) business books and records, operating systems, or any other information base (including lists or other information with respect to current or prospective customers), §197(d)(1)(C)(ii)

    (iii) any patent, copyright, formula, process, design, pattern, knowhow, format, or other similar item, §197(d)(1)(C)(iii)

    (iv) any customer-based intangible,§197(d)(1)(C)(iv)

    (v) any supplier-based intangible, §197(d)(1)(C)(v)

    (vi) any other similar item,§197(d)(1)(C)(vi)

    (vii) any license, permit, or other right granted by a governmental unit or an agency or instrumentality thereof, §197(d)(1)(D)

    (viii) any covenant not to compete (or other arrangement to the extent such arrangement has substantially the same effect as a covenant not to compete) entered into in connection with an acquisition (directly or indirectly) of an interest in a trade or business or substantial portion thereof, §197(d)(1)(E)

    (ix) any franchise, trademark, or trade name. §197(d)(1)(F)

Intangibles that are always subject to 15-year amortization under § 197. This group includes governmental licenses, franchises, trademarks, trade names, covenants in connection with the acquisition of all or part of a business, and know-how. § 197(d)

Intangibles that are never subject to 15-year amortization under § 197. These include off-the-shelf computer software, interests in tangible property leases, and interests in debt obligations. These are subject to the usual write-offs. For example, self-produced goodwill is not an amortizable section 197 intangible, so it is outside § 197 and not amortizable. § 197(e)

Intangibles that are subject to 15-year amortization under § 197 if transferred in connection with the transfer of all or a substantial part of a business. These consist of goodwill and going concern value, customized computer software, contract rights to receive tangible property or services, patents, copyrights, films, and mortgage servicing rights. This grouping is the primary target of § 197. § 197(c)

Covenants not to compete. These are subject to § 197 where there is a related acquisition of a business by a purchase of either assets or stock. This is a big change and highly disadvantageous to sellers compared to prior law. § 197(d)

To illustrate: P Corp. buys T Corp.'s seed business for $10 million. The parties properly allocated the purchase price on a Form 8594 as follows:

Trademark	$ 1.5M
Goodwill	$ 3.0M
Nonsection 197 assets	$ 5.5M
Total	$10.0M

Section 197 allows P Corp. annual amortization deductions of $100,000 for fifteen years with respect to the trademark and $200,000 with respect to the goodwill. If the president/former owner of the company also enters into a covenant not to compete. Covenants not to compete are written off over fifteen years rather than over the life of the covenant.

Abandonment of Intangibles. Aside from lengthening the amortization lives of many intangibles, § 197 carries a heavy stick in that it prevents deductions for abandonments of intangibles unless and until the taxpayer disposes of all its § 197 intangibles in the acquired business. If there is an abandonment, there is no loss, and the "disappearing basis" is assigned to the remaining intangibles. § 197(f)

To illustrate: At the end of the fourth year following the acquisition, when P's remaining basis in the trademark is $1.1 million, P abandons the trademark. P cannot claim a $1.1 million loss for the abandonment of the trademark unless P establishes that the goodwill acquired from T has become entirely worthless. P will continue to amortize the cost of the abandoned trademark over § 197's 15-year amortization period.

To illustrate: P buys all of T's stock for $9 million and also pays T's sole shareholder $1 million for a three-year covenant not to compete. Under § 197, P is allowed amortization deductions for 15 years of only $66,667 per year with respect to the covenant. At the end of three years when the covenant expires, P cannot deduct the unamortized balance of the covenant's purchase price unless P also disposes of its entire interest in T's business (assets and stock); rather, P continues to amortize the price of the expired covenant over the remainder of § 197's fifteen-year amortization period (or, if earlier, when P disposes of its entire interest in T's business).

E. TRANSACTIONAL GUIDE TO NEW CODE SECTION 197

Because § 197 amortizes both purchased goodwill and a noncompete over 15 years, from a tax standpoint buyer no longer benefits from allocating purchase price to a noncompete rather than to goodwill in a [taxable] acquisition. Moreover, depending on the circumstances, there are two potential benefits to allocating purchase price to goodwill rather than to a noncompete:

First, seller's gain on the sale of goodwill generally is taxable as LTCG whereas a noncompete payment is taxed as ordinary income ("OI"). Given the difference between the new highest marginal OI rate (39.6 percent)[5] and the LTCG rate (generally 20 percent)[6] for individuals, the tax savings can be significant where seller is an S corporation, a partnership of individuals, or a sole proprietor. However, where seller is a C corporation, it may still prefer a noncompete payment to its shareholders (although taxed to the shareholders as OI) rather than a goodwill payment to the corporate seller, because the noncompete payment would be taxed only at the shareholder level and thus avoid corporate-level tax.

Because a C corporation is taxed at the same rate on LTCG and OI, a C corporation receiving a noncompete payment often will be indifferent to this issue, unless it has an available capital loss which can only be used against CG.

Second, for GAAP purposes, [the] buyer can amortize goodwill over a period of up to 40 years, whereas a noncompete payment is amortized for GAAP purposes over the life of the noncompete agreement. Therefore, goodwill has a less adverse impact on GAAP earnings in the early years, and hence, is a more attractive GAAP asset than a short-lived noncompete agreement. The favorable GAAP earnings result produced by goodwill is particularly important for a publicly traded buyer (or a buyer which anticipates an IPO).

Given the high level of goodwill in the balance sheets of U.S. corporations, there is a chance to amortize or depreciate a large part of the purchase price of a corporation, making the taxable acquisition much more attractive (compared with a tax-free reorganization). One can project that § 197 will increase the demand for high-intangible businesses, and the associated deductions will partially offset the initial tax cost of choosing a taxable acquisition. The only apparent disadvantage of § 197 is the length of the amortization period. It will be interesting to see if lobbying forces arise to press for a shortening of the § 197 lives. A strong counter argument to allowing such a shortening is that the expenses of developing goodwill are often currently deductible, the most important of which is advertising expenses. *See* C. Johnson, *The Mass Asset Rule Is Not the Blob That Ate Los Angeles, 15 Tax Notes 1603 (1992), and C. Johnson, Newark Morning Ledger: Intangibles Are Not Amortizable*, 57 Tax Notes 691 (1992). In other words, the system is too lavish already to justify sweetening it any more.

NOTE

Allocation agreements between buyer and seller. Assuming that the buyer and seller prepare their Form 8594 as required, can the IRS knock it over by quarrelling with the allocations? Sections 1060(b) and 1.1060-1 suggest so.

---

[5] As of late 2018, the highest marginal OI rate is 37%.

[6] As of late 2018, the LTCG rate is generally 20%.

PROBLEM 19-1

Eastern Enterprises is a corporation that operates various businesses including a retail store. Mr. Pimm is a minority shareholder of Eastern. In complete redemption of Pimm's stock within the meaning of § 302(b)(3), Eastern distributes to Pimm all of the assets of its retail store, which is not a trade or business in Pimm's hands, but was a separate trade or business in Eastern's hands. The assets have a gross value of $3 million. Is this an "applicable asset acquisition?" *See* Reg. § 1.1060-1(b)(1).

PROBLEM 19-2

Aggressor Corp. approaches Target, Inc. with an offer to purchase all of Target's business assets, so as to make it a new division of Aggressor, which include:

- Manufacturing equipment with a fair market value of $50 and a basis of $30;
- A tract of real estate with a fair market value of $500 and a basis of $300;
- A patent for a new machine that will double the speed of production with an estimated fair market value of $200 and a basis of $50; and
- Office furniture with a basis and value of $200.

Aggressor Corp. pays Target, Inc. $1,000 as the entire purchase price.

1) How many classes of assets are there in this transaction §1060 and what are they?

2) How will Target, Inc. compute its gain or loss on the transaction, asset-by-asset or in the aggregate?

3) Will the parties have to report the prices consistently? If so, how must they report the prices?

4) How will any purchase price in excess of the total fair market values of the assets listed above be treated?

5) How much of the purchase price will be allocated to goodwill and going concern value?

6) What amount of gain or loss will Target, Inc. recognize on the transaction?

7) Can Aggressor write off any of the goodwill? If so, over what period?

    a.   If instead Target's shareholders, who were all active employees, signed a covenant not to compete for an amount equal to what would otherwise have been the value of the goodwill and going concern value payable in years 1-3, does this change the tax benefits to the buyer?

    b.   Are the sellers better or worse off, all things otherwise being equal?

8) If the parties allocated part of the purchase price to customer-based intangibles that suddenly become worthless in year four, can Aggressor deduct them in year four?

9) If Aggressor developed its own patent after the acquisition at a cost of $100, over how many years would it be able to write off the patent? Compare §§ 197 and 167(f).

10) What if the party with whom the covenant not to compete was entered into dies? Can Aggressor write off the covenant at that time? Just use your imagination to answer the question.

F. STOCK PURCHASES

1. THE § 338(g) ELECTION

Suppose that a buyer is compelled for business reasons to acquire assets but the seller is only willing to sell stock. Under pre-1983 law, if the corporate buyer bought 80% control of the target's stock and then liquidated the target within a short period of time, the rules of §§ 332/337 did not apply, and the buyer could step up the basis of the target's assets to fair market value just as if it had bought the assets of the liquidating corporation (even though it was not taxed on the liquidating distribution, under then § 337).

The prior rules were useless to a buyer who could not liquidate the target, say because the target owned irreplaceable franchises or other licenses to do business. This seemed unduly rigid, and, as a result, Congress enacted § 338, which enabled a corporate buyer in this situation to elect to change the basis of assets owned by a newly-purchased controlled subsidiary to their fair market values without the necessity of actually liquidating the subsidiary. This was very welcome to taxpayers because the election produced a cost basis for the target's assets for purposes of depreciation and avoided tax on resale of unwanted assets owned by the target. If the target's assets had built-in loss rather than gain, the buyer simply did not make the election and preserved the subsidiary's inside losses.

As a result of the legislative repeal of *General Utilities* in 1986, however, § 338 and its seemingly endless Regulations became what are probably the largest pieces of deadwood in the Internal Revenue Code. Section 338 was passed as part of the Tax Equity and Fiscal Responsibility Act of 1982, at a time when distributions of assets of liquidating corporations were not taxed to the corporation, that is, while the *General Utilities* doctrine was in full bloom.

The original heart of § 338 is the § 338(g) election whereby a corporation, the control of which was recently purchased, can electively hypothesize that it went through a complete liquidation in which it sold all its assets to its shareholders at midnight of day one and repurchased those assets on the dawn of the following day at fair market value. This avoids all the problems inherent in making actual transfers of assets as part of an actual liquidation, and as such it is a great improvement over prior law.

The difficulty is that § 338(g) rarely offers an appetizing outcome because of the repeal of the *General Utilities* doctrine, which exposes the gains that the corporation recognizes in the course of its liquidation to taxation. It makes no sense for the target to pay tax on its built-in gains now in order to obtain depreciation in the same amount later. In some situations the election may still be valuable, however, such as where the target has a large loss carryforward that can neutralize the *General Utilities* tax imposed by § 336.

The mechanics of § 338(g) can be extremely elaborate, but the basic idea is that an acquiring corporation can elect to treat the purchase price of the stock (which may have been bought in different batches at different times) as the purchase price of the assets of the acquired corporation.

Section 338 applies only if certain preconditions are satisfied. The basic requirement is that a corporate purchaser must, within a twelve-month period beginning with its first purchase of stock, buy at least 80% of the target corporation's stock by vote and by value. This produces a "qualified stock purchase." In turn, § 338(g) allows the purchasing corporation to elect the deemed liquidation.

The government has graciously produced Form 8023, which the corporation files to make the election. The corporation must file the form not later than the fifteenth day of the ninth month following the acquisition date, meaning the date when the acquiring corporation got 80% control of the target corporation. § 338(g). The election is irrevocable. § 1.338-2(d). Notice that even though the purchaser might only get 80% of the stock, the § 338(g) election affects all the assets – no different from buying 100% of the stock.

2. DEEMED ELECTIONS UNDER § 338

Section 338(e) provides that there is a *deemed* § 338 election if the purchasing corporation (or any of its affiliates) bought any of the target (or target affiliate) assets before, or in addition to, buying the target's stock. This was designed to prevent acquirors from selectively purchasing some assets and enjoying a cost basis in them while taking the rest of the targets assets with carryover basis by not electing a § 338(g) deemed sale. "All or nothing" became the new rule, and if any asset was purchased at cost, all of them were deemed purchased pursuant to the deemed election. This was capable of producing catastrophic results.

Fortunately, the final Regulations have eliminated the former deemed § 338 election by providing that a deemed election generally cannot arise as a result of the asset consistency rules. Reg. § 1.338-8(a). Rather, if an asset is acquired from a target that is a member of a consolidated group, the acquiring corporation gets a carryover basis in that asset.

PROBLEM 19-3

P Corp. wants to acquire T Corp., but T Corp. is unwilling to sell its assets to P Corp. However, T Corp.'s shareholders are willing to sell P Corp. 100% of their T Corp. stock. P Corp. is concerned that buying the T Corp. stock rather than T Corp.'s assets will not allow P Corp. to depreciate the T Corp. assets as it would like.

1) P Corp. visits you, wanting to know whether there is any way it can structure the transaction so as to be suitable for all parties.

2) Would your answer to P Corp. change if T Corp.'s shareholders were only willing to sell 75% of their T Corp. stock to P Corp?

3) Assume T Corp. had a large net operating loss carryover from prior years. Could the NOL be used in connection with the transaction?

3. SECTION 338(h)(10) BILATERAL ELECTION
Read § 338(h)(10).

What you are about to read is important for several reasons. One is that it reflects a progressive approach to the taxation of corporate restructurings by means of elections as opposed to actual transactions. Second, the materials operate as a review of concepts you have already read.

Now, a word about consolidated returns again. An affiliated group of corporations can elect to file a single *consolidated tax return* under the authority of § 1501 and its legislative Regulations authorized under § 1502. The consolidated return treats the corporation much as if the group were just one large corporation. The possible advantages include offsetting capital or operating losses of one corporation against the gains or operating profits of another, and of deferring income on intercompany transactions.

An *affiliated group* is a parent-subsidiary chain or brother-sister group (with a common parent) of corporations in which at least 80% of the combined voting power and at least 80% of the total value of stock (except nonvoting preferred stock) are owned in so-called "includible corporations." § 1504(a). The latter limit ensures that foreign corporations, insurance companies, and charities cannot file consolidated returns with business corporations.

Now, assume that Parent owns all the stock of Target, and that Parent and Target file a consolidated return. Assume that Acquiror wants to buy the stock of Target. If Parent and Acquiror elect under § 338(h)(10), and Acquiror's purchase of stock was a "qualified stock purchase," then the transaction is treated for tax purposes as if:

1. Target sells its assets to Acquiror's theoretical "new" subsidiary ("new S");

2. Target reports a gain or loss; and

3. Target liquidates into Parent under § 332/337.

Note that although subsidiary (and therefore Parent) reports a gain or loss on the imaginary sale of assets to new S, Parent will report no gain or loss on the actual sale of Target stock. That is the point of the § 338(h)(10) election. It permits buyer and seller to agree that the tax results are the same as steps 1-3 above, but without having to go through the trouble of an actual liquidation and sale of assets. This also preserves the Target's corporate existence for nontax purposes.

4. SECTION 336(e) UNILATERAL ELECTION
Read § 336(e).

Section 336(e) is the "country cousin" of § 338(h)(10). Section 336(e) is intended to produce the same tax result as § 338(h)(10), and it simply extends it to situations where the subsidiary was at least 80%-owned by the seller corporation but did not file a consolidated return. This is sensible because the seller could have avoided gain on the sale of stock by liquidating the controlled subsidiary first under § 332 and then selling the target's assets in order to recognize that gain instead.

A mystifying difference from § 338(h)(10) is that the seller can elect § 336(e) unilaterally, as opposed to the mandatory joint election under § 338(h)(10).

Thus, if the buyer of target's stock wants the target's assets to have a fair market value basis, the buyer presumably must bind the seller to make a § 336(e) election as part of the sales contract. The regulations affirm this requirement. Treas. Reg. § 1.336-2(h)(1)(i).

5. REVIEW OF SOME OPTIONS

An acquiring corporation has a number of choices of what to do with a target subsidiary it purchases:

- It can do nothing, and perhaps file a consolidated return with the new subsidiary;

- It can liquidate the target company under §§ 332/337 and take a carryover basis in the target's assets, along with the target's other tax attributes. This is nontaxable to both the target and acquiror corporations;

- It can make the § 338(g) election on the target subsidiary's behalf and, in most cases, cause the target to pay taxes on the hypothetical liquidation; or

- If the subsidiary was a member of a consolidated group, the acquiring corporation can elect § 338(h)(10) together with the seller, which produces the equivalent of a taxable acquisition of the target's assets, thus affecting the basis of the target's assets and extinguishing its tax history, with any taxes due borne by the selling parent corporation.

- Further, the acquiring corporation can achieve the same result, even if the target was an unconsolidated 80%-owned subsidiary, by means of the § 336(e) election. Keep in mind that in both cases, the transaction is a sale of target stock for state law purposes.

- If the buyer acquires somewhat less than 80% of the sub's stock by vote or by value, it can put the subsidiary through a taxable liquidation and §§ 331 and 336 would apply to buyer and subsidiary, respectively.

PROBLEM 19-4

Target Corp. and Parent Corp. are members of an affiliated group of corporations, filing a consolidated federal income tax return under § 1501. Parent owns 100% of Target stock, in which Parent has a basis of $10. Target Corp. has E & P of $15 and a basis of $90 in its assets, but they are worth $110. Acquiso, Inc. wants to buy the stock of Target Corp. for $110.

1) If Parent sells its Target stock, how much gain will it report?

2) If Parent sells the Target stock, will it have any impact on the basis of the assets of Target?

3) If, instead, Target Corp. liquidates into Parent Corp., what would be the income tax and basis effects? Glance at § 381 for information about the survival of Target's tax attributes in Parent's hands.

4) If as a next step (after "3)") Parent sold the former Target assets to Acquiso, Inc., how much gain or loss would Parent report?

5) Is there any reason to believe that in the transaction described in "4)" Acquiso, Inc. would get the tax attributes of Target?

6) If Acquiso, Inc. then contributed the assets it bought from Parent to a newly formed subsidiary, what basis would the newly formed subsidiary take in the assets?

7) Is there a way for Parent and Acquiso, Inc. to structure this transaction without having to first liquidate Target, and if so, what will be the tax consequences to Parent Corp?

8) Assuming the necessary election is made, which corporation winds up with Target Corp's earnings and profits?

9) Must both entities elect to get a § 338(h)(10) result?

10) If Parent Corp. and Target Corp. do not file a consolidated return, is there an alternative route to the same tax result? If so, at whose election is it available? *Consider* § 336(e).

11) In order for § 338(h)(10) to apply, how much of Target Corp.'s stock must the Acquiso Inc. obtain and over what period of time? *See* § 1504(a)(2) and § 338(g) & (h)(1), Reg. § 1.338(h)(10)-1(c)(1).

Chapter 20

TAX-FREE CORPORATE DIVISIONS

There are many sound business reasons for dividing up a single corporation's lines of business into several corporations. For example, it may be a good business judgment to separate a risky enterprise from a more stable one so that if a lawsuit is brought against the risky enterprise the other corporation will be free of liability. Another reason to break up a company might be to put an end to warfare between different groups of shareholders, or one might want to separate one division in connection with preparing for a sale of that or another division. Sometimes it is necessary to spin off a newly-formed division or subsidiary in order to comply an with an antitrust decree.

These corporate separations may be done solely at the corporate level and on a pro-rata basis or they may be arranged so that only one group of shareholders winds up with the stock of a particular corporation. Tax-free corporate divisions break down into three groupings:

1. *A spin-off.* This is a distribution by one corporation of the stock of its subsidiary corporation to the parent's shareholders with respect to their shares, much like a simple distribution of assets. The subsidiary may already be in existence or may be newly created to accommodate the transaction;

2. *A split-off.* This is the same as the spin-off, except that the shareholders of the parent corporation give up part of their stock in the parent corporation in exchange for stock of the subsidiary, much like a redemption; and

3. *A split-up.* Here the parent corporation distributes the stock of two or more of its subsidiaries, whether newly-created or previously existing, in complete liquidation of the parent corporation.

Technically speaking, there are two categories of tax-free corporate separations:

a) The so-called corporate "divisions" involving a spin-off, split-off or split-up of preexisting subsidiaries, using the rules of §§ 355, 356, and 358 alone; and

b) The "divisive reorganizations" that involve two steps under § 368(a)(1)(D), namely the transfer of assets to one or more subsidiaries and the distribution of the subsidiary stock as in the pure corporate divisions described above. The two-step division is the divisive form of what is known in tax parlance as a "Type D" reorganization.

This Chapter emphasizes the corporate divisions under § 355 alone; the two-step divisive reorganization uses § 355 plus the law of tax-free acquisitive reorganizations are covered later in Chapter 21. The hard part is understanding § 355.

ILLUSTRATIVE PROBLEM

Individuals A and B are equal shareholders of X Corporation, which has conducted two active businesses for more than five years, one in X Corporation and one in a wholly-owned subsidiary, Y Corporation. A and B want to go their separate ways, or at least, and first, to make Y Corporation a sister (not a subsidiary) of X Corporation, owned directly by A and B.

A. To this end, X Corporation distributes all its stock in Y Corporation to A and B, pro-rata. If that is all, it amounts to a spin-off, a distribution of the subsidiary's stock to the two shareholders of X Corporation with respect to their shares (not in exchange for anything). Now, X and Y are brother-sister corporations directly (and jointly) owned by A and B. What are the tax issues? Suppose the stock in Y Corporation had a basis to X Corporation of $150x but was worth $300x at the time of distribution.

1. Will gain or loss be recognized to the distributing corporation (X Corporation)? The answer is that while gain is realized by X Corporation, it is not recognized. *See* § 355(c). Section 361 only applies if this is part of a "D reorganization," as defined in § 368. A subject of study in Chapter 21.

2. Will gain or loss be recognized to the distributee shareholders, A and B? No, if everything is done right, by virtue of § 355. If X Corporation also distributed "boot" (other property) then § 356 requires gain recognition up to the amount of boot, perhaps as a dividend, to the extent § 301 would provide. *See* § 357 if liabilities were assumed or property taken subject to debt by A and B.

3. What basis do A and B take in the Y Corporation shares distributed to them by X? The answer is that their basis is determined under § 358 by allocating the appropriate amount (according to relative fair market values) of A and B's basis in their X Corporation shares to their newly-received Y Corporation shares. *See* § 358(b), (c).

4. What basis effects will the division have on the distributing corporation? None, except X Corporation no longer owns $300x worth of shares in Y Corporation and no longer has any basis in those shares (formerly it had a $150x basis in them).

5. What are the collateral consequences? The earnings and profits and other tax characteristics internal to Y Corporation will generally continue with Y Corporation in the hands of its new owners. The holding periods for A and B in their Y Corporation shares will include (tack onto) the holding periods of the X Corporation shares they held before (and still hold). *See* § 1223(1).

B. Now suppose, as a simple variant based on the original facts of this illustration, that A and B knew that they wanted to go their separate ways and A wanted to take with him the X Corp. division's assets and business and B wanted the Y Corp. subsidiary's assets and business. To that end, suppose X Corp. distributed all its shares in Y Corp. to B in return for all his shares in X Corp. A simply remains the holder of his shares (now 100%) of X Corp. This is a split-off. As a result, each individual has the business he or she wants, in separate corporate form. There has been a separation at both the corporate and shareholder levels. Assume A and B each has a basis of $50x in his shares in X Corp. before the transaction.

1. Must gain or loss be recognized by the distributing corporation, X Corp.? No. *See* § 355(c) (§ 336(c) if this were a split-up). If this were also part of a "D reorganization," § 361 could apply.

2. Must gain or loss be recognized to the distributee shareholders, A and B? No. *See* § 354. Exceptions for boot are in § 356, and other limitations in § 357 (liabilities). A simply rides through this transaction, perhaps not even realizing gain or loss.

3. What basis do A and B have in their shares? A's basis remains the same in his shares in X Corp., which merely remain in his hands. B's basis in his X Corp. shares (which he surrendered in the exchange) becomes his basis in the Y Corp. shares that he received in the tax-free exchange. *See* § 358.

4. What are the basis effects to X Corp.? X Corp. no longer owns stock in Y Corp. and therefore has lost its basis in those shares. Its basis in other assets does not change.

5. What collateral tax issues ensue? There isn't much change because X Corp. and Y Corp. both preexisted the split-off and also survive it. B's basis and holding period (tacked) in Y shares will equal what he had in the X Corp. shares he formerly owned. *See* §§ 358, 1223(1). The earnings and profits of each corporation stay with that corporation.

C. If Y Corp.'s business was previously conducted by X Corp. as a division, it is necessary for X Corp. to incorporate that division in a separate subsidiary. Section 351 provides nonrecognition and carryover basis. In fact, that incorporation, if coupled with the division distribution, would qualify as a "D reorganization" under § 368(a)(1)(D), with the same operative nonrecognition and basis rules applying, namely §§ 355-57, 358, and 361 as to X Corp.

D. If X Corp. had formed or had owned two subsidiaries, Y Corp. and Z Corp., and distributed Y Corp. and Z Corp. stock to A and B, respectively, in exchange for all their shares in X Corp., that would have been a split-up (alone, or as part of a "D reorganization") subject to the same sets of nonrecognition rules.

SPINOFFS

The law prior to 1954 was generous with respect to spin-offs, allowing them to occur tax-free as long as property was passed from one corporation to another and the first corporation, its shareholders, or both combined, controlled the second corporation. If these conditions were met the shareholders of the first corporation paid no tax when they received the stock of the second corporation in connection with the plan of reorganization. *See* Revenue Act of 1924, Pub. L. No. 176, § 203(c), 43 Stat. 253, 256. The tax policy presupposition was that the corporate rearrangement was a mere change in the form of ownership of the same assets by the same owners (known as continuity of proprietary interest and continuity of business enterprise) and therefore was entitled to nonrecognition treatment – much as in the case of a plain § 351 incorporation. This unusually generous provision virtually invited shareholders to put liquid assets into newly-formed corporations and then distribute the stock of the newly-formed corporations to shareholders, leaving the shareholders free to claim that the whole transaction was a tax-free reorganization, rather than a taxable dividend. Those shareholders could then liquidate the recently distributed corporation and take out the cash or liquid assets at long-term capital gain rates under the predecessor of § 331(a).

The following landmark decision considered such a transaction and in so doing added an important judicial limitation to the corporate acquisition and the division rules. It is such an important case that it is known to most tax lawyers by name.

GREGORY v. HELVERING
293 U.S. 465 (1935)

MR. JUSTICE SUTHERLAND delivered the opinion of the Court.

Petitioner in 1928 was the owner of all the stock of United Mortgage Corporation. That corporation held among its assets 1,000 shares of the Monitor Securities Corporation. For the sole purpose of procuring a transfer of these shares to herself in order to sell them for her individual profit, and, at the same time, diminish the amount of income tax which would result from a direct transfer by way of dividend, she sought to bring about a "reorganization" under §112(g) of the Revenue Act of 1928, set forth later in this opinion [the predecessor of §§ 354 and 368]. To that end, she caused the Averill Corporation to be organized under the laws of Delaware on September 18, 1928. Three days later, the United Mortgage Corporation transferred to the Averill Corporation the 1,000 shares of Monitor stock, for which all the shares of the Averill Corporation were issued to the petitioner. On September 24, the Averill Corporation was dissolved, and liquidated by distributing all its assets, namely, the Monitor shares, to the petitioner. No other business was ever transacted, or intended to be transacted, by that company. Petitioner immediately sold the Monitor shares for $133,333.33. She returned [reported] for taxation, as capital net gain, the sum of $76,007.88, based upon an apportioned cost of $57,325.45. Further details are unnecessary. It is not disputed that if the interposition of the so-called reorganization was ineffective, petitioner became liable for a much larger tax as a result of the transaction.

The Commissioner of Internal Revenue, being of opinion that the reorganization attempted was without substance and must be disregarded, held that petitioner was liable for a tax as though the United corporation had paid her a dividend consisting of the amount realized from the sale of the Monitor shares. In a proceeding before the Board of Tax Appeals, that body rejected the commissioner's view and upheld that of petitioner, 27 B.T.A. 223. Upon a review of the latter decision, the Circuit Court of Appeals sustained the commissioner and reversed the board, holding that there had been no "reorganization" within the meaning of the statute. 69 F. (2d) 809. Petitioner applied to this court for a writ of certiorari, which the government, considering the question one of importance, did not oppose. We granted the writ. . . .

[T]he Revenue Act of 1928 . . . deals with the subject of gain or loss resulting from the sale or exchange of property. Such gain or loss is to be recognized in computing the tax, except as provided in that section. The provisions of the section, so far as they are pertinent to the question here presented, follow:

. . . [The predecessor of § 354(a)] Distribution of Stock on Reorganization. If there is distributed, in pursuance of a plan of reorganization, to a shareholder in a corporation a party to the reorganization, stock or securities in such corporation or in another corporation a party to the reorganization, without the surrender by such shareholder of stock or securities in such a corporation, no gain to the distributee from the receipt of such stock of securities shall be recognized. . . .

(i) Definition of Reorganization. As used in this section . . .

The term "reorganization" under [§ 368(a)(1)(D)] means a transfer by a corporation of all or a part of its assets to another corporation if immediately after the transfer the transferor or its stockholders or both are in control of the corporation to which the assets are transferred.

It is earnestly contended on behalf of the taxpayer that since every element required by [current § 368(a)(1)(D)] is to be found in what was done, a statutory reorganization was effected; and that the motive of the taxpayer thereby to escape payment of a tax will not alter the result or make unlawful what the statute allows. It is quite true that if a reorganization in reality was effected . . . the ulterior purpose mentioned will be disregarded. The legal right of a taxpayer to decrease the amount of what otherwise would be his taxes, or altogether avoid them, by means which the law permits, cannot be doubted . . .

But the question for determination is whether what was done, apart from the tax motive, was the thing which the statute intended. The reasoning of the court below in justification of a negative answer leaves little to be said.

When [§ 368(a)(1)(D)] speaks of a transfer of assets by one corporation to another, it means a transfer made "in pursuance of a plan of reorganization" . . . of corporate business; and not a transfer of assets by one corporation to another in pursuance of a plan having no relation to the business of either, as plainly is the case here. Putting aside, then, the question of motive in respect of taxation altogether, and fixing the character of the proceeding by what actually occurred, what do we find? Simply an operation having no business or corporate purpose – a mere device which put on the form of a corporate reorganization as a disguise for concealing its real character, and the sole object and accomplishment of which was the consummation of a preconceived plan, not to reorganize a business or any part of a business, but to transfer a parcel of corporate shares to the petitioner. No doubt, a new and valid corporation was created. But that corporation was nothing more than a contrivance to the end last described. It was brought into existence for no other purpose; it performed, as it was intended from the beginning it should perform, no other function. When that limited function had been exercised, it immediately was put to death.

In these circumstances, the facts speak for themselves and are susceptible of but one interpretation. The whole undertaking, though conducted according to the terms of [§ 368(a)(I)(D)], was in fact an elaborate and devious form of conveyance masquerading as a corporate reorganization, and nothing else. The rule which excludes from consideration the motive of tax avoidance is not pertinent to the situation, because the transaction upon its face lies outside the plain intent of the statute. To hold otherwise would be to exalt artifice above reality and to deprive the statutory provision in question of all serious purpose.

Judgment affirmed.

A. TAX-FREE CORPORATE DIVISIONS UNDER CURRENT LAW
Read § 355(a), (b)(1).

Achieving a tax-free corporate division requires satisfying a cumulative set of tests. If, and only if, all the tests are met, the tax law allows a tax-free distribution by one corporation – known as the "distributing corporation" – of stock or securities (or both combined) of another corporation known as the "controlled corporation" – to shareholders of the distributing corporation with respect to (or in exchange for) their stock, or to security (debt) holders of the distributing corporation in exchange for their securities. Those requirements are discussed under the following headings.

1. CONTROL
Read § 368(c).

The distributing corporation must control the corporation whose stock or securities are being distributed. § 368(c). It is the same definition of "control" as is used in connection with § 351. Control need exist only immediately before the distribution, and the IRS has been generous in allowing pre-distribution restructurings to meet the control requirement. *See, e.g.,* Rev. Rul. 70-18, 1970-1 C.B. 74 (merger of sibling corporations to ensure that the survivor got control).

2. DISTRIBUTION THRESHOLD

The distributing corporation must distribute all of its stock and securities in the controlled corporation, or failing that, distribute enough stock to constitute control. § 368(c). In the latter case the distributing corporation must satisfy the Treasury Department that the retention of stock or securities of the controlled corporation did not occur for reasons having to do with tax avoidance. § 355(a)(1)(D)(ii). Presumably, the concern is that the distributing corporation might make occasional distributions of modest amounts of retained stock and securities instead of paying ordinary dividends. A retention may be justified as a way to satisfy obligations such as those arising under a stock option plan. *See* Rev. Proc. 91-62, 1991-2 C.B. 864, which facilitates private letter ruling requests with respect to retentions of stock.

PROBLEM 20-1

P Corp., a large manufacturing company, owns 90% of the stock of S Corp., a boutique firm that sells only P Corp. products. The other 10% of S Corp. stock is owned by unrelated individuals. P Corp. decides for valid business reasons to distribute all of its S Corp. stock to the P Corp. shareholders at the end of the P Corp.'s tax year. The shareholders of P Corp. each receive 1 share of S Corp. stock for each share of P Corp. stock they hold, and no other transactions or distributions between P Corp. and its shareholders take place regarding P Corp. or S Corp. stock.

1) What type of tax-free corporate division does this transaction resemble, if any?

2) Assuming the transaction did qualify for § 355 treatment:

   (a) How would the basis of the P Corp. stock that each shareholder held be divided between the P stock the shareholder continues to hold and the just received S Corp. stock? *See* Reg. §§ 1.358-2(a) and 1.358-2(c), Example 12.

   (b) Does the shareholder take a fresh holding period in the S Corp. stock? *See* § 1223(1).

3) Would your answer to "(1)" differ if some P Corp. shareholders were required to transfer back their P Corp. stock in exchange for the S Corp. stock they were receiving?

4) Suppose P Corp. also owns 100% of X Corp. stock. Rather than distributing the S Corp. stock to all of its shareholders, P Corp. distributes only S Corp. stock to half of its shareholders. To the other half, P Corp. distributes all of its X Corp. stock. (X Corp. is a 100%-owned subsidiary.) P Corp. then completely liquidates. The S Corp. and X Corp. stock constituting the entirety of its assets. What type of tax-free corporate division, if any, is this?

5) If the transaction in "(4)" failed the non-taxability requirements, how might you classify the transaction?

3. BUSINESS PURPOSE
Read Reg. § 1.355-2(b)(1)-(2).

The Regulations under § 355 demand a business purpose for the distribution at the corporate level. A common difficulty in this realm is that, in the case of closely-held corporations, it is often difficult to differentiate the interests of the corporation from those of its shareholders.

RAFFERTY v. COMMISSIONER
452 F.2d 767 (1st Cir. 1971). *cert. denied*, 408 U.S. 922 (1972)

MCENTEE, CIRCUIT JUDGE.

Taxpayers, Joseph V. Rafferty and wife, appeal from a decision of the Tax Court, 55 T.C. 490, which held that a distribution to them of all the outstanding stock of a real estate holding corporation did not meet the requirements of § 355 of the Internal Revenue Code of 1954 and therefore was taxable as a dividend. Our opinion requires a construction of § 355 and the Regulations thereunder.

The facts, some of which have been stipulated, are relatively simple. The taxpayers own all the outstanding shares of Rafferty Brown Steel Co., Inc. (hereinafter RBS), a Massachusetts corporation engaged in the processing and distribution of cold rolled sheet and strip steel in Longmeadow, Massachusetts. In May 1960, at the suggestion of his accountant, Rafferty organized Teragram Realty Co., Inc., also a Massachusetts corporation. In June of that year RBS transferred its Longmeadow real estate to Teragram in exchange for all of the latter's outstanding stock. Thereupon Teragram leased back this real estate to RBS for ten years at an annual rent of $42,000. In 1962 the taxpayers also organized Rafferty Brown Steel Co., Inc., of Connecticut (RBS Conn.), which corporation acquired the assets of Hawkridge Brothers, a general steel products warehouse in Waterbury, Connecticut. Since its inception the taxpayers have owned all of the outstanding stock in RBS Conn. From 1962 to 1965 Hawkridge leased its real estate in Waterbury to RBS Conn. In 1965 Teragram purchased some unimproved real estate in Waterbury and built a plant there. In the same year it leased this plant to RBS Conn. for a term of fourteen years. Teragram has continued to own and lease the Waterbury real estate to RBS Conn. and the Longmeadow realty to RBS, which companies have continued up to the present time to operate their businesses at these locations.[1]

During the period from 1960 through 1965 Teragram derived all of its income from rent paid by RBS and RBS Conn. Its earned surplus increased from $4,119.05 as of March 31, 1961, to $46,743.35 as of March 31, 1965. The earned surplus of RBS increased from $331,117.97 as of June 30, 1959, to $535,395.77 as of June 30, 1965. In August 1965, RBS distributed its Teragram stock to the taxpayers. Other than this distribution, neither RBS nor Teragram has paid any dividends. Joseph V. Rafferty has been the guiding force behind all three corporations, RBS, RBS Conn., and Teragram. He is the president and treasurer of Teragram which, while it has no office or employees, keeps separate books and records and filed separate tax returns for the years in question.

On various occasions Rafferty consulted his accountant about estate planning, particularly about the orderly disposition of RBS. While he anticipated that his sons would join him at RBS, he wanted to exclude his daughters (and/or his future sons-in-law) from the active management of the steel business. He wished, however, to provide them with property which would produce a steady income. The accountant recommended the formation of Teragram, the distribution of its stock, and the eventual use of this stock as future gifts to the Rafferty daughters. The taxpayers acted on this advice and also on the accountant's opinion that the distribution of Teragram stock would meet the requirements of § 355.

---

[1] Both properties are also suitable for use by other companies in other types of business.

In their 1965 return the taxpayers treated the distribution of Teragram stock as a nontaxable transaction under § 355. The Commissioner viewed it, however, as a taxable dividend and assessed a deficiency. He claimed (a) that the distribution was used primarily as a device for the distribution of the earnings and profits of RBS or Teragram or both, and (b) that Teragram did not meet the active business requirements of § 355.

We turn first to the Tax Court's finding that there was no device because there was an adequate business purpose for the separation and distribution of Teragram stock. In examining this finding we are guided by the rule that the taxpayer has the burden of proving that the transaction was not used principally as a device. *Wilson v. Commissioner*, 42 T.C. 914, 922 (1964). *rev'd on other grounds*, 353 F.2d 184 (9th Cir. 1965). Initially, we are disturbed by the somewhat uncritical nature of the Tax Court's finding of a business purpose. Viewing the transaction from the standpoint of RBS, RBS Conn., or Teragram, no immediate business reason existed for the distribution of Teragram's stock to the taxpayers. Over the years the businesses had been profitable, as witnessed by the substantial increase of the earned surplus of every component, yet none had paid dividends. The primary purpose for the distribution found by the Tax Court was to facilitate Rafferty's desire to make bequests to his children in accordance with an estate plan. This was a personal motive. Taxpayers seek to put it in terms relevant to the corporation by speaking of avoidance of possible interference with the operation of the steel business by future sons-in-law, pointing to *Coady v. Commissioner*, 33 T.C. 771 (1960). . . .

In *Coady*, however, the separation was in response to a seemingly irreconcilable falling-out between the owners of a business. This falling-out had already occurred and manifestly, the separation was designed to save the business from a substantial, present problem . . . In the case at bar there was at best, only an envisaged possibility of future debilitating nepotism. If avoidance of this danger could be thought a viable business purpose at all, it was so remote and so completely under the taxpayers' control that if in other respects the transaction was a "device," that purpose could not satisfy the taxpayers' burden of proving that it was not being used "principally as a device" within the meaning of the statute.

Our question, therefore, must be whether taxpayers' desire to put their stock holdings into such form as would facilitate their estate planning, viewed in the circumstances of the case, was a sufficient personal business purpose to prevent the transaction at bar from being a device for the distribution of earnings and profits. While we remain of the view, which we first expressed in *Lewis v. Commissioner.* 176 F.2d 646 (1st Cir. 1949) that a purpose of a shareholder, qua shareholder, may in some cases save a transaction from condemnation as a device, we do not agree with the putative suggestion in *Estate of Parshelsky v. Commissioner*, 303 F.2d 14, 19 (2d Cir. 1962), that any investment purpose of the shareholders is sufficient. Indeed, in *Lewis,* although we deprecated the distinction between shareholder and corporate purpose, we were careful to limit that observation to the facts of that case and to caution that the business purpose formula "must not become a substitute for independent analysis." 176 F.2d at 650. For that reason we based our decision on the Tax Court's finding that the transaction was "undertaken for reasons germane to the continuance of the corporate business." *Id.* at 647.

This is not to say that a taxpayer's personal motives cannot be considered, but only that a distribution which has considerable potential for use as a device for distributing earnings and profits should not qualify for tax-free treatment on the basis of personal motives unless those motives are germane to the continuance of the corporate business. *Cf. Commissioner v. Wilson*, 353 F.2d 184 (9th Cir. 1965); Treas. Reg. § 1.355-2(c). We prefer this approach over reliance upon formulations such as "business purpose" and "active business." See generally, Whitman. Draining the Serbonian Bog.- A New Approach to Corporate Separations Under the 1954 Code, 81 Harv. L. Rev. 1194 (1968). The facts of the instant case illustrate the reason for considering substance. Dividends are normally taxable to shareholders upon receipt. Had the taxpayers received cash dividends and made investments to provide for their female descendants, an income tax would, of course, have resulted. Accordingly, once the stock was distributed, if it could potentially be converted into cash without thereby impairing taxpayers' equity interest in RBS the transaction could easily be used to avoid taxes. The business purpose here alleged, which could be fully satisfied by a bail-out of dividends, is not sufficient to prove that the transaction was not being principally so used.

Given such a purpose, the only question remaining is whether the substance of the transaction is such as to leave the taxpayer in a position to distribute the earnings and profits of the corporation away from, or out of the business. The first factor to be considered is how easily the taxpayer would be able, were he so to choose, to liquidate or sell the spun-off corporation. Even if both corporations are actively engaged in their respective trades, if one of them is a business based principally on highly liquid investment-type, passive assets, the potential for a bail-out is real. The question here is whether the property transferred to the newly organized corporation had a readily realizable value, so that the distributee-shareholders could, if they ever wished, "obtain such cash or property or the cash equivalent thereof, either by selling the distributed stock or liquidating the corporation, thereby converting what would otherwise be dividends taxable as ordinary income into capital gain . . . " *Wilson v. Commissioner, supra,* 42 T.C. at 23. In this connection we note that the Tax Court found that a sale of Teragram's real estate properties could be "easily arranged." . . . Indeed, taxpayers themselves stressed the fact that the buildings were capable of multiple use.

There must, however, be a further question. If the taxpayers could not effect a bail-out without thereby impairing their control over the on-going business, the fact that a bail-out is theoretically possible should not be enough to demonstrate a device because the likelihood of it ever being so used is slight. "[A] bail-out ordinarily means that earnings and profits have been drawn off without impairing the shareholder's residual equity interest in the corporation's earning power, growth potential, or voting control." B. Bittker & J. Eustice, Federal Income Taxation of Corporations and Shareholders (3d ed. 1971) § 13.06. If sale would adversely affect the shareholders of the on-going company, the assets cannot be said to be sufficiently separated from the corporate solution and the gain sufficiently crystallized as to be taxable. See *Lewis v. Commissioner, supra* 176 F.2d at 650. In this case, there was no evidence that the land and buildings at which RBS carried on its steel operations were so distinctive that the sale of Teragram stock would impair the continued operation of RBS, or that the sale of those buildings would in any other way impair Rafferty's control and other equity interests in RBS.[2]

In the absence of any direct benefit to the business of the original company, and on a showing that the spin-off put saleable assets in the hands of the taxpayers, the continued retention of which was not needed to continue the business enterprise or to accomplish taxpayers' purposes, we find no sufficient factor to overcome the Commissioners determination that the distribution was principally a device to distribute earnings and profits.

[The portion of the decision addressing the need for an active trade or business is limited to the following paragraph.]

It is our view that in order to be an active trade or business under § 355 a corporation must engage in entrepreneurial endeavors of such a nature and to such an extent as to qualitatively distinguish its operations from mere investments. Moreover, there should be objective indicia of such corporate operations. Prior to 1965 Teragram's sole venture was the leasing lack to its parent of its only asset for a fixed return, an activity, in economic terms, almost indistinguishable from an investment in securities. Standing by itself this activity is the type of "passive investment" which Congress intended to exclude from § 355 treatment. Furthermore there are hardly any indicia of corporate operations. Prior to 1965 Teragram paid neither salaries nor rent. It did not employ independent contractors, and its only activity appears

---

[2] Our conclusion is reinforced by the fact that RBS and RBS Conn. were guaranteed occupancy of Teragram property under long term leases at fixed rents.

to have been collecting rent, paying taxes, and keeping separate books. Prior to 1965 it failed to meet either set of criteria for an active trade or business. We need not reach the more difficult question of whether its activities in 1965 constituted an active trade or business.

Affirmed.

NOTES

1. **Rafferty is now embodied in the Regulations**. Reg. § 1.355-2(d)(2)(ii) in essence says that if a distribution serves a corporate business purpose, the business purpose is evidence that the prohibited device is lacking. However, if the distribution also indicated the presence of a device, then one must weigh the business purpose against the evidence of a device in order to determine whether the prohibited device exists. Is this the same standard as the one *Rafferty* developed?

2. **The IRS concedes**. In Rev. Rul. 75-337, 1975-2 C.B. 124, the IRS ruled that estate planning that had the effect of preserving a business constituted a business purpose under § 355.

3. **Scope of business purpose requirement.** According to Reg. § 1.355-2(b)(5), Example 3, the business purpose requirement covers both the formation of the new corporation that is about to be distributed and also the distribution of the stock of the controlled corporation. For example, as indicated in the regulation, although it may make good sense to form a new subsidiary to insulate the parent company from risks associated with the subsidiary, that business purpose does not necessarily include a distribution of the controlled corporation's stock to the distributing company shareholders. An independent business purpose is required for that second step.

4. **Realty companies**. These corporations are often organized for the purpose of draining off income via management fees and rents from an affiliated corporation that has retained so much of its earnings that it might become liable for the confiscatory accumulated earnings tax (§§ 531-537). Unincorporated realty companies are also used to keep real estate out of the operating company so as to make it possible to sell the real estate with only a shareholder-level tax. The corporations in *Rafferty* seemed to be this kind of realty company.

5. **Management "fit and focus" as a business purpose.** In Rev. Proc. 2003-48, the IRS announced that it will no longer issue rulings based on disagreements as to whether a distribution is a prohibited device. Instead, it will issue Revenue Rulings of general guidance. *See* Rev. Rul. 2003-74 and 2003-75.

4. DEVICE FOR DISTRIBUTING EARNINGS AND PROFITS
Read Reg. §§ 1.355-2(d)(2)(ii), -(iii)(A), and (E) and ___ (iv).

The corporate division must not be principally a "device" for the distribution of earnings and profits of the distributing corporation or of the controlled corporation or of both combined. § 355(a)(1)(B). The Code takes a hostile view of prearranged sales of stock of the distributing or controlling corporation following the division. § 1.355-2(d)(2)(iii)(B). The Regulations identify various other evidences of a "device" or a "bailout" of earnings and profits. One obvious factor is that if the distribution is pro-rata, the probability of a "device" is enhanced because it looks like a dividend. § 1.355-2(d)(2)(ii). The same is true if either the controlled or distributing corporation winds up particularly rich with liquid assets that can easily be sold off. § 1.355-

2(d)(2)(iv). This kind of search for factors is a common feature of a tax provision that metes out its results on the basis of taxpayer's motives. Because it is impossible to know what is occurring in taxpayers' minds, their motives must be inferred from external factors.

Even if the facts indicate the presence of a prohibited device, the taxpayer may nevertheless have a legitimate business purpose for undertaking the transaction as well. What then? The answer is that there is some blanket relief in specific cases.

If no one directly or indirectly owns over 5% of a publicly-traded corporation, that indicates the absence of a device. Reg. § 1.355-2(d)(3)(iii). There is also counter-evidence of a device if the distributees are all corporations that can use the benefits of the dividends-received deduction. Reg. § 1.355-2(d)(3)(iv). A lack of a "device" is implied if the distributing and controlled corporations lack earnings and profits and are low on appreciated assets. Reg. § 1.355-2(d)(5)(ii). In addition, if in the absence of § 355, all of the distributees would have qualified for sale *or* exchange treatment under § 302(a) or 303(a), that is also evidence of lack of a device. Reg. § 1.355-2(d)(5)(iii) and (iv).

5. ACTIVE TRADE OR BUSINESS REQUIREMENT
Read § 355(b) and Reg. § 1.355-3(b)(2).

To qualify for nonreorganization treatment, the parent distributing corporation and the subsidiary must both be engaged in the active conduct of a trade or business immediately after the distribution. § 355(a)(1)(c) and § 355(b)(1)(A). The untrained eye can see whether this requirement has been met. A more difficult issue is determining whether each trade or business has been actively conducted throughout the five-year period prior to the distribution. § 355(b)(1)(B). In addition, the active trade or business must not have been acquired by either the parent or subsidiary in a taxable transaction during that five-year period. § 355(a)(3)(B). Notice how these requirements echo those of § 302(e) governing partial liquidations and distributions of assets as opposed to stock.

For this purpose, the Regulations require that a trade or business include every operation that forms part of the process of earning income or profit, including the collection of income and the payment of expenses. § 1.355-3(b)(2)(iii). To be "active," the corporation must perform "active and substantial management and operational functions." This excludes activities undertaken by outside contractors, or the mere holding of stock, securities, royalties, land, or other passive investment activities with respect to owning or leasing property used in the trade or business unless the owner of the property performs significant services with respect to the operation and management of the property. For example, a taxpayer who owns and operates her own hotel or motel business on a full time basis would be engaged in the active conduct of a trade or business, whereas someone who leases a warehouse to a manufacturing company almost surely would not be if the management of the warehouse were the obligation of the tenant under a net lease.

Rafferty held that the passive warehouse operation was not an active trade or business, but it seems that owner-occupied real estate can qualify as an active business if there are enough activities connected with the real estate. *See,* especially, *Gada v. US.,* 460 F. Supp. 859 (D. Conn. 1978), involving a corporation that rented property to a sister corporation. The court ruled that absence of significant activities connected with the real estate meant there was no active trade or business, but found the absence of rents from third parties was merely "some evidence" that the corporation has not engaged in a separate active trade or business. Keep in mind that even if one can show that renting or operating real estate is an active trade or business, there is still the independent "device" issue to contend with. *See* Reg. § 1.355-2(d)(2)(iv)(C).

PROBLEM 20-2

Alpha Corp. has owned 85 shares of Beta Corp. stock for 7 years. Alpha Chapter paid $5 per share. Alpha Corp. acquired the remaining 15 shares of Beta Corp. stock 3 years ago when it purchased those shares for $150 (i.e., $10/share) from an unrelated individual. Alpha Corp. engages in an otherwise valid §355 spin-off, distributing to its shareholders all its stock in Beta Corp. At the time of the distribution, Beta Corp. shares are being traded on a national stock exchange for $20 per share. Will Alpha Corp. recognize any gain on the distribution?

6. VERTICAL DIVISION OF A SINGLE BUSINESS

Although one might imagine that § 355 demands the existence of two different businesses prior to the breakup, the opposite is true. A single active business can be divided in half (or theoretically even into smaller groupings) as long as each half is a free-standing business. The leading case is *Coady v. Commissioner,* 33 T.C. 771 (1960), *acq., affd.* 289 F.2d 490 (6th Cir. 1961). The facts involved a construction business held by two feuding owners. As a result of the corporate division, each was allowed to walk away, tax-free, with a separate, free-standing construction business with several ongoing projects. The divided business had been active for over five years. The Court held that the five-year active business test was met, in effect tacking the five-year history of the whole to each of the parts. The Regulations confirm that this is a viable approach. *See* Reg. § 1.355-3(c), Example 4. *Coady* remains the leading example of a so-called "vertical division" of one business and company into two smaller twins.

It is also possible to move a supporting function of a business into a separate corporation and to have the separation meet the five-year active business test. The trouble is that such a division may be evidence of a device to avoid tax. *See* Reg. § 1.355-2(d)(2)(iv)(C). The Regulations provide an example of a separation of a research department into a newly-formed subsidiary that continued its research activities under contract with the company from which it was spun off or with that company and outside organizations as well; as a result the active business test was met, but the transaction may evidence a "device." *See* Reg. § 1.355-3(c), Examples 9-12.

7. HORIZONTAL DIVISION OF A SINGLE BUSINESS

Successful businesses often expand geographically as well as by expanding their product lines. On occasion they may decide that it is desirable to spin off a recently-opened store or to incorporate a new product line into a separate company and distribute the new corporation to its shareholders. These ideas raise the question of whether a new location or product line constitutes a new business or whether it is instead just an expansion of an existing business such that the extension inherits the maturity of the original business.

A leading example is *Estate of Lockwood v. Commissioner,* 350 F.2d 712 (8th Cir. 1965). There, one corporation sold portable potato sorting machines in various potato-producing states in the West. Later it went into the business of selling other kinds of farming equipment, and in 1954 it established a branch in Maine by internal expansion, which it later incorporated and spun off to its shareholders in 1956. The Court was faced with the question of whether to apply a geographical test to determine the existence and duration of a business, which was rejected, or a functional test, which was accepted. Under the functional test the corporation was viewed as having carried on a farm equipment sales business since the late 1940`s and the business in Maine was merely an extension of the same business. As a result, the five-year test was met, and the spin-off was treated as the nontaxable "horizontal division" of a single business. The Regulations treat even the purchase of a new branch in the same line of business as an expansion of a pre-existing business thereby giving the purchased branch the longevity of the acquiror. *See* Reg. § 1.355-3(b)(3)(ii).

NIELSEN v. COMMISSIONER
61 T.C. 311 (1973)

IRWIN. JUDGE.

The partnership of Riener C. Nielsen and Gene E. Moffatt was located in Los Angeles, Calif. and filed Forms 1065 – U.S. Partnership Return of Income, for the taxable years ending 1964 and 1965.

Oak Park Community Hospital, Inc. (Oak Park), a California corporation, was organized on November 8, 1956, for the purpose of conducting a hospital business. From its inception until its dissolution on March 31, 1964, the 7 outstanding shares of Oak Park were held by the following individuals:

	Shares
Riener C. Neilsen. Los Angeles, Calif	1
Gene E. Moffatt. Los Angeles, Calif	1
Michael F. LoPresti. North Hollywood. Calif	1
L. W. Gaertner. North Hollywood, Calif	1
Lloyd Boettger. Stockton, Calif	1
Theodore P. Pulas. Stockton, Calif	1
John A. Cook. Stockton, Calif	1
Total	7

A successful and profitable hospital business was actively conducted by Oak Park in Stockton, Calif., from its organization in 1956 until August 14, 1961, when it acquired an additional hospital in Los Angeles, Calif. Prior to August 14, 1961, South Side Community Hospital, Inc., a corporation, owned and operated a hospital business located in Los Angeles, Calif. The owners of this corporation were not related in any manner to any of the seven individuals who owned the stock of Oak Park.

On August 14, 1961, Oak Park, in a taxable transaction, purchased all the assets and properties both real and personal, of every kind and character, of South Side Community Hospital, Inc. The assets acquired by Oak Park included the hospital building, furniture, fixtures and equipment therein, stock in trade including drugs, medicine, and surgical supplies, goodwill, accounts receivable, books of account, and existing licenses and permits, and the right to conduct the business of operating a hospital in and/or upon the acquired property.

Oak Park's acquisition of these assets was made from its corporate funds and no outside capital was employed. After this purchase, Oak Park Community Hospital Inc., took over the operation of South Side Community Hospital, Inc., at 7 a.m. on August 15, 1961.

During the 2 1/2-year period, August 15, 1961 to March 31, 1964, Oak Park operated the hospital in Stockton and the hospital in Los Angeles. This operation included the following details:

a. The Stockton hospital primarily served the medical needs of the Stockton region and its patients came mainly from that area, whereas the Los Angeles hospital served primarily the medical needs of the central Los Angeles region and its patients came mainly from that area.
b. Each hospital had a separate staff of doctors who performed services for patients.
c. The same accounting firm and the same attorney represented Oak Park in all its accounting and legal matters with respect to both hospitals.
d. The same insurance company wrote the hospital malpractice insurance and hospital employee dishonesty insurance policies for both hospitals.

360

e. Nonperishable food served to patients and employees in both hospitals was obtained from the same institutional supplier; however, no common warehouse or supply of food was maintained for the two hospitals and the food was ordered by the hospital administrator as needed, pursuant to an old contract with the institutional supplier.

f. Oak Park consistently presented financial statements to respective creditors on a consolidated basis without differentiating the Stockton hospital from the Los Angeles hospital; however, separate profit-and-loss statements were prepared monthly for each hospital.

g. Ethel G. George was the administrator of Oak Park and in this capacity she served as the administrator for both the Stockton and the Los Angeles hospitals, commuting between them in order to perform her duties.

h. Patient accounts were maintained at each hospital by employees thereof; also, each hospital maintained subsidiary invoice records relating to its own expenses: however, Ethel G. George supervised the maintenance of the patient accounts at both hospitals and expenditures at each hospital were required to be approved by her.

i. Each hospital maintained a separate commercial bank account; however, only Ethel G. George, as president and secretary-treasurer of Oak Park, had authority to sign checks on these bank accounts; also, Ethel G. George reconciled the bank accounts.

j. Separate profit-and-loss statements were prepared monthly for each hospital. The operations of the Stockton hospital were generally profitable, whereas the operations of the Los Angeles hospital were initially unprofitable. The operations of the Los Angeles hospital thereafter became profitable but substantially less than operations of the Stockton hospital. After the corporate split-up the operation of the Los Angeles hospital again became unprofitable.

k. The board of directors of Oak Park met alternately in the cities of Stockton and Los Angeles from the fall of 1961 until March 31, 1964.

The cities of Los Angeles Calif., and Stockton Calif. are 344 miles apart. During the course of Oak Park's operation of the two hospitals, a dispute arose among the stockholders concerning matters relating to the Los Angeles hospital. In this dispute, Riener C. Nielsen, Gene E. Moffatt, and Michael F. LoPresti maintained one position, while the other four stockholders maintained another. As a result of this dispute, the stockholders agreed to split up the Los Angeles hospital business and the Stockton hospital business into two separate corporations. In order to accomplish this purpose the stockholders of Oak Park negotiated an agreement regarding the split-up. This dispute became bitter and at one point legal action was threatened to resolve it. By a letter dated January 10, 1964, the three dissident shareholders (Riener C. Nielsen, Gene E. Moffatt, and Michael F. LoPresti) offered in effect that they would take the Los Angeles hospital while Lloyd Boettger, Theodore P. Pulas, John A. Cook, and L. W. Gaertner would take the Stockton hospital. Based on this letter offer, an "agreement" regarding split-up (hereinafter referred to as the agreement) was executed by the stockholders of Oak Park.

Pursuant to the agreement two new California corporations were formed, Oak Park Community Hospital Inc. of Northern California (hereinafter referred to as Oak Park North) and Germ Hospital Inc. (hereinafter referred to as Germ). Thereafter, Oak Park transferred the assets of the Stockton hospital to Oak Park North in exchange for its stock and transferred the assets related to the Los Angeles hospital to Germ in exchange for all its stock.

On March 31, 1964, pursuant to the agreement, Oak Park Community Hospital, Inc., distributed the stock of Germ Hospital, Inc., pro rata to Riener C. Nielsen, Gene E. Moffatt, and Michael F. LoPresti in return for and respect to their stock in Oak Park. Oak Park controlled Oak Park North and Germ immediately before the distribution described above. At this time Oak Park had owned no assets other than the stock of these two corporations. . .

Pursuant to section 355 a distribution of the stock of a controlled corporation enjoys tax-free status if the following conditions are met: (1) The distributing corporation distributes stock of corporations of which it has, immediately prior to the distribution, 80-percent control; (2) the distribution is not principally a device for distributing earnings and profits of either the distributing or controlled corporations; (3) the 5-year active business requirements of section 355(b) are satisfied; and (4) the distributing corporation distributes all the stock it has of the controlled corporation. *Albert W. Badanes*, 39 T.C. 410 (1962); *Edmund P. Coady,* 33 T.C. 771 (1960), *affd.* 289 F.2d 490 (C.A. 6, 1961).

The only dispute between the parties is whether the distribution of the stock of Germ to petitioners satisfied the 5-year active business requirement of section 355(b). Generally, section 355(b) requires in the case of a corporate split-up that each of the corporations resulting from the split-up be actively engaged in the conduct of a trade or business immediately after the split-up and that such trade or business have been conducted actively for the 5-year period immediately preceding the split-up. The 5-year period only includes the active conduct of the business by the distributing corporation; by a corporation controlled by the distributing corporation, or by a person from whom the business was acquired by the distributing corporation in a transaction in which gain or loss was not recognized in whole or in part.

Petitioner contends that for more than 5 years preceding the March 31, 1964, distribution Oak Park conducted a single hospital business of which the Los Angeles hospital was a part. It is well established that a corporation engaged in a single business may be divided into two corporations without recognition of gain under section 355 as long as the two resulting corporations continue to engage in the same business carried on by their predecessor. *Edmund P. Coady, supra.; United States v. Marett*, 325 F.2d 28 (C.A. 5, 1963); Rev. Rul. 64-147, 1964-1 C.B. (Part 1) 136. The 5-year active-business requirement is even satisfied where a corporation expands its business by purchasing assets within the 5-year period preceding the division and these assets become the principal assets of one of the corporations resulting from the division. *Patricia W. Burke*, 42 T.C. 1021 (1964); *Estate of Lockwood v. Commissioner*, 350 F.2d 712 (C.A. 8, 1965).

Respondent claims that Oak Park did not conduct a single business as of March 31, 1964, but two distinct hospital businesses of which only one, the Stockton hospital, had the requisite 5-year history. If a corporation engaged in the conduct of two separate businesses, both must have a 5-year history at the time of a corporate division in order to qualify under section 355. *Isabel A. Elliott*, 32 T. C. 283 (1959). After careful consideration of all of the facts in the stipulated record, we are of the opinion that the operations of Stockton and Los Angeles hospitals constituted two separate businesses. Accordingly, the distribution of the stock of Germ to petitioners pursuant to the agreement to split up Oak Park failed to meet the 5-year active-business requirement of section 355(b) because the Los Angeles hospital business was acquired by purchase only 2 ½ years prior to the distribution.

Although the two hospitals shared the same top management, there was no integration of the income-producing activities of each hospital. The medical staff and patients of each hospital were mutually exclusive. One hospital could hardly be called the branch operation of the other. We think this fact distinguishes the present case from *Patricia W. Burke, supra*, and *Lockwood's Estate v. Commissioner, supra*, upon which petitioners rely. Each hospital had the requisite assets and employees for the production of income, and each was a self-sufficient operation. *See* sec. 1.355-1(c). Income Tax Regs. The things which the hospitals had in common – representation by the same attorneys and accountants and the use of the same insurance company and the same suppliers for some items – might have been shared by any two totally dissimilar businesses owned by one person. Accordingly, we hold that as of March 31, 1964, Oak Park was engaged in the conduct of two separate businesses of which only one, the Stockton Hospital, had been conducted actively for 5 years preceding that date as required by section 355(b).

We have noted that in *Lloyd Boettger, supra*, we also considered the application of section 355 to the split-up of Oak Park with respect to the distributions received by shareholders other than petitioners. Although we have reached the same result that obtained in *Boettger*, we admit that our analysis of section 355 is somewhat different. Irrespective of the rationale of *Boettger*, we believe our analysis of section 355 is well founded on cases like *Patricia W. Burke, supra*, and *Lockwood's Estate v. Commissioner, supra*.

In view of the foregoing,
Decisions will be entered for the respondent.

NOTES AND QUESTIONS

1. **What were the facts again?** Is it true that the only things the hospitals had in common were the same lawyers, accountants, insurance company, and some suppliers? In *Boettger,* cited in *Nielsen,* the Tax Court held that, on exactly the same facts, another of the individuals involved in the same investments and transactions also was taxable on the distribution to him of Oak Park North stock worth $67,937.59 as a dividend, without any offset for his basis of $9,700 in the stock he surrendered in the parent corporation. The Court decided that the acquired hospital was a business that had not been actively conducted for the required five-year period and so the distribution was not entitled to tax-free treatment. The statutory terms had not been met, so the distribution was taxable even though it did not constitute a purposeful attempt to "bail out" earnings by acquisition of a business for later distribution. The record established a valid business purpose for the distribution, and the IRS made no argument that it was a device for distributing earnings and profits.

2. **How would the Regulations (as revised in 1989) treat these cases**? *See* especially Reg. § 1.355-3(d), Example 8 and § 1.355-3(b)(3)(ii) (last sentence). Could a single business in *Boettger* reconcile that case with *Lockwood*?

3. **Which rationale strikes you as preferable, the one in *Nielsen* or the one in *Boettger*?**

4. ***But see* Rev. Rul. 2003-18.** P Corp. had been operating Y Car Dealership (selling A-type cars) for more than five years. P Corp. acquired Z Car Dealership (selling B-type cars) and operated it for two years before spinning it off to shareholders. The IRS ruled that, because Y and Z both are car dealerships, Z was a mere extension of its current operations. Thus, the spin-off was tax-free.

5. **Interdependent and functionally integrated.** If a newly-created division is "interdependent and functionally integrated" with the main company, it will qualify as a mere extension. *See Peterson Produce v. U.S.*, 313 F.2d 609 (8th Cir. 1963). For a modern example, *see* Rev. Rul. 2003-38. In this ruling, P Corp., which had been a shoe store for more than five years, created a website with different know-how. Two years later, it placed the website business into a subsidiary and spun it off. The IRS ruled that this was a tax-free spin-off.

PROBLEM 20-3

AB Corp. is a closely held corporation. It owns 100% of a tennis shoe division and 100% of a treadmill division. AB Corp. has been owned equally by two shareholders, Allen and Bob, for the past 15 years. Allen and Bob used to be great friends; however, lately they have had serious disagreements over the way that AB Corp. should be managed, and as a result have sworn to never set foot in the same room again. Allen and Bob do not want to be co-managers of AB Corp., but they want to continue the businesses. They decide that Allen should take over the tennis shoe manufacturing division, and Bob should take over the treadmill division, and liquidate AB Corp.

1) Allen and Bob come to you, wanting to know if they can split the corporation under this plan without incurring adverse tax consequences. What do you tell them? *See* § 355(b), Reg. § 1.355-2(b)(1) and (2), and Rev. Proc. 2017-52, 2017-41 IRB 283.

2) Assume they decided the right plan was to distribute the tennis shoe division to Allen in the form of a newly incorporated subsidiary that takes that division's assets. The tennis shoe company's assets have greatly appreciated since the start of the company. Before the division takes place, Allen signs a contract with Charlie, agreeing to sell Charlie his tennis shoe company stock following the division. Will this agreement affect the non-taxability of the transaction as to Allen and Bob? *See* § 355(a)(1)(B) and Reg. § 1.355-2(d)(2)(iii).

3) Same facts as "(1)," but AB Corp. had acquired the treadmill and tennis shoe assets in a taxable §1060 acquisition of assets four years prior to the decision to liquidate and divide the corporation. Will this in itself render the breakup of AB Corp. taxable?

4) Would your answer to "(3)" differ if only the treadmill company assets had been acquired in a §1060 transaction in the past 4 years, but the shoe company had been run by AB Corp. for 15 years?

5) Same as "(4)" but one company is in the sneaker business and the other is in the leather shoe business.

B. TAX TREATMENT OF DISTRIBUTING CORPORATION, ASIDE FROM §§ 355(d) AND (e)

1. GENERAL RULES

The outcome is the same no matter whether the distribution is a simple § 355 transaction involving a preexisting subsidiary that is "old and cold," or the distribution is part of a type D reorganization in which the assets of a line of business are first incorporated into a controlled subsidiary. In both cases the distributing corporation recognizes no gain or loss on the distribution of subsidiary stock or subsidiary obligations (known as "qualified property") to its shareholders. §§ 361(c)(1), 355(c)(1). In both cases the distributing corporation will recognize a gain if it distributes appreciated boot but will not be entitled to recognize any loss on such a distribution. §§ 361(c)(2), 355(c)(2). Section 355(e) may pose a problem to the distributing corporation, as may § 355(d). Those provisions are discussed later in this Chapter.

2. IMPACT ON TAX ATTRIBUTES OF DISTRIBUTING CORPORATION

The distributing corporation in a § 355 transaction that is part of a qualifying D reorganization divides its earnings and profits between itself and the controlled corporation in proportion to relative fair market value of the assets that each holds after the distribution. Reg. § 1.312-10(a). If the distribution is kicked off by the formation of a new subsidiary, the subsidiary takes the same basis in its assets as its parent corporation had. The distributing corporation retains all its other tax attributes, such as net operating losses, and does not share them with the newly-formed controlled corporation. In a split-up, the distributing corporation liquidates and its tax attributes disappear entirely.

3. SPIN-OFF OF UNWANTED ASSETS FOLLOWED BY TAX-FREE ACQUISITION

Read § 368(a)(1)(D) and §§ 354(a) and (b)(1).

An acquiring corporation may refuse to accept certain assets of the target corporation and insist that the target dispose of the unwanted assets before the tax-free acquisition. In that case, the target's shareholders may be forced to take the unwanted assets. The question then arises, how to distribute the unwanted assets to shareholders at the smallest tax cost. Basically there are two options: (1) spin off the unwanted assets and then combine the remaining (original) corporation with the acquiring company; or (2) spin off the wanted assets into a new corporation and combine the new corporation with the acquiring corporation.

COMMISSIONER v. MORRIS TRUST
367 F.2d 794 (4th Cir. 1966)

HAYNSWORTH, CHIEF JUSTICE.

Its nubility impaired by the existence of an insurance department it had operated for many years, a state bank divested itself of that business before merging with a national bank. The divestiture was in the form of a traditional "spin-off," but, because it was a preliminary step to the merger of the banks, the Commissioner treated their receipt of stock of the insurance company as ordinary income to the stockholders of the state bank. We agree with the Tax Court, that gain to the stockholders of the state bank was not recognizable under § 355 of the 1954 Code.

In 1960, a merger agreement was negotiated by the directors of American Commercial Bank, a North Carolina corporation with its principal office in Charlotte, and Security National Bank of Greensboro, a national bank. American was the product of an earlier merger of American Trust Company and a national bank, the Commercial National Bank of Charlotte. This time, however, though American was slightly larger than Security, it was found desirable to operate the merged institutions under Security's national charter, after changing the name to North Carolina National Bank. It was contemplated that the merged institution would open branches in other cities.

For many years, American had operated an insurance department. This was a substantial impediment to the accomplishment of the merger, for a national bank is prohibited from operating an insurance department except in towns having a population of not more than 5,000 inhabitants. To avoid a violation of the national banking laws, therefore, and to accomplish the merger under Security's national charter, it was prerequisite that American rid itself of its insurance business.

The required step to make it nubile was accomplished by American's organization of a new corporation, American Commercial Agency, Inc., to which American transferred its insurance business assets in exchange for Agency's stock which was immediately distributed to American's stockholders. The merger of the two banks was then accomplished.

365

Though American's spin-off of its insurance business was a "D" reorganization, as defined in § 368(a)(1), provided the distribution of Agency's stock qualified for non-recognition of gain under § 355, the Commissioner contended that the active business requirements of § 355(b)(1)(A) were not met, since American's banking business was not continued in unaltered corporate form. He also finds an inherent incompatibility in substantially simultaneous divisive and amalgamating reorganizations.

Section 355(b)(1)(A) requires that both the distributing corporation and the controlled corporation be "engaged immediately after the distribution in the active conduct of a trade or business." There was literal compliance with that requirement, for the spin-off, including the distribution of Agency's stock to American's stockholders, preceded the merger. The Commissioner asks that we look at both steps together, contending that North Carolina National Bank was not the distributing corporation and that its subsequent conduct of American's banking business does not satisfy the requirement.

A brief look at an earlier history may clarify the problem. Initially, the active business requirement was one of several judicial innovations designed to limit nonrecognition of gain to the implicit, but unelucidated, intention of earlier Congresses.

Nonrecognition of gain in "spin-offs" was introduced by the Revenue Act of 1924. Its § 203(b)(3), as earlier Revenue Acts, provided for nonrecognition of gain at the corporate level when one corporate party to a reorganization exchanged property solely for stock or securities of another, but it added a provision in subsection (c) extending the nonrecognition of gain to a stockholder of a corporate party to a reorganization who received stock of another party without surrendering any of his old stock. Thus, with respect to the nonrecognition of gain, treatment previously extended to "split-offs" was extended to the economically indistinguishable "spin-off."

The only limitation upon those provisions extending nonrecognition to spin-offs was contained in § 203(h) and (i) defining reorganizations. The definition required that immediately after the transfer, the transferor or its stockholders or both be in control of the corporation to which the assets had been transferred, and "control" was defined as being the ownership of not less than eighty per cent of the voting stock and eighty per cent of the total number of shares of all other classes of stock.

With no restriction other than the requirement of control of the transferee, these provisions were a fertile source of tax avoidance schemes. By spinning off liquid assets or all productive assets, they provided the means by which ordinary distributions of earnings could be cast in the form of a reorganization within their literal language.

The renowned case of *Gregory v. Helvering,* 293 U.S. 465, 55 S. Ct. 266, 79 L. Ed. 596, brought the problem to the Supreme Court. The taxpayer there owned all of the stock of United Mortgage Corporation which, in turn, owned 1000 shares of Monitor Securities Corporation. She wished to sell the Monitor stock and possess herself of the proceeds. If the sale were effected by United Mortgage, gain would be recognized to it, and its subsequent distribution of the net proceeds of the sale would have been a dividend to the taxpayer, taxable as ordinary income. If the Monitor stock were distributed to the taxpayer before sale, its full value would have been taxable to her as ordinary income. In order materially to reduce that tax cost, United Mortgage spun off the Monitor stock to a new corporation, Averill, the stock of which was distributed to the taxpayer. Averill was then liquidated, and the taxpayer sold the Monitor stock. She contended that she was taxable only on the proceeds of the sale, reduced by an allocated part of her cost basis of United Mortgage, and at capital gain rates.

The Supreme Court found the transaction quite foreign to the congressional purpose. It limited the statute's definition of a reorganization to a reorganization of a corporate business or businesses motivated by a business purpose. It was never intended that Averill engage in any business, and it had not. Its creation, the distribution of its stock and its liquidation the court concluded was only a masquerade for the distribution of an ordinary dividend as of course, it was.

In a similar vein, it was held that the interposition of new corporations of fleeting duration, though the transactions were literally within the congressional definition of a reorganization and the language of a nonrecognition section, would not avail in the achievement of the tax avoidance purpose when it was only a mask for a transaction which was essentially and substantively the payment of a liquidating dividend, a sale for cash, or a taxable exchange.

Such cases exposed a number of fundamental principles which limited the application of the nonrecognition of gain sections of the reorganization provisions of the Code. Mertens defines them in terms of permanence, which encompasses the concepts of business purpose and a purpose to continue an active business in altered corporate form. As concomitants to the primary principle and supplements of it, there were other requirements that the transferor, or its stockholders, retain a common stock interest and that a substantial part of the value of the properties transferred be represented by equity securities.

Underlying such judicially developed rules limiting the scope of the nonrecognition provisions of the Code, was an acceptance of a general congressional purpose to facilitate the reorganization of businesses, not to exalt economically meaningless formalisms and diversions through corporate structures hastily created and as hastily demolished. Continuation of a business in altered corporate form was to be encouraged, but immunization of taxable transactions through the interposition of short-lived, empty, corporate entities was never intended and ought not to be allowed.

While these judicial principles were evolving and before the Supreme Court declared itself in *Gregory v. Helvering*, an alarmed Congress withdrew nonrecognition of gain to a stockholder receiving securities in a spin-off. It did so by omitting from the Revenue Act of 1934, a provision comparable to § 203(c) of the Revenue Act of 1924.

Nonrecognition of gain to the stockholder in spin-off situations, however, was again extended by § 317(a) of the Revenue Act of 1951, amending the 1939 Code by adding § 112(b)(11). This time, the judicially developed restrictions upon the application of the earlier statutes were partially codified. Nonrecognition of gain was extended "unless it appears that (A) any corporation which is a party to such reorganization was not intended to continue the active conduct of a trade or business after such reorganization, or (B) the corporation whose stock is distributed was used principally as a device for the distribution of earnings and profits to the shareholders of any corporation a party to the reorganization."

If this transaction were governed by the 1939 Code, as amended in 1951, the Commissioner would have had the support of a literal reading of the A limitation, for it was not intended that American, in its then corporate form, should continue the active conduct of the banking business. From the prior history, however, it would appear that the intention of the A limitation was to withhold the statute's benefits from schemes of the *Gregory v. Helvering* type. It effectively reached those situations in which one of the parties to the reorganization was left only with liquid assets not intended for use in the acquisition of an active business or in which the early demise of one of the parties was contemplated, particularly, if its only office was a conduit for the transmission of title. The B limitation was an additional precaution intended to encompass any other possible use of the device for the masquerading of a dividend distribution.

The 1954 Code was the product of a careful attempt to codify the judicial limiting principles in a more particularized form. The congressional particularization extended the principles in some areas, as in the requirement that a business, to be considered an active one, must have been conducted for a period of at least five years ending on the distribution date and must not have been acquired in a taxable transaction during the five-year period.[3] In other areas,

---

[3] Section 355(b)(2).

it relaxed and ameliorated them, as in its express sanction of non-pro/rata distributions. While there are such particularized variations, the 1954 Code is a legislative re-expression of generally established principles developed in response to definite classes of abuses which had manifested themselves many years earlier. The perversions of the general congressional purpose and the principles the courts had developed to thwart them, as revealed in the earlier cases, are still an enlightening history with which an interpretation of the reorganization sections of the 1954 Code should be approached.

Section 355(b) requires that the distributing corporation be engaged in the active conduct of a trade or business "immediately after the distribution." This is in contrast to the provisions of the 1951 Act, which, as we have noted, required an intention that the parent, as well as the other corporate parties to the reorganization, continue the conduct of an active business. It is in marked contrast to § 355(b)'s highly particularized requirements respecting the duration of the active business prior to the reorganization and the methods by which it was acquired. These contrasts suggest a literal reading of the post-reorganization requirement and a holding that the Congress intended to restrict it to the situation existing "immediately after the distribution."

Such a reading is quite consistent with the prior history. It quite adequately meets the problem posed by the *Gregory v. Helvering* situation in which, immediately after the distribution, one of the corporations held only liquid or investment assets. It sufficiently serves the requirements of permanence and of continuity, for as long as an active business is being conducted immediately after the distribution, there is no substantial opportunity for the stockholders to sever their interest in the business except through a separable, taxable transaction. If the corporation proceeds to withdraw assets from the conduct of the active business and to abandon it, the Commissioner has recourse to the back-up provisions of § 355(a)(1)(B) and to the limitations of the underlying principles. At the same time, the limitation, so construed, will not inhibit continued stockholder conduct of the active business through altered corporate form and with further changes in corporate structure, the very thing the reorganization sections were intended to facilitate.

Applied to this case, there is no violation of any of the underlying limiting principles. There was no empty formalism, no utilization of empty corporate structures, no attempt to recast a taxable transaction in nontaxable form and no withdrawal of liquid assets. There is no question but that American's insurance and banking businesses met all of the active business requirements of § 355(b)(2). It was intended that both businesses be continued indefinitely, and each has been. American's merger with Security, in no sense, was a discontinuance of American's banking business, which opened the day after the merger with the same employees, the same depositors and customers. There was clearly the requisite continuity of stockholder interest, for American's former stockholders remained in 100% control of the insurance company, while, in the merger, they received 54.385% of the common stock of North Carolina National Bank, the remainder going to Security's former stockholders. There was a strong business purpose for both the spin-off and the merger, and tax avoidance by American's stockholders was neither a predominant nor a subordinate purpose. In short, though both of the transactions be viewed together, there were none of the evils or misuses which the limiting principles and the statutory limitations were designed to exclude.

We are thus led to the conclusion that this carefully drawn statute should not be read more broadly than it was written to deny nonrecognition of gain to reorganizations of real businesses of the type which Congress clearly intended to facilitate by according to them nonrecognition of present gain.

The Commissioner, indeed, concedes that American's stockholders would have realized no gain had American not been merged into Security after, but substantially contemporaneously with, Agency's spin-off. Insofar as it is contended that § 355(b)(l)(A) requires the distributing corporation to continue the conduct of an active business, recognition of gain to American's stockholders on their receipt of Agency's stock would depend upon the economically irrelevant technicality of the identity of the surviving corporation in the merger. Had American been the survivor, it would in every literal and substantive sense have continued the conduct of its banking business.

Surely, the Congress which drafted these comprehensive provisions did not intend the incidence of taxation to turn upon so insubstantial a technicality. Its differentiation on the basis of the economic substance of transactions is too evident to permit such a conclusion.

This, too, the Commissioner seems to recognize, at least conditionally, for he says that gain to the stockholders would have been recognized even if American had been the surviving corporation. This would necessitate our reading into § 355(b)(1)(A) an implicit requirement that the distributing corporation, without undergoing any reorganization whatever, whether or not it resulted in a change in its corporate identity, continue the conduct of its active business.

We cannot read this broader limitation into the statute for the same reasons we cannot read into it the narrower one of maintenance of the same corporate identity. The congressional limitation of the post-distribution active business requirement to the situation existing "immediately after the distribution" was deliberate. Consistent with the general statutory scheme, it is quite inconsistent with the Commissioner's contention.

The requirement of § 368(a)(1)(D) that the transferor or its stockholders be in control of the spun-off corporation immediately after the transfer is of no assistance to the Commissioner. It is directed solely to control of the transferee, and was fully met here. It contains no requirement of continuing control of the transferor. Though a subsequent sale of the transferor's stock, under some circumstances, might form the basis of a contention that the transaction was the equivalent of a dividend within the meaning of § 355(a)(1)(B) and the underlying principles, the control requirements imply no limitation upon subsequent reorganizations of the transferor.

There is no distinction in the statute between subsequent amalgamating reorganizations in which the stockholders of the spin-off transferor would own 80% or more of the relevant classes of stock of the reorganized transferor, and those in which they would not. The statute draws no line between major and minor amalgamations in prospect at the time of the spin-off. Nothing of the sort is suggested by the detailed control-active business requirements in the five-year predistribution period, for there the distinction is between taxable and nontaxable acquisitions, and a tax free exchange within the five-year period does not violate the active business-control requirement whether it was a major or a minor acquisition. Reorganizations in which no gain or loss is recognized, sanctioned by the statute's control provision when occurring in the five years preceding the spin-off, are not prohibited in the post-distribution period.

As we have noticed above, the merger cannot by any stretch of imagination be said to have affected the continuity of interest of American's stockholders or to have constituted a violation of the principle underlying the statutory control requirement. The view is the same whether it be directed to each of the successive steps severally or to the whole.

Nor can we find elsewhere in the Code any support for the Commissioner's suggestion of incompatibility between substantially contemporaneous divisive and amalgamating reorganizations. The 1954 Code contains no inkling of it; nor does its immediate legislative history. The difficulties encountered under the 1924 Code and its successors, in dealing with formalistic distortions of taxable transactions into the spin-off shape, contain no implication of any such incompatibility. Section 317 of the Revenue Act of 1951 and the Senate Committee Report, to which we have referred, did require an intention that the distributing corporation continue the conduct of its active business, but that transitory requirement is of slight relevance to an interpretation of the very different provisions of the 1954 Code and is devoid of any implication of incompatibility. If that provision, during the years it was in effect, would have resulted in recognition of gain in a spin-off if the distributing corporation later, but substantially simultaneously, was a party to a merger in which it lost its identity, a question we do not decide, it would not inhibit successive reorganizations if the merger preceded the spin-off.

The Congress intended to encourage six types of reorganizations. They are defined in § 368 and designated by the letters "A" through "F." The "A" merger, the "B" exchange of stock for stock and the "C' exchange of stock for substantially all of the properties of another are all amalgamating reorganizations. The "D" reorganization is the divisive spin-off, while the "E" and "F" reorganizations, recapitalizations and reincorporations, are neither amalgamating nor divisive. All are sanctioned equally, however. Recognition of gain is withheld from each and successively so. Merger may follow merger, and an "A" reorganization by which Y is merged into X corporation may proceed substantially simultaneously with a "C" reorganization by which X acquires substantially all of the properties of Z and with an "F" reorganization by which X is reincorporated in another state. The "D" reorganization has no lesser standing. It is on the same plane as the others and, provided all of the "D" requirements are met, is as available as the others in successive reorganizations.

We have not placed our reliance upon that provision of the National Banking Act which continues the identity of each merging bank in the consolidated banking association which is deemed the same bank as each of the merging constituents. We have not done so, for, at best, it would supply an answer only to the Commissioner's most limited contention. Moreover, we have had previous occasion to point out the narrow purpose of that statute. It was enacted to secure the continuing efficacy of previous fiduciary appointments of each of the constituent banks. It was not intended, as we held in *Fidelity-Baltimore*, to exempt merging banks from stamp taxes to which all other merging corporations are subject. Nor do we think it was intended, when enacted in 1959, to amend the reorganization sections of the 1954 Code or to accord to the stockholders of reorganizing banks more favorable tax treatment than that accorded the stockholders of other corporations undergoing comparable reorganizations. The comprehensive scheme of the 1954 Code was intended to have a uniform application. The courts should not import artificial distinctions into it.

Our conclusion that gain was not recognizable to American's stockholders as a result of the spin-off, therefore, is uninfluenced by the fact that the subsequent merger was under the National Banking Act. It would have been the same if the merger had been accomplished under state laws.

In a substantive sense, however, in every merger there is a continuation of each constituent. Each makes its contribution to the continuing combination, and the substantiality of that contribution is unaffected by such technicalities as a choice to operate under the charter of one constituent rather than that of another. After the merger, North Carolina National Bank was as much American as Security. It was not one or the other, except in the sense of the most technical of legalisms; it was both, and with respect to the Charlotte operation, old American's business, it was almost entirely American. North Carolina National Bank's business in the Charlotte area after the merger was American's business conducted by American's employees in American's banking houses for the service of American's customers. Probably the only change immediately noticeable was the new name.

While we reject the technical provision of the National Banking Act as a basis for decision, therefore, it is important to the result that, as in every merger, there was substantive continuity of each constituent and its business. In framing the 1954 Code, the Congress was concerned with substance, not formalisms. Its approach was that of the courts in the *Gregory v. Helvering* series of cases. Ours must be the same. The technicalities of corporate structure cannot obscure the continuity of American's business, its employees, its customers, its locations or the substantive fact that North Carolina National Bank was both American and Security.

370

A decision of the Sixth Circuit[4] appears to be at odds with our conclusion. In *Curtis*, it appears that one corporation was merged into another after spinning off a warehouse building which was an unwanted asset because the negotiators could not agree upon its value. The Court of Appeals for the Sixth Circuit affirmed a District Court judgment holding that the value of the warehouse company shares was taxable as ordinary income to the stockholders of the first corporation.

A possible distinction may lie between the spin-off of an asset unwanted by the acquiring corporation in an "A" reorganization solely because of disagreement as to its value and the preliminary spin-off of an active business which the acquiring corporation is prohibited by law from operating. We cannot stand upon so nebulous a distinction, however. We simply take a different view. The reliance in *Curtis* upon the Report of the Senate Committee explaining § 317 of the Revenue Act of 1951, quite dissimilar to the 1954 Code, reinforces our appraisal of the relevant materials. . .

For the reasons which we have canvassed, we think the Tax Court, which had before it the opinion of the District Court in Curtis, though not that of the affirming Court of Appeals, correctly decided that American's stockholders realized no recognizable taxable gain upon their receipt in the "D" reorganization of the stock of Agency.

Affirmed.

NOTES

1. **The IRS concedes the battle.** In Rev. Rul. 68-603, 1968-2 C.B. 148, the IRS accepted the decision in *Morris Trust* to the extent that it held that a merger of the distributing corporation into the acquiring corporation after the division does not fail the "active business" test of § 355(b)(1)(A) or the control test of § 368(a)(1)(D). Reg. § 1.355-2(d)(2)(iii)(A) and (E), issued in 1989, states that a spin-off followed by a sale indicates a device, but a spin-off followed by a reorganization does not (because the reorganization exchange is not a "sale"), thus validating *Morris Trust* and opening the door to a wide variety of transactions.

2. **Then the tables turn.** In 1997, Congress enacted § 355(e), described below in this Chapter, threatening many *Morris Trust* transactions. It is now necessary to prepare in advance, by making the spin-off distribution well before the acquisition and before the acquiror is identified. These requirements are discussed below.

C. RECENT LIMITS ON TAX-FREE DIVISIONS: §§ 355(d) AND (e)

1. SECTION 355(d) LIMITATION
Read § 355(d).

In 1990 Congress added § 355(d) to the IRC. Under § 355(d), the distributing corporation must recognize gain on the distribution of certain "disqualified stock." The shareholders do not recognize any gain as long as the rest of 355 is satisfied. The reason for the change was a Congressional belief that tax-free divisions were being used as fig leaves to cover asset purchases. Section 355(d) is targeted at a narrow class of transactions and is much less important than § 355(e), which is discussed later.

Section 355(d) is designed to isolate disguised asset acquisitions from legitimate spin-offs by identifying "disqualified distributions." A "disqualified distribution" is a distribution to

---

[4] *Curtis v. United States*, 6 Cir., 336 F.2d 714.

any person pursuant to § 355 if that person (or concerted group) holds "disqualified stock" constituting after the distribution at least a 50 percent interest in either the distributing or controlled corporation. § 355(d)(2). "Disqualified stock" is stock in the distributing or controlled corporation that was bought in the past five years ending on the date of the distribution. § 355(d)(3).

Having identified the disqualified distribution, § 355(d)(1) treats any stock or securities in the controlled corporation as not "qualified property" under § 355(c)(2)(B). The result is that such stock or securities are treated like boot as to the distributing corporation (only), so that the distributing corporation must recognize gain on the difference between the value of the stock or securities it distributed and the basis of the stock or securities in the distributing corporation's hands. § 355(d)(1). The recipients of the stock or securities can enjoy nonrecognition treatment under § 355(a)(1), as long as all the other requirements of § 355 are met. Note that § 355(d) only applies if the distribution is within § 355(a).

To illustrate: A group of corporate raiders recently bought 55% of the stock of Creaky Co., which owns a silver mine that the raiders think is worth $1.5 million. The purchase price of the 55% interest in Creaky was $1 million. The basis of the mine in Creaky Co.'s hands is $100,000. Creaky Co. owned the mine for over fifty years. To get rid of the raiders, Creaky incorporates the silver mine into Mines. Inc., distributes the Mines Inc. stock to the raiders, and, in exchange, the raiders hand back their Creaky stock to Creaky Co. The raiders claim that the exchange is a tax-free split-off under § 355 and understandably assign a $1 million basis to the Mines, Inc. stock. The raiders sell the Mines, Inc. stock to another party for $1.5 million and report a $500,000 long-term capital gain when the combined holding periods of the Creaky and Mines, Inc. stock exceed one year. The transaction resembles an outright sale of a newly formed mining subsidiary but with no corporate-level tax on the seller. This was the scheme in the bad old days.

In the terminology of the Code, the distributing corporation – Creaky Co. – is subject to income tax on its "disqualified distributions" of "disqualified stock" of Mines, Inc., in effect as if it sold the silver mine on the open market. The raiders will indirectly bear a tax if Mines, Inc. later sells the silver mine because Mines, Inc. will have to pay a tax on that sale. That is the same as under prior law.

2. SECTION 355(e) LIMITATION
Read § 355(e).

In 1997, Congress dramatically trimmed back opportunities to restructure the target company in advance of an acquisition of either the distributing corporation or the distributed corporation. Now, if stock of a controlled corporation is distributed in an otherwise tax-free division as part of a plan under which there is an "acquisition" of either the distributed or distributing corporation, then the distributing corporation recognizes gain as if it had sold the stock or securities that it distributed.

An "acquisition" occurs if one or more persons obtain a 50% or greater interest (measured by vote or value of stock) in the controlled corporation or the distributing corporation. The forbidden "plan" is rebuttably presumed to exist if stock constituting an acquisition is acquired within two years before or after the distribution. § 355(e)(2)(B). Why this new rule? The answer is that, if either corporation is disposed of, then the real purpose of the distribution was to set the stage for a disposition to an outside party. The plan becomes something similar to a sale, as opposed to a mere restructuring. Not everyone would agree that there is a need for § 355(e).

To be more specific, if a parent corporation distributes stock or securities of a controlled corporation in a transaction that qualifies as a tax-free corporate division and either the distributing corporation or the controlled corporation is acquired in a certain fashion, then stock or securities of the controlled corporation are not treated as "qualified property." § 355(e). As a result, § 355(c)(2) forces the distributing corporation to recognize any gain as if it had sold the stock or securities of the controlled corporation to the distributee for its fair market value immediately before the distribution. This could even include a public offering of stock of the parent or the subsidiary. *See* Conf. Rep. No. 105-220 (PL 105-34), at 533. The acquisition of the parent or the subsidiary can be taxable or tax-free; all that matters is that there is an acquisition.

To illustrate: P owns all of the stock of S which has a basis of $100 and a value of $200 in P's hands. P distributes all of the S stock to its shareholders in a transaction that qualifies as a tax-free division. S is promptly acquired by an unrelated acquiror in a tax-free reorganization. The stock of S loses its status as qualified property, so P recognizes $100 of gain on the distribution.

To illustrate: P owns 100% of the stock of S with a basis of $100 and a value of $200. An unrelated corporation buys all the stock of P, and, within two years, P distributes S to its shareholders in a transaction that qualifies as a tax-free division. As a result, the stock of S is not treated as qualified property, with the consequence that P recognizes $100 of gain.

There are two primary exceptions to § 355(e). All they do is limit § 355(e) to its purposes. First, the gain recognition rule does not apply to distributions to which § 355(d) applies, a small comfort. § 355(e)(2)(D). Section 355(d) applies where a 50% stock interest in either P or S was purchased within the five years preceding the distribution; it provides for corporate-level gain recognition for P with respect to appreciation in S. Thus, this exception avoids double-counting of the same gain under two different provisions. Second, there are exceptions for cases where the acquisition does not result in a 50% decline in the direct and indirect ownership of T by the target shareholders. § 355(e)(3)(A)(iv). This covers situations such as where T is formally acquired by a smaller corporation, such that T shareholders get control of the acquiror.

To illustrate*:* P corporation distributes all the stock of S to P shareholders in a tax-free division. Under the plan, Mini-Grabber Corp. next acquires all the stock of P in exchange for Mini-Grabber stock in a tax-free stock swap under § 368(a)(1)(B). Because Mini-Grabber is smaller than P, the former P shareholders wind up with indirect control of Mini-Grabber – that is, over 50% of the stock of P via its ownership of most of the stock of Mini-Grabber. This acquisition does not trigger gain recognition under § 355(e).

In general, the IRS believes that the following facts and circumstances tend to show that a distribution and an acquisition are part of a "plan" under § 355(e): [*]

(1) In the case of an acquisition (other than one involving a public offering) after a distribution, at some time during the two-year period ending on the date of the distribution, there was an agreement, understanding, arrangement, or substantial negotiations regarding the acquisition or a similar acquisition.

---

[*] Reg. § 1.355-7(b)(3).

(2) In the case of an acquisition involving a public offering after a distribution, at some time during the two-year period ending on the date of the distribution, there were discussions by the distributing or controlled corporation with an investment banker regarding the acquisition or a similar acquisition.

(3) In the case of an acquisition (other than involving a public offering) before a distribution, at some time during the two-year period ending on the date of the acquisition, the distributing or controlled corporation held discussions with the acquirer regarding a distribution. The weight to be accorded this fact depends on the nature, extent, and timing of the discussions. Also, in the case of an acquisition (other than involving a public offering) before a distribution where a person other than the distributing or controlled corporation intends to cause a distribution and, as a result of the acquisition, can meaningfully participate in the decision regarding whether to make a distribution.

(4) In the case of an acquisition involving a public offering before a distribution, at some time during the two-year period ending on the date of the acquisition, the distributing or controlled corporation held discussions with an investment banker regarding a distribution. The weight to be accorded this fact depends on the nature, extent, and timing of the discussions.

(5) In the case of an acquisition either before or after a distribution, the distribution was motivated by a business purpose to facilitate the acquisition or a similar acquisition.

Conversely, the IRS believes that the following facts and circumstances tend to show that a distribution and an acquisition were *not* part of a "plan" under § 355(e):

(1) In the case of an acquisition involving a public offering after a distribution, during the two-year period ending on the date of the distribution, there were no discussions by the distributing or controlled corporation with an investment banker about the acquisition or a similar acquisition.

(2) In the case of an acquisition after a distribution, there was an identifiable, unexpected change in market or business conditions following the distribution that resulted in the acquisition that was otherwise unexpected at the time of the distribution.

(3) In the case of an acquisition (other than involving a public offering) before a distribution, during the two-year period ending on the date of the acquisition, the distributing and controlled corporation had no discussions with the acquirer about a distribution. This does not apply if the acquisition occurred after the date of the public announcement of the planned distribution. Also, this does not apply in the case of an acquisition where a person other than the distributing or controlled corporation intends to cause a distribution and, as a result of the acquisition, can meaningfully participate in the decision regarding whether to make a distribution.

(4) In the case of an acquisition before a distribution, there was an identifiable, unexpected change in market or business conditions after the acquisition that resulted in a distribution that was otherwise unexpected.

(5) In the case of an acquisition either before or after a distribution, the distribution was motivated in whole or substantial part by a corporate business purpose other than one to facilitate the acquisition or a similar acquisition.

374

(6) In the case of an acquisition either before or after a distribution, the distribution would have occurred at about the same time and in similar form regardless of the acquisition.

PROBLEM 20-4

P Corp. has two business divisions, I and II. Both divisions have been held for over 5 years. Business I consists of assets with a basis of zero and a fair market value of $100. Business II consists of assets with a basis and a fair market value of $100. (This means that if P incorporates Business II as S, any freshly issued stock of S will have a basis and a value of $100.) Acquiso International, Inc. wants to obtain only Business I in a tax-free corporate acquisition in exchange for Acquiso Stock. The directors of P Corp. are impressed with Acquiso and would like to do the deal.

1) How should P Corp. proceed so as to minimize its federal income tax liabilities?

2) What if Acquiso is much smaller than P?

3) If P goes through the corporate separation before Acquiso communicates with P, how long must the takeover by Acquiso be deferred?

4) What if there were a good business purpose for the distribution aside from facilitating a takeover, and the negotiations to buy one of the corporations did not start until 8 months after the distribution? *See* Reg. 1.355-7(d)(1).

5) Assume that P Corp. incorporated the two divisions, calling them SubOne and SubTwo and that Big Co. bought 10% of SubTwo three years ago and it bought 20% of P Corp. eight months ago. Last month, P Corp. redeemed all of Big Co.'s P Corp. stock in exchange for 40% of the stock of SubTwo. The stock of SubTwo has appreciated greatly over the years.

   a) Is P taxed on the distribution of SubTwo stock? *See* § 335(d).

   b) Would P be allowed to recognized a loss if the stock of SubTwo had declined in value?

   c) Assuming P is taxed on the distribution, does that mean that Big Co.'s redemption is a taxable transaction?

   d) Now assume that P Corp. distributed all its subsidiary stock (*i.e.*, all of its stock in SubOne and SubTwo) in redemption of all of Big Co.'s stock in P Corp. How does this affect your conclusions?

Questions: Should American corporations begin forming and spinning off new entities now, so that the businesses are easier to dispose of on a tax-free basis? Can one negotiate informally, then do a nontaxable division and then go back to the table and be able to say that there was no "plan" to do a post-division acquisition? Perhaps, but one thing is for sure, there is no guarantee of protection from an IRS attack under § 355(e), even if the acquisition occurs outside the four-year period described in § 355(e)(2)(B).

D. SPIN-OFF, SPLIT-OFF, OR SPLIT-UP FOLLOWED BY A TAXABLE ACQUISITION

Whereas the law has developed reasonably favorably toward combining divisive transactions with tax-free acquisitive ones, the same cannot be said where the second step is a taxable sale of either the distributing or distributed company's stock.

First, the taxable transaction is evidence of a device under Reg. § 1.355-2(d)(2).

Second, the divisive transaction is taxable because there is a lack of continuity of proprietary interest on the part of the shareholders of whichever entity is sold. This violates the requirement that the historic shareholders of the original corporation must continue to have a majority equity stake in both companies after the corporate division. *See* Reg. § 1.355-2(c). Note that this is distinct from § 355(d). All becomes clearer after the readings on corporate acquisitions.

E. TAX TREATMENT OF DISTRIBUTEES IN A CORPORATE DIVISION

If it is done right, the shareholders and the security holders of the distribution will recognize no gain or loss when they receive stock or securities of the spun-off corporation. Instead, shareholders will allocate their basis in the distributing corporation stock between that stock and the stock of the subsidiary in proportion to their relative fair market values, just as in the case of a tax-free stock dividend. Similarly, shareholders can "tack" the holding period of their old stock onto the new stock. *See* §§ 358(a) and 1223(1). Securities enjoy similar treatment.

If "boot" is distributed, § 356 steps in. Taxable boot includes cash and the fair market value of any distributed property other than stock and securities of the corporation, as well as stock rights and warrants, nonqualified preferred stock, and any stock of the controlled corporation that the distributing corporation acquired in a taxable transaction within the past five years. *See* § 355(a)(3)(B). If the corporation distributes securities with a principal amount (meaning face amount) that is greater than the total principal amount of the securities that the distributee gave up, the fair market value of the difference between the principal amount of the distributed securities and the principal amount of the securities surrendered (if any) constitutes boot. § 355(a)(3) and § 356(d).

To illustrate: An individual shareholder exchanges a security in the principal amount of $1,000 for another security in the principal amount of $1,200 with fair market value of $1,080. The fair market value of the $200 excess principal amount is $180, and that is the amount of taxable boot. This figure is obtained by multiplying the ratio of fair market value to face amount ($1,080/$1,200 = 90%) of the new security times the excess face amount (90% of $200 = $180). Reg. § 1.356-3(c), Example 5.

It is worth going through this small technical detour now because one uses the same calculation of boot in connection with the distribution of additional principal amounts of debt as part of acquisitive reorganizations discussed in the following Chapter. Shareholders and security holders cannot recognize losses in otherwise qualifying tax-free distributions under § 355, whether or not they receive "boot." *See* § 356(c).

1. BOOT IN A SPIN-OFF

In a spin-off, boot is treated as a § 301 distribution regardless of the shareholder's realized gain. This will result in a dividend to the extent of the distributing corporation's earnings and profits, and any excess of the distribution above earnings and profits first reduces basis and then produces capital gain. §§ 356(b) and 301(c). Now that individual shareholders are taxed on dividends at not over 15%, the outcome is more acceptable.

2. BOOT IN A SPLIT-OFF OR SPLIT-UP

In a split-off or split-up, an exchange of stock for boot resembles a redemption under § 302. Under § 356(a)(1) and (2), boot in such transactions is given sale or exchange treatment unless it "has the effect of the distribution of a dividend." Even then, there are two limitations to the dividend: (1) it is limited to the amount of gain recognized, and (2) it is limited to the recipient shareholder's ratable share of earnings and profits of the distributing corporation. § 356(a)(2). The remainder of recognized gain, if any, is capital gain under § 356(a)(1). This is known as the "dividend within gain rule."

PROBLEM 20-5

National Tile Corporation (NTC) is owned in equal shares by George and Henrietta, both of whom are individuals. NTC has abundant E & P. Henrietta has a basis of $30,000 in her NTC stock. NTC transfers the assets of one of its two divisions to a controlled corporation (Spun) in exchange for stock of Spun. NTC then distributes the stock of Spun, worth $150,000, plus $50,000 in cash, to Henrietta in redemption of all her stock in NTC. Assuming that the requirements of § 335 are met:

1) How much gain does she realize? How much does she recognize?

2) What is the character of the gain, if any? Capital gain, ordinary? Something else?

3) How would the result differ, if at all, if Henrietta and George were married?

F. DISTRIBUTIONS IN CONNECTION WITH TAXABLE DIVISIONS

It is clear that a spin-off that falls outside § 355 will constitute a distribution of property under § 301 with the result that there can be a tax on the distributing corporation under § 311(b) and a dividend to the recipient under § 301.

A nonqualifying split-off should be treated as a redemption of the stock of the distributing corporation, which is taxable to the distributing corporation under § 311(b) and to the shareholders under § 302. This would force one to consult § 302 in order to determine whether the distribution qualifies as an exchange or as a distribution under § 301.

A nonqualifying split-up, however, looks like a complete liquidation under §§ 331(a) and 336, which means that, although the liquidating corporation could owe a *General Utilities* tax, the shareholders will normally report capital gains or losses to the extent that the value of what they receive exceeds the basis of their stock in the distributing corporation that they surrender. A nonqualifying split-up ought to be taxed as a regular liquidation under § 331 even if the subsidiaries were recently formed.

Chapter 21

CORPORATE REORGANIZATIONS

A. INTRODUCTION

The corporate reorganization rules are an exception to the general rule that realized gains and losses from exchanges of stock for stock or stock for assets must be recognized. The corporate reorganization provisions of §§ 354-368 carve out a major exception from § 1001 for corporate transactions that fit into one of several pigeonholes. The operative nonrecognition rules are keyed to § 368's definitional rules, and can transform what would otherwise be taxable acquisitions into nontaxable ones. An individual shareholder cannot make a tax-free exchange of stock in one corporation for stock or assets of another unless the transaction qualifies at the corporate level as a reorganization.[1]

The tax policy assumption underlying these non-recognition provisions appears in Reg. § 1.1002-1(c), namely that the tax-free exchange provisions apply in cases where "the new enterprise, the new corporate structure and the new property are substantially continuations of the old still unliquidated;" this is consistent with other tax-deferral provisions in the Code that depend on the fundamental assumption that the taxpayer's investment has not been cashed out. The reorganization provisions grant tax deferral by requiring that the unrecognized gains and losses remain embedded in the taxpayer's property for future taxation. To do this, various basis rules, particularly in §§ 358 and 362, complement the income-tax-deferral rules of §§ 354-57, § 361 and § 1032. As usual, this principle is thwarted in the case of stock held until the taxpayer's death. At death, the stock receives a fair market value basis under § 1014.

The earliest reorganization provisions were enacted as part of the Revenue Act of 1918 in anticipation of the end of World War I and of the need to restructure American industry from its wartime footing to a world at peace. As the Senate Finance Committee put it, the legislation would "negative the assertion of tax in the case of certain purely paper transactions." S. Rep. No. 617, 65th Cong., 3d Sess. 5-6 (1918), Senate Finance Committee report on § 202(b) of the Revenue Act of 1918.

Under prior law, even an exchange that was purely technical could be held taxable, such as where a New Jersey corporation did nothing more than reincorporate itself as a Delaware corporation and issue new Delaware shares to its shareholders in exchange for their old New Jersey shares in the otherwise identical company. *See Marr v. US.*, 268 U.S. 536 (1925). Such an exchange would now be tax-free under § 368(a)(1)(F) as a "mere change in identity, form, or place of organization of one corporation."

The legislative history of the 1918 Act provided little guidance as to what the term "reorganization" might mean. As a result, the courts were forced to develop some of the most important doctrines in the area in an effort to contain the term "reorganization" to what the courts considered its intended meaning. Their fundamental purpose is to ensure that the reorganization provisions are limited to bona fide cases and, above all, to prevent "astute tax lawyers" from converting what is in substance a taxable sale into a tax-free reorganization by skillful maneuvering of form. *See, e.g.,* H.R. Rep. No. 179, 68th Cong., 1st Sess. (1924), reprinted in 1939-1 C.B. (Pt. 2), 142, 252, 554, 556.

Subsequent Revenue Acts provided more fine-grained definitions of the term "reorganization" and expanded the kinds of transactions that could qualify, but did not explicitly codify these judicial doctrines. Even today the definition of a "reorganization" consists of two elements. One consists of the mechanical description of various types of qualifying exchanges

---

[1] § 351 admittedly looks like an exception, but it is rarely a practical acquisition technique.

of stock and assets in § 368 of the Code. The other consists of three substance-over-form requirements derived from case law that operate independently of the definitions in § 368, namely:

1. The reorganization must have a corporate business purpose;

2. The target company's business must continue to some minimum extent after the reorganization, known as the "continuity of business enterprise" requirement; and

3. The owners of the target company must have a continuing stake in the acquiring company, known as the "continuity of proprietary interest" requirement.

These requirements were not all included in the Regulations until 1980. *See* Reg. § 1.368-1. Despite the Regulations' attempt to define these requirements, case law remains an important independent source of interpretation.

B. CODE STRUCTURE
Read §§ 368(a)(1), 354(a) and 361(a).

If a transaction meets both the statutory definition of a "reorganization" under § 368(a)(1) and the three judicial requirements discussed above, then the transaction will generally be tax-free at the shareholder, security holder and corporate levels.

At the shareholder and security holder level, § 354 ensures that gain or loss will go unrecognized if stock or securities in a corporation that is "a party to a reorganization" (as defined in § 368(b)) is exchanged solely for stock or securities in that same corporation or in another corporation that is also a party to the reorganization. This provision protects shareholders and security holders from current income taxation. If "boot" property or liabilities are involved, there may be some recognition of gain under §§ 356-57.

Corporate parties to the reorganization are protected by § 361 and § 1032, which also provide for nonrecognition of gains or losses on a corporate exchange of property solely for stock or securities of another corporation that is a party to the reorganization. These provisions are not elective, so that a taxpayer who desires to recognize a loss for tax purposes may discover to his disappointment that the loss is barred because it arose in the context of an unexpected "reorganization." On the other hand, large corporations almost always seek an advance ruling from the IRS or an opinion of a top law firm to ensure the expected tax treatment. It is the smaller businesses that are likely to run into trouble.

C. STATUTORY MERGERS AND CONSOLIDATIONS
Read § 368(a)(1)(A).

Section 368(a)(1)(A) contemplates two similar kinds of transactions, a statutory merger or a consolidation. A merger arises under specific state statutes pursuant to which one corporation absorbs another corporation and becomes the sole survivor, comprising the assets and liabilities of both. That is, the absorbed corporation goes out of existence in a merger, and as a matter of corporate law the acquiring corporation obtains all the assets and liabilities of the target corporation automatically. That greatly diminishes the need for deeds and other transfer documents.

A consolidation occurs when two (or more) free-standing corporations combine and become a third corporation. The old corporations disappear but the shareholders and creditors of the disappearing corporations automatically become the shareholders and creditors of the new corporation by operation of state law. Recent changes in the Regulations now permit tax-deferred mergers of U.S. corporations with foreign corporations. That subject is beyond the scope of this course because it entails a network of further Code provisions.

The merger was the first form of reorganization to be explicitly recognized in the Code. It is also the most popular form due to its great flexibility. For example, unlike the other forms of reorganization under § 368(a), a merger freely allows the use of nonvoting stock or preferred stock of the acquiring corporation as consideration paid to the shareholders of the target, and it is generous in its permission to use money or other "boot" as consideration as well.

1. MINIMUM CONTINUITY OF PROPRIETARY INTEREST

The riskiest feature of the Type A reorganization concerns the minimum amount of equity that must be issued in connection with the reorganization. This is often expressed in terms of "continuity of propriety interest." The question presented by this issue is, "how much of the consideration that the acquiring corporation pays to the shareholders of the target corporation must be in stock of the acquiring corporation?" The rule of thumb for practitioners is 50%, and this is derived from the fact that the IRS will not issue a ruling in advance of a merger unless this 50% requirement is met. Rev. Proc. 77-37, 1977- 2 C.B. 568.

Note that the 50% rule has nothing to do with percentage ownership of the acquiring corporation or with the relative sizes of the two corporations. A minnow may swallow a whale in a valid Type A reorganization just as a whale may swallow a minnow.

To illustrate: T Corporation ("T") is a target of a takeover by A Corporation ("A") by means of a merger under state law. T is owned by one shareholder, Mr. T. He owns stock with a value of $10 and holds $90 of T bonds. As long as he receives at least $5 worth of A stock in the merger, the continuity of proprietary interest test will be met under the standard "bright line" rule. The size of A is irrelevant, and it does not matter whether A's $5 worth of A stock represents 0.001% of A or 99% by value. If T had several shareholders who collectively owned $10 of T stock, the question would be whether as a group they received at least $5 worth of A Corporation stock. The particular distribution of the A stock among the T shareholders does not matter and need not be pro rata.

The courts, at least in some older cases, have allowed much lower percentages. In *Miller v. Commissioner*, 84 F.2d 415 (6th Cir. 1936), 25% was held to be sufficient. In a merger or consolidation, any kind of stock of the acquiror (but not warrants or other rights) counts, including even nonvoting preferred which has no interest in future growth and is in this respect more like debt than equity. Thus, in *John A. Nelson Corp. v. Helvering,* 296 U.S. 374 (1935), the Supreme Court decided that continuity of interest was present where the consideration paid for the target's voting common stock consisted of 38% nonvoting preferred stock and 62% cash.

At the other end of the spectrum, the lowest reported level of continuity that failed to qualify appears to be that in *Kass v. Commissioner*, 60 T.C. 218 (1973), *aff'd* 491 F.2d 749 (3d Cir. 1974), holding that 16% in the form of voting common stock was not "tantalizingly high."

In determining continuity of interest for purposes of avoiding income in a Type A reorganization, taxpayers are sometimes forced to classify what they receive as debt or equity. Where debt received in exchange for equity is treated as equity, the usual consequence is to confer reorganization status on the acquisition. In contrast, if an alleged equity interest is treated as debt, those amounts do not count towards continuity of interest. Hybrid debt/equity interests may cause difficulty, as in the decision below.

ESTATE OF MOSE SILVERMAN v. COMMISSIONER
98 T.C. 54 (1992)

RUWE, JUDGE:

[In 1982, pursuant to a plan of merger the taxpayers exchanged their shares of stock in a State-chartered stock S&L for passbook savings accounts and certificates of deposit in the acquiring federally chartered mutual S&L. No part of the principal of the certificates of deposit could be withdrawn for 6 years. The taxpayer treated the gain realized on the transaction as the nontaxable proceeds of a § 368(a)(1)(A) reorganization. In 1985, the U.S. Supreme Court decided *Paulsen v. Commissioner*, 469 U.S. 131 (1985),which held that exchanges of this type did not qualify as tax-free reorganizations, so the taxpayers filed an amended federal income tax return for 1982, treating the exchange as an installment sale. They paid taxes on the gain attributable to passbook savings accounts received, but treated the certificates of deposit as delayed payment obligations. The IRS claimed the transaction did not qualify for installment sale treatment.]

Opinion

Respondent contends that Mr. and Mrs. Silverman were required to include the entire gain on disposition of their Olympic stock in their 1982 income. Petitioners concede that the exchange is not entitled to treatment as a tax-free reorganization. They argue, however, that the gain on the exchange may be reported on the installment method. We must decide whether the Silvermans were entitled to report the exchange under the installment method.

Section 1001(a) provides that the gain from the sale of property (there is no question that the term accounts in the instant case constitute property within the meaning of § 1001) shall be the excess of the amount realized there from over the adjusted basis. Amount realized is defined as the sum of any money received plus the fair market value of property (other than money) received. Sec. 1001(b). All gain realized under section 1001 must be recognized absent a statutory exception. Sec. 1001(c).

Section 453 provides such an exception. It allows income from an installment sale to be reported in the year "payment" is received. The amount of income to be recognized for any taxable year is the "proportion of the payments received in that year which the gross profit (realized or to be realized when payment is completed) bears to the total contract price." Sec. 453(c).

An "installment sale" is defined as "a disposition of property where at least 1 payment is to be received after the close of the taxable year in which the disposition occurs." Sec. 453(b)(l). Generally, and for purposes of this case, the term "payment" does not include the receipt of evidences of indebtedness of the person acquiring the property." Sec. 453(f)(3).

Mr. and Mrs. Silverman disposed of property (Olympic stock) to Coast [the acquiring S&L]. Coast was thus "the person acquiring the property." In return, the Silvermans received withdrawable statement savings accounts and term accounts that could not be withdrawn for 6 years. If the Coast term accounts which Mr. and Mrs. Silverman received in the exchange are "evidences of indebtedness of the person acquiring the property," then Mr. and Mrs. Silverman's receipt of the term accounts would not constitute "payment" for purposes of section 453, and they would therefore be entitled to report the disposition of their Olympic stock on the installment method.

Whether certificates of deposit are "evidences of indebtedness" of the issuing savings and loan association was answered by the Supreme Court in *Paulsen v. Commissioner,* 469 U.S. 131(1985). In that case, involving practically identical facts, the Court was called upon to determine whether a transaction wherein the taxpayer received savings accounts and certificates of deposit from a federally chartered mutual savings and loan association in exchange for stock in a State-chartered savings and loan association, qualified as a tax-free reorganization under sections 354(a)(1) and 368(a)(1)(A). One requirement for such a tax-free exchange was that the taxpayer's ownership in the prior organization must continue in a meaningful fashion in the reorganized enterprise, i.e., "the seller must acquire an interest in the affairs of the purchasing company more definite than that incident to ownership of its short-term purchase-money notes." *Pinellas Ice & Cold Storage Co. v. Commissioner,* 287 U.S. 462, 470 (1933); *Paulsen v. Commissioner,* 469 U.S. at 136. In *Paulsen,* the Court recognized that the certificates of deposit had both "equity and debt characteristics," *Paulsen,* 469 U.S. at 138, but found that the debt characteristics predominated, and that the equity characteristics were insubstantial.

> "[T]here are substantial debt characteristics to the Citizens shares that pre-dominate. Petitioners' passbook accounts and certificates of deposit are not subordinated to the claims of creditors, and their deposits are not considered permanent contributions to capital. Shareholders have a right on 30 days' notice to withdraw their deposits, which right Citizens is obligated to respect. While petitioners were unable to withdraw their funds for one year following the merger, this restriction can be viewed as akin to a delayed payment rather than a material alteration in the nature of the instruments received as payment. . . .
>   In our view, the debt characteristics of Citizens' shares greatly outweigh the equity characteristics. The face value of petitioners' passbook accounts and certificates of deposit was $210,000. Petitioners have stipulated that they had a right to withdraw the face amount of the deposits in cash, on demand after one year or at stated intervals thereafter. Their investment was virtually risk free and the dividends received were equivalent to prevailing interest rates for savings accounts in other types of savings institutions. The debt value of the shares was the same as the face value, $210,000; because no one would pay more than this for the shares, the incremental value attributable to the equity features was, practically, zero. . . . *Paulsen v. Commissioner,* supra at 139, 140."

We perceive no meaningful distinction between the certificates of deposit in *Paulsen* and those involved here. The certificates of deposit received by Mr. and Mrs. Silverman represent "evidences of indebtedness" of the person acquiring their property. Petitioners meet all of the literal statutory requirements of section 453 so as to entitle them to report income from the disposition of Olympic stock using the installment method.

Respondent argues that the term accounts are "cash equivalents" and therefore must be included in income in the year of sale. Respondent points out that the Court in *Paulsen* characterized the accounts as cash equivalents. . . .

The result of satisfying either the cash equivalence or the ascertainable fair market value tests is that gain is realized under section 1001(b). See *Warren Jones Co. v. Commissioner,* supra at 791, n.6. Petitioners do not dispute that gain was realized in 1982. Such realized gain under section 1001 must be recognized absent a statutory exception, but, as previously pointed out, section 453 provides such an exception. A finding that a transaction may be reported under section 453 assumes there has been a realization event and makes any further consideration of the cash equivalence doctrine redundant. See *Warren Jones Co. v. Commissioner,* 68 T.C. 837 (1977), aff'd. 617 F.2d 536 (9th Cir. 1980). Thus, despite the inclusion of the value of the buyer's obligation in the amount realized under section 1001(b), a taxpayer is entitled to report gain from the transaction under the installment method. *Warren Jones Co. v. Commissioner,* 524 F.2d 788 (9th Cir. 1975). . . .

The legislative history of section 453 indicates that Congress believed that the cash equivalence characteristics of certain types of debt instruments made it inappropriate to allow them to be reported under the installment method. As a result, it enacted specific provisions to preclude certain debt instruments from being reported under the installment method. See S. Rept. 91-552 (1969), 1969-3 C.B. 423, 515. These provisions, section 453(f)(4) and (5), first became part of the installment sale section in 1969 as paragraph 453(b)(3). These paragraphs provide:

"(3) Payment. – Except as provided in paragraph (4), the term "payment" does not include the receipt of evidences of indebtedness of the person acquiring the property (whether or not payment of such indebtedness is guaranteed by another person).

(4) Purchaser evidences of indebtedness payable on demand or readily tradable. – Receipt of a bond or other evidence of indebtedness which is (A) payable on demand, or (B) is issued by a corporation or a government or political subdivision thereof and is readily tradable, shall be treated as receipt of payment.

(5) Readily tradable defined. – For purposes of paragraph (4), the term "readily tradable" means a bond or other evidence of indebtedness which is issued –

(A) with interest coupons attached or in registered form (other than one in registered form which the taxpayer establishes will not be readily tradable in an established securities market), or

(B) in any other form designed to render such bond or other evidence of indebtedness readily tradable in an established securities market."

These provisions were a Congressional response to the increasing number of acquisitive corporate reorganizations in which shareholders received corporate debentures for shares. Such an exchange was not exempt from taxation under the sections of the Code governing reorganizations, but tax deferral could otherwise be secured under section 453.

The Senate Finance Committee report stated:

"Debentures, however, in most cases can be readily traded on the market and, therefore are a close approximation of cash. Thus, the problem of the seller not having the cash with which to pay the tax due would not appear to be present where he receives debentures or other readily marketable securities. [S. Rept. 91-552 (1969), 1969-3 C.B. 423, 515.] Consequently, Congress directed that certain types of indebtedness be treated as payment received in the year of sale." S. Rept. 91-552 at 516.

The type of indebtedness to be treated in this manner are bonds or debentures with interest coupons attached, in registered form, or in any other form designed   to make it possible to readily trade them in an established securities market . . . "[S. Rept. 91-552 at 516.]

However, the report goes on to state that:

"The committee amendments also provide that bonds in registered form which the taxpayer establishes will not be readily tradable [sic] in an established securities market are not to be treated as payments received in the year of sale, since because of their lack of ready marketability they do not possess the characteristics which would render them essentially similar to cash." [S. Rept. 91-552 at 516.]

Therefore, while Congress has created an exception to installment reporting based on the cash equivalence characteristics of certain obligations, it specifically enumerated the type of debt obligations which fell within the exception. We conclude that cash equivalence is not an exception to the installment method except as specifically provided in the statute. The term accounts in issue in this case were not readily tradable in an established securities market, and, thus, were not within the aforementioned statutory exception. . . .

During 1982, the Silvermans never possessed the right to receive payment of the amounts represented by the term accounts. The term accounts were not withdrawable until 1988, were not readily tradable in an established securities market, and were not assignable except upon the death of a joint owner, in which case title could only be vested in the decedent's personal representative or the surviving joint owner. The passbooks evidencing the accounts stated on their face that transferability was limited. In short, it is difficult to see how the Silvermans received the economic benefits of payment when the term accounts could not be withdrawn, sold, or borrowed against during the year in issue. . . .

Decision will be entered for petitioners.

NOTE

Installment sale treatment in a valid reorganization. *Silverman* involved a fully taxable merger (not a § 368(a)(1) "reorganization" for tax purposes). What if the transaction were a "reorganization" and the target company shareholder got paid "boot" in the form of an installment obligation payable over time? The answer under Reg. § 1.453-11(a) and (c)(1) is that the boot can be reported under § 453. This means that the shareholder is assured of being able to match his tax bill with his cash proceeds, which is the purpose of § 453, subject to a fairly complex calculation. Reg. § 1.453-11(c)(4)(iv) provides an example of how the calculation is performed.

The following General Counsel Memorandum was prepared by the Office of the Chief Counsel of the IRS and was sent to the Director of the Corporation Tax Branch at the National Office of the IRS. It is part of a chain of in-house official communications that grew out of a Regulations project and a proposed Revenue Ruling. G.C.M's are now subject to mandatory public disclosure.

G.C.M. 39404
September 4, 1985

Issues

1. Does the statutory merger of S into P result in sufficient continuity of interest to constitute a "reorganization" within the meaning of section 368(a)(1)(A) if P owns a 70 percent "old and cold" stock interest in S?

2. If the statutory merger does qualify as an "A" reorganization, does P recognize gain or loss on the transaction?

CONCLUSION

The proposed revenue ruling concludes that the merger does not qualify as a reorganization because the continuity of interest requirement is not satisfied. The transaction is viewed instead as a complete liquidation of S, and P is required to recognize gain or loss pursuant to section 331(a)(1) on the receipt of the assets of S.

The proposed ruling is based on G.C.M. 31228, *** A-629558 (May 14, 1959). Upon reconsideration we believe G.C.M. 31228 is in error. We are therefore unable to concur in the proposed ruling. G.C.M. 31228 is revoked.

In connection with this case we have reconsidered G.C.M. 35653 I-451-73 (Feb. 4, 1974), which concludes that because there is no "solely for voting stock" requirement for "D" reorganizations, the rationale of Rev. Rul. 54-396, 1954-2 C.B. 147, and Bausch & Lomb Optical Company v. Commissioner, 267 F.2d 75 (2d Cir.), cert. denied, 361 U.S. 835 (1959), does not apply to such reorganizations. G.C.M. 35653 is reaffirmed.

1.   The conversion of P's indirect stock interest in S into a direct interest in the S assets should be viewed as preserving continuity of interest for purposes of section 368(a)(1)(A). It is only in those cases in which the receipt of solely voting stock is required that the conversion of an indirect interest into a direct interest will cause the transaction to fail to qualify as a reorganization.

2.   In view of our conclusion that the merger qualifies as a reorganization under section 368(a)(1)(A), we conclude that no gain or loss will be recognized to either P or S as a result of the transaction. The basis of the S assets in the hands of P is determined by section 362(b). The exchange of the minority shareholders' S stock is governed by sections 354 or 356.

Facts

P, a publicly owned corporation, owns 70 percent of the only class of stock of S corporation. All of the S stock owned by P was purchased in the over-the-counter market more than twenty years ago. The remaining 30 percent of S stock is owned by M corporation. In order to achieve a result that was advantageous to P and M a plan of reorganization was adopted under which S was merged into P in a statutory merger pursuant to state law. Under the plan M received 400x dollars and 100 shares of P stock trading at 1x dollars per share, in a value-for-value exchange, for the S stock held by M. Thereafter, P used the assets of S in its business.

Analysis

The proposed revenue ruling is based on the facts of a private letter ruling considered by this office in G.C.M. 31228, (May 14, 1959). Following G.C.M. 31228, the proposed ruling concludes that the upstream merger of a less than 80 percent subsidiary does not qualify as a reorganization. The transaction is viewed instead as a complete liquidation of S in which P recognizes gain or loss pursuant to section 331(a)(1).

I. The Statutory Merger of S into P Constitutes a Section 368 (a)(1)(A) Reorganization.

A. Section 332

Section 332 provides that no gain or loss will be recognized where an 80 percent subsidiary is liquidated into its parent corporation. The flush language of section 332(b) states that this result will not be affected by the fact that assets are transferred to the taxpayer corporation (parent) in an exchange described in section 361, and by the fact that shares not owned by the taxpayer (parent corporation) are surrendered in an exchange described in section 354. Section 332 overrides the reorganization rules to the extent that the two overlap. But see *Eastern Color Printing Co. v. Commissioner*, 63 T.C. 27 (1974), acq., 1975-1 C.B. 1, and cases cited therein holding that an "F" reorganization that met the provisions of section 332 could nonetheless be excluded from section 381(b)(3); Rev. Rul. 75-561, 1975-2 C.B. 129. This means that a transaction may qualify as a reorganization as to minority shareholders while still being treated as a section 332 liquidation for purposes of the controlling parent. See Treas. Reg. §§ 1.332-2(d) and (e), 1.332-5. If the acquiring corporation owns less than 80 percent of the acquired corporation at the time of the adoption of the plan of merger, section 332 is inapplicable. However, nothing in section 332 or the Regulations there under requires that a transfer of assets from a less than 80 percent subsidiary to be characterized as a liquidation.

In addition, the legislative history of section 332 does not indicate that Congress intended to preclude tax-free treatment in an upstream merger of a less than 80 percent subsidiary into its parent. . . "[T]he statutory predecessor of section 332, was adopted to encourage the simplification of corporate structures and the elimination of holding companies." Testimony before the Committee on Finance disclosed that there was some uncertainty in the business community as to the tax-free status of a liquidation of a subsidiary into its parent by merger, inhibiting desirable corporate restructuring . . . It was felt that the clarifying legislation would cure the uncertainty in the area. Nowhere does it appear, however, that Congress intended to limit the scope of the definitions relating to corporal, reorganizations, or to foreclose the possibility that an upstream merger could qualify for reorganization treatment. . .

In summary, the legislative history of the predecessor of section 332 indicates that Congress was aware that the liquidation of a subsidiary into its parent by merger might qualify as a tax-free reorganization under existing law and desired to insure this nonrecognition for 80 percent controlled subsidiaries.

B. Continuity of Interest

In view of the above, where the acquiring corporation's interest in the acquired corporation is old and cold and the merger is pursuant to state law, as in the instant case, the question arises whether the merger should be treated as a section 368(a)(1)(A) reorganization, rather than a liquidation . . . Treas. Reg. § 1.368-1(b) provides that requisite to a reorganization is a continuity of interest in the new corporation on the part of those persons who directly or indirectly were the owners of the enterprise prior to the reorganization. Treas. Reg. § 1.368-2(a) provides that the term "reorganization" does not embrace the mere purchase by one corporation of the properties of another. These Regulations embody a well-developed judicial gloss on the statutory definition of reorganizations, the purpose of which is to exclude from the scope of the reorganization provisions those transactions that are in fact sales . . .

The court in *Southwest Natural Gas Company* summarized the continuity of interest test as follows:

While no precise formula has been expressed for determining whether there has been retention of the requisite interest, it seems clear that . . . [there must be] a showing: (1) that the transferor corporation or its shareholders retained a substantial proprietary stake in the enterprise represented by a material interest in the affairs of the transferee corporation, and, (2) that such retained interest represents a substantial part of the value of the property transferred. 189 F.2d at 334 (footnote omitted).

The court held that the continuity of interest test was applicable to an "A" reorganization although not specifically mandated by the statute.

In G.C.M. 31228, we disagreed with your proposed conclusion and held that the statutory merger of a 66 percent subsidiary into its parent fails to qualify as a section 368(a)(1)(A) reorganization because the transaction does not meet the continuity of interest requirement. Continuity was analyzed by looking solely to the consideration received by the minority shareholders of the subsidiary, and since the parent's stock received by the minority shareholders represented less than 15 percent in value of the stock surrendered by such shareholders, continuity of interest was lacking. The instant cases require reconsideration of that position.

In an upstream merger, the indirect stock interest of the parent in its subsidiary is converted into a direct interest in the subsidiary's assets, assuming the parent's prior stock interest is old and cold, as in the instant case since the parent's original investment remains at the risk of the business.

The historic purpose of the continuity of interest requirement is to distinguish sales from reorganizations. In an upstream merger only the form of the parent's investment has been changed, and its prior equity interest has been intensified and not "cashed out." Although the previous corporate relationship has been terminated, this is not the same as a cash sale of the subsidiary's assets. We believe that denying the existence of continuity of interest under such circumstances misapprehends the purpose of the rule . . .

Published positions of the Service do not resolve whether the continuity of interest requirement is satisfied under the facts of the instant case, because the minority shareholders do not receive a sufficient amount of parent stock. . .

More recently the Service concluded that the statutory merger of a 79 percent subsidiary into its parent constituted a reorganization under section 368(a)(1)(A) and (a)(2)(C). In Rev. Rul. 58-93, 1958-1 C.B. 188, considered in this ruling, X corporation held 79 percent of Y corporation; Y transferred its assets to newly formed Z corporation in exchange for all the stock of Z. Y was then merged into X in a statutory merger. The minority shareholders of Y received X stock in exchange for their Y shares. The transaction was characterized as a merger of Y into X under section 368(a)(l)(A) followed by a transfer of the acquired Y assets to Z pursuant to section 368(a)(2)(C), and the ruling concludes that gain or loss will not be recognized by X, Y, or Z, or the minority shareholders of Y. Because the minority shareholders of Y received only X stock continuity of interest is satisfied under the standard of G.C.M. 31228.

The Regulations under section 332 stated that a transaction may be treated as a liquidation of an 80 percent subsidiary with respect to the parent corporation, and yet be a reorganization with respect to minority shareholders. Treas. Reg. § 1.332-2(d) states:

> If a transaction constitutes a distribution in complete liquidation within the meaning of the Internal Revenue Code of 1954 and satisfies the requirements of section 332, it is not material that it is otherwise described under the local law. If a liquidating corporation distributes all of its property in complete liquidation and if pursuant to the plan for such complete liquidation a corporation owning the specified amount of stock in the liquidating corporation received property constituting amounts distributed in complete liquidation within the meaning of the Code and also receives other property attributable to shares not owned by it, the transfer of the property to the recipient corporation shall not be treated, by reason of the receipt of such other property, as not being a distribution (or one of a series of distributions) in complete cancellation or redemption of all of the stock of the liquidating corporation within the meaning of section 332, even though for purposes of those provisions relating to corporate reorganizations the amount received by the recipient corporation in excess of its ratable share is regarded as acquired upon the issuance of its stock or securities in a tax-free exchange as described in section 361 and the cancellation or redemption of the stock not owned by the recipient corporation is treated as occurring as a result of a tax-free exchange described in section 354.

Since in a section 332 liquidation by merger no more than twenty percent of the total value of the acquired corporation can be acquired for stock of the acquiring (parent) corporation, it follows that continuity is preserved in this situation by ownership of assets. We do not believe it is reasonable to consider a parent's eighty percent indirect interest to be continuity preserving while treating a lesser percentage indirect interest as not continuity preserving. . . .

II. *Nonrecognition to Parent Corporation*

The Service has argued on at least two occasions that although an upstream merger could qualify as a reorganization, the parent's acquisition is not tax-free, because there is no provision that literally provides nonrecognition treatment to exchanges by a corporation of stock in another corporation for property of such other corporation. In *Rogan v. Starr Piano Company*, 139 F.2d 671 (9th Cir. 1943), *cert. denied*, 322 U.S. 728 (1944), the court accepted this position and rejected the parent's argument that a statutory merger could not be both a reorganization and a liquidation. Thus the court held that although the statutory merger of a wholly-owned subsidiary into its parent constituted a reorganization under section 112(g)(1)(A) of the Revenue Act of 1934, gain should be recognized to the parent as on a distribution in complete liquidation. The predecessors to sections 354(a) and 361(a) were inapplicable since there had been no actual exchange of stock or securities for stock or securities, and no exchange by a corporation of property for stock or securities in another corporation. The court refused to find a constructive exchange of parent stock for subsidiary assets sufficient for purposes of qualifying the acquisition under the predecessor to section 354(a).

The Second Circuit arrived at a contrary result in *Gutbro Holding Company v. Commissioner*, 138 F.2d 16 (2d Cir. 1943). There, a parent and its wholly-owned subsidiary were consolidated under state law, pursuant to a plan providing that upon consolidation, the stock of the parent should represent the stock of the consolidated corporation. The court held that the substance of the transaction was a reorganization, and it did not possess the characteristics of a liquidation. Although acquisition of the subsidiary's assets did not literally fall within the reorganization nonrecognition provisions, the court was willing to view the transaction as constructively involving an exchange within the meaning of the predecessor to section 354(a), since a formal stock-for-stock exchange under these circumstances would have been an "idle act". . . .

On reconsideration of this question it is our opinion that, since the [parent] exchanged the stock which it owned in the [subsidiary] for shares of its own stock held by the latter company in pursuance of a plan of reorganization to which reorganization both corporations were parties, the transaction comes within the express language of [the predecessor of section 354(a)(l)] and the profit derived is not recognizable for tax purposes. 29 B.T.A. 905, 909 non-acq., XIII-1 C.B. 32 (1934). . . .

We do not believe the absence of a section 1032 exchange preceding the merger [is the right way to dispose of the *Starr Piano* problem because] [s]uch an exchange is a purely formal transaction, an "idle act" . . . so that to insist upon it as a condition for nonrecognition would serve only to set a trap for the unwary. Moreover, the strict requirement of a stock-for-stock exchange would be contrary to the characterization of the transaction in Rev. Rul. 58-93. . . .

George H, Jelly
Director

The following ruling illustrates a cash merger combined with a unique twist.

REV. RUL. 84-71
1984-1 C.B. 106

The Internal Revenue Service has reconsidered Rev. Rul. 80-284, 1980-2 C.B. 117, and Rev. Rul. 80-285, 1980-2 C.B. 119, in which transfers that satisfied the technical requirements of section 351(a) of the Internal Revenue Code were nevertheless held to constitute taxable exchanges because they were part of larger acquisitive transactions that did not meet the continuity of interest test generally applicable to acquisitive reorganizations.

In Rev. Rul. 80-284, fourteen percent of T corporation's stock was held by A, president and chairman of the board, and eighty-six percent by the public. P, an unrelated, publicly held corporation wished to purchase the stock of T. All the T stockholders except A were willing to sell the T stock for cash. A wished to avoid recognition of gain.

In order to accommodate these wishes, the following transactions were carried out as part of an overall plan. First, P and A formed a new corporation, S. P transferred cash and other property to S in exchange solely for all of S's common stock; A transferred T stock to S solely in exchange for all of S's preferred stock. These transfers were intended to be tax-free under section 351 of the Code. Second, S organized a new corporation, D, and transferred to D the cash it had received from P in exchange for all the D common stock. Third, D was merged into T under state law. As a result of the merger, each share of T stock, except those shares held by S, were surrendered for cash equal to the stock's fair market value and each share of D stock was converted into T stock.

Rev. Rul. 80-284 concluded that if a purported section 351 exchange is an integral part of a larger transaction that fits a pattern common to acquisitive reorganizations, and if the continuity of shareholder interest requirement of section 1.368-1(b) of the Income Tax Regulations is not satisfied with respect to the larger transaction, then the transaction as a whole resembles a sale and the exchange cannot qualify under section 351 because that section is not intended to apply to sales. Rev. Rul. 80-285 reached a similar conclusion with respect to an asset, rather than stock, acquisition in which a purported section 351 exchange was also part of a larger acquisitive transaction.

Upon reconsideration, the Service has concluded that the fact that "larger acquisitive transactions," such as those described in Rev. Rul. 80-284 and Rev. Rul. 80-285, fail to meet the requirements for tax-free treatment under the reorganization provisions of the Code does not preclude the applicability of section 351(a) to transfers that may be described as part of such larger transactions, but also, either alone or in conjunction with other transfers, meet the requirements of section 351(a).

NOTES

1. **The importance of the ruling**. To appreciate the importance of the ruling, put yourself in the position of the 14% shareholder. What did he accomplish? In what respect did he come out ahead of his fellow shareholders?

2. **Impact on tax attributes**. If this were a taxable liquidation, the subsidiary's tax attributes could disappear, and both corporations would be taxed under §§ 336 and 331. That might be a high price to pay. Nevertheless, under some circumstances, taxable treatment is acceptable. For example the subsidiary might have enough losses from other sources to offset its own § 336 gain, and the parent might have its own losses to offset the § 331 gain that it recognized on getting the sub's assets. By contrast, both a § 332 liquidation and a Type A reorganization result in no tax to either corporation and the parent inherits the tax attributes of the target. Take a glance at § 381(a)(1) to confirm this.

3. **Downstream mergers**. What about the merger of a parent into a subsidiary company? In *Edwards Motor Transit Co. v. Commissioner, T.C.* Memo 1964-317 (1964), a parent company merged into its subsidiary in a transaction that formally met the requirements of

§ 368(a)(1)(A). The case does not seem surprising unless you ask yourself whether the practical result is not really a liquidation of the parent company. In *Edwards Motor Transit*, the parent was a mere holding company and it is difficult to see what distinguished the transaction from a liquidation of the parent other than the fact that it met the technical definition of a reorganization. On the other hand, reorganization treatment promotes the simplification of corporate structures by eliminating unnecessary layers of corporations on a tax-deferred basis.

4. **Drop-downs**. Section 368(a)(2)(C) allows the acquiring corporation in a Type A, B, or C reorganization to "drop down" the acquired stock or assets to a corporation that it controls. In Rev. Rul. 64-73, 1964-1 C.B. 142 (in connection with a Type C reorganization) the IRS interpreted "control" as allowing a drop-down to a second-tier or presumably even lower-tier corporation as long as the acquiring corporation directly or indirectly controls the lowest-tier subsidiary within the meaning of § 368(c).

5. **"Creeping" mergers.** Any acquisition can be made either in a single transaction or over time by gradual acquisitions of stock followed by a final stock or asset acquisition that resembles a reorganization or perhaps liquidations (perhaps under § 332 if the acquiror has requisite control). It is often difficult to determine whether such creeping acquisitions qualify partly or wholly as reorganizations because of the lack of Congressional attention to them. One of the big problems, already addressed, is whether a less-than-80% stock purchase followed by a liquidation in a state-law merger can constitute a Type A reorganization or whether it is necessarily a taxable purchase combined with a taxable liquidation. An analysis of creeping reorganizations depends primarily on whether each step of the acquisition is respected as a separate transaction or is treated as part of a single "plan" so that all the planned steps are collapsed into a single transaction. For example, if pursuant to a plan, an acquiring company buys all of the stock of a target company for cash and then immediately merges the target subsidiary into itself, it is fairly obvious that there is no "reorganization" because the target shareholders lack any continuing proprietary stake in the continuing former business and can fairly be said to have sold their stock. By contrast, if the upstream merger takes place after the cash acquisition is "old and cold," the parent corporation has become the genuine shareholder and the merger can qualify as an A reorganization. It will not matter whether the initial step is "old and cold" if the consideration paid to the target shareholders contains sufficient continuity of interest (i.e., sufficient stock of the acquiring corporation) because continuity of interest will be present in either case.

6. **What is an equity interest?** Warrants and rights to purchase stock do not carry continuity of interest, nor does debt that is convertible into stock until it is actually converted. However, if the corporation is insolvent, there is authority for the position that the debt holders should be treated as having become de facto the equity shareholders. *See Helvering v. Alabama Asphaltic Limestone Co.,* 315 U.S. 179 (1942). Nonqualified preferred stock (NQP) exists in a twilight zone; it counts for purposes of determining if there is continuity of proprietary interest, but is taxed as boot in the recipient's hands, except where it is swapped for other NQP or in certain reorganizations of family corporations. See H.R. Conf. Rep. 105-220, 105th Cong., 1st Sess. 544 (1997). Preferred stock subject to classification as "boot" should be limited and preferred as to dividends, and "capped" as to growth. In 2004, Congress narrowed the definition of "preferred stock" in order to meet these requirements. Now, § 351(g)(3)(A) provides that preferred stock does not participate in corporate earnings and growth unless the shareholders have a real and meaningful likelihood of actual participation. In addition, § 351(g)(2)(A) defines nonqualified

preferred stock as either: (1) mandatorily redeemable (2) stock that the insurer is required to redeem, (3) subject to a call by the issuer (or a related party) that is more likely than not to be exercised, or (4) stock with a floating dividend rate.

7. **Accounting treatment of mergers and acquisitions**. The accounting treatment for these transactions is not consistent with the tax results. The accounting analog of a nontaxable corporate restructuring is a *pooling of interests*, under which the acquiring corporation picks up the Target's assets, liabilities, and net worth at the same book values as they had on the target's balance sheet and is entitled to report the target's earnings as its own. However, it is hard to achieve a pooling result because, in simplified terms, the accounting rules require that:

- At least 90% of the consideration received by Target (T) shareholders is voting common stock of the acquiror (P);

- Before the acquisition, P and T were autonomous entities;

- P and T did not engage in stock redemptions of voting stock, spin-offs, or any other changes in capital stock in connection with the P-T plan of combination;

- The consideration paid by T is fixed in amount; and

- P will not dispose of T assets or reacquire P stock from T shareholders.

If any requirement is not met, the result is a *purchase*, which results in P taking a cost basis in T's assets and treating the excess of the purchase price over the value of the assets as goodwill to be amortized over forty years. This is generally undesirable, because amortization of goodwill creates an annual financial expense on P's books that reduces P's reported earnings. Notice how the purchase often favors the acquirer by (in effect) boosting the book value of the target's assets.

8. **Combining steps**. Subchapter C describes a large number of separate transactions, such as tax-free organizations under §351, spin-offs under §355, and forward triangular mergers under §368(a)(1)(A). Taxpayers can manipulate these pieces like children's building blocks by establishing back-to-back transactions. The taxpayer may or may not want to combine for income tax purposes. How to know whether steps should be combined or left separate? The answer is the "step transaction doctrine." If it applies, then the step transaction doctrine looks only at the first and last steps to characterize the transaction. There are three different versions of the step transaction doctrine. To be safe, apply all three. The courts are not consistent and sometimes apply only one test.
One is the "binding commitment test." This applies only if the steps are legally bound together.
The second is the "mutual interdependence" test. This combines steps that would not have been undertaken but for the next steps. The third test is the "end result" test. This collapses the steps if the taxpayer intended the outcome that resulted from the steps. Without this knowledge of the step transaction doctrine, you cannot competently deal with subchapter C.

9. **The step-transaction doctrine as a taxpayer's sword**. In *King Enterprises v. United States*, 418 F.2d 511 (Ct. Cl. 1969), the acquiring corporation paid cash for approximately

49% of target company's stock and its own stock for the balance, and in a later but prearranged second step merged the newly-acquired subsidiary into itself. The upstream merger was held a Type A reorganization and the initial acquisition was held to be part of the same transaction so that the target shareholders were entitled to reorganization treatment on the exchange of stock (the cash was taxable boot). The target shareholders used the step-transaction doctrine to salvage a potentially taxable stock acquisition (a failed "B" reorganization) and turned it into a nontaxable "Type A" reorganization. In a wonderful example of a whipsaw, the acquiring corporation obtained a step-up in the basis of the target's assets because it was protected by a private letter ruling that guaranteed (former) § 334(b)(2) treatment of the transaction as a purchase of assets. Thus the two sides of the transaction were given inconsistent treatment and each side got the best of both worlds: it was a taxable transaction on the buyer's side, but a tax-free reorganization to the sellers. To top it all off, the sellers were corporations, and the boot was treated as a dividend qualifying for the § 243 dividends-received deduction.

10. **The concept of the historic shareholder.** Assume a group of individuals decide they want to get control of T. They buy 84% of the stock, leaving Mrs. Kass, the only remaining T shareholder, owning 16%. Next, the raiders cause a corporation they own, called P, to acquire T by merger. All the shareholders of T get P stock, including Mrs. Kass. It used to be clear that the merger failed the continuity of proprietary interest test because the historic shareholders (here Mrs. Kass) only got 16% of the stock, which is far less than the necessary 50%. *See Kass v. Commissioner*, 60 T.C. 218 (1973), aff'd CA3 (1974). The doctrine was often stated in terms of only the consideration issued to shareholders whose holdings were "old and cold." The doctrine's competitor is the notion that all that counts is whether enough equity was issued, ignoring who got the equity. The Regulations have moved to this second theory, subject to some restrictions that are not important now. *See* Reg. § 1.368-1(e)(1) and § 1.368-1(e)(6). These changes to the Regulations occurred after the *Seagrams* decision, which appears immediately below.

11. **The "plan of reorganization" requirement.** Although one can view this as a mere application of the step transaction doctrine, it is really a separate requirement for any reorganization. *See* Reg. § 1.368-2(g). Handshake agreements may be good enough to constitute a "plan," but they are imprudent. Wise practitioners make sure to "paper the deal" with documents.

Before you read the following case, read Reg. § 1.368-1(e)(1) and (e)(6).

J.E. SEAGRAM CORP. v. COMMISSIONER
104 T.C. 75 (1995)

[This was a famous, controversial and complicated deal. Basically two corporate giants competed to acquire another giant. To be specific, Seagrams, a large publicly-traded corporation, bought a 32% block of the stock of Conoco, also a publicly-traded corporation. Shortly thereafter, Conoco agreed with DuPont Holdings, Inc. (DH), a subsidiary of DuPont, to a competing tender offer for all of the stock of Conoco and DuPont got about 46% of the Conoco stock. Seagrams knew it was beaten. Next, Conoco merged into DH, and Seagrams exchanged its Conoco stock for DuPont stock. DuPont asserted the acquisition of Conoco was a good reorganization because in the competing transaction it acquired the Conoco stock for stock of DuPont (54%) and cash (46%). Seagrams claimed a loss on the exchange, theorizing that its ownership of the 32% block was transitory. If Seagrams was right, then the merger was probably taxable because DuPont only got 22% of Conoco from the historic public shareholders for DuPont stock. The IRS asserted that it was a good reorganization because the 32% block of Seagram's stock should also be counted (creating 54% continuity) and denied the Seagrams loss, treating it as target shareholder that gave up Conoco stock for DuPont stock.]

We first address the question of whether Conoco's merger into DuPont was pursuant to a plan of reorganization, as contemplated by section 354(a)(1). Simply stated, petitioner [Seagrams] claims that DuPont's tender offer and the subsequent merger squeezing out the remaining Conoco shareholders were separate and independent transactions. Consequently, petitioner argues that the exchange of Conoco stock for DuPont stock pursuant to DuPont's tender offer rather than pursuant to the merger could not have been in pursuance of a plan of reorganization, as section 354 requires.

Petitioner argues at length that (1) the DuPont tender offer had independent significance from the DuPont-Conoco merger in that the tender offer had a separate business motive apart from the merger; separate and permanent legal, economic, and business consequences; and a strategically critical role in the contest for control of Conoco; (2) there were material conditions and contingencies which could have been serious impediments to the consummation of the merger; (3) the tender offer was a legally binding contract that closed prior to the merger and irrespective of whether the subsequent merger would ever close; and (4) the tender offer, not the merger, was the essential transaction by which DuPont obtained control of Conoco. We can agree with most of these assertions, and yet disagree with petitioner's conclusion that there was no reorganization. Since petitioner's points are all variations on a single theme, we will deal with them together as a single issue.

Petitioner insists that the DuPont tender offer was a legally binding contract that closed prior to the merger and irrespective of whether the subsequent merger would even be consummated. Petitioner argues that the tender offer was "plainly not a 'step' engaged in by DuPont for tax planning reasons. Rather the tender offer was the essential transaction by which DuPont obtained control of Conoco."

Petitioner asks us to apply the rationale of *Esmark, Inc. v. Commissioner*, 90 T.C. 171 (1988), affd. without published opinion 886 F.2d 1318 (7th Cir. 1989), to sustain the argument that the DuPont tender offer, standing alone, controls the outcome of this case. However, *Esmark, Inc.* did not involve a reorganization, so the facts of that case are not apposite. Furthermore, the result in *Esmark, Inc.* is antithetical to petitioner's position in this case.

Esmark, Inc. involved a series of related transactions culminating in a tender offer and redemption of a part of the taxpayer's stock in exchange for certain property. The Commissioner, seeking to apply the step transaction doctrine, sought to recharacterize the tender offer/redemption as a sale of assets followed by a self-tender. While it is true that we held that each of the preliminary steps leading to the tender offer/redemption had an independent function, we also held that the form of the overall transaction coincided with its substance, and was to be respected. In the case before us, petitioner would have us respect the independent significance of DuPont's tender offer, but disregard the overall transaction, which included the merger. That result would, of course, be inconsistent as an analogy with the result in *Esmark, Inc*. We therefore decline petitioner's request that we apply *Esmark, Inc.* to the facts of this case.

Petitioner makes much of the fact that there were significant contingencies that might have prevented the completion of the merger even after the tender offer had closed, citing in support, among other cases, *Dunlap & Associates, Inc. v. Commissioner*, 47 T.C. 542 (1967). But the facts of *Dunlap & Associates, Inc.* are far from apposite to those of this case.

As preliminary steps looking toward a public offering of its stock, the taxpayer in *Dunlap & Associates, Inc.* undertook to change its State of incorporation, in what we held to be an "F" reorganization (section 368(a)(1)(F)), and to acquire by an exchange of stock, in what we held to be two "B" reorganizations (section 368(a)(1)(B)) the minority holdings in two of its subsidiaries. For reasons not germane here, the taxpayer argued that there was "one integrated plan of reorganization," an argument we rejected since, among other things, "we [failed] to see how the end result would come within . . . any one of the definitions [of reorganization] "contained in section 368(a)(1)." Id. at 551. In dictum, we also stated that the transactions were not interdependent because there was no "provision in the merger agreements that the transfer of the New York corporation's assets to [taxpayer] would be undone if the minority stockholders were not responsive to the offers." *Id.* at 551.

Petitioner maintains that, as in *Dunlap & Associates, Inc.*, there were "significant legal contingencies that could well have resulted in DuPont's tender offer closing but not the merger." We list some of these from petitioner's memorandum of law in support of its motion for summary judgment (petitioner's memorandum):

1. After DuPont waived its precondition that it receive tenders of at leapt 51 percent of the Conoco shares, DuPont opened up the possibility, if its option to acquire 15,900,000 shares from Conoco were declared invalid, that it would not acquire enough Conoco stock to be able to effectuate the Merger.

2. Minority Conoco shareholders might successfully sue to enjoin the Merger on the grounds of fairness and breach of fiduciary duty.

3. The proposed Merger might not comply with applicable procedural and substantive requirements of Delaware law.

The fatal defect in petitioner's "contingencies" argument, however, is that whatever the contingencies (and any contemplated merger involving public companies like DuPont and Conoco is bound to be fraught with contingencies), the merger did in fact take place, just as contemplated in the DuPont/Conoco agreement.

As respondent correctly states in her memorandum of law in opposition to petitioner's motion for summary judgment and in support of respondent's motion for summary judgment (respondent's memorandum), taxation depends on actual events, not on what might have happened. The Court of Appeals for the Ninth Circuit, in *Walt Disney Inc. v. Commissioner*, 4 F.3d 735, 740 (9th Cir. 1993), *rev'g* 97 T.C. 221 (1991), on grounds other than a step transaction analysis, emphasized this point when it said: "That there were numerous conditions and contingencies which could have prevented the completion of the ["D"] reorganization is irrelevant; as the Commissioner asserts, the point is that the transaction was in fact closed as planned," pursuant to the taxpayer's "undisputed legal obligation" to do so. As discussed infra, DuPont had an indisputable legal obligation to complete the merger with Conoco, notwithstanding the possibility of intervening legal impediments, or contingencies, which in fact, never materialized.

The concept of "plan of reorganization," as described in section 1.368-2(g), Income Tax Regs., quoted above, is one of substantial elasticity. See *International Tel. & Tel. Corp. v. Commissioner*, 77 T.C. 60, 75 (1981), affd. per curiam 704 F.2d 252 (2d Cir. 1983). One commentator has stated that:

> The courts, and the Service where it has served its purposes, have adopted a functional approach to the problem that is undoubtedly consistent with congressional intent. They have held that a plan of reorganization is a series of transactions intended to accomplish a transaction described as a reorganization in section 368, regardless of how and in what form the plan is expressed and whether the parties intended tax-free treatment . . . [Faber, "The Use and Misuse of the Plan of Reorganization Concept," 38 Tax L. Rev. 515, 523 (1983).]

The DuPont/Conoco agreement was the definitive vehicle spelling out the interrelated steps by which DuPont would acquire 100 percent of Conoco's stock. To explain the mechanics of the type of procedure utilized by DuPont and Conoco, respondent submitted an "Expert Affidavit" of Bernard S. Black. Black is a professor of law at the Columbia University School of Law, where he teaches courses in corporate finance, securities and capital markets Regulations, and corporate acquisitions. He is coauthor of, among other treatises, The Law and Finance of Corporate Acquisitions. We found his affidavit, although on occasion somewhat argumentative, to be cogent, apparently well informed, and generally convincing.

In the affidavit, Professor Black states that:

> In substance, DuPont's bid for Conoco was a minor variant on a standard two-step acquisition, in which the parties sign a merger agreement that contemplates a first-step cash tender offer, to be followed by a second-step merger. The parties to an acquisition often use this transaction form, rather than a single-step merger (without a tender offer), because a tender offer can close faster than a merger, which increases the likelihood that the acquisition will be completed . . .

Professor Black goes on to observe that "DuPont added a third step to this transaction form – an exchange offer of DuPont stock for Conoco stock." The DuPont/Conoco agreement, which definitively states the terms for "the acquisition of [Conoco] by [DuPont Tenderor] (and thus by DuPont)" sets out the steps referred to by Professor Black in his affidavit – the series of transactions which in their totality were intended to accomplish a section 368 reorganization. Article I of the agreement relates to "THE OFFER," and provides the terms of the acquisition of Conoco stock by DuPont Tenderor in exchange for the combined cash/DuPont stock package.

Article II relates to "THE OPTION," granting DuPont Tenderor an option to purchase up to 15,900,000 shares of authorized but unissued Conoco stock. Article III relates to "THE MERGER," and provides in part:

> SECTION 3.01. (a) As promptly as practicable following the consummation or termination of the Offer, subject to the terms and conditions of this Agreement, the Company shall be merged into the Subsidiary in accordance with Delaware General Corporation Law. . .

(c) The parties hereto shall take all action necessary in accordance with applicable law and their respective Certificates of Incorporation and Bylaws to cause such Merger to be consummated prior to March 31, 1982 . . .

As we have previously noted, the agreement originally provided that the obligation of DuPont Tenderor to accept shares for exchange was, among other things, subject to the condition that at least 51 percent of Conoco's outstanding shares be tendered. Due to the exigencies created by the competing tender offers of petitioner and Mobil, DuPont subsequently found it expedient to reduce the 51 percent minimum to 41 percent. However, on August 5, 1981, DuPont Tenderor exercised the option provided in the agreement to buy 15,900,000 authorized but unissued Conoco shares, which would give DuPont an absolute majority of Conoco shares.

It has been said that "reorganizations, like other commercial events, must have a discrete start and a finish." *See* Bittker & Eustice, Federal Income Taxation of Corporations and Shareholders, par. 12.21. [10]. Uncertainty in this regard can present questions as to whether various steps can be considered together as a unified transaction constituting a reorganization. See, e.g., *Commissioner v. Gordon*, 391 U.S. 83, 96 (1968); *King Enters., Inc. v. United States*, 189 Ct. Cl. 466, 418 F.2d 511, 514 (1969).

The agreement provides a discrete start and finish, and the record discloses no steps agreed to outside the agreement, or preagreement activity by DuPont or its shareholders, that would invalidate the contemplated reorganization. Cf., e.g., *Superior Coach of Fla., Inc. v. Commissioner*, 80 T.C. 895 (1983), discussed infra. We do not view DuPont's increase in the price it was willing to pay for the Conoco shares, or the reduction in the percentage of Conoco shares acceptable under the DuPont tender offer, to be vitiating steps, since both steps benefited the Conoco shareholders and were steps taken to assure the success of the plan of reorganization, not to enlarge it outside its initial confines.

In *Commissioner v. Gordon*, supra at 96, the Supreme Court held that the requirement that the character of a transaction be determinable means that "if one transaction is to be characterized as a `first step' there must be a binding commitment to take the later steps." This requirement has been met. While DuPont's acquisition of control of Conoco by means of the tender offer unquestionably had economic significance, "independent" or not, and unquestionably was not a "meaningless step," DuPont and DuPont Tenderor were under a binding and irrevocable commitment to complete the culminating merger – the second step – upon the successful completion of the DuPont tender offer – the first step.

Petitioner argues that DuPont had a "plan" to engage in a series of transactions that "ultimately may include a reorganization," but not a "plan of reorganization." For reasons already discussed, we disagree. We hold that, because DuPont was contractually committed to undertake and complete the second step merger once it had undertaken and completed the first step tender offer, these carefully integrated transactions together constituted a plan of reorganization within the contemplation of section 354(a).

Petitioner also argues that even if the DuPont tender offer and merger were to be treated as an integrated transaction, the merger does not qualify as a reorganization because it fails the "continuity of interest" requirement.

In *Penrod v. Commissioner*, supra at 1427-1428, we stated…:[I]t is well settled that, in addition to meeting specific statutory requirements, a reorganization under section 368(a)(1)(A) must also satisfy the continuity of interest doctrine. See sec. 1.368-1(b), Income Tax Regs. . . . Because the reorganization provisions are based on the premise that the shareholders of an acquired corporation have not terminated their economic investment, but have merely altered its form, the continuity of interest doctrine limits the favorable nonrecognition treatment enjoyed by reorganizations to those situations in which (1) the nature of the consideration received by the acquired corporation or its shareholders confers a proprietary stake in the ongoing enterprise, and (2) the proprietary interest received is definite and material and represents a substantial part of the value of the property transferred . . .

On the date of the Conoco/DuPont agreement, July 6, 1981, there were approximately 85,991,896 Conoco shares outstanding. Petitioner is essentially arguing that because it acquired approximately 32 percent of these shares for cash pursuant to its own tender offer, and DuPont acquired approximately 46 percent of these shares for cash pursuant to its tender offer, the combined 78 percent of Conoco shares acquired for cash after the date of the agreement destroyed the continuity of interest requisite for a valid reorganization. We think petitioner's argument, and the logic that supports it, miss the mark.

Pursuant to its two-step tender offer/merger plan of reorganization, DuPont acquired approximately 54 percent of the "initial" 85,991,896 shares of Conoco stock in exchange for DuPont stock, which included petitioner's recently acquired Conoco shares that it tendered pursuant to DuPont's tender offer. If the 54 percent had been acquired by DuPont from Conoco shareholders in a "one-step" merger type acquisition, there would be little argument that continuity of interest had been satisfied. Sec. 368(a)(1)(A).

In *Helvering v. Minnesota Tea Co.*, 296 U.S. 378 (1935), the Supreme Court held that an equity interest in the transferee equal to about 56 percent of the value of the transferor's assets was adequate. In *John A. Nelson Co. v. Helvering*, 296 U.S. 374 (1935), the Supreme Court considered 38-percent equity continuity to be sufficient. For advance ruling purposes, the IRS considers a 50-percent equity continuity of interest, by value, to be sufficient. Rev. Proc. 77-37, 1977-2 C.B. 568. On the other hand, the U.S. Court of Appeals for the Fifth Circuit has held that a 16.4-percent continuing common stock interest, representing less than 1 percent of the total consideration (consisting of cash, bonds, and common stock) paid by the acquiring corporation, did not evidence sufficient continuity of interest to bring a transaction within the requirements of the predecessor of section 368(a)(1)(A). *Southwest Natural Gas Co. v. Commissioner*, 189 F.2d 332 (1951), affg. 14 T.C. 81 (1950).

Where sufficient continuity is lacking, the acquired corporation will not be a "party to a reorganization," thus causing the overall transaction to fail as a reorganization under section 368(a)(1)A). Section 368(b) provides in relevant part:

SEC. 368(b). PARTY TO A REORGANIZATION. – For purposes of this part, the term "a party to a reorganization" includes –

(1) a corporation resulting from a reorganization, and

(2) both corporations, in the case of a reorganization resulting from the acquisition by one corporation of stock or properties of another.

In the case of a reorganization qualifying under paragraph (1)(A) of subsection (a) by reason of paragraph (2)(D) of that subsection, the term "a parry to a reorganization" includes the controlling corporation referred to in such paragraph (2)(D). . . .

Thus the question petitioner raises is whether there is sufficient continuity of interest so as to qualify Conoco, DuPont, and DuPont Tenderor (by virtue of section 368(a)(2)(D)) as parties to a reorganization under this section.

The parties stipulated that petitioner and DuPont, through their wholly owned subsidiaries, were acting independently of one another and pursuant to competing tender offers. Furthermore, there is of course nothing in the record to suggest any prearranged understanding between petitioner and DuPont that petitioner would tender the Conoco stock purchased for cash if petitioner by means of its own tender offer failed to achieve control of Conoco.

Consequently, it cannot be argued that petitioner, although not a party to the reorganization, was somehow acting in concert with DuPont, which was a party to the reorganization. If such had been the case, the reorganization would fail because petitioner's cash purchases of Conoco, stock could be attributed to DuPont, thereby destroying continuity.

The cases cited by petitioner in support of its argument that DuPont's plan of reorganization failed for lack of continuity of interest are not germane. For example, petitioner quotes *Superior Coach of Fla., Inc. v. Commissioner*, 80 T.C. at 904, as stating that "[the continuity of interest requirement is] based upon the fundamental statutory purpose of providing for the carryover of tax attributes only if the reorganization is distinguishable from a sale." In *Superior Coach of Fla., Inc.,* the majority shareholders of P purchased all of the shares of T and merged T into P. We held that the P shareholders' acquisition of the T stock was "inextricably interwoven" with the intent to effect the merger, and since the "historic shareholders" of T retained no proprietary interest in P, the merger did not qualify as a reorganization under section 368(a)(1)(A). In other words, the reorganization failed because the majority shareholders of P were acting on its behalf when they bought the T stock for cash, and there was no continuity of interest on the part of the acquired corporation's previous shareholders. In the case before us, DuPont's shareholders did not purchase Conoco stock for cash (or for any other consideration) to facilitate the merger, and except for approving the plan of reorganization and the merger did not act on DuPont's behalf. Superior Coach of Fla., Inc. is therefore not apposite on its facts.

Petitioner cites *Yoc Heating Corp. v. Commissioner*, 61 T.C. 168, 177 (1973), for the proposition that continuity requires looking at shareholders "immediately prior to the inception of the series of transactions" in an integrated transaction. Again, we look at the facts: R, the acquiring corporation, purchased for cash over 85 percent of the stock of O, and then caused O to transfer its assets, subject to its liabilities, to R's wholly owned subsidiary, N. N issued 1 share of its stock to R in exchange for every 3 shares of O held by R plus cash to be paid to the minority shareholders of O.

The Commissioner argued in *Yoc Heating* that the taxpayer's series of transactions constituted a reorganization within the meaning of section 368(a)(1)(F) or, alternatively, section 368(a)(1)(D). We held, however, that the acquisition by N of O's assets constituted a purchase under the "integrated transaction" (step transaction) doctrine, rather than a reorganization under either section proposed by the Commissioner. Id. at 177-178. Thus *Yoc Heating*'s comparison of stock ownership immediately prior to and immediately after the series of transactions is perfectly appropriate to the facts of that case, where the acquiring corporation acquired control of the target for cash and then effected the corporate combination, because the shareholders of O before the acquisition by R lacked the requisite continuing interest in the affairs of O after the acquisition.

Respondent points out, correctly we believe, that the concept of continuity of interest advocated by petitioner would go far toward eliminating the possibility of a tax-free reorganization of any corporation whose stock is actively traded. Because it would be impossible to track the large volume of third party transactions in the target's stock, all completed transactions would be suspect. Sales of target stock for cash after the date of the announcement of an acquisition can be neither predicted nor controlled by publicly held parties to a reorganization. A requirement that the identity of the acquired corporation's shareholders be tracked to assume a sufficient number of "historic" shareholders to satisfy some arbitrary minimal percentage receiving the acquiring corporation's stock would be completely unrealistic.

Such a mandate to look only to historic shareholder identity to determine continuity was rejected by the Supreme Court in *Helvering v. Alabama Asphaltic Limestone Co.*, 315 U.S. 179 (1942). In *Alabama Asphaltic*, unsecured note holders of an insolvent corporation commenced a bankruptcy proceeding against the corporation. The note holders bought the corporate assets from the trustee and transferred them to a newly formed corporation in exchange for its stock. In discussing these facts, the Supreme Court stated:

> "When the equity owners are excluded and the old creditors become the stockholders of the new corporation, it conforms to realities to date their equity ownership from the time when they invoked the processes of the law to enforce their rights of full priority. At that time they stepped into the shoes of the old stockholders. The sale did nothing but recognize officially what had before been true in fact. . ."

Some contention, however, is made that this transaction did not meet the statutory standard because the properties acquired by the new corporation belonged at that time to the committee and not to the old corporation. That is true. Yet, the separate steps were integrated parts of a single scheme. Transitory phases of an arrangement frequently are disregarded under these sections of the revenue acts where they add nothing of substance to the completed affair. *Gregory v. Helvering*, 293 U.S. 465; *Helvering v. Bashford*, 302 U.S. 454. Here they were no more than intermediate procedural devices utilized to enable the new corporation to acquire all the assets of the old one pursuant to a single reorganization plan.[Id. at 184-185; citation omitted . . .]

In reaching this conclusion, the Supreme Court upheld the finding of a valid "A" reorganization by this Court. *Alabama Asphaltic Limestone Co. v. Commissioner*, 41 B.T.A. 324, 336 (1940), affd. 119 F.2d 819 (5th Cir. 1941), affd. 315 U.S. 179 (1942).

In the "integrated" transaction before us petitioner, not DuPont, "stepped into the shoes" of 32 percent of the Conoco shareholders when petitioner acquired their stock for cash via the JES competing tender offer, held the 32 percent transitorily, and immediately tendered it in exchange for DuPont stock. For present purposes, there is no material distinction between petitioner's tender of the Conoco stock and a direct tender by the "old" Conoco shareholders themselves. Thus, the requirement, of continuity of interest has been met.

Petitioner extended its tender offer even after DuPont had been tendered a "significant majority" of the outstanding shares of Conoco and withdrawal rights had closed. At that time petitioner announced that it was accepting the shares tendered to it and "was seeking additional shares to increase its investment in Conoco." And as we recited earlier, petitioner, in connection with its tender of its just-acquired Conoco stock, issued a press release quoting Edgar M. Bronfman, Seagram's chairman and CEO, as saying that Seagram was pleased at the prospect of becoming "a large stockholder of the combined DuPont and Conoco." (Emphasis added.) We also noted that petitioner did not report a loss on the exchange of its Conoco stock for DuPont stock for financial accounting purposes. Instead, petitioner ascribed its carrying cost for its Conoco stock to the DuPont stock. None of these acts is consistent with the recognized loss petitioner claimed on its tax return.

For the reasons stated in this opinion, we hold that a loss cannot be recognized by petitioner on its exchange of Conoco stock for DuPont stock, made pursuant to the DuPont-Conoco plan of reorganization. To reflect this holding and concessions by the parties,

An order will be issued denying petitioner's motion for summary judgment and granting respondent's motion for summary judgment, and directing the parties to submit computations under Rule 155 in anticipation of a decision to be entered thereunder.

ISSUE

On the facts described below, is the control-for-voting-stock requirement of § 368(a)(2)(E) of the Internal Revenue Code satisfied, so that a series of integrated steps constitutes a tax-free reorganization under §§ 368(a)(1)(A) and 368(a)(2)(E) and § 354 or § 356 applies to each exchanging shareholder?

FACTS

SITUATION 1. Corporation P and Corporation T are widely held, manufacturing corporations organized under the laws of state A. T has only voting common stock outstanding, none of which is owned by P. P seeks to acquire all of the outstanding stock of T. For valid business reasons, the acquisition will be effected by a tender offer for at least 51 percent of the stock of T, to be acquired solely for P voting stock, followed by a merger of a subsidiary of P into T. P initiates a tender offer for T stock conditioned on the tender of at least 51 percent of the T shares. Pursuant to the tender offer, P acquires 51 percent of the T stock from T's shareholders for P voting stock. P forms S and S merges into T under the merger laws of state A. In the statutory merger, P's S stock is converted into T stock and each of the T shareholders holding the remaining 49 percent of the outstanding T stock exchanges its shares of T stock for a combination of consideration, two-thirds of which is P voting stock and one-third of which is cash. Assume that under general principles of tax law, including the step transaction doctrine, the tender offer and the statutory merger are treated as an integrated acquisition by P of all of the T stock. Also assume that all nonstatutory requirements for a reorganization under §§ 368(a)(1)(A) and 368(a)(2)(E) and all statutory requirements of § 368(a)(2)(E), other than the requirement under § 368(a)(2)(E)(ii) that P acquire control of T in exchange for its voting stock in the transaction, are satisfied.

SITUATION 2. The facts are the same as in Situation 1, except that S initiates the tender offer for T stock and, in the tender offer, acquires 51 percent of the T stock for P stock provided by P.

LAW AND ANALYSIS

Section 368(a)(1)(A) states that the term "reorganization" means a statutory merger or consolidation. Section 368(a)(2)(E) provides that a transaction otherwise qualifying under § 368(a)(1)(A) will not be disqualified by reason of the fact that stock of a corporation (the "controlling corporation") that before the merger was in control of the merged corporation is used in the transaction, if (1) after the transaction, the corporation surviving the merger holds substantially all of its properties and of the properties of the merged corporation (other than stock of the controlling corporation distributed in the transaction), and (2) in the transaction, former shareholders of the surviving corporation exchanged, for an amount of voting stock of the controlling corporation, an amount of stock in the surviving corporation that constitutes control of such corporation (the "control-for-voting-stock requirement"). For this purpose, control is defined in § 368(c).

In *King Enterprises, Inc. v. United States*, 418 F.2d 511 (Ct. Cl. 1969), as part of an integrated plan, a corporation acquired all of the stock of a target corporation from the target corporation's shareholders for consideration, in excess of 50 percent of which was acquiring corporation stock, and subsequently merged the target corporation into the acquiring corporation. The court held that, because the merger was the intended result of the stock acquisition, the acquiring corporation's acquisition of the target corporation qualified as a reorganization under § 368(a)(1)(A).

Section 354(a)(1) provides that no gain or loss will be recognized if stock or securities in a corporation a party to a reorganization are, in pursuance of the plan of reorganization, exchanged solely for stock or securities in another corporation a party to the reorganization.

Section 356(a)(1) provides that, if § 354 would apply to the exchange except for the receipt of money or property other than stock or securities in a corporate party to the reorganization, the recipient shall recognize gain, but in an amount not in excess of the sum of the money and the fair market value of the other property.

Section 1.368-1(c) of the Income Tax Regulations provides that a plan of reorganization must contemplate the bona fide execution of one of the transactions specifically described as a reorganization in § 368(a) and the bona fide consummation of each of the requisite acts under which nonrecognition of gain is claimed. Section 1.368-2(g) provides that the term plan of reorganization is not to be construed as broadening the definition of reorganization as set forth in § 368(a), but is to be taken as limiting the nonrecognition of gain or loss to such exchanges or distributions as are directly a part of the transaction specifically described as a reorganization in § 368(a).

As assumed in the facts, under general principles of tax law, including the step transaction doctrine, the tender offer and the statutory merger in both Situations 1 and 2 are treated as an integrated acquisition by P of all of the T stock. The principles of *King Enterprises* support the conclusion that, because the tender offer is integrated with the statutory merger in both Situations 1 and 2, the tender offer exchange is treated as part of the statutory merger (hereinafter the "Transaction") for purposes of the reorganization provisions. Cf. *J. E. Seagram Corp. v. Commissioner*, 104 T.C. 75 (1995) (treating a tender offer that was an integrated step in a plan that included a forward triangular merger as part of the merger transaction). Consequently, the integrated steps, which result in P acquiring all of the stock of T, must be examined together to determine whether the requirements of § 368(a)(2)(E) are satisfied. Cf. § 1.368-2(j)(3)(i); § 1.368-2(j)(6), Ex. 3 (suggesting that, absent a special exception, steps that are prior to the merger, but are part of the transaction intended to qualify as a reorganization under §s 368(a)(1)(A) and 368(a)(2)(E), should be considered for purposes of determining whether the control-for-voting-stock requirement is satisfied).

In both situations, in the Transaction, the shareholders of T exchange, for P voting stock, an amount of T stock constituting in excess of 80 percent of the voting stock of T. Therefore, the control-for-voting-stock requirement is satisfied. Accordingly, in both Situations 1 and 2, the Transaction qualifies as a reorganization under § 368(a)(1)(A) and 368(a)(2)(E).

Under §§ 1.368-1(c) and 1.368-2(g), all of the T shareholders that exchange their T stock for P stock in the Transaction will be treated as exchanging their T stock for P stock in pursuance of a plan of reorganization. Therefore, T shareholders that exchange their T stock only for P stock in the Transaction will recognize no gain or loss under § 354. T shareholders that exchange their T stock for P stock and cash in the Transaction will recognize gain to the extent provided in § 356. In both Situations 1 and 2, none of P, S, or T will recognize any gain or loss in the Transaction, and P's basis in the T stock will be determined under § 1.358-6(c)(2) by treating P as acquiring all of the T stock in the Transaction and not acquiring any of the T stock before the Transaction.

HOLDING

On the facts set forth in Situations 1 and 2, the control-for-voting-stock requirement is satisfied in the Transaction, the Transaction constitutes a tax-free reorganization under §§ 368(a)(1)(A) and 368(a)(2)(E), and § 354 or § 356 applies to each exchanging shareholder.

NOTES

1. **The concept of "independent significance" and the "functionally unrelated" doctrine**. Where two or more transactions carried out pursuant to an overall plan have economic significance that are independent of each other, they will not be stepped together, unless perhaps there is a binding commitment to undertake the second transaction. This is a limitation on the interdependence test. For example, in Rev. Rul. 79-250, 1979-2 CB 156, an acquisition of a target company in a subsidiary merger was followed by a reorganization of the subsidiary in a new state. The reorganization was found "real and substantial" and so the last transaction was ignored in characterizing and testing the prior steps. But see Rev. Rul. 96-29, 1996-1 CB 50 (limiting Rev. Rul. 79-250 to § 368(a)(1)(F) (reorganizations). In *Reef Corporation v. Commissioner*, 368 F.2d 125 (5th Cir. 1966), cert. denied (1967), the court basically replaced the words "independent significance" with "functionally unrelated" in declaring a certain step (namely a pre-reorganization redemption of a major shareholding group) should be ignored. Predicting when this will occur is difficult. Notwithstanding §368(b), starting in 2005, a continuity of the business enterprise and a continuity of interest is no longer required for reorganizations under section 368(a)(1)(E) or (F). Instead, the Code recognizes the amalgamation of two corporate enterprises under a single corporate structure as a reorganization if there exists among the holders of the stock and securities of either of the old corporations the requisite continuity of interest in the new corporation. However, there is not a reorganization if the holders of the stock and securities of the old corporation are merely the holders of short-term notes in the new corporation.

2. **Post-reorganization continuity of proprietary interest**. Until 1996, the IRS took the position that, for purposes of determining continuity of proprietary interest, a target company shareholder had to hold her acquiring corporation stock for a respectable period of time after the reorganization. Many commentators disagreed, considering that what counted was the consideration used (equity of the acquiror or its parent) and not how long it was held. The IRS now agrees with the commentators even if the sale of acquiring company stock was arranged before the merger. *See* Reg. § 1.368-1(e)(1)(i)(6), Example 1.

Moreover, continuity of proprietary interest is not just measured by the continuation of equity. It can also be measured in terms of business activities or assets of the target company that fall into the transferee corporation's hands. This is what is meant in Reg. § 1.368-1(e)(l)(i) by the words, "it is exchanged by the acquiring corporation for a direct interest in the target corporation." This allows an acquisition of assets of the target to count for continuity of proprietary interest. This variation is often confusing, because it is the continuation of the assets or business of the target that one tests to see if the separate requirement of continuity of proprietary interest is met.

To illustrate: T corporation has two corporate shareholders, A and P. A owns 30% and P owns 70%. T merges into P. In connection with the merger, A gets $30x of cash. This satisfies the continuity of proprietary interest test because P got the business assets of T in exchange for the stock P held in T (which is now canceled). Thus, P's 70% continuity manifests itself in the form of an equivalent share of assets of T. *See* Reg. § 1.368-1(e)(8), Example 7. This does not mean the continuity of business enterprise test is necessarily met, because that is an independent issue. For example, if all the operating assets of T had then been sold to raise the cash to pay A, and T's historic business ended, the reorganization would fail for lack of continuity of business enterprise.

To illustrate: If, in contrast, A had been the acquiror and P had been taken out for cash, A would have failed the 50% test and there would have been no reorganization for lack of continuity of proprietary interest.

The Regulations address the problematic issue of major stock redemptions of target company stock, or major distributions to target company shareholders, that take place in connection with the intended reorganization. Reg. § 1.368-1(e)(1)(i). The trouble is there are no "bright line" tests to know when a redemption or dividend is "too big" to ensure continuity of proprietary interest, just a vague statement that one has to consider all the facts and circumstances and some terse examples. Reg. § 1.368-1(e)(8).

PROBLEM 21-1

In all cases, assume that the transaction is otherwise a valid reorganization under § 368(a)(1) and concentrate on the narrow issue the problem presents. A is the acquiring corporation, T is the target corporation, P is a parent corporation, and S is a subsidiary.

1) P owns 90% of the stock of T. P agrees to a merger in which T will merge into S, a subsidiary of A, in exchange for common stock of A. P has agreed before the merger to sell all the A stock that it receives in the merger to the Friendly Bank. Does the agreement to sell the stock to the bank violate the continuity of proprietary interest rules? *See* Reg. § 1.368-1(e)(1), (e)(3), (e)(8) Example (1).

2) Same as "(1)", but P agrees in advance to sell 51% of the A stock received in the acquisition back to A. *See* Reg. § 1.368-1(e)(1)(i) and (e)(8), Example 4. What result?

3) Same as "(2)", except that instead of agreeing to sell the stock to A, P will sell the stock to X, another subsidiary of A. What result? Reg. § 1.368-1(c)(8) Example 4(iii).

4) Same as "(1)", but the A stock is preferred stock that P can force A to buy at will after six years have elapsed. If you had to make a policy decision that was consistent with what you have read so far, what would you decide as to whether the preferred stock gives rise to adequate continuity of proprietary interest?

5) Mrs. B owns all the stock of T. A owns all the stock of S1. T merges into S1, and Mrs. B gets S1 stock as consideration. She immediately transfers the SI stock to A in exchange for cash. Is it a good reorganization as to her? As to T and S1?

2. CONTINUITY OF BUSINESS ENTERPRISE IN A REORGANIZATION

This independent requirement has to be satisfied in every reorganization. The basic notion is that unless either one of the historic businesses of the target company, or a significant portion of its historic business assets continue to be used by the acquiror or survivor, there is no reorganization. Reg. § 1.368-1(d)(1)-(2). Rather, the transaction is comparable to a liquidation of the target. The focus is on the business, not on the consideration paid for the company. The rules are generally quite relaxed.

An example in the Regulations suggests that one third of the assets are apt to constitute the requisite "significant portion" of the historic assets. Reg. § 1.368-1(d)(5) Example 1. The Regulations ultimately avoid commitments to specific proportions. If the target company has subsidiaries that are at least 80%-owned (using the measure found in § 368(c)), then the assets and businesses of the target include the assets and businesses of the subsidiaries of the target. This will help a great deal if the target is a holding company with no business of its own. Lower-tier subsidiaries are counted as well, but only if they are at least 80%-owned by the upper-tier corporation; that means that the business or assets of a second-tier sub as to which the parent corporation owns only 64% indirectly is still counted for continuity of business enterprise purposes. *See* Reg. § 1.368-1(d)(4).

The Regulations accommodate retransfers from the acquiring corporation to a partnership. For example, if A acquired the assets of T in a merger, A can immediately retransfer the assets to a partnership with an unrelated party without failing to meet the continuity of business enterprise test. Reg. §§ 1.368-1(d)(4). However, this kind of transfer must result in A (or an affiliate) either owning a significant interest in the partnership, or performing "active and substantial management functions." Reg. § 1.368-1(d)(4)(iii)(B).

Drop-downs of stock or assets into endless tiers of subsidiaries, including splitting the business or assets up into numerous subsidiaries, are evidently permissible as long as the subsidiary that acts as the resting place is in a chain of at least 80%-owned by the next higher tier subsidiaries. Reg. § 1.368-1(d)(2)-(3). For example, if T merges into P and its business is passed to S, which is 80%-owned by P, and S in turn passes the business to SI, which is 80%-owned by S, the continuity of business enterprise test is still met.

PROBLEM 21-2

1) P owns 100% of the stock of T Corp. T has three equally significant lines of business. T merges into A in exchange for A stock. A instantly transfers its assets of T to X, one of its subsidiaries. X discontinues two of the lines of T's business. Is the continuity of business enterprise test met? *See* Reg. §§ 1.368-1(d)(4)(i) and -1(d)(5), Example 1.

2) What if the facts are same as "(1)", but all three businesses wind up in a partnership of which X is a 40% partner? *See* Reg. § 1.368-1(d)(5), Example 9.

D. TYPE B REORGANIZATIONS
Read § 368(a)(1)(B).

1. GENERAL

A Type B reorganization, as defined in § 368(a)(1)(B), is an acquisition by one corporation, in exchange solely for its voting stock (or voting stock of its parent) of stock of another corporation, if the acquiror thereafter has "control" of the acquired corporation. It is a stock-for-stock exchange, but only where the acquiror is a corporation.

The Type B reorganization is fairly uncommon. It is most frequently seen in the form of a so-called tender offer in which an acquiring company publicly invites the shareholders of a target company to tender (deliver) their stock to a particular institutional agent by a certain deadline. If the shareholders of the target company acquiesce by mailing in their certificates in a sufficient volume, the deal closes, and they receive stock of the acquiring company. If they do not tender enough stock, then the offer is typically terminated and the tendered shares are returned to the target company shareholders who responded to the offer. The acquiring company may use common or preferred stock, but it must be voting stock alone and cannot, for example, include warrants or stock options. *See Helvering v. Southwest Consol. Corp.*, 315 U.S. 194 (1942).

The most formidable difficulty with using a B reorganization is that no boot of any kind may be paid to the target shareholders directly or indirectly to acquire their shares. The acquisition must be made "solely" for voting stock of the acquiring corporation (or its controlling parent). There is plenty of room here for disastrous accidents, especially when all the transactions which precede and follow the acquisition of control are considered together.

NOTES

1. **Cash payments that can be made without destroying a Type B reorganization.** The acquiring company can pay script or cash for a target company shareholders' fractional shares. Richard Mills v. Com., 381 F.2d 321 (CA5 1964). Rev. Rul. 55-59, 1955-1 C.B. 35. For example, if the acquiring company stock were worth only $10.00 a share and it had to acquire the stock of a particular shareholder who held only one target company share worth $12.00, in a perfect world the acquiring company would issue one and one-fifth of its shares to the target company's shareholder in exchange for her share. The Fifth Circuit allows the shareholder to take $2.00 in cash in lieu of the fractional share without disqualifying the B reorganization.

    Dissenting shareholders of the target cannot be bought out for cash or other property by the acquiring company, but the target company can redeem stock from such shareholders for cash or other property without upsetting the Type B reorganization, provided the cash does not derive from the acquiring corporation. See Rev. Rul. 68-285 1968-1 C.B. 147. The acquiring company may safely buy bonds or notes issued by the target corporation because that does not entail a payment of boot in exchange for stock. *See Stockton Harbor Indus. Co. v. Commissioner,* 216 F.2d 638 (9th Cir. 1954), cert. denied, 349 U.S. 904 (1955).

    Obviously, the acquiring company cannot pay for the target company shareholders' personal expenses in connection with the reorganization, but the IRS has ruled that it can pay the target corporation's expenses, provided they are directly related to the reorganization. Rev. Rul. 73-54, 1973-1 C.B. 187 (involving an acquisition of target assets for acquiring corporation stock).

2. **Issuance of additional shares.** Sometimes an acquiring company will promise to issue more stock to the sellers in the event that the target company performs especially well. In such cases, the "solely for voting stock" requirement is not considered violated unless the target company shareholders receive a negotiable instrument evidencing their rights. Rev. Proc. 84-42, 1984-1 C.B. 521.

3. **Overlap with other transactions.** Assume that all of Tiny Corporation's stock is held by Mr. B. A large corporation contributes a very large amount of its voting stock to Tiny Corp. in exchange for 80% or more of the voting stock of Tiny Corp., thus giving it control of Tiny. Is this a § 368(a)(1)(B) transaction, or is it a § 351 transaction?

4. **Triangular Type B reorganization.** The parenthetical language in the definition of a Type B reorganization clearly allows the acquiring company to use its parent corporation's stock. As a result, when the dust settles, there may be a three-tier structure in which the target company is in the third tier and the former shareholders of the target company will own stock of the corporation in the top tier. Note that one cannot use the stock of both corporations as consideration. *See* Reg. § 1.368-2(c).

5. **Drop-downs.** Section 368(a)(2)(C) specifically allows the acquiring corporation to take the target company's stock and to drop it into a subsidiary producing the same three-tier structure described above. If the acquiror is a first-tier subsidiary using its parent's stock, it can continue the process by dropping down the target stock to a still lower tier.

6. **Nonqualified preferred stock**. Receiving this kind of stock, even if it votes, ruins a B reorganization for all the target shareholders. *See* §§ 351(g), 354(a)(2)(C)(i), and 356(e).

2. CREEPING "B" REORGANIZATIONS

The "solely for voting stock" (or "no boot") requirement makes it difficult for the acquiring corporation to acquire the stock of the target over time in a "creeping B" reorganization if doing so involves paying cash or other nonstock consideration to any seller. For example, if the acquiring company previously acquired any of the target company stock for consideration other than the acquiror's own voting stock, the exchange after which the acquiror meets the 80% control requirement will not qualify as a Type B reorganization unless the prior acquisition of target stock is "old and cold."

It is not necessary to immediately acquire control in a qualifying B reorganization; it is only necessary for the acquiror to have control immediately after an exchange. Thus the acquiring corporation may already own some or even a controlling stock interest before a valid B reorganization provided the earlier stock acquisitions – if for other than stock of the acquiror – were not made by purchase as part of the same plan.

Even if the acquiror went from 0% to 80% control of the target solely for voting stock in a single transaction, if any other stock was obtained by purchase and can be linked to an overall plan, the B reorganization is invalid. *See Chapman v. Commissioner*, 618 F.2d 856 (1st Cir. 1980). There, International Telephone and Telegraph Corporation ("ITT") purchased 8% of Hartford Fire Insurance Company's common stock for cash. Fourteen months later, it attempted to acquire the rest of Hartford's stock in exchange for its own voting stock in a B reorganization. Before the exchange, ITT sold the previously-purchased 8% interest to a third party in order to comply with a condition of its private letter ruling.

The shareholders of Hartford tendered the requisite 80% amount, but some time later the IRS asserted that the previously-purchased 8% had been "parked" in friendly hands and never fully disposed of. The attempted B reorganization was therefore invalid. In a proceeding for summary judgment that did not decide the facts, ITT argued that even if the previously-purchased stock formed part of the larger acquisition, there was still a valid B reorganization because it obtained control (80%) of Hartford solely in exchange for its voting stock, and that it did not matter whether it also acquired additional shares by purchase.

The court ruled that, as a matter of law, if the initial cash purchase and the later stock-for-stock exchange were part of a single integrated series of transactions, then the B reorganization was defective. That laid to rest one of the intriguing issues about the Type B reorganization that Congress had never fully clarified.

The effect of a failed B reorganization is a taxable exchange of stock.

To illustrate: If ITT had purchased 30% of Hartford as an investment and then 10 years later decided to take over Hartford, it could engage in the following tax-deferred transaction: ITT could issue voting (preferred or common) stock to Hartford shareholders, obtaining at least another 50% of the outstanding Hartford stock. This second transaction would qualify as a Type B reorganization because ITT had control immediately after the exchange and did not transfer any consideration to ITT's shareholders other than voting stock. Conversely, if the 30% purchase were part of a plan that included the 50% stock swap, that stock swap would be a taxable exchange. Even if ITT got 90% of Hartford in stock swaps, but later, as part of the same plan, bought the last 10%, the entire set of transactions would be rendered taxable.

PROBLEM 21-3

Big Co. and Little Co. negotiate a stock-for-stock exchange, in which Little Co. shareholders will receive 1 share of Big Co. common stock for every 2 Little Co. shares they exchange. The companies would like to structure this transaction so as to receive Type B reorganization treatment under § 368(a)(1)(B).

1) Can either Big Co. or Little Co. buy the shares of the Little Co. shareholders who dissent to the transaction?

2) Can Big Co. provide the Little Co. shareholders a mixture of Big Co. stock and debentures for their Little Co. stock?

3) Must Big Co. acquire 100% of the Little Co. stock to receive Type B reorganization treatment?

4) If Little Co. has two classes of stock, one common voting class made up of 100 outstanding shares, and one non-voting preferred class, made up of 50 outstanding shares, how much of each class must Big Co. acquire to have access to Type B reorganization treatment?

5) Can Big Co. offer Little Co. shareholders the voting common stock of its parent corporation, P Corp., in exchange for their Little Co. stock?

6) Big Co. is contemplating dropping the Little Co. stock it acquires down into a wholly owned subsidiary, Biggie, Inc., will this drop down ruin the reorganization characterization?

7) What will be the effect if the transaction fails to meet the Type B reorganization requirements?

8) Can Big Co. pay cash to Little Co. bondholders for their bonds without preventing the stock swaps from being a Type B reorganization?

9) Which of the following can Big Co. pay for without harming a Type B reorganization?

   a) Little Co.'s legal and accounting fees?

   b) Transfer taxes on issuance of stock issued to Little Co. shareholders?

   c) Little Co.'s shareholders' investment expenses?

10) Could part of the consideration paid by Big. Co. for stock of Little Co. be warrants? *See* Reg. §1.354-1(e).

11) Might it be possible for Big Co. to trade its warrants for Little Co. warrants held by Little Co.'s shareholders tax-free?

12) Would the exchange of warrants wreck the intended Type B reorganization?

13) Assume Big Co. engaged in the following unrelated transactions in which it swapped its voting stock for stock of Little Co. as follows:

18 months ago	25%
12 months ago	30%
3 months ago	35%
last week	10%

a) Which of these transactions, if any, qualify as a type B reorganization?

b) What if all the transactions were bound together by a single plan? *See* Reg. § 1.368-2(c).

c) Same as "(b)" immediately above but in the third transaction Big Co. used stock of its parent, which owns all of Big Co.?

14) Assuming the acquisition of Little Co. is done by means of a valid Type B reorganization, does Big Co. inherit Little Co.'s tax attributes?

15) What if Big Co. uses voting nonqualified preferred stock for Little Co's stock, will voting nonqualified preferred stock destroy the Type B reorganization?

PROBLEM 21-4

1) Country Music, Inc. ("CMI") is 100% owned by Mel Gilley. Gilley recently agreed to exchange all his CMI stock (all of which is voting stock) for voting stock of an unrelated publicly-owned corporation, Bronx Recording Corporation ("BRC") issued by BRC. The parties entered into the deal because they felt that by combining skills, they could develop a new musical art form, "country rap." As it turned out, CMI is so valuable that Gilley wound up owning 82% by vote and value of BRC. CMI stayed in the same business as before. What is the nature of this transaction?

2) Assume Gilley wound up owning only 40% of BRC's stock. Then BRC contributed its CMI stock to a partnership consisting of BRC and an unrelated party. Would the transfer to the partnership disturb the "B" reorganization? Consider Reg. § 1.368-1(e)(5).

3) This time the facts are quite different. CMI proposes to redeem 90% of Gilley's CMI stock, after which BRC will issue Gilley a block of BRC voting stock to acquire his 100% stake in CMI. Is the redemption a problem? Assume the steps are all part of a single plan of CMI, BRC, and Gilley. *See* Reg. § 1.368-1(e)(8) Example 9.

4) What if instead of a redemption, LA Music, Inc. a 100%-owned subsidiary of BMC, bought the 90% block in "(3)" for cash? *See* Reg. § 1.368-1(e)(3) and (4).

5) What if instead of a redemption, CMI paid Gilley a dividend equal in value to the 90% redemption in "(3)" above? In your view, should he affect the continuity of Gilley's interest for purposes of determining if the overall transaction is a reorganization? Reg. § 1.368-1(e)(1)(ii).

3. ACQUIRING COMPANY'S BASIS IN TARGET COMPANY STOCK
Read § 362(b).

The acquiring company takes as its basis in the target company's stock the same basis that the target company shareholders had in stock. See § 362(b). This presents difficulties if the target company is widely held and the target company shareholders do not cooperate in providing information as to their stock basis. The IRS has sensibly allowed acquiring corporations to use statistical sampling techniques in order to make a reasonable approximation to be used as the acquiring company's basis in the target company stock. Rev. Proc. 2011-35, 2011-25 IRB 890.

PROBLEM 21-5

Parent Corporation owns 100% of the stock of Subsidiary Corporation. Parent Corporation has a $5 basis in its Subsidiary Corporation stock. Parent wants to acquire all of the stock of Target Company and wishes to place it in a subsidiary of Subsidiary Corporation. Assume that Parent contributes Parent Corporation voting stock to Subsidiary Corporation and that Subsidiary Corporation uses that stock to acquire all of the stock of Target Company in a Type B reorganization. Assume that Target Company's shareholders have a basis of $85 in their Target Company stock.

1) Can Subsidiary Corporation form its own subsidiary to which it contributes the stock of Target Company without disqualifying the reorganization?

2) Assume, instead, that Subsidiary Corporation does not form its own subsidiary. Instead, assume that, after the reorganization, Subsidiary Corporation owns all of the stock of Target Company. What is Parent Corporation's basis in Subsidiary Corporation? *See* Reg. § 1.358-6(c)(2)(ii).

E. TYPE C REORGANIZATIONS
Read §§ 368(a)(1)(C) and 368(a)(2)(B).

In a "C" reorganization the acquiring corporation must obtain "substantially all the properties" of the target corporation in exchange solely for voting stock of the acquiring company or its parent. These transactions are often called "practical mergers" because the effects of a merger and a Type C reorganization are so similar. In a taxable form, this would be an acquisition of assets in exchange for stock.

1. SUBSTANTIALLY ALL THE PROPERTIES

Failure to acquire substantially all of the target's assets implies that the transaction may be divisive in character. If the transaction is divisive, it should be tested under the rules of § 355, which are quite restrictive. By contrast, if substantially all of the properties are acquired, it is logical to use standards that are more similar to those that apply in a merger. For purposes of obtaining a private letter ruling, the IRS requires that the acquiring company obtain at least 70% of the target's gross assets and 90% of the net assets. Also, the taxpayer must represent that it intends no pre-reorganization spin-offs, sales, or redemptions that are related to the acquisition and might deplete T's assets for purposes of the 70%/90% rule. Rev. Proc. 77-37, 1977-2 C.B. 568.

In the past, there was a difficult question of how many and what kind of assets the target company could retain. Rev. Rul. 57-518, 1957-2 C.B. 253 took the position that what mattered most was that the target not be able to retain assets that would let it slip back into business. Because § 368(a)(2)(G) now insists that the target liquidate, this issue has disappeared.

2. PERMISSIBLE CONSIDERATION

Voting stock of the acquiring company's parent company can be used as consideration instead of its own. Section 368(a)(1)(C) (parenthetical language). In addition, the acquiror can assume any amount of the transferor's liabilities and accept any amount of property subject to liabilities without violating the "solely for voting stock" rule. Unlike a B reorganization, a C reorganization does permit the acquiring corporation to pay boot in addition to voting stock under the so-called "boot relaxation rule" of § 368(a)(2)(B). The amount of permissible boot is a maximum of 20% of the fair market value of all the target's property, provided the remainder is paid for with voting stock.

This 20% boot concession can be a land mine. The reason is that, if the acquiring company pays any form of boot, then any liabilities that it assumes or takes subject to are also treated as boot. It is the combination of liabilities and boot that creates the greatest anxiety for tax planners.

To illustrate: Target corporation has property with a total value of $100,000, and the property is subject to liabilities of $15,000. This means that the acquiring corporation can pay not more than $5,000 in money or other boot in addition to assuming the liabilities or taking the properties subject to the liabilities. *See* § 368(a)(2)(B), last sentence.

Note the high risks involved here. One must be accurate and precise about the $100,000 value of the Target's assets and the $15,000 amount of its liabilities. If it turns out that the assets are worth less, or that the liabilities are more than anticipated, then the transaction does not qualify as a Type C reorganization because the 20% test is violated.

The acquiring corporation can use its parent's stock but not both the stock of itself and of its parent. Reg. § 1.368-2(d)(1). However, if the 80% standard is met, it seems likely that one could use parent company stock as if it were cash under the boot relaxation rule.

3. OVERLAPS

Suppose that one corporation acquires another in a valid B reorganization and then promptly liquidates the target into itself. According to Rev. Rul. 67-274, 1967-2 C.B. 141, this is, if anything, a C reorganization. This has positive and negative features.

The positive feature is that some boot can apparently be transferred, and thus an attempted B reorganization that has failed due to a minor transfer of boot can be saved from taxability by a related liquidation and conversion to a C reorganization. The negative feature is that in a B reorganization, nothing prevents the target from disposing of unwanted assets by sale, redemption, or otherwise in preparation for the acquisition, but if the corporation does dispose of assets and is later liquidated by the acquiror, then the transactions might fail the "substantially all the properties" rule when tested as a C reorganization.

Section 368. – Definitions Relating to Corporate Reorganizations, *26 CFR 1.368-1: Purpose and scope of exception of reorganization exchanges.*

Section 338. This ruling discusses an integrated transaction where stock of a target corporation is acquired in a taxable reverse subsidiary merger, followed by liquidation of target. The ruling addresses the proper treatment and application of the step transaction doctrine in light of the policies behind section 338 of the Code.

ISSUE

What is the proper Federal income tax treatment of the transaction described below?

FACTS

T is a corporation all of the stock of which is owned by individual A. T has 150x dollars worth of assets and 50x dollars of liabilities. P is a corporation that is unrelated to A and T. The value of P's assets, net of liabilities, is 410x dollars. P forms corporation X, a wholly owned subsidiary, for the sole purpose of acquiring all of the stock of T by causing X to merge into T in a statutory merger (the "Acquisition Merger"). In the Acquisition Merger, P acquires all of the stock of T, and A exchanges the T stock for 10x dollars in cash and P voting stock worth 90x dollars. Following the Acquisition Merger and as part of an integrated plan that included the Acquisition Merger, T completely liquidates into P (the "Liquidation"). In the Liquidation, T transfers all of its assets to P and P assumes all of T's liabilities. The Liquidation is not accomplished through a statutory merger. After the Liquidation, P continues to conduct the business previously conducted by T.

LAW

Section 368(a)(1)(A) of the Internal Revenue Code provides that the term "reorganization" means a statutory merger or consolidation. Section 368(a)(2)(E) provides that a transaction otherwise qualifying under § 368(a)(1)(A) shall not be disqualified by reason of the fact that stock of a corporation in control of the merged corporation is used in the transaction, if (i) after the transaction, the corporation surviving the merger holds substantially all of its properties and of the properties of the merged corporation (other than stock of the controlling corporation distributed in the transaction), and (ii) in the transaction, former shareholders of the surviving corporation exchanged, for an amount of voting stock of the controlling corporation, an amount of stock in the surviving corporation which constitutes control of the surviving corporation. Further, § 1.368-2(j)(3)(iii) of the Income Tax Regulations provides that "[i]n applying the 'substantially all' test to the merged corporation, assets transferred from the controlling corporation to the merged corporation in pursuance of the plan of reorganization are not taken into account."

Section 368(a)(1)(C) provides in part that a reorganization is the acquisition by one corporation, in exchange solely for all or part of its voting stock, of substantially all of the properties of another corporation, but in determining whether the exchange is solely for stock, the assumption by the acquiring corporation of a liability of the other shall be disregarded. Section 368(a)(2)(B) provides that if one corporation acquires substantially all of the properties of another corporation, the acquisition would qualify under § 368(a)(1)(C) but for the fact that the acquiring corporation exchanges money or other property in addition to voting stock, and

411

the acquiring corporation acquires, solely for voting stock described in § 368(a)(1)(C), property of the other corporation having a fair market value which is at least 80 percent of the fair market value of all of the property of the other corporation, then such acquisition shall (subject to § 368(a)(2)(A)) be treated as qualifying under § 368(a)(1)(C). Section 368(a)(2)(B) further provides that solely for purposes of determining whether its requirements are satisfied, the amount of any liabilities assumed by the acquiring corporation shall be treated as money paid for the property.

Section 1.368-1(a) generally provides that in determining whether a transaction qualifies as a reorganization under § 368(a), the transaction must be evaluated under relevant provisions of law, including the step transaction doctrine.

Section 1.368-2(k) provides, in part, that a transaction otherwise qualifying as a reorganization under § 368(a) shall not be disqualified or recharacterized as a result of one or more distributions to shareholders (including distribution(s) that involve the assumption of liabilities) if the requirements of §1.368-1(d) are satisfied, the property distributed consists of assets of the surviving corporation, and the aggregate of such distributions does not consist of an amount of assets of the surviving corporation (disregarding assets of the merged corporation) that would result in a liquidation of such corporation for Federal income tax purposes.

Rev. Rul. 67-274, 1967-2 C.B. 141, holds that an acquiring corporation's acquisition of all of the stock of a target corporation solely in exchange for voting stock of the acquiring corporation, followed by the liquidation of the target corporation as part of the same plan, will be treated as an acquisition by the acquiring corporation of substantially all of the target corporation's assets in a reorganization described in § 368(a)(1)(C). The ruling explains that, under these circumstances, the stock acquisition and the liquidation are part of the overall plan of reorganization and the two steps may not be considered independently of each other for Federal income tax purposes. *See also* Rev. Rul. 72-405, 1972-2 C.B. 217.

Rev. Rul. 2001-46, 2001-2 C.B. 321, holds that, where a newly formed wholly owned subsidiary of an acquiring corporation merged into a target corporation, followed by the merger of the target corporation into the acquiring corporation, the step transaction doctrine is applied to integrate the steps and treat the transaction as a single statutory merger of the target corporation into the acquiring corporation. Noting that the rejection of step integration in Rev. Rul. 90-95, 1990-2 C.B. 67, and § 1.338-3(d) is based on Congressional intent that § 338 replace any nonstatutory treatment of a stock purchase as an asset purchase under the Kimbell-Diamond doctrine, the Service found that the policy underlying § 338 is not violated by treating the steps as a single statutory merger of the target into the acquiring corporation because such treatment results in a transaction that qualifies as a reorganization in which the acquiring corporation acquires the assets of the target corporation with a carryover basis under § 362, rather than receiving a cost basis in those assets under § 1012. (In *Kimbell-Diamond Milling Co. v. Commissioner*, 14 T.C. 74, *aff'd per curiam*, 187 F.2d 718 (1951), *cert. denied*, 342 U.S. 827 (1951), the court held that the purchase of the stock of a target corporation for the purpose of obtaining its assets through a prompt liquidation should be treated by the purchaser as a purchase of the target corporation's assets with the purchaser receiving a cost basis in the assets.)

Section 338(a) provides that if a corporation makes a qualified stock purchase and makes an election under that section, then the target corporation (i) shall be treated as having sold all of its assets at the close of the acquisition date at fair market value and (ii) shall be treated as a new corporation which purchased all of its assets as of the beginning of the day after the acquisition date. Section 338(d)(3) defines a qualified stock purchase as any transaction or series of transactions in which stock (meeting the requirements of § 1504(a)(2)) of one corporation is acquired by another corporation by purchase during a 12-month acquisition period. Section 338(h)(3) defines a purchase generally as any acquisition of stock, but excludes acquisitions of stock in exchanges to which § 351, § 354, § 355, or § 356 applies.

412

Section 338 was enacted in 1982 and was "intended to replace any nonstatutory treatment of a stock purchase as an asset purchase under the Kimbell-Diamond doctrine." H.R. Conf. Rep. No. 760, 97th Cong, 2d Sess. 536 (1982), 1982-2 C.B. 600, 632. Stock purchase or asset purchase treatment generally turns on whether the purchasing corporation makes or is deemed to make a § 338 election. If the election is made or deemed made, asset purchase treatment results and the basis of the target assets is adjusted to reflect the stock purchase price and other relevant items. If an election is not made or deemed made, the stock purchase treatment generally results. In such a case, the basis of the target assets is not adjusted to reflect the stock purchase price and other relevant items.

Rev. Rul. 90-95 (Situation 2), holds that the merger of a newly formed wholly owned domestic subsidiary into a target corporation with the target corporation shareholders receiving solely cash in exchange for their stock, immediately followed by the merger of the target corporation into the domestic parent of the merged subsidiary, will be treated as a qualified stock purchase of the target corporation followed by a § 332 liquidation of the target corporation. As a result, the parent's basis in the target corporation's assets will be the same as the basis of the assets in the target corporation's hands. The ruling explains that even though "the step-transaction doctrine is properly applied to disregard the existence of the [merged subsidiary]," so that the first step is treated as a stock purchase, the acquisition of the target corporation's stock is accorded independent significance from the subsequent liquidation of the target corporation and, therefore, is treated as a qualified stock purchase regardless of whether a § 338 election is made. Thus, in that case, the step transaction doctrine was not applied to treat the transaction as a direct acquisition by the domestic parent of the assets of the target corporation because such an application would have resulted in treating a stock purchase as an asset purchase, which would be inconsistent with the repeal of the Kimbell-Diamond doctrine and § 338.

Section 1.338-3(d) incorporates the approach of Rev. Rul. 90-95 into the regulations by requiring the purchasing corporation (or a member of its affiliated group) to treat certain asset transfers following a qualified stock purchase (where no § 338 election is made) independently of the qualified stock purchase. In the example in § 1.338-3(d)(5), the purchase for cash of 85 percent of the stock of a target corporation, followed by the merger of the target corporation into a wholly owned subsidiary of the purchasing corporation, is treated (other than by certain minority shareholders) as a qualified stock purchase of the stock of the target corporation followed by a § 368 reorganization of the target corporation into the subsidiary. As a result, the subsidiary's basis in the target corporation's assets is the same as the basis of the assets in the target corporation's hands.

ANALYSIS

If the Acquisition Merger and the Liquidation were treated as separate from each other, the Acquisition Merger would be treated as a stock acquisition that qualifies as a reorganization under § 368(a)(1)(A) by reason of § 368(a)(2)(E), and the Liquidation would qualify under § 332. However, as provided in § 1.368-1(a), in determining whether a transaction qualifies as a reorganization under § 368(a), the transaction must be evaluated under relevant provisions of law, including the step transaction doctrine. In this case, because T was completely liquidated, the § 1.368-2(k) safe harbor exception from the application of the step transaction doctrine does not apply. Accordingly, the Acquisition Merger and the Liquidation may not be considered independently of each other for purposes of determining whether the transaction satisfies the statutory requirements of a reorganization described in § 368(a)(1)(A) by reason of § 368(a)(2)(E). As such, this transaction does not qualify as a reorganization described in § 368(a)(1)(A) by reason of § 368(a)(2)(E) because, after the transaction, T does not hold substantially all of its properties and the properties of the merged corporation.

413

In determining whether the transaction is a reorganization, the approach reflected in Rev. Rul. 67-274 and Rev. Rul. 2001-46 is applied to ignore P's acquisition of the T stock in the Acquisition Merger and to treat the transaction as a direct acquisition by P of T's assets in exchange for 10x dollars in cash, 90x dollars worth of P voting stock, and the assumption of T's liabilities.

However, unlike the transactions considered in Revenue Rulings 67-274, 72-405 and 2001-46, a direct acquisition by P of T's assets in this case does not qualify as a reorganization under § 368(a). P's acquisition of T's assets is not a reorganization described in § 368(a)(1)(C) because the consideration exchanged is not solely P voting stock and the requirements of § 368(a)(2)(B) are not satisfied. Section 368(a)(2)(B) would treat P as acquiring 40 percent of T's assets for consideration other than P voting stock (liabilities assumed of 50x dollars, plus 10x dollars cash). *See* Rev. Rul. 73-102, 1973-1 C.B. 186 (analyzing the application of § 368(a)(2)(B)). P's acquisition of T's assets is not a reorganization described in § 368(a)(1)(D) because neither T nor A (nor a combination thereof) was in control of P (within the meaning of § 368(a)(2)(H)(i)) immediately after the transfer. Additionally, the transaction is not a reorganization under § 368(a)(1)(A) because T did not merge into P. Accordingly, the overall transaction is not a reorganization under § 368(a).

Additionally, P's acquisition of the T stock in the Acquisition Merger is not a transaction to which § 351 applies because A does not control P (within the meaning of § 368(c)) immediately after the exchange.

Rev. Rul. 90-95 and § 1.338-3(d) reject the step integration approach reflected in Rev. Rul. 67-274 where the application of that approach would treat the purchase of a target corporation's stock without a § 338 election followed by the liquidation or merger of the target corporation as the purchase of the target corporation's assets resulting in a cost basis in the assets under § 1012. Rev. Rul. 90-95 and § 1.338-3(d) treat the acquisition of the stock of the target corporation as a qualified stock purchase followed by a separate carryover basis transaction in order to preclude any nonstatutory treatment of the steps as an integrated asset purchase.

In this case, further application of the approach reflected in Rev. Rul. 67-274, integrating the acquisition of T stock with the liquidation of T, would result in treating the acquisition of T stock as a taxable purchase of T's assets. Such treatment would violate the policy underlying § 338 that a cost basis in acquired assets should not be obtained through the purchase of stock where no § 338 election is made. Accordingly, consistent with the analysis set forth in Rev. Rul. 90-95, the acquisition of the stock of T is treated as a qualified stock purchase by P followed by the liquidation of T into P under § 332.

HOLDING

The transaction is not a reorganization under § 368(a). The Acquisition Merger is a qualified stock purchase by P of the stock of T under § 338(d)(3). The Liquidation is a complete liquidation of a controlled subsidiary under § 332.

PROBLEM 21-6

Mega Corp. seeks to acquire the assets of one of its customers, Target Corp., which has a dominant share of the market for selling Mega Corp's products. Mega Corp. proposes to exchange its voting stock for the assets of Target Corp. Target Corp. owns assets with a value of $500,000 and a basis of $300,000, along with liabilities of $100,000. Mega Corp., after acceptance of the deal by shareholders of Target Corp., exchanges its voting stock worth $400,000 for all the assets of Target Corp., subject to or assuming liabilities, as part of a plan of reorganization.

1) Will the exchange of Target Corp's assets for Mega Corp. stock under the plan of reorganization meet the requirements of § 368(a)(l)(C)?

2) What if Mega Corp. also paid cash of $1,000?

3) Assuming that Mega Corp did not want one of Target's lines of business and it persuaded Target to distribute the assets of that line of business, would that prevent a Type C reorganization?

4) Suppose that Mega already owned 20% of the stock of Target before the exchange ($80,000 worth out of the total $400,000 value). How would that affect the viability of the attempted tax-free Type C reorganization?

F. TRIANGULAR MERGERS
See §§ 368(a)(2)(D) and (E).

In a forward triangular merger, the target corporation merges into a subsidiary of a parent company, and the shareholders of the target receive stock of the parent company. In a reverse triangular merger the acquiring corporation's subsidiary disappears into the target company by means of a merger. The practical results are the same, because in both transactions the target company shareholders wind up holding parent company stock and the parent owns either all of the stock of the target itself (reverse merger) or of the acquisition subsidiary which has become the target's alter ego (forward merger). The advantage of the reverse merger is that it ensures that the name of the target company is unchanged, it prevents any debate with creditors about the continuation of the target's liabilities, and otherwise leaves the target intact just as in a B reorganization.

If minority shareholders of the company protest, state law generally limits their rights to an appraisal proceeding pursuant to which they are entitled to the cash value of their stock of the target company. These are called dissenters' rights. In order to simplify the process for all concerned, triangular mergers often provide for a "cash option" pursuant to which the target company's shareholders can elect to take cash in lieu of stock. As you already know from your previous readings, if too many target shareholders elect to take cash, then the merger will not qualify as a Type A reorganization. As a result of this danger, cash options are often restricted to some fraction of the total consideration, 50% being a traditional number in the case of a forward merger. A reverse merger is more restrictive as to boot.

Both of these forms of acquisitive reorganizations are highly popular with corporate planners. Not only does a subsidiary insulate the parent from the target's hidden liabilities, but if the parent is publicly held, it is far more convenient to use the subsidiary as the acquiror. State corporate law generally requires either a majority or a super-majority vote of all the shareholders before a corporation may engage in a merger. This is clearly impractical for a large diversified corporation that may engage in many acquisitions each year. By using acquisition subsidiaries, a corporation can engage in acquisitions without going to shareholders for permission.

1. FORWARD TRIANGULAR MERGERS

A forward triangular merger requires the same 50% continuity of interest as mergers under § 368(a)(l)(A) but with two additional restrictions that are not applicable to plain A reorganizations. The first is borrowed from the C reorganization. Under § 368(a)(2)(D) the acquisition subsidiary (S) (which may be a newly-formed shell or a preexisting S) must obtain "substantially all the properties" of the target corporation (T), which has the usual 90%/70% meaning for ruling purposes. Just as with a C reorganization, pre-merger spin-offs, sales or redemptions of assets from T may upset compliance with this requirement. The second restriction (the reason for which is far from apparent) is that no stock of S can be used as consideration. The parent (P) of S can issue its stock directly to T shareholders; it does not have to contribute the stock to its subsidiary first. P.L.R. 8925087 (March 30, 1989). As in an A reorganization, there is no limit on the amount of T's liabilities that S can assume. This is a substantial improvement over the baroque rules governing C reorganizations. Section 368(a)(2)(D)(ii) demands that the merger would have qualified if done directly with the parent corporation. This evidently means that the subsiding merger must meet the continuity of business enterprise test and continuity of proprietary interest test excepting the use of parent stock.

To illustrate: P forms wholly-owned S and contributes P stock to S. T, which is worth $100, merges into S under state law, and S pays the T shareholders P stock worth $100 for surrendering of all their shares of T. The transaction is a valid forward triangular merger under § 368(a)(2)(D) provided: (1) S receives substantially all T's assets and (2) the judicial requirements for a reorganization are met. (If instead the consideration consisted of $90 worth of P stock and $10 worth of S stock, the transaction would be outside § 368(a)(2)(D) despite an apparent 100% continuity of interest). T shareholders will be taxed as if they went through a typical type A merger or consolidation. That means the former T shareholders will take a basis in P stock that equals their basis in their former T stock, modified for the impact of boot. § 358. S takes T's basis in T's assets, plus any gain that T recognized. § 362(b).

P's basis in the S stock will consist of its pre-merger basis in S stock, plus further basis equal to T's inside basis in its assets minus the liabilities acquired from T, as if P first acquired T's assets and then dropped them down to S. Reg. § 1.358-6(c)(1).

Overlap with a reorganization: If the consideration were $40 worth of P stock and $60 worth of S stock, then the transaction would not qualify under § 368(a)(2)(D), but should nevertheless qualify as an A reorganization directly into S with the P stock treated as permissible (taxable) boot because this time there is enough S stock for continuity of proprietary interest to exist in the direct S-T merger.

2. REVERSE TRIANGULAR MERGERS

A reverse triangular merger strongly resembles a B reorganization, because the result in both cases is that T becomes a controlled subsidiary of P, and T's shareholders receive P voting stock in exchange. It is useful in situations where it is necessary to preserve the corporate existence of T. Although its mechanical requirements are more stringent than those of a forward triangular merger, they are somewhat more flexible than for a B reorganization.

Section 368(a)(2)(E) requires that (1) the shareholders of T transfer control of T solely for voting stock of S's controlling parent (P); and (2) that after the transaction T will hold substantially all the properties of both T and S (except for any P stock that S transferred to T's shareholders in the exchange). In addition, two requirements are borrowed from the rules for C reorganizations: (1) only up to 20% boot may be paid to T's shareholders (but without the C reorganization concern that permissible boot is reduced by assumption of T's liabilities); and (2) T must hold "substantially all the properties" of S after the merger and retain substantially all of its own properties as well. Unlike a B reorganization, 80% control of T must be obtained in a single transaction. Thus, preexisting ownership by S or P of more than 20% of T's stock will prevent the use of § 368(a)(2)(E). There is little if anything to justify these complications.

It is not necessary for P to transfer its stock to S so that S can distribute the P stock to T's shareholders. The IRS has allowed a direct transfer from P to the shareholders of T in P.L.R. 9125013 (March 21, 1991).

P's basis in the T stock is calculated in precisely the same way as for a forward triangular merger except that, if P acquires less than 100% of S, then a corresponding basis reduction is made to reflect that fact. *See* Reg. § 1.358-6(c)(4), Examples 2(d) and (e). After all, it will not have all of the T stock, so P's basis in its block of T stock should reflect that fact. If P already owned some T stock, P can elect to hypothesize that it acquired the stock in the reorganization for purposes of determining its basis in S stock. Reg. § 1.358-6.

As in all reorganizations, T's shareholders will take a substituted basis in their P stock that will equal their former basis in their T stock, modified for the impact of boot. § 358.

"Forced B" Reorganization as a Safety Net

If an attempted reverse triangular merger fails to meet one or more of the technical requirements of § 368(a)(2)(E), it may nevertheless qualify as a B reorganization. For example, suppose that in connection with an otherwise valid reverse triangular merger using P stock as the sole consideration, T shears off some operating assets immediately before the merger, so that T fails the "substantially all the properties" rule. If the transaction had been structured as a B reorganization it would have been tax-free because there is no "substantially all" rule in a B reorganization. The IRS applied the step transaction doctrine to such a transaction in Revenue Ruling 67-448, 1967-2 C.B. 144 to the taxpayers' advantage and held that the intervening merger could be ignored because the end result was tantamount to a valid B reorganization. Note that the forced B reorganization facilitates squeeze-outs of minority shareholders, so it is not a source of pleasure to everyone.

PROBLEM 21-7

T has 10,000 shares of voting common stock outstanding, all in one class. Assume that P bought 2,000 shares of T in December of year 0. In an unrelated transaction in year 9, P merged transitory S into T and received 7,900 shares (out of the total of 8,000 remaining shares) of T. The T shareholders received solely voting stock of P as consideration. In connection with the merger, the directors of T acquiesced to the demands of some angry shareholders and agreed that T would buy their 100 shares of stock at a fair price.

a)   Is this a successful reverse triangular merger?

b)   Can this qualify as a Type B reorganization? *See* Reg. § 1.368-2(j)(6), Example 5.

G. ACQUISITIVE TYPE D REORGANIZATIONS
Read § 368(a)(1)(D).

417

A D reorganization can be either divisive or acquisitive in form and in result. In Chapter 20 you saw that § 368(a)(1)(D) comprehends a divisive reorganization in which the distributing corporation first forms a controlled subsidiary (or subsidiaries) to which it transfers part of its assets and then distributes the stock of the subsidiaries to its shareholders with respect to their shares under § 355. If the distributing corporation transfers substantially all its assets to a corporation which it thereafter controls and then distributes the controlled corporation's stock together with any retained properties, however, the transactions form an acquisitive reorganization under § 368(a)(1)(D) governed by § 354 instead of § 355. The required level of control of the transferee corporation is reduced from the usual 80% standard to the 50% standard (using the § 318(a) attribution rules) of § 304(c). *See* § 368(a)(2)(H).

Acquisitive D reorganizations are rare in practice. They have historically been imposed on taxpayers by the government in its effort to combat the liquidation-reincorporation abuse in which a corporation's owners attempt to withdraw cash from the business without paying taxes on dividends at ordinary income rates. To accomplish this, the owners choose the alternative path of liquidating the corporation with a view to retaining some of the proceeds of the liquidation, typically cash, and later contributing the operating assets to another operating company which they control. The practice can take various forms. In the simple case of an abusive liquidation with a major retention of cash by the shareholder-taxpayer, the taxpayer benefits by what amounts to a withdrawal of cash from a going concern at long-term capital gains rates and enjoying the secondary benefits of a stepped-up basis in reincorporated assets together with the elimination of the earnings and profits account. The IRS is aware of the revenue loss resulting from these practices, and has fashioned two primary counterattacks. The first is that the steps, taken together, constitute a corporate reorganization of some sort (usually an acquisitive D reorganization), with the result that the withdrawn cash is taxable at ordinary income rates, and the second (alternative) is that there was no bona fide complete liquidation.

To illustrate: National Accumulator Corporation has a long history of profitability and has accumulated cash. The founders would like to extract the cash at long-term capital gain rates. To carry out their wishes, the corporation liquidates and distributes all of its assets to the founders in turn. The founders report capital gain under § 331 when they receive the assets of the corporation. The founders next contribute the manufacturing assets (with likely stepped-up basis) plus a small amount of cash to a newly formed corporation (Newco) which carries on National Accumulator Corporation's business and later changes its name to National Accumulator Corporation. If this scheme works, the founders will manage to extract a large amount of cash and claim the benefit of long-term capital gain rates. This was a big deal before dividend taxes were capped at 20%. Now the tax utility is limited to wiping out E& P and obtaining stepped-up basis in assets.

Section 368(a)(1)(D) became the weapon of choice for combating the liquidation-reincorporation abuse. In the above illustration, the IRS was likely to argue that the transaction is not a liquidation at all, but rather a D reorganization with the results that the liquid assets constitute boot that is taxable as a dividend, the operating assets retain their original basis as if they had never left corporate solution, and the old earnings and profits account is similarly carried over to the new corporation. Notice how recently-enacted § 368(a)(2)(H)'s lower 50% measure of control made qualification as a D reorganization relatively easy compared with the 80% control requirement for an incorporation or a Type B reorganization. This was deliberately inserted to make it easier for the IRS to fight the liquidation-reincorporation abuse.

The IRS would win in the above illustration. But suppose the newly-reincorporated Newco's shareholders are not identical to the former shareholders of National because 21% of Newco shares are purchased by newcomers in the reincorporation? Before the 1984 enactment

418

of § 368(a)(2)(H) the transaction would succeed in wiping out e&p and obtaining stepped up basis because Newco would not be controlled by National or its former shareholders at the 80% level then required for a D reorganization. See *Berghash v. Commissioner*, 43 T.C. 743 (1965), *aff'd*, 361 F.2d 257 (2d Cir. 1966). Under current law, the former shareholders of National must own less than 50% of Newco (after applying the § 318 attribution rules) for the transaction to avoid being a D reorganization.

The courts have generally ignored the other requirements of § 368(a)(1)(D) in their eagerness to squelch abusive liquidation-reincorporations. For example, in *Smothers v. US.*, 642 F.2d 894 (5th Cir. 1981), the "substantially all" rule was held to be met by a sale of only 15% of the assets of one corporation (a service company) to a commonly-controlled sister corporation followed by liquidation of the transferor on the ground that the assets constituted substantially all the operating assets of a service business, and because the sister corporation hired the former employees of the liquidated corporation. The requirement of a distribution of all the stock of the transferee (service) corporation under § 354(b)(l)(B) was held unnecessary on the ground that the shareholders of the transferor already owned all the stock of the transferee.

The reorganization and liquidation sections have generally been held to be mutually exclusive. A transaction is either one or the other. The IRS has occasionally argued to the contrary in order to combat liquidation-reincorporations on a theory of "incomplete liquidation." The courts have generally refused to accept this doctrine, except for the Tax Court's decision (of uncertain reach) in *Telephone Answering Serv. Co. v. Commissioner*, 63 T. C. 423 (1974), *aff'd* by order, 546 F.2d 423 (4th Cir. 1976), cert. denied, 431 U.S. 914 (1977) ("TASCO"). In TASCO a shell parent corporation transferred its operating assets to an alter ego subsidiary and liquidated. The court held that the putative liquidation of the parent was "incomplete" because the parent's business continued in the form of another corporation.

NOTES

1. **Alter ego theory.** The so-called alter ego theory is best illustrated in *Telephone Answering Serv. Co. v. Commissioner,* 63 T.C. 423 (1974), *affd*, 546 F. 423 (4th Cir. 1976), cert. denied, 431 U.S. 914 (1977), which was briefly described above. Parts of this case were quite dramatic. A telephone answering company went through a split-up in which all of its assets found their way into a second corporation that was identical in every respect to the first corporation, including the name. The only differences were the legal event of dissolution of the first corporation and a new bank account. The government successfully asserted that in effect there was no liquidation and that the surviving corporation was merely an alter ego of the allegedly liquidated corporation.

2. **Overlap.** Assume that a parent corporation contributes all of its assets to a wholly-owned subsidiary, and in exchange it receives stock of the subsidiary. This looks like a § 351 exchange. To qualify under § 354(b) as a D reorganization, the subsidiary must receive substantially all of the parent's assets (achieved) and the parent company must distribute all of its properties, including the stock of the subsidiary, in pursuance of the plan of reorganization. Is this a D reorganization or § 351 exchange? If it is a reorganization, § 381 applies and the tax attributes of the parent company will be shifted to the subsidiary company. These would include such things as its earnings and profits account, net operating losses and capital loss carryovers. By contrast, if it is a § 351 exchange, there will be no carryover of tax attributes.

3. **More overlap questions**. Assume the same facts given immediately above. Why is this not also a C reorganization? The subsidiary acquired all of the assets of the transferor in exchange for voting stock and meets the distribution requirements of § 368(a)(2)(G)(i). This

transaction qualifies as *both* a C and a D reorganization, but a special rule covering this situation requires that it must be treated as a D reorganization. § 368(a)(2)(A).

H. TYPE E REORGANIZATIONS
Read § 368(a)(l)(E).

An E reorganization is simply stated to be a "recapitalization." § 368(a)(I)(E). There are numerous reasons to engage in a recapitalization. Probably the most common reason is to shift control of a closely-held corporation from the older generation to the next generation by a selective recapitalization exchange of common stock for preferred stock. The older generation then gives away a generous amount of the remaining common stock to the children. If this is done shrewdly, the common stock will have little immediate value, but it will represent the value of the corporation's future growth if the younger generation can manage the corporation effectively. The lack of any clear definition of the E reorganization other than a "recapitalization" has caused some difficulties, but it is clear that not every reshuffling of the corporation's capital structure will result in a tax-free reorganization.

BAZLEY v. COMMISSIONER
331 U.S. 737, 67 S. Ct. 1489 (1947)

MR. JUSTICE FRANKFURTER delivered the opinion of the Court:

In the *Bazley* case, no. 289, the Commissioner of Internal Revenue assessed an income tax deficiency against the taxpayer for the year 1939. Its validity depends on the legal significance of the recapitalization in that year of a family corporation in which the taxpayer and his wife owned all but one of the Company's one thousand shares. These had a par value of $100. Under the plan of reorganization the taxpayer, his wife, and the holder of the additional share were to turn in their old shares and receive in exchange for each old share five new shares of no par value, but of a stated value of $60, and new debenture bonds, having a total face value of $400,000, payable in ten years but callable at any time. Accordingly, the taxpayer received 3,990 shares of the new stock for the 798 shares of his old holding and debentures in the amount of $319,200. At the time of these transactions the earned surplus of the corporation was $855,783.82.

The Commissioner charged to the taxpayer as income the full value of the debentures. The Tax Court affirmed the Commissioner's determination, against the taxpayer's contention that as a "recapitalization" the transaction was a tax-free "reorganization" and that the debentures were "securities in a corporation a party to a reorganization," "exchanged solely for stock or securities in such corporation" "in pursuance of a plan of reorganization," and as such no gain is recognized for income tax purposes. Internal Revenue Code, [§ 368(a)(1)(E)]. The Tax Court found that the recapitalization had "no legitimate corporate business purpose" and was therefore not a "reorganization" within the statute. The distribution of debentures, it concluded, was a disguised dividend, taxable as earned income under [§§ 61(a)(7), 301 and 302]. The Circuit Court of Appeals for the Third Circuit, sitting en banc, affirmed, two judges dissenting. 155 F.2d 237.

Unless a transaction is a reorganization contemplated by [§ 368(a)(1)], any exchange of "stock or securities" in connection with such transaction, cannot be "in pursuance of the plan of reorganization" under [§ 368(a)(1)]. While [§ 368(a)(1)] informs us that "reorganization" means, among other things, "a recapitalization," it does not inform us what "recapitalization" means. "Recapitalization" in connection with the income tax has been part of the revenue laws since 1921. . . . Congress has never defined it and the Treasury Regulations shed only limited light. One thing is certain. Congress did not incorporate some technical concept, whether that of accountants or of other specialists, into § 368, assuming that there is agreement among specialists as to the meaning of recapitalization. And so, recapitalization as used in [§ 368(a)(1)(E)] must draw its meaning from its function in that section. It is one of the forms of reorganization which obtains the privileges afforded by [§ 354(a)(1)] Therefore, "recapitalization" must be construed with reference to the presuppositions and purpose of [the reorganization rules]. It was not the purpose of the reorganization provision to exempt from payment of a tax what as a practical matter is realized gain. Normally, a distribution by a corporation, whatever form it takes, is a definite and rather unambiguous event. It furnishes the proper occasion for the determination and taxation of gain. But there are circumstances where a formal distribution, directly or through exchange of securities, represents merely a new form of the previous participation in an enterprise, involving no change of substance in the rights and relations of the interested parties one to another or to the corporate assets. As to these, Congress has said that they are not to be deemed significant occasions for determining taxable gain.

These considerations underlie [§ 368] and they should dominate the scope to be given to the various sections, all of which converge toward a common purpose. Application of the language of such a revenue provision is not an exercise in framing abstract definitions. In a series of cases this Court has withheld the benefits of the reorganization provision in situations which might have satisfied provisions of the section treated as inert language, because they were not reorganizations of the kind with which [§ 368], in its purpose and particulars, concerns itself.

Congress has not attempted a definition of what is recapitalization and we shall follow its example. The search for relevant meaning is often satisfied not by a futile attempt at abstract definition but by pricking a line through concrete applications. Meaning frequently is built up by assured recognition of what does not come within a concept the content of which is in controversy. Since a recapitalization within the scope of [§ 368] is an aspect of reorganization, nothing can be a recapitalization for this purpose unless it partakes of those characteristics of a reorganization which underlie the purpose of Congress in postponing the tax liability.

No doubt there was a recapitalization of the Bazley corporation in the sense that the symbols that represented its capital were changed, so that the fiscal basis of its operations would appear very differently on its books. But the form of a transaction as reflected by correct corporate accounting opens questions as to the proper application of a taxing statute; it does not close them. Corporate accounting may represent that correspondence between change in the form of capital structure and essential identity in fact which is of the essence of a transaction relieved from taxation as a reorganization. What is controlling is that a new arrangement intrinsically partake of the elements of reorganization which underlie the Congressional exemption and not merely give the appearance of it to accomplish a distribution of earnings. In the case of a corporation which has undistributed earnings, the creation of new corporate obligations which are transferred to stockholders in relation to their former holdings, so as to produce, for all practical purposes, the same result as a distribution of cash earnings of equivalent value, cannot obtain tax immunity because cast in the form of a recapitalization-reorganization. The governing legal rule can hardly be stated more narrowly. To attempt to do so would only challenge astuteness in evading it. And so it is hard to escape the conclusion that whether in a particular case a paper recapitalization is no more than an admissible attempt to avoid the consequences of an outright distribution of earnings turns on details of corporate affairs, judgment on which must be left to the Tax Court. *See Dobson v. Commissioner*, 320 U.S. 489.

What have we here? No doubt, if the Bazley corporation had issued the debentures to Bazley and his wife without any recapitalization, it would have made a taxable distribution. Instead, these debentures were issued as part of a family arrangement, the only additional ingredient being an unrelated modification of the capital account. The debentures were found to be worth at least their principal amount, and they were virtually cash because they were callable at the will of the corporation which in this case was the will of the taxpayer. One does not have to pursue the motives behind actions, even in the more ascertainable forms of purpose, to find, as did the Tax Court, that the whole arrangement took this form instead of an outright distribution of cash or debentures, because the latter would undoubtedly have been taxable income whereas what was done could, with a show of reason, claim the shelter of the immunity of a recapitalization-reorganization.

The Commissioner, the Tax Court and the Circuit Court of Appeals agree that nothing was accomplished that would not have been accomplished by an outright debenture dividend. And since we find no misconception of law on the part of the Tax Court and the Circuit Court of Appeals, whatever may have been their choice of phrasing, their application of the law to the facts of this case must stand. A "reorganization" which is merely a vehicle, however elaborate or elegant, for conveying earnings from accumulations to the stockholders is not a reorganization under [§ 368]. This disposes of the case as a matter of law, since the facts as found by the Tax Court bring them within it. And even if this transaction were deemed a reorganization, the facts would equally sustain the imposition of the tax on the debentures under [§ 356(a)(1) and (2)]. . . .

NOTES

1. **The impact of § 354(a)(2)**. *Bazley* was decided before the passage of § 354(a)(2). If that section had been in force when *Bazley* was decided, would it have made any difference? If there is no reorganization, what Code section applies to the receipt of additional consideration, including additional securities?

2. **Bond for bond exchanges**. A corporation may choose to redeem old bonds and substitute new ones if interest rates have changed. This can be a complex area because it implicates § 108 and the original issue discount rules.

3. **Continuity of interest**. Assume that a taxpayer exchanges common stock for a combination of bonds and common stock in the same corporation. Does the recapitalization fail if the 50% continuity of proprietary interest standard is not satisfied? The answer is "no." Neither continuity of the business enterprise nor continuity of interest is required in a recapitalization exchange. *See* Reg. § 1.368-1(b).

4. **Relationship to § 305**. A transaction might be an E reorganization and also fit within the list of taxable transactions under § 305(b). If that is the case, what are the results? Is it a nontaxable reorganization or a distribution of stock? The answer appears to be a taxable stock distribution except in a "classic recapitalization" in which an older generation of founders swaps its common stock for newly preferred stock while the younger generation of executives correspondingly increase their share of common stock. The underlying basis for this is a statement by Senator Long in the course of the Senate Floor Debate on the bill incorporating session § 305. *See* 115 Cong. Rec. 37807 at 37902 (1969). *See also* Reg. § 1.305-3(e), Example 12, which formalizes the statement.

REV. RUL. 55-112
1955-1 C.B. 344

Six stockholders owning 54 percent of the common stock of a corporation (which had only common then outstanding) surrendered all of their common stock for newly issued nonvoting preferred stock of the same book value and same fair market value. After the exchange, none of the preferred stockholders was an officer, director, or employee of the corporation, and none of such stockholders had any direct or indirect economic interest in the affairs of the corporation except that evidenced by his preferred stock. *Held*, the transaction is a nontaxable reorganization (recapitalization) within the terms of section 112(g)(l)(E) of the Internal Revenue Code of 1939.

Advice has been requested with respect to the tax consequences, for Federal income tax purposes, of a change in the capital structure of M Corporation.

All the stock of the M Corporation (which had only common stock outstanding) was held by 5 men interested in its management and operation and by the wives of these individuals. Three of these men, due to ill-health and other reasons, desired to cease all activity in connection with the corporate business, while the other 2 desired to remain active in the business. The 2 who wished to remain active wanted complete control of the corporation and the others were willing to let them have such control.

Accordingly, all the interested parties agreed that the stockholders who did not wish to remain active would exchange their common stock for preferred stock. Therefore, the corporate charter was amended to authorize the issuance of nonvoting stock, preferred as to dividends and on liquidation, having no pre-emptive rights and redeemable at the option of the corporation. The 3 stockholders who desired to cease being active, and their wives, surrendered all their common stock (totaling 54 percent of all the stock) and received in exchange preferred stock of equal fair market value and of equal book value (such book value being determined by the corporation's basis for its assets for tax purposes). The corporation redeemed and canceled all the common stock received by it in the exchange. After the transaction all the preferred stockholders owned no common stock, and were not officers, directors or employees of the corporation. None of the preferred stockholders was related by blood or marriage to any common stockholder, or to any officer, director or employee of the corporation, and no preferred stockholder had any economic interest whatever in the affairs of the corporation, except that evidenced by his preferred stock shares.

Section 112(a) of the Internal Revenue Code of 1939 provides, in effect, that upon the sale or exchange of property, the entire amount of the gain or loss resulting shall be recognized, unless the results of such exchanges are expressly exempted by the provisions of section 112(b) of such Code. Among the exchanges, the results of which are exempted, is an exchange in connection with a recapitalization (reorganization).

Section 112(b)(3) provides:

(b) EXCHANGES SOLELY IN KIND. –

(3) STOCK FOR STOCK ON REORGANIZATION. – No gain or loss shall be recognized if stock or securities in a corporation a party to a reorganization are, in pursuance of the plan of reorganization, exchanged solely for stock or securities in such corporation or in another corporation a party to the reorganization.

Section 39.112(g)-1(b) of Regulations 118 provides that the purpose of the reorganization provisions of the Internal Revenue Code is to except from the general rule certain specifically described exchanges incident to such readjustments of corporate structures, made in one of the particular ways specified in the Code, as are required by business exigencies, and which effect only a readjustment of continuing interests in property under modified corporate forms. The same subsection also provides that a continuity of the business enterprise under the modified corporate form, and a continuity of interest therein on the part of those persons who were the owners of the enterprise prior to the transaction, are requisite to a reorganization under the Code.

Section 39.112(e) of Regulations 118 provides that a recapitalization and therefore a reorganization, takes place if, for example a corporation issues preferred stock, previously authorized but unissued, for outstanding common stock.

Accordingly, the described transaction is a recapitalization as defined by section 112(g)(1)(E) of the Internal Revenue Code of 1939 and under section 112(b)(3) no gain or loss is recognized to the stockholders upon the exchanges by them of their common stock for new preferred stock. The basis of the preferred stock received by each shareholder is the same as the cost or other basis of the common stock surrendered by him. The exchanges of common stock for preferred stock have no effect upon the accumulated earnings and profits. . . .

NOTES

1. **Section 306 effect**. Assuming the corporation had earnings and profits at the time of this transaction, is the preferred stock § 306 stock?

2. **The burden of § 306**. What result if the senior shareholders were to cause some of their stock to be redeemed? The older shareholders might decide to give away their § 306 stock so as to strip their estates. If the redemption is complete, the corporation can redeem their stock in full at their death, and the § 306 taint will not apply. § 306(b)(1). The donees might later be able to persuade the corporation to recapitalize the preferred back into common, thereby eliminating the § 306 taint entirely. Wait a minute! What if the person holding the preferred agreed to convert it to common and then promptly redeemed the common? Would that not open up a loophole? The answer is "yes." However, the IRS is aware of it. In Rev. Rul. 76-387, 1976-2 C.B. 96, a recapitalization exchange of all the outstanding § 306 stock for nonvoting common was ruled to qualify under § 368(a)(1)(E), provided there was no plan to redeem the common.

3. **The § 1036 alternative.** Read § 1036 and note how it overlaps with the recapitalization provisions. However, it is narrow because it only extends to exchanges of the same grade of stock (common for common or preferred for preferred).

4. **Nonqualified preferred stock ("NQP stock").** Look at § 354 to see how NQP stock is handled.

I. TYPE F REORGANIZATIONS
Read § 368(a)(1)(F).

This form of reorganization is typically used when a corporation wishes to move from one state to another. It will normally do so by forming a new corporation with the same name in a different state and then transferring all its assets and liabilities to the new corporation in exchange for stock of the new corporation, after which the old corporation liquidates. Even though this involves two corporations, as long as only one of them is an operating company there can still be a nontaxable Type F reorganization. Legislative History of the Tax Equity and Fiscal Responsibility Act of 1982, P.L. 97-248. H. Rep. 760, 97th Cong., 2d Sess. At page 541 (1982). Except for this situation (where there is only one active corporation), the F reorganization does not apply if more than one corporation is involved.

The advantage of an F reorganization is that the survival of tax attributes in the hands of the surviving corporation is granted far more generously than for reorganizations under A, B, C, and D.

Which of the following transactions qualifies as an F reorganization?

1) X Corporation changes state of incorporation, its name, and key elements of its charter.

2) X Corporation, which is an operating company, merges into Y Corporation, a completely inert company, in order to get the benefit of the name "Y Corporation."

3) What impact does § 381 have on the taxable years of Y in "b)"? *See* § 381(b).

4) X merges into Y. Both X and Y are active business corporations with exactly the same shareholders.

J. TYPE G REORGANIZATIONS
Read § 368(a)(1)(G).

This class of reorganization accommodates corporations going through restructurings in bankruptcy. The key feature of § 368(a)(I)(G) is that it opens the door to treating creditors who receive stock as persons with respect to whom there is continuity of proprietary interest. If it were not for this provision, a corporation whose net worth was wiped out could never go through a reorganization because, as a practical matter, its shareholders would never receive enough stock to constitute continuity of proprietary interest under the general meaning of that term. Section 368(a)(1)(G) is infrequently used in practice and is only mentioned in passing here.

K. TREATMENT OF THE PARTIES TO A REORGANIZATION
Read §§ 354(a), 361, 362(a) and (b).

In a qualifying reorganization §§ 354, 361, and 362 dictate the bulk of the outcomes at the corporate and the shareholder levels. The result is generally that income taxes are deferred by means of a continuation of basis. Similarly, under § 1223, there will also be a continuation of holding periods. The problem is that §§ 354, 361, and 362 are not well organized and use unfamiliar language to express Congress' intent. Because the initial steps in a reorganization generally occur at the corporate level, the corporate-level effects are discussed first below.

1. IMPACT ON CORPORATIONS

The central feature of the acquisitive reorganization is that the stock or assets of one corporation are transferred to another corporation. The Code uses the term "transferor" generally to mean the target corporation, that is the company that transfers its assets to the acquiring "transferee."

a. As to the Transferor (Target) Corporation

Section 361(a) prevents the target from recognizing gain or loss on the exchange of its assets to the acquiring corporation for acquiring corporation stock, and thus overrides §§ 311 and 336. The same is true under § 361(b) for the target's transfer of both the acquiring corporation's stock and boot to its shareholders, but only if the entire boot is either distributed to its shareholders or used to pay creditors, or both combined. § 361(b)(1)(B). The transferor is not permitted to recognize any loss in the exchange even if it is due to boot received from the acquiring corporation (transferee). § 361(b)(2). The transferor does recognize gain (but not loss) however, if it distributes boot to its shareholders in the form of its own appreciated property. § 361(c). Basis issues for the acquiring corporation are a bit complicated, and are discussed separately below.

Section 358 governs the basis results for the target company, but these are marginal issues, because the target generally liquidates as part of the plan of reorganization.

b. As to the Transferee (Acquiring) Corporation

The acquiring corporation does not recognize gain on the issuance of stock for assets. § 1032. However, if the acquiring corporation transfers boot in kind, its inherent gain or loss in the boot is part of a taxable exchange, even though the exchange arises in the context of an otherwise nontaxable reorganization. § 351(f). The acquiror's transfer of cash boot would not be taxed because the basis of cash is always equal to its face amount.

In general, there is no problem if the acquiring company assumes the liabilities of the target company. § 357(a). However, if tax avoidance motives were at work, § 357(b) turns all liabilities into boot.

What if the subsidiary uses parent corporation's stock to acquire the assets of the target in a merger? Does § 1032 apply? Formally, the answer is "no," but in Rev. Rul. 57-278, 1957-1 C.B. 124, the IRS ruled that the subsidiary recognizes no gain or loss on the theory that there would have been none had there been a merger at the parent level followed by a drop down to the subsidiary. This is an admirable example of the application of common sense to Subchapter C.

c. The Acquiring Company's Basis in Acquired Assets

Section 362(b) says that property that a corporation acquires "in connection with a reorganization" normally takes a basis equal to the transferor's (target company's) basis plus any gain that the target company recognized on the transfer. So, for example, where the target's distribution of boot causes it to recognize gain, the acquiring corporation benefits from an upward adjustment to basis. If the transaction is not a reorganization, the acquiring company takes a cost basis in the target's assets as, for example, in a cash merger.

d. Foreign Corporations

If a reorganization or incorporation involves a transfer of appreciated assets to a foreign corporation, Congress is understandably concerned that the transferred assets might escape tax permanently and has installed a safeguard, § 367, which generally taxes gains (but not losses) on such "outbound" (i.e., to a foreign country) transfers by the curious mechanism of declaring the transferee corporation "not a corporation." § 367(a)(1). Therefore, the nonrecognition rules of §§ 354-356, § 361, § 1032, and the definitions of § 368 do not apply because they require transfers to and from a "corporation." There are various exceptions for transfers of assets that will be used in an active business, and the Treasury has regulatory authority to relax the rules even further.

2. TAXATION OF SHAREHOLDERS AND SECURITY HOLDERS
Read §§ 354(a), 355(a)(1), 356, and 358.

Section 354(a)(l) and § 355(a)(1) generally prevent recognition of gain to the target's shareholders on exchanges or distributions in a qualifying reorganization. However, if boot is distributed, § 354(a)(3) directs the reader to § 356, which requires the target shareholder to recognize any realized gain (but not loss) to the extent of the amount of the boot received. § 356(a) and (c). Securities received are boot except to the extent that securities of the target are given up in the same face amount in the exchange. If a greater face amount is received than given up, the value of the excess face amount is boot. § 356(d)(2)(B).

To illustrate: Mrs. Klinger owns one share of T stock with a basis of $105 and a value of $175. T merges into P in an A reorganization in which she receives stock of T worth $100, $50 in cash, and a note (a security) with face amount and value of $25 in exchange for her one share of stock. Assume the exchange does not have the flavor of a distribution, so that there is no disguised dividend issue. Her realized gain is $70 ($175 total consideration received less her basis of $105). The note is boot. The recognized gain is also $70, because § 356(a)(1) necessarily limits recognized gain to realized gain. As long as neither the T stock nor the note is "readily tradable," she can report $25 of the gain on the installment method. *See* Reg. § 1.453-11(c)(1), allowing boot in the form of an installment obligation be reported under § 453.

The gain is treated as being from a sale or exchange unless the boot distribution "has the effect of the distribution of a dividend," but even then dividend treatment applies only to the extent of the distributee's ratable share of earnings and profits. § 356(a)(2). The *Clark* case explores the issue of exactly when boot "has the effect of a dividend."

Section 358 prescribes the basis of property received by shareholders in a reorganization, and it is identical to the rules for § 351 exchanges. The basis of the shareholder's stock received is the same as that of the target stock given up, less any boot received and plus any gain recognized. As always, boot receives a fair market value basis at the time of the merger.

COMMISSIONER OF INTERNAL REVENUE v. CLARK
489 U.S. 726 (1989)

[In 1979 taxpayer, the sole shareholder of Basin Surveys, Inc. (Basin), entered into a triangular merger agreement with NL Industries, Inc. ("NL"), pursuant to which he transferred all of Basin's stock to NL's wholly owned subsidiary in exchange for 300,000 NL shares, being approximately 0.92% of NL's outstanding common stock, and a significant amount of cash. Taxpayer reported the cash as a capital gain, but the IRS asserted that the result was a distribution. The Commissioner assessed a deficiency of $972,504.74.]

JUSTICE STEVENS delivered the opinion of the Court.

This is the third case in which the Government has asked us to decide that a shareholder's receipt of a cash payment in exchange for a portion of his stock was taxable as a dividend. In the two earlier cases, *Commissioner v. Estate of Bedford*, 325 U.S. 283 (1945), and *United States v. Davis*, 397 U.S. 301 (1970), we agreed with the Government largely because the transactions involved redemptions of stock by single corporations that did not "result in a meaningful reduction of the shareholder's proportionate interest in the corporation." *Id.*, at 313. In the case we decide today, however, the taxpayer in an arm's-length transaction exchanged his interest in the acquired corporation for less than 1% of the stock of the acquiring corporation and a substantial cash payment. The taxpayer held no interest in the acquiring corporation prior to the reorganization. Viewing the exchange as a whole, we conclude that the cash payment is not appropriately characterized as a dividend. We accordingly agree with the Tax Court and with the Court of Appeals that the taxpayer is entitled to capital gains treatment of the cash payment.

I

In determining tax liability under the Internal Revenue Code of 1954, gain resulting from the sale or exchange of property is generally treated as capital gain, whereas the receipt of cash dividends is treated as ordinary income. The Code, however, imposes no current tax on certain stock-for-stock exchanges. In particular, § 354(a)(1) provides, subject to various limitations, for nonrecognition of gain resulting from the exchange of stock or securities solely for the other stock or securities, provided that the exchange is pursuant to a plan of corporate reorganization and that the stock or securities are those of a party to the reorganization. 26 U.S.C. § 354(a)(1).

Under § 356(a)(1) of the Code, if such a stock-for-stock exchange is accompanied by additional consideration in the form of a cash payment or other property –something that tax practitioners refer to as "boot" – "then the gain, if any, to the recipient shall be recognized, but in an amount not in excess of the sum of such money and the fair market value of such other property." 26 U.S.C. § 356(a)(1). That is, if the shareholder receives boot, he or she must recognize the gain on the exchange up to the value of the boot. Boot is accordingly generally treated as a gain from the sale or exchange of property and is recognized in the current tax year.

Section 356(a)(2), which controls the decision in this case, creates an exception to that general rule. It provided in 1979:

"If an exchange is described in paragraph (1) but has the effect of the distribution of a dividend, then there shall be treated as a dividend to each distribute such an amount of the gain recognized under paragraph (1) as is not in excess of his ratable share of the undistributed earnings and profits of the corporation accumulated after February 28, 1913. The remainder, if any, of the gain recognized under paragraph (1) shall be treated as gain from the exchange of property." 26 U.S.C. §356(a)(2)(1976 ed.).

Thus, if the "exchange . . . has the effect of the distribution of a dividend," the boot must be treated as a dividend and is therefore appropriately taxed as ordinary income to the extent that gain is realized. In contrast, if the exchange does not have "the effect of the distribution of a dividend," the boot must be treated as a payment in exchange for property and, insofar as gain is realized, accorded capital gains treatment. The question in this case is thus whether the exchange between the taxpayer and the acquiring corporation had "the effect of the distribution of a dividend" within the meaning of § 356(a)(2).

The relevant facts are easily summarized. For approximately 15 years prior to April 1979, the taxpayer was the president of Basin Surveys, Inc. (Basin). In January 1978, he became sole shareholder in Basin, a company in which he had invested approximately $85,000. The corporation operated a successful business providing various technical services to the petroleum industry. In 1978, N.L. Industries, Inc. (NL), a publicly owned corporation engaged in the manufacture and supply of petroleum equipment and services, initiated negotiations with the taxpayer regarding the possible acquisition of Basin. On April 3, 1979, after months of negotiations, the taxpayer and NL entered into a contract.

The agreement provided for a "triangular merger," whereby Basin was merged into a wholly owned subsidiary of NL. In exchange for transferring all of the outstanding shares in Basin to NL's subsidiary, the taxpayer elected to receive 300,000 shares of NL common stock and cash boot of $3,250,000, passing up an alternative offer of 425,000 shares of NL common stock. The 300,000 shares of NL issued to the taxpayer amounted to approximately 0.92% of the outstanding common shares of NL. If the taxpayer had instead accepted the pure stock-for-stock offer, he would have held approximately 1.3% of the outstanding common shares. The Commissioner and the taxpayer agree that the merger at issue qualifies as a reorganization under §§ 368(a)(1)(A) and (a)(2)(D).

Respondents filed a joint federal income tax return for 1979. As required by § 356(a)(1), they reported the cash boot as taxable gain. In calculating the tax owed, respondents characterized the payment as long-term capital gain. The Commissioner on audit disagreed with this characterization. In his view, the payment had "the effect of the distribution of a dividend" and was thus taxable as ordinary income up to $2,319,611, the amount of Basin's accumulated earnings and profits at the time of the merger.

Respondents petitioned for review in the Tax Court, which, in a reviewed decision, held in their favor. 86 T.C. 138 (1986). The court started from the premise that the question whether the boot payment had "the effect of the distribution of a dividend" turns on the choice between "two judicially articulated tests." Id. at 140. Under the test advocated by the *Commissioner* and given voice in *Shimberg v. United States,* 577 F.2d 283 (CA5 1978), cert. denied, 439 U.S. 1115 (1979), the boot payment is treated as though it were made in a hypothetical redemption by the acquired corporation (Basin) immediately prior to the reorganization. Under this test, the cash payment received by the taxpayer indisputably would have been treated as a dividend. The second test, urged by the taxpayer and finding support in *Wright v. United States,* 482 F.2d 600 (CA8 1973), proposes an alternative hypothetical redemption. Rather than concentrating on the taxpayer's pre-reorganization interest in the acquired corporation, this test requires that one imagine a pure stock-for-stock exchange, followed immediately by a post-reorganization redemption of a portion of the taxpayer's shares in the acquiring corporation (NL) in return for a payment in an amount equal to the boot. Under § 302 of the Code, which defines when a redemption of stock should be treated as a distribution of dividend, NL's redemption of 125,000 shares of its stock from the taxpayer in exchange for the $3,250,000 boot payment would have been treated as capital gain.

The Tax Court rejected the pre-reorganization test favored by the Commissioner because it considered it improper "to view the cash payment as an isolated event totally separate from the reorganization." 86 T.C., at 151. Indeed, it suggested that this test requires that courts make the "determination of dividend equivalency fantasizing that the reorganization does not exist." Id. at 150 (footnote omitted). The court then acknowledged that a similar criticism could be made of the taxpayer's contention that the cash payment should be viewed as a post-reorganization redemption. It concluded, however, that since it was perfectly clear that the cash payment would not have taken place without the reorganization, it was better to treat the boot "as the equivalent of a redemption in the course of implementing the reorganization," than "as having occurred prior to and separate from the reorganization." Id. at 152. . . .

The Court of Appeals for the Fourth Circuit affirmed. 828 F.2d 221 (1987). Like the Tax Court, it concluded that although "[s]ection 302 does not explicitly apply in the reorganization context," Id. at 223, and although § 302 differs from § 356 in important respects, Id at 224, it nonetheless provides "the appropriate test for determining whether boot is ordinary income or a capital gain," Id. at 223. Thus, as explicated in § 302(b)(2), if the taxpayer relinquished more than 20% of his corporate control and retained less than 50% of the voting shares after the distribution, the boot would be treated as capital gain. However, as the Court of Appeals recognized, "[b]ecause § 302 was designed to deal with a stock redemption by a single corporation, rather than a reorganization involving two companies, the section does not indicate which corporation [the taxpayer] lost interest in." Id. at 224. Thus, like the Tax Court, the Court of Appeals was left to consider whether the hypothetical redemption should be treated as a prereorganization distribution coming from the acquired corporation or as a postreorganization distribution coming from the acquiring corporation. It concluded:

> "Based on the language and legislative history of § 356, the change in ownership principle of § 302, and the need to review the reorganization as an integrated transaction, we conclude that the boot should be characterized as a post reorganization stock redemption by N. L. that affected [the taxpayer's]. interest in the new corporation. Because this redemption reduced [the

taxpayer's] N. L. holdings by more than 20%, the boot should be taxed as a capital gain." *Id.* at 224-225."

This decision by the Court of Appeals for the Fourth Circuit is in conflict with the decision of the Fifth Circuit in *Shimberg v. United States,* 577 F.2d 283 (1978), in two important respects. In Shimberg, the court concluded that it was inappropriate to apply stock redemption principles in reorganization cases "on a wholesale basis." Id. at 287; see also *ibid.* n. 13. In addition, the court adopted the prereorganization test, holding that "§ 356(a)(2) requires a determination of whether the distribution would have been taxed as a dividend if made prior to the reorganization or if no reorganization had occurred." *Id.* at 288.

To resolve this conflict on a question of importance to the administration of the federal tax laws, we granted certiorari. 485 U.S. 933 (1988).

II

We agree with the Tax Court and the Court of Appeals for the Fourth Circuit that the question under § 356(a)(2) whether an "exchange . . . has the effect of the distribution of a dividend" should be answered by examining the effect of the exchange as a whole. We think the language and history of the statute, as well as a commonsense understanding of the economic substance of the transaction at issue, support this approach.

The language of § 356(a) strongly supports our understanding that the transaction should be treated as an integrated whole. Section 356(a)(2) asks whether "an exchange is described in paragraph (1)" that "has the effect of the distribution of a dividend." . . . The statute does not provide that boot shall be treated as a dividend if its payment has the effect of the distribution of a dividend. Rather, the inquiry turns on whether the "exchange" has that effect. Moreover, paragraph (1), in turn, looks to whether "the property received in the exchange consists not only of property permitted by section 354 or 355 to be received without the recognition of gain but also of other property or money" . . . Again, the statute plainly refers to one integrated transaction and, again, makes clear that we are to look to the character of the exchange as a whole and not simply its component parts. Finally, it is significant that § 356 expressly limits the extent to which boot may be taxed to the amount of gain realized in the reorganization. This limitation suggests that Congress intended that boot not be treated in isolation from the overall reorganization. See Levin, Adess, & McGaffey, *Boot Distributions in Corporate Reorganizations – Determination of Dividend Equivalency*, 30 Tax Lawyer 287, 303 (1977).

Our reading of the statute as requiring that the transaction be treated as a unified whole is reinforced by the well-established "step-transaction" doctrine, a doctrine that the Government has applied in related contexts, *see, e.g.*, Rev. Rul. 75-447. 1975-2 Cum. Bull 113, and that we have expressly sanctioned, see *Minnesota Tea Co. v. Helvering*, 302 U.S. 609, 613 (1938); *Commissioner v. Court Holding Co.*, 324 U.S. 331, 334 (1945). Under this doctrine, interrelated yet formally distinct steps in an integrated transaction may not be considered independently of the over all transaction. By thus "linking together all interdependent steps with legal or business significance, rather than taking them in isolation," federal tax liability may be based "on a realistic view of the entire transaction." 1 B. Bittker, Federal Taxation of Income, Estates and Gifts para. 43.5, p. 4-52 (1981).

Viewing the exchange in this case as an integrated whole, we are unable to accept the Commissioner's prereorganization analogy. The analogy severs the payment of boot from the context of the reorganization. Indeed, only by straining to abstract the payment of boot from the context of the overall exchange, and thus imagining that Basin made a distribution to the taxpayer independently of NL's planned acquisition, can we reach the rather counterintuitive conclusion urged by the Commissioner – that the taxpayer suffered no meaningful reduction in his ownership interest as a result of the cash payment. We conclude that such a limited view of

430

the transaction is plainly inconsistent with the statute's direction that we look to the effect of the entire exchange.

The prereorganization analogy is further flawed in that it adopts an overly expansive reading of § 356(a)(2). As the Court of Appeals recognized, adoption of the prereorganization approach would "result in ordinary income treatment in most reorganizations because corporate boot is usually distributed pro rata to the shareholders of the target corporation." 828 F.2d, at 227; see also Golub, *"Boot" in Reorganizations – The Dividend Equivalency Test of Section 356(a)(2)*, 58 Taxes 904, 911 (1980); Note, 20 Boston College L. Rev. 601, 612 (1979). Such a reading of the statute would not simply constitute a return to the widely criticized "automatic dividend rule" (at least as to cases involving a pro rata payment to the shareholders of the acquired corporation), see n.8, *supra,* but also would be contrary to our standard approach to construing such provisions. The requirement of § 356(a)(2) that boot be treated as dividend in some circumstances is an exception from the general rule authorizing capital gains treatment for boot. In construing provisions such as § 356, in which a general statement of policy is qualified by an exception, we usually read the exception narrowly in order to preserve the primary operation of the provision. See *Phillips, Inc. v. Walling,* 324 U.S. 490, 493 (1945) ("To extend an exemption to other than those plainly and unmistakably within its terms and spirit is to abuse the interpretative process and to frustrate the announced will of the people"). Given that Congress has enacted a general rule that treats boot as capital gain, we should not eviscerate that legislative judgment through an expansive reading of a somewhat ambiguous exception.

The post reorganization approach adopted by the Tax Court and the Court of Appeals is, in our view, preferable to the Commissioner's approach. Most significantly, this approach does a far better job of treating the payment of boot as a component of the overall exchange. Unlike the prereorganization view, this approach acknowledges that there would have been no cash payment absent the exchange and also that, by accepting the cash payment, the taxpayer experienced a meaningful reduction in his potential ownership interest.

Once the post reorganization approach is adopted, the result in this case is pellucidly clear. Section 302(a) of the Code provides that if a redemption fits within any one of the four categories set out in § 302(b), the redemption "shall be treated as a distribution in part or full payment in exchange for the stock," and thus not regarded as a dividend. As the Tax Court and the Court of Appeals correctly determined, the hypothetical post reorganization redemption by NL of a portion of the taxpayer's shares satisfies at least one of the subsections of § 302(b). In particular, the safe harbor provisions of subsection (b)(2) provide that redemptions in which the taxpayer relinquishes more than 20% of his or her share of the corporation's voting stock and retains less than 50% of the voting stock after the redemption shall not be treated as distributions of a dividend. See n.6, *supra.* Here, we treat the transaction as though NL redeemed 125,000 shares of its common stock (i.e., the number of shares of NL common stock forgone in favor of the boot) in return for a cash payment to the taxpayer of $3,250,000 (*i.e.,* the amount of the boot). As a result of this redemption, the taxpayer's interest in NL was reduced from 1.3% of the outstanding common stock to 0.9%. *See* 86 T.C., at 153. Thus, the taxpayer relinquished approximately 29% of his interest in NL and retained less than a 1% voting interest in the corporation after the transaction, easily satisfying the "substantially disproportionate" standards of § 302(b)(2). We accordingly conclude that the boot payment did not have the effect of a dividend and that the payment was properly treated as capital gain.

III

The Commissioner objects to this "recasting [of] the merger transaction into a form different from that entered into by the parties," Brief for Petitioner 11, and argues that the Court of Appeals' formal adherence to the principles embodied in § 302 forced the court to stretch to "find a redemption to which to apply them, since the merger transaction entered into by the parties did not involve a redemption," *id.,* at 28. There are a number of sufficient responses to this argument. We think it first worth emphasizing that the Commissioner overstates the extent to which the redemption is imagined. As the Court of Appeals for the Fifth Circuit noted in *Shimberg,* "[t]he theory behind tax-free corporate reorganizations is that the transaction is merely a 'continuance of the proprietary interests in the continuing enterprise under modified corporate form'. *Lewis v. Commissioner of Internal Revenue,* 176 F. 2d 646, 64 8 (CA 1 1949); Treas. Reg. § 1.368-1(b). *See generally* Cohen, *Conglomerate Mergers and Taxation,* 55 A.B.A. J. 40 (1969)." 577 F.2d, at 288. As a result, the boot-for-stock transaction can be viewed as a partial repurchase of stock by the continuing corporate enterprise – i.e., as a redemption. It is, of course, true that both the prereorganization and post reorganization analogies are somewhat artificial in that they imagine that the redemption occurred outside the confines of the actual reorganization. However, if forced to choose between the two analogies, the post reorganization view is the less artificial. Although both analogies "recast the merger transaction," the post reorganization view recognizes that a reorganization has taken place, while the prereorganization approach recasts the transaction to the exclusion of the overall exchange.

Moreover, we doubt that abandoning the prereorganization and post reorganization analogies and the principles of § 302 in favor of a less artificial understanding of the transaction would lead to a result different from that reached by the Court of Appeals. Although the statute is admittedly ambiguous and the legislative history sparse, we are persuaded – even without relying on § 302 – that Congress did not intend to except reorganizations such as that at issue here from the general rule allowing capital gains treatment for cash boot. 26 U. S. C. § 356(a)(1). The legislative history of § 356(a)(2), although perhaps generally "not illuminating," *Estate of Bedford,* 325 U.S., at 290, suggests that Congress was primarily concerned with preventing corporations from "siphon[ing] off" accumulated earnings and profits at a capital gains rate through the ruse of a reorganization. *See* Golub, 58 Taxes, at 905. This purpose is not served by denying capital gains treatment in a case such as this in which the taxpayer entered into an arm's-length transaction with a corporation in which he had no prior interest, exchanging his stock in the acquired corporation for less than a 1% interest in the acquiring corporation and a substantial cash boot.

Section 356(a)(2) finds its genesis in § 203(d)(2) of the Revenue Act of 1924. See 43 Stat. 257. Although modified slightly over the years, the provisions are in relevant substance identical. The accompanying House Report asserts that § 203(d)(2) was designed to "prevent evasion." H. R. Rep. No. 179, 68th Cong., 1st Sess., 15 (1924). Without further explication, both the House and Senate Reports simply rely on an example to explain, in the words of both Reports, "the necessity for this provision." *Ibid*; S. Rep. No. 398, 68th Cong., 1st Sess., 16 (1924). Significantly, the example describes a situation in which there was no change in the stockholders' relative ownership interests, but merely the creation of a wholly owned subsidiary as a mechanism for making a cash distribution to the shareholders:

> "Corporation A has capital stock of $100,000, and earnings and profits accumulated since March 1, 1913, of $50,000. If it distributes the $50,000 as a dividend to its stockholders, the amount distributed will be taxed at the full surtax rates.

> "On the other hand, Corporation A may organize Corporation B, to which it transfers all its assets, the consideration for the transfer being the issuance by B of all its stock and $50,000 in cash to the stockholders of Corporation A in exchange for their stock in Corporation A. Under the existing law, the $50,000 distributed with the stock of Corporation B would be taxed, not as a dividend, but as a capital gain, subject only to the 12 ½ per cent rate. The effect of such a distribution is obviously the same as if the corporation had declared out as a dividend its $50,000

earnings and profits. If dividends are to be subject to the full surtax rates, then such an amount so distributed should also be subject to the surtax rates and not to the 12 1/2 per cent rate on capital gain." *Ibid.*; H. R. Rep. No. 179, at 15.

The "effect" of the transaction in this example is to transfer accumulated earnings and profits to the shareholders without altering their respective ownership interests in the continuing enterprise.

Of course, this example should not be understood as exhaustive of the proper applications of § 356(a)(2). It is nonetheless noteworthy that neither the example, nor any other legislative source, evinces a congressional intent to tax boot accompanying a transaction that involves a bona fide exchange between unrelated parties in the context of a reorganization as though the payment was in fact a dividend. To the contrary, the purpose of avoiding tax evasion suggests that Congress did not intend to impose an ordinary income tax in such cases. Moreover, the legislative history of § 302 supports this reading of § 356(a)(2) as well. In explaining the "essentially equivalent to a dividend" language of § 302(b)(1) – language that is certainly similar to the "has the effect . . . of a dividend" language of § 356(a)(2) – the Senate Finance Committee made clear that the relevant inquiry is "whether or not the transaction by its nature may properly be characterized as a sale of stock . . . " S. Rep. No. 1622, 83d Cong., 2d Sess., 234 (1954); cf. *United States v. Davis,* 397 U.S., at 311.

Examining the instant transaction in light of the purpose of § 356(a)(2), the boot-for-stock exchange in this case "may properly be characterized as a sale of stock." Significantly, unlike traditional single corporation redemptions and unlike reorganizations involving commonly owned corporations, there is little risk that the reorganization at issue was used as a ruse to distribute a dividend. Rather, the transaction appears in all respects relevant to the narrow issue before us to have been comparable to an arm's-length sale by the taxpayer to NL. This conclusion, moreover, is supported by the findings of the Tax Court. The court found that "[t]here is not the slightest evidence that the cash payment was a concealed distribution from BASIN." 86 T.C., at 155. As the Tax Court further noted, Basin lacked the funds to make such a distribution:

"Indeed, it is hard to conceive that such a possibility could even have been considered, for a distribution of that amount was not only far in excess of the accumulated earnings and profits ($2,319,611), but also of the total assets of BASIN ($2,758,069). In fact, only if one takes into account unrealized appreciation in the value of BASIN's assets, including good will and/or going-concern value, can one possibly arrive at $3,250,000. Such a distribution could only be considered as the equivalent of a complete liquidation of BASIN . . . " *Ibid.*

In this context, even without relying on § 302 and the post-reorganization analogy, we conclude that the boot is better characterized as a part of the proceeds of a sale of stock than as a proxy for a dividend. As such, the payment qualifies for capital gains treatment.

The judgment of the Court of Appeals is accordingly

Affirmed.

[Justice White's dissent is omitted. Ed.]

NOTES

1. **Consider the choices**. The *Wright* decision evaluated the effect of a hypothetical redemption of stock of the acquiring corporation after the reorganization. *Shimberg*

considered whether a hypothetical redemption from the target corporation would have been taxed as a dividend if it had been made before the reorganization. The third possibility is to compare the taxpayer's level of ownership of the target company with her level of ownership of the acquiring company. The last theory is most likely to find a redemption treated as an exchange. The *Shimberg* theory is least likely to find a redemption treated as an exchange, and the *Wright* theory lies somewhere in between. Congress should have specified what § 356(a)(2) means instead of leaving the issue to the courts.

2. **Application.** Is the dividend-within-gain principle still relevant to individual shareholders? How about corporate shareholders?

REV. RUL. 93-62
1993-30 I.R.B. 10

In Revenue Ruling 93-62, the Service has concluded that gain recognized on the receipt of cash in an exchange of stock that otherwise qualifies under section 355 is not treated as a dividend distribution under section 356(a)(2).

Facts

Distributing is a corporation with 1,000 shares of a single class of stock outstanding. Each share has a fair market value of $1x. A, one of five unrelated individual shareholders, owns 400 shares of Distributing stock. Distributing owns all of the outstanding stock of a subsidiary corporation, Controlled. The Controlled stock has a fair market value of $200x.

Distributing distributes all the stock of Controlled plus $200x cash to A in exchange for all of A's Distributing stock. The exchange satisfies the requirements of section 355 but for the receipt of the cash.

Law and Analysis

Section 355(a)(1) of the Code provides, in general, that the shareholders of a distributing corporation will not recognize gain or loss on the exchange of the distributing corporation's stock or securities solely for stock or securities of a controlled subsidiary if the requirements of section 355 are satisfied.

Section 356(a)(1) of the Code provides for recognition of gain on exchanges in which gain would otherwise not be recognized under section 354 (relating to tax-free acquisitive reorganizations) or section 355 if the property received in the exchange consists of property permitted to be received without gain recognition and other property or money ("boot"). The amount of gain recognized is limited to the sum of the money and the fair market value of the other property.

Under section 356(a)(2) of the Code, gain recognized in an exchange described in section 356(a)(1) that "has the effect of the distribution of a dividend" is treated as a dividend to the extent of the distributee's ratable share of the undistributed earnings and profits accumulated after February 28, 1913. Any remaining gain is treated as gain from the exchange of property.

Determinations of whether the receipt of boot has the effect of a dividend are made by applying the principles of section 302 of the Code. *Commissioner v. Clark*, 489 U.S. 726 (1989), 1989-2 C.B. 68. Section 302 contains rules for determining whether payments in redemption of stock are treated as payments in exchange for the stock or as distributions to which section 301 applies.

Under section 302(a) of the Code, a redemption will be treated as an exchange if it satisfies one of the tests of section 302(b). Section 302(b)(2) provides exchange treatment for substantially disproportionate redemptions of stock. A distribution is substantially disproportionate if (1) the shareholder's voting stock interest and common stock interest in the corporation immediately after the redemption are each less than 80 percent of those interests immediately before the redemption, and (2) the shareholder owns less than 50 percent of the voting power of all classes of stock immediately after the redemption.

In *Clark*, the Supreme Court determined whether gain recognized under section 356 of the Code on the receipt of boot in an acquisitive reorganization under section 368(a)(1)(A) and (a)(2)(D) should be treated as a dividend distribution. In that case, the sole shareholder of the target corporation exchanged his target stock for stock of the acquiring corporation and cash. In applying section 302 to determine whether the boot payment had the effect of a dividend distribution, the Court considered whether section 302 should be applied to the boot payment as if it were made (i) by the target corporation in a prereorganization hypothetical redemption of a portion of the shareholder's target stock, or (ii) by the acquiring corporation in a post-reorganization hypothetical redemption of the acquiring corporation stock that the shareholder would have received in the reorganization exchange if there had been no boot distribution.

The Supreme Court stated that the treatment of boot under section 356(a)(2) of the Code should be determined "by examining the effect of the exchange as a whole," and concluded that treating the boot as received in a redemption of target stock would improperly isolate the boot payment from the overall reorganization by disregarding the effect of the subsequent merger. Consequently, the Court tested whether the boot payment had the effect of a dividend distribution by comparing the interest the taxpayer actually received in the acquiring corporation with the interest the taxpayer would have had if solely stock in the acquiring corporation had been received in the reorganization exchange.

Prior to the decision in *Clark*, the Service considered the facts and issue presented in this revenue ruling in Rev. Rul. 74-516, 1974-2 C.B. 121. The determination of whether the exchange of Distributing stock for Controlled stock and boot under section 355 of the Code had the effect of a dividend distribution under section 356(a)(2) was made by comparing A's interest in Distributing prior to the exchange with the interest A would have retained if A had not received Controlled stock and had only surrendered the Distributing stock equal in value to the boot. The Court's decision in *Clark* does not change the conclusion in Rev. Rul. 74-516, because, like *Clark*, the ruling determined whether the exchange in question had the effect of a dividend distribution based on an analysis of the overall transaction.

The exchange of A's Distributing stock for stock of Controlled qualifies for non-recognition treatment under section 355 of the Code in part because the overall effect of the exchange is an adjustment of A's continuing interest in Distributing in a modified corporate form. See section 1.355-2(c) of the Income Tax Regulations. The Controlled stock received by A represents a continuing interest in a portion of Distributing's assets that were formerly held by A as an indirect equity interest. The boot payment has reduced A's proportionate interest in the overall corporate enterprise that includes both Distributing and Controlled. Thus, the boot is treated as received in redemption of A's Distributing stock, and A's interest in Distributing immediately before the exchange is compared to the interest A would have retained if A had surrendered only the Distributing shares equal in value to the boot.

Under the facts presented here, before the exchange, A owned 400 of the 1,000 shares, or 40 percent, of the outstanding Distributing stock. If A had surrendered only the 200 shares for which A received boot, A would still hold 200 of the 800 shares, or 25 percent, of the Distributing stock outstanding after the exchange. This 25 percent stock interest would represent 62.5 percent of A's pre-exchange stock interest in Distributing. Therefore, the deemed redemption would be treated as an exchange because it qualifies as substantially disproportionate under section 302(b)(2) of the Code.

Holding

In an exchange of stock that otherwise qualifies under section 355 of the Code, whether the payment of boot is treated as a dividend distribution under section 356(a)(2) is determined prior to the exchange. This determination is made by treating the recipient shareholder as if the shareholder had retained the distributing corporation stock actually exchanged for controlled corporation stock and received the boot in exchange for distributing corporation stock equal in value to the boot.

NOTE

Boot always takes a fair market value basis and its holding period will begin on the date of the exchange. § 358(a)(2). The presence of boot does not affect the favorable tax treatment of qualifying stock and securities received in the transaction.

PROBLEM 21-9

X Corp.'s stock is owned equally by two shareholders, A and B. X Corp. has two lines of business, Hardware worth $1,300 and Pizza worth $700. X Corp. has ample earnings and profits and 2,000 shares, each worth $1.00. Due to management disagreements, A and B decide to split X Corp. into two corporations. In a valid split-off under §§ 368(a)(1)(D) and 355, X Corp. first forms Y Corp. and transfers to it the Pizza division, and then in exchange for all of A's stock in X Corp., it distributes all the Y Corp. stock to A. As part of the transaction, X Corp. also distributes $300 cash to A as an equalization payment. What is the tax result to A from receipt of the $300 boot?

PROBLEM 21-10

As part of a merger, Acquiso Corp. transfers 65 share certificates of Acquiso voting common stock worth $1 each, plus $15 of cash to Target, Inc. in exchange for all of Target's assets, having a basis of $50. Target, Inc. is also saddled with $20 of nonrecourse debt. Target, Inc. immediately distributes the 65 share certificates of Acquiso stock and the $15 in cash to its shareholders. Assume the transaction qualifies as a Type A reorganization and that Target, Inc. did not incur the liabilities for tax-avoidance reasons. Also, assume that the Target shareholders all have a basis of $0 in their stock.

1) Will Target, Inc. recognize any gain on the transaction? *See* § 361.

2) What basis will Acquiso, Inc. have in the Target, Inc.'s assets? *See* § 362.

3) Will Acquiso, Inc. face any tax consequences in taking assets subject to the $20 of Target, Inc. liabilities? *See* § 357.

4) Will Acquiso, Inc. recognize any gains or losses on the transaction?

5) What if, instead of cash, Acquiso, Inc. provided IBM bonds with a basis of $10 and a value of $15?

6) Do Target shareholders realize any gain on the reorganization?

436

7) What basis will the Target shareholders take in their newly acquired Acquiso stock? *See* § 358.

8) What basis will Target shareholders take in their boot, whatever its form?

L. CONTINGENT PAYOUTS

It is fairly common business practice to provide for further consideration if the target corporation is especially prosperous in the post-reorganization period. The IRS and the courts have accommodated these needs.

REV. PROC. 77-37
1977-2 C.B. 568

SECTION 1. PURPOSE

.01 The purpose of this Revenue Procedure is to update Rev. Proc. 74-26, 1974-2 C.B. 478, which sets forth certain operating rules of the Internal Revenue Service pertaining to issuing ruling letters and in determining whether it should decline to issue ruling letters.

* * *

OPERATING RULES FOR ISSUING RULING LETTERS

* * *

.03 In reorganizations under sections 368(a)(1)(A), 368(a)(1)(B), and 368(a)(1)(C) of the Code where the requisite stock or property has been acquired, it is not necessary that all of the stock of the acquiring corporation or a corporation in "control" thereof, which is to be issued in exchange therefore be issued immediately provided (1) that all of the stock will be issued within five years from the date of the transfer of assets in the case of reorganizations under sections 368(a)(1)(A) and 368(a)(1)(C), or within five years from the date of the initial distribution in the case of reorganization under section 368(a)(1)(B); (2) there is a valid business reason for not issuing all of the stock immediately, such as the difficulty in determining the value of one or both of the corporations involved in the reorganization; (3) the maximum number of shares which may be issued in the exchange is stated; (4) at least fifty percent of the maximum number of shares of each class of stock which may be issued is issued in the initial distribution; (5) the agreement evidencing the right to receive stock in the future prohibits assignment (except by operation of law) or, in the alternative, if the agreement does not prohibit assignments, the right must not be evidenced by negotiable certificates of any kind and must not be readily marketable; and (6) such right can give rise to the receipt of only additional stock of the acquiring corporation or a corporation in "control" thereof, as the case may be. Stock issued as compensation, royalties or any other consideration other than in exchange for stock or assets will not be considered to have been received in the exchange. Until the final distribution of the total number of shares of stock to be issued in the exchange is made, the interim basis of the stock of the acquiring corporation received in the exchange by the shareholders of the acquired corporation (not including that portion of each share representing interest) will be determined, pursuant to section 358(a), as though the maximum number of shares to be issued (not including that portion of each share representing interest) had been received by the shareholders.

* * *

.06 In reorganizations under sections 368(a)(1)(A), 368(a)(1)(B), and 368(a)(1)(C) of the Code where the requisite stock or property has been acquired, a portion of the stock of the acquiring corporation, or a corporation in "control" thereof, that is issued in the exchange may be placed in escrow by the exchanging shareholders, or may otherwise be made subject to a condition pursuant to the agreement or plan of reorganization, for possible return to the acquiring corporation under specified conditions provided (1) there is a valid business reason for establishing the arrangement; (2) the stock subject to such arrangement appears as issued and outstanding on the balance sheet of the acquiring corporation and such stock is, in fact, legally outstanding under applicable state law; (3) all dividends paid on such stock will be distributed currently to the exchanging shareholders; (4) all voting rights of such stock (if any) are exercisable by or on behalf of the shareholders or their authorized agent; (5) no shares of such stock are subject to restrictions requiring their return to the issuing corporation because of death, failure to continue employment or similar restrictions; (6) all such stock is released from the arrangement within 5 years from the date of consummation of the reorganization (except where there is a bona fide dispute as to whom the stock should be released to); and (7) at least 50 percent of the number of shares of each class of stock issued initially to the shareholders (exclusive of shares of stock to be issued at a later date as described in.03 above) is not subject to the arrangement.

Chapter 22

CARRYOVERS OF TAX ATTRIBUTES AND RESTRICTIONS ON CARRYOVERS
Read §§ 381(a), (b)(3), and (c)(2).

The basic theme of a tax-free asset acquisition, whether it be a § 368(a)(l) reorganization or a § 332 subsidiary liquidation, is that transactions that are a mere reshuffling of continuing businesses within corporate forms should not be impeded by taxes. Consistent with that approach, § 381(a) states the general rule that the acquiring corporation "shall succeed to and take into account" the tax attributes of the acquired corporation specified in § 381(c), including earnings and profits, accounting methods, capital loss carryovers, and net operating loss carryovers. Notice how this includes all the attributes even if the acquirer or transferee winds up with less then all of the target corporation's stock or assets.

Section 381 provides an extensive list of mechanical directions to make sure that the target corporation's (or liquidated subsidiary's) tax attributes shift to the acquiring corporation, just as the tax histories of the assets themselves are transferred by means of the carryover basis rules of § 362 and the holding period rules of § 1223. Both the earnings and profits account of the target and its net operating losses (NOLs) are carried over to the acquiror by operation of § 381(c).

The fact that NOLs carry over to the acquiror (together with built-in losses in assets) has caused friction between taxpayers and the government. Acquirors have been quick to see opportunities to shelter their own incomes by offsetting losses of the target against them. If it were not for the elaborate safeguards Congress has enacted, prosperous corporate taxpayers would acquire failed corporations (even corporate "shells") for no other reason than to enjoy this sheltering. This is called "trafficking" in NOLs.

Sheltering in the opposite direction is restricted as well, so that losses of the *acquiring* corporation are often ineligible for offset against target corporation's gains. After all, Gainco can merge into Lossco just as easily as the other way around. Some safeguards are built directly into § 381 itself, and a variety of other hurdles appear in §§ 269 and 382-384, which are the subject of this Chapter.

Section § 381 generally forbids offsets in both directions for gains and losses of either corporation that occurred before the acquisition. Section 381(c)(l) prevents the target's preexisting NOLs from offsetting profits of the acquiring corporation that accrued before the acquisition, and thus the target's NOLs can only be used to offset post-acquisition earnings of the acquiror. Similarly, § 381(b)(3) forbids an acquiring corporation to carry back its NOLs to offset the target's earnings from years prior to the acquisition (except in an F reorganization). This overrides the usual rules of § 172 that let a corporation carry losses back for two years to offset its prior gains and to obtain a refund of tax. There are similar barriers against using deficits in earnings and profits of either corporation to offset positive earnings and profits from pre-acquisition years. *See* § 381(c)(2).

PROBLEM 22-1

A Corp. acquires the assets of T Corp. in a type C reorganization on June 30. Both corporations are accrual method taxpayers operating on the calendar taxable year. At the time of the reorganization, T Corp. had an unused $100 NOL. A Corp. ended the current taxable year with a $50 profit. The operating division of A that used to be T Corp. also ended this year with a $50 profit. (For purposes of this problem, ignore potential limitations posed by § 382).

1)   Must T Corp. file a short year return? § 381(b)(1)?

2) Can A Corp. use any of T's NOL to offset any of A's profit incurred *prior* to its acquisition of T Corp.?

3) What amount of A Corp.'s profit will be deemed to have been earned *after* the time of its T Corp. acquisition?

4) What amount of T Corp.'s profit will be deemed to have been earned *prior* to the time of its acquisition by A Corp.?

5) Can A Corp. use any of T Corp.'s NOL to offset any A Corp. profit earned *after* the acquisition of T Corp.?

6) Can A Corp. use any of the NOL to offset the profit earned by T Corp. *prior* to its acquisition?

7) Can A Corp. use any of the NOL to offset the profit earned by the T division *after* its acquisition?

8) Will any portion of the NOL be carried forward to be used in future years?

9) If T Corp. acquired A Corp., could T Corp. carry back T Corp.'s NOLs to A Corp.'s pre-reorganization years?

A. SECTION 269: THE SUBJECTIVE APPROACH TO DENYING LOSSES
Read § 269.

Section 269 permits the IRS to disallow any deduction or other tax benefit that may flow from an acquisition of 50% or more control of a corporation (or of its assets in a tax-free transaction) if the "principal purpose for which such acquisition was made is evasion or avoidance of Federal income tax." The provision applies potentially to all A and C reorganizations, as well as to B reorganizations in which the acquiror had less than 50% control before the exchange. It also applies to taxable purchases of stock, but not to taxable purchases of assets. It has even been held that obtaining the benefit of the acquiror's own NOLs by acquiring a profitable business can violate § 269. *See Commissioner v. British Motor Car Distributors, Ltd.,* 278 F.2d 392 (9th Cir. 1960).

On its face, this rule may look like a blank check to the IRS, but in practice it is limited by the need to demonstrate the taxpayer's forbidden state of mind. There are nearly always multiple reasons for acquiring a corporation or its assets. Section 269 applies only if "the principal purpose" was to secure tax benefits not otherwise available. The following case presses the question of how bad one has to be to suffer a tax forfeiture under § 269.

CANAVERAL INTERNATIONAL CORP v. COMMISSIONER

61 T.C. 520 (1974), *acq.*, 1974-2 C.B. 1

[Canaveral International Corp., the publicly-traded parent of an affiliated group of corporations, negotiated to buy a yacht which could be converted to business use as a charter vessel. On learning that Norango, Inc. owned the yacht and that the yacht had an undepreciated basis of $769,632.75, Canaveral instead acquired all of Norango's stock in exchange for some of Canaveral's nonvoting preferred stock. Thereafter, Norango improved the yacht and unsuccessfully tried to charter it for commercial purposes until Norango finally sold it for $250,000. On its consolidated return, Canaveral reported depreciation deductions and an ordinary loss under § 1231 on the sale computed with reference to Norango's undepreciated basis.]

FEATHERSTON, JUDGE.

Respondent determined a deficiency in petitioner's Federal income tax and that of its affiliated companies for the taxable year ended September 30, 1966, in the amount of $159,431.48. By stipulation the parties have settled most of the issues outlined in the notice of deficiency, leaving for decision the following questions:

(1) Whether the principal purpose motivating petitioner's acquisition of the stock of Norango, Inc., was the evasion or avoidance of Federal income tax within the meaning of section 269. . . .

Opinion

1. The Applicability of Section 269 to the Acquisition of the Stock of Norango, Inc.

(a) Tax-avoidance purpose. – 269(a) provides, in pertinent part, that if any person acquires control of a corporation, and the "principal purpose" for which such acquisition is made is evasion or avoidance of Federal income tax by securing the benefit of a deduction, credit, or other allowance which such person or corporation would not otherwise enjoy, such deduction, credit, or other allowance shall not be allowed. More simply, the section "states in effect that, if A acquires B for the principal purpose of tax avoidance, then A cannot have the tax benefit which the ownership of B would otherwise entail." *Bobsee Corporation v. United States*, 411 F. 2d 231, 234 (C.A. 5, 1969).

For the section to be operative, the tax evasion or avoidance purpose must outrank, or exceed in importance, any other one purpose. S. Rept. No. 627, 78th Cong., 1st Sess. (1943), 1944 C.B. 1017. The determination of the purpose of an acquisition requires a scrutiny of the entire circumstances in which the transaction or course of conduct occurred, including the relationship of the transaction to the claimed consequent tax result. Sec. 1.269-3(a), Income Tax Regs. The burden of proof rests with petitioner. "Theoretically the question of purpose is purely subjective; pragmatically, however, the trier of fact can only determine purpose from objective facts.*" Bobsee Corporation v. United States, supra* at 238.

The enactment in 1943 of the predecessor of section 269(a) was prompted by a desire to curb a growing market for defunct corporate shells with a history of large amounts of invested capital coupled with subsequent net operating losses. Such characteristics were effective income and excess profits tax shields for booming war enterprises. H. Rept. No. 871, 78th Cong., 1st Sess. (1943), 1944 C.B. 938; S. Rept. No. 627, 78th Cong., 1st Sess. (1943), 1944 C.B. 1016. But the section was intended to be broader in concept than a measure merely to prevent the trafficking in loss corporations. Its grander design, as expressed by Congress, was –

441

"to codify and emphasize the general principle set forth in *Higgins v. Smith,* (308 U.S. 473 . . .), and in other judicial decisions, as to the ineffectiveness of arrangements distorting or perverting deductions, credits, or allowances so that they no longer bear a reasonable business relationship to the interests or enterprises which produced them and for the benefit of which they were provided." S. Rept. No. 627, 1944 C.B. at 1016.

We think the evidence in the instant case, weighed in the light of the foregoing principles, requires a holding that petitioner's principal purpose in acquiring Norango's stock was to receive the tax benefits of the vessel's sizable basis which otherwise would not have been enjoyed by petitioner and its affiliated group. Legitimate business reasons may have motivated petitioner to seek a vessel suitable for oceanographic and geodetic charter purposes. However, once petitioner's representatives became aware of Norango's corporate existence, viewed Norango's books, and discovered the yacht's undepreciated $769,632.75 cost basis, we think the overriding reason for acquiring Norango's stock was to, reduce petitioner's consolidated income tax liability, present and prospective. *See* Industrial Suppliers, Inc., 50 T.C. 635, 646 (1968); *Temple Square Mfg. Co.,* 36 T.C. 88, 94 (1961).

The evidence is unmistakably clear that petitioner's representatives, not the Woolworth estate, were responsible for casting the transaction in the form of an acquisition of Norango's stock. The evidence shows that Woolworth had advertised a yacht for sale, not a corporation owning a yacht, and that petitioner had decided to acquire a vessel for use in an oceanographic and geodetic charter business, not a corporation engaged in such business. There is some dispute as to whether Woolworth, prior to his death, had agreed to a stock-for-stock exchange. But the evidence is clear that after examining Norango's books, petitioner's representatives, including a New York attorney-accountant versed in tax matters, proposed to Malcolm, the representative of the Woolworth estate, that the transaction be cast in the form of an exchange of some of petitioner's stock for Norango's stock and the notes payable to Woolworth.[1]

Petitioner's representatives made this proposal notwithstanding the risk of undisclosed liabilities ordinarily attendant upon the acquisition of the stock of a small corporation. Also, the notes payable in the amount of $961,484.89, recorded on Norango's books, ordinarily would have dictated that only the corporation's assets be acquired. However, by purchasing Norango's notes payable and stock and contributing the notes to the capital of the corporation, petitioner tailored the transaction to make the purchase of Norango's stock economically feasible. It would have been simpler to have acquired the yacht directly, and petitioner has given no worthwhile explanation as to why the more roundabout route was taken. The most reasonable inference is that petitioner's representatives wanted the transaction cast in this form for tax-avoidance reasons.

---

[1] Malcolm, representative of the Woolworth estate, testified that petitioner's representatives proposed that the transaction take the form of a sale of stock:

Q. Did you bring up the possibility of selling the stock of Norango, Inc.?
A. I didn't bring it up.
Q. Did you suggest that?
A. I didn't bring it up. They asked me for it.

Though Henry Dubbin's testimony on the issue is evasive, he testified at one point:

"[Mr. Field, the New York attorney-accountant who assisted in the negotiations] may have been called in on tax matters. I don't really recall him being called in specifically on tax matters. I recall him being – discussing them with our comptroller and our auditing division."

The potential tax benefits from the stock acquisition were so disproportionate in relation to the consideration paid for the stock as to cause a major distortion in petitioner's income. For the Norango stock, petitioner traded 949 shares of its non-dividend-bearing, non-voting preferred stock which were convertible to 20,878 shares of petitioner's common shares. The conversion could not take place until sometime between December 31, 1966, and February 1, 1967. On the day of the closing of the sale, petitioner's common stock was selling at a high of 11 ¼ and a low of 10 ¾. Due to the restrictions on the preferred stock's convertibility, the non-dividend-bearing character of the preferred stock, and the uncertainty of the number of shares of preferred stock allocable to the notes acquired in the transaction, we have found that the value of the yacht and of the shares of stock petitioner exchanged for the Norango stock was $177,500.[2]

For this outlay of property worth $177.500, petitioner's consolidated group obtained potential tax deductions in the form of depreciation over the life of the vessel or a loss on a subsequent sale, computed by use of an adjusted basis of $769,632.75 (the cost of the yacht and furniture and fixtures as carried over from the books of Norango). At the prevailing corporate tax rates, the tax windfall from Norango's high basis in the yacht so far exceeded petitioner's investment in Norango's stock that the consolidated group could have realized a net profit even if the newly acquired yacht had sunk on its first voyage. This is the kind of subversion of the basis-loss provisions to distort income that section 269 was enacted to prevent. Sec. 1.269-2(b), Income Tax Regs.; *Scroll, Inc. v. Commissioner,* 447 F. 2d 612, 618-619 and fn. 15 (C.A. 5, 1971).

Petitioner hammers away on the point that it intended to, and did, use the vessel for business purposes. However, the fact that petitioner would have acquired the yacht in the absence of a tax-avoidance motive is not determinative. Sec. 1.269-3(a), Income Tax Regs. *See F. C. Publication Liquidating Corporation v. Commissioner,* 304 F 2d 779, 780-781 (C.A. 2, 1962), affirming 36 T.C. 836 (1961); *Industrial Suppliers, Inc.,* 50 T.C.at 646. Section 269 is directed to the principal purpose for the acquisition of control of a corporation, not the absence of a business purpose in acquiring a corporation's assets. That petitioner planned to use the yacht for business reasons does not alone explain the principal purpose underlying its acquisition of the stock.

In *Industrial Suppliers, Inc., supra,* Caldwell and associates acquired for $20,000 the stock of a corporation which had a merchandise inventory with a book value of $165,475 and which had a long history of net operating losses. The purchasers thereupon used the corporation in carrying out a highly profitable joint venture. Rejecting a contention that section 269 was not applicable because the purchaser's principal purpose was to acquire the corporation's inventory, this Court said (50 T.C.at 646):

> We have no doubt that Caldwell was interested in acquiring petitioner's inventory at what he considered to be a bargain price and, on first impression, this would appear to be a valid, business purpose for the acquisition of petitioner's stock. We are not convinced, however, that the tax benefits to be derived from the carryover of previous net operating losses was not the principal purpose for acquiring the inventory through the purchase of petitioner's stock rather than by a simple purchase of the inventory itself. The purchase of the stock and the various manipulations which

---

[2] We have found the value of the yacht at the time of petitioner's acquisition of the Worango [sic] stock in August 1962 was $177,500, the value of the stock given in the exchange. We recognize that petitioner sold the yacht in December 1963 for $250,000. However, this sale followed extensive renovations and refurbishment and a demonstration of the feasibility of the use of the vessel – described by one of the witnesses as a "white elephant" – for commercial purposes.

this involved, as well as the subsequent utilization of petitioner in the * * * (joint) venture, thereby creating additional profits against which the loss carryovers could be applied, belies Caldwell's testimony that the tax benefits were not a consideration for the purchase of the stock.

Similarly, in *Bobsee Corporation v. United States, 411 F.2d at 239,* the court dismissed an argument that section 269 did not apply because each of seven corporations was created for a business purpose, stating: 'To establish a principal non-tax motive * * * (the owner of the taxpayer) had to justify the creation of seven corporations; however, the reason she gave would only justify the formation of a single corporation.' By analogy, that petitioner wanted to acquire a vessel for business purposes does not show that its principal reason for acquiring the stock of Norango was not tax avoidance.

Petitioner argues that the claimed loss on the sale of the yacht occurred after the Norango stock was acquired and that there in substantial disagreement among the Courts of Appeals as to whether section 269 is applicable at all to postacquisition losses. The disagreement petitioner refers to is whether section 269 applies to losses which accrue economically after affiliation. . . . The economic loss in the instant case, *i.e.,* the difference between the basis of the yacht carried on Norango's books and the value of the consideration exchanged by petitioner for Norango's stock, had already accrued at the time of Norango's affiliation, and the Courts of Appeals all agree that section 269 may be used to disallow such 'built-in' losses.

In holding against petitioner, we do not suggest that section 269 requires a taxpayer to acquire a corporation's assets rather than its stock merely because a stock acquisition produces more favorable tax results. In given cases, the courts have recognized that acquiring the stock of a corporation may be the only, or the most feasible, way of handling the transaction. *Hawaiian Trust Co., Ltd. v. United States*, 291 F.2d 761 (C.A. 9, 1961). See e.g., *Glen Raven Mills, Inc.,* 59 T.C. 1, 15 (1972); *Clarksdale Rubber Co.,* 45 T.C. 234, 240-241 (1965); *Baton Rouge Supply Co.,* 36 T.C. 1, 13 (1961). But when section 269 is placed in issue, it does require a showing that the most favorable tax route, when that route involves the acquisition of a corporation, was principally motivated by non-tax related business reasons. Petitioner has shown no substantial business reasons for acquiring Norango's stock rather than the yacht. The evidence is persuasive that the transaction was so cast in an effort to obtain the tax benefits of the yacht's high basis which petitioner otherwise would not have enjoyed.

In cases where the purchase price paid for the stock of a corporation is substantially less than the aggregate basis of the corporation's assets, the burden of proof imposed on the taxpayer can be difficult to sustain. . . . In the instant case, petitioner exchanged preferred stock worth $177,500 for stock in a corporation with assets having a $769,632.75 basis. Through such use of Norango's basis, unrelated to petitioner's cost, petitioner sought, among other things, to reduce its consolidated tax liability by taking excessive depreciation deductions and by converting an economic gain on the sale of the yacht into a deductible tax loss. The practical effect of the transaction, if section 269 does not apply, was to enable petitioner's consolidated group to offset current business earnings from other sources against a preacquisition economic loss suffered by Norango while the yacht was used for nonbusiness purposes. . . . Such a distortion of petitioner's tax liability is by itself prima facie evidence of the principal purpose of tax evasion or avoidance, and petitioner has failed to produce convincing evidence proving otherwise.

(b) *Determination of basis.*- Having concluded that petitioner acquired Norango's stock for tax-avoidance purposes within the meaning of section 269 we must now decide the tax consequences of that conclusion. In its consolidated income tax returns for its taxable years ended September 30 of 1962, 1963, and 1964, petitioner claimed depreciation deductions on the yacht, and in the 1964 return claimed a loss on the vessel's sale. Both the depreciation and the loss deductions were computed by using the $769,632.75 basis of the yacht, as shown on

444

Norango's books, with some minor adjustments. In the notice of deficiency, respondent reduced the depreciation deductions and determined that petitioner realized a gain of $74,855.71 rather than a loss of $511,726 on the sale of the vessel. In making these computations, respondent used a basis of $177,500, with adjustments, for the vessel.

Section 269(a) disallows, in the described circumstances, the full amounts of a 'deduction, credit, or other allowance (which the taxpayer) would not otherwise enjoy.' Section 269(b) however, permits the Secretary or his delegate, in any case to which section 269 (a) applies, to allow any part of the deduction, credit, or allowance and to disallow the remainder, if he determines that such allowance will not result in the proscribed evasion or avoidance of Federal income taxes. That is what was done in the instant case. Respondent used the cost to petitioner of the Norango stock ($177,500) as the cost basis of the yacht and then, in computing depreciation and gain or loss, made appropriate adjustments to basis for the cost of improvements and for allowable depreciation. In making this determination, respondent treated petitioner's acquisition of the stock as if petitioner had directly acquired the yacht, consistent with the following explanation of the predecessor of section 269(b) in S. Rept. No. 627, 78th Cong., 1st Sess. (1943), 1944 C.B. 1018:

> Subsection (a) provides for the disallowance in its entirety of the deduction, credit, or allowance which was the objective of the tax avoidance and evasion devices, but in order that the disallowance may be consistent with the purpose and appropriate scope of the section, subsection (b) authorizes the allowance of such part of the deduction, credit, or allowance as will not result in the avoidance or evasion of taxes sought by the acquisition. A proper result can be simply reached under paragraph (1) of subsection (b) in the more widely advertised schemes by reflecting in the deductions, credits, and allowances the purchase in substance by the acquiring interests of the assets which it was the design of the scheme so artfully to conceal.

Accordingly, respondent looked through the corporation Norango and determined petitioner's cost basis for the yacht to be reflected by the value of the stock which petitioner exchanged to acquire control of Norango. This procedure gives petitioner a tax benefit equal to the full amount of its investment but denies it any tax benefits it would not have enjoyed had it acquired the yacht directly. This treatment of the transaction accords with subsections (a) and (b) of section 269. Respondent's determinations in this respect, therefore, ARE SUSTAINED.

QUESTION

Whom does § 269 scare? Is it possible that § 269 does as much harm as good by scaring off well-intentioned taxpayers? Do we really need such *in terrorem* rules?

B. SECTION 382: THE OBJECTIVE APPROACH TO LOSSES
Read § 382(a), (b)(1)-(2), (c).

1. INTRODUCTION

The purpose of § 382 is to discourage "trafficking" in loss corporations. It is designed to limit the extent to which net operating loss carryovers (NOLs) may be enjoyed after a change of ownership of a "loss corporation." The fundamental idea is quite simple: if more than 50% of the stock of any corporation changes hands within a three-year period, the corporation's NOLs survive but they are restricted so as to offset future income only at an annual rate of interest, namely the federal "long-term tax exempt rate." § 382(f). In addition, the target business enterprise must continue for at least two years; otherwise, the NOLs are forfeited. §382(c).

Congress' intent was to let the loss corporation use its losses at the same rate that it theoretically could have generated income if, rather than being taken over, it instead sold all its assets and invested the proceeds in long-term tax-exempt debt. This ownership-based approach is in some respects a radical departure from pre-1986 law, which was chiefly concerned with preventing losses from one business from offsetting profits from another.

To illustrate: If A Corporation is profitable and it acquires unrelated T Corporation (which has large NOLs) in a tax-free reorganization, § 382 will limit the extent to which A Corporation can use T Corp.'s pre-acquisition NOL's. The more A paid for T and the higher the hypothetical earnings rate on T's assets, the more rapidly T's NOL's become available.

Even a simple change of ownership of a single loss corporation will trigger the § 382 limitation. So if A and B, the original shareholders of T Corporation, sell their shares to C and D, this change of ownership of T will limit the extent to which T can carry forward and use its NOLs from pre-change of ownership years to post-change years compared to what T could have done if it had not changed hands. If the new owners turn the loss corporation around with new management and/or infusion of fresh capital, § 382 applies despite the fact that the NOLs would offset income derived solely from the same business that produced the losses. In such a case, the NOLs would merely perform their intended income-averaging function.

It is difficult to see any policy reason for subjecting the energetic new owners to worse tax treatment than T's original owners. In fact, a loss corporation that has been successfully turned around under new ownership may have greater value if it is resold because, if § 382 is deliberately triggered a second time, the increased sales price will free up the remaining NOLs at a faster rate.

a.   Ownership Change
   § 382(g)

The annual "section 382 limitation" of § 382(b) is triggered by an "ownership change" as defined under § 382(g)(1). There are two ways in which an ownership change may occur. The first is through an "owner shift" involving one or more 5% shareholders. § 382(g)(2). The second is through an "equity structure shift." § 382(g)(3).

b.   Owner Shift Involving 5% Shareholders
   § 382(g)(2)

There is an *owner shift involving a 5% shareholder* if there is any change in the ownership of the stock of the corporation that affects the percentage of stock owned by any person who is a 5% shareholder before or after the change. § 382(g)(2). There is a fatal *ownership change* if, just after any owner shift involving a 5% shareholder, the percentage of the stock of the loss corporation owned by one or more 5% shareholders has increased by more than 50 percentage points over the lowest percentage of stock of the loss corporation (or any predecessor corporation) owned by such shareholders at any time during the testing period. § 382(g)(1). The testing period is the three-year period ending on the day of any owner shift involving a 5% shareholder or equity structure shift (discussed below). § 382(i)(1).

This basically forces one to identify every stock-related transaction for increases in ownership by major shareholders, and then to see if – looking back three years from each such transaction – there has been more than a 50 percentage point rise in ownership by all such

446

shareholders. This requires looking at subtle transactions, such as stock redemptions, as well as the obvious ones.

To illustrate: A owns 100% of the stock of L Corp. On January 1, year one, A sells 51% of L Corp. to B. Two "owner shifts" occur on that date because both A and B are 5% shareholders immediately after the sale and both have altered their holdings. B's owner shift causes an "ownership change" triggering the § 382 limitation because B's ownership of L Corp. has increased by more than fifty percentage points (from zero to 51%) within the three-year period ending immediately after the sale.

The shareholder's stock ownership percentage is determined by the value of the stock owned by the shareholder, not the number of shares. § 382(k)(6)(C). Nonvoting nonconvertible preferred shares are not treated as "stock," but warrants, options, and convertible debt are generally treated as "stock." § 382(k)(6)(A)-(B). A strikingly one-sided rule provides that such rights to acquire stock are treated as "stock" only if it will result in an ownership change – *i.e.*, only when it benefits the government. § 382(l)(3)(A)(iv).

For the purpose of testing whether an ownership change has occurred, all less-than-5% shareholders are treated as a single 5% shareholder. § 382(g)(4)(A). The result is that changes in ownership of less-than-5% shareholders are not normally counted except where such shareholders are acting in concert. This rule avoids the problem of keeping track of all purchases and sales of publicly traded stock, and prevents accidental triggering of an ownership change if 50% of the stock changes hands over a three-year period through countless anonymous sales on a public exchange. If all the public shareholders are less-than-5% shareholders, no matter how many sales take place, the public shareholders count as a single 5% shareholder and their aggregate ownership remains unchanged.

To illustrate: 1,000 shareholders own 49% of the stock of T. None of them own as much as 5% of T stock. P owns 51% of the stock of T. The public group that includes the public shareholders of T is treated as a 5% shareholder that owns 49% of T. Reg. § 1.382-2T(j)(1)(vi) Example (2). Alternatively, the 1,000 shareholders own all the stock of P. None of the 1,000 shareholders owns as much as 5% of P stock. P owns all the stock of T. Next year. P distributes all of the T stock pro rata to its shareholders. The 1,000 shareholders are now members of a public group that is treated as a 5% shareholder that owns 100% of the stock of T. *Id.*

Stock owned by any members of the same family (as defined by § 318(a)(1)) is also treated as owned by a single individual, which means that sales and other transfers within a family are ignored, as are gifts, bequests, and transfers of stock between spouses or incident to divorce. § 382(l)(3)(A)-(B).

To illustrate: A has owned all 100 shares of T Corp. for four years. In the only sale in the pertinent period, A sells 45 shares to B, who is unrelated to A, on July 1, year five. Both A and B are 5% shareholders whose ownership has changed on July 1, year five, and that date becomes the testing date to determine whether (scanning back over the 3-year period) an ownership change has occurred. The sale does not result in an ownership change because B, the only other shareholder, did not increase his percentage of stock in the loss corporation by more than 50 percentage points over his lowest percentage of ownership during the three-year testing period B has increased his ownership only 45 percentage points (from zero to 45% of the value of all shares).

Note that subsequent stock transactions may become more risky as a result. For example, if on January 1, year six, A sells 30 shares to C, then January 1, year six becomes a new testing date, and the testing period is again three years because the previous transaction on July

1, year five did not result in an ownership change. The sale to C does result in an ownership change, because both B and C are 5% shareholders and their combined ownership in T Corp. increased from zero to 75% during the three-year testing period. The use of T Corp.'s NOLs is subject to the annual limitation of § 382. (The Code refers to T after the ownership change as the "New Loss Corporation").

In contrast, if A is related to B or C, no ownership change occurs, and the same would be true if any of the transfers were by gift, bequest, or pursuant to divorce.

c. Equity Structure Shift

An ownership change also occurs if there is an "equity structure shift" resulting in an increase of more than 50% ownership within the testing period. An equity structure shift is a tax-free reorganization under § 368 (except for divisive § 368(a)(1)(D) or (G) reorganizations and F reorganizations involving a mere change in form). § 382(g)(3)(A). Equity structure shifts also include taxable reorganizations, public offerings and similar transactions. § 382(g)(3)(B). Any combination of equity structure shift(s) and/or owner shifts within the testing period will trigger an ownership change if the total new ownership increases by more than 50%.

When an equity structure shift occurs, the less-than-5% shareholders of each corporation that was a party to the reorganization are kept apart and each is treated as a separate less-than-5% shareholder. § 382(g)(4)(B)(1). Whether an ownership change has occurred is measured by comparing the ownership of the loss corporation (whether it is the target or the acquirer) before and after the reorganization. The surviving corporation possessing the NOLs is a "new loss corporation." § 382(k)(3).

To illustrate: If Loss Corp., which has 1,000 small shareholders, merges into Gain Corp. and the former shareholders of Loss Corp. receive 25% of Gain Corp. stock, an ownership change occurs that subjects Gain Corp. (the "new loss corporation") to the § 382 limitation. The Gain Corp. shareholder group, considered as a single less-than-5% shareholder, has increased its ownership in Loss Corp. from zero to 75%. If the acquisition of Loss Corp. were effected through an exchange of 25% of Gain Corp. stock for all the stock of Loss Corp. in a "B" reorganization, the outcome under § 382 would be the same.

Absent the rule of § 382(g)(4)(B), which separates the less than 5% shareholders of each corporation into two different groups, most reorganizations would escape the grasp of § 382. In the above illustration, if no shareholder of either corporation is a 5% shareholder, and the less-than-5% shareholders of both Loss Corp. and Gain Corp. were treated as a single less-than-5% shareholder, that less than-5% shareholder's holdings would be unchanged by the merger.

d. Constructive Ownership

Stock held by partnership, estate, trust, or corporation is considered to be held by the partners. beneficiaries, or shareholders, respectively, in proportion to their interest in the entity, ignoring the 50% corporate ownership threshold in § 318. § 382(l)(3)(A)(ii). In effect, these constructive ownership rules look through entities to treat all stock as owned by individuals. Only ultimate ownership by individuals matters. This may require looking through a maze of entities to determine the ultimate individual ownership of all shares of stock.

One purpose of these look-through rules is to prevent easy avoidance of § 382 by interposing an entity as owner of a loss corporation's stock. Consider a variation of the above illustration of the acquisition of Loss Corp. by means of a "B" reorganization. If the Loss Corp. stock is held by Holding Co. and Holding Co. stock is exchanged for 25% of Gain Corp. stock,

448

Loss Corp. is 100% owned by Holding Co. before and after the exchange. The look-through rules appropriately treat the Gain Corp. shareholders as proportionate owners of Loss Corp. stock, however, and because their indirect ownership has increased from zero to 75%, § 382 applies.

The look-through rules can also prevent § 382 from applying where it otherwise might. If loss corporation stock is transferred to another corporation that has the same owner, common ownership will prevent § 382 from applying.

2. LIMITS ON THE USE OF NOL AFTER AN OWNERSHIP CHANGE

a. Business Continuity Requirement

The new loss corporation must continue the business enterprise of the old loss corporation at all times for the two-year period after the ownership change. § 382(c). The "continuity of business enterprise" requirement is satisfied if the new loss corporation continues the old loss corporation's historic business or if it uses a significant portion of the old loss corporation's assets in some other line of business. If this requirement is not met, the loss corporation's NOLs are completely eliminated and the § 382 annual limitation for any post-change year is zero. There is a special rule under which certain recognized built-in gains (discussed below) may still be offset against the NOLs despite lack of business continuity. § 382(c)(2).

b. Annual Income Limitation

If an ownership change occurs, the "Section 382 limitation" then applies so that the new loss corporation can deduct "pre-change losses" for a "post-change year" only to the extent of the "section 382 limitation" for that post-change year. The limitation is based on a formula: the value of the old loss corporation multiplied by the "long-term tax-exempt rate." § 382(b)(1) and (f). The value of the old loss corporation is the fair market value of its stock immediately before the ownership change, including the value of any nonparticipating, nonvoting preferred stock which was omitted in determining whether a change of ownership occurred. §§ 382(e)(1) and 1504(a)(4).

To illustrate: Loss Corp. has $1,000,000 of NOLs at the change date when all its stock is sold to new owners. The stock is sold for $200,000 which is its fair market value. The applicable long-term tax-exempt interest rate is 10%. The § 382 annual limitation on income the NOL can offset is thus $200,000 times 10%, or $20,000 per year. Loss Corp. will be permitted to use its NOLs to offset post-change income at a maximum rate of $20,000 per year.

Question: Does it strike you that the right rate is the higher taxable AFR?

Multiplying $20,000 per year of the $1 million of NOLs takes 50 years to recapture and is in effect largely disallowed.

If Loss Corp. does not have sufficient income in a post-change year to use the entire $20,000 allowable deduction, the remainder may be carried over and increases the following year's § 382 annual limitation. Using the above example, if Loss Co. has only $10,000 of income and cannot use the full $20,000 allowable deduction, the $10,000 unused amount is added to the following year's limitation, which is thereby increased to $30,000. § 382(b)(2).

If the ownership change occurs in mid-year, the § 382 limitation applies only to income of the post-change portion of the taxable year, calculated on a ratable daily basis. As a result, income that is allocable to the pre-change portion of the year may be offset by the pre-change

NOLs without limitation. § 382(b)(3)(A). Post-change income may be offset only by a prorated amount of the § 382 annual limitation that is proportional to the number of days remaining after the change. § 382(b)(3)(B). Thus if the change occurs precisely at mid-year, precisely half of the $20,000 limitation, or $10,000, will become the allowable § 382 limitation for the post-change period of the year. Finally, it should be remembered that the § 382 limitation applies only to NOLs in existence on the change date. Losses incurred subsequent to a change of ownership are unimpeded by § 382.

To illustrate: Continuing the previous example, suppose Loss Corp.'s change date is April 1, year one and that at the end of year one, Loss Corp. has a $40,000 operating loss for the year. This $40,000 is separated into the pre-change and post-change short years on a pro rata daily basis. Because the change date occurs after 1/4 of the year, 1/4 of the $40,000 loss, or $10,000, would be added to the pre-change NOL resulting in a carryforward of $1,010,000, which is subject to the § 382 annual limitation of $20,000. The remaining $30,000 of the year one loss allocable to the last 3/4 of year one is attributed to the post-change tax year and is not subject to the § 382 annual limitation. The unused portion of the § 382 annual limitation for year one is $15,000 (3/4 times the $20,000 § 382 annual limitation).

If, instead, Loss Corp. had $400,000 of taxable income for year one, 1/4 of the income ($100,000) allocable to the pre-change portion of the year would be fully offset by the pre-change NOLs without limitation. This reduces the NOLs from $1 million to $900,000 as of the change date. The remaining 3/4 of Loss Corp.'s year one income ($300,000) is subject to the § 382 annual limitation, which is 3/4 of $20,000, or $15,000. Thus only $15,000 of the post-change NOLs may be used to offset the $300,000 post-change income for year one.

c. Anti-Stuffing Rules

Because the § 382 limitation is dependent upon the value of the loss corporation at the change date, taxpayers might be tempted to increase its value in order to increase the limitation. Again using the example of Loss Corp., if the original owners were to contribute $800,000 worth of Treasury bonds to its capital before selling Loss Corp.'s stock, the stock would be worth $1 million, and the § 382 annual limitation would become $100,000 (10% times $1 million) rather than $20,000. This ploy is forestalled by an "anti-stuffing" rule.

The "anti-stuffing" rule of § 382(l)(1) requires the value of any capital contributions to be disregarded if made pursuant to a plan to increase the § 382 annual limitation. Section 382 presumes such a forbidden plan if the contributions are made within two years before the change date. § 382(l)(1)(B). Another anti-stuffing rule requires reduction of the value of the loss corporation if at least one-third of the value of its assets consist of nonbusiness (investment) assets, regardless of when or why the assets were acquired. § 382(l)(4)(B)(i). The loss corporation's value must then be reduced by the value of its nonbusiness assets, less an allocable portion of loss corporation's indebtedness. § 382(l)(4)(A). Under either or both of the anti-stuffing rules, the contribution of $800,000 worth of Treasury bonds to Loss Corp. would not increase the § 382 annual limitation.

d. Built-in Gains and Losses

Section 382(h) provides that if a loss corporation has "net unrealized built-in gain" on the change date, the § 382 limitation amount is increased by any "recognized built-in gain" during the five-year "recognition period" following the change date. In effect, the loss corporation is given credit for major unrealized gains that accrued before the change date, and if such gains are later recognized through a taxable sale or other disposition, they may be fully offset by pre-change NOLs despite the § 382 annual limitation. § 382(h)(1)(A). When a pre-change appreciated asset is sold during the recognition period, only the pre-change built-in gain qualifies for offset by increasing the § 382 limitation. § 382(h)(2)(A). Thus any taxable profit due to further post-change appreciation does not increase the § 382 limitation.

Conversely, "net unrealized built-in losses" recognized during the five-years post-change period are treated in the same way as pre-change NOLs, and their deductibility is subject to the § 382 limitation. § 382(h)(l)(B). This rule reflects Congress' concern that a corporation with unrealized losses in its assets might be an attractive acquisition for tax purposes for the same reason as a corporation with NOLs, i.e., an acquiring corporation could offset its own gains against the built-in losses by causing them to be recognized after the acquisition.

However, there is a "threshold requirement" before either of the gain or loss rules can apply. The "net unrealized built-in gain" (or loss) must exceed the *lesser* of: (1) 15% of the fair market value of the loss corporation's assets immediately prior to the ownership change, or (2) $10 million. § 382(h)(3)(B). "Net unrealized built-in gain" (or loss) means the amount by which the fair market value of all the assets is more (or less, respectively) than their aggregate basis immediately before the change date. § 382(h)(3)(A)(i). If the threshold is not met, the net unrealized gain (or loss) is treated as zero. § 382(h)(3)(B). The effect of applying this de minimis rule is that recognized built-in gains do not increase the § 382 limitation, and built-losses are disconnected from § 382 considerations.

To illustrate: Again using the Loss Corp. example, suppose that the pre-change aggregate value of its assets is $200,000 and the aggregate basis is $250,000. There is a net aggregate built-in loss of $50,000 that exceeds the threshold requirement of $30,000 (viz., 15% of value of Loss Corp.'s $200,000 worth of assets). The threshold is met. If Loss Corp. sells asset A within the five-year recognition period and recognizes a $20,000 loss, and asset A as of the change date had a value of $50,000 and basis of $70,000, the loss deduction is subject in its entirety to the § 382 annual limitation. This would use up Loss Corp.'s entire $20,000 annual limitation. If the change date value of asset A had been $60,000 instead, only $10,000 of the loss (the amount of loss built in at the change date) would reduce the annual limitation, and the remaining $10,000 of loss would be freely deductible.

PROBLEM 22-2

A and T are corporations owned by unrelated people. Nine months ago, A bought 49% of T stock. T was experiencing difficulties, and had built up a $500 unused NOL from prior years. T is worth $5,000 (the aggregate value of all classes of its outstanding stock). According to a plan intended to boost T's profits, A now purchases another 3% of T stock.

1) Has an ownership change occurred that will prompt the invocation of the § 382 limitation? *See* § 382(g)(2).

2) Would your answer to "(1)" change if A had purchased the additional T stock in a series of transactions carried out over 30 months following the acquisition of the 49%?

3) What if A instead purchased an additional 3% of T's non-voting, non-convertible preferred stock?

4) What if A and T were at all times owned by the same married couple?

5) Suppose it is three years since the change date, and T is still maintaining the same business operations. T has been operating at a loss until this past taxable year, in which it ended at a $3,500 profit. The pertinent long-term tax-exempt rate is 20%. What is the maximum amount of the pre-ownership change loss that T can apply to offset this year's profits?

6) What difference, if any, would it make to your answer in "(5)" if 50% of T's assets were in the form of municipal stocks and bonds being held for investment purposes?

7) What if T was previously only worth $4,000, but A contributed an additional $1,000 in property six months prior to the acquisition of the additional stock?

PROBLEM 22-3

1) On January 1, year one, Samantha bought 49% of X Corp. from its sole shareholder, Ted, an unrelated person. Ted died, and X Corp. redeemed the 51% of X Corp. stock held by Ted's estate for $550,000 cash on January 1, year two. At the date of the redemption, X Corp. had a $300,000 NOL carryforward. Immediately before the redemption, the value of X Corp. was $1,000,000. Does the § 382 limitation apply? Why or why not?

2) Assume the § 382 limit does apply and that in year two, X Corp. has taxable income of $75,000. Assume the relevant federal long-term tax-exempt rate is 10%. What is the § 382 limitation, and how much of X Corp.'s Year two taxable income can be offset by its NOL carryforward? *See* §§ 382(b), 382(e)(1), 382(e)(2), and 382(g)(1).

3) Assume the same facts as in "(1)" and that the § 382 limit applies. Assuming that X Corp. had $25,000 of taxable income in year two. How does this change the § 382 limitation?

4) Assume the same facts as "(1)" and that the § 382 limit applies, but that Samantha made a $300,000 capital contribution to X Corp. on December 1, year one, in order to increase the value of X Corp. before the corporation redeemed its stock from Ted's estate on January 1, year two. What are the tax implications of Samantha's capital contribution with respect to the § 382 limitation?

5) Same as "(1)", except that Samantha and Ted are married.

PROBLEM 22-4

A Corp. acquired all the stock of T Corp. ("T") on January 1, year one. On that date, T Corp. had a $200,000 NOL carryforward and T's § 382 limitation was determined to be $100,000. For year one, T had taxable income of $50,000, which was fully offset against T's $200,000 NOL carryforward because the § 382 limitation was $100,000. On April 1, year two, A Corp. decides to discontinue T's business and sells T's historic operating assets. What are the tax implications of the sale?

452

PROBLEM 22-5

1) Sid was the sole shareholder of Loss Corp. On January 1, year one, Sid sold his stock in Loss Corp. to Big Corp. for $3,000,000, at which time Loss Corp. had a $1,000,000 loss carryforward and the federal long-term tax exempt rate was 10%. At the acquisition date, Loss Corp's assets, excluding cash and cash equivalents, had an aggregate fair market value of $3,500,000 and an aggregate basis of $2,500,000. Loss Corp. had held all of its assets for more than two years before the January 1, year one, acquisition date. On January 1, year one, Loss Corp. owned a manufacturing plant with a fair market value of $400,000 and a basis of $300,000. Loss Corp. sold the manufacturing plant on June 1, year three, when its fair market value was $400,000 and its adjusted basis was $250,000. What is the tax implication of the sale? *See* § 382(h)(1).

2) Assume the same facts as in "(1)," except that Loss Corp.'s assets had an aggregate basis of $5,000,000 and the plant had a basis of $500,000 on January 1, year one, and on June 1, year one, as well.

C. SECTION 384: LIMITATION ON USE OF PREACQUISITION LOSSES TO OFFSET TARGET'S OR ACQUIROR'S BUILT-IN GAINS
Read § 384(a)-(c).

Section 384 further restricts the ability of a corporation to acquire another corporation or its assets in order to offset the pre-acquisition losses of one corporation against the built-in gains of the other. The principal purpose of § 384 is to foreclose "trafficking" in gain corporations, i.e., acquisition by a loss corporation of a corporation with built-in gains. Section 382 would not cover this situation because there is no ownership change of the loss corporation that meets the threshold requirement of Section 382(h). If § 384(a) applies, built-in gains of a "gain corporation" may not be offset by preacquisition losses of the other corporation.

The following two kinds of acquisitions activate § 384: (1) a corporation acquires directly, or through one or more other corporations, 80% (not the usual 50% for § 382) control of another corporation, or (2) the assets of a corporation are acquired by another corporation in a Type A, C, or acquisitive D reorganization. In either kind of acquisition, one of the corporations must be a "gain corporation." § 384(a). A "gain corporation" is a corporation with built-in gains on the acquisition date that are large enough to meet the threshold requirement of § 382(h)(3)(B). §§ 384(a), (c)(4),(8).

It does not matter whether the loss corporation acquires the gain corporation or the gain corporation acquires the loss corporation. In either event § 384 may apply. Also, if there is an ownership change of a loss corporation, both §§ 382 and 384 may apply at the same time.

Section 384 mercifully does not apply if both corporations were members of a "controlled group" at all times during the five-year period prior to the acquisition date. § 384(b). "Controlled group" is defined in § 1563(a), but dropped the ownership requirement from 80% to "over 50%" by vote and value of stock. If one or both of the corporations has been in existence less than five years, the period of actual existence is substituted for the usual five-year period. This means after five years, the assets can be sold free of § 384.

PROBLEM 22-6

Mr. Big has owned all the stock of P for over ten years. Early this year, when P had a cumulative $5,000 NOL, P bought all of T's outstanding stock from unrelated parties. Just before the acquisition, the total value of T's assets (aside from cash and some marketable securities it owned) was $10,000, and their total basis amounted to $6,000.

1) Does § 384 apply to this acquisition? If so, what is the effect?

2) Same as "(1)" but P acquired 80% of T's stock (all of which is voting common stock) in a Type B reorganization in which T's shareholders received 40% of P's voting common stock in the exchange. Does § 384 apply to this acquisition? If so, what is the effect of its application?

PROBLEM 22-7

Loss Co. (Loss) has NOLs. Loss Co. obtains 90% of the assets of the landholding partnership (LHP) in a § 351 transaction. LHP expects large profits, perhaps large enough to fully offset Loss Co.'s NOLs. In exchange, Loss issues 35% of its stock for the land. The existing shareholders of Loss contribute enough cash to constitute 10% of the stock they previously owned, so that they become transferors under the accommodation transferor rules. The shareholders of Loss are unrelated to the partners of LHP.

Is this transaction vulnerable to attack under § 269, 382, 384, or 482?

PROBLEM 22-8

Beta Boat Corporation ("Beta") sold its assets and went out of business about three months ago; its sole remaining asset is a $3 million NOL. Mr. Lomax owns 100% of Beta and is keeping the company alive to prevent the inadvertent loss of the NOL. He also owns 55% of Delta Boat Corporation ("Delta"), which owns three ferries (each of which has a basis of $100,000 and a value of $1 million). He was the founder of both corporations and has been a dominant figure for twenty years. The other 45% is owned by Leona Lomax, his daughter and current CEO of Beta Boat.

Offshore Rigs, Inc. has signed a letter of intent with Delta to buy two of Delta's ferries at $1 million each. All three corporations are on the calendar year and use the accrual method of accounting. Realizing that Beta Boat's loss is an asset that should be used to offset the $900,000 gain on each boat, the accounting firm has advised the Lomax family to merge Delta into Beta as soon as possible so that Beta can be the seller of the boats. The deal is about to close. Leona thinks there is something fishy about the deal and wants your advice on whether the deal will work. Make sure to mention the effect, if any, of §§ 269 and 384.

Chapter 23

SPECIAL CORPORATE PENALTY OR REGULATORY TAXES

A. INTRODUCTION

This chapter briefly covers two sets of Code provisions that perform a policeman's role, namely:

- The accumulated earnings tax; and

- The personal holding company tax.

The taxes patrol corporations that retain their profits in a corporation instead of distributing them.

B. ACCUMULATED EARNINGS TAX
Read §§ 531, 532(a), 532(b), and 533.

1. INTRODUCTION

In addition to the regular corporate income tax and the corporate alternative minimum tax, Congress has imposed the accumulated earnings surtax of § 531 on the undistributed income of some corporations. If § 531 applies, the tax bite is serious because the tax itself is nondeductible for federal income tax purposes. § 275(a). The purpose of § 531 is to penalize a corporation that excessively accumulates its earnings beyond the reasonable needs of its business in order to defer or avoid shareholder-level income taxes on dividends.

When individual rates are much higher than corporate rates, a corporation that accumulates its earnings beyond the needs of its business can advantageously shelter income by retaining it. Now that the top individual rate is 37% and the top corporate rate is 21%, this penalty tax has become more important. Rate relationship changes could alter that condition. The § 531 tax is enforced even against publicly-held corporations. It has a general exemption-equivalent (of $250,000) and some legitimate escape routes, and thus room for argument in many instances. The current rate is 20%.

If the corporation is organized outside the United States, it may seek to accumulate its business profits indefinitely, but it must battle a special network of rules designed to prevent shifting income from intercorporate activities into low tax countries and to prevent the accumulation of investment income in foreign corporations in an attempt to defer application of the U.S. (perhaps higher) regular corporate income tax. That subject is for the course on international taxation.

As you can see from the following case, if the taxpayer can show that the accumulation is not unreasonable, then the IRS loses, and vice versa. As a result, litigation tends to revolve around the *bona fides* of the accumulation. The following case is an old favorite.

MYRON'S ENTERPRISES v. UNITED STATES
548 F. 2d 331 (9th Cir. 1977)

SNEED, CIRCUIT JUDGE

Taxpayer-corporations sued in district court below for a refund of accumulated earnings taxes imposed by the Commissioner. The Commissioner had based the tax on his determination that for taxpayers' fiscal years 1966 through 1968 the reasonable needs of the business stemmed entirely from working capital needs and never exceeded $21,272. The taxpayers contended that their retained earnings for the years in question of $316,000, $374,316, and $415,766 respectively were needed to cover both working capital requirements of $100,000 and the planned purchase and remodeling of the ballroom operated by taxpayers. at an estimated cost of $375,000.

The district court, in *Myron's Ballroom v. United States*, 382 F. Supp. 582 (C.D. Cal. 1974), held that taxpayers had accumulated earnings in excess of the reasonable needs of their business, but not to the extent claimed by the Commissioner. The court also found that the taxpayers had been availed of for the purpose of avoiding income taxes. Thus, the court upheld the surtax, but required a partial refund in light of the Commissioner's underestimation of taxpayers' reasonable business needs.

The taxpayers argue on appeal that they are entitled to a full refund (i) because all of the retained earnings in the years in question were required to meet the reasonable needs of their business, and (ii) because they proved by the preponderance of the evidence that they were not availed of to avoid taxes, despite the contrary finding by the district court. The Government argues, in response, that taxpayers were not even entitled to a partial refund – that the Commissioner's initial determination of the reasonable needs of the business was correct and that taxpayers failed to prove lack of tax-avoidance motivation. We conclude that the taxpayers are entitled to the full refund they seek. Therefore, we reverse and remand for such necessary proceedings as are consistent with this opinion.

I

Taxpayer-corporations operate a ballroom and adjoining cocktail lounge. At all times since taxpayers were formed, they have leased their operating premises from Miss Pearl Rose, an elderly lady who has owned the property for approximately 30 years. The taxpayers began inquiring into the possibilities of purchasing the property in 1957, in part because they did not wish to make needed improvements unless they owned the building. Taxpayers made offers to Miss Rose of $100,000 and $150,000 for the property in the late 1950s-early 1960s, neither of which was accepted. However, at the time of the second offer, Miss Rose told taxpayers that they would have "first choice" if and when she decided to sell the ballroom.

In 1963, taxpayers learned that Russ Morgan, a former orchestra leader at the ballroom, had offered Miss Rose $300,000 cash for the property in an attempt apparently to take over the ballroom operation. The price offered by Morgan probably reflected the goodwill that taxpayers had built up in their operations and therefore was considerably higher than the value of the ballroom property by itself. Morgan's actions convinced taxpayers that their business could be involuntarily "acquired" by someone purchasing the ballroom from

Miss Rose.[1] Taxpayers therefore, promptly offered Miss Rose the identical sum of $300,000. This, offer was renewed in 1964, 1965, 1966, 1967, 1968 and 1970. While Miss Rose never

---

[1] While taxpayers had a lease and an option to renew on the ballroom property at the time Morgan made his $300,000 offer to Miss Rose, there was always the possibility that the lease could he broken or

objected to the terms of the offers, she never sold and still owned the ballroom at the time of trial.

As the Government points out, Miss Rose was never particularly clear as to when and if she would sell her building. Nevertheless, the district court found (a) that taxpayers "expected at any time during the years 1966, 1967 and 1968 that [they] would be able to purchase the ballroom property from Pearl Rose for a price of $300,000 cash no less than that amount, and maybe more," 382 F. Supp. at 587, and moreover (b) that the "expectation that the ballroom property would be acquired at any time during the years in issue was a reasonable expectation," *Id.* at 588. Thus, during the years in issue the acquisition of the ballroom property and the planned improvements and repairs were reasonably anticipated business needs of [taxpayers], and said needs were directly connected with the business of the corporations." *Id.*

The district court further concluded that, "[c]onsidering the reasonably anticipated business need of the corporations to purchase the ballroom property, the corporations combined required at least $375,000, in addition to their combined working capital needs of $100,000." *Id.* However, the court went on to hold that in light of taxpayers' sole shareholder Mrs. Myrna Myron's willingness to loan up to $200,000 to her corporations for purchase of the ballroom "if the corporations did not have sufficient funds to consummate the transactions . . . a reasonable accumulation [for the purchase] would be $250,000 with Mrs. Myron loaning the balance of funds required," *id.,* thus leading to an excess accumulation in 1967 and 1968.

II

Section 537 of the Internal Revenue Code provides that the reasonable needs of a business, for purposes of determining whether there has been an excess accumulation of earnings, include "the reasonably anticipated needs of the business." Treas. Reg. § 1.537-1(b)(1) provides that to justify an accumulation of earnings on grounds of reasonably anticipated business needs, a corporation must have "specific definite, and feasible plans for the use of such accumulation" and must not postpone execution of the plan "indefinitely."

The Government contends that the district court erred in concluding that the taxpayers had a "specific, definite, and feasible plan" to acquire and remodel the ballroom. The Government notes that Miss Rose never agreed to sell the ballroom and argues that taxpayers could not have reasonably expected Miss Rose to so agree within the taxable years in question after nearly a decade of unsuccessful negotiations.

We agree with other circuits that a determination by the trial court of the reasonably anticipated business needs of a corporation is a finding of fact which must he sustained unless clearly erroneous…. A court should be particularly wary of overturning a finding of a trial court supporting the taxpayer's determination of its anticipated business needs, since, in the first instance, the "reasonableness of the needs is necessarily for determination by those concerned with the management of the particular enterprise. This determination must prevail unless the facts show clearly the accumulations were for prohibited purposes." *Henry Van Hummell. Inc. v. Commissioner of Internal Revenue*, 364 F.2d 746, 749 (10th Cir. 1966). *cert. denied,* 386 U.S. 956. 87 S. Ct. 1019, 18 L. Ed. 2d 102 (1967). We conclude that the district court was not clearly erroneous in finding that taxpayers' expected purchase and remodeling of the ballroom for $375,000 was a "reasonably anticipated need of the business."

---

evaded. According to Mrs. Myron, Morgan had asked his attorney and Miss Roses agent "to review [the lease] line by line to see if there was some way or some word – something that could break the lease." *Id.* at 73. This possibility of a loophole in the lease left the door open for involuntary "acquisition."

The Government argues that if the instant plan to purchase the ballroom is held to be a reasonably anticipated business need, "any individual could organize a one-man corporation, lease a building and discuss with the lessor the purchase of the building at some future time, and then assert that in the meantime business needs required accumulation of corporate earnings." *I.A. Dress Co. v. Commissioner of Internal Revenue*, 273 F.2d 543, 544 (2d Cir.), *cert. denied*, 362 U.S. 976. 80 S. Ct. 1060, 4 L. Ed. 2d 1011 (1960).

Such fears of artificially constructed needs were well-founded in the quoted case of *I.A. Dress Co.;* there, the owner of the building that the taxpayer sought to purchase, "was willing to sell but at a price some $300,000 more than the taxpayer was willing to pay." Id. The offer of the taxpayer lacked substance and could easily have been a facade. In the instant case, however, the taxpayers were extremely diligent in their attempts to purchase the ballroom; the taxpayers agreed to all of Miss Rose's stated terms – including payment in all cash; the price offered, far from being criticized by Miss Rose as too low, was apparently in excess of the property's fair market value.[2]

Neither do we have a situation where taxpayers' planned purchase of the ballroom was clearly infeasible. *See Colonial Amusement Corp.*, 1948 Tax. Ct. Mem. Dec. (PH) P 48,149 (building restrictions and priorities prevented carrying out of expansion plans). Here, as in *Universal Steel Co.*, 5 T.C. 627 (1945) (war priority restrictions temporarily blocked purchase of pickling plant), the taxpayers "had a right to hope, if not expect" *id.* at 638 that Miss Rose would sell to them in the near future. Miss Rose never foreclosed the possibility of sale on the terms offered by taxpayers; she merely wanted to "think it over some more." As expressed by Miss Rose's agent at one point during the negotiations, Miss Rose "was an elderly lady and had a very definite mind" her answers according to the agent, would differ depending on how she felt on getting up in the morning. Taxpayers were encouraged at several points in the negotiations: in 1965, Miss Rose's agent had told taxpayers. "Be prepared and ready to go." In light of the reasonable possibility that Miss Rose might have decided to accept the offer at any time during the taxable years in issue, calling for quick collection of $375,000 in cash, it would have been unreasonable to force taxpayers to pay out all of their earnings in dividends. Section 537 allows taxpayers to provide for "reasonably anticipated needs," not merely for certainties.

The district court's finding is supported by several tax court cases. In *Magic Mart, Inc.,* 51 T.C. 775 (1969), *acq.,* 1969-2 C.B. xxiv. the Tax Court held that the taxpayer's accumulation of earnings for 1959 through 1962 was reasonable in light of taxpayer's plan to acquire enlarged and expanded facilities, even though it had tried unsuccessfully to buy larger facilities since 1957 and was not able to close a deal until 1967, five years after the taxable years in question. In *Breitfeller Sales, Inc.*, 28 T.C. 1164 (1957), *acq.*, 1958-2 C.B. 4. the Tax Court held that a General Motors dealership's accumulation of earnings was justified, inter alia, by "the continuing possibility that it might [to avoid harmful competition] be required to finance a new dealership in [a neighboring community]." *Id.* at 1168 . . . *See also Universal Steel Co., supra.*

---

[2] The Government argues that in addition to these steps the taxpayers also should have investigated purchasing other property in the general area once Miss Rose did not prove totally disposing. *Cf. Magic Mart., Inc.*, 51 T.C. 775 (1969), *acq.*, 1969-2 C.B. xxiv. We agree that the failure of a taxpayer to look into the possibility of purchasing alternative properties generally will be a relevant factor in determining whether the taxpayer actually had a reasonably anticipated business need to purchase the sought-after property. However, other factors also must be considered, including the uniqueness of the sought property. Here, as was testified to at trial, a substantial amount of good will was tied up in the ballroom occupied by taxpayers; given that this value would have been lost if taxpayer had moved to another location, we do not believe that taxpayers' failure to pursue other possible properties (if other ballrooms even existed) calls for reversing the finding of the district court.

III

The Government rests its entire case upon the argued lack of a specific, definite, and feasible plan. No attempt is made to support the trial court's use of Mrs. Myrna Myron's capacity to loan to the taxpayers to reduce the amount of the reasonable accumulation. The Government thus agrees with taxpayers that, assuming a feasible plan, the district court, in determining whether taxpayers unreasonably accumulated earnings, erred in subtracting from the cash needed to purchase the ballroom an amount that Mrs. Myron stated that she would be willing to loan to the taxpayers if necessary. We also agree. Having found that the reasonably anticipated business need of the taxpayers to purchase the ballroom property required at least $375,000 in cash, the district court erred in concluding that a reasonable accumulation was any less.

Having determined that the reasonable business needs of taxpayers, within the meaning of section 535, equaled or exceeded the accumulated earnings of tax payers for the taxable years in question, it is unnecessary for us to consider whether the district court was correct in holding that taxpayers had been availed of to avoid taxes within the meaning of section 531. Taxpayers are entitled to a full refund. The case is [reversed and] remanded to the district court for such necessary proceedings as are consistent with this opinion.[3]

---

[3]   That the reasonableness of accumulations should be judged without regard to the borrowing capabilities of the corporation-taxpayer is well established by the case law. *See, e.g., General Smelting Co.*, 4 T.C. 313, 323 (1944), *acq.*, 1945 C.B. 3; B. Bittker & J. Eustice, Federal Income Taxation of Corporations and Shareholders 8-20 to 8-21 & n. 42 (3rd ed. 1971). In computing "accumulated taxable income." which forms the base for the needs of the business." There is no authority for reducing the credit to reflect the lending capacity of taxpaver's shareholders. If the reasonable business needs of taxpayer equal or outstrip the retained earnings no surtax can be imposed, even though the needs could be financed by borrowing from outside – such financing decisions are for the taxpayer not the courts to make.

The district court's logic could conceivably be extended to the point of totally nullifying Congress' expressed policy of allowing corporate taxpayers to accumulate earnings necessary for reasonable business needs. A sole shareholder can always loan back any cash distributed by his corporation dividends if the corporation later needs the money (minus, of course, any income taxes paid). Therefore, to take into account the ability of a shareholder to loan money to the corporation could be construed as virtual authority "for denying all sole stockholder corporations the right ever to maintain accumulations even for reasonable needs. The test expressed by the statute would then be completely abandoned." *Smoot Sand & Gravel Corp. v. Commissioner of Internal Revenue*, 241 F.2d 197, 206 (4th Cir.). *cert. denied*, 354 U.S. 922, 77 S. Ct. 1383, 1 L. Ed. 2d 1437 (1957). . . .

PROBLEM 23-1

Alpha Corp., a manufacturer, has earned $500,000 of income thus far in the current taxable year. It wants to retain the entirety of this income until next year when it will face the maturity date on a $500,000 promissory note Alpha Corp. executed several years ago.

1)   Will Alpha Corp. potentially be subject to the accumulated earnings tax if it holds onto the income, not distributing it to its shareholders? *See* § 531 and Reg. § 1.537-2(b)?

2)   Would your answer to "1)" change if you knew that the note was in connection with a loan made by Bob Builder, an 80% shareholder and CEO of the company? What would the note have to contain in order to survive the accumulated earnings tax?

3)   What if Alpha Corp. wanted to keep the income because its officers had concocted a scheme by which they were planning to try to convince the owner of a rare art collection worth $1 million to exchange the collection for $500,000 and a public thank you?

4)   Assume the $500,000 is not deemed to be retained for reasonably anticipated business needs and, as such, is subject to the accumulated earnings tax. Would Alpha Corp. be taxed on the entire amount withheld? Can the company deduct any tax actually paid? *See* § 535(a).

2.   CALCULATING THE TAX

The base for the accumulated earnings tax is so-called accumulated taxable income, which is determined under § 535. To compute the number, one begins with taxable income and then makes various adjustments, such as the elimination of the dividends-received deduction, in order to arrive at something in the nature of real economic income.

Next, one moves to § 535(c), which provides that a credit will be provided for in the amount "retained for the reasonable needs of the business." The "credit" amounts to a minimum exemption of $250,000 for most corporations. The figure is $150,000 for personal service corporations and $250,000 for holding or investment corporations capped at the same figure (*i.e.*, not a penny more). §§ 535(c)(2)-(3). The cumulative "credit" increases to the extent the corporation can tell a good story to justify its further accumulations. Holding and investment companies are excluded from story-telling. A controlled group of corporations is entitled to only one credit.

PROBLEM 23-2

PSC Corp. is a personal service company solely owned by Adam. The principal activity of PSC Corp. is providing architectural services. PSC Corp. is a calendar year taxpayer. PSC Corp. filed its year one corporate income tax return in January of year two. In February of year two, the IRS audited PSC Corp's year one tax return and the agent determined that the company had accumulated earnings beyond the reasonable needs of the business. PSC Corp's accumulated taxable income as of December 31 year one was $1,000,000.

1)   How can PSC Corp. avoid the accumulated earnings tax? *See* §§ 561(a), 563(a), and 565.

2)   Can PSC Corp. deduct a deficiency dividend paid to PSC Corp.'s sole shareholder, Adam, under § 547(a)? *See* Reg. § 1.565-1(B)(3).

3) Explain how the accumulated earnings credit is applied to these facts.

C. PERSONAL HOLDING COMPANIES

1. INTRODUCTION
Read § 541.

The Personal Holding Company ("PHC") tax provisions are supposed to prevent taxpayers from shifting income to closely-held corporations (perhaps taxable at lower rates) in lieu of having the shareholder earn the money directly. One can avoid the tax by having the corporation pay dividends. The tax is directed at three "sins," which are often described in terms of the following memorable characterizations:

1. The incorporated talent;

2. The incorporated pocketbook; and

3. The incorporated yacht.

The federal income tax return forces the tax return preparer to disclose whether the corporation is a PHC. If it is, it is subject to a separate tax under § 541. The tax is calculated on personal holding company income under § 543, a key feature of which is that it exempts long-term capital gains. Like the accumulated earnings tax, the PHC tax is nondeductible and can be mitigated by paying dividends, including deficient dividends.

2. DETERMINATION OF PERSONAL HOLDING COMPANY STATUS

This 20% tax falls only on the undistributed income of a personal holding company, meaning a company controlled by a limited number of shareholders and deriving a large percentage of its income from specified sources. In order to be treated as a PHC, a corporation must meet a tainted income test under § 542(a)(1) and a stock ownership test under § 542(a)(2).

Under § 542(a)(1), the tainted income test requires that at least 60% of the corporation's adjusted ordinary gross income for a taxable year constitute PHC income, as defined in § 543(a). The IRS ruled in P.L.R 8043098 (July 19, 1980) that because a limited partnership interest is not one of the items enumerated in § 543(a) as comprising PHC income, and because a limited partnership interest represents the limited partner's distributive share of the partnership's income, it is the nature of the underlying income generated by the partnership that determines whether there is PHC income – a "look through" rule.

The stock ownership test is met if, "at any time during the last half of the taxable year more than fifty percent in value of the corporation's outstanding stock is owned directly or indirectly, by or for not more than five individuals." § 542(a)(2). A specific set of attribution rules applies in determining whether the stock ownership test is met.

Under § 544(a)(1), each partner is considered to own a proportionate share of the stock held by his partnership. Under § 544(a)(2), an individual is considered to own the stock owned directly or indirectly by or for his family or by or for his partners; and § 544(a)(5) provides reattribution rules. As a result of the attribution rules, a partner is always deemed to own all of the stock held by his partnership and any other stock held by his fellow partners outside the partnership.

a. The Incorporated Talent
Read § 543(a)(7).

The following ruling illustrates the § 543 tax issues when the income arises from rendering personal services.

REV. RUL. 75-67
1975-1 C.B. 169

Advice has been requested whether, under the circumstances described below, a corporation will be considered to have received personal holding company income within the meaning of section 543(a)(7) of the Internal Revenue Code of 1954. B, a doctor specializing in a certain area of medical services, owns 80 percent of the outstanding stock of L, a domestic professional service corporation. B is the only officer of L who is active in the production of income for L, and he is the only medical doctor presently employed by L. B performs medical services under an employment contract with L. L furnishes office quarters and equipment, and employs a receptionist to assist B. P, a patient solicited the services of and was treated by B.

Section 543(a)(7) of the Code provides, in part, that the term personal holding company income includes amounts received under a contract whereby a corporation is to furnish personal services if some person other than the corporation has the right to designate, by name or description, the individual who is to perform the services, or if the individual who is to perform the services is designated, by name or description, in the contract.

In dealing with a professional service corporation providing medical services, an individual will customarily solicit and expect to receive the services of a particular physician, and he will usually he treated by the physician sought.

A physician-patient relationship arises from such a general agreement of treatment. Either party may terminate the relationship at will, although the physician must give the patient reasonable notice of his withdrawal and may not abandon the patient until a replacement, if necessary, can be obtained. C. Morris & A. Moritz, Doctor and Patient and the Law 135 (5th ed. 1971). Moreover, if a physician who has entered into a general agreement of treatment is unable to treat the patient when his services are needed, he may provide a qualified and competent substitute physician to render the services. C. Morris & A. Moritz, *supra*, at 138. 374-75.

Thus, when an individual solicits, and expects, the services of a particular physician and that physician accepts the individual as a patient and treats him, the relationship of physician-patient established in this manner does not constitute a designation of the individual who is to perform the services under a contract for personal services within the meaning of section 543(a)(7) of the Code.

If, however, the physician or the professional service corporation contracts with the patient that the physician personally will perform particular services for the patient, and he has no right to substitute another physician to perform such services, there is a designation of that physician as the individual to perform services under a contract for personal services within the meaning of section 543(a)(7) of the Code.

The designation of a physician as an individual to perform services can be accomplished by either an oral or written contract. See Rev. Rul. 69-299, 1969-1 C.B. 165.

Moreover, if L agreed to perform the type of services that are so unique as to preclude substitution of another physician to perform such services, there is also a designation.

Accordingly, since in the instant case there is no indication that L has contracted that B will personally perform the services or that the services are so unique as to preclude substitution, it is held that income earned by L from providing medical service contracts will not be considered income from personal service contracts within the meaning of section 543(a)(7) of the Code.

b. The Incorporated Pocketbook

The notion here is that taxpayers should not be allowed to generate investment income and hide it in a low-bracket corporation, where it is split off from the taxpayer's other income losses, expenses, and tax-filing characteristics. The trouble is that some special purpose corporations such as those formed to hold real estate or oil and gas interests are formed for legitimate nontax reasons. How does one sort them out? The answer is that § 543(a)(2)-(6) describe a series of corporations that are rich with some special type of passive income, but low on other passive income. The Code in effect declassifies their income from being personal holding company income. Now scan §§ 543(a)(2)-(6) to see how the concept is applied, and note that there is another test relating to the extent to which the corporation has § 162 deductions. Congress views the existence of significant § 162 deductions as evidence that there really is a business under the microscope.

c. The Incorporated Yacht
Read § 543(a)(6).

The sin here is putting a yacht, along with some income-producing investment property, into the hands of a corporation and then personally renting the yacht from the corporation. The fiscal scheme would be to generate tax deductions (for business or profit-seeking costs, such as depreciation) where none would otherwise be available and offsetting the investment income with such deductions. Section 543(a)(6) comes to the Treasury's rescue by turning such income into personal holding company income. Nowadays, the passive loss rules in §469 make the scheme harder to implement.

d. Miscellaneous

(1) In the Foreign Sphere

Subpart F (§§ 951-964) does a similar thing in the international context. There is more to it than this, but the unique feature of Sub-part F is that it levies a tax on the owner of stock with respect to distributions that were never received. Devotees of a strict reading of the Sixteenth Amendment may find this startling.

(2) Overlap

If a corporation is subject to both the accumulated earnings tax and the personal holding company tax, the personal holding company tax rules prevail. § 532(b)(1).

(3) Deficiency Dividends

Look at the deficiency dividend rules in § 547. Do they mean that the § 541 tax should never be paid, or is never paid? Keep in mind that the tax is designed not to raise revenue, but rather to regulate conduct and to force offending corporations to make distributions to shareholders so that the right kind of tax will be collected and not deferred or ultimately escaped. If § 541 is sometimes a trap for the unwary, § 547 is the escape for the unwary who have become wary.

(4) Realism

Do we still need this tax, now that dividends are generally taxed at a mere 20%?

PROBLEM 23-3

Beta Co., a Delaware corporation, just ended its first taxable year with adjusted ordinary gross income of $11,000 and § 162 deductions totaling $1,000. $2,000 of the income was in the form of patent royalties; $2,000 was in the form of rentals paid for the use of an office building owned by Beta Co.; $2,500 was in the form of dividends paid by Delta, Inc., a company in which Beta Co. owns a significant block of preferred stock; and the remaining income was from the ordinary operation of Beta Co.'s shoe store.

The only series of Beta Co. stock, common voting stock, has been owned by the following unrelated individuals in the following proportions since the company's inception one year ago:

Adam	12%
Bob	9%
Carla	25%
David	5%
Ellen	14%
Frank	2%
George	20%
Hannah	8%
Isabelle	5%

1) Does Beta Co. meet the stock ownership requirement for determining whether it is a personal holding company? *See* § 542(a)(2).

2) Does Beta Co. meet the income requirement in determining if it is a personal holding company? *See* §§ 542(a)(1) and 543(a), (b).

3) Assume Beta Co. is classified as a personal holding company, subject to the personal holding company tax of § 541. If Beta retains its $10,000 taxable income, will it be subject to the § 541 tax on the entire $10,000? If not, what portion would potentially be subject to the tax? *See* §§ 541, 545(a), (b), 561.

4) Is there a way Beta Co. could avoid the personal holding company tax even after a determination that a PHC tax is due? Is there a time limitation during which the action must be taken? *See* § 547.

D. LIMITATIONS ON THE USE OF MULTIPLE CORPORATIONS

Corporations pay graduated income taxes. In theory, a single business could fragment itself into a large number of corporations in order to pay taxes in lower brackets. At the high water mark of the practice, it was common for taxpayers to form corporations distinguished only by their last names to do things like build tract homes, with A Corp. owning one home, B Corp. owning the next home, and so forth. By doing so, the gain on each home that was sold was taxed at the bottom of the tax rate "ladder." Section 1561 pinches off this strategy by treating a group of commonly controlled corporations as a single taxpayer.

Section 1563(a)(2) defines the key term "controlled group of corporations" as including both parent-subsidiary and brother-sister groups. Various other Code provisions strive to ensure the same result on an *ad hoc* basis. *See*, for example, § 179(d)(6).

A "controlled group" of corporations may consist of a parent-subsidiary group or brother-sister group. A parent-subsidiary group exists where a parent corporation owns at least 80% of a subsidiary corporation, by vote or by value. § 1563(a)(1).

A brother-sister group is more complicated. It exists where five or fewer individuals, estates, or trusts own over 50% of each corporation by vote or value, counting stock ownership of each person only to the extent it is identical or overlapping in each corporation. This remarkably rigid rule appears in Reg. § 1.1563-1(a)(3) and was affirmed in *United States v. Vogel Fertilizer Co.*, 455 U.S. 16 (1982).

To illustrate: The one class of outstanding stock of Corporations X and Y are owned by individual shareholders A and B as follows:

Identical/Overlapping Individuals' Ownership	Corporation	
	X	**Y**
A (35%)	65%	35%
B (35%)	35%	65%
Total: (70%)	100%	100%

Corporations X and Y are members of a brother-sister controlled group., because individuals A and B meet the "more than 50% identical or overlapping" ownership requirement. The identical or overlapping ownership by each shareholder is the minimum percentage common to corporations, which in this case is 35%. Combining the identical ownership percentages results in 70%.

In contrast, the following grouping would not be a brother-sister controlled group because there would only be 20% identical or overlapping ownership.

Identical/Overlapping Individuals' Ownership	Corporation	
	X	**Y**
A (10%)	90%	10%
B (10%)	10%	90%
Total: (20%)	100%	100%

PROBLEM 23-4

The one class of outstanding stock of corporations U and V (both of which are domestic manufacturing companies) is owned by the following unrelated individuals:

Individuals	U (Percent)	V (Percent)
A	24	0
B	11	13

C	11	13
D	12	11
E	14	12
F	13	14
G	15	11
H	0	26
Total:	100	100

1) Is this a brother-sister controlled group?

2) What is the practical impact of being found a brother-sister controlled group?

E. CONSOLIDATED RETURNS

Although Congress is hostile to fragmenting income among multiple corporations, it is generally receptive to allowing affiliated corporations to file a single consolidated federal income tax return. §§ 1501-1504. This calls for preparing a separate imaginary or tentative return for each member corporation and then, among other things, eliminating intercompany transactions and deferring their recognition until one of the parties to the transaction leaves the group, say because the common parent corporation sold the stock of a member that sold property to another member, or until an asset is sold, services are ultimately rendered, or profits are distributed, to someone outside the group. Section 1502 is an all powerful source of authority because it gives the Treasury Department a quasi-legislative grant of authority.

1. QUALIFYING TO FILE A CONSOLIDATED RETURN

The privilege of filing a consolidated return applies to parent corporations and chains of subsidiaries as to which they have specified levels of control. Once the election is made, it is irrevocable except with the consent of the IRS, or unless the common parent goes out of existence. Once the election is made, the group will pay consolidated income taxes and the parent will act as the agent for the group – the mastermind – in federal income tax matters as if it were the management of a single corporation.

An "affiliated group" is defined in § 1504. It has two basic standards. First, only "includible corporations" can join and they must be under sufficient control. Section 1504(b) defines the key term "includible corporation." Please take a moment to scan the list. Most of the exclusions are based on the incompatibility of the tax computations that apply to specialized corporations, such as life insurance companies, as opposed to traditional business corporations.

Second, the ownership test requires that the parent own at least 80% of the stock of the subsidiary by vote and value ignoring "plain vanilla" preferred stock. Ignoring this kind of stock frees the subsidiary to issue preferred stock to outsiders to raise capital without imperiling the consolidation. Looking down the chain of ownership, each lower-tier subsidiary must also be at least 80%-owned, directly. § 1504(a)(2). Thus, for example, a second tier subsidiary that is only 64%-owned indirectly by the ultimate parent corporation can be included in the affiliated group, but less than 64% is insufficient. Stock options are generally ignored. Some courts have held that there must be a business purpose for a consolidation. *See, e.g., Elko Realty Co. v. Commissioner,* 29 T.C. 1012, *aff'd per curium,* 260 F.2d 949 (3d Cir. 1958).

Notice that a nonincludible corporation might still be a subsidiary, but the chain of affiliation stops where the chain of includible corporations ends. So, for example, one might want to put a 100%-owned life insurance company at the bottom of the chain to maximize the opportunity to file consolidated returns with all the other members.

When a member leaves or enters a group (except at year-end) it must file a short period return for the nonconsolidated period, and its income for the consolidated period must be identified and apportioned.

The price of admission to the group is fairly high. Each corporation is severally liable for the group's federal income taxes. The group has one tax rate, one accumulated earnings tax exemption and other similar "one company" restrictions. Moreover, the complications of filing a consolidated return are themselves significant, as the following materials will show.

On the other hand, there are some big advantages, the key one being the ability to offset income and losses among group members and to defer profits in dealings between members of the group.

2. COMPUTING CONSOLIDATED INCOME AND LOSS

Each corporation has to prepare its own tax return using its own accounting method, but must use the group's taxable year. Once that is done, the returns are merged and the lesser-included items, such as charitable contributions, are combined for purposes of imposing any special limitation that might apply to the particular kind of item, such as the 10% of taxable income limit on charitable contributions made by corporations. § 170(a)(2). So, for example, if only one of the affiliated corporations made a charitable contribution, that contribution would be limited to 10% of consolidated income, not merely 10% of the contributing corporation's income. After that, consolidated tax credits reduce the group's consolidated federal income tax liability.

Consolidated returns are often inches thick. To make it worse, not all states acknowledge the concept of the consolidated return.

3. DEFERRAL AND ELIMINATION OF INTERCOMPANY TRANSACTIONS

The consolidated group can be likened to divisions of a single company. Consistent with that model, sales of goods or the provision of services among members are not taxable events. Instead, gains and losses on sales to insiders are deferred until the property is transferred to an outsider under what is known as the "deferred intercompany transaction" concept. At that point, the income tax falls on the selling member and the member that sold to the selling member.

For example, if A and B are members of an affiliated group and A sells a hat to B for $10, representing a $4 mark-up, there is no taxable gain, but when B sells the hat to an unrelated merchant for $12, A reports a $4 gain and B reports a $2 gain. This deferred intercompany transaction approach can result in a gain to one member and a loss to the other member.

Consistent with the income tax effect, E & P effects also are symmetrically deferred. Deferred intercompany transactions can be triggered by more subtle events, such as the departure from the group of the buying or selling member before the property is sold to an outsider, or the worthlessness of a debt obligation that arose between members.

If the intra-group payment is of the currently deductible variety, such as the provision of deductible repair services, the rule is easy. One simply eliminates the income from the seller and denies the buyer a deduction within the consolidated group.

4. INTERCOMPANY DISTRIBUTIONS

Consistent with the "one company" model, inter-company distributions are eliminated from the taxable income of the group. Reg. § 1.1502-13(a)(1). Under proposed regulations, a partnership model applies within the group in that distributions from a subsidiary reduce the recipient's basis in the subsidiary stock under what are known as the "investment basis adjustment" rules. Prop. Reg. § 1.1502-32. The downward adjustment appropriately reduces the potential loss that would occur if the parent corporation later sold its stock in the distributing corporation. It is also a natural corollary of the rule that forces the parent to increase its basis in the subsidiary by the subsidiary's E & P increase for the year if it had a profitable year (also like a partnership).

If the distribution is not out of E & P, the parent must still reduce its basis in the payor's stock. If the distribution would have been taxable if it had occurred outside a consolidated group (such as a distribution of appreciated property), the gain is put on ice under the deferred inter-company transaction rules. Reg. § 1.1502-13. This means that, for example, a later deconsolidation of the payor subsidiary from the group would trigger the deferred gain.

5. BASIS IN SUBSIDIARY STOCK

As you have already seen, the investment basis adjustment rules run along partnership lines. The essential idea is to increase basis in subsidiary stock annually for profits, reduce it for losses, increase it for capital contributions, and reduce it for distributions. Reg. § 1.1502-32.

This is one of the rare areas where quasi-negative basis can occur. For example, if a parent had a basis of $100 in its wholly-owned subsidiary and the subsidiary paid a dividend of $110 and if the subsidiary were only 79%-owned, then the parent corporation would have to pay tax on a $10 gain. § 301(c)(3). If the subsidiary files a consolidated return with the parent, then the parent reduces its basis in the subsidiary to $0, and establishes an "excess loss account" of $10.00 Reg. § 1.1502-32(e)(1) Example 4. This is tantamount to allowing a negative basis of $10. If, for example, the parent were to sell the stock for $0, the parent would report a $10 gain. Reg. § 1.1502-19(b).

The changes in basis go all the way up and down the chain of members. For example, if SI earned $100 and it was owned by an intervening sub (S), which neither made nor lost money during the year, S would increase its basis in SI by $100 and P would equally increase its basis in S stock. This prevents artificial gains if the stock of either subsidiary is later sold. P's basis in loss-producing subsidiaries is conversely affected, losses likewise go up the chain. As you can see, to make the investment basis adjustments, the bookkeeper has to start this process at the bottom and work all way up the chain, making adjustments for profits, losses, contributions, and distributions for each link.

6. IMPLICATIONS OF ADMITTING AND ELIMINATING MEMBERS

In general, losses and deductions that occurred in an economic sense before a subsidiary was consolidated are quarantined in the new subsidiary. The idea is that the new subsidiary's attributes from prior ("separate return") years should not be blended into the results of the consolidated group.

Thus, under the so-called "separate return limitation year" (SRLY) rule, NOLs, certain built-in (property) losses, and built-in (current) deductions from transactions occurring before the consolidation, only offset income or gains of the new member itself and not of others in the new group. Reg. §§ 1.1502-1(f), 1.1502-15, 1.1502-21 and 1.1502-22. This generally prevents the SRLY rules from being confiscatory. If the newly acquired subsidiary had remained free-standing, it would have been in the same position as a quarantined member of an affiliated group. The restrictions on built-in losses and built-in deductions only last for 5 years, consistent with § 384.

If the new member had an NOL when it was acquired, § 382 can also apply. Reg. § 1.1502-92. Relatively recent Regulations have generally eliminated application of the SRLY limitation rules as unnecessarily duplicative where § 382 applies as well, and § 382 alone will now apply in such situations. *See* 64 FR 36092-01, T.D. 8823 (July 2. 1999).

WOLTER CONSTRUCTION COMPANY, INC. v. COMMISSIONER
634 F.2d 1029 (6th Cir. 1980)

CELEBREZZE, J.

[Taxpayer claimed the losses of a subsidiary it acquired, despite the separate return limitation year. The taxpayer's justification was that it acquired the subsidiary from its own shareholders, who formerly owned all the stock of the subsidiary, River Hills Golf Club, Inc. The taxpayer lost in the Tax Court.]

II.

Section 1501 of the Internal Revenue Code (Code) allows an "affiliated group" of corporations to file a consolidated income tax return for a taxable year instead of filing separate income tax returns. An "affiliated group" of corporations, as defined in Section 1504(a) of the Code, consists of a common parent corporation and one or more other corporations. Each corporation in the "affiliated group," except the common parent, must be 80 percent directly owned by another corporation in the group. The common parent corporation must directly own a minimum of 80 percent of at least one of the other corporations in the group. On March 2, 1970, Wolter and River Hills became an affiliated group eligible to file a consolidated return by virtue of Wolters acquisition of 80 percent of the common stock of River Hills. I.R.C. Sec. 1501.

The calculus for computing the consolidated income for an affiliated group and the corresponding income tax is not spelled out within the Code. Rather, Congress in §1502 of the Code has authorized the Secretary of the Treasury to promulgate Regulations that outline the requisites for and effects of filing a consolidated income tax return . . .

* * *

Reg. 1.1502-21(b)(1) is concerned with the use of net operating losses on a consolidated return. That regulation permits an affiliated group to use net operating losses sustained by any members of the group in "separate return years" if the losses could be carried over pursuant to the general principles of § 172 of the Code. A "separate return year" is defined as any year in which a company filed a separate return or in which it joined in the filing of a consolidated return by another group. Reg. 1.1502-1(e).

As a general rule, then, net operating losses reported on a separate return can be carried over to and used on a consolidated return. An important exception to this rule is found in Reg. 1.1502-21(c). That section provides that the net operating loss of a member of an affiliated group arising in a "separate return limitation year" which may be included in the consolidated net operating loss deduction of the group shall not exceed the amount of consolidated taxable income contributed by the loss-sustaining member for the taxable year at issue. The term "separate return limitation year" is defined in Reg. 1.1502-1(f), in essence, as a separate return year in which the member of the group (except, with qualifications, the common parent) was either: 1) not a member of the group for its entire taxable year; or 2) a member of the group for its entire taxable year, that enjoyed the benefits of multiple surtax exemptions. In summary, losses incurred by a brother or sister corporation or by a corporation which is unrelated at the time of its losses to its subsequent affiliates, before it becomes a member of an affiliated group filing a consolidated return, can only be carried forward and used on the consolidated return to the extent that the corporation that incurred the losses has current income reflected on the consolidated return.

Prior to River Hills becoming part of an affiliated group by virtue of Wolter's procurement of 80 percent of its stock, (that is, during River Hills' separate return years 1968, 1969, short year 1970) River Hills had incurred $125,255.43 in net operating losses. If, during the consolidated return years River Hills had had net income of $125,255.43 to report on the consolidated return, it could have used its earlier losses – incurred before becoming a member of the affiliated group – as a "consolidated net loss carryover" on the consolidated return. Reg. 1.1502-21(b). However, River Hills had no net income during the consolidated return years in question, and therefore any carry forward of its net operating losses to the consolidated return years would operate to offset only Wolter's income. This is precisely the type of net operating loss carryover prohibited by Reg. 1.1502-21(c).

The Tax Court in the present case concluded that because Wolter and River Hills were not members of an affiliated group in the loss years (1968, 1969, short year 1970), as required by Reg. 1.1502-1(f)(2)(ii), the loss years were separate return limitation years. Because River Hills had no separate taxable income and therefore did not contribute to the consolidated taxable income for the tax years in question, (1970 and 1971) the carryover of the net operating losses sustained by River Hills prior to affiliation with Wolter was barred by Section 1.1502-21(c) of the Treasury Regulations.

III.

Wolter's principal argument is that the net operating loss (NOL) carryover should be allowed under the Common Parent rule of Reg. 1.1502-1(f)(2) since Wolter and River Hills were commonly controlled when the losses were sustained. In the alternative taxpayer contends that Section 1.1502-2(c) of the Treasury Regulations is invalid to the extent that it prohibits the carryforward of River Hills' net operating losses from separate return limitation years.

To repeat, the carryover of net operating losses sustained by a member of an affiliated group in a separate return year is subject to the limitation imposed by Reg. 1.1502-21(c). Under that regulation the amount of a NOL of an affiliated group member arising in a separate return limitation year which may be carried forward on a consolidated return cannot exceed the income generated by the loss sustaining member for the taxable year in question. This regulation prevents the affiliated group from obtaining any advantage from the carryover losses. A loss is usable only to the extent the loss corporation adds an equivalent amount of income to the consolidated tax return of the group.

Notwithstanding this general restriction on the carryover of NOL's arising in a separate return limitation year, Reg. 1.1502-1(f)(2) provides that a separate return year for the corporation which is the common parent of the affiliated companies for the consolidated return year is not generally considered a separate return limitation year (the so-called "lonely parent" rule). Accordingly, a NOL sustained in a separate return year by the common parent of an affiliated group is not subject to the limitation of Reg. 1.1502-21(c). The net effect is to allow pre-affiliation NOL's of the common parent to be used to offset post-affiliation profits of any member of the group.

Were the relationship between Wolter and River Hills different in a few critical respects the Regulations would allow the River Hills' losses to be employed to offset Wolter's income. For instance, if Wolter had possessed 80 percent control of River Hills when the losses were incurred, but a consolidated return was not filed. River Hills could have carried forward those losses to the consolidated return years. Similarly, if the losses in question were losses incurred by Wolter (which is now the "parent" of the affiliated group) in pre-affiliation years, the losses could be carried forward onto the consolidated return regardless of Wolter's current income.

Both of these hypothetical situations would exempt the early net operating loss years from the definition of "separate return limitations year" and it is only those losses from separate return limitation years which cannot be carried forward to consolidated return years unless the corporation which incurred the losses has sufficient consolidated return income to offset them.

Wolter argues that the common parent rule should he construed to permit the carryover of River Hills' NOL's, since both companies were commonly controlled when the losses occurred. Underlying the common parent rule, appellant asserts, is a Congressional intent to make the use of NOL carryovers dependent upon the identity of the individuals involved rather than the form of the reorganization. Wolter asks this court to . . . make the tax consequences turn on the substance of the transaction . . . This is appropriate, Wolter continues, because the common parent rule is designed to permit the free use of loss carryovers when the party which suffered the past NOL's will be the same party which benefits from the NOL carryovers.

A.
* * *

The Commissioner and the taxpayer agree that Wolter was and is the common parent of the affiliated group. Appellant's position is that River Hills should receive the same advantageous tax treatment which is generally given to the common parent, i.e. exemption from separate return limitation year treatment. Significantly, this exemption is not always available to the common parent and is not given only to the common parent. It is from the exceptions to the favorable treatment generally accorded the common parent that Wolter extracts the policy that, by looking at the corporate law structure of the group, the separate return limitation year rules look beyond the corporate framework to the ownership of the corporations so as to permit use of a subsidiary's NOLs when the individuals who experienced the losses will reap the tax benefits from the carryover.

In support of its argument, taxpayer points to the fact that, under the Regulations, the common parent corporation's exclusion from the limitation on net operating loss carryforwards set forth in Section 1.1502-21(c) is itself subject to an exception in the case of a so-called "reverse acquisition." In a typical reverse acquisition in the loss carryover context, substantially all the assets or stock of a profit corporation are nominally acquired by a loss corporation in exchange for more than 50 percent of the latter's stock, so that control of the loss corporation has shifted to the shareholders of the profit corporation as they existed prior to the acquisition. The Regulations essentially treat the loss corporation as having been acquired, and under Section 1.1502-1(f)(3) of the Treasury Regulations, all taxable years of the loss corporation prior to the reverse acquisition are treated as separate return limitation years, notwithstanding its status as the common parent corporation of the new affiliated group consisting of it and the profit corporation. Conversely, the separate return years of the profit corporation prior to the acquisition are not treated, in general, as separate return limitation years. Accordingly, the net operating losses sustained by the loss corporation, but not the profit corporation, in its separate return years are subject to the carryover limitation contained in Section 1.1502-21(c). The purpose and effect of the reverse acquisition rules is to prevent trafficking in loss corporations. This is accomplished by redirecting the SRLY limitation to the ostensibly acquiring corporation. This "simple mechanical rule thwarts the attempts of those who would seek to present that the ailing David is trying to improve its financial strength by drawing on the earning power of Goliath." . . .

* * *

While a focus on the identity of the taxpayer can be viewed as a common thread running through the consolidated return Regulations, careful examination reveals that the Regulations are designed to prevent "trafficking" in loss corporations. As an example, the CRCO limitation is aimed at the acquisition of a loss group by the owners of a profitable corporation who then seek to apply the former's loss carryovers against the latter's income on a consolidated return.

The reverse acquisition Regulations reverse the substance of the acquisition for tax purposes so that acquisition by loss groups are limited by the relative size test of the rules to see which party to the acquisition is to be subject to the SRLY strictures of Reg. 1.1502-1(f). The Regulations also impede the acquisition of a corporation with "built-in" losses (such as depreciated stock in trade, plant or capital assets and debts that are about to become worthless) for the purpose of utilizing these losses to offset post-affiliation consolidated income attributable to other members of the group. Reg. 1.1502-15. The SRLY limitation at issue here is designed to discourage an affiliated group of corporations from acquiring a loss corporation merely for the NOL carryover. Basically, Reg. 1.1502-21 (c) refuses to allow commonly controlled corporations which chose to be treated as separate corporations prior to affiliation to undo retroactively that decision when it would benefit the group tax-wise. The consolidated return Regulations thus distinguish between affiliation and non-affiliation years. The principle of drawing the line between affiliated and non-affiliated years is appropriate because it allows greater flexibility and avoids the disadvantages of "trafficking in loss corporations. . . ."

* * *

To conclude that River Hills is entitled to an exemption from the SRLY restriction would require us to make a leap that we are unwilling to take. First, it would require an assumption that an exception to the SRLY rule for commonly controlled brother-sister corporations was inadvertently omitted from the consolidated return Regulations. Second, it would require us to overrule a legislative regulation so as to permit a deduction based only upon a generalized policy distilled from the Regulations and symbiotic Code provisions.

The decision of the Tax Court is *Affirmed.*

PROBLEM 23-5

X Corp. owns all of Y Corp. They have filed a consolidated return for the past nine years. X Corp. acquires Z Corp. in a type B reorganization at the beginning of year ten. Z Corp. has a NOL from prior years of $6. X, Y, and Z Corps. all use the calendar year. The shareholders of X owned all the stock of Z since it inception.

1) Does § 382 prevent Z's losses from being carried forward against the X-Y group's income in year ten?

2) Does the separate return limitation year rule of Reg. §§ 1.1502-1(f) and 1.1502-21(c) prohibit the offset described in "1)"?

3) Would the result in "2)" differ if Z was at all pertinent times an unconsolidated subsidiary of X?

4) Might § 269 preclude using Z's loss against the X-Y group's income?

PROBLEM 23-6

1) Sprawling Industries, Inc. (SII) has a seemingly endless array of subsidiaries with which it files a consolidated return. Which of the following corporations can be consolidated with SII?

    a.   A French auto-maker?

    b.   An S corporation?

    c.   A domestic corporation that makes hub caps. SII owns 90% of its common stock by vote but only 79% by value. Its name is Glitzy Hubs, Inc. (GHI).

    d.   Same as "(c)", but SII also owned all the preferred stock of the hub cap company (being 10% of the value of the equity of the sub), and the preferred stock, in addition to getting its normal dividend, is also entitled to dividends that amount to half of what the common stock dividends are?

    e.   Assuming SII and GHI can file consolidated returns, are they obligated to?

    f.   If they do file consolidated returns, must all members use the same tax year and accounting method?

    g.   Must all affiliated group members join in filing a consolidated return if the other members file such a return?

2) You are responsible for preparing SII's consolidated return. How would you handle the following transactions?

    a.   GHI, which correctly files a consolidated return with SII, manufactured 10,000 Dynaflow hubcaps at a cost of $50,000, all of which it sold to SII this year for $45,000 (an arm's-length price).

    b.   SII has an accounting subsidiary that provides accounting services for pay. GHI paid the accounting sub $90,000 for routine accounting assistance.

    c.   SII acquired all the stock of a small new subsidiary (TSub) in a tax-free B reorganization. TSub has operated at a loss since its inception. Can the SII group offset its group profits with TSub's loss carryforwards?

    d.   Same as "(c).", but TSub has always been profitable and the SII group has a history of losing money. Can the SII group's post-consolidation losses offset TSub's profits?

    e.   At the beginning of the year, SII had a basis of $1 million in its GHI stock. GH1 earned $900,000 of taxable income, but its E & P rose by only $850,000. What is SII's basis in the GHI stock?

    f.   What would its basis in GHI stock be if GHI also paid SII a dividend of $300,000?

g. SII has another subsidiary, Fast-Lube, Inc. (FLI), which has not done well. At the beginning of the year SII had a basis of $1 million in its FLI stock, but FLI lost $1.6 million this year (the E & P decline is the same as the operating loss). What is SII's basis in the FLI stock at year end? Need there be an excess loss account? If so, what would its amount be?

h. A year has passed, and SII sold the 10,000 hubcaps to an unrelated wholesaler for $48,000. What result, if any, to GHI and SII?

i. Assume SII only owns 80% of GHI, just enough to file a consolidated return. Will the consolidated return include 80% or 100% of GHI's taxable income?

Chapter 24

S CORPORATIONS: DEFINITION AND QUALIFICATIONS

A. INTRODUCTION

Most tax practitioners would tell you that an S corporation is basically an American corporation that makes an election to be taxed much like a partnership, with the result that S corporations are treated as conduits and that taxable income or loss of an S corporation, as well as the tax credits it generates, "pass through" the corporation and are subject to a single shareholder level tax. They will also tell you that the "S" stands for the subchapter of the Code that contains the specialized rules relating to these corporations. These statements are helpful in a general way, but dangerously misleading in their details, hence much of this chapter will concentrate on the areas of divergence from the supposedly simple "pure conduit" model that applies to partnerships.

The practitioner will point out that S corporations have the advantage of not being subject to the personal holding company tax or the tax on unreasonable accumulations, or the alternative minimum tax. § 1363(a). The practitioner might pause and point out that there is no guarantee that there would not be a significant state income or franchise tax, but many states have subchapter S elections available in their state income taxes.

The practitioner might even point out that the entity can use the cash method of accounting for taxation, unless it is a tax shelter as defined in § 448, and that his wealthy clients who act only as investors have been gratified to learn that profitable S corporations can generate passive income that can be used to offset passive losses under § 469. Taxpayers holding tax shelter investments have a great interest in "passive income generators" (PIGs) because a PIG can produce income that is absorbed by otherwise suspended passive activity losses and credits. This makes the S corporation extraordinary, as it lets a passive investor in an S corporation generate income that can sop up suspended losses arising out of tax shelter investments, something § 469 generally strives to prevent. Conversely, if the investor is passive and the S corporation loses money, § 469 applies and the investor's losses from the S corporation may be put on ice. If the investor becomes impatient and sells his stock, the sale frees up the suspended losses for deduction, and any losses on the stock sale may qualify for ordinary loss treatment under § 1244.

When top individual income tax rates are higher than corporate tax rates, it is common business strategy to run new businesses as an S corporation while it loses money, and then drop the election once the corporation operates in the black. Thus, a great many corporations owned by small groups of shareholders operate as S corporations. Some of them are mammoth enterprises.

The S corporation is a fairly recent arrival on the tax scene. In 1954, the Senate made a legislative initiative to allow small corporations to be taxed as partnerships, partly to eliminate the influence of taxes on the choice of business form. S. Rept. No. 1622, 83rd Cong., 2d Sess., 119 (1954). The initiative failed in 1954, but succeeded in 1958. The 1958 rationales included a desire to allow small business people to be taxed at their rate brackets rather than the frequently higher rates imposed on their corporations and to allow them to flow their losses through to their owners so that the owners could offset them against their personal income. S. Rept. No. 1983, 85th Cong., 2d Sess., 87 (1958).

There was yet another major revision in 1982, which eliminated many defects in the 1958 legislation, as a result of which the more general goal of equating the federal income taxation of S corporations with partnerships has largely been achieved. However, the S corporation is far from a pure conduit. It is a separate entity for a variety of purposes and makes almost all the tax elections that affect the preparation of its (information) tax return. (The shareholders elect only as to the treatment of certain mining exploration costs under § 617, and as to deducting or crediting of foreign taxes. § 1363(c)(2)). Like a partnership it pays its own excise and employment taxes. The limits on forming S Corporation's have gradually become more relaxed.

The primary differences between S corporations and partnerships are that, whereas partnership status for federal income tax purposes is readily achieved, one can only achieve S corporation status via an election procedure that is ringed with restrictions. Also, corporate liabilities are not included in a shareholder's basis in his or her S corporation stock, and special allocations are not a feature of S corporations. Moreover, a transferee of S corporation stock cannot modify his or her "inside basis" to reflect the value of its share of the entity's assets in order to take account of the disparity between the purchase price of the stock and the corporation's basis in its assets. Compare this to § 754, which allows a periodic realignment of inside and outside basis in a partnership. Worse, from the owner's perspective, S corporations that used to be C corporations may have to pay a specialized income tax on excessive passive investment income as well as a major tax on certain built-in gains that existed at the time of making the S election. These are discussed in detail later in the Chapter.

There are also two minor taxes that are merely alluded to here and never again. One is the tax from recomputing a prior-year investment tax credit (ITC), and the other is a LIFO (Last-In, First-Out accounting) recapture tax. *See* Reg. § 1.47-4(a)(1) for ITC recapture. The LIFO recapture amount is computed and included in the gross income of the corporation's last taxable year as a C corporation. § 1363(d)(1). In light of the purposes of this book, it is not worth looking up those Code sections.

B. ELIGIBILITY TO ELECT STATUS
Read § 1361.

Section 1361(a)(1) contains an easy generic rule:

> [T]he term "S corporation" means, with respect to any year, a small business corporation for which an election under section 1362(a) is in effect for such year.

In turn, subsection 1361(b) defines a small business corporation as a domestic (*i.e.*, U.S.) corporation that is not an ineligible corporation (more on that shortly) and that does not violate a series of standards. The concept of an ineligible corporation generally concerns the corporation's industry.

Section 1361(b)(2) excludes a financial institution that uses the reserve method of accounting for bad debts, an insurance company that is subject to tax under subchapter L of the Code, or a DISC (Domestic International Sales Corporation) or former DISC. The latter are export promotion companies that are all but defunct now.

1. SUBSIDARY CORPORATIONS
Read § 1361(a)-(b).

An S corporation cannot have a corporation as a shareholder, but it can certainly own stock in other corporations. However, an S corporation cannot file a consolidated return with another corporation. § 1504(b)(8). Section 1361(b)(3) extends a special opportunity to S corporations, allowing them to treat 100%-owned subsidiaries as if they were division of their S corporation parents. The stock must be of an electing "qualified subchapter S subsidiary" (QSSS), pronounced "KWISS", which is defined as any domestic corporation if: (1) 100% of the stock of the corporation is held by a parent S corporation, (2) if the corporation is not an ineligible corporation under section 1361(b)(2); and (3) if the S corporation parent elects (on Form 966) to treat the subsidiary S corporation as a "qualified subchapter S subsidiary."

The definition of a QSSS contemplates multiple tiers of subsidiaries. This means an S corporation may act as a holding company for a chain of qualified subsidiary corporations, or may form a structure of brother/sister subsidiaries for the S corporation. There is further flexibility in that the QSSS election need not be made for all subsidiaries eligible for QSSS treatment.

The implications of making the QSSS election include the following: (1) that all the assets, liabilities, and items of income, deduction, and credit of a QSSS must be treated as assets, liabilities, and items of income, deduction and credit of the parent S corporation; (2) transactions between the S corporation and the QSSS are disregarded for income/loss calculations; (3) debts issued by the QSSS to shareholders of the parent S corporation are treated as debt of the parent. § 1361(b)(3)(A)(ii). This can help support further loss deductions for shareholders under § 1366(d), discussed later. The election generally produces a deemed § 332 liquidation of the QSSS, with the parent taking over the QSSS' tax attributes tax-free. *See* P.L.R. 9801015 (Sept. 30, 1997).

2. ONE HUNDRED SHAREHOLDER LIMIT

Over the years the availability of the S corporation has gradually seen a progressive growth in the number of people who can be shareholders. Going over the 100 shareholder limit results in instantaneous termination of the Subchapter S election and therefore instant C corporation status. The same "sudden death rule" applies to any other event that violates the requirements for being a "small business corporation." § 1362(d)(2).

Defining "a shareholder" is not a cut-and-dried matter. When counting shareholders, the Code imposes the following rules, not because they are particularly clever, but because definitional clarification is needed.

- Count each beneficiary of a voting trust or of an electing small business trust as a shareholder.

- Treat the grantor of a grantor trust as the shareholder. Likewise, one treats a § 678 beneficiary as an owner. § 1361(c)(2)(A)(ii), (B)(i). This is consistent with the concept of ignoring the existence of these trusts for federal income tax purposes.

- Count a husband and wife, and their estates, as one shareholder even if they own stock separately. § 1361(c)(1)(A)(i).

- Combine family members and their estates and treat them as one shareholder. § 1361(c)(1). This is extraordinarily broad because, for example, it treats family beneficiaries of QSSTs and of ESBTs and certain foster children as "family members."

- Otherwise, count everyone who owns any stock, even if the stock is owned jointly with another person.

3. LIMITS ON TYPES OF SHAREHOLDERS

a. Nonresident Aliens

A nonresident alien is a noncitizen who is also not a resident of the United States. *See* § 7701(b) and Reg. § 1.871-2. An alien becomes a resident alien either by obtaining a so-called "green card," which confers formal admission to the U.S. as a resident, or by being present in the U.S. for a significant period of time. § 7701(b)(1)(A).

A nonresident alien cannot be a shareholder of an S corporation. § 1361(b)(1)(C). One strategy for dropping S corporation status in a hurry is to sell to just such a person. Conversely, one can avoid the problem by inserting language on the stock certificates to state that the charter or by-laws of the company treat such transfers (as well as other disqualifying transfers) as void. Naturally, the charter or by-laws should bear out the threat. No legislative history accompanies this discriminatory provision. Perhaps Congress thought that nonresident aliens could too easily avoid U.S. taxes on their share of the corporation's profits.

b. Trusts

(1) Trusts Other Than Qualified Subchapter S Trusts and Electing Small Business Trusts

The following domestic trusts, among a few others can be shareholders of an S corporation under § 1361(c)(2):

- A grantor trust may continue to be an S corporation shareholder of stock held by the trust when the owner died, but not for more than two years.

- A trust created primarily to exercise the voting power of stock transferred to it. Each beneficiary of the trust is treated as a shareholder.

- Any trust to which stock is transferred according to the terms of a will, but only for two years, beginning with the day the stock was transferred to the trust under the will. The estate of the person leaving the will is treated as the shareholder.

(2) Qualified Subchapter S Trusts (§ 1361(d))

The beneficiaries of so-called qualified Subchapter S trusts (QSSTs, pronounced like "twists") can elect to have their trusts qualify as shareholders. A qualified Subchapter S trust is a trust described in § 1361(d). Review the requirements on your own. It is an important provision. As you read it, you might want to imagine a closely-held S corporation, the stock of which has to date been owned by the founder, who has two minor children. Consider the power of the QSST as a tax planning device, given that it can enable the founder to shift an S corporation's profits to the QSSTs, thence to the children, with no need to make corporate distributions to cover the profits attributed, and taxed, to the children via their QSSTs. To avoid his children's wrath, the founder might exercise his power over the corporation to make sure the children will be distributed enough cash to cover the income taxes the QSSTs burden them with. Of course, the Kiddie tax of I.R.C. § 1(g) will limit the tax-reducing advantages of splitting income with minor children.

(3) Electing Small Business Trust § 1361(e)

The Electing Small Business Trust (ESBT) is yet another relatively recent addition to the population of legitimate owners of an S corporation. The term means any trust if the following three requirements are met:

1) Generally, the trust does not have as a beneficiary anyone other than an individual, an estate, or a charity;

2) No interest in the trust was acquired by purchase; and

3) The trustee elects ESBT status for the trust.

The stock of each S corporation held in trust constitutes a separate trust. §§ 641(c)(1) and (5). The trust cannot be a charitable remainder unitrust or charitable remainder annuity trust. § 1361(e)(l)(B). The ESBT is taxed as a separate taxpayer on its income and allows the trustee the power to distribute income from the trust in different proportions among the beneficiaries from year to year.

Unlike a QSST, an ESBT is not "invisible" for tax purposes. Instead, it is a true taxpayer taxable at top trust tax rates. Distributions come out tax-free to the beneficiary.

An ESBT is actually divided into the following two parts: (1) the part consisting of S corporation stock (the S portion taxable at top rates) and; (2) the rest of the assets of the trust, if any (the non-S portion). *See* § 641(c)(1)-(2). The S portion is taxed on income attributable to the S corporation stock held by the trust. § 641(c). Each of the ESBT's beneficiaries is treated as a separate shareholder for purposes of the 100 shareholder limit and the requirements for eligible shareholders, but the ESBT is the person taxed on the S corporation income.

The non-S portion of the ESBT is subject to the usual Subchapter J trust rules. For example, trust distributions that are not attributable to S corporation stock are taxed under the normal trust rules, which tax the beneficiary on amounts the trust deducted.

The S portion items are excluded in determining the distributable net income (DNI) of the entire trust. § 641(c)(3). Since the S portion items are not included in the computation of the ESBT's DNI, they are treated for purposes of determining the treatment of trust distributions the same way as any other item that does not enter into the DNI computation, such as capital gains and losses allocated to corpus.

c. Estates

Estates, including bankruptcy estates, can be shareholders. § 1361(b)(1)(B), (c)(3). A corporation's S election is not terminated because of the commencement of a bankruptcy case involving someone who is a shareholder in the corporation. The surviving spouse and the estate of the decedent count as one shareholder under § 1361(c)(1).

d. Charities

Section 501(c)(3) says charities and organizations exempt from taxation under § 501(a) can now be shareholders of an S corporation. §§ 1361(b)(l)(B), 1361(c)(6). Before this change, it was impossible to make a charitable contribution of S corporation stock without wrecking the S election. Although a charitable organization may hold S corporation stock, income attributable to the stock will be unrelated business taxable income (UBTI), which is taxed to the otherwise tax-exempt organization. § 512(e)(1).

PROBLEM 24-1

1) P is an S corporation that used to own 100% of a 'qualified subchapter S subsidiary' ("Sub"). P sold 25% of its Sub stock to an unrelated party on March 1 of this year. At that time, the assets of Sub had a basis of $100 and value of $120.

    a.   Does the sale terminate Sub's S election?

    b.   As of what date does Sub cease to be a QSSS? *See* § 1361(b)(3).

    c.   What is deemed to occur transactionally after a cessation of a QSSS election with respect to Sub?

    d.   Will there be any tax to P as a result of the stock sale, aside from gain or loss on the sale of the stock?

2) Which of the following attributes is unique to a qualified subchapter S trust (§ 1361(d)) or to an electing small business trust (§ 1361(e))? *See* Reg. § 1.1361-5(b)(3).

    a.   The trust may not accumulate income.

    b.   Distributions to a beneficiary are not taxable to a beneficiary because they have already been taxed to the trust.

    c.   The trust can "sprinkle" or "spray" trust income among beneficiaries.

    d.   A beneficiary is taxed directly on income earned by the trust.

3) Which of the following are inherently ineligible to elect to be taxed as an S corporation:

    a.   A bank using the reserve method of accounting.

    b.   A US ("domestic") corporation running a clothing store in France?

    c.   A domestic corporation that is 20% owned by a partnership consisting of individuals?

    d.   A foreign corporation owned by US individuals running a clothing store in New York?

    e.   Same as "(b)," but the store also owns all the stock of a Florida corporation that runs a clothing store in Palm Beach?

    f.   Same as "(b)," but the store is owned by a private college, which is a § 501(c)(3) organization? If the ownership is permissible, how would the college be taxed on its share of the profits? *See* § 1361(b)(1)(B), (c)(6) and § 512.

    g.   A domestic S corporation that owns 100% of the stock of a bank?

    h.   Same as "(g)." Is the parent able to make the "qualified Subchapter S subsidiary" election as to the bank? *See* § 1361(b)(2).

4. ONE CLASS OF STOCK

a. General Rule

One of the most troubling provisions is the so-called "one-class-of-stock" rule under § 1361(b)(1)(D). One class of stock generally means that the outstanding shares of the corporation must be identical with respect to the rights of the holders in the profits and in the assets of the corporation. Stock can have differences in voting rights and still be considered one class of stock. Regs. § 1.1361-1(l)(1). For example, one may have Class A voting stock owned by the adults and Class A nonvoting stock held by QSSTs for their children.

Authorized but unissued stock and treasury stock are not considered in determining if a corporation has more than one class of stock. Regs. § 1.1361-1(l)(1). The existence of outstanding options, warrants to acquire stock, or convertible debentures does not constitute a second class of stock. Once they are exercised into a novel class of stock, however, the risk of a second class becomes immediate and potentially catastrophic from a tax perspective.

Note the downside; if the corporation turns out to have had two classes of stock from the time it was formed, it is a C corporation *ab initio*. The following cases exemplify and explore some of the policies underlying the one-class-of-stock rule.

PAIGE v. UNITED STATES
580 F.2d 960 (9th Cir. 1978), *aff'g* 75-2 USTC P9587 (C.D. Cal. 1975)

SKOPIL, DISTRICT JUDGE:

Plaintiff-taxpayers appeal from the denial of their claim for a tax refund. The issue involved is whether taxpayers' corporation qualified for the subchapter S election provided in 26 U.S.C. § 1371 (1954). We hold that it did not . . . Tackmer made the subchapter S election in 1965. The government now contends that Tackmer Corporation had more than one class of stock.

Tackmer is a small California company that was first incorporated in 1965 When Tackmer first issued stock, it received two different kinds of consideration, Plaintiffs and another party assigned their rights to an exclusive license agreement in exchange for Tackmer stock ("property shareholders"). Eight other parties paid cash ("cash shareholders").

The Articles of Incorporation state that "No distinction shall exist between the shares of the corporation (or) the holders thereof." . . . The applicable California Corporation Code, § 304 (West 1949), stated that there could be no distinction between shares unless specified in the Articles.

Before Tackmer could issue any stock, it was required to obtain a permit from the California Department of Corporations. The California Corporation Code gave the Department authority to impose conditions on corporations for the protection of the public.[1] Pursuant to this authority the Department had a policy of imposing certain conditions on small corporations such as Tackmer which were capitalized with both cash and property that had an indeterminate value. The purpose of the conditions was to protect the shareholders who paid with cash from having their interests diluted by an over issue of stock to the shareholders who paid with property.

---

[1] Cal. Corp. Code § 25508 (West 1949) provided: "AUTHORITY TO IMPOSE CONDITIONS FOR PROTECTION OF PUBLIC. The commissioner may impose conditions requiring the deposit in escrow of securities . . . the waiver of assets and dividends by holders of promotional securities, and such other conditions as he deems reasonable and necessary or advisable for the protection of the securities." This section was repealed by 1968 Cal. Stat. c. 88 p. 243, § 1 (1969). Former § 25508 is similar to Cal. Corp. Code § 25141 (West 1977).

The conditions imposed by the Department of Corporations were as follows:

The stock had to be deposited in escrow and could not be sold without the Department's consent;

a) If the company defaulted on dividend payments for two years, the cash shareholders would have irrevocable power of attorney to vote the property shareholders' shares for the board of directors;

b) On dissolution, the property shareholders had to waive their rights to the distribution of assets until the cash shareholders had received the full amount of their purchase price plus any unpaid accumulated dividends at 5% per year;

c) The property shareholders had to waive their rights to any dividends until the cash shareholders annually received cumulative dividends equal to 5% of the purchase price per share;

d) The conditions were to remain in effect until the shares were released from escrow . . . The conditions were in effect from 1965 to 1970.

The property shareholders signed an agreement with the company stating that they would abide by the conditions. The taxpayers admit that the conditions could have been waived by the cash shareholders . . . Notwithstanding the conditions, the differences between the two kinds of shareholders were never taken into account and all dividends were distributed on a pro rata basis.

A corporation must meet six requirements in order to qualify for subchapter S tax treatment. The applicable statute reads: "For purposes of . . . subchapter [S, a qualifying corporation is] a domestic corporation which is not a member of an affiliated group . . . and which does not "(1) have more than [today, 100] shareholders"; (2) have as a shareholder a person (other than an estate) who is not an individual; (3) "have a nonresident alien as a shareholder"; and "(4) have more than one class of stock." 26 U.S.C. § 1371 (1954) . . .

The taxpayers filed a timely joint tax return in 1970 . . . On January 14, 1973, the Commissioner of Internal Revenue . . . assessed additional taxes of $244.64 plus $37.30 interest (total: $281.94). The reason stated for the disallowance was that the conditions imposed by the California Department of Corporations created more than one class of stock, disqualifying Tackmer for subchapter S treatment.

* * *

The taxpayers contend that because the Articles and state law authorized only one class of stock, there can be only one class for subchapter S purposes. We hold, however, that the interpretation of subchapter S qualifications is a federal question. *Kean v. Commissioner of Internal Revenue,* 469 F.2d 1183 (9th Cir. 1972).

Treas. Reg. § 1.1371-1(g) provides that "If the outstanding shares of stock of the corporation are not identical with respect to the rights and interests which they convey in the control, profits, and assets of the corporation, then the corporation is considered to have more than one class of stock." . . . The cash shareholders had preferred rights over property shareholders, notwithstanding that the cash shareholders chose not to exercise those rights. The possibility of the exercise of differing rights is enough to disqualify a corporation for subchapter S tax treatment.

Taxpayers' assertion that Tackmer in fact made all distributions on a pro rata basis is irrelevant. A corporation's qualifications for subchapter S status is judged at the date of election. *See, Barnes Motor & Parts Co. v. United States,* 309 F. Supp. 298 (E.D.N.C. 1970). The court may not consider Tackmer's actual distributions after its election. The language in the statute is clear. Tax planners must be able to assume that the court will give it its plain meaning.

482

Taxpayers assert that Treas. Reg. § 1.1371-1(g) has been overturned as applied to them by *Parker Oil Company*, 58 T.C. 985 (1972) and the Service's acquiescence in Rev. Rul. 73-611, 1973-2 C.B. 312. Taxpayers contend that the Regulation was found to be inconsistent with the basic purpose of the requirement that there be one class of stock. We disagree. *Parker Oil* involved only voting rights arising out of shareholder agreements. It did not involve distributions from the corporations. Control of distributions is at the heart of the one class of stock requirement. This aspect of Treas. Reg. § 1.1371-1(g) was untouched by *Parker Oil*.

There is a strong policy behind the requirement that subchapter S corporations have only one class of stock. The corporations themselves pay no corporate income tax. The shareholders pay individual income tax on a pro rata share of all corporate income, regardless of whether any money or property has actually been distributed to the shareholder. If the statute allowed more than one class of stock, complicated allocation problems could arise . . . This would introduce substantial complexity in the administration of subchapter S. It was this type of potential difficulty which Congress sought to avoid by limiting subchapter S corporations to one class of stock.

We agree with the taxpayers that the purpose of subchapter S is to benefit small corporations such as the one here. It is unfortunate that a requirement of state law has caused a result that no one intended. However, the taxpayers' subjective intent to create one class of stock cannot be allowed to override statutory requirements. *Cf. Gamman v. Commissioner of Internal Revenue*, 46 T.C. 1 (1966). Congress has set forth specific objective requirements for subchapter S qualification, and we must follow the mandate of the statute.

We affirm.

PORTAGE PLASTICS CO. v. UNITED STATES
486 F.2d 632 (7th Cir. 1973)

CUMMINGS, CIRCUIT JUDGE.

This appeal presents the question whether plaintiff qualified as a small business corporation within the meaning of Section 1371(a) of the Internal Revenue Code, thus supporting its timely elections under Section 1372(a) not to be subject to corporate income taxes for the fiscal years 1961, 1962 and 1963. The district court upheld plaintiffs qualification (301 F. Supp. 684), but a panel of this Court reversed by divided vote (470 F.2d 308). On en banc consideration, we now affirm the district court's refund judgment.

The facts were largely stipulated, but other facts were found after a bench trial. There is no dispute as to the facts, and only the essential ones reflected in the testimony or found by the district court will be stated in this opinion.

Plaintiff, a plastics manufacturer, is a Wisconsin corporation with its principal place of business in Portage, Wisconsin. It adopted the accrual method of accounting, with its fiscal year ending May 31. It was organized on June 1, 1957, and its Articles of Incorporation authorized 1,000 shares of common stock with a par value of $10 per share. Effective January 23, 1962, the Articles were amended to increase the authorized shares to 20,000 shares of common stock of the same par value. No other class of common stock was authorized.

During the first of the fiscal years in question, plaintiffs stockholders were William G. Hamilton, Ann Hamilton Kirk, Eugene Palmbach and William Hamilton, Jr., and in the latter two fiscal years, Armand Cimaroli was an additional stockholder.

According to the testimony of the secretary-treasurer of plaintiff, its organizers "did not want to sacrifice any of the equity of the corporation" to obtain working capital but found a very unfavorable reception from banks in regard to loans. As a result, on June 1, 1957, William G. Hamilton's mother, Mrs. Elizabeth Berst, and his aunt, Miss Sara Garnett, agreed to advance the plaintiff $12,500 each and in exchange received standard business note forms. These instruments obligated plaintiff to pay Mrs. Berst and Miss Garnett $12,500 apiece on June 1, 1962, in Portage, Wisconsin, and contained the following provision for "Interest: 5% of the net profit before taxes." At the time of issuance, the parties verbally agreed that on June 1, 1962, either or both of the ladies could renew the June 1, 1957 instruments at their request for a similar 5-year period. Both ladies exercised their renewal options, and accordingly, on June 1, 1962, two identical renewal instruments were executed. In June of 1963, Mrs. Berst and Miss Garnett exchanged those instruments for 245 shares each of common stock of plaintiff.

There was no oral or written agreement for the repayment of the $25,000 advanced by the ladies in the event of default in payment of the stipulated "interest." Plaintiff did not establish a sinking fund to provide for the retirement of the obligations within the time periods provided.

Mrs. Berst and Miss Garnett executed separate agreements in June 1959, subordinating for a year all their rights pertaining to the instruments in favor of the City Bank of Portage, Wisconsin, a lender to plaintiff. On February 8 and March 26, 1962, respectively, they agreed to subordinate their rights in the instruments in favor of the First National Bank of Chicago, another lender to plaintiff.

The original and renewal instruments were recorded as Notes Payable on the books and records of the corporation and were shown as Long-Term Debt and as Notes Payable on the annual audit reports prepared by its certified public accountants and on financial statements furnished to banks and other creditors. The accrual and payment of the amounts denoted as "interest" in the instruments were recorded on the books and records of the corporation in the Accrued Interest Payable account. The payments to each lady were as follows: $957.87 in 1959; $4,916.05 in 1960; $4,737.31 in 1961; $3,323.79 in 1962; and $2,245.03 in 1963. These payments reflected the unexpectedly fast growth of the corporation.

In the first year of operation, plaintiff lost $13,485.08, but thereafter earned substantial sums in each fiscal year. During the years in question, plaintiff had a relatively high debt to equity ratio because it found it necessary to borrow funds to fulfill the increasing needs for capital engendered by rapid expansion. No actual distributions were made with respect to the common stock until fiscal year 1962, when $40,000 was distributed, and in fiscal year 1963, when $36,000 was distributed. The primary reason for such distributions was to enable the shareholders to meet their tax obligations brought about as a result of plaintiff's timely election to be taxed pursuant to the provisions of Subchapter S of the Internal Revenue Code for the fiscal years ending in 1961, 1962 and 1963.

The Commissioner of Internal Revenue determined that plaintiff was ineligible to make the statutory election not to be subject to corporate income taxes for these three fiscal years on the ground that it had more than one class of stock and was therefore not a small business corporation as defined in Subchapter S. Accordingly, in January 1965, the Commissioner first notified plaintiff that he was claiming deficiencies in the amount of what he decided was the proper corporate income tax for the years 1961 through 1963. Plaintiff paid the deficiencies asserted and thereafter sued to recover income taxes and statutory interest in the amount of $164,733.13, plus interest. The district court held that plaintiff was entitled to such a refund because it "qualified as a small business corporation within the meaning of Section 1371(a) so as to be eligible to elect under Section 1372(a) not to be subject to corporate income taxes for its fiscal years 1961, 1962 and 1963." 301 F. Supp. at 694. We affirm. Section 1371(a) of the Internal Revenue Code provides as follows:

> "Small business corporation. – For purposes of this subchapter, the term "small business corporation" means a domestic corporation which is not a member of an affiliated group (as defined in section 1504) and which does not – (1) have more than [100] shareholders; (2) have as a shareholder a person

(other than an estate) who is not an individual; (3) have a nonresident alien as a shareholder; and (4) have more than one class of stock. . . ."

It is conceded that plaintiff met the first three requirements of the statute, but the Commissioner contends that the instruments issued to Mrs. Berst and Miss Garnett in exchange for their advances of $12,500 apiece were contributions to plaintiffs capital rather than loans and constituted a second class of stock, thus disqualifying plaintiff as a small business corporation. On the other hand, plaintiff contends that the advances were loans, but in any event did not constitute another class of stock within the meaning of the statute.

Applying the traditional tests of the thin capitalization doctrine, the district court held that the advances in question constituted contributions to capital. The court was impressed by the fact that the rate of interest was fixed at a percentage of net profits, thus placing the risks of the venture upon Mrs. Berst and Miss Garnett. The court was also impressed by the following factors: on two occasions their rights under the instruments were subordinated to bank loans; plaintiff had a comparatively high ratio of debt to equity; there was no provision for acceleration of payment of principal in case of default in interest payments; and plaintiffs plastics business had been a marginal operation, rendering its anticipated returns speculative in nature. In the aggregate, these factors were found clearly to outweigh those suggesting that the advances constituted loans. The entire panel of this Court agreed with the district court's conclusion that the advances were contributions to capital rather than loans under the criteria of the thin capitalization doctrine, but that decision is unnecessary to review here. The point at issue is whether the criteria heretofore developed to determine the debt versus equity question in other contexts are determinative of the question whether another "class of stock" exists within the meaning of Section 1371(a)(4).

Both in the district court and here, the Government relied on Treasury Regulation § 1.1371-1(g), which provides in pertinent part:

"Obligations which purport to represent debt but which actually represent equity capital will generally constitute a second class of stock. However, if such purported debt obligations are owned solely by the owners of the nominal stock of the corporation in substantially the same proportion as they own such nominal stock, such purported debt obligations will be treated as contributions to capital rather than a second class of stock." T.D. 6904, 1967-1 Cum. Bull. 219).

The Government of course points to the inapplicability of the second sentence of the Regulation because Mrs. Berst and Miss Garnett were then not stockholders of the plaintiff corporation, so that the proportionality exception of the Regulation was inapplicable. It is the Government's position that the tests of the thin capitalization doctrine determine the existence of a second class of stock if the instruments in question do not come within the exception of the Regulation's second sentence. The underlying argument does little more than postulate the ubiquitous utility of those tests. Then the Government simply states: "Every instrument representing an advance to a corporation is either stock or debt. There is no such thing as non-stock equity. Corporate obligations that have been recharacterized as equity, are preferred stock for tax purposes."

While holding that these advances constituted contributions to capital rather than loans, the district court concluded that "it does not appear that the traditional debt-equity tests applied in other areas of tax litigation are relevant to the general purpose of Subchapter S or to the two conceivable purposes of the one class of stock requirement . . . " (301 F. Supp. at 692). Consequently, the court analyzed the instruments in question in the light of the statutory purposes to ascertain whether they would be served by a conclusion that they constituted a second class of stock, disqualifying plaintiff from eligibility for Subchapter S status. The judge's perceptive analysis led him to conclude: " . . . that the general purpose of Subchapter S to permit small businesses to select a form of organization without regard to tax consequences would be served by a conclusion that plaintiff was eligible to elect to be taxed as a small business corporation during the years in question. It further appears that the purposes of the one class of stock requirement, to avoid administrative complexities and to limit the advantages of Subchapter S status to small corporations, would not be served by a conclusion that the instruments in question constituted a second class of stock within the meaning of § 1371(a)(4)." (301 F. Supp. at 694).

In the panel's prior opinion herein, the majority was of the view that the criteria heretofore developed to determine the debt versus equity question under the thin capitalization doctrine and used by the district court to conclude that the advances by Mrs. Berst and Miss Garnett were contributions to capital rather than loans were determinative of the existence of a second class of stock. Thus the majority upheld the validity of Treasury Regulation § 1.1371-1(g) and held that there under, once the district court had concluded the advances were contributions to capital, that ipso facto meant they constituted a class of stock, the proportionality exception being inapplicable.

For the reasons detailed in the dissenting opinion . . . , incorporated herein by reference, we conclude that the traditional thin capitalization doctrine tests for determining whether a purported loan should be treated as an equity contribution in order to prevent improper tax avoidance in other contexts are not suitable for determining whether a purported loan constitutes a second class of stock within the meaning of Section 1371(a)(4).[2]

As can best be divined, the purpose of the single class of stock requirement was none other than to avoid the administrative complexity in the allocation of income which would result with more than one class of stock when preferred dividends were paid in excess of current earnings from undistributed but taxed prior earnings.[3] Because the shareholders of a Subchapter S corporation are pro rata taxed on the corporation's undistributed taxable income for any year, if in a subsequent year dividends in excess of current earnings are distributed to preferred shareholders, the common stockholders will have already been taxed on the excess going to the preferred shareholders. But under the existing provisions of the Code, the common shareholders could only receive a capital loss benefit for the previously taxed income which they did not receive. Section 1376(a). Consequently, some sort of refund mechanism would be necessary to prevent the inequity to the common shareholders, and this is the administrative problem Congress evidently sought to avoid through the single class of stock requirement.

Although the district court accurately pointed out that this problem could not occur in the instant case because "interest" on the advances was to be paid only out of net profits before taxes, it further appears that the problem is not encountered in any case so long as interest is treated as interest. This is because shareholders are permitted a deduction for the excess of interest payments over earnings in any year, and hence they are adequately compensated for having been previously taxed on the earnings out of which interest payments may later be made.[4]

---

[2] As emphasized in the prior dissenting opinion. this conclusion in no way forecloses use of the thin capitalization doctrine tests to recharacterize purported debt as equity where appropriate to deny particular tax benefits wrongfully taken in those cases where tax avoidance through the use of debt is still available in the Subchapter S context and in those cases where it is peculiarly available within the confines of Subchapter S. 470 F.2d at 318 and n. p.9.

[3] 12 S. Rep. No. 1622, 83d Cong., 2d Sess. 453-454 (1954).

[4] Whatever problems that exist with "leakage" of previously taxed but undistributed earnings, when a shareholder transfers stock before interest is paid out of them in a year giving rise to a net operating loss, these problems are inherent in the provisions of Subchapter S and exist regardless of the nature of the loan. *See* Note. 41 N.Y.U. L. Rev. 1012, 1018-1019 (1966); Note, 67 Colum L. Rev. 494, 513-514 (1967).

26 U.S.C. § 1374(a), (d)(1); see 26 U.S.C. § 1376(b). Indeed, assuming that the general problem of allocation of earnings and losses between various classes of stock was a Congressional concern in enacting the single class of stock requirement, the district court recognized that the problem arises only if the interest payments are first recharacterized as dividends . . . The same principle applies to the particular administrative problem which occurs when dividends are paid to preferred shareholders in excess of current earnings – it is a problem only if the payments are recharacterized as dividends in the first place. The Government concedes as much when it states,

> "Once the notes have been recharacterized as equity, they present the same tax accounting problems with respect to the Subchapter S treatment of the corporation's undistributed taxable income and net operating loss as are presented by preferred stock." (Principal appellate brief for the United States, p. 13.)

The earlier dissenting opinion in this cause and the Fifth Circuit's opinion in *Shores Realty, supra*, have demonstrated that just because the purported loans come out on the capital contribution end on the thin capitalization test scale is not a sufficient reason to make that initial recharacterization. In enacting the single class of stock requirement, there is no evidence of a Congressional design to ensure that what is debt for corporate purposes be insulated from the risks of the business venture to such an extent that the doctrine's tests would not recharacterize it as equity if used for tax avoidance. And generally, in enacting Subchapter S, Congress has evinced no concern with the manner in which a small business corporation is capitalized in terms of how the contributors furnish money or property to the corporation. Quite the contrary, for the primary policy underlying the enactment of Subchapter S is "to permit businesses to select the form of business organization desired without the necessity of taking into account major differences in tax consequences."[5] Moreover, in seeking to approximate partnership tax treatment, it is difficult to understand why Congress would view differentiation among participants in the venture as to the form and extent of their participation as inherently bad from an economic policy standpoint.

The Government argues that if the taxpayer's denomination of the advances is to control, the corporation can avoid the single class of stock requirement by simply attaching a label of debt to any instruments different from the common stock of the corporation. But this argument is nothing else than a contention that a corporation should not be able to secure Subchapter S treatment through a sham in a scheme of improper tax avoidance. Assuming the advantage of Subchapter S election itself can properly be considered improper tax avoidance, this case hardly fits the Government's hypothetical. It does not exemplify an instance of masquerading instruments as debt in order to evade any qualification requirement for Subchapter S status. The capital structure of the plaintiff was established and its common stock and the instruments in question were issued in 1957 when Subchapter S did not exist. Even considering Mrs. Berst and Miss Garnett as shareholders, plaintiff would have had no more than seven shareholders during any of the taxable years in question, would not have had a corporation, trust, or partnership as a shareholder, and would have had no alien shareholders. § 1371(a)(1)-(3). The existence of a business purpose for the issuance of debt instruments to Mrs. Berst and Miss Garnett is not questioned. And, simply stated, the Commissioner has never contended that the capital structure of the plaintiff was adopted with a view toward taking advantage of Subchapter S by evading the requirements for qualification thereunder.

Furthermore, it ill suits the Government to argue that the tests of the thin capitalization doctrine are justified to prevent the above, hypothetical "evasion" because those tests were

---

[5] S. Rep. No. 1983, 85th Cong., 2d Sess. 87 (1958), U.S. Code Cong. & Admin. News 1958, p 4791; see
    S. Rep. No. 830, 88th Cong., 2d Sess. 146 (1964), U.S. Code Cong. & Admin. News 1964 p. 1313.

designed to prevent tax avoidance through the use of debt in contexts where treatment as debt would subvert underlying congressional policy to afford benefits for debt when "the funds were advanced with reasonable expectations of repayment regardless of the success of the venture . . . [and were not] placed at the risk of the business . . . " *Gilbert v. Commissioner*, 248 F.2d 399, 406 (2d Cir. 1957). The Government does not have a comparable economic policy underlying its desire to thwart supposed spurious labeling through use of the thin capitalization doctrine tests. Apparently the Government is concerned solely with a nefarious tax avoidance motive in denominating certain advances as debt, but if that is a justifiable concern, it would seem only logical to attack the problem directly, instead of through the blunderbuss application of the thin capitalization doctrine tests. Moreover, it seems that Treasury Regulation § 1.1371-1(g) cannot be justified on the Government's argument, since that Regulation would apparently allow a corporation seeking to qualify for or retain Subchapter S status deliberately to put a label of debt on instruments that otherwise would have been denominated preferred stock in order to evade the single class of stock requirement – so long as the purported debt obligations were held by the shareholders in substantially the same proportion that they owned the nominal stock.

Finally, it is unnecessary to decide whether the advances in question were properly recharacterized as equity contributions under the tests of the thin capitalization doctrine, for in determining whether the instruments held by these ladies constituted a second class of stock, there is no occasion to utilize those tests. Even if they constituted contributions to capital according to those criteria, the Commissioner has not persuaded us that they must be considered as a second class of stock within the meaning of the statute. To the extent that Treasury Regulation 1.1371-1(g) calls for a contrary result, it is arbitrary and beyond the power of the Commissioner.

Affirmed.

b. Straight Debt Safe Harbor

As we have seen, the big problem with issuing debt is the perpetual risk that the IRS might attempt to reclassify debt as equity, thereby potentially creating a prohibited second class of stock. There is a special safe harbor rule for so-called "straight debt," which ensures that even if such debt is found to be equity, it will not be a second class of stock. § 1361(c)(5).

"Straight debt" means any written unconditional promise to pay a fixed amount on demand or on a specific date, with three special features. First, the interest rate, and interest payment dates are not contingent on profits, the borrower's discretion, or similar factors. Second, the debt cannot be converted directly or indirectly into stock. Third, the creditor must be an individual, estate, or trust eligible to hold stock in an S corporation or a person actively and regularly engaged in lending money. *See* § 1361(c)(5)(B).

This means that a simple bank loan is inside the safe harbor and is unlikely to make trouble as long as it is "plain vanilla" debt. On the other hand, in the event that the debt provided by a bank turns out to be equity, the S election would fail because of the existence of a corporate shareholder.

c. Treasury Views on Debt and Hybrid Instruments

The IRS and practitioners are persistently troubled by the one-class-of-stock rule. From the taxpayer's point of view, the provision causes needless restrictions on the company's ability to finance itself creatively. As you know already, from the Treasury Department's point of view, a relaxation of the rules would lead to complexity. S. Rep. No. 1622, 83d Cong. 2d Sess. 453 (1954). The following Notice of Proposed Rule Making appeared in the Federal Register in mid-1991 as an attempt to calm down a hornet's nest of angry reactions of practitioners to a previous set of proposed Regulations on the second-class-of-stock issue. 26 C.F.R. 1, [PS-4-731], R1N 1545-AC37. 56 Fed. Reg. 38,391 (August 13, 1991). What follows is an edited form of the notice of proposed Regulations and some comments, set off in brackets, as to how the much more pro-taxpayer final (November 1992) Regulations came out:

Explanation of Provisions

General Rules

Under the proposed Regulations, a corporation is treated as having only one class of stock if all outstanding shares of stock of the corporation confer identical rights to distribution and liquidation proceeds and if the corporation has not issued any instrument or obligation, or entered into any arrangement, that is treated as a second class of stock.

The determination of whether all outstanding shares of stock confer identical rights to distribution and liquidation proceeds is based on the corporate charter, articles of incorporation, bylaws, applicable State law, and any binding agreements relating to distribution or liquidation proceeds (collectively, the "governing provisions"). It is the rights conferred by the governing provisions that are taken into account in determining whether the corporation has more than one class of stock. A . . . commercial contractual arrangement such as a lease, employment agreement, or loan agreement is not a "binding agreement relating to distribution and liquidation proceeds" and thus is not a governing provision, unless such an agreement is entered into [with a principal purpose] to circumvent the one class of stock requirement of § 1361(b)(1)(D) and the proposed Regulations.

Although a corporation is not treated as having more than one class of stock if the governing provisions provide for identical distribution and liquidation rights, any distributions (including actual, constructive, or deemed distributions) that differ in timing or amount are to be given appropriate tax effect in accordance with the facts and circumstances. For example, a payment of excessive compensation may be recharacterized as a distribution by the corporation for which no deduction is allowed; however, neither the payment nor the distribution created by the recharacterization results in a second class of stock. Similarly, a distribution may be recharacterized in whole or in part as deductible compensation (on which FICA and FUTA taxes may be due), but any difference in distribution rights resulting from such a recharacterization will not result in a second class of stock.

Exceptions to General Rules

The proposed Regulations provide that certain types of state laws and binding agreements are disregarded in determining whether all of a corporation's outstanding shares of stock confer identical rights to distribution and liquidation proceeds. State laws that require a corporation to pay or withhold state income taxes on behalf of some or all of the corporation's shareholders are disregarded, provided that, when the constructive distributions resulting from the payment or withholding of taxes by the corporation are taken into account, the outstanding shares confer identical rights to the distribution and liquidation proceeds. The difference in timing between the constructive distributions and the actual distributions to the other shareholders does not create a second class of stock.

Agreements to redeem or purchase stock at the time of death, disability, [divorce] or termination of employment are disregarded in determining whether a corporation's outstanding shares of stock confer identical distribution and liquidation rights (regardless of the stock price or other terms of the agreement). In addition, bona fide buy-sell agreements among shareholders, agreements to restrict the transferability of stock, and certain redemption agreements are disregarded in determining whether a corporation's outstanding shares of stock confer identical

489

distribution and liquidation rights unless (i) the agreement is entered into to circumvent the one class of stock requirement of § 1361(b)(1)(D) and the proposed Regulations and (ii) the agreement establishes a redemption or purchase price that, at the time the agreement is entered into, is significantly in excess of or below the fair market value of the stock. Under the proposed Regulations, agreements described in the preceding sentence that provide for the purchase or redemption of stock at book value or at a price between fair market value and book value are disregarded.

[The Regulations generally treat buy-sell agreements, and options and the like as not a second class of stock, but that if these arrangements (1) constitute equity or otherwise result in the holder being treated as the stock owner under general federal tax principles and (2) are created for the purpose of circumventing the one-class-of-stock requirement, they will result in a second class of stock, except in certain safe harbor situations. [Reg. § 1.1361-(l)(4)(ii).]

The proposed Regulations also address situations in which there has been a change of stock ownership and the corporation determines the amount of its post-change distributions to its shareholders based on the allocation of income in the immediately preceding year. Agreements that provide for distributions in this manner do not result in a second class of stock. If distributions pursuant to the agreement are not made within a reasonable time after the close of the taxable year in which the ownership change occurs, however, the distributions may be recharacterized depending on the facts and circumstances.

Shares Taken into Account

Under the proposed Regulations, all outstanding shares of stock are taken into account in determining whether a corporation has a second class of stock. The proposed Regulations provide that, for purposes of subchapter S stock that is substantially nonvested within the meaning of § 1.83-3(b) is not treated as outstanding stock unless the holder makes an election with respect to the stock under § 83(b). Substantially nonvested stock with respect to which an election under § 83(b) has been made, however, is taken into account in determining whether a corporation has a second class of stock. Such stock is not treated as a second class of stock if the stock confers rights to distribution and liquidation proceeds that are identical to rights conferred by the other outstanding shares of stock . . .

Rules Relating to Debt Obligations, Call Options, and Similar Instruments In General

Under the proposed Regulations, instruments, other obligations, or arrangements may be treated as a class of stock in certain circumstances. The proposed Regulations provide a number of safe harbors or exceptions for certain ordinary business arrangements entered into by S corporations and their shareholders.

Obligations Designated as Debt

The proposed Regulations generally provide that an obligation (whether or not designated as debt) is not treated as a second class of stock unless two conditions are met: (1) the obligation constitutes equity or otherwise results in the holder being treated as the owner of stock under general principles of Federal tax law, and (2) the obligation is used to contravene the rights conferred by the corporation's outstanding stock with regard to distribution or' liquidation proceeds or to contravene the limitation on eligible shareholders contained in this subchapter. This rule is consistent with case law holding that purported debt which would ordinarily be recharacterized as equity does not always constitute a second class of stock for purposes of subchapter S.

[Convertible debt is a second class of stock if (1) it would be treated as a second class of stock under the general rules relating to an instrument, obligation, or arrangement being treated as equity under general principles or (2) it is essentially equivalent to a call option that is treated as a second class of stock under the rules applicable to call options. [Reg. § 1.1361-(l)(4)(iv).]

Certain Safe Harbors for Obligations Designated as Debt

The proposed Regulations also set forth certain safe harbors for obligations issued by a corporation. First, unwritten advances from a shareholder that do not exceed $10,000 in the aggregate at any time, are treated as debt by the parties, and are expected to be repaid within a reasonable time are not treated as a second class of stock [for that year], even if the advances are considered equity under general principles of Federal tax law. Second, proportionately-held obligations are not treated as a second class of stock. Proportionately-held obligations are any class of obligations that are considered equity under general principles of Federal tax law, but are owned solely by the owners of, and in the same proportion as, the outstanding stock of the corporation. Obligations owned by the sole shareholder of a corporation are always held proportionately to the corporation's outstanding stock.

The failure of an obligation to meet either of these safe harbors will not necessarily result in a second class of stock. As stated above, an unwritten advance or another obligation will not be treated as a second class of stock unless it is considered equity under general principles of Federal tax law and is used to contravene the rights conferred by the outstanding stock or the limitation on eligible shareholders.

Safe Harbor for Call Options

The proposed Regulations also provide that a call option (or similar instrument) is not treated as a second class of stock unless, taking into account all the facts and circumstances, the call option is substantially certain to be exercised and has a strike price substantially below the fair market value of the underlying stock (*See* Reg. § 1.1361-1(1)(4)(iii)(C) for a description of "substantially below fair market value") on the date that the call option is issued, transferred [by an eligible shareholder] to a person who is not an eligible shareholder, or materially modified. For purposes of this rule, if an option is issued in connection with a loan and the time period in which the option may be exercised is extended in connection with (and consistent with) a modification of that loan, the extension of the time period in which the option may be exercised is not a material modification. The determination of whether an option is substantially certain to be exercised takes into account not only the likelihood that the holder may exercise the option, but also the likelihood that a subsequent transferee may exercise the option. For example, a corporate holder may be unlikely (or unable) to exercise an option, but the option would still be substantially certain to be exercised if it could be transferred to an individual who would be substantially certain to exercise the option. A call option does not have a strike price substantially below fair market value if the price at the time of exercise cannot, pursuant to the terms of the instrument, be substantially below the fair market value of the underlying stock at that time.

If a convertible debt instrument embodies rights equivalent to those of a call option, it is evaluated both as debt and as a call option under the proposed Regulations.

Exceptions for Certain Call Options

[A call option, warrant, or similar instrument issued by a corporation is generally a second class of stock if the call option is substantially certain to be exercised and has a strike price substantially below the fair market value of the underlying stock on the date of issue, transfer, or material modification of the option. Reg. § 1.1361-(l)(4)(iii)(A).]

The proposed Regulations offer two exceptions for call options. First, a call option is not treated as a second class of stock if it is issued by a corporation to a person that is actively and regularly engaged in the business of lending and is issued in connection with a loan to the corporation that is commercially reasonable. [A transfer of a call option from one lender to another, along with the loan, qualifies for the lender exemption.] Second, a call option that is issued to an individual who is an employee or an independent contactor in connection with the performance of services [for the corporation of a related corporation] (and that is not excessive by reference a services performed) is not treated as a second class of stock if the call option is nontransferable within the meaning of § 1.83-3(d) and the call option does not have a readily ascertainable fair market value as defined in § 1.83-7(b) at the time the option is issued. If the call option becomes transferable, however, the exception ceases to apply. In this event, the option is tested under the general option rule if and when it is transferred to a person who is not an eligible shareholder or is materially modified.

5. ELECTION PROCEDURE
Read § 1362(a)-(c).

a. Effect of Election

The S election is not a taxable event to the corporation making the election, except for the comparatively trivial LIFO and ITC recapture taxes mentioned earlier on. By the way, at times legislation has been proposed to make the S election a (taxable) constructive liquidation of the preceding C corporation followed by a nontaxable reincorporation, but these proposals have not become the law. Accordingly, all the attributes of a C corporation that existed prior to the election continue after the election. The big exception is that net operating losses of the C corporation are suspended and cannot be used again until the corporation reverts to C corporation status. § 1363(b)(2).

b. Shareholder Consents For Obtaining S Corporation Status

The corporation's election of S corporation status is valid only if all shareholders consent to the election. The process of gathering up the consents is much simplified by IRS Form 2553, which puts the consent and election on the same page. *See* Form 2553, which is in the appendices. The difficulty is timely filing. An election made during the first 2 ½ months of the tax year can be effective for the full year in which it was made. However, if the consent is filed after the beginning of the year for which it is to be effective, all shareholders in the corporation who held stock on any day in the election year, but before the election is made, must also consent, no matter where they might reside at the moment. Reg. § 1.1362-6(b)(3)(i). This puts tax advisors in the position of warning clients teetering on the brink of making an S election against exotic travel by any of the shareholders, including those who sold their stock early in the year. In addition, the entity itself must have been a "small business corporation" for the part of the year preceding the election. § 1362(b)(2). The corporation's S election is invalid if any consent is filed late, except that a late-filing shareholder may apply to the Internal Revenue Service Center for an extension of time to file the consent. Reg. § 1.1363-6(b)(3)(iii). The IRS is authorized to waive lateness if there is a reasonable cause for the delay. § 1362(b)(5).

c. Corporate Election

The shareholders consent; the corporation elects. This qualification process is again simplified by the existence of Form 2553, which in a gesture of rare efficiency also includes the place to indicate the corporation's election, and a means for selecting the taxable year. Having elected, the corporation must file the form at a time when it qualifies for the election. § 1361(b); § 1362(b)(l). This can be a challenging problem because of the number of requirements that must be met in order to be an S corporation. S corporation status is effective for the next tax year if Form 2553 is filed any time during the previous tax year, or by the fifteenth day of the third month of the tax year to which the election is to apply, e.g., by March 15 for a calendar year S corporation, as most are provided it was a "small business corporation" from the very beginning of its tax year. Once the election and consents are perfected, the enterprise can continue as an S corporation indefinitely. If the election to claim S corporation status is otherwise valid, and it is made before the sixteenth day of the third month of the taxable year, but the election or consent is flawed, the election is treated as made for the next taxable year. § 1362(b)(2).

PROBLEM 24-2

You are an associate at a law firm that has a new client by the name of Jiffy Products, Inc. You have driven out to visit the offices of Jiffy Products to prepare it for the filing of an S election. So far, you have learned that Jiffy Products is an accrual method, calendar year C corporation that has been around for thirty years. Jiffy has accumulated "earnings and profits" (*see* § 316) of $150,000 and is owned by several shareholders, including the ABC partnership, which holds 15% of the common stock.

A and B are U.S. citizens, both of whom reside in Jiffy's home state, but C only recently arrived in the U.S.A. The remaining 85% of the common stock is owned by 30 U.S. citizens. Jiffy has issued some stock warrants to its executives and has a shadow stock plan that gives executives extra money if the company's stock performs well. Jiffy has two classes of common stock, which differ only in that one class votes and the other does not. Its preferred stock is nonvoting and nonconvertible. Jiffy's accounts, which you were just shown, look like this:

Accounts payable	$300,000
Note due to president	$30,000
Long-term bonds	$800,000
Paid-in-capital for common stock	$345,000
Class A	$5,000
Class B	$5,000
Paid-in-capital for preferred stock	$40,000
Retained earnings	$150,000
Paid-in capital for warrants (convertible into common stock)	$1,000

You also learned that the shareholder-officers of the corporation have a buy-sell agreement under which Jiffy Products, Inc. will redeem their stock on retirement or death for a price equal to the book value of each share at the time of death or retirement. Book value under the agreement is essentially the basis of the corporation's assets minus its liabilities.

What steps need to be taken to ensure that Jiffy's effort to become an S corporation can be achieved, starting next year? Assume it is now October 15. As to the warrants, *see* Reg. §§ 1.1361-1(l)(4)(iii)(B)(2) and (C).

C. LOSS OF STATUS VIA TERMINATION OR REVOCATION OF THE ELECTION

1. REVOCATION
Read § 1362(d)(1).

The corporation can revoke its S election for any taxable year. This process requires that shareholders who collectively own more than 50% of the outstanding stock in the S corporation consent to the revocation. The consenting shareholders must own their stock in the S corporation at the time the corporation makes the revocation. The corporation must provide the IRS with a statement to that effect and, if the corporation wants to pick a particular revocation date that will take effect in the future and should specify the date the revocation will take effect. The corporation is supposed to attach a statement of consent, signed by each shareholder who consents to the revocation to its statement.

If the corporation does not specify a prospective revocation date, the revocation is effective on the first day of the tax year if the revocation is made during the first 2 ½ months of the same tax year. If the corporation waits past that deadline the revocation is effective on the first day of the following taxable year, unless the revocation specifies some particular future date that the revocation will take effect. If the corporation specifies a prospective date for revocation that is other than the first day of the tax year, the result will be a so-called "S termination year," a matter taken up later in this Chapter.

2. TERMINATION
Read § 1362(d)(2).

Revocation is a voluntary act. Termination is not, unless the corporation deliberately uses a termination as a shortcut for a revocation. There are several ways a termination of a valid S election can come about.

a. By Cessation of Small Business Corporation Status

S corporation status terminates the moment the corporation ceases to qualify as an S corporation. If the corporation inadvertently ceases to qualify, there is a chance the IRS will, with appropriate begging and pleading from the taxpayer, relent and disregard the fault. § 1362(f). The IRS may also waive an inadvertent failure to qualify as a result of not getting the needed shareholder consents. If the IRS refuses to overlook the flaw, the corporation cannot make another S election for five years. § 1362(g).

There is no shortage of ways to lose S corporation status. For example, there might be more than 100 shareholders; a shareholder might transfer stock to a nonresident alien, a C corporation or a partnership; or the company might issue a second class of stock.

A termination of S corporation status is effective as of the date the terminating event occurred. If this occurs other than on the first day of the tax year the result is an "S termination year."

If a corporation does terminate its status as an S corporation, it generally must wait five tax years before it can again become an S corporation, although if it gets the permission of the IRS, the waiting period may be shortened. § 1362(g). One might wonder if the owners could form a new company and cause the terminated S corporation to be acquired by merger or asset purchase so as to let the new company make the S election. The answer is negative. The Treasury has identified the scam and has promulgated a regulation that treats the successor corporation as the continuation of the old S corporation. Reg. § 1.1362-5. A successor corporation is one that acquires a substantial part of the S corporation assets or whose assets were in large measure owned by the S corporation, provided at least half its stock is directly or indirectly owned by the same persons whose election terminated the old corporation and either the new corporation acquired a substantial portion of the assets of the olds corporation, or a substantial portion of the assets from the new corporation were assets of the old corporation. Reg. § 1.1362-5(b).

PROBLEM 24-3

The president of an incorporated client recently called to say that the company was expecting to have a very bad year next year. The client wondered if, assuming it met the requirements to be an S corporation, it could make the S election, flow the losses through to its owners, and then drop the election for the following year. The client also wondered if it could do the same thing again in the future. How would you answer? *See* § 1362(g).

PROBLEM 24-4

Alpha Co. is a small New Jersey manufacturing corporation owned by 85 shareholders (all of whom are U.S. citizens) of its only class of stock. Alpha Co. is engaged in the business of manufacturing and selling widgets. It uses the accrual method and calendar year.

1) Alpha Co.'s director and CEO, Adams, comes to you for advice as to whether Alpha Co. could make the S corp. election. What do you tell him? *See* § 1361.

2) Would your answer to "1)" change if one of the shareholders was a trust created by under New Jersey law, qualifying as a grantor trust under the Code? The grantor is a US citizen residing in France.

3) What if Alpha Co., in an attempt to raise additional capital to fund an expansion of its offices, decided to make a public offering of nonconvertible bonds with a $100 face value, 10% interest rate, and a maturity date of July 4, 2014? Would this cause Alpha Co. to lose its ability to make the S Corp. election? *See* §§ 1361(b)(1)(D) and 1361(c)(5).

4) Could Alpha Co., in a shareholders' meeting on March 1st, successfully propose to make the S Corp. election and apply it to the current year? *See* § 1362(b)(1).

5) Assume Raul, a Latin American, owned one share of Alpha Co. until January 10 of this year, when he sold it to one of the existing United States shareholders. Can Alpha Co. make the election for this year?

6) What IRS form is used to make the election?

7) What percentage of the shareholders must consent to the election? *See* § 1362(a).

8) If Alpha Co. later decides that the S Corp. election is not the best route for its business, may the corporation revoke its election? If so, what percentage of shareholders must vote for revocation to be effective? *See* § 1362(d)(1)(B).

9) Can Alpha Co. vote to revoke its S Corp. election on April 1st, with the revocation to not take effect until September 25th? *See* § 1362(d)(1)(C),(D).

10) What if no effective date of revocation is specified when the vote is taken on March 1st? *See* § 1362(d)(1)(C),(D).

495

11) What steps need to be taken to allow executives of the company to maximize their stock options?

b. By Violating Passive Income Limitation
Read § 1362(d)(3).

This way of losing S corporation status is fairly easy to bumble into because there are few obvious signals of a problem. Under § 1362(d)(3), an S corporation's status terminates if both of the following conditions occur for three consecutive taxable years:

- The corporation has pre-S corporation earnings and profits at the end of each such taxable year, and

- Its passive investment income for each such year is more than 25% of its gross receipts. The terms "passive investment income" and "gross receipts" are discussed later under the heading "Tax on Excess Net Passive Income."

This rule is evidently intended to prevent a regular C corporation from electing S status and converting into a passive investment company, rather than liquidating and incurring an income tax at the shareholder level on liquidation proceeds from the period that it operated as a C corporation.

It is important to not lose sight of the converse. If there are no earnings and profits from pre-S corporation years, then the S corporation can act as an investment company without losing its status as an S corporation, and without paying federal income taxes. The income tax on passive investment income only applies if the S Corp. has earnings and profits (E & P) from a time when it operated as a C corporation or obtained the E & P in a reorganization. In other words, a corporation that has been an S corporation since its formation (a "virgin" S corporation in the lingo of the trade) is not susceptible to termination for excessive passive income.

3. S TERMINATION YEAR
Read § 1362(e)(1)-(4).

A termination that takes effect on any day other than the first day of the taxable year creates an S termination year. The part of the tax year ending on the day before the effective date of the termination is a Form 1120S (S corporation) short tax year. The part of the S termination year beginning on the next day is the start of an 1120 (C corporation) short tax year. § 1362(e)(1). After the S termination year is divided into an 1120S short year and an 1120 short year, the corporation's income and deductions are generally prorated on a daily basis between the two years, unless it and its shareholders elect an imaginary closing of the books, as with partnerships. § 1362(e)(2),(3). One must use the exact method if one-half or more of the corporation's stock is sold or exchanged during the S termination year. § 1362(e)(6)(D).

The S termination year counts as only one tax year for figuring carrybacks and carryforwards, even though two returns are filed for the year. The result is favorable to taxpayers, because it reduces the risk that suspended net operating losses (NOLs) will be obliterated.

4. RELIEF FOR INADVERTENT TERMINATIONS
Read § 1362(1).

Imagine an S corporation whose accountants concluded that it had no accumulated pre-S corporation earnings and profits, and that the corporation was audited by the IRS some years later. In the course of the audit it turned out that the corporation did indeed have undistributed earnings and profits left over from its years as a C corporation. Given the right facts, that could easily lead to a conclusion that the corporation had violated the passive investment income test of § 1362(d)(3).

As you will see later, it can also result in the imposition of a tax on the corporation under § 1375. In that case, the company would owe corporate taxes, plus interest and perhaps penalties, and the shareholders would have to amend their returns to remove income or losses flowed through to them in past years, a messy proposition for all concerned. This problem is worsened by the possibility that some of their years might be closed and that the mitigation provisions of § 1311 *et seq.* do not extend to S corporations and their shareholders. § 1313(c).

Section 1362(f) provides that if the corporation inadvertently terminated its election because it ceased to qualify as an S corporation or because it violated the restriction on passive investment income, the IRS may waive the termination if it concludes that the termination was inadvertent, the corporation takes steps to correct the event within a reasonable period of time, and the corporation and its shareholders agree to be treated as if the event had not occurred.

The format for asking for this help is apparently to seek a private letter ruling from the National Office of the IRS. The request should state all relevant facts pertaining to the terminating event, including when the corporation's election to be an S corporation took place, a detailed explanation of the event causing termination, when and how the event was discovered, and what steps were taken to return the corporation to S corporation status.

Chapter 25

TAXATION OF THE ENTITY AND ITS OWNERS

A. CONDUIT MODEL
Read §§ 1366(a)-(c); § 1367.

The basic model of pass-through taxation of an S corporation and its shareholders is generally the same as that for partnerships. Each shareholder reports a pro rata share of each item of income, loss, deduction, or credit that is separately stated on the information return filed by the entity and a pro rata share of non-separately stated income or loss on his or her income tax return, with the character of each item determined at the S corporation level and flowed through to the shareholder. This is taxed to the shareholder, using the corporation's accounting method. § 1366(a)(1); Reg. § 1.1363-1(b). The corporation's operating results are computed on the basis of its own taxable year, as with partnerships. The shareholder's stock basis rises with corporate profits and shareholder contributions, and declines with corporate losses and distributions. § 1367. Distributions are taken into account in computing stock basis before taking into account the impact of losses. § 1366(d)(1); § 1368(d). This tends to preserve the nontaxability of distributions from the corporation to its shareholders.

However, do not be fooled into thinking the S corporation is as pure a conduit as a partnership. Instead, as with C corporations, regular and liquidating distributions of appreciated property are recognition events and the appreciation is taxable to the owners. In the case of S corporations with earnings and profits accumulated from C corporation years, there is a risk of incurring a corporate-level tax on excessive passive investment income under § 1375, and, regardless of E & P, on sales and distributions of property with certain built-in gains (also known as the "BIG tax") under § 1374. The shareholders alone pay the tax on distributions, unless the BIG tax of § 1374 applies, in which case the corporation pays a separate tax. Sections 1374 and 1375 are discussed later in the text.

B. COMPUTATION OF CORPORATE TAX BASE

1. ACCOUNTING METHOD
Read § 448(a).

An S corporation can use the cash method unless it is a tax shelter. § 448. Congress considers use of the cash method a privilege, and to some extent it is. If it prefers, the S corporation is free to use the accrual method. In either case, the corporation will calculate its income on the basis of its selected accounting method, and the choice may have a major impact on the shareholders. To take a simple example, if the company can accrue a large interest expense deduction, the result may be significant tax savings for the shareholders. Conversely, shareholders of an accrual method engineering firm with a big backlog of receivables may incur an undue amount of taxes, subject to later bad debt deductions in the event of nonpayment.

2. TAXABLE YEAR
Read § 1378; §§ 444(a), (b)(l), (2), and (4) and § 1366(a)(1).

Congress has made a general effort to force S corporations onto the calendar year. In form, one can still choose between a calendar year or a fiscal year. § 1378. However, a fiscal year will have to be a so-called "permitted year," for which the corporation establishes a substantial business purpose to the satisfaction of the IRS. Otherwise, the corporation can elect under § 444 to have a tax year other than a permitted tax year, but in that case it will have to pay a toll charge in the form of accelerated payments of income taxes that rob the company of the benefit of making a fiscal year election; this puts most S corporations and partnerships in the same boat.

The shareholder will report the corporation's results in the shareholder's year in which, or with which, the corporation's tax year ends. If the years overlap, the shareholder reports the results of the overlapping year. § 1366(a)(1). Nowadays, the corporation and its shareholders will normally both be on the calendar year.

To illustrate: A and B are the equal shareholders of AB Corp. ("AB"), an S corporation. A and B both use the calendar year. AB uses the June 30 fiscal year. The operating results of AB, as determined on June 30 of this year, were a profit of $100. A and B will each include $50 of income for their tax year ending December 31 of this year. If AB's year closed on December 31 of this year and the profits were $120, then A and B would each report $60 of that profit on their tax returns for the year ending December 31 of this year.

If the shareholder terminates his or her interest in the S corporation, generally speaking, the annual income is prorated to each shareholder on an average daily basis. However, if the shareholders who are affected by the change (normally, the buyer and seller of the block of stock) and the corporation all consent, the proration can be done on an exact basis, with a "closing of the books" as of the date of the change. § 1377(b)(2). This can open the door to tax planning opportunities, such as selling all one's stock to a family member in a lower tax bracket than one's own just before the S corporation starts making money.

3. TAXABLE INCOME AND DISTRIBUTIVE SHARES
Read §§ 1363(b) and 1366(a)-(d)(2).

To calculate an S corporation's income, one divides its items of income, loss, expense, and credit into two groups: separately stated items, and items used to figure non-separately stated income or loss. Both groups are often called "pass thru items" because they are passed through to the shareholders on a pro rata basis. §§ 1363(b), 1366. This is the same rule as applies for partnerships.

The concept here is the same as for partnerships under § 702(a), namely that one must separately state items of income, loss, expense, and credit to the extent that, when separately treated on the shareholder's income tax return, they could affect the shareholder's tax liability. Examples include interest income, dividend income, short-term capital gain or loss, long-term capital gain or loss, and items needed to calculate the shareholder's alternative minimum tax.

As with partnerships, the entity prepares its own return and a separate Schedule K-1 that it mails to each shareholder so he or she can prepare his or her own tax return. The share of income attributable to each owner depends on his or her proportionate ownership of the company's common stock, using a daily per-share proration to apportion the results, so the sum of the results on the Forms K-1 will equal the S corporation's results.

C. ELECTIONS
Read § 1363(c).

Most tax elections are made by the entity. Note that there is no analog to § 754, so stock transfers cannot affect the S corporation's basis in its assets in any way.

D. BUILT-IN GAINS TAX ON S CORPORATIONS THAT FORMERLY WERE C CORPORATIONS

Read §§ 1374(a), (b)(1)-(2), (c), (d)(l)-(5).

This is an absolutely critical problem with respect to the S election. The legislative purpose of the built-in gains (BIG) tax is to remove the benefit of using S corporations to duck the anti-*General Utilities* rules enacted in 1986. *See* § 311(b); § 336(a). If it were not for the BIG tax, a C corporation could launder gains from property that had appreciated during the C corporation years by making the S election, then promptly sell or distribute appreciated property, and shift the gain to the shareholders alone, with no corporate-level tax. Consistent with the Congressional concern, the BIG tax does not reach a corporation that has been an S corporation all its life (a so-called "virgin" S corporation). The following description is adapted from a Joint Committee report regarding technical corrections to the built-in gain rules:

[P]resent law (as modified by the 1986 Act) also provides that a corporate-level tax is imposed on certain gains of an S corporation that was formerly a C corporation. The corporate-level tax applies to any gain that arose prior to the conversion of the corporation to S status (built-in gain) and is recognized by the S corporation, through sale, distribution or other disposition within five years after the date on which the S election took effect (sec. 1374). The total amount of gain subject to corporate-level tax, however, is limited to the aggregate net built-in gain of the corporation at the time of conversion to S corporation status. See House Explanation Comrep ¶ 13741.005 (88 TMRA, PL 100-647, 11/10/88)."

The Code taxes built-in gains at the top corporate rate of 21%. Congress hit hard with the BIG tax, in that it imposed an immediate tax on *both* the S corporation and on the shareholder (whose tax base is reduced by the tax the corporation paid). By contrast, if a C corporation distributes appreciated property,[1] although the corporation will be taxable on the appreciation, there is no assurance of a shareholder-level gain; it might well be that the distribution constituted a return of capital because the corporation had no current or accumulated E & P (hence no dividend) and the shareholder had a high enough stock basis that the distribution would not be taxable under § 301. Moreover, if the C corporation merely sells an appreciated asset there is no shareholder level tax until a distribution is made.

The amount of net recognized built-in gain for any taxable year is limited to the amount that would be taxable income of the corporation if it were not an S corporation. § 1374(d)(2). The gain that escapes the BIG tax via this limit is suspended. For this purpose, taxable income means gross income of the corporation minus most deductions, including the amortization deduction for corporate organization costs allowed a corporation, but not the net operating loss deduction or other special deductions for corporations. Although this limit ensures that the BIG tax will not kick economically weak companies when they are down, the BIG tax reapplies when they get back up. That is because under § 1374 the suspended amount is treated as recognized built-in gain in the following tax year. § 1374(d)(2)(B). The computations become surprisingly complicated.

Any BIG tax (*i.e.*, the check written to the IRS) is passed through to the shareholders as a loss for the year in which the tax arises. § 1366(f)(2). The character of the loss depends on the character of the built-in gain on which the BIG tax was imposed. Consider the inequity if the tax did not flow out as a deduction and the shareholder later sold stock. Here is a simple example of the BIG tax:

---

[1] The same result occurs if the C corporation sells the assets and then distributes the sales proceeds to its shareholders.

To illustrate: C Corp. elected to be an S corporation this year, at a time when it had one asset, an item of inventory having a value of $10 and a basis of $0. It soon thereafter sold the asset, incurring a corporate tax of 21% on $10, or taxes of $2.10. The shareholder was also taxed on $10 gain, but got to deduct the $2.10 tax; thus, the shareholder's federal income tax base (the amount to be included in income) is $7.90. Assuming a 37% tax rate, the shareholder pays a tax of $2.92. Total taxes are $5.02.

Now read (or re-read) §§ 1374(a), (b)(1)-(2), (c)(1), (d)(8), and § 1375(a). You might want to try this as a self-test:

Self-Test: Suppose ABC Corporation is a small business corporation that qualifies for and elects S corporation status for its first tax year beginning in Year 1; having operated profitably as a C corporation since its inception. All of its outstanding shares of common stock are owned equally by mother and daughter, Anne and Marie, each of whom has a basis of $25,000 in her stock. In its first S corporation year, ABC earns $250,000, $100,000 of which is long-term capital gain, and $100,000 of which is rental income. ABC Corp. incurred no capital loss. It does not distribute anything to its shareholder. Consider these questions, with minimum concern for the numbers.

1) Will ABC Corporation have to pay a tax for this year? *See* §§ 1363, 1374, 1375.

2) What amounts will Anne and Marie each have to include in income? *See* § 1366(a). Could the fact that Anne worked full-time as a rental property manager for ABC and received a large annual salary from the corporation affect the allocation of income to the shareholders? *See* § 1366(e).

Answers to Self-Test:

1) ABC Corporation will not have to pay any tax on ordinary corporate income (§ 1363), but it is subject to an entity-level tax if (1) any of its income were from realizing built-in gain, which at least part of the $100,000 gain is, to the extent that the gain was from appreciated property owned at the time of converting to S corporation status (§ 1374) or (2) if it had excess passive investment income and had any leftover Subchapter C earnings and profits (§ 1375). If the entire $100,000 were subject to the BIG tax, the bill would be $21,000.

2) Anne and Marie would each have to include her pro-rata share of the corporation's income, with the long-term capital gain (less the BIG tax) and (possibly passive) rental income. § 1366. The rates of tax on each type of income (with its character passed through) will depend on the individual circumstances of each shareholder. § 1366. The salaries can serve to reduce the corporation's taxable income, thereby deferring the BIG tax.

PROBLEM 25-1

Xeno Corp. is a prosperous cash method incorporated architectural firm that elects to be an S corporation. It has $10,000 of receivables, by face amount and value, from clients at the beginning of its first tax year as an S corporation, which was last year. Xeno and its shareholders are all in the 37% bracket.

1) Are the receivables built-in gain items? *See* §§ 1374(a), (d).

2) Knowing that Xeno and its shareholders are in the 37% bracket, what is the tax to Xeno and its shareholders if it sells the receivables for $10,000 within five years?

3) What if the receivables were sold for $12,000?

4) Would the result be any different if instead of holding the receivables directly, the receivables were the sole asset of a 100%-owned subsidiary that the S corporation recently acquired and as to which a QSSS election was made? Think back to the model as to how QSSSs are viewed. *See* H.R. Rep. No. 104-586, 104th Cong., 2d Sess. 89 (1996).

PROBLEM 25-2

Alpha Corp. is a cash method, calendar year S corporation that recently elected S corporation status. At the time of the election, it had two assets, one with a value of $20,000 and an adjusted basis of $0, and the other with a value of $0 and an adjusted basis of $10,000. There are no other assets. In its first year as an S corporation (year one), it sold both assets for their (unchanged) fair market values. Alpha also had a $10,000 loss from other activities after it became an S corporation.

1) Is Alpha subject to the BIG tax? What is its tax bill if it only sells the gain asset?

2) Same as "(1)", but the sales were instead in year two. In that year Alpha had taxable income of $5,000, none of which is attributable to recognized built-in gains. Is it subject to the BIG tax?

3) Would the result in "(1)" differ if Alpha had a $10,000 net operating loss that arose during its prior existence as a C corporation? *See* § 1374(b)(2).

4) If Alpha waits until the very beginning of year six, can it avoid the BIG tax on the sales of the gain asset?

5) Can Alpha avoid the BIG tax by selling on the installment method, with the first payment due after the ten-year "recognition period." *See* Reg. § 1.1374-4(h).

E. TAX ON EXCESS NET PASSIVE INCOME
Read § 1375.

An S corporation that has earnings and profits at the end of a taxable year may be subject to a tax on its excess net passive income. § 1375. Moreover, if passive investment income is more than 25% of gross receipt for three consecutive taxable years and the corporation has earnings and profits at the end of each of those years, the corporation's S corporation status terminates, and the corporation would not be able to reelect S status for five years. § 1362(d)(3).

There is no minimum amount of earnings and profits; it appears that one cent would do. (Note that earnings and profits can only exist for a former C corporation that elected S corporation status or one that reorganized with a C corporation that had E & P. It could not arise in a "virgin" S corporation. Thus, virgin S corporations make handy investment companies.)

The base on which the tax is imposed is "excess passive net income." § 1375(a). The tax rate is the top corporate rate, currently 21%. § 11(b). Section 1375(b)(3) indirectly defines the term "gross receipts" as the total amount an S corporation receives or accrues under its method of tax accounting, including the proceeds of sales or exchanges of most property.

Section 1375(b)(3) defines "passive income" by reference to § 1362(d)(3), and is generally a gross figure, rather than a net figure.

Proceeds from the sale or exchange of stock or securities are included in "gross receipts" only to the extent of net gain; losses are disregarded. § 1375(b)(3); § 1362(d)(3)(C)(i). Certain amounts received in exchange for stock in a corporate liquidation are also disregarded if the S corporation owned over one-half of each class of the liquidating corporation's stock as of the first distribution with respect to the liquidation. § 1362(d)(3)(C)(iv).

The term "passive investment income" includes gross receipts from royalties, rents, dividends (other than dividends from qualified subchapter S subsidiaries), interest, annuities, and gains from sales or exchanges of stock or securities. § 1362(d)(3)(C)(i). Each of the listed terms has its own definition, but the details are beyond the scope of this book.

"Net passive investment income" is passive investment income minus allowable deductions directly connected with the production of the income. § 1375(b)(2). The §172 net operating loss deduction and special deductions under §§ 241-250 are not allowed. § 1375(b)(2)(B). There are some further esoteric restrictions.

Calculating the tax. The 21% tax falls on excess net passive income for the taxable year. To compute the amount of excess net passive income, one must multiply net passive income by a fraction consisting of passive investment income minus 25% of gross receipts *over* passive investment income. Once this jumble of words is turned into a formula, it is much less daunting. Excessive net passive income equals:

$$\text{Net passive investment income for the year} \quad \times \quad \frac{\text{Passive investment income in excess of 25\% of gross receipts for the year}}{\text{Passive investment income for the year}}$$

The tax is softened three ways. First, excess net passive income cannot be more than the S corporation's taxable income for the year, as calculated without allowance for dividends-received deductions and net operating loss deductions. § 1375(b)(1)(B). Second, the S corporation may be able to talk its way out of the tax if it can show that it believed it did not in fact have earnings and profits at the end of the taxable year and it disgorges its earnings and profits within a reasonable time after discovering the error. Reg. § 1.1375-1(d). Third, the tax reduces the amount of passive investment income that is taxed to the shareholders, thereby modestly reducing shareholder level taxes. § 1366(f)(3).

The next couple of problems explore how the tax operates.

PROBLEM 25-3

The Gilmore Corporation, a cash method, calendar year taxpayer, has operated a profitable warehouse business since 1957 in Big City, USA. Its books clearly show that it has earnings and profits of $800,000 as of the end of this year. It made the S election two years ago. It has rented out one of its properties on a "net lease" basis (*i.e.*, the tenant pays local taxes, etc.) to be used as a parking lot. At the same time, it is only breaking even on the warehouse business. The net lease income is $1 million this year. Its gross receipts from the warehouse business were $1 million, but its related expenses were also $1 million. The corporation incurred $250,000 of professional fees in connection with a dispute with the net lease tenant this year.

1) What, if anything, is its § 1375 tax?

2) What defenses or limitations can the corporation raise to the tax?

3) Is the S election forfeited?

PROBLEM 25-4

Delta, Inc., an accrual method, calendar year manufacturing company, is an S corporation that has ended its taxable year with $700 taxable income, and large amount of real estate rental income from properties the corporation owns. The CEO asks you whether the company might face the possibility of a tax on excess net passive investment income. *See* § 1375(d).

1) If Delta, Inc. has no E & P, is there no such risk?

2) If E & P is a problem, can the E & P be eliminated somehow?

3) Is there a *de minimis* exemption available to Delta?

F. PASS THROUGH OF INCOME AND LOSS: TIMING OF PASS-THROUGH AND CHARACTER OF INCOME

1. PRO RATA SHARE RULE
Read §§ 1366(a) and 1377(a).

The general rule is that every shareholder reports a daily prorata share of the S corporation's annual net income or loss, except to the extent components of net income or loss are separately stated because of their possible differential effect on the tax liability of any shareholder. Those separately stated items are also includable on a prorata, per-day basis. This is the same pattern as applies for partnerships.

Although earnings or losses from an S corporation are normally apportioned among shareholders on a daily per-share basis, if (1) any shareholder terminated his or her interest in an S corporation during a taxable year, and (2) (as was mentioned earlier) the affected shareholders – meaning the transferors and transferees – sign consents, and (3) the corporation also elects, then the taxable year of the corporation with respect to the new and to the departing shareholder is treated as if it were composed of two taxable years, the first of which ends on the date the shareholder's interest in the corporation terminates.

This split tax year opens powerful tax planning opportunities. For example, a high-bracket shareholder can sell all her stock just before the company turns profitable and, via the election, repel all future income and dump it in the lap of a low-bracket related buyer. See § 1377(a)(2). Note that whether or not the § 1377(a)(2) election is made, the seller's tax liability for the part of the year when she held her stock is affected by what the corporation's tax return reports, and that if the buyer bought all the stock, the tax return will probably be prepared by the buyer, at the end of the year. This creates risk. For example, if there is no election to close the year, the buyer may be able to exaggerate income in the year of the sale so as to ascribe a disagreeable amount of income to the seller.

PROBLEM 25-5

S Corporation was organized two years ago. It is on the cash method and uses the calendar year. Its shareholders are all cash method U.S. citizens or estates of deceased U.S. citizens. The Estate of A owns 60% of the stock and has a May 31 year-end. B, who is on the calendar year, used to own 40%, but sold his stock to C (also a calendar year U.S. citizen) on June 30 of year two. S Corporation had $20,000 of ordinary income in year two, and it distributed $1,500 to B and $1,500 to the Estate of A on February 1 of year two. No § 1377(a)(2) election was made.

1) How much income should B, C, and the Estate of A report for year two?

2) Can S corporation use the cash method of accounting? *See* § 448.

PRIV. LTR. RUL. 9026005
(June 29, 1990)

Issue

Has X, an S corporation that intended to elect to treat the tax year at issue as if it consisted of two tax years pursuant to section 1377(a)(2) of the Internal Revenue Code, substantially complied with the election requirements of section 18.1377-1 of the Temporary Income Tax Regulations [current cite of final Regulations: Reg. § 1.1377-1(b)(5)(i)], even though it did not include a statement of election with the tax return for the tax year at issue?

Facts

X, a subchapter S corporation, had two fifty percent shareholders during 1985, A and B. X was on a fiscal year ending February 28. On April 1, 1985, A sold all of his stock in X to B for $1,300,000. On January 27, 1986, X sold all its assets to another corporation and completely liquidated to the sole remaining shareholder, B.

The Form 1120S tax return for X for the tax year ending January 27, 1986, stated ordinary income of $655,810 and a net long-term capital gain of $2,786,466. The Schedule K-1 for B, attached to X's tax return, stated $666,430 of ordinary income and $2,786,466 of net long-term capital gain. The Schedule K-1 for A, attached to X's tax return, stated an ordinary loss of $10,620. However, no statement of election with accompanying statement of consent as specified in section 18.1377-1 of the temporary Regulations was included with X's tax return.

On A's individual income tax return, he reported the $10,620 ordinary loss from the Schedule K-1 attached to X's tax return. On B's individual income tax return, he reported the $666,430 of ordinary income and the $2,786,466 of net long-term capital gain from the Schedule K-1 attached to X's tax return.

Law and Analysis

Section 1377(a)(1) of the Code provides that for purposes of subchapter S, except as provided in section 1377(a)(2), each shareholder's pro rata share of any item for any tax year shall be the sum of the amounts determined with respect to the shareholder (A) by assigning an equal portion of such item to each day of the tax year, and (B) then by dividing that portion pro rata among the shares outstanding on such day.

Section 1377(a)(2) of the Code provides that under Regulations prescribed by the Secretary, if any shareholder terminates his interest in the corporation during the tax year and all persons who are shareholders during the tax year agree to the application of this paragraph, section 1377(a)(l) shall be applied as if the tax year consisted of two tax years the first of which ends on the date of the termination.

Section 18.1377-1 of the temporary Regulations provides that in the case of a tax year of an S corporation during which any shareholder terminates his or her entire shareholder interest in the corporation, the corporation may elect under section 1377(a)(2) to have the rules in section 1377(a)(2) applied as if the tax year consisted of two tax years. The election can be made only with the consent of all persons who are or were shareholders in the corporation at any time during such tax year. Such election shall be made by the corporation by filing a statement that the corporation elects . . . to have the rules provided in section 1377(a)(1) applied as if the tax year consisted of two tax years, which statement shall set forth the manner of the termination (e.g., the sale of a shareholder's entire shareholder interest) and the date thereof and shall be filed with the return for such tax year. The statement to be filed with the return for such tax year shall be signed by any person authorized to sign the return required to be filed under section 6037. In addition, there shall be attached to the statement of election a statement of consent, signed by each person who is or was a shareholder in the corporation at any time during the tax year, in which each such shareholder consents to the corporation making the election under section 1377(a)(2).

Because X did not include the statement of election required by section 18.1377-1 of the temporary Regulations, we must determine if the filing of the Form 1120S with accompanying Schedules K-1 together with X's shareholders filing their individual tax returns consistent with the Schedules K-1 is enough to "substantially comply" with section 18.1377-1 of the temporary Regulations.

Literal compliance with procedural directions in Treasury Regulations is not always required. "[S]ubstantial compliance may be sufficient if the regulatory requirements in dispute are procedural or directory in that they are not of the essence of the thing to be done but are given with a view to the orderly and prompt conduct of business, and if the omission of the required material has not operated to the Commissioner's prejudice." *Tipps v. Commissioner*, 74 T.C. 458 at 468 (1980), acq., 1981-2 C.B. 2 (Citations omitted).

For substantial compliance to exist one need not comply with all the formal requirements set forth in the Code and Regulations; however, it must be clear from the return as filed that the election is being made, what the election covers, and that the taxpayers understand and accept the consequences of the election. *Tipps v. Commissioner, supra.* The taxpayer must not be left room to argue later that he had never intended to make the election and must not be permitted to "wait and see" or use hindsight to the Commissioner's disadvantage. *Young v. Commissioner*, 83 T.C. 831, 839 (1984), and *Taylor v. Commissioner*, 67 T.C. 1071, 1080 (1977); *acq.* 1979-2 C.B. 2.

The doctrine of substantial compliance applies to the present case because the requirements in section 18.1377-1 of the temporary Regulations are "procedural and directory" and not the essence of the thing to be done. The statement of election required by section 18.1377-1 facilitates the conduct of business in a prompt and orderly manner by stating that the section 1377(a)(2) election is being made, stating the manner and date of the terminating event, and providing a statement of consent for each shareholder. However, it is not the essence of the statutory and regulatory scheme. The essence of section 1377(a)(2) of the Code and accompanying Regulations is to have the shareholders agree to treat the tax year as if it consisted of two tax years, the first of which ends on the date of the termination of the shareholder's interest. If the taxpayers indicate from the return, accompanying schedules, and in the case of an S corporation, their corresponding individual returns, that they have agreed to treat the tax year as if it consisted of two tax years, then the essence of the statutory and regulatory scheme has been satisfied. The failure to file the election and consent statement as set forth in section 18.1377-1 of the temporary Regulations has not operated to the Commissioner's prejudice because an examination of the return, accompanying Schedules K-1, and the shareholders' corresponding individual returns would indicate that the election was made, what the election covered, and that the shareholders understood and accepted the consequences of the election. There was not an opportunity to use hindsight to the Commissioner's prejudice because the shareholders indicated their intent to be bound by the election. If the taxpayers did not intend to make the section 1377(a)(2) election, the Schedules K-1 for A and B would have stated ordinary income and capital gain for both shareholders because under section 1377(a)(1) of the Code each shareholder would have been assigned a pro rata portion of the S corporation items that would have been assigned equally to each day of the tax year. Thus, neither shareholder would have been allocated a loss for the tax year because for the tax year as a whole there was ordinary income and net long-term capital gain. If the shareholders did not agree to be bound by the section 1377(a)(2) election, they would not have reported the items from the Schedules K-1 attached to X's tax return consistently on their individual returns.

Conclusion

Although X failed to file a statement of election with the tax return for the tax year at issue in the precise manner required by section 18.1377-1 of the temporary Regulations, X has substantially complied with the requirements of section 1.1377-1 of the temporary Regulations.

NOTES

1. **Line Drawing.** Some compliance is substantial, some is not. As usual, the courts are dragged in and asked to draw lines. Judges must feel as if they are being forced to handle the Greek paradox of the heap. The paradox goes like this:

   Imagine a modest sized heap of sand. Now take away a grain of sand from the heap. It is still a heap. Now remove another grain of sand, and then another. There is still a heap. If you keep doing it long enough, you know there will be only one grain of sand left. Is that grain a heap? If it is not, when did it stop being a heap?

2. **Reconciling the Differences.** *Rockwell Inn, Ltd. v. Commissioner*, 65 T.C.M. 2374 (1993) is more challenging. There, the Tax Court ruled the S election invalid where the corporation failed to file its Form 2553 on time, even though the corporation filed its tax return indicating that it had previously elected to be treated as an S corporation and issued a Schedule K-1 to each of its shareholders, showing each shareholder's distributive share of the corporation's income, and each shareholder reported the information shown on the K-1 on his or her individual tax return. The court rejected the taxpayer's assertion that Form 2553 is not mandatory in order to make the S election. It also rejected the contention that the corporation and its shareholders had substantially complied with the requirements for making an S election because the corporation's federal income tax return, including the Schedules K-1, contained essentially all the information sought by Form 2553. The court

said that the corporate income tax return did not clearly and firmly elect S status, and, therefore, the corporation did not substantially comply with the essence of the statute.

Can you reconcile *Rockwell* with Private Letter Ruling 9026005? Is there some difference in the risk of prejudice to the IRS in the two cases? Is there a difference in the degree of notice provided by taxpayers in the two cases? Can one articulate what substantial compliance means? Might it be a good idea to leave the concept of substantial compliance vague to prevent taxpayers from playing fast and loose with their obligations?

Read Reg. § 1.1377-1. Does it seem to you that there would be any difference between a redemption of the shareholder's stock by the corporation as opposed to a sale to another person?

PROBLEM 25-6

Mrs. Friendly is a 33% shareholder in the Dynamo Corporation ("Dynamo"), which, like her, uses the cash method and the calendar year. Dynamo has $1 million of accounts receivable and very little other income and few expenses. Dynamo is an S corporation. Mrs. Friendly is just about to sell her stock to Edward ("Fast Eddy") Zapp for $400,000 near the end of the year. Fast Eddy will take over as CEO and will be able to do just about anything he wants to do once he has the stock. Mrs. Friendly is a bit worried that Fast Eddy might do something with the receivables that somehow harm her. She wants your advice as to what to do. Assume the sales price of the stock and the closing date are negotiable. What do you suggest?

2. BASIS OF STOCK
Reread §§ 1367(a), (b) and 1366(a)-(b).

The Code readings should seem fairly familiar if you have already completed the materials on partnership taxation. If not, be especially sure to read them closely, then consider the following problem.

PROBLEM 25-7

Gamma Corp. ("Gamma") is a calendar year, cash method S corporation. It has the following items of income, credit and deductions. Assume Gamma has one shareholder (L) who has a basis of $10,000 in her stock as of the end of the prior year.

What is L's basis in Gamma's stock after the following adjustments are made?

Operating revenues	$10,000.00
Business deductions	$5,000.00
Nondeductible expenses	$1,000.00
Income tax credits	$2,000.00
Tax-exempt interest	$7,000.00

3. REALLOCATION AMONG FAMILY GROUPS
Read § 1366(e).

Misallocations of income and losses from S corporations require great ingenuity because Subchapter S contains no equivalent of § 704(b). There are several reasons to do so, aside from merely shifting income to low-bracket family members. For example, one might use an S corporation to convert salary income that is otherwise subject to Social Security taxes into investment earnings that can be used to sop up losses from a tax shelter investment that are otherwise suspended by the passive loss rules of § 469. A share of profits from an S corporation is not subject to Social Security ("payroll") taxes. Rev. Rul. 59-221, 1959-1 C.B. 225. Because Social Security taxes on income from self-employment are 15.3% up to the annual threshold amount (over $118,000 as of this writing), this is a serious consideration. See § 1401. If an S corporation pays compensation to shareholder-employees, the IRS can be expected to try to recharacterize the compensation as salary. On the other hand, if the S corporation pays reasonable compensation, extra amounts should qualify as distributions. *See Radtke v. United States*, 895 F.2d 1196 (7th Cir. 1990) and *Spicer Accounting, Inc. v. United States*, 918 F.2d 90 (9th Cir. 1990).

Another important point is that § 704(e) requires appropriate allocations with respect to services and capital in family partnership settings. Section 1366(e) performs a similar job, but unlike § 704(e), it is not self-executing.

DAVIS v. COMMISSIONER
64 T.C. 1034 (1975)

GOFFE, JUDGE:

The petitioner, Dr. Davis, is an orthopedic surgeon who was engaged in a complete medical practice in that specialty. In his diagnostic work he relied upon x-rays made in his office and in cases where treatment was administered, the physical therapy was performed in his office. He organized two corporations, one of which performed the X-ray function and the other carried out physical therapy treatment which he prescribed. He made gifts of 90 percent of the stock of each of the corporations to his three minor children and they and the corporations elected to be taxed as small business corporations under the provisions of Subchapter S.

The Commissioner determined that the income of the corporations should be taxed to Dr. Davis under three distinct principles: (1) that under section 61 Dr. Davis attempted to assign the income or "fruit of the tree" when, in reality, Dr. Davis earned the income reported by the corporations; (2) section 482 required allocation of the income from the corporations to Dr. Davis in order to prevent avoidance of tax; and (3) Dr. Davis performed services for the corporations and section [1366(e)], therefore, required allocation back to him of the income reported by the corporations.

Respondent has limited the scope of his challenge to the reporting of the income by apparently conceding that X-ray and Therapy were not "shams or fictions in the purest sense." Likewise, respondent concedes that Dr. Davis' transfer of the stock to his children had substance and should, therefore, be recognized . . . We are urged, on the authority of *Gregory v. Helvering*, 293 U.S. 465, 470 (1935); *Commissioner v. Court Holding Co.*, 324 U.S. 331, 334 (1945); *Kimbrell v. Commissioner*, 371 F.2d 897, 902 (5th Cir. 1967), to find that the economic practicalities and substance of the arrangement requires taxation of the income to Dr. Davis rather than to the corporations.

Respondent further submits that the transfer of the X-ray and therapy facilities by Dr. Davis to the corporations followed by his transfer of the stock to his children constituted an anticipatory assignment of a portion of his future income. *See, e.g., Lucas v. Earl*, 281 U.S. 111 (1930); *Helvering v. Clifford*, 309 U.S.331, 335 (1940); *Commissioner v. Sunnen*, 333 U.S. 591 (1948). Alternatively, respondent advocates an allocation of the entire net taxable income of the corporations to Dr. Davis on the theory that the corporate contributions to the earning of the net taxable income were de minimis as compared to the services rendered by Dr. Davis. In this regard, he relies on the presumption accorded his determination under section 482, *Grenada Industries, Inc.*, 17 T.C. 231 (1951), *affd.* 202 F.2d 873 (5th Cir. 1953), cert. denied 346 U.S. 819 (1953), and, in the main, upon the inferences that may be drawn from all the circumstances where income is generated by a controlled business activity dependent upon the direction of patients, clients, or consumers from a controlling business activity which is closely related. Respondent also contends that the net taxable income of the corporations should be allocated to Dr. Davis pursuant to section [1366(e)] to reflect the value of his services to the corporations.

Respondent does not contend that X-Ray and Therapy were not viable business entities. Instead, respondent relies upon *Gregory v. Helvering*, 293 US. 465 (1935), and challenges taxation of the income to the corporations rather than to Dr. Davis on the grounds that his purpose in organizing the corporations was solely tax motivated. The primary reasons given by Dr. Davis for the transfers of the X-ray and physical therapy functions to the corporations and gifts of the stock to his children were as follows:

1. To provide security for his children in view of his marital difficulties and his personal health problems;

2. To insulate him personally from damage suits arising from negligent use of the potentially dangerous X-ray and physical therapy equipment; and

3. To separate the personnel problems into the X-ray and physical therapy functions and away from the personnel problems of his medical practice. Respondent counters with alternative remedies to the concerns of Dr. Davis. He could have made cash gifts to his children; he could have purchased liability insurance to insulate him from liability arising from the negligent use of the X-ray and physical therapy equipment; and he could have issued mandates to resolve the personnel problems.

We do not agree with respondent that Dr. Davis' purposes were tenuous. The transfer of valuable property rights with a known potential to produce income seems a logical reason to establish the corporations and give the stock to his children instead of giving cash which would have to be invested. Using the corporate form to insulate the taxpayer from liability has long been recognized as a valid reason for incorporating. *Sam Siegel*, 45 T.C. 566 (1966). It is especially applicable here because Dr. Davis had recently experienced the possibility of liability caused by serious burns received by a patient who was receiving heat therapy. We find Dr. Davis' explanation of resolving personnel differences by separation of the operations a plausible and satisfactory reason.

Respondent's reliance upon *Commissioner v. Kimbrell, supra*, is unavailing. In that case the corporations merely executed contracts, hired employees, negotiated loans, and collected interest thereon, and filed income tax returns. In the instant case the corporations X-rayed patients and administered physical therapy to patients.

Moreover, a taxpayer is not required to continue one form of business organization which results in the maximum tax on business income. *Polak's Frutal Works, Inc.,* 21 T.C. 953, 974-975 (1954).

Respondent contends that the earnings of the corporations should be taxed to Dr. Davis because he had control over the earning of the profits by performing the services. The facts are otherwise. Dr. Davis prescribed the type of X-ray or X-rays to be made for each patient and he prescribed the physical therapy, to be administered. The X-ray prescriptions to the corporation were no different than were those to a radiologist he referred patients to before he owned X-ray equipment or those given to the hospital when he would prescribe X-rays for a patient who was admitted to the emergency room. We see little difference in prescribing X-rays or physical therapy and prescribing drugs to be compounded by a pharmacist. Dr. Davis' division of his endeavors is not particularly unusual. It is common knowledge that an orthopedic surgeon does not himself normally take X-rays nor does he administer physical therapy. If, on the other hand, Dr. Davis attempted to separate his diagnostic work from his surgery, this would be unusual because a doctor personally performs both of these services for a patient. The income of the corporations was generated by the services of persons employed by the corporations not by the services performed by Dr. Davis. Dr. Davis direct services to the corporations were minimal. Under section 61, we conclude that the corporations controlled the capacity to produce the income through their employees and they, not Dr. Davis, are taxable on that income. *Ronan State Bank*, 62 T.C. 27 (1974).

Section 482 authorizes the Commissioner to allocate income and other items among related taxpayers in order to clearly reflect income or to prevent evasion of taxes.[2]

In his notices of deficiency the Commissioner allocated the net taxable income of the corporations to Dr. Davis. In his brief the Commissioner contends that the corporate employees were adequately compensated for the services they performed and that he advocates allocation only of the net taxable income of the corporations to Dr. Davis because the corporations' contributions of earning that portion of the income were minimal. This line of reasoning is fallacious. The corporations were paid fees comparable to those charged by other X-ray laboratories and physical therapists in the community and those fees were received by the corporations for the services performed by their employees, not Dr. Davis. Again, the analogy to the pharmacist is appropriate. The X-ray technician, the physical therapist and the pharmacist all carry out prescriptions made by the doctor. Respondent's blanket characterization of the tasks of the employees of the corporations which include the X-ray technician and the physical therapist as "routine" is not warranted. Both are specialists trained to carry out a doctor's order just as a pharmacist fills a prescription. As pointed out above in our discussion of section 61, the division of Dr. Davis' practice into medical practice, X-ray and physical therapy is not unusual in that the different endeavors are frequently engaged in by separate persons or entities. It is also not unusual in the respect that X-ray laboratories and physical therapists rely on referrals for their business. Again, we see a close analogy to the better known relationship of doctor and pharmacist. The entire arrangement was comparable to others in the community except that Dr. Davis was in a position to forward business to the corporations. For example, before he owned X-ray equipment, he referred his patients to a radiologist which did not give him a referral fee in return. The radiologist performed no service for the patient different from what the X-ray corporation now performs; i.e., in both instances the X-rays were interpreted and acted upon by Dr. Davis. Based on all the evidence we conclude that petitioners have made an adequate showing that the Commissioner abused the discretion granted to him by section 482 in allocating the net taxable income of the corporations to Dr. Davis.

Respondent relies upon *Pauline W. Ach*, 42 T.C. 114 (1964), *affd*. 358 F.2d 342 (6th Cir. 1966). That case is factually distinguishable. *Ach* involved the transfer of a lucrative dress shop business from one member of a family to a related family-owned corporation which had operated a losing dairy business. The transfer was for a promissory note equal to the book value of the assets of the dress shop business. The income of the dress shop business was absorbed by net operating loss carryovers of the dairy business. We sustained disallowance of the net operating loss carryovers under the provisions of section 269 and we approved allocation under section 482 of 70 percent of the dress business profits to Pauline Ach because that portion was attributable to her services. In the instant case we have found as a fact that the gross income of the corporations was not generated by Dr. Davis but, instead, by the employees of the corporations. The referrals, because they are not unusual as explained above, do not constitute services rendered by Dr. Davis to the corporations.

Respondent points to the failure of Dr. Davis to charge rent for the first six months of 1966, the failure to charge Dr. Davis for use of the X-ray machine and the failure to share

---

[2] Petitioner seeks to distinguish management and control by directing our attention to a series of decisions, which are concerned with the assignment of income question under *Lucas v. Earl*, 281 U.S. 111 (1930). Accordingly, we find those decisions distinguishable. We find the reality of control obvious. Sec. 1.482-1(a)(3)-(4), Income Tax Regs.

common overhead expenses as indicative that his reallocation was proper. As explained above, we have held the reallocation of the Commissioner to be unreasonable. Respondent has not pleaded in the alternative that the specific items described above should be allocated nor did he request amendment of his pleadings following the trial to conform them to the proof. It is obvious that there is some basis for reallocation of the three items, minimal as they are. We will not voluntarily attempt to make such an allocation at this point because the pleadings never apprised petitioners of that issue in order that they could offer proof of the proper allocation of those specific items. The issue presented at trial was allocation of net taxable income upon the broad concept that Dr. Davis generated the income. The size of these three items in relation to the gross income and other expenses cannot justify allocation of the entire net taxable income to Dr. Davis.

As a final "string to his bow" the Commissioner relies upon section [1366(e)] which permits him to allocate from one shareholder in a "Small Business Corporation" (Subchapter S corporation) amounts treated as dividends which should be allocated to other shareholders who are members of the shareholders' family to reflect the value of services rendered to the corporation by such shareholders. The purpose of section [1366(e)] is to tax each shareholder of a Subchapter S corporation on the full value of the income he earns. No deflection of that income is to be permitted through artificial salary or dividend payments. S. Rept. No. 1983, 85th Cong., 2d Sess. (1958), 1958-3 C.B. 1143-1144; *Charles Rocco*, 57 T.C. 826, 831 (1972).

In determining the value of services rendered by a shareholder, consideration shall be given to all the facts and circumstances of the business, including the managerial responsibilities of the shareholder, and the amount that would ordinarily be paid in order to obtain comparable services from a person not having an interest in the corporation . . . [Sec. 1.1375-3(a), Income Tax Regs. This provision continues to appear in the Regulations beginning "1.1375," but the Code has been reshuffled to put the subject in 1366(e), at least until the next reshuffling. Eds.]

The determination is factual and tests applied to ascertain the value of the shareholder's services include "the nature of the services performed, the responsibilities involved, the time spent, the size and complexity of the business, prevailing economic conditions, compensation paid by comparable firms for comparable services, and salary paid to company officers in prior years . . . " *Walter J. Roob,* 50 T.C. 891, 898, 899 (1968).

As in *Charles Rocco, supra*, at 832, we need not decide whether section [1366(e)] requires petitioner to merely overcome the presumptive correctness of the Commissioner's determination or requires him to prove that the Commissioner abused his discretion (if section [1366(e)] provides the Commissioner with the same authority he possesses under section 482) because here we find that petitioners have satisfied both tests.

The Commissioner allocated 100 percent of the net taxable income of the Subchapter S corporations to Dr. Davis. The undisputed testimony is that he did not actually spend more than 20 hours per year in direct duties to the corporations, which is minimal.

Respondent would have us consider the referral activities of Dr. Davis as being personal services rendered by him to the corporations. This we will not do. As stated above, one of the tests we enumerated above from *Roob*, supra, is compensation paid by comparable firms for comparable services. When Dr. Davis referred X-ray patients to a radiologist before he acquired X-ray equipment, the radiologist did not pay him a fee. The same is true as to referrals to a physical therapist. The fees earned by the corporations were the result of the use of the equipment which they owned and the services of their employees, not as a result of services performed by Dr. Davis for the corporations. Respondent's theory, therefore, fails under the comparability test and our holding under section [1366(e)] is consistent with our holdings under section 61 and 482. The Commissioner erred in allocating the net taxable income of the corporations to Dr. Davis under section [1366(e)].

Accordingly, we find that none of the net taxable income of X-Ray and Therapy was taxable to Petitioners Edwin D. Davis and Sandra W. Davis for the taxable years 1966 and 1967.

Decisions will be entered under Rule 155.

NOTES

Assuming the transactions with the related corporations are at arm's length, what has Dr. Davis achieved from a tax perspective? Assuming it is desirable to coordinate Subchapter S and Subchapter K, should § 1366(e) be made self-executing, or should § 704(e) perhaps be made not self-executing?

Note that if one successfully shifts income to children, even if the children pay taxes at income tax rates as high as their parents' on income from the S corporation, the parent will still have saved federal estate or gift taxes compared to being taxed on the S corporation's income and making gifts of the net proceeds to children, if federal transfer taxes apply to the gifts. Because top transfer tax rates exceed top income tax rates, they are an important planning consideration for the owner of a prosperous business.

Observe that § 704(e) only covers cases where interests in the partnership have been shifted by gift or by sale to family members. There is no such limit upon § 1366(e).

Note that salaries and wages from an S corporation are subject to Social security taxes but that distributive shares of profits are not. This has led IRS auditors to attempt to recharacterize distributive shares as wages or salaries with respect to undercompensated employees.

G. LIMITS ON USE OF LOSSES AND DEDUCTIONS

1. GENERAL LIMITATION
Read §§ 1366(d)(l) and (2) and 1367(a), (b).

The amount of losses and deductions a shareholder of an S corporation can claim is limited to the adjusted basis of the shareholder's stock, plus any loans the shareholder has made to the corporation. § 1366(d)(l). To compute these limits, a shareholder computes the upward adjustments to basis of the shareholder's stock at year-end, then reduces basis in the stock for distributions made during the year, and then reduces basis by losses and separately stated deductions. *See* § 1366(d)(1)(A), § 1367(a), Reg. § 1.1367-1(f).

After the basis in the S corporation stock declines to zero, the shareholder next reduces her basis in the debt. §§ 1367(a)(2), § 1366(d)(1)(B). There is a trap here with respect to debt, namely that if the holder of the debt sells it before its basis is replenished, the holder will suffer a taxable gain if the debt is sold for an amount greater than its basis. Another trap is that if the corporation makes a distribution with respect to its stock at a time when the holder's basis in the debt has not been replenished, the result is a gain with respect to the stock, because the stock has a zero basis. *See* § 1368(b)(2). This problem could arise if the tax advisor forgot that S corporation income replenishes basis first in debt, then stock, not vice-versa.

When the rule limiting shareholder deductions of pass-through items to stock and debt basis limits a shareholder's loss or deduction, the excess deduction is suspended and deemed incurred by the S corporation in the next taxable year for that shareholder and carries forward indefinitely until that shareholder uses up the suspended amount, disposes of the stock or dies. *See* § 1366(d)(2).

The shareholder's loss may be further limited by some other restriction, such as the "at-risk" restriction of § 465 or the passive-activity loss rules of § 469. An S corporation shareholder's basis in stock of the corporation is reduced under § 1367(a)(2)(B) by a passive activity loss passed through to the shareholder even though the shareholder's claim to that loss may be suspended by the passive activity loss limitation. To prevent double counting, the basis is not again reduced when the loss ultimately is allowed under § 469. S. Rep. No. 313, 99th

513

Cong., 1986-3 C.B. 723. Thus, several restrictions may operate at once, and those losses are the shareholder's alone and cannot be transferred away.

PROBLEM 25-8

George is a 50% shareholder in S Corp. Both George and S Corp. are cash method, calendar year taxpayers. At the beginning of the year, George had a $30 basis in his S Corp. stock. During the past taxable year, S Corp. distributed $20 to George. S Corp. ended the year with a $50 operating loss, but has no outstanding debt.

1) What is George's share of the operating losses of S Corp.?

2) Does one compute the corporation's losses for the year before or after the determining how distributions are taxed to shareholders?

3) What is George's outside basis in his shares after the distribution, but prior to the allocation of losses?

4) What is George's outside basis in his shares after the distribution and the allocation of losses?

5) Is any portion of the loss allocated to George disallowed? If so, what happens to it? *See* §§ 1366, 1367.

6) How would the results in "(2)" and "(3)" differ if the rules as to the timing of losses versus distributions were reversed?

2. MANIPULATION OF DEBT AND GUARANTEES

One can easily see that shareholders have an incentive for tax purposes to classify business debts as their own obligations and not the corporation's, because they get no "outside" basis in the company's debt, quite unlike the case for partnerships (under § 752). This has led to a lot of tax planning and occasional major blunders by taxpayers and their advisors.

ESTATE OF LEAVITT v. COMMISSIONER
875 F.2d 420 (4th Cir. 1989), *cert. denied*, 493 U.S. 958 (1989)

MURNAGHAN, CIRCUIT JUDGE.

The appellants, Anthony D. and Marjorie F. Cuzzocrea and the Estate of Daniel Leavitt, Deceased, et al., appeal the Tax Court's decision holding them liable for tax deficiencies for the tax years 1979, 1980 and 1981. Finding the appellants' arguments unpersuasive, we affirm the Tax Court.

I.

As shareholders of VAFLA Corporation, a subchapter S corporation during the years at issue, the appellants claimed deductions under §1374 of the Internal Revenue Code of 1954 to reflect the corporation's operating losses during the three years in question. The Commissioner disallowed deductions above the $10,000 bases each appellant had from their original investments.

514

The appellants contend, however, that the adjusted bases in their stock should be increased to reflect a $300,000 loan which VAFLA obtained from the Bank of Virginia ("Bank") on September 12, 1979, after the appellants, along with five other shareholders ("Shareholders-Guarantors"), had signed guarantee agreements whereby each agreed to be jointly and severally liable for all indebtedness of the corporation to the Bank. At the time of the loan, VAFLA's liability exceeded its assets, it could not meet its cash flow requirements and it had virtually no assets to use as collateral. The appellants assert that the Bank would not have lent the $300,000 without their personal guarantees.

VAFLA's financial statements and tax returns indicated that the bank loan was a loan from the Shareholders-Guarantors. Despite the representation to that effect, VAFLA made all of the loan payments, principal and interest, to the Bank. The appellants made no such payments. In addition, neither VAFLA nor the Shareholders-Guarantors treated the corporate payments on the loan as constructive income taxable to the Shareholders-Guarantors.

The appellants present the question whether the $300,000 bank loan is really, despite its form as a borrowing from the Bank, a capital contribution from the appellants to VAFLA. They contend that if the bank loan is characterized as equity, they are entitled to add a pro rata share of the $300,000 bank loan to their adjusted bases, thereby increasing the size of their operating loss deductions. Implicit in the appellants' characterization of the bank loan as equity in VAFLA is a determination that the Bank lent the $300,000 to the Shareholders-Guarantors who then contributed the funds to the corporation. The appellants' approach fails to realize that the $300,000 transaction, regardless of whether it is equity or debt, would permit them to adjust the bases in their stock if, indeed, the appellants, and not the Bank, had advanced VAFLA the money. The more precise question, which the appellants fail initially to ask, is whether the guaranteed loan from the Bank to VAFLA is an economic outlay of any kind by the Shareholders-Guarantors. To decide this question, we must determine whether the transaction involving the $300,000 was a loan from the Bank to VAFLA or was it instead a loan to the Shareholders-Guarantors who then gave it to VAFLA, as either a loan or a capital contribution.

Finding no economic outlay, we need not address the question, which is extensively addressed in the briefs, of whether the characterization of the $300,000 was debt or equity.

II.

To increase the basis in the stock of a subchapter S corporation, there must be an economic outlay on the part of the shareholder. *See Brown v. Commissioner,* 706 F.2d 755, 756 (6th Cir. 1983*), affg,* T.C. Memo 1981-608 (1981) ("In similar cases, the courts have consistently required some economic outlay by the guarantor in order to convert a mere loan guarantee into an investment"); *Blum v. Commissioner,* 59 T.C. 436, 440 (1972) (bank expected repayment of its loan from the corporation and not the taxpayers, i.e., no economic outlay from taxpayers).[3] A guarantee, in and of itself, cannot fulfill that requirement. The guarantee is merely a promise to pay in the future if certain unfortunate events should occur. At the present time, the appellants have experienced no such call as guarantors, have engaged in no economic outlay, and have suffered no cost.

The situation would be different if VAFLA had defaulted on the loan payments and the Shareholders-Guarantors had made actual, disbursements on the corporate indebtedness. Those payments would represent corporate indebtedness to the shareholders which would increase their bases for the purpose of deducting net operating losses under § 1374(c)(2)(B). *Brown,* 706

---

[3] Even the Eleventh Circuit case on which the appellants heavily rely applies this first step. *See Selfe v. United States,* 778 F.2d 769, 772 (11th Cir. 1985) ("We agree with *Brown* inasmuch as that court reaffirms that economic outlay is required before a stockholder in a Subchapter S corporation may increase her basis.").

F.2d at 757. See also *Raynor v. Commissioner*, 50 T.C. 762, 770-71 (1968) ("No form of indirect borrowing, be it guaranty, surety, accommodation, co-making or otherwise, gives rise to indebtedness from the corporation to the shareholders until and unless the shareholders pay part or all of the obligation.").

The appellants accuse the Tax Court of not recognizing the critical distinction between § 1374(c)(2)(A) (adjusted basis in stock) and § 1374(c)(2)(B) (adjusted basis in indebtedness of corporation to shareholder). They argue that the "loan" is not really a loan, but is a capital contribution (equity). Therefore, they conclude, § 1374(c)(2)(A) applies and § 1374(c)(2)(B) is irrelevant. However, the appellants once again fail to distinguish between the initial question of economic outlay and the secondary issue of debt or equity. Only if the first question had an affirmative answer, would the second arise.

The majority opinion of the Tax Court, focusing on the first issue of economic outlay, determined that a guarantee, in and of itself, is not an event for which basis can be adjusted. It distinguished the situation presented to it from one where the guarantee is triggered and actual payments are made. In the latter scenario, the first question of economic outlay is answered affirmatively (and the second issue is apparent on its face, i.e., the payments represent indebtedness from the corporation to the shareholder as opposed to capital contribution from the shareholder to the corporation). To the contrary is the situation presented here. The Tax Court, far from confusing the issue by discussing irrelevant matters, was comprehensively explaining why the transaction before it could not represent any kind of economic outlay by the appellants.

The Tax Court correctly determined that the appellants' guarantees, unaccompanied by further acts, in and of themselves, have not constituted contributions of cash or other property which might increase the bases of the appellants' stock in the corporation.

The appellants, while they do not disagree with the Tax Court that the guarantees, standing alone, cannot adjust their bases in the stock, nevertheless argue that the "loan" to VAFLA was in its "true sense" a loan to the Shareholders-Guarantors who then theoretically advanced the $300,000 to the corporation as a capital contribution. The Tax Court declined the invitation to treat a loan and its uncalled-on security, the guarantee, as identical and to adopt the appellants' view of the "substance" of the transaction over the "form" of the transaction they took. The Tax Court did not err in doing so.

Generally, taxpayers are liable for the tax consequences of the transaction they actually execute and may not reap the benefit of recasting the transaction into another one substantially different in economic effect that they might have made. They are bound by the "form" of their transaction and may not argue that the "substance" of their transaction triggers different tax consequences. *Don E. Williams Co. v. Commissioner,* 429 U.S. 569, 579-80, 51 L. Ed. 2d 48, 97 S. Ct. 850 (1977); *Commissioner v. National Alfalfa Dehydrating & Milling Co.,* 417 U.S. 134, 149, 40 L. Ed. 2d 717, 94 S. Ct. 2129 (1974). In the situation of guaranteed corporate debt, where the form of the transaction may not be so clear, courts have permitted the taxpayer to argue that the substance of the transaction was in actuality a loan to the shareholder. *See Blum,* 59 T.C. at 440. However, the burden is on the taxpayer and it has been a difficult one to meet. That is especially so where, as here, the transaction is cast in sufficiently ambiguous terms to permit an argument either way depending on which is subsequently advantageous from a tax point of view.

In the case before us, the Tax Court found that the "form" and "substance" of the transaction was a loan from the Bank to VAFLA and not to the appellants:

The Bank of Virginia loaned the money to the corporation and not to petitioners. The proceeds of the loan were to be used in the operation of the corporation's business. Petitioners submitted no evidence that they were free to dispose of the proceeds of the loan as they wished. Nor were the payments on the loan reported as constructive dividends on the corporation's Federal income tax returns or on the petitioners' Federal income tax returns during the years in issue. Accordingly, we find that the transaction was in fact a loan by the bank to the corporation guaranteed by the shareholders.

Whether the $300,000 was lent to the corporation or to the Shareholders/Guarantors is a factual issue which should not be disturbed unless clearly erroneous. Finding no error, we affirm.

It must be borne in mind that we do not merely encounter naive taxpayers caught in a complex trap for the unwary. They sought to claim deductions because the corporation lost money. If, however, VAFLA had been profitable, they would be arguing that the loan was in reality from the Bank to the corporation, and not to them, for that would then lessen their taxes. Under that description of the transaction, the loan repayments made by VAFLA would not be on the appellants' behalf, and, consequently, would not be taxed as constructive income to them. *See Old Colony Trust Co. v. Commissioner,* 279 U.S. 716, 73 L. Ed. 918, 49 S. Ct. 499 (1929) (payment by a corporation of a personal expense or debt of a shareholder is considered as the receipt of a taxable benefit). It came down in effect to an ambiguity as to which way the appellants would jump, an effort to play both ends against the middle, until it should be determined whether VAFLA was a profitable or money-losing proposition. At that point, the appellants attempted to treat the transaction as cloaked in the guise having the more beneficial tax consequences for them.

Finally, the appellants complain that the Tax Court erred by failing to apply debt-equity principles to determine the "form" of the loan. We believe that the Tax Court correctly refused to apply debt-equity principles here, a methodology which is only relevant, if at all, to resolution of the second inquiry – what is the nature of the economic outlay.[4] Of course, the second inquiry cannot be reached unless the first question concerning whether an economic outlay exists is answered affirmatively. Here it is not.

The appellants, in effect, attempt to collapse a two-step analysis into a one-step inquiry which would eliminate the initial determination of economic outlay by first concluding that the proceeds were a capital contribution (equity). Obviously, a capital contribution is an economic outlay so the basis in the stock would be adjusted accordingly. But such an approach simply ignores the factual determination by the Tax Court that the Bank lent the $300,000 to the corporation and not to the Shareholders-Guarantors.

The appellants rely on *Blum v. Commissioner*, 59 T.C. 436 (1972), and *Selfe v. United States,* 778 F.2d 769 (11th Cir. 1985), to support their position. However, the appellants have misread those cases. In *Blum,* the Tax Court declined to apply debt-equity principles to determine whether the taxpayer's guarantee of a loan from a bank to a corporation was an indirect capital contribution. The Tax Court held that the taxpayer had failed to carry his burden of proving that the transaction was in "substance" a loan from the bank to the shareholder rather than a loan to the corporation. The *Blum* court found dispositive the fact that "the bank expected repayment of its loan from the corporation and not the petitioner." *Blum*, 59 T.C. at 440.

---

[4] The appellants correctly state that the First, Fifth and Ninth Circuits have all applied traditional debt-equity principles in determining whether a shareholder's guarantee of a corporate debt was in substance a capital contribution. *See Casco Bank & Trust Co. v. United States,* 544 F.2d 528 (1st Cir. 1976), cert. denied, 430 U.S. 907, 97 S. Ct. 1176, 51 L. Ed. 2d 582 (1977); *Plantation Patterns v. Commissioner,* 462 F.2d 712 (5th Cir. 1972), *cert. denied*, 409 U.S. 1076, 93 S. Ct. 683, 34 L. Ed. 2d 664 (1972); *Murphy Logging Co. v. United States*, 378 F.2d 222 (9th Cir. 1967). What the appellants fail to point out, however, is that those cases each involved activated guarantees, i.e., actual advances or payments on defaults. Therefore, the issue in those cases was not whether the taxpayer had made an "investment" – an economic outlay – in the corporation. The investment was admitted. The issue in those cases asked what was the nature of the investment – equity or debt. None of those cases involved the disallowance of deductions claimed by a shareholder pursuant to § 1374 for his or her share of an electing corporation's operating losses where there had simply been no economic outlay by the shareholder under the guarantee).

With regard to *Selfe,* the Tax Court stated:

> The Eleventh Circuit applied a debt-equity analysis and held that a shareholder's guarantee of a loan made to a subchapter S corporation may be treated for tax purposes as an equity investment in the corporation where the lender looks to the shareholder as the primary obligor. We respectfully disagree with the Eleventh Circuit and hold that a shareholder's guarantee of a loan to a subchapter S corporation may not be treated as an equity investment in the corporation absent an economic outlay by the shareholder.

The Tax Court then distinguished *Plantation Patterns,* 462 F.2d 712 (5th Cir. 1972), relied on by *Selfe,* because that case involved a C corporation, reasoning that the application of debt-equity principles to subchapter S corporations would defeat Congress' intent to limit a shareholder's pass-through deduction to the amount he or she has actually invested in the corporation.

The Tax Court also distinguished *In re Lane,* 742 F.2d 1311 (11th Cir. 1984), relied on by the *Selfe* court, on the basis that the shareholder had actually paid the amounts he had guaranteed, i.e., there was an economic outlay. In *Lane,* which involved a subchapter S corporation, the issue was "whether advances made by a shareholder to a corporation constitute debt or equity . . . "*Id.* at 1313. If the advances were debt, then Lane could deduct them as bad debts. On the other hand, if the advances were capital, no bad debt deduction would be permitted. Thus, the issue of adjusted basis for purposes of flow-through deductions from net operating losses of the corporation was not at issue. There was no question of whether there had been an economic outlay.

Although *Selfe* does refer to debt-equity principles, the specific issue before it was whether any material facts existed making summary judgment inappropriate. The Eleventh Circuit said:

> At issue here, however, is not whether the taxpayer's contribution was either a loan to or an equity investment in Jane Simon, Inc. The issue is whether the taxpayer's guarantee of the corporate loan was in itself a contribution to the corporation [as opposed to a loan from the bank] sufficient to increase the taxpayer's basis in the corporation.

The *Selfe* court found that there was evidence that the bank primarily looked to the taxpayer and not the corporation for repayment of the loan. Therefore, it remanded for "a determination of whether or not the bank primarily looked to Jane Selfe [taxpayer] for repayment [the first inquiry] and for the court to apply the factors set out in *In re Lane* and I.R.C. section 385 to determine if the taxpayer's guarantee amounted to either an equity investment in or shareholder loan to Jane Simon, Inc. [the second inquiry]." *Id.* at 775. The implications are that there is still a two-step analysis and that the debt-equity principles apply only to the determination of the characterization of the economic outlay, once one is found.

Granted, that conclusion is clouded by the next and final statement of the *Selfe* court: "In short, we remand for the district court to apply *Plantation Patterns* and determine if the bank loan to Jane Simon, Inc. was in reality a loan to the taxpayer." *Id.* To the degree that the *Selfe* court agreed with *Brown* that an economic outlay is required before a shareholder may increase her basis in a subchapter S corporation, *Selfe* does not contradict current law or our resolution of the case before us. Furthermore, to the extent that the *Selfe* court remanded because material facts existed by which the taxpayer could show that the bank actually lent the money to her rather than the corporation's, we are still able to agree. It is because of the *Selfe* court's suggestion that debt-equity principles must be applied to resolve the question of whether the bank actually lent the money to the taxpayer/shareholder or the corporation, that we must part company with the Eleventh Circuit for the reasons stated above.

In conclusion, the Tax Court correctly focused on the initial inquiry of whether an economic outlay existed. Finding none, the issue of whether debt-equity principles ought to apply to determine the nature of the economic outlay was not before the Tax Court. The Tax Court is

Affirmed.

QUESTIONS

Does it make sense to deny a shareholder-guarantor basis for a loan made by a third party to the S corporation, especially if the lender is really looking to the guarantor's credit and not the corporation's? Does this rigidity trap the unwary who use guarantees, while forcing those who can afford good tax advice to go through the extra step of borrowing the money and then lending it on to the S corporation? Also, why deny a guarantor basis for an S corporation debt, but grant basis in nonrecourse debt if a partnership is the borrower?

H. QUALIFIED BUSINESS INCOME (QBI) 20% OF INCOME DEDUCTION ("PASS-THROUGH DEDUCTION") FOR TAX YEARS 2018–2025. §199A
Read: Code Sec. 199A

Sole proprietorship, partnerships, S corporations, REITS or LLCs receive a 20% Qualified business income deduction for tax years 2018–2025 against their qualified business income. The QBI deduction is not an itemized deduction. Taxpayers who take the standard deduction still get the 20% deduction. A highly distilled refresher follows. For a more in-depth discussion, please see page __.

Qualified Business Income is the net amount of items of income, gain, deduction, and loss with respect to the trade or business. Section 199A excludes certain types of business income such as capital gains or losses, dividends, interest income, employee compensation and guaranteed payments to a partner.

Taxpayers with taxable income above $157,500 ($315,000 for joint filers), exclude income from "specified service" trades or businesses from QBI. These trades or businesses involve the performance of services, such as in health, law, consulting, athletics, financial or brokerage or where the principal asset of the business is the reputation or skill of one or more employees or owners.

In addition, for taxpayers with taxable income above t$157,500 ($315,000 for joint filers), a limit on the deduction phases in based either on wages paid or wages paid plus capital.

PROBLEM 25-9

1) Alice, an unmarried individual, owns and operates a computer repair shop as a sole proprietorship. The business generated $100,000 in net taxable income from operations in 2018. Alice has no capital gains or losses. After allowable deductions not relating to the business, Alice's total taxable income for 2018 is $81,000.

    a. What is the business' Qualified Business Income?

    b. What is the amount of Alice's §199A deduction?

2) Assume the same facts as in "(1)" except that Alice also has $7,000 in net capital gain for 2018 and that, after allowable deductions not relating to the business, Alice's taxable income for 2018 is $74,000. What is the amount of Alice's §199A deduction?

I. CURRENT DISTRIBUTIONS: INTRODUCTION
Read §§ 1368(a) and (b).

A shareholder is generally not subject to tax on actual distributions of cash or property by the S corporation unless the distributions exceed the shareholder's basis in the corporation's stock or, in general, unless the corporation was formerly a C corporation and still has earnings and profits. § 1368. The details in this area are not simple, but not overwhelmingly difficult either.

1. CORPORATIONS WITHOUT E & P
Read §§ 1368(a) and (b).

At the end of an S corporation's taxable year, each shareholder must determine the tax treatment of any distributions actually received during the S corporation's taxable year, and their effect on the shareholder's basis in his shares. This must be done before making adjustments in the shareholder's basis in his shares for purposes of both determining the limit on the pass-through of losses to the shareholder and the effects on basis of such losses passed through. § 1366(d)(1)(A).

Any distribution that a shareholder receives from an S corporation that has no earnings and profits simply reduces the adjusted basis of the shareholder's stock in the S corporation. If the distribution does not exceed the shareholder's adjusted basis, it is treated as a nontaxable return of capital and stock basis is adjusted downward by that amount. § 1368(b)(1); § 1367(a)(2)(A). (A shareholder's basis in debt cannot be used to affect tax on distributions, although it can be used to affect the allowance of losses passed through.)

If and to the extent the distributions exceed the adjusted basis of the shareholder's stock, the excess is treated as a gain from the sale or exchange of stock. See § 1368(b)(2). Thus, the gain is generally long or short-term capital gain. The next year's opening adjusted basis for shareholder's stock will be affected not only by the distributions, but also by adjustments for passed through gains and losses.

To illustrate: Erica Wharton owns all the stock of S Corp. S Corp. has no E & P. Her year-end stock basis is $60,000, before adjustments for income, losses, and distributions. S Corp. incurs a $60,000 loss this year and distributes $10,000 to her at the very end of the year. As a result, the $10,000 distribution is tax-free, but her loss deduction is limited to $50,000, because her basis in her stock has been reduced by the $10,000 distribution. The year-end basis is $0 and her loss carry forward is $10,000.

PROBLEM 25-10

You are the sole shareholder of an S corporation that is faring poorly. In year one, you invested $10,000 of cash and loaned the company $30,000. It then quickly lost $40,000. However, it is now the very end of year one, and, some months ago, the company borrowed $10,000 from a bank, which money you suddenly need for your personal use.

How would you characterize the $10,000 you are about to get so as to minimize your tax burden? Assume that you will not actually receive the $10,000 until next year (*i.e.*, in year two, when the corporation is inert).

2. CORPORATIONS WITH E & P

Read §§ 1368(c) through (e)(2).

S corporations with E & P have more complicated tax lives than those without E & P.

a. Impact

Although S corporations themselves cannot use their operating results to generate or reduce E & P for taxable years beginning after 1982 in which they were S corporations, an S corporation can still have earnings and profits from various sources, including:

- Taxable years when the corporation was a C corporation;

- A corporate acquisition that caused a carryover of earnings and profits from the acquired corporation under § 381; and

- The acquisition of a subsidiary with E & P, which is made the subject of a QSSS election.

To determine the source of a distribution, the Code sets forth a priority list of sources in § 1368(c). Specifically, if the corporation has accumulated earnings and profits, it must maintain separate accounts for three separate sources of distributions:

(1) The accumulated adjustments account (AAA), which is post-1982 earnings of an S corporation that have been taxed to shareholders;

(2) Previously taxed income (PTI), which is undistributed income of an S corporation that was taxed to shareholders under pre-1983 law; and

(3) Accumulated E & P.

The ordering rules tend to favor basis reductions instead of producing ordinary income. A distribution is deemed first to come out of the accumulated adjustments account (AAA). Such a distribution reduces the shareholder's adjusted basis in his or her stock and is not taxable up to that amount. A distribution out of AAA that exceeds the shareholder's adjusted basis in the stock is gain from the sale or exchange of stock, unless there are further sources, as described in the following sentences.

If and to the extent distributions in the taxable year exceed the AAA at the end of the taxable year (calculated before the distributions), the AAA is generally allocated to each distribution made during the year in proportion to the amount of each distribution. If the S corporation has previously taxed income (PTI), the PTI is the next source for distributions. Any distribution out of PTI reduces the shareholder's basis in his or her stock and is not taxable up to that basis. A distribution out of PTI in excess of the shareholder's stock basis is also deemed a gain from the sale of stock.

Third, after the prior two sources are exhausted, a distribution is deemed to come from the S corporation's E & P, if any. Any such distribution is a taxable dividend up to the amount of the corporation's earnings and profits; these distributions do not reduce stock basis. *See* § 1367(a)(2).

Fourth, after the prior three sources are exhausted, a distribution is applied against and reduces the shareholder's basis in stock and possibly produces additional gain. *See* §§ 1368(b)-(c).

Finally, any further distribution is deemed taxable as from a sale of stock. Stock basis is never reduced below zero by these rules.

b. Election to Purge Earnings and Profits

An S corporation can elect to treat its distributions as coming first from E & P, if all shareholders who receive a distribution during the taxable year consent to the S corporation election. § 1368(e)(3). In effect, the corporation can do this by paying out less actual cash than would otherwise be necessary if it had to pay out all the AAA account in order to reach the E & P account. This can only be done in the year of the S election.

The effect of the election is that each shareholder reports a taxable dividend in the amount of the distribution that is treated as coming from E & P. Once earnings and profits are fully disgorged, subsequent distributions are treated as having been paid by an S corporation without earnings and profits. The benefits can be significant; if the corporation has no E & P, there can be no § 1375 tax on excess passive income and no loss of S corporation status because of having too much of such income. At the current 20% rate on most dividends, the pain is not great.

c. The Accumulated Adjustments Account ("AAA") Revisited
Read § 1368(e)(l).

The AAA begins at zero (unless the company is the product of a restructuring that resulted in picking up another firm's AAA account) and is adjusted annually for income, losses, and expenses. On the first day of an S corporation's first tax year that begins after 1982, the balance of its AAA is zero. This accommodates the law that created the concept of the AAA. One makes no adjustment to the AAA for tax-exempt income or related expenses, whereas such amounts do entail adjustments to the basis of the stock. *See* § 1368(e)(l)(A).

The AAA can be negative, in which case later income will make the account positive, but only after the negative balance has been restored.

PROBLEM 25-11

Bob owns 60% and Ray owns 40% of the stock of Einbinder Flypaper Corporation, which is an S corporation. The stock constitutes a capital asset in each of their hands. The AAA is zero at the beginning of the year. As of the end of the year, Bob's basis for his stock was $80,000, and Ray's basis for his stock was $30,000 because he recently bought the stock on the cheap from Bob's nephew.

At a time when it had accumulated E & P from a C corporation year of $10,000, Einbinder Flypaper Corporation distributed cash of $90,000 to Bob and $60,000 to Ray. The following items had been allocated to Einbinder Flypaper Corporation's shareholders during its period of operating as an S corporation:

(1) Tax-exempt interest of $40,000;

(2) § 1231 gains of $30,000;

(3) Non-separately-computed income from domestic sources of $110,000;

(4) Short-term capital losses of $10,000;

(5) Long-term capital losses of $15,000; and

(6) Foreign losses of $25,000.

Assume that all these amounts were already accounted for in computing Bob and Ray's basis in their stock.

1)   What is Einbinder Flypaper Corporation's AAA account?

2)   What is the post-distribution basis of the stock held by Bob? By Ray?

3)   How are the distributions to Bob and Ray taxed?

4)   How is the tax-exempt income accounted for? *See* §§ 1367(a) and 1366(a).

5)   If Bob had allocable losses in excess of his stock basis, could he claim basis for a loan from a bank to Einbinder Flypaper Corporation where the bank really looked to Bob's credit-worthiness for comfort and not to the corporation?

3. DISTRIBUTIONS OF PROPERTY
Read § 1371(a).

If an S corporation distributes property, currently or in liquidation, the amount of the distribution is its fair market value. If it distributes property with a value in excess of basis, the S corporation is treated as if it had sold the property to its shareholders at fair market value. §§ 311 and 1371(a)(1). The corporation must recognize the gain (it does not recognize a loss) and it will pass that gain through to its shareholders. § 311. Thus, the corporation *generally* does not actually pay a tax; the shareholders do. The exception is the § 1374 BIG tax, which falls on the corporation itself at top corporate rates.

The shareholder uses that same hypothetical fair market value sales price to report the tax treatment of the property distribution.

To illustrate: Sam Shareholder owns all the stock of S Corp. His basis in his stock is $2,000. S Corp. owns an asset with a basis of $0 and a fair market value of $1,000. S Corp. distributes the asset to Sam. Assume the asset has been held for eleven years, which means that the BIG tax cannot apply. The results are that S Corp. pays no tax, but it does report that S Corp. and, therefore, Sam had a $1,000 gain. This momentarily increases Sam's stock basis to $3,000. The $1,000 distribution, however, reduces his basis back down to $2,000. Sam's basis in the asset is $1,000.

Because it was a current distribution, the corporation was forced to recognize gains, but will not be allowed to report losses. S. Rep. No. 445, 100th Cong, 2d Sess. 65 (1988). The shrewd S corporation will sell loss assets rather than distribute them, in order to be able to recognize, and all its shareholders to deduct, the loss on sale.

Again, unless the BIG tax of § 1374 applies, the practical effect is that the corporation as such pays no tax; rather, the gain flows through to its shareholders. If § 1374 applies, the story is different. The corporation will in fact pay tax at top corporate rates.

If the distribution is part of a liquidation, § 336 applies, and the company reports gains *and losses* on its constructive sale of appreciated or loss property, which will in turn flow through to its shareholders. Again, if § 1374 applies, there may be a corporate level tax. If the distribution occurred in liquidation, § 331 treats shareholders as if they sold their stock; thus the shareholder's gain is almost invariably a capital gain.

Returning to the example of a current liquidation, if the BIG tax applied, the differences are dramatic. Sam will get soaked.

To illustrate: The facts are the same, except that the asset was contributed nine years ago, before the election was made. This time S Corp. will pay a tax of 21% on $1,000, viz. $210. Sam also pays a tax on the gain under § 1366(a), but it is only on the amount deemed distributed after taxes, $790, because the S corporation's payment of the § 1374 BIG tax gives rise to a loss deduction under § 1366(f)(2) for Sam. Sam's stock basis will increase by the gain recognized under § 1367(a)(l) ($1,000), and the distribution of $1,000 value of the asset will reduce it in equal measure. § 1367(a)(2)(A).

4. POST-TERMINATION DISTRIBUTIONS
Read §§1366(d)(3), 1371.

The day an S corporation loses its status, it becomes a C corporation. Its income ceases to flow through to the shareholders under § 1366(a). The shareholders can elect to close the corporation's taxable year on the last day of the S corporation's short taxable year rather than to prorate the income between the taxable years of the S corporation and the C corporation on an average daily basis. § 1362(e)(2), (3). Tax planning considerations would drive that decision.

When an S corporation becomes a C corporation, its AAA might devolve into an E & P account, a fairly nasty thought to a shareholder trying to get his already-taxed money out of a former S corporation. Indeed, that was the law until it was changed in 1996. Now, during the "post-termination" period, shareholders can generally withdraw, free of tax, money (but not property) up to the corporation's AAA. § 1371(e). (The withdrawals do reduce the adjusted basis of stock.). After doing so, subsequent distributions are the same as those from any C corporation.

If the shareholder has losses in excess of basis, she may use the losses after termination only if she acquires basis during the post-termination transition period. §§ 1366(d)(3) and 1377(b). This means that a shareholder whose losses were suspended as a result of not having sufficient basis in debt and equity in prior periods can infuse the corporation with extra cash equity (and only equity) and thereby salvage those losses. This may not hurt much, because the buyer may be willing to pay for the extra infusion, dollar-for-dollar, because a buyer indirectly gets to keep the seller's infusion. The same thing is true of losses suspended by the "at risk" rules (§ 465). There is a chance to revive them in the post-termination transition period. § 1366(d)(3)(D).

The "post-termination transition period" begins the day after losing S corporation status and ends on the later of:

- One year after the last day as an S corporation; or

- The due date for filing the return for the last year as an S corporation, including extensions.

In the interest of helping putative S corporations caught in controversies over their status, the post-termination transition period is a 120-day period beginning on the date of a determination that the corporation's election of S corporation status had terminated for a previous tax year.

For this purpose, a "determination" means: (1) a court decision that becomes final; (2) a closing agreement between taxpayer and the I.R.S.; (3) the final disposition of a claim for refund or credit; or (4) an agreement between the corporation and the IRS that the corporation did not qualify as an S corporation. § 1377(b).

Any one of these choices gives the tax advisor plenty of time to compute the AAA and to tell shareholders how to pull out their shares of the account tax-free.

PROBLEM 25-12

Sal owns all the stock of S Corp. Her basis in the stock is $12,000. S Corp. has a $9,000 AAA and no E & P or PTI. Sal causes S Corp. to revoke its S election as of the beginning of this year. She also causes it to distribute $8,000 in cash nine months later.

1) How is the $8,000 taxed? What is her stock basis after the distribution?

2) What is S Corp.'s (now a C corporation) E & P after the distribution?

J. RELATIONSHIP OF SUBCHAPTER S TO REST OF CODE
Read §§ 1363(a) and 1371(a).

Subchapter S occupies only a small corner of the Internal Revenue Code. S corporations regularly have to contend with a mass of issues raised by the remainder of the Code, including the definition of gross income, availability of deductions, timing rules, capital gains versus ordinary income, and merger and acquisition effects, to name just a few. Unfortunately, as one might expect, Subchapter S is not entirely coordinated with the rest of the Code.

One area of interaction between Subchapter S and Subchapter C that is well-coordinated concerns net operating losses (NOLs). A C corporation that becomes an S corporation passes its post-election NOLs through to its shareholders. The corporation cannot apply carryovers from tax years when it was not an S corporation to years when it is an S corporation. § 1371(b)(1). By making the S election, NOLs are put on a kind of death row and can be reinstated only if and when the corporation reverts to being a C corporation. Conversely, an S corporation's losses cannot be used by the corporation after it terminates its S election. The only relief is that during the magical post-termination transition period shareholders may use up the corporation's suspended loss carryovers by contributing to equity. § 1366(d)(3).

1. SPECIAL INTERACTIONS OF SUBCHAPTER S AND SUBCHAPTER C

Section 1371(a) states that, except as otherwise provided and except as inconsistent with Subchapter S, Subchapter C applies to an S corporation and its shareholders. Thus, for example, one looks to § 351 to see how to perform a tax-deferred incorporation, § 331 for the impact of liquidations on shareholders, § 368(a) and its compatriots to determine the implications of mergers and acquisitions, § 355 and § 368(a)(1)(D) for divestitures, and so forth.

Again, the rules are not fully coordinated, but the basic congressional directive is clear. The materials that follow illustrate some of the issues taxpayers must face in this area.

a. Liquidations

PRIV. LTR. RUL. 9218019
(May 1, 1992)

Dear [Taxpayer]:

We received your letter on July 30, 1991, requesting a ruling on behalf of A about the tax consequences to a shareholder on a sale by an S corporation of its assets followed by a liquidating distribution of the proceeds of the sale in the same taxable year as the sale. This letter is in reply to your request.

In 1969, X was incorporated under the laws of Z. X elected S corporation status under section 1362(a) of the Internal Revenue Code on December 23, 1986, for its January 1, 1987, taxable year. Since 1969, X has owned, as its sole capital asset, a commercial building located in Z. On December, 31, 1990, X's adjusted basis for the commercial building was about $100,000. Depreciation on X's commercial building has been calculated on the straight line method.

At the time of death, B owned all of X corporation's stock. On B's death, B's estate, A, became the owner of all X corporation's stock. C, who is B's only beneficiary, does not wish to operate the commercial building that is the sole asset of X. Thus, the executors of A propose to sell the commercial building owned by X, and to distribute the cash proceeds to A in complete liquidation of X.

In connection with proposed transaction, the taxpayer represents the following: (a) No formal or informal plan of liquidation has ever been adopted by X, except for the proposed plan in which the sale of the building is contemplated. (b) The liquidation of X will not be preceded or followed by the reincorporation in, or transfer or sale to, a recipient corporation (Recipient) of any of the business or assets of X, if persons holding more than 20 percent in value of the stock in X also hold more than 20 percent in value of the stock in Recipient. For purposes of this representation, ownership has been determined by application of the constructive ownership rules of section 318 of the Internal Revenue Code as modified by section 304(c)(3). (c) All assets of X will be distributed in complete liquidation of X within the 12-month period beginning on the date of adoption of the plan of liquidation. (d) No part of the consideration to be received by any shareholder of X will be received by the shareholder of X as a creditor, employee, or in some capacity other than that of a shareholder. (e) Pursuant to the proposed plan of liquidation, X will cease to be a going concern and its activities will be limited to the winding up of its affairs, paying its debts, and distributing any balance of its assets to its shareholders. (f) The fair market value of X's assets will exceed its liabilities both on the date of adoption the plan of liquidation and at the time the first liquidating distribution is made. (g) No distribution of assets representing earned but unreported income will be made by X to its shareholders in the liquidation. (h) The liquidating distribution described in this ruling request is an isolated transaction and is not related to any other past or future transaction. (i) X does not maintain a reserve for bad debts.

Section 1014(a) of the Code provides, generally, that the basis of property in the hands of a person acquiring the property from a decedent is the fair market value of the property at the date of the decedent's death. Section 1001(a) of the Code provides, generally, that the gain from the sale or other disposition of property is the excess of the amount realized from the sale or disposition over the adjusted basis of the property.

Section 1367(a) of the Code provides, generally, that the basis of each shareholder's stock in an S corporation is increased for any period by the sum of items of income described in section 1366(a)(1)(A) and (B) of the Code.

Section 1374(a) of the Code provides, generally, that if an S corporation has a net recognized built-in gain for any taxable year beginning in a S corporation's recognition period, a tax is imposed on the income of such corporation for such taxable year.

Section 1371(a)(1) of the Code provides, generally, that except as otherwise provided in the Internal Revenue Code, and except to the extent inconsistent with subchapter S, subchapter C applies to S corporations and S corporation shareholders. Section 1.1372-1(c) of the Income Tax Regulations provides, generally, that to the extent that provisions of subchapter C of the Code are not inconsistent with the provisions and regulation under subchapter S such provisions will apply to an S corporation and its shareholders.

Section 336(a) requires, generally, that a liquidating corporation recognize gain or loss on the distribution of property in complete liquidation as if the property were sold to a distributee at its fair market value.

Section 331(a) of the Code provides that amounts received by a shareholder in a distribution in complete liquidation of a corporation are treated as in full payment in exchange for stock.

Based on the information submitted and the above representations made by the taxpayer, we reach the following conclusions.

Under section 1014(a), A's basis in the stock of X will be stepped-up to the fair market value of the property as of the date of B's death. Under section 1001 (a), X's gain from the sale of its commercial building will be measured by the difference between the amount realized on the sale of the building and X's adjusted basis in the building. Section 1366 requires all items of an S corporation's income to pass-through to the S corporation shareholders. Thus, we conclude that the gain realized by X on the sale of its commercial building will pass-through to and be recognized by A, its sole shareholder. Further, we conclude that under section 1367(a)(1), A's stepped-up basis under section 1014(a) will be increased by the amount realized and passed-through to A on X's sale of its building.

Under section 336(a) of the Code, a liquidating corporation recognizes gain or loss on the distribution of property in complete liquidation. However, X is not a taxable entity under section 1363(a)(1), and any gain or loss recognized would be recognized by X's shareholder. In addition, X is distributing cash not appreciated assets. Thus, we conclude that section 336(a) does not require recognition of gain or loss on the distribution of cash in complete liquidation of X.

In addition, assuming the liquidation of X qualifies as a complete liquidation under section 331(a) of the Code, we conclude that the amounts received by A in the distribution in complete liquidation of X are treated as in full payment in exchange for A's stock in accordance with section 331(a). We further conclude that A's gain or loss, under section 1001, will be measured by the difference between the amount of cash received and A's adjusted basis in its X stock surrendered.

Finally, assuming X has been continuously an S corporation, within the meaning of section 1361(a)(1) of the Code, as of the effective date of its above-described S corporation election, and further assuming that X's election is not subject to a terminating event, within the meaning of section 1362(d) of the Code, prior to the date of the complete liquidation, we reach the following conclusion. X will not be subject to the tax on net built-in gains imposed by section 1374 of the Code . . . for assets held by X on December 31, 1986. . . . The provisions of section 1374 of the Code will apply to X for any asset held by X that was acquired after December 31, 1986, and is described in section 1374(d)(8) of the Code. . . .

Except as specifically ruled on above, we express no other opinion about the federal tax consequences of any aspects of the above-described transaction. More specifically, no opinion is expressed about whether X met the requirements of section 1361(b) of the Code, or whether its S election was terminated under section 1362(d) as a result of any events not specifically addressed and ruled on by this letter ruling. . . .

Sincerely,
William P. O'Shea
Chief, Branch 3
Office of the Assistant Chief Counsel
(Passthroughs and Special Industries)

NOTES

1. **De facto § 754 results**. Private Letter Ruling 9218019 (May 1, 1992), *supra*, states that S corporation stock takes a fair market value at death basis, with the result that if the corporation has appreciated assets, they can be sold at a taxable gain, increasing stock basis. However, if the stock is then sold, the stock's basis (now exaggerated) will likely be more than the amount realized, with the result that the loss will offset the prior gain. This results in a de facto § 754 election at the S corporation level. The estate planning advice is to hang on to valuable assets in the S corporation and to sell the loss assets.

2. **Income in respect of a decedent (IRD)**. Anyone who inherits S corporation stock must treat as IRD the pro-rata portion of any item of income that would have been IRD if acquired directly from the decedent. The usual deduction for the extra estate tax attributable to IRD items as a result of death will be allowed under § 691(c). Any step-up in basis of S corporation stock as a result of death must be reduced to the extent of the stock's value attributable to IRD. This aligns the tax treatment of S corporation stock with that of partnership interests. *See* § 1367(b)(4).

b. Corporate acquisitions

Nontaxable reorganizations involving S corporations are a regular occurrence, but they do involve some special issues. Common trouble spots are the risk that the S corporation that survives a reorganization will lose its election because it has too many shareholders, or shareholders of the wrong type, or that the acquired assets will be subject to the BIG tax if they are sold within a decade. Keep in mind that the BIG tax only applies to assets owned by the S corporation when the S election takes effect. This can get complicated. *See* M. Ginsburg & J. Levin, Mergers, Acquisitions and Leveraged Buyouts ¶ 1105.031 (2018).

To illustrate: T is a C corporation. Acquiso, an S corporation, acquires all the assets of T in a tax-free reorganization. Assuming T has appreciated assets, these assets are subject to § 1374 if they are sold or distributed in the decade beginning with Acquiso's receipt of T's assets. Ann. 86-128, 1986-51 IRB 22.

c. S Corporation as a Shareholder

Former § 1371(a)(2) used to provide that for purposes of Subchapter C, if an S corporation was a shareholder in another corporation, the S corporation was treated as an individual. This simple statement caused a good deal of confusion, and was eventually narrowed to mean something much simpler, namely that S corporations do not get the dividends-received deduction. That makes sense, because an S corporation (unlike a C corporation) is generally not a taxpayer, so there is no fiscal justification for a dividends-received deduction, and there is no need to deduct dividends received because they flow through to the shareholders tax-free at the corporate level.

Another important simplification that has not made it into the Code, but which the IRS has staked out in private letter rulings, is that transitory ownership of S corporation stock by disqualified shareholders does not terminate the S election. *See, e.g.,* Private Letter Ruling 9245004 (November 6, 1992), ruling that an S corporation's transitory ownership of a C corporation (which would have disqualified the § 338 election) should be disregarded because it was part of a larger acquisition plan. The larger plan, which the IRS approved, was that the C corporation target was programmed to be purchased, then to make a § 338(g) (hypothetical taxable liquidation) election, after which the target would be liquidated into the S corporation tax-free.

NOTES

1. **Who participates in Private Letter Rulings?** Even though taxpayers are formally not allowed to rely on other people's private letter rulings, these rulings are watched with great interest by the practicing bar. An unexpected change of position on the government's part is likely to reverberate inside and outside the National Office of the IRS in Washington. So who participates in this process on the government's part? The answer is (1) tax experts in the Technical Branch of the IRS who specialize in the particular Code section or sections at issue, and (2) if requested by "Technical," the people from the Interpretative, General Litigation, and Legislation and Regulations ("L&R") Divisions of the Office of the Chief Counsel of the IRS. See M. Saltzman, IRS Practice and Procedure para. 3.03[5]. Note that P.L.R. 9245004 is actually a Technical Advice Memorandum, meaning an opinion issued by the IRS National Office to a taxpayer and the IRS (in the field) to help resolve an audit issue. The same personnel participate in TAMs as in a regular private letter ruling.

2. **Spin-offs involving S corporations**. In Private Letter Ruling 9321006 (November 30, 1992) the IRS reviewed a divisive type D reorganization and ruled, among other things, that the newly-formed subsidiary which elected S status after being distributed, would be subject to the BIG tax to the same extent the distributing parent corporation was, but with the favorable result that the parent's holding period for the built-in gain assets would be added to the subsidiary's holding period, as opposed to beginning anew. In the second ruling, the IRS also found that, consistent with Reg. § 1.1368-2(d)(3), the AAA of the distributing corporation would be split between it and the controlled corporation(s). This directive called for applying the principles of § 312(h), which generally relies on relative fair market values.

3. **Does § 1244 apply to S corporations?** What if an S corporation holds stock in another corporation that goes belly up? Can the S corporation pass a § 1244 loss through to its shareholders? The answer is "no" according to *Rath v. Commissioner*, 101 T.C. 196 (1993), because Congress did not mean to extend the benefits of § 1244 that far. Section 1244 does apply to a loss on the sale of S corporation stock itself, however.

PROBLEM 25-13

Acquiso, Inc., an S corporation, wants to acquire the assets of T Corp., a subsidiary of P Corp. T and P have been filing consolidated returns for many years; both are C corporations. T's assets have a basis of $60 and a value of $100.

Acquiso buys all the stock of T from P, paying P with a note with a face amount of $100 plus an appropriate rate of interest. The note is Acquiso's only debt. Acquiso's total equity (meaning the value of all its assets minus all its liabilities) after the purchase of T is $120. Acquiso and P properly make the joint § 338(h)(10) election to treat the sale of the T stock as a deemed sale of T's assets. The transaction occurs in the middle of the tax year of all pertinent corporations. T and Acquiso are both profitable corporations.

1) Will Acquiso get the E & P account of T?

2) Does P report a gain or loss on the sale of T stock?

3) If Acquiso immediately liquidates T in a liquidation qualifying under § 332, what will be the basis of the former assets of T in Acquiso's hands?

4) Assuming T had an E & P account of $15 and P, an S corporation (having no E & P prior to the transaction, but having a large AAA account) distributes $10 to its shareholders after the sale of the T stock, is the distribution taxable as a dividend?

5) Might the $100 note to P imperil Acquiso's status as an S corporation? If so, why? What if, instead of using a note, Acquiso paid with preferred stock of Acquiso?

Now change the facts in the following way: T merges into Acquiso in exchange for stock of Acquiso that is paid to the T shareholders. T has 15 shareholders, all of whom are U.S. citizens. The 15 shareholders receive the Acquiso stock worth $100 in total. Assume the merger qualifies as a type A reorganization.

6) If Acquiso sells T's former assets to an unrelated party six years later for $120, how will the sale be taxed? Will § 1374 apply?

7) What would be your answer to "(4)" be under these circumstances?

8) Would the tax-free status of the merger be jeopardized if T were owned by P, not by the 15 shareholders?

9) Would the S election of Acquiso be jeopardized on the facts of "(8)"?

10) Assuming the reorganization in "(6)" were instead a B reorganization, how would your answer change?

11) Would Acquiso have to make a QSSS election in order to retain its status as an S corporation?

PROBLEM 25-14

The Friendly Corporation is a cash-method calendar-year S corporation. On June 30, year one, for good business reasons and not to avoid taxes, it acquired all the stock of the National Hatblocking Corporation, a C corporation that manufactures hat-shaping equipment, which is also on the cash method and uses the calendar year. The consideration for the acquisition was voting stock of Friendly Corporation.

On the same day, Friendly Corporation purported to make a § 338(g) election on National Hatblocking Corporation's behalf. It then liquidated National Hatblocking into itself in a § 332 liquidation.

Prior to the acquisition, National Hatblocking redeemed all the stock of its founder, Harold Hatman, for $600,000 in cash it did not need. After the redemption, National

Hatblocking had assets with a value of $5 million and a basis of $2 million and no liabilities. It also had a net operating loss carryover of $4 million.

The time between the acquisition of the stock and the liquidation into Friendly Corporation was fourteen days.

1) Does Friendly Corporation lose its S election?

2) Are the §§ 332 and 338 elections valid?

3) Assuming the § 338(g) election is valid, would gains on the hypothetical sale of the assets pursuant to § 338 of S corporation be taxable to the shareholders or to National Hatblocking? If so, when? *See* Reg. § 1.338-4.

4) What is the character of the reorganization? *See* Rev. Rul. 76-123, 1976-1 C.B. 94, discussed in connection with type B reorganizations earlier in this book.

5) What becomes of National Hatblocking's NOL? *See* § 338(a), (b) and (g)(3).

d. Fringe Benefits
Read § 1372.

No founder will organize an S corporation for its fringe benefit advantages; there are none. This is because people owning 2% or more of the common stock of an S corporation are treated like partners in a partnership. § 1372. This status arises if there is direct or indirect ownership on any day of the taxable year. The 2% refers either to voting stock or to total outstanding stock; thus, there is no hiding out from the rule by issuing a lot of nonvoting stock to third parties.

The intended implication is that 2% shareholders cannot be "employees." Because various fringe benefit plans are available only to "employees," the result is fatal to some key fringe benefits, especially medical reimbursement plans. *See* §§ 105 and 106. Other examples include the exclusions for meals and lodging (§ 119) and certain life insurance coverage (§ 79) furnished by an employer.

e. At-Risk Rules

Losses that pass through to shareholders may be limited by the at-risk rules of § 465. The restriction is measured activity-by-activity at the shareholder level. § 465(a)(1)(A). A special rule combines businesses in which the taxpayer actively manages, provided at least 65% of the losses are allocated to active managers. § 465(c)(3)(B). The at-risk rules apply before the passive-loss rules. Reg. § 1.469-2T(d)(6)(i).

f. Hobby Loss Rules

S corporations are subject to the hobby loss rules at the corporate level. Reg. § 1.183-1(f).

g. Passive Activity Loss Rules

These apply at the shareholder level, activity-by-activity. Each shareholder who materially participates (or who actively participates, in the case of certain rental real estate) is free of the restrictions of § 469. Reg. § 1.469-2T(e)(1). Operating income earned qua passive shareholder in an S corporation is considered passive income, a good thing from the point of view of a shareholder with net passive losses, but losses the S corporation generates are suspended unless the shareholder is active in the business. *Id.* Those losses can be used to offset passive activity income from other activities.

Another advantage of being active in the business is that interest paid to buy the S corporation stock will be free of the § 163(d) limit on investment interest expenses. *See* § 163(d)(4)(D). Section 163(d) limits current interest expense deductions to net current investment income, and defers the nondeductible portion to future years.

h. Alternative Minimum Tax

This tax applies at the shareholder level. §§ 1363(a) and 55. The entity reports the AMT items on the annual Form K-1 distributed to owners, and they in turn combine the AMT amounts from all sources for the year to determine whether the items generate an AMT liability.

i. Transactions with Related Taxpayers

S corporations can deal with their shareholders as if they were strangers to the entity, the same as with C corporations. There is no analog to the guaranteed payment by a partnership to a partner. The same basic rules apply to denial of losses and deferral of deductions in dealings with shareholders as apply in the case of partnerships. There is no unique set of provisions under Subchapter S. Thus, one must look to § 267 for these limitations. They are discussed with respect to partnerships in the pertinent chapters of this book.

j. Audits of S Corporations

Section 6937 imposes an important procedural requirement: the shareholders of an S corporation must report their shares of the S corporation's results ("S corporation items") on their personal returns consistently with the way the corporation prepared its own tax return, or else notify the IRS of the inconsistent treatment.

If the taxpayer reports inconsistently and fails to point out the issue, the IRS can make adjustments to the taxpayer's return as if they were arithmetic or clerical mistakes, which means the IRS can assess the deficiency at once, and the taxpayer loses the procedural defense of a notice of deficiency. He or she simply owes the money. Period. § 6037. Note that the shareholder should use Form 8082 (Notice of Inconsistent Position) to explain the inconsistency.

Although the S corporation's income or loss generally flows to its shareholders, it is responsible for a few taxes of its own, such as the tax on excess investment income under § 1375, and the S corporation is audited directly on those items, but disputes about items passed through the shareholders are audited at the shareholder level. This is in contrast to the former "unified proceedings" process under which the IRS audited the S corporation pursuant to former § 6241.

S corporations can be a member of a partnership or limited liability company. For post-2017 tax returns, any adjustment to items of income, gain, loss, deduction, or credit of a partnership for a partnership tax year (and any partner's distributive share thereof) is determined, any tax attributable thereto are assessed and collected, and the applicability of any penalty, addition to tax, or additional amount which relates to an adjustment to any such item or share is determined, at the partnership level. Certain partnerships are allowed to elect out of the partnership audit rules. In the post-2017 version of §§ 6221(b)(1)(C), 6221(b)(2), S corporations may, under specified conditions, become a partner in a partnership electing out of unified audit procedures.

The acceptance of a proposed audit adjustment or settlement by a partnership, estate, trust, S corporation or DISC is made on Form 875.

Effective Dec. 22, 2017, any Code Sec. 481(a) adjustment of an eligible terminated S corporation attributable to the revocation of its S corporation election (i.e., a change from the cash method to an accrual method) is taken into account ratably during 6-tax year period beginning with the year of change. An eligible terminated S corporation is any C corporation which (1) is an S corporation the day before Dec. 22, 2017; (2) during the 2-year period beginning on Dec. 22, 2017 revokes its S corporation election; and (3) all of the owners of which on the date the S corporation election is revoked are the same owners (and in identical proportions) as the owners on Dec. 22, 2017.

2. MULTIFORM S CORPORATIONS

It should come as no surprise that practicing lawyers have found ways to combine S corporations with other entities. As you may recall, a partnership cannot hold stock in an S corporation. § 1361(b)(1). However, the reverse is not true. S corporations can combine to form partnerships.

PRIV. LTR. RUL. 9017057
(January 30, 1990)

This is in response to a request for a private letter ruling, dated September 22, 1989, submitted on your behalf by your authorized representative, regarding the treatment of the above-referenced corporations as small business corporations.

The information submitted states that X1, X2, X3, X4, X5, X6, X7, X8, X9, X10, X11, X12, X13, X14, X15, X16, X17, X18, and X19 are corporations, all of which were incorporated between 1979 and 1988. The shareholders of each corporation have filed an election, under section 1362(a) of the Internal Revenue Code, for the corporation to be treated as an S corporation for federal income tax purposes. Each S corporation election has been in effect since the inception of each corporation. Stock in the corporations is held by a total of 136 individuals, with several individuals holding stock in more than one corporation.

Each corporation owns one or two restaurant sites and in connection therewith owns the land, improvements, equipment and furnishings necessary for the operation of the restaurant or restaurants. None of the corporations have pledged assets to secure the indebtedness of another corporation, and no corporation has guaranteed or otherwise agreed to assume liability for the indebtedness of another corporation.

Each corporation entered into a management agreement with W, a corporation. W has not made an election to be treated as an S corporation for federal income tax purposes. Under the management agreement, W is responsible for providing bookkeeping, accounting and payroll services, personnel training, management services and direction, advertising and maintenance services. In return, W generally receives a fee for each of these management functions, based on a percentage of the corporation's gross receipts, or it bills the corporation directly for the cost of providing the services. The stock of W is wholly-owned by A, an individual.

The Corporations and W have proposed forming a limited partnership for the purpose of acquiring, owning and operating additional restaurants. W will be the general partner of the partnership and each of the corporations will be a limited partner. W will contribute organizational and management services for its interest in the partnership and each corporation will contribute cash. Each corporation will continue to own and operate the restaurant site or sites it currently owns, and will remain liable for its current liabilities. In certain cases, a corporation may acquire additional restaurant sites.

It has been represented that the partnership can acquire new restaurant sites more easily and economically by using cash contributed to the partnership, rather than raising the equity for each future restaurant from the proceeds of the sale of stock in newly-created corporations. In addition, the shareholders of the corporations wish to avoid the dilution of their ownership in their directly-held sites. Finally, the proposed limited partnership form will not subject the restaurants directly-held by the corporations to the liabilities associated with the restaurants acquired by the partnership.

Section 1361 (a)(1) of the Code defines an "S corporation" as a small business corporation for which an election is in effect for the taxable year. Section 1361(b)(1) defines "small business corporation," in part, as a corporation that has no more than [100] shareholders and that has as shareholders no persons other than individuals, estates, or trusts described in section 1361(c)(2).

Rev. Rul. 71-455, 1971-2 C.B. 318, implies that an S corporation can own a partnership interest without losing its status as an S corporation. In Rev. Rul. 71-455, the S corporation owned and operated motion picture theaters and was also an equal partner with another in a joint venture that owned and operated a motion picture theater. However, in Rev. Rul. 77-220, 1977-1 C.B. 263, the Service announced that it would disregard a form of business organization that lacks economic substance and that is established principally to circumvent the provisions of subchapter S of the Code. In that ruling, thirty unrelated individuals who jointly operated a single business divided themselves into three groups of ten. Each group organized a separate corporation that held equal amounts of capital. The corporations then organized a partnership to carry on the joint business. The shareholders set up three separate corporations principally so that each corporation could elect to be taxed under subchapter S. The predecessor of section 1361 limited to ten the number of shareholders of a small business corporation. The ruling held that the separate corporations were in substance a single corporation that could not elect to be an S corporation.

Unlike the parties in Rev. Rul. 77-220, the parties in the present case are existing S Corporations who will contribute cash to the partnership while retaining their existing operating assets. Like Rev. Rul. 71-455, each corporation in the present case has valid business reasons for the transaction and each corporation will continue to operate its directly-owned restaurant or restaurants independently of the business of the partnership.

Based on the above, we conclude that the mere formation of partnership and the acquisition of interests therein by X1, X2, X3, X4, X5, X6, X7, X8, X9, X10, X11, X12, X13, X14, X15, X16, X17, X18, and X19 will not cause X1 to violate the [100] shareholder limitation contained in section 1361(b)(1)(A) of the Code. . . .

NOTE

Aggressive tax planning. A more provocative model involves using an S corporation to operate a business at a loss and a low-bracket C corporation to lend money to it. One might imagine a yacht leasing company that the owner ("0") actively manages, thereby avoiding the passive loss rules as to that owner. The leasing company loses money because of interest expense deductions and depreciation. 0 owns the lending company. The lending company reports interest income. This raises the specter of § 267(a)(2), but there is no deferral or disallowance of the interest expenses as long as the payments are made in a timely manner.

Chapter 26

LIMITED LIABILITY COMPANIES

A. BACKGROUND

For many years, sophisticated natural resource corporations used the *limitada*, a form of Hispanic or Brazilian law entity, to undertake risky projects here and abroad. The charm of the *limitada* is that its owners' liabilities are limited in the same way as are those of typical shareholders, but the enterprise is taxed as a partnership for federal income tax purposes. In effect, the flow-through benefits offered by S corporations (which are, of course, not available to corporate shareholders) without the usual S Corporation restrictions.

B. THE WYOMING RESPONSE

The State of Wyoming was the first to recognize the opportunity to legislate a homegrown form of the *limitada*, the so-called limited liability company ("LLC"). In Rev. Rul. 88-76, 1988-2 C.B. 360, the IRS opened the flood gates of tax planning by conceding that a well-formed Wyoming LLC should be classified as a partnership for federal income tax purposes.

The following is an illustrative ruling that classified LLCs before the "check-the-box" Regulations made the analysis unnecessary. Under the new rules, the normal default result is that a domestic multi-member LLC is taxable as a partnership and a one-member LLC is treated as a sole proprietorship. An election against the default outcome makes the entity a corporation. Reg. § 301.7701-3(b). Probably the hardest part is that the election (which is made on Form 8832) cannot take a retroactive effect over a period of more than 75 days. Reg. § 301.7701-3(c)(iii).

To illustrate: Ms. R and Mrs. S formed an LLC under Nevada law on January 1 of year one planning to elect to treat the LLC as a corporation for federal income tax purposes. On June 15 their accountant pointed out that the Form 8832, election was never filed. They can still file the Form 8832 on June 15, but it will be retroactive only back to April 1 of year one. The LLC will be a partnership for federal income tax purposes for the period January 1-March 31 of year one.

C. CURRENT STATUS

Although called a "company," the LLC is an *unincorporated* form of business association formed under state (or D.C.) laws that are separate from state corporation laws. All the states have passed limited liability company acts, and the IRS has gracefully issued rulings on those acts. An LLC can have just one member, in which case the owner can decide whether to elect to treat it as a corporation or do nothing and let it be a sole proprietorship by default.

Under current Regulations, a new, domestic one-person LLC is to be treated as a sole proprietorship unless it elects to be taxed as a corporation. A new two-or-more-member domestic LLC is to be treated as a partnership unless it elects to be taxed as a corporation for federal income tax purposes. Regs. § 301.7701-3(b).

The various limited liability company acts diverge greatly in their details. For example, some permit a majority of the shareholders to reconstitute the company on the withdrawal of a shareholder while others require a unanimous approval. Some statutes, such as Delaware's, permit mergers involving limited liability companies. Del. Code § 18-209.

Other statutes allow shareholders agreements to control LLCs and allow disproportionate distributions. See, e.g., Del. Code § 18-101(6) (shareholders' agreements) and Ga. Code § 14-11-404 (disproportionate distributions). One can expect state legislatures gradually to modify their limited liability statutes in light of the need to coordinate federal income tax statutes with the legal features of limited liability companies. For the time being, the coordination is partial and mysteries abound.

NOTES

1. **What is a limited liability partnership (LLP)?** The answer is that it is a professional partnership, commonly a law firm, that qualifies (generally by paying money and showing minimum insurance coverage) under a state law that prevents vicarious liability for malpractice from one professional to another. It has no independent tax significance. The LLP clearly helps protect general partners; what it does for limited partners is less clear.

2. **Employment taxes.** A limited partner is not subject to social security taxes except as to salaries and guaranteed payments; a member of an LLC is treated the same way. As a result, limited partners and LLC members often strive to substitute distributive shares of income for salaries, so as to avoid these taxes. In turn, the IRS commonly audits such arrangements in order to recharacterized distributive shares as salaries or guaranteed payments. *See* § 1402(a)(13) and Prop. Reg. § 1.1402(a)-2(h)(2)(individual member treated as a limited partner unless she has personal liability for the debts of the LLC, has authority to contract on behalf of the LLC, or participates in the LLC's trade or business for more than 500 hours during the tax year).

PROBLEM 26-1

Imagine for a moment that an accountant on the other end of the phone line tells you that she plans to have a client of yours form a corporation and make the S corporation election. You wish to point out some of the advantages of using a limited liability company. What particular benefits would you point out, in comparison to the S election? What would be the income tax impact if one of her clients elected to treat his old LLC (which is presently taxed as a corporation) as a partnership? The client's LLC is rich with appreciated assets. Might the client be better off with an S election instead of shifting to partnership status? What about fringe benefits; can she offer superior fringe benefits if the LLC chooses to be taxed as a partnership?

D. SELECTED COMPLICATIONS

Coordinating the limited liability company acts and federal income tax laws, especially Subchapter K, is not easy.

1. Can a qualified income offset be installed in an LLC, and if so, how? How does one install a "minimum-gain charge back provision"? If LLC liabilities are nonrecourse, this becomes an issue. This may be tied to the corporate law question of whether the Board of the LLC can differentiate among members when making distributions.

2. If there is to be a special allocation, in general each partner must have a duty to restore any deficit in his or her capital account after liquidation of the partnership or of the partnership interest. How does one accomplish this in an LLC where the expectation is that there is no duty to make further contributions?

3. What is the impact of recourse debt on a member's basis in the LLC interest, assuming the LLC is taxed as a partnership?

4. What would be the impact of a member of such an LLC issuing a guarantee of an LLC debt?

APPENDIX
FLOW CHART AND IRS FORMS

Page

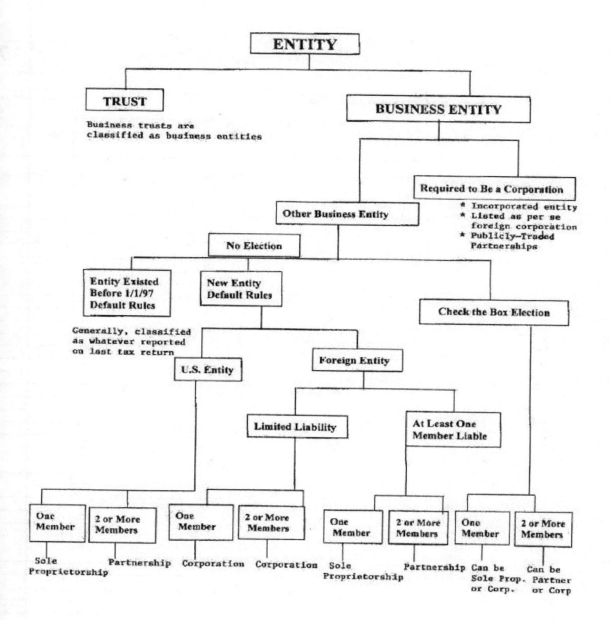

539

Form 1065

Department of the Treasury
Internal Revenue Service

U.S. Return of Partnership Income

For calendar year 2017, or tax year beginning _____ , 2017, ending _____ , 20 ____

▶ Go to www.irs.gov/Form1065 for instructions and the latest information.

OMB No. 1545-____

2017

A Principal business activity		Name of partnership	D Employer identification
B Principal product or service	Type or Print	Number, street, and room or suite no. If a P.O. box, see the instructions.	E Date business started
C Business code number		City or town, state or province, country, and ZIP or foreign postal code	F Total assets (see the instructions) $

G Check applicable boxes: (1) ☐ Initial return (2) ☐ Final return (3) ☐ Name change (4) ☐ Address change (5) ☐ Amended
(6) ☐ Technical termination - also check (1) or (2)

H Check accounting method: (1) ☐ Cash (2) ☐ Accrual (3) ☐ Other (specify) ▶ _____

I Number of Schedules K-1. Attach one for each person who was a partner at any time during the tax year ▶ _____

J Check if Schedules C and M-3 are attached . . . .

Caution. *Include only trade or business income and expenses on lines 1a through 22 below. See the instructions for more information.*

Income	1a	Gross receipts or sales	1a	
	b	Returns and allowances	1b	
	c	Balance. Subtract line 1b from line 1a	1c	
	2	Cost of goods sold (attach Form 1125-A)	2	
	3	Gross profit. Subtract line 2 from line 1c	3	
	4	Ordinary income (loss) from other partnerships, estates, and trusts (attach statement) . .	4	
	5	Net farm profit (loss) (attach Schedule F (Form 1040))	5	
	6	Net gain (loss) from Form 4797, Part II, line 17 (attach Form 4797)	6	
	7	Other income (loss) (attach statement)	7	
	8	**Total income (loss).** Combine lines 3 through 7	8	
Deductions (see the instructions for limitations)	9	Salaries and wages (other than to partners) (less employment credits)	9	
	10	Guaranteed payments to partners	10	
	11	Repairs and maintenance	11	
	12	Bad debts	12	
	13	Rent	13	
	14	Taxes and licenses	14	
	15	Interest	15	
	16a	Depreciation (if required, attach Form 4562) 16a		
	b	Less depreciation reported on Form 1125-A and elsewhere on return 16b	16c	
	17	Depletion (**Do not deduct oil and gas depletion.**)	17	
	18	Retirement plans, etc.	18	
	19	Employee benefit programs	19	
	20	Other deductions (attach statement)	20	
	21	**Total deductions.** Add the amounts shown in the far right column for lines 9 through 20 .	21	
	22	**Ordinary business income (loss).** Subtract line 21 from line 8	22	

Sign Here

Under penalties of perjury, I declare that I have examined this return, including accompanying schedules and statements, and to the best of my knowledge and belief, it is true, correct, and complete. Declaration of preparer (other than partner or limited liability company member) is based information of which preparer has any knowledge.

May the IRS discuss this return with the preparer shown below (see instructions)? ☐ Yes

▶ _____   ▶ _____
Signature of partner or limited liability company member   Date

Paid Preparer Use Only	Print/Type preparer's name	Preparer's signature	Date	Check ☐ if self-employed	PTIN
	Firm's name ▶			Firm's EIN ▶	
	Firm's address ▶			Phone no.	

For Paperwork Reduction Act Notice, see separate instructions.   Cat. No. 11390Z   Form 1065

540

Schedule B	**Other Information**

		Yes	No
1	What type of entity is filing this return? Check the applicable box:		

a ☐ Domestic general partnership   **b** ☐ Domestic limited partnership

c ☐ Domestic limited liability company   **d** ☐ Domestic limited liability partnership

e ☐ Foreign partnership   **f** ☐ Other ▶

2   At any time during the tax year, was any partner in the partnership a disregarded entity, a partnership (including an entity treated as a partnership), a trust, an S corporation, an estate (other than an estate of a deceased partner), or a nominee or similar person? . . . .

3   At the end of the tax year:

a   Did any foreign or domestic corporation, partnership (including any entity treated as a partnership), trust, or tax-exempt organization, or any foreign government own, directly or indirectly, an interest of 50% or more in the profit, loss, or capital of the partnership? For rules of constructive ownership, see instructions. If "Yes," attach Schedule B-1, Information on Partners Owning 50% or More of the Partnership . . . .

b   Did any individual or estate own, directly or indirectly, an interest of 50% or more in the profit, loss, or capital of the partnership? For rules of constructive ownership, see instructions. If "Yes," attach Schedule B-1, Information on Partners Owning 50% or More of the Partnership . . . .

4   At the end of the tax year, did the partnership:

a   Own directly 20% or more, or own, directly or indirectly, 50% or more of the total voting power of all classes of stock entitled to vote of any foreign or domestic corporation? For rules of constructive ownership, see instructions. If "Yes," complete (i) through (iv) below . . . .

(i) Name of Corporation	(ii) Employer Identification Number (if any)	(iii) Country of Incorporation	(iv) Percentage Owned in Voting Stock

b   Own directly an interest of 20% or more, or own, directly or indirectly, an interest of 50% or more in the profit, loss, or capital in any foreign or domestic partnership (including an entity treated as a partnership) or in the beneficial interest of a trust? For rules of constructive ownership, see instructions. If "Yes," complete (i) through (v) below . .

(i) Name of Entity	(ii) Employer Identification Number (if any)	(iii) Type of Entity	(iv) Country of Organization	(v) Maximum Percentage Owned in Profit, Loss, or Capital

		Yes	No
5	Did the partnership file Form 8893, Election of Partnership Level Tax Treatment, or an election statement under section 6231(a)(1)(B)(ii) for partnership-level tax treatment, that is in effect for this tax year? See Form 8893 for more details		
6	Does the partnership satisfy **all four** of the following conditions?		
a	The partnership's total receipts for the tax year were less than $250,000.		
b	The partnership's total assets at the end of the tax year were less than $1 million.		
c	Schedules K-1 are filed with the return and furnished to the partners on or before the due date (including extensions) for the partnership return.		
d	The partnership is not filing and is not required to file Schedule M-3		
	If "Yes," the partnership is not required to complete Schedules L, M-1, and M-2; Item F on page 1 of Form 1065; or Item L on Schedule K-1.		
7	Is this partnership a publicly traded partnership as defined in section 469(k)(2)?		
8	During the tax year, did the partnership have any debt that was cancelled, was forgiven, or had the terms modified so as to reduce the principal amount of the debt?		
9	Has this partnership filed, or is it required to file, Form 8918, Material Advisor Disclosure Statement, to provide information on any reportable transaction?		
10	At any time during calendar year 2017, did the partnership have an interest in or a signature or other authority over a financial account in a foreign country (such as a bank account, securities account, or other financial account)? See the instructions for exceptions and filing requirements for FinCEN Form 114, Report of Foreign Bank and Financial Accounts (FBAR). If "Yes," enter the name of the foreign country. ▶		

Schedule B	Other Information *(continued)*		
		Yes	**No**
11	At any time during the tax year, did the partnership receive a distribution from, or was it the grantor of, or transferor to, a foreign trust? If "Yes," the partnership may have to file Form 3520, Annual Return To Report Transactions With Foreign Trusts and Receipt of Certain Foreign Gifts. See instructions		
12a	Is the partnership making, or had it previously made (and not revoked), a section 754 election? . . . . See instructions for details regarding a section 754 election.		
b	Did the partnership make for this tax year an optional basis adjustment under section 743(b) or 734(b)? If "Yes," attach a statement showing the computation and allocation of the basis adjustment. See instructions		
c	Is the partnership required to adjust the basis of partnership assets under section 743(b) or 734(b) because of a substantial built-in loss (as defined under section 743(d)) or substantial basis reduction (as defined under section 734(d))? If "Yes," attach a statement showing the computation and allocation of the basis adjustment. See instructions		
13	Check this box if, during the current or prior tax year, the partnership distributed any property received in a like-kind exchange or contributed such property to another entity (other than disregarded entities wholly owned by the partnership throughout the tax year) . . . . ▶ ☐		
14	At any time during the tax year, did the partnership distribute to any partner a tenancy-in-common or other undivided interest in partnership property?		
15	If the partnership is required to file Form 8858, Information Return of U.S. Persons With Respect To Foreign Disregarded Entities, enter the number of Forms 8858 attached. See instructions ▶		
16	Does the partnership have any foreign partners? If "Yes," enter the number of Forms 8805, Foreign Partner's Information Statement of Section 1446 Withholding Tax, filed for this partnership. ▶		
17	Enter the number of Forms 8865, Return of U.S. Persons With Respect to Certain Foreign Partnerships, attached to this return. ▶		
18a	Did you make any payments in 2017 that would require you to file Form(s) 1099? See instructions		
b	If "Yes," did you or will you file required Form(s) 1099?		
19	Enter the number of Form(s) 5471, Information Return of U.S. Persons With Respect To Certain Foreign Corporations, attached to this return. ▶		
20	Enter the number of partners that are foreign governments under section 892. ▶		
21	During the partnership's tax year, did the partnership make any payments that would require it to file Form 1042 and 1042-S under chapter 3 (sections 1441 through 1464) or chapter 4 (sections 1471 through 1474)?		
22	Was the partnership a specified domestic entity required to file Form 8938 for the tax year (See the instructions for Form 8938)?		

Designation of Tax Matters Partner (see instructions)
Enter below the general partner or member-manager designated as the tax matters partner (TMP) for the tax year of this return:

Name of designated TMP ▶		Identifying number of TMP ▶	
If the TMP is an entity, name of TMP representative ▶		Phone number of TMP ▶	
Address of designated TMP ▶			

Form **1065** (2017)

Schedule K		Partners' Distributive Share Items			Total amount	

	1	Ordinary business income (loss) (page 1, line 22)		1		
	2	Net rental real estate income (loss) (attach Form 8825)		2		
	3a	Other gross rental income (loss)	3a			
	b	Expenses from other rental activities (attach statement)	3b			
	c	Other net rental income (loss). Subtract line 3b from line 3a		3c		
	4	Guaranteed payments		4		
	5	Interest income		5		
	6	Dividends: a Ordinary dividends		6a		
		b Qualified dividends	6b			
	7	Royalties		7		
	8	Net short-term capital gain (loss) (attach Schedule D (Form 1065)) . . .		8		
	9a	Net long-term capital gain (loss) (attach Schedule D (Form 1065))		9a		
	b	Collectibles (28%) gain (loss)	9b			
	c	Unrecaptured section 1250 gain (attach statement) . .	9c			
	10	Net section 1231 gain (loss) (attach Form 4797)		10		
	11	Other income (loss) (see instructions) Type ▶		11		
	12	Section 179 deduction (attach Form 4562)		12		
	13a	Contributions		13a		
	b	Investment interest expense		13b		
	c	Section 59(e)(2) expenditures: (1) Type ▶_____ (2) Amount ▶		13c(2)		
	d	Other deductions (see instructions) Type ▶		13d		
	14a	Net earnings (loss) from self-employment		14a		
	b	Gross farming or fishing income		14b		
	c	Gross nonfarm income		14c		
	15a	Low-income housing credit (section 42(j)(5))		15a		
	b	Low-income housing credit (other)		15b		
	c	Qualified rehabilitation expenditures (rental real estate) (attach Form 3468, if applicable)		15c		
	d	Other rental real estate credits (see instructions) Type ▶		15d		
	e	Other rental credits (see instructions) Type ▶		15e		
	f	Other credits (see instructions) Type ▶		15f		
	16a	Name of country or U.S. possession ▶				
	b	Gross income from all sources		16b		
	c	Gross income sourced at partner level		16c		
		Foreign gross income sourced at partnership level				
	d	Passive category ▶_____ e General category ▶_____ f Other ▶		16f		
		Deductions allocated and apportioned at partner level				
	g	Interest expense ▶_____ h Other . . . . ▶		16h		
		Deductions allocated and apportioned at partnership level to foreign source income				
	i	Passive category ▶_____ j General category ▶_____ k Other ▶		16k		
	l	Total foreign taxes (check one): ▶ Paid ☐ Accrued ☐		16l		
	m	Reduction in taxes available for credit (attach statement)		16m		
	n	Other foreign tax information (attach statement)				
	17a	Post-1986 depreciation adjustment		17a		
	b	Adjusted gain or loss		17b		
	c	Depletion (other than oil and gas)		17c		
	d	Oil, gas, and geothermal properties—gross income		17d		
	e	Oil, gas, and geothermal properties—deductions		17e		
	f	Other AMT items (attach statement)		17f		
	18a	Tax-exempt interest income		18a		
	b	Other tax-exempt income		18b		
	c	Nondeductible expenses		18c		
	19a	Distributions of cash and marketable securities		19a		
	b	Distributions of other property		19b		
	20a	Investment income		20a		
	b	Investment expenses		20b		
	c	Other items and amounts (attach statement)				

Row groups (left margin labels): Income (Loss); Deductions; Self-Employment; Credits; Foreign Transactions; Alternative Minimum Tax (AMT) Items; Other Information

Form **1065** (2017)

543

Analysis of Net Income (Loss)

| 1 | Net Income (loss). Combine Schedule K, lines 1 through 11. From the result, subtract the sum of Schedule K, lines 12 through 13d, and 16l . . . . | **1** | | |

2	Analysis by partner type:	(i) Corporate	(ii) Individual (active)	(iii) Individual (passive)	(iv) Partnership	(v) Exempt Organization	(vi) Nominee/Other
a	General partners						
b	Limited partners						

Schedule L — Balance Sheets per Books

	Assets	Beginning of tax year (a)	(b)	End of tax year (c)	(d)
1	Cash				
2a	Trade notes and accounts receivable . . .				
b	Less allowance for bad debts				
3	Inventories				
4	U.S. government obligations				
5	Tax-exempt securities				
6	Other current assets (attach statement) . . .				
7a	Loans to partners (or persons related to partners)				
b	Mortgage and real estate loans				
8	Other investments (attach statement) . . .				
9a	Buildings and other depreciable assets . .				
b	Less accumulated depreciation				
10a	Depletable assets				
b	Less accumulated depletion				
11	Land (net of any amortization)				
12a	Intangible assets (amortizable only)				
b	Less accumulated amortization				
13	Other assets (attach statement)				
14	Total assets				
	Liabilities and Capital				
15	Accounts payable				
16	Mortgages, notes, bonds payable in less than 1 year				
17	Other current liabilities (attach statement) .				
18	All nonrecourse loans				
19a	Loans from partners (or persons related to partners)				
b	Mortgages, notes, bonds payable in 1 year or more				
20	Other liabilities (attach statement)				
21	Partners' capital accounts				
22	Total liabilities and capital				

Schedule M-1 — Reconciliation of Income (Loss) per Books With Income (Loss) per Return

Note. The partnership may be required to file Schedule M-3 (see instructions).

1	Net Income (loss) per books			6	Income recorded on books this year not included on Schedule K, lines 1 through 11 (itemize):	
2	Income included on Schedule K, lines 1, 2, 3c, 5, 6a, 7, 8, 9a, 10, and 11, not recorded on books this year (itemize):			a	Tax-exempt interest $ _____	
3	Guaranteed payments (other than health insurance)			7	Deductions included on Schedule K, lines 1 through 13d, and 16l, not charged against book income this year (itemize):	
4	Expenses recorded on books this year not included on Schedule K, lines 1 through 13d, and 16l (itemize):			a	Depreciation $ _____	
a	Depreciation $ _____			8	Add lines 6 and 7	
b	Travel and entertainment $ _____			9	Income (loss) (Analysis of Net Income (Loss), line 1). Subtract line 8 from line 5 .	
5	Add lines 1 through 4					

Schedule M-2 — Analysis of Partners' Capital Accounts

1	Balance at beginning of year			6	Distributions: a Cash	
2	Capital contributed: a Cash . . .				b Property	
	b Property . .			7	Other decreases (itemize):	
3	Net Income (loss) per books					
4	Other increases (itemize): _____			8	Add lines 6 and 7	
5	Add lines 1 through 4			9	Balance at end of year. Subtract line 8 from line 5	

Form **1065** (2017)

Schedule K-1
(Form 1065)
Department of the Treasury
Internal Revenue Service

2017

For calendar year 2017, or tax year

beginning / / 2017 ending / /

Partner's Share of Income, Deductions, Credits, etc.
▶ See back of form and separate instructions.

☐ Final K-1   ☐ Amended K-1   OMB No. 1545-0123

Part III	Partner's Share of Current Year Income, Deductions, Credits, and Other Items

1	Ordinary business income (loss)	15	Credits
2	Net rental real estate income (loss)		
3	Other net rental income (loss)	16	Foreign transactions
4	Guaranteed payments		
5	Interest income		
6a	Ordinary dividends		
6b	Qualified dividends		
7	Royalties		
8	Net short-term capital gain (loss)		
9a	Net long-term capital gain (loss)	17	Alternative minimum tax (AMT) items
9b	Collectibles (28%) gain (loss)		
9c	Unrecaptured section 1250 gain		
10	Net section 1231 gain (loss)	18	Tax-exempt income and nondeductible expenses
11	Other income (loss)		
12	Section 179 deduction	19	Distributions
13	Other deductions		
		20	Other information
14	Self-employment earnings (loss)		

Part I   Information About the Partnership

A Partnership's employer identification number

B Partnership's name, address, city, state, and ZIP code

C IRS Center where partnership filed return

D ☐ Check if this is a publicly traded partnership (PTP)

Part II   Information About the Partner

E Partner's identifying number

F Partner's name, address, city, state, and ZIP code

G ☐ General partner or LLC member-manager   ☐ Limited partner or other LLC member

H ☐ Domestic partner   ☐ Foreign partner

I1 What type of entity is this partner? _____

I2 If this partner is a retirement plan (IRA/SEP/Keogh/etc.), check here ☐

J Partner's share of profit, loss, and capital (see instructions):

	Beginning	Ending
Profit	%	%
Loss	%	%
Capital	%	%

K Partner's share of liabilities at year end:

Nonrecourse . . . . $ _____
Qualified nonrecourse financing . $ _____
Recourse . . . . $ _____

L Partner's capital account analysis:

Beginning capital account . . . $ _____
Capital contributed during the year $ _____
Current year increase (decrease) . $ _____
Withdrawals & distributions . . $ (_____)
Ending capital account . . . . $ _____

☐ Tax basis   ☐ GAAP   ☐ Section 704(b) book
☐ Other (explain)

M Did the partner contribute property with a built-in gain or loss?
☐ Yes   ☐ No
If "Yes," attach statement (see instructions)

*See attached statement for additional information.

For IRS Use Only

For Paperwork Reduction Act Notice, see Instructions for Form 1065.   www.irs.gov/Form1065   Cat. No. 11394R   Schedule K-1 (Form 1065) 2017

545

This list identifies the codes used on Schedule K-1 for all partners and provides summarized reporting information for partners who file Form 1040. For detailed reporting and filing information, see the separate Partner's Instructions for Schedule K-1 and the Instructions for your income tax return.

1. Ordinary business income (loss). Determine whether the income (loss) is passive or nonpassive and enter on your return as follows.

	Report on
Passive loss	See the Partner's Instructions
Passive income	Schedule E, line 28, column (g)
Nonpassive loss	See the Partner's Instructions
Nonpassive income	Schedule E, line 28, column (j)

2. Net rental real estate income (loss) — See the Partner's Instructions
3. Other net rental income (loss)

Net income	Schedule E, line 28, column (g)
Net loss	See the Partner's Instructions

4. Guaranteed payments — Schedule E, line 28, column (j)
5. Interest income — Form 1040, line 8a
6a. Ordinary dividends — Form 1040, line 9a
6b. Qualified dividends — Form 1040, line 9b
7. Royalties — Schedule E, line 4
8. Net short-term capital gain (loss) — Schedule D, line 5
9a. Net long-term capital gain (loss) — Schedule D, line 12
9b. Collectibles (28%) gain (loss) — 28% Rate Gain Worksheet, line 4 (Schedule D instructions)
9c. Unrecaptured section 1250 gain — See the Partner's Instructions
10. Net section 1231 gain (loss) — See the Partner's Instructions
11. Other income (loss)

Code
A	Other portfolio income (loss)	See the Partner's Instructions
B	Involuntary conversions	See the Partner's Instructions
C	Sec. 1256 contracts & straddles	Form 6781, line 1
D	Mining exploration costs recapture	See Pub. 535
E	Cancellation of debt	Form 1040, line 21 or Form 982
F	Other income (loss)	See the Partner's Instructions

12. Section 179 deduction — See the Partner's Instructions
13. Other deductions

A	Cash contributions (50%)	
B	Cash contributions (30%)	
C	Noncash contributions (50%)	
D	Noncash contributions (30%)	
E	Capital gain property to a 50% organization (30%)	See the Partner's Instructions
F	Capital gain property (20%)	
G	Contributions (100%)	
H	Investment interest expense	Form 4952, line 1
I	Deductions—royalty income	Schedule E, line 19
J	Section 59(e)(2) expenditures	See the Partner's Instructions
K	Deductions—portfolio (2% floor)	Schedule A, line 23
L	Deductions—portfolio (other)	Schedule A, line 28
M	Amounts paid for medical insurance	Schedule A, line 1 or Form 1040, line 29
N	Educational assistance benefits	See the Partner's Instructions
O	Dependent care benefits	Form 2441, line 12
P	Preproductive period expenses	See the Partner's Instructions
Q	Commercial revitalization deduction from rental real estate activities	See Form 8582 Instructions
R	Pensions and IRAs	See the Partner's Instructions
S	Reforestation expense deduction	See the Partner's Instructions
T	Domestic production activities information	See Form 8903 instructions
U	Qualified production activities income	Form 8903, line 7b
V	Employer's Form W-2 wages	Form 8903, line 17
W	Other deductions	See the Partner's Instructions

14. Self-employment earnings (loss)

Note: If you have a section 179 deduction or any partner-level deductions, see the Partner's Instructions before completing Schedule SE.

A	Net earnings (loss) from self-employment	Schedule SE, Section A or B
B	Gross farming or fishing income	See the Partner's Instructions
C	Gross non-farm income	See the Partner's Instructions

15. Credits

A	Low-income housing credit (section 42(j)(5)) from pre-2008 buildings	
B	Low-income housing credit (other) from pre-2008 buildings	
C	Low-income housing credit (section 42(j)(5)) from post-2007 buildings	See the Partner's Instructions
D	Low-income housing credit (other) from post-2007 buildings	
E	Qualified rehabilitation expenditures (rental real estate)	
F	Other rental real estate credits	
G	Other rental credits	
H	Undistributed capital gains credit	Form 1040, line 73; check box a
I	Biofuel producer credit	
J	Work opportunity credit	See the Partner's Instructions
K	Disabled access credit	

Code		Report on
L	Empowerment zone employment credit	
M	Credit for increasing research activities	
N	Credit for employer social security and Medicare taxes	See the Partner's Instructions
O	Backup withholding	
P	Other credits	

16. Foreign transactions

A	Name of country or U.S. possession	
B	Gross income from all sources	Form 1116, Part I
C	Gross income sourced at partner level	

Foreign gross income sourced at partnership level

D	Passive category	
E	General category	Form 1116, Part I
F	Other	

Deductions allocated and apportioned at partner level

G	Interest expense	Form 1116, Part I
H	Other	Form 1116, Part I

Deductions allocated and apportioned at partnership level to foreign source income

I	Passive category	
J	General category	Form 1116, Part I
K	Other	

Other information

L	Total foreign taxes paid	Form 1116, Part II
M	Total foreign taxes accrued	Form 1116, Part II
N	Reduction in taxes available for credit	Form 1116, line 12
O	Foreign trading gross receipts	Form 8873
P	Extraterritorial income exclusion	Form 8873
Q	Other foreign transactions	See the Partner's Instructions

17. Alternative minimum tax (AMT) items

A	Post-1986 depreciation adjustment	
B	Adjusted gain or loss	See the Partner's Instructions and the Instructions for Form 6251
C	Depletion (other than oil & gas)	
D	Oil, gas, & geothermal—gross income	
E	Oil, gas, & geothermal—deductions	
F	Other AMT items	

18. Tax-exempt income and nondeductible expenses

A	Tax-exempt interest income	Form 1040, line 8b
B	Other tax-exempt income	See the Partner's Instructions
C	Nondeductible expenses	See the Partner's Instructions

19. Distributions

A	Cash and marketable securities	
B	Distribution subject to section 737	See the Partner's Instructions
C	Other property	

20. Other information

A	Investment income	Form 4952, line 4a
B	Investment expenses	Form 4952, line 5
C	Fuel tax credit information	Form 4136
D	Qualified rehabilitation expenditures (other than rental real estate)	See the Partner's Instructions
E	Basis of energy property	See the Partner's Instructions
F	Recapture of low-income housing credit (section 42(j)(5))	Form 8611, line 8
G	Recapture of low-income housing credit (other)	Form 8611, line 8
H	Recapture of investment credit	See Form 4255
I	Recapture of other credits	See the Partner's Instructions
J	Look-back interest—completed long-term contracts	See Form 8697
K	Look-back interest—income forecast method	See Form 8866
L	Dispositions of property with section 179 deductions	
M	Recapture of section 179 deduction	
N	Interest expense for corporate partners	
O	Section 453(l)(3) information	
P	Section 453A(c) information	
Q	Section 1260(b) information	
R	Interest allocable to production expenditures	See the Partner's Instructions
S	CCF nonqualified withdrawals	
T	Depletion information—oil and gas	
U	Reserved	
V	Unrelated business taxable income	
W	Precontribution gain (loss)	
X	Section 108(i) information	
Y	Net investment income	
Z	Other information	

546

Form **2553**

(Rev. December 2017)

Department of the Treasury
Internal Revenue Service

Election by a Small Business Corporation

(Under section 1362 of the Internal Revenue Code)

(Including a late election filed pursuant to Rev. Proc. 2013-30)

▶ You can fax this form to the IRS. See separate instructions.
▶ Go to www.irs.gov/Form2553 for instructions and the latest information.

OMB No. 1545-0123

Note: This election to be an S corporation can be accepted only if all the tests are met under *Who May Elect* in the instructions, all shareholders have signed the consent statement, an officer has signed below, and the exact name and address of the corporation (entity) and other required form information have been provided.

Part I   Election Information

Type or Print	Name (see instructions)	A Employer identification number
	Number, street, and room or suite no. If a P.O. box, see instructions.	B Date incorporated
	City or town, state or province, country, and ZIP or foreign postal code	C State of incorporation

D Check the applicable box(es) if the corporation (entity), after applying for the EIN shown in A above, changed its ☐ name or ☐ address

E Election is to be effective for tax year beginning (month, day, year) (see instructions) . . . . ▶ _____

Caution: A corporation (entity) making the election for its first tax year in existence will usually enter the beginning date of a short tax year that begins on a date other than January 1.

F Selected tax year:

(1) ☐ Calendar year

(2) ☐ Fiscal year ending (month and day) ▶ _____

(3) ☐ 52-53-week year ending with reference to the month of December

(4) ☐ 52-53-week year ending with reference to the month of ▶ _____

If box (2) or (4) is checked, complete Part II.

G If more than 100 shareholders are listed for item J (see page 2), check this box if treating members of a family as one shareholder results in no more than 100 shareholders (see test 2 under *Who May Elect* in the instructions) ▶ ☐

H Name and title of officer or legal representative whom the IRS may call for more information | Telephone number of officer or legal representative

I If this S corporation election is being filed late, I declare I had reasonable cause for not filing Form 2553 timely. If this late election is being made by an entity eligible to elect to be treated as a corporation, I declare I also had reasonable cause for not filing an entity classification election timely and the representations listed in Part IV are true. See below for my explanation of the reasons the election or elections were not made on time and a description of my diligent actions to correct the mistake upon its discovery. See instructions.

_____

_____

_____

_____

_____

_____

_____

_____

Sign Here

Under penalties of perjury, I declare that I have examined this election, including accompanying documents, and, to the best of my knowledge and belief, the election contains all the relevant facts relating to the election, and such facts are true, correct, and complete.

▶ _____   _____   _____
Signature of officer   Title   Date

For Paperwork Reduction Act Notice, see separate instructions.   Cat. No. 18629R   Form **2553** (Rev. 12-2017)

Name

Employer identification number

| **Part I** | Election Information *(continued)* **Note:** If you need more rows, use additional copies of page 2. |

J Name and address of each shareholder or former shareholder required to consent to the election. (see instructions)	K Shareholder's Consent Statement Under penalties of perjury, I declare that I consent to the election of the above-named corporation (entity) to be an S corporation under section 1362(a) and that I have examined this consent statement, including accompanying documents, and, to the best of my knowledge and belief, the election contains all the relevant facts relating to the election, and such facts are true, correct, and complete. I understand my consent is binding and may not be withdrawn after the corporation (entity) has made a valid election. If seeking relief for a late filed election, I also declare under penalties of perjury that I have reported my income on all affected returns consistent with the S corporation election for the year for which the election should have been filed (see beginning date entered on line E) and for all subsequent years.		L Stock owned or percentage of ownership (see instructions)		M Social security number or employer identification number (see instructions)	N Shareholder's tax year ends (month and day)
	Signature	Date	Number of shares or percentage of ownership	Date(s) acquired		

Form **2553** (Rev. 12-2017)

548

Part II Selection of Fiscal Tax Year (see instructions)

Note: All corporations using this part must complete item O and item P, Q, or R.

O   Check the applicable box to indicate whether the corporation is:

1. ☐   A new corporation **adopting** the tax year entered in item F, Part I.

2. ☐   An existing corporation **retaining** the tax year entered in item F, Part I.

3. ☐   An existing corporation **changing** to the tax year entered in item F, Part I.

P   Complete item P if the corporation is using the automatic approval provisions of Rev. Proc. 2006-46, 2006-45 I.R.B. 859, to request (1) a natural business year (as defined in section 5.07 of Rev. Proc. 2006-46) or (2) a year that satisfies the ownership tax year test (as defined in section 5.08 of Rev. Proc. 2006-46). Check the applicable box below to indicate the representation statement the corporation is making.

1. Natural Business Year ▶ ☐   I represent that the corporation is adopting, retaining, or changing to a tax year that qualifies as its natural business year (as defined in section 5.07 of Rev. Proc. 2006-46) and has attached a statement showing separately for each month the gross receipts for the most recent 47 months. See instructions. I also represent that the corporation is not precluded by section 4.02 of Rev. Proc. 2006-46 from obtaining automatic approval of such adoption, retention, or change in tax year.

2. Ownership Tax Year ▶ ☐   I represent that shareholders (as described in section 5.08 of Rev. Proc. 2006-46) holding more than half of the shares of the stock (as of the first day of the tax year to which the request relates) of the corporation have the same tax year or are concurrently changing to the tax year that the corporation adopts, retains, or changes to per item F, Part I, and that such tax year satisfies the requirement of section 4.01(3) of Rev. Proc. 2006-46. I also represent that the corporation is not precluded by section 4.02 of Rev. Proc. 2006-46 from obtaining automatic approval of such adoption, retention, or change in tax year.

Note: If you do not use item P and the corporation wants a fiscal tax year, complete either item Q or R below. Item Q is used to request a fiscal tax year based on a business purpose and to make a back-up section 444 election. Item R is used to make a regular section 444 election.

Q   Business Purpose—To request a fiscal tax year based on a business purpose, check box Q1. See instructions for details including payment of a user fee. You may also check box Q2 and/or box Q3.

1. Check here ▶ ☐   If the fiscal year entered in item F, Part I, is requested under the prior approval provisions of Rev. Proc. 2002-39, 2002-22 I.R.B. 1046. Attach to Form 2553 a statement describing the relevant facts and circumstances and, if applicable, the gross receipts from sales and services necessary to establish a business purpose. See the instructions for details regarding the gross receipts from sales and services. If the IRS proposes to disapprove the requested fiscal year, do you want a conference with the IRS National Office?

☐ Yes   ☐ No

2. Check here ▶ ☐   to show that the corporation intends to make a back-up section 444 election in the event the corporation's business purpose request is not approved by the IRS. See instructions for more information.

3. Check here ▶ ☐   to show that the corporation agrees to adopt or change to a tax year ending December 31 if necessary for the IRS to accept this election for S corporation status in the event (1) the corporation's business purpose request is not approved and the corporation makes a back-up section 444 election, but is ultimately not qualified to make a section 444 election, or (2) the corporation's business purpose request is not approved and the corporation did not make a back-up section 444 election.

R   Section 444 Election—To make a section 444 election, check box R1. You may also check box R2.

1. Check here ▶ ☐   to show that the corporation will make, if qualified, a section 444 election to have the fiscal tax year shown in item F, Part I. To make the election, you must complete **Form 8716**, Election To Have a Tax Year Other Than a Required Tax Year, and either attach it to Form 2553 or file it separately.

2. Check here ▶ ☐   to show that the corporation agrees to adopt or change to a tax year ending December 31 if necessary for the IRS to accept this election for S corporation status in the event the corporation is ultimately not qualified to make a section 444 election.

Name	Employer identification number

Part III   Qualified Subchapter S Trust (QSST) Election Under Section 1361(d)(2)* **Note:** If you are making more th one QSST election, use additional copies of page 4.

Income beneficiary's name and address	Social security number

Trust's name and address	Employer identification number

Date on which stock of the corporation was transferred to the trust (month, day, year) . . . . ▶

In order for the trust named above to be a QSST and thus a qualifying shareholder of the S corporation for which this Form 2553 is filed, I hereby make the election under section 1361(d)(2). Under penalties of perjury, I certify that the trust meets the definitional requirements of section 1361(d)(3) and that all other information provided in Part III is true, correct, and complete.

Signature of income beneficiary or signature and title of legal representative or other qualified person making the election	Date

* Use Part III to make the QSST election only if stock of the corporation has been transferred to the trust on or before the date on which the corporation makes its election to be an S corporation. The QSST election must be made and filed separately if stock of th corporation is transferred to the trust **after** the date on which the corporation makes the S election.

Part IV   Late Corporate Classification Election Representations (see instructions)

If a late entity classification election was intended to be effective on the same date that the S corporation election was intended to b effective, relief for a late S corporation election must also include the following representations.

1   The requesting entity is an eligible entity as defined in Regulations section 301.7701-3(a);

2   The requesting entity intended to be classified as a corporation as of the effective date of the S corporation status;

3   The requesting entity fails to qualify as a corporation solely because Form 8832, Entity Classification Election, was not timely filed under Regulations section 301.7701-3(c)(1)(i), or Form 8832 was not deemed to have been filed under Regulations section 301.7701-3(c)(1)(v)(C);

4   The requesting entity fails to qualify as an S corporation on the effective date of the S corporation status solely because the S corporation election was not timely filed pursuant to section 1362(b); **and**

5a   The requesting entity timely filed all required federal tax returns and information returns consistent with its requested classification as an S corporation for all of the years the entity intended to be an S corporation and no inconsistent tax or information returns have been filed by or with respect to the entity during any of the tax years, **or**

b   The requesting entity has not filed a federal tax or information return for the first year in which the election was intended to be effective because the due date has not passed for that year's federal tax or information return.

550

Form **8832**

(Rev. December 2013)

Department of the Treasury
Internal Revenue Service

Entity Classification Election

OMB No. 1545-1516

▶ Information about Form 8832 and its instructions is at *www.irs.gov/form8832.*

Type or Print	Name of eligible entity making election — Employer identification number
	Number, street, and room or suite no. If a P.O. box, see instructions.
	City or town, state, and ZIP code. If a foreign address, enter city, province or state, postal code and country. Follow the country's practice for entering the postal code.

▶ Check if: ☐ Address change   ☐ Late classification relief sought under Revenue Procedure 2009-41
☐ Relief for a late change of entity classification election sought under Revenue Procedure 2010-32

Part I — Election Information

1 Type of election (see instructions):

a ☐ Initial classification by a newly-formed entity. Skip lines 2a and 2b and go to line 3.
b ☐ Change in current classification. Go to line 2a.

2a Has the eligible entity previously filed an entity election that had an effective date within the last 60 months?

☐ **Yes.** Go to line 2b.
☐ **No.** Skip line 2b and go to line 3.

2b Was the eligible entity's prior election an initial classification election by a newly formed entity that was effective on the date of formation?

☐ **Yes.** Go to line 3.
☐ **No.** Stop here. You generally are not currently eligible to make the election (see instructions).

3 Does the eligible entity have more than one owner?

☐ **Yes.** You can elect to be classified as a partnership or an association taxable as a corporation. Skip line 4 and go to line 5.
☐ **No.** You can elect to be classified as an association taxable as a corporation or to be disregarded as a separate entity. Go to line 4.

4 If the eligible entity has only one owner, provide the following information:

a Name of owner ▶ _____
b Identifying number of owner ▶ _____

5 If the eligible entity is owned by one or more affiliated corporations that file a consolidated return, provide the name and employer identification number of the parent corporation:

a Name of parent corporation ▶ _____
b Employer identification number ▶ _____

For Paperwork Reduction Act Notice, see instructions.   Cat. No. 22598R   Form **8832** (Rev. 12-2013)

Part I   Election Information (Continued)

6   **Type of entity** (see instructions):

a   ☐ A domestic eligible entity electing to be classified as an association taxable as a corporation.
b   ☐ A domestic eligible entity electing to be classified as a partnership.
c   ☐ A domestic eligible entity with a single owner electing to be disregarded as a separate entity.
d   ☐ A foreign eligible entity electing to be classified as an association taxable as a corporation.
e   ☐ A foreign eligible entity electing to be classified as a partnership.
f   ☐ A foreign eligible entity with a single owner electing to be disregarded as a separate entity.

7   If the eligible entity is created or organized in a foreign jurisdiction, provide the foreign country of
organization ▶ _____

8   Election is to be effective beginning (month, day, year) (see instructions) . . . . ▶ _____

9   Name and title of contact person whom the IRS may call for more information | 10   Contact person's telephone number

Consent Statement and Signature(s) (see instructions)

Under penalties of perjury, I (we) declare that I (we) consent to the election of the above-named entity to be classified as indicated above, and that I (we) have examined this election and consent statement, and to the best of my (our) knowledge and belief, this election and consent statement are true, correct, and complete. If I am an officer, manager, or member signing for the entity, I further declare under penalties of perjury that I am authorized to make the election on its behalf.

Signature(s)	Date	Title

Form **8832** (Rev. 12-2013)

Part II   Late Election Relief

11   Provide the explanation as to why the entity classification election was not filed on time (see instructions).

_____

_____

_____

_____

_____

_____

_____

_____

_____

Under penalties of perjury, I (we) declare that I (we) have examined this election, including accompanying documents, and, to the best of my (our) knowledge and belief, the election contains all the relevant facts relating to the election, and such facts are true, correct, and complete. I (we) further declare that I (we) have personal knowledge of the facts and circumstances related to the election. I (we) further declare that the elements required for relief in Section 4.01 of Revenue Procedure 2009-41 have been satisfied.

Signature(s)	Date	Title

Form **8832** (Rev. 12-2013)

553

General Instructions

Section references are to the Internal Revenue Code unless otherwise noted.

Future Developments

For the latest information about developments related to Form 8832 and its instructions, such as legislation enacted after they were published, go to www.irs.gov/form8832.

What's New

For entities formed on or after July 1, 2013, the Croatian Dicnicko Drustvo will always be treated as a corporation. See Notice 2013-44, 2013-29, I.R.B. 62 for more information.

Purpose of Form

An eligible entity uses Form 8832 to elect how it will be classified for federal tax purposes, as a corporation, a partnership, or an entity disregarded as separate from its owner. An eligible entity is classified for federal tax purposes under the default rules described below unless it files Form 8832 or Form 2553, Election by a Small Business Corporation. See Who Must File below.

The IRS will use the information entered on this form to establish the entity's filing and reporting requirements for federal tax purposes.

Note. An entity must file Form 2553 if making an election under section 1362(a) to be an S corporation.

 A new eligible entity should not file Form 8832 if it will be using its default classification (see Default Rules below).

Eligible entity. An eligible entity is a business entity that is not included in items 1, or 3 through 9, under the definition of corporation provided under Definitions. Eligible entities include limited liability companies (LLCs) and partnerships.

Generally, corporations are not eligible entities. However, the following types of corporations are treated as eligible entities:

1. An eligible entity that previously elected to be an association taxable as a corporation by filing Form 8832. An entity that elects to be classified as a corporation by filing Form 8832 can make another election to change its classification (see the 60-month limitation rule discussed below in the instructions for lines 2a and 2b).

2. A foreign eligible entity that became an association taxable as a corporation under the foreign default rule described below.

Default Rules

Existing entity default rule. Certain domestic and foreign entities that were in existence before January 1, 1997, and have an established federal tax classification generally do not need to make an election to continue that classification. If an existing entity decides to change its classification, it may do so subject to the 60-month limitation rule. See the instructions for lines 2a and 2b. See Regulations sections 301.7701-3(b)(3) and 301.7701-3(h)(2) for more details.

Domestic default rule. Unless an election is made on Form 8832, a domestic eligible entity is:

1. A partnership if it has two or more members.

2. Disregarded as an entity separate from its owner if it has a single owner.

A change in the number of members of an eligible entity classified as an **association** (defined below) does not affect the entity's classification. However, an eligible entity classified as a partnership will become a disregarded entity when the entity's membership is reduced to one member and a disregarded entity will be classified as a partnership when the entity has more than one member.

Foreign default rule. Unless an election is made on Form 8832, a foreign eligible entity is:

1. A partnership if it has two or more members and at least one member does not have limited liability.

2. An association taxable as a corporation if all members have limited liability.

3. Disregarded as an entity separate from its owner if it has a single owner that does not have limited liability.

However, if a qualified foreign entity (as defined in section 3.02 of Rev. Proc. 2010-32) files a valid election to be classified as a partnership based on the reasonable assumption that it had two or more owners as of the effective date of the election, and the qualified entity is later determined to have a single owner, the IRS will deem the election to be classified as a disregarded entity provided:

1. The qualified entity's owner and purported owners file amended returns that are consistent with the treatment of the entity as a disregarded entity;

2. The amended returns are filed before the close of the period of limitations on assessments under section 6501(a) for the relevant tax year; and

3. The corrected Form 8832, with the box checked entitled: Relief for a late change of entity classification election sought under Revenue Procedure 2010-32, is filed and attached to the amended tax return.

Also, if the qualified foreign entity (as defined in section 3.02 of Rev. Proc. 2010-32) files a valid election to be classified as a disregarded entity based on the reasonable assumption that it had a single owner as of the effective date of the election, and the qualified entity is later determined to have two or more owners, the IRS will deem the election to be classified as a partnership provided:

1. The qualified entity files information returns and the actual owners file original or amended returns consistent with the treatment of the entity as a partnership;

2. The amended returns are filed before the close of the period of limitations on assessments under section 6501(a) for the relevant tax year; and

3. The corrected Form 8832, with the box checked entitled: Relief for a late change of

entity classification election sought under Revenue Procedure 2010-32, is filed and attached to the amended tax returns. See Rev. Proc. 2010-32, 2010-36 I.R.B. 320 for details.

Definitions

Association. For purposes of this form, an association is an eligible entity taxable as a corporation by election or, for foreign eligible entities, under the default rules (see Regulations section 301.7701-3).

Business entity. A business entity is any entity recognized for federal tax purposes that is not properly classified as a trust under Regulations section 301.7701-4 or otherwise subject to special treatment under the Code regarding the entity's classification. See Regulations section 301.7701-2(a).

Corporation. For federal tax purposes, a corporation is any of the following:

1. A business entity organized under a federal or state statute, or under a statute of a federally recognized Indian tribe, if the statute describes or refers to the entity as incorporated or as a corporation, body corporate, or body politic.

2. An association (as determined under Regulations section 301.7701-3).

3. A business entity organized under a state statute, if the statute describes or refers to the entity as a joint-stock company or joint-stock association.

4. An insurance company.

5. A state-chartered business entity conducting banking activities, if any of its deposits are insured under the Federal Deposit Insurance Act, as amended, 12 U.S.C. 1811 et seq., or a similar federal statute.

6. A business entity wholly owned by a state or any political subdivision thereof, or a business entity wholly owned by a foreign government or any other entity described in Regulations section 1.892-2T.

7. A business entity that is taxable as a corporation under a provision of the Code other than section 7701(a)(3).

8. A foreign business entity listed on page 7. See Regulations section 301.7701-2(b)(8) for any exceptions and inclusions to items on this list and for any revisions made to this list since these instructions were printed.

9. An entity created or organized under the laws of more than one jurisdiction (business entities with multiple charters) if the entity is treated as a corporation with respect to any one of the jurisdictions. See Regulations section 301.7701-2(b)(9) for examples.

Disregarded entity. A disregarded entity is an eligible entity that is treated as an entity not separate from its single owner for income tax purposes. A "disregarded entity" is treated as separate from its owner for:

• Employment tax purposes, effective for wages paid on or after January 1, 2009; and

• Excise taxes reported on Forms 720, 730, 2290, 11-C, or 8849, effective for excise taxes reported and paid after December 31, 2007.

See the employment tax and excise tax return instructions for more information.

Limited liability. A member of a foreign eligible entity has limited liability if the member has no personal liability for any debts of or claims against the entity by reason of being a member. This determination is based solely on the statute or law under which the entity is organized (and, if relevant, the entity's organizational documents). A member has personal liability if the creditors of the entity may seek satisfaction of all or any part of the debts or claims against the entity from the member as such. A member has personal liability even if the member makes an agreement under which another person (whether or not a member of the entity) assumes that liability or agrees to indemnify that member for that liability.

Partnership. A partnership is a business entity that has at least two members and is not a corporation as defined above under Corporation.

Who Must File

File this form for an eligible entity that is one of the following:

• A domestic entity electing to be classified as an association taxable as a corporation.

• A domestic entity electing to change its current classification (even if it is currently classified under the default rule).

• A foreign entity that has more than one owner, all owners having limited liability, electing to be classified as a partnership.

• A foreign entity that has at least one owner that does not have limited liability, electing to be classified as an association taxable as a corporation.

• A foreign entity with a single owner having limited liability, electing to be an entity disregarded as an entity separate from its owner.

• A foreign entity electing to change its current classification (even if it is currently classified under the default rule).

Do not file this form for an eligible entity that is:

• Tax-exempt under section 501(a);

• A real estate investment trust (REIT), as defined in section 856; or

• Electing to be classified as an S corporation. An eligible entity that timely files Form 2553 to elect classification as an S corporation and meets all other requirements to qualify as an S corporation is deemed to have made an election under Regulations section 301.7701-3(c)(v) to be classified as an association taxable as a corporation.

All three of these entities are deemed to have made an election to be classified as an association.

Effect of Election

The federal tax treatment of elective changes in classification as described in Regulations section 301.7701-3(g)(1) is summarized as follows:

• If an eligible entity classified as a partnership elects to be classified as an association, it is deemed that the partnership contributes all of its assets and liabilities to the association in exchange for stock in the association, and immediately thereafter, the partnership liquidates by distributing the stock of the association to its partners.

• If an eligible entity classified as an association elects to be classified as a partnership, it is deemed that the association distributes all of its assets and liabilities to its shareholders in liquidation of the association, and immediately thereafter, the shareholders contribute all of the distributed assets and liabilities to a newly formed partnership.

• If an eligible entity classified as an association elects to be disregarded as an entity separate from its owner, it is deemed that the association distributes all of its assets and liabilities to its single owner in liquidation of the association.

• If an eligible entity that is disregarded as an entity separate from its owner elects to be classified as an association, the owner of the eligible entity is deemed to have contributed all of the assets and liabilities of the entity to the association in exchange for the stock of the association.

Note. For information on the federal tax consequences of elective changes in classification, see Regulations section 301.7701-3(g).

When To File

Generally, an election specifying an eligible entity's classification cannot take effect more than 75 days prior to the date the election is filed, nor can it take effect later than 12 months after the date the election is filed. An eligible entity may be eligible for late election relief in certain circumstances. For more information, see *Late Election Relief*, later.

Where To File

File Form 8832 with the Internal Revenue Service Center for your state listed later.

In addition, attach a copy of Form 8832 to the entity's federal tax or information return for the tax year of the election. If the entity is not required to file a return for that year, a copy of its Form 8832 must be attached to the federal tax returns of all direct or indirect owners of the entity for the tax year of the owner that includes the date on which the election took effect. An indirect owner of the electing entity does not have to attach a copy of the Form 8832 to its tax return if an entity in which it has an interest is already filing a copy of the Form 8832 with its return. Failure to attach a copy of Form 8832 will not invalidate an otherwise valid election, but penalties may be assessed against persons who are required to, but do not, attach Form 8832.

Each member of the entity is required to file the member's return consistent with the entity election. Penalties apply to returns filed inconsistent with the entity's election.

If the entity's principal business, office, or agency is located in:	Use the following Internal Revenue Service Center address:
Connecticut, Delaware, District of Columbia, Florida, Illinois, Indiana, Kentucky, Maine, Maryland, Massachusetts, Michigan, New Hampshire, New Jersey, New York, North Carolina, Ohio, Pennsylvania, Rhode Island, South Carolina, Vermont, Virginia, West Virginia, Wisconsin	Cincinnati, OH 45999

If the entity's principal business, office, or agency is located in:	Use the following Internal Revenue Service Center address:
Alabama, Alaska, Arizona, Arkansas, California, Colorado, Georgia, Hawaii, Idaho, Iowa, Kansas, Louisiana, Minnesota, Mississippi, Missouri, Montana, Nebraska, Nevada, New Mexico, North Dakota, Oklahoma, Oregon, South Dakota, Tennessee, Texas, Utah, Washington, Wyoming	Ogden, UT 84201
A foreign country or U.S. possession	Ogden, UT 84201-0023

Note. Also attach a copy to the entity's federal income tax return for the tax year of the election.

Acceptance or Nonacceptance of Election

The service center will notify the eligible entity at the address listed on Form 8832 if its election is accepted or not accepted. The entity should generally receive a determination on its election within 60 days after it has filed Form 8832.

Care should be exercised to ensure that the IRS receives the election. If the entity is not notified of acceptance or nonacceptance of its election within 60 days of the date of filing, take follow-up action by calling 1-800-829-0115, or by sending a letter to the service center to inquire about its status. Send any such letter by certified or registered mail via the U.S. Postal Service, or equivalent type of delivery by a designated private delivery service (see Notice 2004-83, 2004-52 I.R.B. 1030 (or its successor)).

If the IRS questions whether Form 8832 was filed, an acceptable proof of filing is:

• A certified or registered mail receipt (timely postmarked) from the U.S. Postal Service, or its equivalent from a designated private delivery service;

• Form 8832 with an accepted stamp;

• Form 8832 with a stamped IRS received date; or

• An IRS letter stating that Form 8832 has been accepted.

Specific Instructions

Name. Enter the name of the eligible entity electing to be classified.

Employer identification number (EIN). Show the EIN of the eligible entity electing to be classified.

Do not put "Applied For" on this line.

Note. Any entity that has an EIN will retain that EIN even if its federal tax classification changes under Regulations section 301.7701-3.

If a disregarded entity's classification changes so that it becomes recognized as a partnership or association for federal tax purposes, and that entity had an EIN, then the entity must continue to use that EIN. If the entity did not already have its own EIN, then the entity must apply for an EIN and not use the identifying number of the single owner.

A foreign entity that makes an election under Regulations section 301.7701-3(c) and (d) must also use its own taxpayer identifying number. See sections 6721 through 6724 for penalties that may apply for failure to supply taxpayer identifying numbers.

If the entity electing to be classified using Form 8832 does not have an EIN, it must apply for one on Form SS-4, Application for Employer Identification Number. The entity must have received an EIN by the time Form 8832 is filed in order for the form to be processed. An election will not be accepted if the eligible entity does not provide an EIN.

Do not apply for a new EIN for an existing entity that is changing its classification if the entity already has an EIN.

Address. Enter the address of the entity electing a classification. All correspondence regarding the acceptance or nonacceptance of the election will be sent to this address. Include the suite, room, or other unit number after the street address. If the Post Office does not deliver mail to the street address and the entity has a P.O. box, show the box number instead of the street address. If the electing entity receives its mail in care of a third party (such as an accountant or an attorney), enter on the street address line "C/O" followed by the third party's name and street address or P.O. box.

Address change. If the eligible entity has changed its address since filing Form SS-4 or the entity's most recently-filed return (including a change to an "in care of" address), check the box for an address change.

Late-classification relief sought under Revenue Procedure 2009-41. Check the box if the entity is seeking relief under Rev. Proc. 2009-41, 2009-39 I.R.B. 439, for a late classification election. For more information, see Late Election Relief, later.

Relief for a late change of entity classification election sought under Revenue Procedure 2010-32. Check the box if the entity is seeking relief under Rev. Proc.

2010-32, 2010-36 I.R.B. 320. For more information, see Foreign default rule, earlier.

Part I. Election Information

Complete Part I whether or not the entity is seeking relief under Rev. Proc. 2009-41 or Rev. Proc. 2010-32.

Line 1. Check box 1a if the entity is choosing a classification for the first time (i.e., the entity does not want to be classified under the applicable default classification). Do not file this form if the entity wants to be classified under the default rules.

Check box 1b if the entity is changing its current classification.

Lines 2a and 2b. 60-month limitation rule. Once an eligible entity makes an election to change its classification, the entity generally cannot change its classification by election again during the 60 months after the effective date of the election. However, the IRS may (by private letter ruling) permit the entity to change its classification by election within the 60-month period if more than 50% of the ownership interests in the entity, as of the effective date of the election, are owned by persons that did not own any interests in the entity on the effective date or the filing date of the entity's prior election.

Note. The 60-month limitation does not apply if the previous election was made by a newly formed eligible entity and was effective on the date of formation.

Line 4. If an eligible entity has only one owner, provide the name of its owner on line 4a and the owner's identifying number (social security number, or individual taxpayer identification number, or EIN) on line 4b. If the electing eligible entity is owned by an entity that is a disregarded entity or by an entity that is a member of a series of tiered disregarded entities, identify the first entity (the entity closest to the electing eligible entity) that is not a disregarded entity. For example, if the electing eligible entity is owned by disregarded entity A, which is owned by another disregarded entity B, and disregarded entity B is owned by partnership C, provide the name and EIN of partnership C as the owner of the electing eligible entity. If the owner is a foreign person or entity and does not have a U.S. identifying number, enter "none" on line 4b.

Line 5. If the eligible entity is owned by one or more members of an affiliated group of corporations that file a consolidated return, provide the name and EIN of the parent corporation.

Line 6. Check the appropriate box if you are changing a current classification (no matter how achieved), or are electing out of a default classification. Do not file this form if you fall within a default classification that is the desired classification for the new entity.

Line 7. If the entity making the election is created or organized in a foreign jurisdiction, enter the name of the foreign country in which it is organized. This information must be provided even if the entity is also organized under domestic law.

Line 8. Generally, the election will take effect on the date you enter on line 8 of this form,

or on the date filed if no date is entered on line 8. An election specifying an entity's classification for federal tax purposes can take effect no more than 75 days prior to the date the election is filed, nor can it take effect later than 12 months after the date on which the election is filed. If line 8 shows a date more than 75 days prior to the date on which the election is filed, the election will default to 75 days before the date it is filed. If line 8 shows an effective date more than 12 months from the filing date, the election will take effect 12 months after the date the election is filed.

Consent statement and signature(s). Form 8832 must be signed by:

1. Each member of the electing entity who is an owner at the time the election is filed; or

2. Any officer, manager, or member of the electing entity who is authorized (under local law or the organizational documents) to make the election. The elector represents to having such authorization under penalties of perjury.

If an election is to be effective for any period prior to the time it is filed, each person who was an owner between the date the election is to be effective and the date the election is filed, and who is not an owner at the time the election is filed, must sign.

If you need a continuation sheet or use a separate consent statement, attach it to Form 8832. The separate consent statement must contain the same information as shown on Form 8832.

Note. Do not sign the copy that is attached to your tax return.

Part II. Late Election Relief

Complete Part II only if the entity is requesting late election relief under Rev. Proc. 2009-41.

An eligible entity may be eligible for late election relief under Rev. Proc. 2009-41, 2009-39 I.R.B. 439, if each of the following requirements is met.

1. The entity failed to obtain its requested classification as of the date of its formation (or upon the entity's classification becoming relevant) or failed to obtain its requested change in classification solely because Form 8832 was not filed timely.

2. Either:

a. The entity has not filed a federal tax or information return for the first year in which the election was intended because the due date has not passed for that year's federal tax or information return; or

b. The entity has timely filed all required federal tax returns and information returns (or if not timely, within 6 months after its due date, excluding extensions) consistent with its requested classification for all of the years the entity intended the requested election to be effective and no inconsistent tax or information returns have been filed by or with respect to the entity during any of the tax years. If the eligible entity is not required to file a federal tax return or information return, each affected person who is required to file a federal tax return or information return must have timely filed all such returns (or if not timely, within 6 months after its due date, excluding extensions) consistent with the

556

COURTS

SECOND EDITION

SAGE Text/Reader Series in Criminology and Criminal Justice

Craig Hemmens, Series Editor

1. Walsh and Hemmens: *Introduction to Criminology: A Text/Reader*, 2nd Edition
2. Lawrence and Hemmens: *Juvenile Justice: A Text/Reader*
3. Stohr, Walsh, and Hemmens: *Corrections: A Text/Reader*, 2nd Edition
4. Spohn and Hemmens: *Courts: A Text/Reader*, 2nd Edition
5. Archbold: *Policing: A Text/Reader* (forthcoming)
6. Barton-Belessa and Hanser: *Community Corrections: A Text/Reader*
7. Greene and Gabbidon: *Race and Crime: A Text/Reader*
8. Tibbetts and Hemmens: *Criminological Theory: A Text/Reader*
9. Daigle: *Victimology: A Text/Reader*
10. Mallicoat: *Women and Crime: A Text/Reader*
11. Payne: *White Collar Crime: A Text/Reader*

Other Titles of Related Interest

Hemmens, Brody, and Spohn: *Criminal Courts*
Spohn: *How Do Judges Decide?* 2nd Edition
Lippman: *Criminal Procedure*
Lippman: *Contemporary Criminal Law,* 2nd Edition
Banks: *Criminal Justice Ethics,* 3rd Edition
Cox, Allen, Hanser, and Conrad: *Juvenile Justice,* 7th Edition
Lawrence and Hesse: *Juvenile Justice: The Essentials*
Scaramella, Cox, and McCamey: *Introduction to Policing*
Stohr and Walsh: *Corrections: The Essentials*
Hanser: *Community Corrections*
Cullen and Jonson: *Correctional Theory*
Pratt: *Addicted to Incarceration*
Hagan: *Introduction to Criminology,* 7th Edition
Lilly, Cullen, and Ball: *Criminological Theory,* 5th Edition
Tibbetts: *Criminological Theory: The Essentials*
Pratt, Gau, and Franklin: *Key Ideas in Criminology and Criminal Justice*
Felson and Boba: *Crime and Everyday Life,* 5th Edition
Boba Santos: *Crime Analysis With Crime Mapping,* 3rd Edition
Gabbidon and Greene: *Race and Crime,* 3rd Edition
Bachman and Schutt: *The Practice of Research in Criminology and Criminal Justice,* 4th Edition
Bachman and Schutt: *Fundamentals of Research in Criminology and Criminal Justice,* 2nd Edition
Gau: *Statistics for Criminal Justice*
Mosher, Miethe, and Hart: *The Mismeasure of Crime,* 2nd Edition
Martin: *Understanding Terrorism,* 4th Edition
Payne: *White Collar Crime: The Essentials*
Howell: *Gangs in America's Communities*
Maguire and Okada: *Critical Issues in Criminology and Criminal Justice*

COURTS
A Text/Reader

SECOND EDITION

Cassia Spohn
Arizona State University

Craig Hemmens
Missouri State University

Los Angeles | London | New Delhi
Singapore | Washington DC

Los Angeles | London | New Delhi
Singapore | Washington DC

FOR INFORMATION:

SAGE Publications, Inc.
2455 Teller Road
Thousand Oaks, California 91320
E-mail: order@sagepub.com

SAGE Publications Ltd.
1 Oliver's Yard
55 City Road
London EC1Y 1SP
United Kingdom

SAGE Publications India Pvt. Ltd.
B 1/I 1 Mohan Cooperative Industrial Area
Mathura Road, New Delhi 110 044
India

SAGE Publications Asia-Pacific Pte. Ltd.
33 Pekin Street #02-01
Far East Square
Singapore 048763

Acquisitions Editor: Jerry Westby
Editorial Assistant: Erim Sarbuland
Production Editor: Catherine M. Chilton
Copy Editor: Diana Breti
Typesetter: C&M Digitals (P) Ltd.
Proofreader: Annette R. Van Deusen
Indexer: Molly Hall
Cover Designer: Janet Kiesel
Marketing Manager: Erica DeLuca
Permissions: Karen Ehrmann

Copyright © 2012 by SAGE Publications, Inc.

Printed in the United States of America

Library of Congress Cataloging-in-Publication Data

Spohn, Cassia.

Courts : a text/reader / Cassia Spohn, Craig Hemmens. — 2nd ed.

p. cm.
Includes bibliographical references and index.

ISBN 978-1-4129-9718-8 (pbk. : alk. paper)

1. Courts—United States. 2. Justice, Administration of—United States. 3. Courts. I. Hemmens, Craig. II. Title.

KF8720.S66 2012347.73'1—dc23 2011023597

This book is printed on acid-free paper.

12 13 14 15 10 9 8 7 6 5 4 3 2